The Collector's Encyclopedia of

SHELLS

edited by

S. PETER DANCE

photographs by

IAN CAMERON

McGraw-Hill
Book Company

NEW YORK ST LOUIS SAN FRANCISCO

TORONTO

**Library of Congress Cataloging in
Publication Data**

Dance, S. Peter.
   The collector's encyclopedia of shells.
   Bibliography: p.
   1. Shells. I. Title.
Q1405.D34   594'.04'7   74-2152
ISBN 0-07-015290-X

Printed in Great Britain

A Carter Nash Cameron book
Design: Tom Carter
Organisation: Ann Nicachi
Copy editing: Jan Miller
Research: John Blatchford
           Peter Fricker
           Judy Ross

The production of this book would not
have been possible without the aid of
those who provided most of the specimens described and photographed.
Over half of the specimens were made
available by the National Museum of
Wales, Cardiff, by kind permission of
the Keeper of Zoology, Mr J. A.
Bateman. We are particularly grateful
to Dr June Chatfield for the unstinting
help which she gave us while we were
working in Cardiff. Many specimens
were provided by Eaton's Shell Shop,
Manette Street London, W.1., where
our thanks are due to Mr F. Mayer and
Mr K. R. Wye who also lent us many
shells from their own collections. Our
other major source of specimens was
the collection of Mr R. P. Scase of
Wisley, Surrey, to whom we also offer
our thanks.

Contents

About this book

The ever-growing interest in shell collecting in recent years has resulted in a spate of books popularising the subject, and the publication of yet another may seem superfluous. Numerous books now available are undeniably designed to help the collector, but most of them deal with the shells of a particular region. The very few attempting to give a world-wide coverage are often inadequately illustrated or contain insufficient textual information to assist the collector who wants to identify shells. This book sets out to satisfy collectors and students whose interest in seashells is not restricted to those from a particular part of the globe. More than that, it does so systematically and gives special attention to higher systematic categories, a feature distinguishing it from most popular shell books available at the present time. Descriptions are given for each family, often stating the number of genera contained within each, and comparable descriptions are provided for each genus except where these would more or less repeat the details given for the parent family.

A volume of this length could be devoted entirely to one species; indeed, such books exist already. Consequently this Encyclopedia cannot be totally encyclopedic in its coverage. It is limited to seashells and does not mention any of the thousands of species living on land or in fresh water. A whole class of exclusively marine molluscs, the Monoplacophora, is also ignored, but as its few members are extremely rare deep-water creatures, its exclusion is justified. Details of molluscan anatomy are mostly ignored, not because they are considered unimportant but because most of those who will use the book will not be seeking such information. It is useful, however, to understand the significance of certain shell features, such as the adductor muscle impressions and pallial sinus imprinted on the inside of a bivalve shell by its former soft-bodied occupant. That kind of information is provided.

The book attempts to illustrate in words and pictures the variety of shells living in the world's seas and should enable anyone to identify the family, if not the genus and species, to which a shell belongs. A pictorial key facilitating identification to family level is a novel feature of the book although, as with all such keys, it will not be an infallible guide. Geographical distribution is indicated on the basis of established zoogeographical provinces. Whether a species occurs very widely or over a very restricted range, its distribution always falls within one or more of these provinces, which are shown on the map provided on page 11. The citation of one of these provinces does not necessarily imply that a species occurs throughout it. The boundaries of the provinces as given on the map are sometimes wider than those laid down in other books. The Caribbean Province, for instance, here embraces the entire area of the Caribbean Sea and all its adjacent coast lines, including the southernmost part of Florida, as well as the South American east coast down to Rio de Janeiro; in other books this province is interpreted less widely.

The frequency of occurrence of a species is indicated by the expressions common, frequent, uncommon, rare. These must not be interpreted too literally. A species abundant in one locality but rare elsewhere may be considered common here. A species known only from deep water in a restricted area may be so readily available in commerce that it may reasonably be considered of frequent occurrence. The size of a species may vary considerably across its distribution or even within a population. The size range is usually that which is general for the species, although an upper measurement may sometimes be abnormally large or a lower abnormally small. Each dimension given here is the largest obtainable from a shell, including spines or other processes. A single measurement preceded by *c* is the size of an average specimen, sometimes the size of the only specimen available. Species attaining a maximum size of less than 0·5cm are almost completely ignored.

The colour photographs, which are integrated with the entries, have all been specially taken for this book. Because the shells illustrated range in size from very small to very large, they cannot be reproduced to a common scale. Each is shown as large as is practicable within the format of the book. Specimens have not been chosen for their beauty or perfection, although many are both beautiful and perfect. Availability of suitable material has dictated the choice. Nearly all the descriptions are based on an examination of actual specimens, but the dimensions often incorporate those given in published sources. When more than one suitable specimen has been available two or more have often been photographed. For many species, however, a single shell has been considered sufficient. Rarely, the details of colour as given in the text differ to some extent from those shown in the illustrations. This is because some of the illustrated shells were not freshly collected and their colours have faded over the years. The illustrations are closely integrated with the entries, and, in most cases, the illustration appears within the text entry for the species. Linear magnification of each illustration is given in the heading of the species description, together with an arrow if the illustration is adjacent to rather than within the entry. Captions appear only when it is not otherwise clear from the layout which species is illustrated. Almost every genus in the book includes at least one illustrated species; most genera are very fully illustrated.

The classification adopted is a composite one based largely on recent published accounts, most of which are listed in the Bibliography. On the whole, a conservative approach has been adopted. If a group has been authoritatively and fully covered in a recent publication, for example the Volutidae, the classification used in that publication has been followed. Other groups not recently covered with such thoroughness, such as the Nassariidae and Cerithiidae, are dealt with conservatively. At family and genus level, *The Treatise of Invertebrate Paleontology* has been followed for the groups so far dealt with in that still unfinished work, which is notably conservative in its approach, particularly among the bivalves. For convenience, species are arranged alphabetically within each genus and not according to a subjective appraisal of their similarity or relationship to each other. Genera with only fossil representatives are excluded from the totals given under families. Generic synonyms do not include subgeneric names as given in the *Treatise* and elsewhere. Specific synonyms are not complete for each species, but include only those of common occurrence in available literature. The use of popular or colloquial names is restricted to those which have general currency. Where popular names apply to different species in different countries, they have been omitted to avoid confusion. Straightforward translations of scientific names are avoided. The name *Thatcheria mirabilis*, for example, might be translated as The Wonderful Thatcher Shell, or Thatcher's Miracle Shell. Even Mr Thatcher, after whom the genus of this strikingly attractive species was named, would probably agree that the shell, already and suitably known as The Japanese Wonder Shell, would lose some of its dignity by being gratuitously labelled with his name in this way.

Introduction

Shell or mollusc?

The essential feature of a seashell, apart from its characteristic shape, is its hardness. It may be thick and heavy or thin and fragile, but it is always more or less hard rather than soft. At the same time it is the product of a soft-bodied, fleshy animal. It is to that animal what the external armour-like carapace is to a crab or the skeleton to a human being. The skeleton supports; the carapace supports and encloses. The seashell sometimes supports, sometimes encloses, frequently does both and occasionally does neither. Depending on its evolutionary history, it may be conspicuous and vital or inconspicuous and useless to the animal which makes it.

In the early days of zoology, soft animal and hard shell were treated as two separate entities, the animal being called a mollusc. In current usage, mollusc describes the animal and shell combined, just as insect denotes all the parts of a creature which may have such appendages as wings, wing coverings, legs and antennae. Many molluscs do not have shells, but that does not make them any less molluscan. All the photographs in this book are of shells. The text, on the other hand, frequently refers, as it must, to features or habits of the entire creature, or mollusc. The expression 'shell-fish', often applied to edible molluscs, is obviously inappropriate as they are in no sense fish-like.

Classification

Molluscs all belong to the phylum Mollusca, one of the larger groups in the animal kingdom. The phylum is divided up into six classes:

AMPHINEURA (chitons) With shells usually of eight pieces, or valves, held together by a surrounding fleshy girdle. Exclusively marine.

MONOPLACOPHORA (gastroverms) With one-piece, limpet-like shells. Exclusively marine.

SCAPHOPODA (tusk shells) With one-piece shells, tubular, tapering and open at both ends. Exclusively marine.

GASTROPODA (limpets, snails, slugs, whelks, etc.) Animals with one-piece shells, usually coiled and usually external, but sometimes absent. Marine, freshwater and terrestrial.

BIVALVIA (cockles, mussels, oysters, clams, etc.) Animals with two-piece shells, hinged at one edge, equal or unequal in size and shape. Marine and freshwater.

CEPHALOPODA (squids, nautiluses, cuttlefish, octopuses) Animals without shells or with one-piece shells which may be coiled or straight and are usually internal. Exclusively marine.

Fuller details of these classes, with one exception, will be found in their relevant places in the main part of this book. The exception is the Monoplacophora, the smallest class, which comprises only one genus with about six species. The most primitive of all molluscs, the monoplacophorans, or gastroverms as they are sometimes called, have segmented bodies with gills and other organs paired. They are inhabitants of very deep water and have been collected only on rare occasions by specially equipped research vessels.

The classes are divided into subclasses, orders, suborders, superfamilies, families, subfamilies, genera, species and sub-species. In this book some of these subdivisions are ignored in favour of a simplified arrangement largely by superfamily, family, genus and species. A superfamily is a major grouping which is very useful curatorially in very extensive collections such as those in large museums and similar institutions. Superfamilies are not defined here because their definitions are founded largely on anatomical features of the animal rather than the shell. A family is a large or small division of a superfamily containing at least one genus and one species. Sometimes a family may include very dissimilar species belonging to various genera, which are grouped together because of anatomical or behavioural similarities. A genus is the smallest grouping used in this book. It contains at least one species but may, as in the genus *Conus*, contain hundreds. A species is the lowest unit used in this book. The term species may be taken to mean all specimens of one kind which resemble each other so closely as to be practically identical. This definition is greatly oversimplified but is close enough for our purpose.

Scientific names

With the exception of the species, all the units which have been mentioned are given a single name each, e.g. superfamily Conacea, family Conidae, genus *Conus*. The species, however, has a two-part name, e.g. *Conus elegans*. The names given to animals are applied according to an internationally agreed set of rules formulated by the International Commission of Zoological Nomenclature which has the power to modify them as necessary. Conventionally only the names of genera and species are italicised. The name of the person or persons who originally proposed the generic or specific name should be added to the scientific name; it is indeed part of the scientific name. Strictly speaking, the date when the scientific name was first published should also be added but it is often, as here, ignored. No generic name may be used to denote more than one group of animals. Similarly a species name, such as *Conus elegans*, should only be applied to one species (although the specific epithet *elegans* may be used in combination with any other generic name). The first half of the species name may be likened to a surname, the second part to a christian name. A scientific name represents an abstract conception. A specimen, however, is a concrete example of a species.

Biology of molluscs

It is impossible to understand the great diversity of shells without some knowledge of molluscan biology. A good starting point is external form of the animals in each of the five classes to be dealt with. The chitons (Amphineura) have a large, sucker-like foot almost as wide as the shell. There is a head but no eyes or tentacles, and the gills are arranged in two series, one on each side of the foot. The tusk shells (Scaphopoda) have a wedge-shaped foot and a mouth but lack eyes and gills. The gastropods (Gastropoda) vary enormously in appearance; they usually have a large, muscular foot, a well developed head with eyes and tentacles and have either gills or a modified 'lung'. Short or long siphons are often present. There may be an operculum on the upper surface of the foot which partially or completely seals the shell aperture when the animal withdraws. The bivalves (Bivalvia) usually have a large elongate or hatchet-shaped foot and a pair of siphons posteriorly; they have gills. There is no head or organ associated with a head. The cephalopods (Cephalopoda) usually have a series of large tentacles surrounding a mouth in which is situated a beak

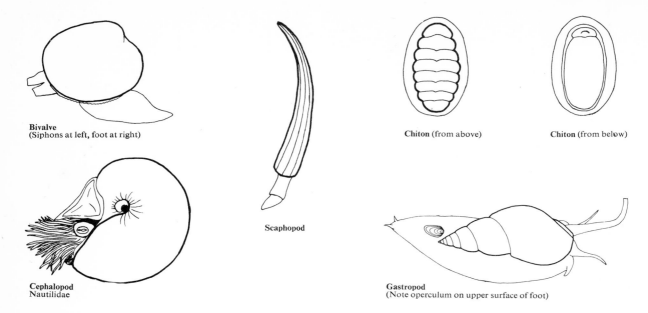

Bivalve
(Siphons at left, foot at right)

Scaphopod

Chiton (from above)

Chiton (from below)

Cephalopod
Nautilidae

Gastropod
(Note operculum on upper surface of foot)

like a parrot's. The long or short, fleshy or leathery body often has a funnel-shaped siphon. The eyes are large and well developed.

The sex life of molluscs varies considerably from group to group. Sexes are separate in a large number of molluscs, but many gastropods (almost all of them non-marine) and some bivalves and cephalopods are hermaphrodite, with male and female reproductive organs in the same individual. Some molluscs have an even more eventful sex life. Beginning as male animals, they pass through a hermaphrodite stage and end up as females. Sexual differences are not necessarily restricted to aspects of the soft anatomy but may also be transmitted to the shells. The shell of the female is often larger than that of the male, and the ornamentation may differ. The shell of a male winkle (*Littorina*) is often smaller than that of the female; the male of some species of scorpion shell (*Lambis*) not only has a smaller shell, but the digitations on its outer lip stick out straight, where those of the female are turned sharply upwards.

Reproduction is achieved in a variety of ways. Fertilisation may be external or internal according to the species. In many marine gastropods and most bivalves, eggs or sperms produced in a gonad are conducted through a special duct to be ejected at spawning time into the water; fertilisation takes place externally. Huge numbers of tiny eggs drift about and develop into swimming larvae. A larva passes through two stages, known respectively as the trochophore and the veliger. The trochophore stage usually lasts only a few hours. Though microscopically small, as a rule, the ensuing veliger stage is much more advanced, having a tiny shell, a foot, eyes and tentacles. It swims by means of a velum, a thin flap bearing relatively large paddle-shaped lobes. The veliger finally drops to the sea floor, casts off the velum and begins life as a recognisable miniature version of its parents. In gastropods with more elaborate reproductive systems, there is internal fertilisation with copulation between male and female, sperms being deposited in the female's reproductive tract. She lays the fertilised eggs in protective capsules. In some species, development is completed within the capsules. In others, the larvae hatch out from their capsules as free-swimming veligers and complete their development externally. Some bivalves incubate their young in brood pouches.

Chitons usually produce a large number of eggs which are either shed freely into the water or are anchored in short strings of mucus. Scaphopods also produce eggs which develop into free-swimming veligers. Cephalopods have a unique and remarkable method of fertilisation. Nearly all of them have separate and often very dissimilar sexes. One of the tentacles, or arms, functions as a male copulatory organ (the hectocotylus) which breaks off inside the female and remains there to fertilise the eggs. These are laid in various ways or left to float. The embryos complete their development within the egg capsules and emerge as baby cephalopods.

The developmental history of a mollusc gives us an insight into its distribution pattern. If it has a lengthy period as a veliger, it is likely to have a wide distribution. Conversely, if it completes its larval development early, or has no free-swimming stage, it is likely to have a restricted distribution or is at least unlikely to traverse great oceans.

Growth

After its larval development is completed, the mollusc begins to feed and to grow. A shelled mollusc grows by adding shelly material to the edge of the tiny coiled shell or valves acquired during the larval stage. Environmental factors affect its rate of growth beneficially or adversely so that it may mature slowly or rapidly. Many molluscs produce shells which differ conspicuously at different growth stages. Some are essentially similar at all stages of growth and have an 'unfinished' appearance at maturity. Shells of juvenile cowries look like thin-shelled olives; juvenile strombs resemble, and are often mistaken for, cones. The appearance of the mature shell is often greatly modified by the final growth stages which terminate in the production of a thicker shell with pronounced apertural features. Periodical cessations of growth may produce varices on gastropods or well-defined growth rings on bivalves. If a mollusc is cemented to a hard substrate or is confined within a crevice or lives in crowded conditions, its growth is more or less impeded and stunting or distortion may result. Shells normally spiny may not develop their spines at all in exposed or turbulent environments. Species which are normally smooth-shelled may develop spines or lamellae under very favourable conditions. Different ecological conditions or different degrees of geographical separation may produce minor or major differences in size, ornament and colour within the same species. This helps explain why some species have several alternative scientific names. In the early days of conchology, shells were often described as new to science on the basis of characters which we now recognise as superficial and attributable to environmental factors.

Shell structure

To a great extent, food influences the appearance of a mollusc's shell. A food-rich environment often helps a mollusc develop a shell which is thicker, more strongly ornamented and more colourful than one developed by a mollusc living under more austere conditions. In the polar regions or the abyssal depths of the sea, such molluscs as exist produce only thin, weakly ornamented, dull and colourless shells. Those frequenting coral reefs in tropical seas tend to have thick, strongly ornamented or highly glossy shells with bright colours and bold patterns. Almost all of them, however, utilise the same substance, calcium carbonate, to form their shells.

Crystals of calcium carbonate, which is the chemical basis of such rocks as limestone and chalk, are the basis of most molluscan shells. The crystals are deposited in layers by the animal's fleshy mantle, either as aragonite – the mother-of-pearl or nacre which appears on the inside of many shells – or as calcite, a lighter form of calcium carbonate. A substance known as conchiolin is associated with the layers and helps strengthen them. Successive layers are structurally different from each other, giving added strength; the layers are sometimes of different colours and clearly distinct when the shell is sectioned or severely abraded.

Shell form

It is the endless variety of shell form among molluscs which, more than anything else, makes us want to collect and study them. A mollusc must continually add new shell growth to old to ensure adequate protection for itself. It does so by adding increments at the mantle edge so that growth is a more or less regular, rhythmical process depending on the maintenance of suitable conditions for growth such as adequate food and optimum water temperature and light. Evidence for the regularity and rhythm of shell growth is provided by the growth lines on a shell. These are axial in a coiled gastropod, concentric in an uncoiled or patelliform one, and concentric also in the valves of chitons and bivalves.

Uncoiled gastropod shells grow only downwards or forwards from the point of origin – a limpet does not add any new growth to its apex. Tusk shells, too, grow only at the broader apertural end. Bivalves add new shell growth only at the edges furthest from the umbones. Chitons enlarge each valve by adding concentric rings of growth. Coiled gastropod shells provide complications to this growth pattern because the act of coiling makes it possible for a late growth stage to come in contact with and to be superimposed upon an earlier one. Fundamentally, however, growth is consistently in one direction only.

Shells which do not coil about an imaginary axis are all more or less flat, cap shaped or tusk shaped. Those which coil can and often do change their appearance at any stage of growth, although most of them do not do so after having formed a thickened outer lip. The principle of coiling has been very little exploited among bivalve shells for the very good reason that it would become progressively more difficult for a bivalve shell to function properly. In an evolutionary sense, bivalves have gone about as far as they can go in exploiting the various combinations of shell form open to them and very few seem to have experimented with the coiling principle. Two of the most extreme examples are found in the genus *Corculum* and the genus *Glossus*. Both have strongly inrolled umbones, but in *Corculum*, the rest of the shell is strongly compressed and the umbones are forced

to slide past each other to allow the valves to open at all. In *Glossus*, the valves have become grossly inflated so that the umbones are far enough apart to prevent them clashing when the valves open. In the genus *Thracia*, the valves are unequal in size and the umbo of the smaller valve sometimes pierces the umbo of the larger, which it must do if the valves are to open wide enough.

Shell ornament

Shells may be smooth externally or may have their surfaces cut into or elevated in various ways. Ornamentation is reasonably constant in disposition within a single species but may vary considerably in strength according to environmental conditions. Most ornamental features are produced at the same time as additions are made to the growing edge of the shell. Spines, scales, tubercles and ridges are not superimposed at a later stage on a previously formed smooth surface. The only exception to this statement is the production of a callus deposit which overlies previously formed shell features. Such a deposit is a conspicuous feature of the gastropod genus *Ancilla* in which the spire is almost or quite covered with a thick glaze laid down long after the spire was formed. In many gastropod shells, such as those of some Naticidae and Trochidae, a previously open umbilicus may become partially or completely obliterated by subsequent addition of callus deposits. Conversely, some molluscs absorb previously laid down surface ornament such as spines. The appearance of a shell may be modified throughout its life by these processes.

Colour and pattern

Very thin shells are sometimes translucent and colourless. Thicker, opaque shells are always coloured, although many of them are entirely white: the colour of their principal constituent. The iridescent surface of some shells makes them appear colourful. This is not due to the presence of pigments but is the result of reflection and refraction of light rays as they pass through the different layers of calcite. All colours other than white are laid down in the shell or its periostracum as pigments, which are also present in the soft parts. Pigment cells are concentrated in the mantle which transfers pigments to the shell as it is being secreted. The main pigments found in shells impart colours ranging from pale to dark brown, pink to crimson, violet to purple, yellow to green. Shells of the same species, even those collected in the same place at the same time, will often vary considerably in colour: some might be all pink, others all yellow or all white, and so on.

Many species have more than one colour and show some kind of colour pattern. The different colours are distributed over the shell as rays, streaks, spots, triangles, stripes, blotches or other configurations. The distribution of colours is entirely the result of a rhythmic deposition of pigments at certain points along the mantle edge. The points of deposition may wander along the mantle edge, may expand or contract and may function intermittently. A pigment continuously deposited at one point on the mantle edge will produce a coloured line spiralling around the whorls of a coiled shell, or one which radiates from the umbo to a point on the ventral margin of a bivalve shell. If deposition is intermittent, the line will be broken up into dots or lines of varying length. In this way fluctuations in the activity of pigment-producing cells at the mantle edge can produce a great variety of patterns.

Sunlight and warmth are as essential to the production of bright and varied colours as they are to the growth of thick and well ornamented shells. Warm water shells are generally more colourful than those from cold water, and those from tropical regions are even more colourful. Areas rich in coral provide the best living conditions for molluscs and other marine animals and produce the most colourful shells of all. It will be obvious from the descriptions in the main part of the book that shells vary more in colour and pattern than they do in form and ornamentation.

Feeding
Nearly all bivalves feed on vegetable and animal matter which is either suspended as particles in the water or is lying on or just below the sea floor. Some of them take in microscopic food particles via the inhalant siphon and pass them over the gills to the mouth. Others use the inhalant siphon to suck up food from the sea floor. A few are virtually carnivorous, drawing in worms and other small invertebrates which they are able to crush and digest. All cephalopods are carnivorous: they catch other animals, sometimes their own kind, with their tentacles and use their strong beak to kill them. Inside a cephalopod's mouth is a rasping organ, the radula, which is a ribbon-like structure studded with sharp teeth. It is used to rasp away and macerate the pieces of flesh bitten out of the prey. Scaphopods burrow through mud and sand, trapping minute animals with sticky-ended filaments; they, too, employ a radula to aid the digestive process.

The feeding habits of gastropods are more diverse. To a great extent, this diversity is reflected in the structure of the radula, for this organ is used in several different ways and is modified accordingly. Herbivorous gastropods rasp away at vegetable matter with a radula which has many teeth arranged in rows of a hundred or more (rhipidoglossate). Top shells and limpets have this kind of radula. Some gastropods, such as winkles and cowries, have a radula with only seven teeth in each row (taenioglossate). This is a more adaptable radula and allows the animal to pick up food particles and to cut and shred them more efficiently than would be possible with a rhipidoglossate radula. Gastropods which have a radula with only three large teeth per row (rachiglossate) are carnivorous; their teeth are necessarily stronger to cope with the tough tissues of living or dead prey. Whelks and volutes have this type of radula. Another carnivorous group of gastropods has developed a radula which, in association with a poison apparatus, acts like a hypodermic needle and is used to paralyse prey before ingestion. This (toxoglossate) radula has a single, harpoon-like tooth which is replaceable. It is best exemplified by the cones, whose poison apparatus is efficient enough to paralyse such prey as small fish. Some species have an impressive capacity for disabling creatures which they cannot hope to devour. Some humans stung by cones have experienced slight discomfort; others have died in agony. Live cones of whatever species must be handled so that the animal's proboscis cannot come in contact with any part of the collector's body. There are also parasitic gastropods which suck the juices or eat the tissues of molluscs or other invertebrates. They do not have a radula.

Locomotion
Molluscs have adopted many different ways of getting about. Chitons and most gastropods crawl or glide by means of a muscular foot which is lubricated by special mucus glands. Some gastropods, such as the Strombidae, progress awkwardly by repeatedly jabbing the sharply pointed operculum into the ground and pulling against it so that the whole animal is jerked forwards. Large side flaps allow some gastropods, such as Bulla, to swim. Some bivalves, including Lima and Chlamys, also swim but do so by rapidly opening and closing their valves to create a kind of jet propulsion. Most other bivalves use the flexible muscular foot for burrowing or ploughing. Tusk shells also burrow by using a flexible foot similar to that of burrowing bivalves. Cephalopods are built for a swimming existence. Water is expelled from the mantle cavity by muscular action and the direction of movement can be controlled by the exhalant funnel. Stabilising fins are present in the fast-moving squids.

Where molluscs live
As well as being present in all the world's seas, molluscs have successfully invaded brackish and fresh water and are abundant on land. Marine molluscs are predominantly inhabitants of relatively shallow water, although there are many adapted to a life spent in the total darkness of ocean abysses. Floating (pelagic) molluscs are found in the open sea: pteropods, tiny creatures with thin and glassy shells, are among the most abundant of all marine invertebrates. Many cephalopods live in the open sea at all depths. Members of the gastropod family Janthinidae drift about on the surface attached to bubble-like rafts of mucus.

Sandy shores or seabeds are ideal for molluscs adapted for a burrowing existence. All tusk shells and most bivalves frequent such places, as do many gastropods. Where the sand is mixed with mud, the molluscan fauna is richer and the shells are often larger and more perfect. In such an environment, molluscs with long siphons and a muscular wedge-shaped foot are better off than those without them because they can burrow deeper and feed more efficiently.

Rocky shores favour an entirely different life-style for molluscs. Here bivalves can survive only by attaching themselves to the rocks, squeezing between them or burrowing into them. They may, like the Chamidae, cement themselves by one valve, or anchor themselves with a byssus formed of strong mucus threads, as do the mussels, or they may, like the Pholadidae, excavate burrows in which they spend their lives. Chitons, clamped down firmly with the sucker-like foot and girdle to resist the waves, are more at home here than anywhere else. Top shells, limpets and ear shells (Haliotidae) are well represented on rocky shores and are largely confined to them. Some live in very exposed situations and are able to withstand heavy battering by rough seas. Other, less robust species prefer the quieter existence of rock pools.

Coral, in one form or another, provides a food-rich environment for a host of different molluscs including many of the world's most beautiful species. Coral reefs, coral rubble and coral sand harbour volutes, mitres, harp shells and other graceful and colourful gastropods. Embedded in the coral are their less handsome, less mobile cousins, Magilus and Coralliophila. Many bivalves bore into or attach themselves to the living coral.

Mangrove swamps are formed where muddy water discharged by rivers meets tidal flats. In these oozy, often noisome places, many burrowing and crawling molluscs find nourishment and refuge. Mangrove roots give anchorage and shelter to oysters and other bivalves which, in turn, are food for predatory gastropods such as Melongena and Busycon. In these places, the water is often brackish and forms a transition zone between salt water and fresh water.

Collecting
The art of collecting molluscs rather than empty shells requires skill, determination, luck and a certain amount of equipment. Shell collecting is so absorbing that it is easy to forget simple rules for self protection. It is clearly necessary to keep warm when collecting in cold places. Less obviously, the whole body, not just the back of the neck, needs protection in the tropics. An unglamorous but efficient outfit incorporates a pair of pyjamas, a broad-brimmed floppy hat and a pair of rope-soled canvas shoes or sneakers. Sometimes as in coral reef areas, it is better to wear thick, rubber-soled footwear to prevent wounds from sharp-edged coral and venomous or spiny creatures such as stone-fish and sea urchins. Always be acquainted beforehand with local conditions such as the vagaries of tides and water currents.

Many a collector has been stranded because he did not envisage (or forgot) that an incoming tide could cut off his escape route.

Never take too much equipment with you and try to carry it so that it leaves the hands free and does not impede progress. It is a good idea to secure useful items so that they cannot be easily dropped and lost; several of them may be carried on loops of cord around the neck – certainly the best way of carrying a low power lens. Larger items may. be carried at the waist. Plastic forceps are more suitable than metal ones for the collector as they float if dropped and will not rust. A plastic bucket is also invaluable because it floats and, suitably anchored, may be used to hold collecting gear as well as the catch. Bags made of nylon or calico are useful for carrying specimens. Plastic containers and small glass tubes will hold small or fragile specimens. Hand dredges can be effective in collecting small molluscs from sandy or muddy places. Copper mesh is recommended as it does not rust or corrode easily in salt water. As the only function of a hand dredge is to act as a sieve, it does not have to be elaborately constructed; a flour sieve is often adequate, although a larger mesh is usually necessary. A glass-bottomed box will open up new dimensions for the collector who is not also a scuba diver or a snorkeller. It should be attached to the wrist by a line. As well as revealing the sea floor in wonderful detail, it may, if it is of generous proportions, also be used for carrying equipment and specimens. A stick with two or three metal hooks at the end is useful for turning over rocks or coral blocks under the water. Chitons and limpets may be dislodged with a knife. Deep-burrowing bivalves have to be dug up with a spade or fork. Boring molluscs may be obtained only by breaking into their burrows with a crowbar or hammer and chisel.

There are times when collecting excursions are likely to be particularly fruitful. Extreme low tides will expose areas which are inaccessible to beachcombers at other times. Consult local tide tables to ensure that an excursion is timed to coincide with low tide rather than high tide. After gales and storms, shells from off-shore areas may be washed up on the beach. Some of the world's rarest shells have been found after hurricanes or other severe weather phenomena. It should also be borne in mind that molluscs are nocturnal animals and tend to hide themselves away in daytime. Collecting at night by torch light may be very rewarding.

If you disturb a habitat, always try to leave it as it was before your arrival. Rocks and coral blocks should not be left overturned but should be put back to their original positions. If a mollusc is found on or near its eggs, resist the temptation to collect it; the survival of those eggs depends on the survival of the mother. Leave immature molluscs to complete their growth; this gives them the chance to reach sexual maturity and to produce offspring. Taking notes about these occurrences is a valuable and praiseworthy enterprise. Never collect more than two or three specimens of a species which is obviously scarce, and always try to ensure that some living specimens are left behind to produce replacements for those you have taken.

Preparation and storage
Empty shells may need only a wash before they take their place in a collection. Live-collected specimens must be killed and cleaned. Plunging them into boiling water is the most frequently adopted killing method, but there are other ways of accomplishing this distasteful part of shell collecting. The soft parts may be allowed to rot in fresh or salt water before flushing them out under the tap. Some collectors drown cowries and other glossy-shelled molluscs in paraffin some time before removing the animal. This method does not harm the glossy surface. Deep freezing and subsequent thawing is a useful but seldom convenient way to prepare a mollusc for cleaning. The animals of some species are easily winkled out after thawing but others are more obstinate. If shells are placed near ant colonies the ants will gradually eat out the contents, a slow but widely used cleaning procedure. The smell of a dead mollusc will also attract flies which lay their eggs in such unsavoury places and, with their larvae, are efficient but obnoxious cleaners. Whatever method is used, remnants of the soft parts often stay lodged inaccessibly within the shell. To eliminate the smells and unsightly liquids to which these remnants give rise, plunge the shell into methylated spirits for a few days. Remove and allow to dry, then plug the aperture with tissue paper. In time, the tissue paper may be removed.

Bivalve molluscs are easily cleaned because they usually gape widely when killed and the animal may be cut and scraped away. To maintain the valves in a closed position tie cotton thread around the freshly cleaned specimen. Chitons demand special treatment or they just curl up and stay curled up when killed. Induce a chiton to crawl on to a flat piece of glass or plastic in a dish containing sea water. Press down on the chiton, pour off the water and replace with alcohol of about 70% strength. After a minute held down in the alcohol, the chiton may be released. It is now dead and should stay in a natural uncurled position. Later on, it may be taken out of the alcohol and the soft parts removed. Chitons may also be tied down to flat sticks with cotton thread to achieve a similar result.

Many shells have disfiguring deposits and growths on them which the collector usually wants to remove. A stiff brush will remove some of them, but the harder incrustations remain. Immersion for a few hours in diluted domestic bleach tends to loosen them. They may then be brushed or chipped away, but do not treat them roughly and be philosophical about the deposits which do not respond to treatment. Shell cleaning is an art which must be cultivated; there are no short cuts.

The cleaned and thoroughly dried shells must be stored. Shells may be kept in open card trays, clear plastic boxes, cardboard boxes, match boxes, glass tubes, tins or other receptacles. They may be tastefully mounted in glass-topped table cases, embedded in clear plastic or simply placed on a shelf. For study purposes, they are best placed in see-through receptacles. Wherever they are stored, protect them from damp and do not over-expose them to light; damp conditions help promote fungal growths which eat into the shell, and over-exposure to light will surely cause their colours to fade.

Labels are essential. Without them, shells are almost valueless scientifically and less desirable commercially. The most important information on a label is of locality, date of collection and the name of the collector. Of secondary importance is the species name because this is subjective information which may be added at any time. Labels should be made of high grade paper to prevent their deterioration. Those accompanying specimens preserved in alcohol or other fluids must be able to retain their strength in those fluids. Indian ink should be used for labelling, although pencil is very suitable for labels kept in fluids. Temporary field collecting labels and notes should also be pencilled.

Identification
The principal objective of this book is to enable shells to be identified by means of descriptions and photographs. Identification down to family or genus level should also be possible for many of the species which are not featured in it. The bibliography gives references to some other books which are useful for identification purposes. It will soon become clear to the collector that even if he owns all the shell books now in print, he will still be unable to put a name to many of the specimens he acquires. It is then that he needs to seek

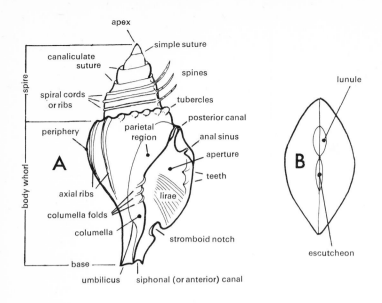
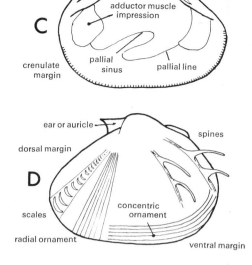
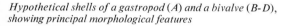

Hypothetical shells of a gastropod (A) and a bivalve (B-D), showing principal morphological features

the help of other collectors. Joining one of the many shell clubs is perhaps the best way to make contact with other collectors. Enquiries at a local library should produce the names and addresses of one or more of these organisations, although some parts of the world are still without shell clubs. Much may be gained from postal contacts, but it is far more helpful to associate with experienced collectors.

A shell may be easily identified by comparing it with a good photograph. Often, however, there are shell features which are not easily seen in a photograph and these must be described in words. The specialised terminology of some of these features is not very obscure, although at first sight some of the terms are puzzling. The text drawings given here show the more important features referred to in this book.

Distribution

Climate, temperature, ocean currents, depth of water, breeding habits and other factors prevent molluscs from spreading haphazardly over the globe. A species which thrives where there is warmth, sunlight, calm water and abundant food is unlikely to be found in cold, sunless, turbulent places with a limited food supply. Between these extremes, of course, there are places which meet the demands of a wide variety of species. It is not surprising, therefore, that the distribution of molluscs and other animals follows a pattern. About the middle of the nineteenth century, S. P. Woodward analysed the distribution patterns of molluscs on a world-wide basis. He discovered that the range of a mollusc was limited to a certain zone, or zoogeographical province, or often to more than one. He distinguished and named about 16 principal provinces, each containing a high proportion (at least 50%) of species which were absent from all other provinces. As molluscs do not recognise political boundaries, it is more scientific and much more convenient to refer to their actual, or zoogeographical range, using the names of the provinces in which they occur. The map indicates the provinces and their names. Their limits are as follows.

Aleutian Aleutian Islands, coasts of Alaska to British Columbia, Sea of Okhotsk.
Arctic All above Arctic Circle, southern end of Greenland, east coast of Kamchatka, east coast of Canada to Gulf of St Lawrence.
Australian Australia south of Brisbane on the east and south of Geraldton on the west, Tasmania, New Zealand.
Boreal North-east coast of North America from Gulf of St Lawrence to Cape Cod, south coast of Iceland, Norway, Shetlands, Faroes, British Isles, Baltic. As used here, the term Boreal always implies that a species occurs in the eastern part of the province but not necessarily the western part, unless there is a qualification to the contrary.
Californian West coast of North America from British Columbia to the Gulf of California.
Caribbean South Florida, Caribbean Sea, Gulf of Mexico, West Indies, Antilles, east coast of South America down to Rio de Janeiro. This is a wider interpretation of the province than is generally accepted.
Indo-Pacific Indian Ocean and Pacific Ocean from Suez and Durban on the west to Clipperton Island on the east and comprising all the island groups of the Indian Ocean, Australia north of Brisbane on the east and north of Geraldton on the west, Polynesia, Melanesia, Indonesia and islands and coasts northwards to Korea and the China Sea.
Japonic Japan and east coast of Korea.
Magellanic Antarctica, Southern Chile, Tierra del Fuego, Falkland Islands, South Georgia and other islands in comparable southern latitudes.
Mediterranean Mediterranean, Black Sea, Azores, Canaries, Atlantic coasts from Bay of Biscay to the Spanish Sahara.
Panamic Gulf of California to Ecuador.
Patagonian East coast of South America from Rio de Janeiro to Tierra del Fuego.
Peruvian West coast of South America between Ecuador and Southern Chile.
South African South African coast.
Transatlantic East coast of North America from Cape Cod to half way down east coast of Florida.
West African West coast of Africa from the Spanish Sahara to southern end of Angola, Cape Verde Islands and islands in the Bight of Biafra.

Shell collecting past and present

As a recreation, shell collecting has ancient roots. In prehistoric times, shells were collected for ornamental purposes and must have been as important and attractive to some cultures as gold and jewels are to us now. The Romans collected shells as playthings for the leisured class. During the Renaissance, shells were treasured collectors' items in Europe. The Netherlands, through its trade with the East Indies, became the acknowledged centre of conchological activity, although shells were not the only natural objects which found their way into cabinets of curiosities belonging to dilettante collectors of that period.

The publication in the late seventeenth century of the first illustrated shell books opened the way to a wider appreciation of shells. Noblemen and wealthy merchants were prepared to spend a lot of money on shells brought back to Europe by Dutch sailors and later by others. By the end of the eighteenth century, many additional species had been brought to Europe by men who sailed on voyages of discovery: the conchological riches of the Central Pacific and Australasia had been tapped for the first time.

The nineteenth century saw a remarkable increase in the numbers of new, or supposedly new, species and many important, often lavishly illustrated books were produced to satisfy the demands of collectors and students who must have thought that the flood of novelties would never cease. In those days, collectors usually wanted examples of every kind of shell obtainable for their collections. Quality rather than scientific accuracy was their watchword. Then, as now, they had to pay high prices for top quality specimens, but most of them would not have contemplated trying to collect exotic shells themselves. Dealers provided them with every-thing. The few who did venture abroad to distant seas risked their lives to collect desirable shells. The scientific aspects of shell collecting appealed to very few. Those few, however, published an astonishing number of books and lesser articles on the subject. By the end of the nineteenth century, conchology had become as much a scientific pursuit as a pleasurable hobby and shell collectors began to demand and to provide more accurate data with their shells.

For economic reasons, Europe after World War I was no longer the centre of conchological activities that it had been before. The United States had steadily increased in stature as a shell collecting nation and began to assume leadership in the conchological world. At the same time, residents in countries as far apart as Japan, the Philippines, Fiji and Mauritius were making collections of their local shells and exchanging them amongst themselves. During and after World War II, interest in shell collecting mushroomed as a direct result of overseas postings of men and women to places in the Pacific and elsewhere. Shell collecting was becoming a popular hobby on a grand scale. Scuba diving and snorkelling extended collecting possibilities and brought into circulation countless specimens of high quality.

Shell collecting has never been out of fashion but it now has an unprecedented number of devotees. Its past is fascinating, its present exciting. Its future could largely depend on the intelligence and foresight of collectors such as those who use this book.

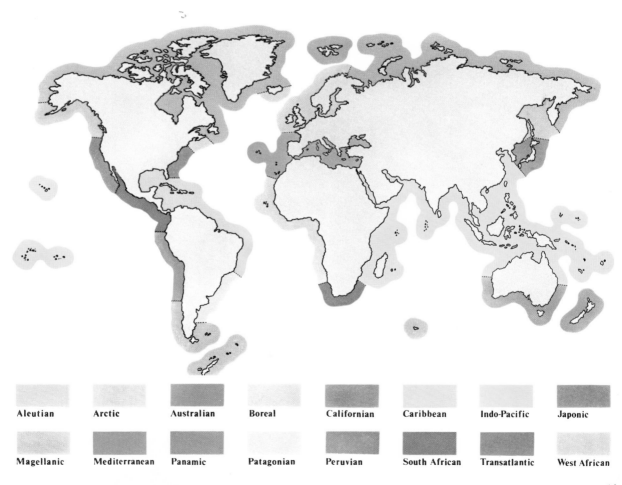

| Aleutian | Arctic | Australian | Boreal | Californian | Caribbean | Indo-Pacific | Japonic |

| Magellanic | Mediterranean | Panamic | Patagonian | Peruvian | South African | Transatlantic | West African |

Identification Key

This key is a general guide to the identification of families based entirely on the shell and covering only the genera and species described in this book. It ignores the soft anatomy of the animal and its accessory hard parts, which are often missing. The section dealing with bivalves, however, assumes that both valves are present and unworn. The key is entirely artificial in character and does not reflect the relationships of the species.

Where a family name is given without qualification, the preceding description should be taken as applying to most but not necessarily all members of the family. Numbers given in parentheses are page references to the family or the first genus mentioned within it.

Shell in more than two pieces: AMPHINEURA — Chitonidae (25), Ischnochitonidae (25).

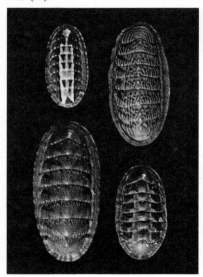

Shell in two pieces of equal or unequal size joined by hinge: BIVALVIA (for key, see p.21).

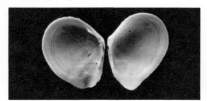

Shell in one piece; if with a calcareous or corneous operculum, then shell clearly spiral.
A. Shell tusk-shaped: **SCAPHOPODA–Dentaliidae (26).**

B. Shell not strongly spiral in external appearance, or very compressed and with body whorl forming almost entire surface: **GASTROPODA** (part).
a) Patelliform: **Patellidae** (34), Acmaeidae (36).

b) Patelliform and emarginate, or with slit or apical hole: **Fissurellidae (31).**

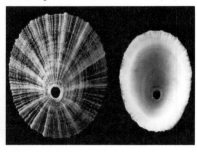

c) Patelliform with tightly coiled apex: **Capulidae (72).**

d) Patelliform with shelf-like or cup-like internal appendage: **Calyptraeidae (72).**

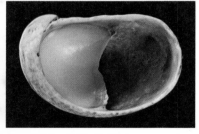

e) Patelliform with strongly recurved spire immersed in body whorl: **Muricidae** (*Concholepas*, 134), **Triviidae** (*Pedicularia*, 87).

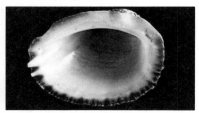

f) Extremely compressed spiral with very wide aperture: **Naticidae** (*Sinum*, 102).

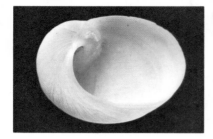

g) As f) but with row of perforations: **Haliotidae** (28).

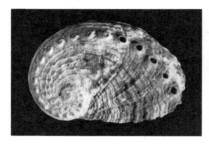

h) Solid and more or less globular with concealed spire and narrow aperture: **Triviidae** (87), **Cypraeidae** (cowries, 88), **Amphiperatidae** (99), **Marginellidae** (some species only, 192).

i) Thin, more or less globular, with sunken spire: **Hydatinidae** (220), **Bullidae** (220), **Scaphandridae** (221).

j) Spindle-shaped with concealed spire: **Amphiperatidae** (*Volva*, 99).

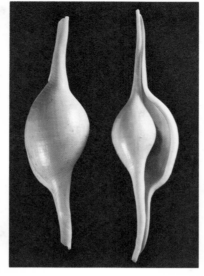

C. Shell coiled only in early stages, then growth irregular: **GASTROPODA** Siliquariidae (63), Coralliophilidae (*Magilus*, 138).

D. Shell coiled, bilaterally symmetrical – no spire: **CEPHALOPODA** – Nautilidae, Argonautidae (275), **Spirulidae** (276).

E. Shell spirally coiled, usually with spire raised: **GASTROPODA.**

a) Without siphonal canal or siphonal notch.
1) Very tall (height at least three times width).
i) spiral ornament only: **Turritellidae** (60).

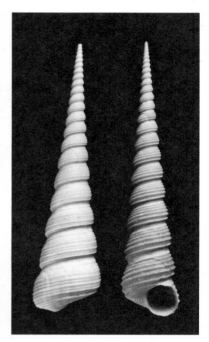

ii) axial or cancellate ornament: **Epitoniidae** (some species, 70).

2) With regular, thin varices: **Epitoniidae** (70).

3) Flat-topped with round aperture, sometimes spiny: **Angariidae** (47).

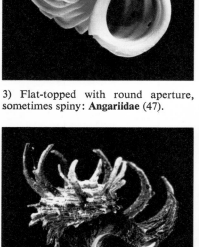

4) Covered with shells and other debris: **Xenophoridae** (*Xenophora*, 74).

5) Very flattened (width at least twice height).

i) With wide 'spiral staircase' umbilicus: **Architectonicidae** (62).

ii) With long peripheral spines or peripheral flange: **Turbinidae** (*Guildfordia*, 52), **Xenophoridae** (*Tugurium, Stellaria*, 74).

6) Body whorl much larger than spire.
i) Shell thin: **Lamellariidae** (86).

ii) Shell thick, with umbilicus (sometimes filled in): **Naticidae** (100).

iii) Shell thick, without umbilicus: **Neritidae** (55), **Littorinidae** (*Littorina littoralis*, 58).

7) Shell more or less top-shaped, with periphery to some extent keeled: **Trochidae** (most species, 37), **Turbinidae** (*Astraea*, 48), **Littorinidae** (*Echininus, Tectarius*, 59).

8) Shell elongate top-shaped: **Trochidae** (*Bankivia*, *Cantharidus*, 37), **Eulimidae** (70).

9) Shell more or less turban-shaped: **Trochidae** (*Cittarium*, *Diloma*, 39), **Turbinidae** (48), **Littorinidae** (*Littorina*, 57).

12) Similar to 9) but with truncate columella: **Planaxidae** (63).

11) Similar to 9) but with tooth on columella: **Modulidae** (64).

10) Similar to 9) but more elongate: **Phasianellidae** (54).

13) Small, elongate shells with widely expanded outer lip: **Rissoidae** (59).

14) Small, thin, ovate shells with one or two curved folds on columella: **Acteonidae** (220).

b) With siphonal canal or siphonal notch.

1) Conical to biconical shells with aperture as long as body whorl and usually narrow: **Cassididae** (*Morum tuberculosum*, 111), **Mitridae** (*Imbricaria*, 178), **Conidae** (200).

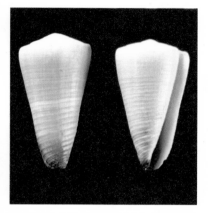

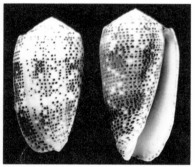

2) Thin shells with sharply angled whorls and broad, flat platform from suture to shoulder: **Thatcheriidae** (200).

3) Elongate to extremely elongate, but not spindle-shaped. With numerous whorls and aperture small in relation to length of shell.

i) Outer lip thickened or expanded; often with reflected or oblique siphonal canal: **Potamididae** (64), **Cerithiidae** (65).

ii) Outer lip not thickened or expanded: **Terebridae** (215).

4) Extremely thin, turban-shaped, always with purple coloration: **Janthinidae** (71).

5) Pear-shaped shells with long, tapering, relatively broad siphonal canal: **Ficidae** (120), **Coralliophilidae** (*Rapa*, 144), **Melongenidae** (some species of *Busycon*, 154).

6) Outer lip widely expanded, or with spines or digitations, but shell without varices: **Aporrhaidae** (75), **Strombidae** (*Lambis*, some species of *Strombus*, 77), **Muricidae** (some species of *Drupa*, 130).

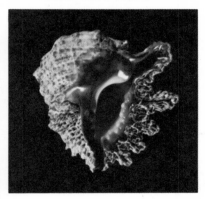

7) Large, thin, globular shells with thin outer lip, and without folds on the columella or varices: **Tonnidae** (*Tonna*, 118).

8) Thick, inflated shells with thickened, reflected, often denticulate outer lip and reflected siphonal canal, with or without strong varices: **Cassididae** (102), **Tonnidae** (*Malea*, 119).

9) Shell with conspicuous varices, but not as 8).
i) With conspicuous posterior siphonal canal at upper edge of outer lip: **Cymatiidae** (some species, 108), **Bursidae** (114).

ii) Without conspicuous posterior siphonal canal: **Strombidae** (*Varicospira*, 77), **Cymatiidae** (some species, 108), **Muricidae** (120).

10) Surface smooth and highly polished.
i) Outer lip conspicuously thickened: **Marginellidae** (192).

ii) Outer lip not conspicuously thickened: **Strombidae** (*Terebellum*, 75), **Olividae** (165), **Mitridae** (*Swainsonia*, 176), **Volutidae** (some species, 182).

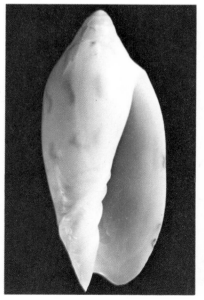

17

11) Siphonal canal forming spine, sometimes very long: **Strombidae** (*Tibia*, 75).

12) With stromboid notch as well as siphonal notch: **Strombidae** (*Strombus*, 80).

13) Thick, globular, nodose or spiny shells with strongly toothed aperture: **Muricidae** (*Drupa*, 130).

14) With true or false umbilicus more or less conspicuous, and not as in 1) to 13): **Trichotropidae** (63), **Muricidae** (*Thais, Acanthina, Rapana*, 132), **Coralliophilidae** (*Latiaxis*, some species of *Coralliophila*, 136), **Buccinidae** (*Neptunea, Penion, Babylonia*, 139), **Fasciolariidae** (some species, 160).

15) Without more or less conspicuous umbilicus and not as 1) to 13).
i) Narrow, spindle-shaped shells with long or moderately long siphonal canal:
— with notch or slit in upper part of outer lip: **Turridae** (197).

— without notch or slit in upper part of outer lip: **Fasciolariidae** (*Fusinus*, some species of *Fasciolaria*, 160).

ii) With elongate, narrow siphonal canal, but shell broader than in i): **Muricidae** (*Columbarium*, *Forreria*, 129), **Fasciolariidae** (*Pleuroploca*, some species of *Fasciolaria*, 160), **Vasidae** (*Tudicula*, *Tudicla*, *Afer*, 179).

iii) Inflated shells with large body whorl and numerous regular axial ribs or lamellae: **Muricidae** (*Trophon*, 130), **Harpidae** (180).

iv) Siphonal canal recurved but not very long and narrow: **Cymatiidae** (*Linatella*, 113), **Buccinidae** (*Siphonalia*, *Penion*, *Euthria*, 139), **Pyrenidae** (some species of *Strombina*, 153), **Melongenidae** (some species of *Busycon*, 154), **Fasciolariidae** (*Peristernia*, some species of *Fasciolaria* and *Latirus*, 160), **Turridae** (*Pusionella*, 197).

v) With small posterior notch or siphonal canal at upper end of outer lip, and with parietal callus or tooth: **Bursidae** (*Bursa marginata*, 116), **Muricidae** (*Morula*, *Vexilla*, 132), **Buccinidae** (*Cominella*, *Burnupena*, some species of *Pisania* and *Cantharus* 144), **Nassariidae** (155).

vi) With strong tooth at base of outer lip, **Muricidae** (*Acanthina*, 134), **Buccinidae** (*Opeatostoma*, 146).

vii) Columella with ten or less folds, and not as i) to vi): **Pyrenidae** (some species, 150), **Fasciolariidae** (*Pleuroploca*, some species of *Latirus*, 161), **Mitridae** (169), **Vasidae** (*Vasum*, 178), **Xancidae** (180), **Volutidae** (181), **Cancellariidae** (some species, 191).

viii) Columella without folds and not as
i) to vi):
—inner margin of outer lip not dentate,
denticulate, crenulate or lirate: **Struthiolariidae** (75), **Cassididae** (*Cassidaria*,
102), **Buccinidae** (*Neptunea*, *Metula*,
Buccinum, some species of *Buccinulum*,
139), **Nassariidae** (*Bullia*, 158), **Melongenidae** (*Melongena*, 154).

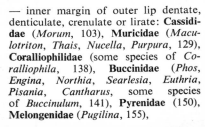

— inner margin of outer lip dentate,
denticulate, crenulate or lirate: **Cassididae** (*Morum*, 103), **Muricidae** (*Maculotriton*, *Thais*, *Nucella*, *Purpura*, 129),
Coralliophilidae (some species of *Coralliophila*, 138), **Buccinidae** (*Phos*,
Engina, *Northia*, *Searlesia*, *Euthria*,
Pisania, *Cantharus*, some species
of *Buccinulum*, 141), **Pyrenidae** (150),
Melongenidae (*Pugilina*, 155),

Shell in two pieces of equal or unequal size, joined by hinge: BIVALVIA.

A. With finger-like internal process projecting from umbonal cavity of each valve: **Pholadidae** (272), **Thraciidae** (274).

B. Umbones terminal or near-terminal: **Mytilidae** (226), **Pinnidae** (229), **Carditidae** (some species, 243), **Solenidae** (253,) **Cultellidae** (*Ensis, Phaxas*, 254), **Pholadidae** (272), **Hiatellidae** (272),

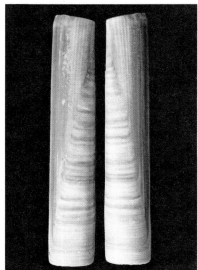

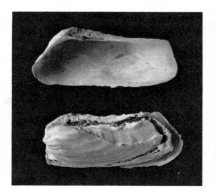

C. Anterior and/or posterior dorsal margin produced into long wing: **Pteriidae** (*Pteria*, 230), **Malleidae** (230).

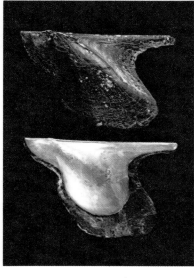

D. With small, more or less triangular projections on each side of umbo: **Pectinidae** (231), **Spondylidae** (some species, 237), **Limidae** (some species, 239).

E. With hole below umbo in one valve (but not smooth, bevelled hole caused by predatory molluscs such as Naticidae): **Anomiidae** (*Anomia*, 238), **Thraciidae** (*Thracia conradi*, 274).

F. Shell with one or more gapes, i.e. points at which valve margins do not meet when shell is closed: **Nuculanidae** (222), **Solemyidae** (223), **Arcidae** (some species of *Arca*, 223), **Limidae** (some species, 239), **Cardiidae** (*Cardium costatum*, 246), **Tridacnidae** (249), **Mactridae** (*Lutraria*, 252), **Psammobiidae** (261), **Solecurtidae** (262), **Myidae** (271), **Lyonsiidae** (273), **Periplomatidae** (274).

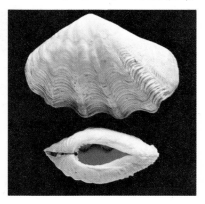

G. Shell clearly inequivalve, not gaping: **Spondylidae** (237), **Ostreidae** (some species, 240), **Chamidae** (242), **Tellinidae** (*Tellidora*, *Macoma*, 238), **Corbulidae** (271), **Myochamidae** (274), **Thraciidae** (274).

H. Shell equivalve, not gaping.
a) Shell with long or short spines or processes: **Spondylidae** (237), **Chamidae** (242), **Cardiidae** (*Acanthocardia*, 246), **Veneridae** (*Pitar lupanaria*, 265).

b) Shell inflated, with conspicuously in-rolled, widely separated umbones: **Glossidae** (263).

c) Shell antero-posteriorly flattened, with inrolled, overlapping umbones: **Cardiidae** (*Corculum*, 248).

d) Single adductor muscle impression in each valve: **Pteriidae** (*Pinctada*, 230), **Limidae** (239), **Anomiidae** (239), **Ostreidae** (240).

e) Not as a) to d) and with pallial line not indented by a sinus.
1) With plate-like process descending from below dorsal margin: **Cucullaeidae** (225).

2) With series of small teeth on hinge line meeting below umbones: **Nuculidae** (222), **Arcidae** (223), **Noetiidae** (225), **Glycymerididae** (225).

3) Not as 1) and 2), and without radial ornament, but often with concentric ornament: **Lucinidae** (*Lucina*, 241), **Astartidae** (245), **Crassatellidae** (245), **Arcticidae** (263).

4) Not as 1) and 2) and with radial, and sometimes also concentric, ornament: **Trigoniidae** (241), **Lucinidae** (241), **Fimbriidae** (242), **Carditidae** (243), **Cardiidae** (246).

f) Not as a) to d) and with pallial line indented with a sinus.
1) With internal rib from umbo to anterior ventral margin: **Cultellidae** (*Siliqua*, 262).

2) At least one valve with three cardinal teeth: **Veneridae** (263), **Petricolidae** (271).

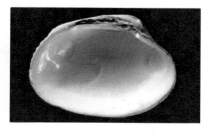

3) With two cardinal teeth in each valve, and often with flexure on posterodorsal slope: **Tellinidae** (255), **Donacidae** (259).

4) At least one valve with only one cardinal tooth; other with not more than two: **Mactridae** (250), **Mesodesmatidae** (253), **Scrobiculariidae** (262), **Semelidae** (262).

23

Class AMPHINEURA

Moderately large class of exclusively marine molluscs comprising two subclasses: the Aplacophora and the Polyplacophora. Members of the Aplacophora have no shells and are ignored here. Members of the Polyplacophora, commonly known as chitons, have a shell consisting of eight articulating pieces (or valves) attached to the back of a soft-bodied animal. Surrounding the valves and binding them together is a muscular band (or girdle) which may be smooth, or ornamented with spines, scales or chitinous hairs. Body of animal bilaterally symmetrical. Radula present but tentacles and cephalic eyes absent. Shell valves variously ornamented. Tiny, eye-like structures present in upper shell layer. Most species live attached to or under rocks and stones in shallow water, where they browse on algae and other small organisms. Many genera have been proposed for the 500 or more species. Found in nearly all seas, but particularly abundant in Australian and Peruvian provinces. Identification largely based on features which cannot be examined without disarticulating the valves. Description of these features, which necessitates complicated nomenclature, is considered unnecessary for the few species described here.

Family CHITONIDAE

Small to large shells with more or less strongly developed ornament on valves. Principal differentiating characteristics not visible without disarticulating valves. Girdle usually prominently ornamented with spines, spicules, hairs or scales. Seven genera.

Genus CHITON Linnaeus

Medium-sized to large shells with lateral areas of valves generally raised and prominent, their surface smooth to radially or concentrically ribbed, sometimes both. Median area of valves smooth or with longitudinal lines. Girdle usually covered by smooth, large scales. Numerous species in most seas.

Chiton cumingi Frembly   × 0·6

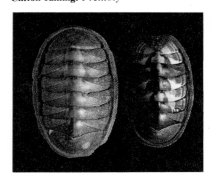

Large, broad, elevated shell. Head and tail valves and lateral areas of intermediate valves strongly ribbed and beaded. Fine, longitudinal lines on median area of valves. Girdle broad and granulose. Very variable colour and pattern. Usually greenish or pale brown with irregular, blackish and yellowish areas on some valves. Often with fine lines encircling whole shell. Girdle light green with dark green, lateral bands. 4–7cm. Peruvian (Chile). Common.

Chiton sulcatus Wood   × 0·8

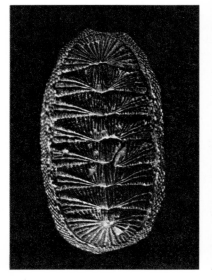

Large, thick, elevated shell. Valves heavily ribbed all over, ribs being closer together on median area. Girdle covered with large, raised granules. Unicolorous black. Granules on girdle brown, green and yellowish. 6–8cm. Panamic (Galapagos Islands). Common.

Genus ONITHOCHITON Gray

Small to large, oval or broadly ovate shells. Usually elevated and rounded rather than arched. Polished surface has fine, longitudinal lines and low nodules. Pale brown, triangular and flattened. Girdle fleshy and ornamented with tiny hairs, spicules or scales. Few species in tropical and warm seas.

Onithochiton neglectus Rochebrune × 0·9
Moderately large, broadly ovate shell with

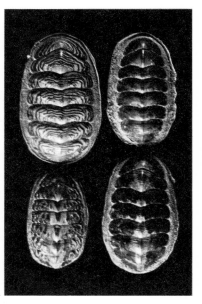

valves rounded and low. Girdle moderately broad, fleshy and scaly. Variable colour and pattern. Yellowish brown with concentric, dark brown lines, sometimes dark brown blotched with red, orange or yellow. Girdle dark brown. 3·0–4·5cm. Australian (New Zealand). Common.

Family ISCHNOCHITONIDAE

Ovate to elongate shells with diagonal ribs on both sides of each of the six intermediate valves which divides them into distinct lateral and central areas. Principal differentiating characteristics not visible without disarticulating valves; girdle bare or ornamented with small or minute scales, bristles or granules. Eight genera.

Genus ISCHNOCHITON Gray

For details, see Family Ischnochitonidae. Numerous species in most seas.

Ischnochiton crispus Reeve ×1·2

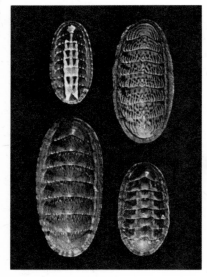

Small, elongate and elevated shell with almost smooth valves and narrow, rough girdle. Considerable variation in colour and pattern. Usually light or dark green with or without white, median zone on all valves. Sometimes unicolorous white, or pale brown with greenish stripes encircling shell. Girdle dull brown, sometimes with darker brown, lateral bands. 2·5–3·5cm. Australian (South Australia). Common.

Genus LEPIDOCHITONA Gray
Trachydermon Carpenter,
Lepidochiton Thiele.
Small to medium-sized shells with moderately elevated valves. Smooth or finely granulose. Girdle ornamented with minute, scaly processes. Numerous species in temperate and cold seas.

Lepidochitona lineata Wood ×0·9

Medium-sized shell with broad girdle. Valves pink or reddish brown, lateral areas decorated with longitudinal, dark brown and white stripes. Ventral area sometimes has central, white band. Girdle dark brown. 2·5–4·0cm. Californian. Common.

Class SCAPHOPODA

Small class of exclusively marine molluscs immediately recognisable by their tubular shells open at both ends. Apertural, or anterior, end is usually wider than anal, or posterior, end. Family Siphonodentaliidae comprises small, translucent and fragile species in which shell is swollen in middle. Family Dentaliidae comprises larger and stronger species, usually called tusk shells. In this family, posterior end is often notched. Tusk shells lie buried on sandy seabed with posterior end exposed above sand. The animals have a radula but lack eyes. Conical foot protrudes from posterior end. Tentacle-like filaments capture small organisms and pass them to the mouth.

Family DENTALIIDAE
Tubular, tapering, usually thin and colourless shells. Anterior opening (aperture) larger than posterior, or anal, opening. Posterior opening often notched. Straight, almost straight, or curved (arcuate). Smooth or ornamented with longitudinal ribs, rarely with spiral, or annular, rings. Shape in cross section usually circular but modified by longitudinal ornament. Numerous genera have been proposed but as species are very similar they may conveniently be grouped under the single genus *Dentalium*. Known as tusk shells. Widely distributed in all seas. Some species live at great depths.

Genus DENTALIUM Linnaeus
For details see Family Dentaliidae. About 300 species varying in size from a few millimetres to about 15cm.

Dentalium aprinum Linnaeus ×0·9

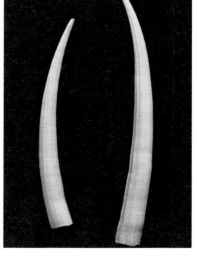

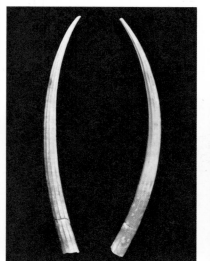

Similar to *D. elephantinum* but thinner-shelled, narrower throughout, paler green. 5·5–7·5cm. Indo-Pacific. Common.

Dentalium bisexangulatum Sowerby ×1·0
Thin, arcuate shell with twelve longitudinal ribs. Round in cross section. No posterior notch. White, porcellaneous surface. 5·2–7·8cm. Indo-Pacific (Philippines). Uncommon.

Dentalium elephantinum Linnaeus ×0·8
Large, thick, arcuate. Longitudinally ribbed. Greenish anterior end fading to

whitish at posterior. Notched posterior opening. 6·2–10·0cm. Indo-Pacific (Philippines). Common.

Dentalium entalis Linnaeus
Slightly arcuate, with fine, irregular, annular growth lines. Posterior end not notched. 3·0–3·5cm. Boreal. Common.

Dentalium ergasticum Fischer   × 0·8

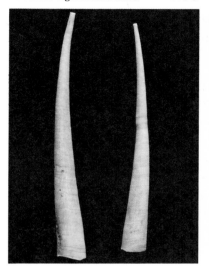

Thick, slightly arcuate. Fine longitudinal striae. Notched posterior end. Dull, whitish or yellow. 7·5–9·0cm. Mediterranean. Uncommon.

Dentalium inaequicostatum Dautzenberg
Slightly arcuate, solid and usually opaque, occasionally translucent. 9–12 longitudinal ridges which tend to become obsolete towards aperture. 3–6cm. Mediterranean. Common.

Dentalium longitrorsum Reeve   × 0·9

Shell thin, long, slightly arcuate. Aperture rounded. Dull, off-white. 6·0–7·5cm. Indo-Pacific. Frequent.

Dentalium lubricatum Sowerby   × 1·2
Shell thin, translucent, slightly arcuate and

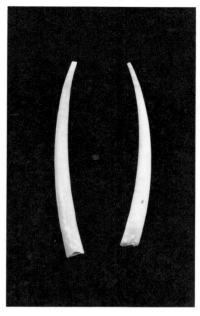

gently tapering. Smooth and moderately glossy. Whitish. 4·0–4·5cm. Indo-Pacific (Pacific). Uncommon.

Dentalium mannarensis Winckworth ×1·6

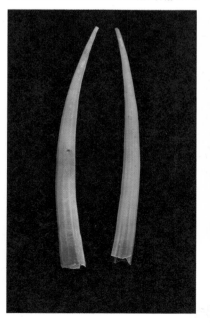

Very thin, almost straight shell. Dull, white and semi-transparent towards polygonal aperture. No posterior notch. 3·0–4·5cm.

Indo-Pacific (Indian Ocean, Gulf of Mannar). Frequent.

Dentalium rectum Gmelin   × 1·0
Shell very thick, slightly arcuate, with broad aperture, narrowing fairly steeply

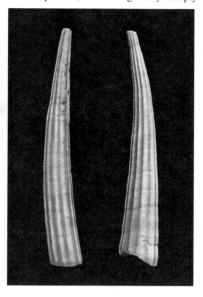

towards posterior. Small notch at posterior end. Strong, thick, longitudinal ribs crossed by fine growth striae. Dull, off-white. 6·5–8·5cm. Mediterranean. Uncommon.

Dentalium sexcostatum Sowerby   × 1·1

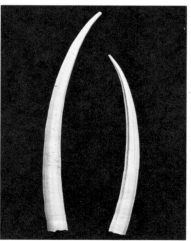

Thin, arcuate, with six strong, longitudinal ribs and three weak ridges in each of the interstices. White, six-sided aperture. Posterior notch. 4·5–6·0cm. Japonic. Uncommon.

Dentalium shoplandi Jousseaume   × 0·9
megathyris Dall.
Thick, almost straight shell with strong,

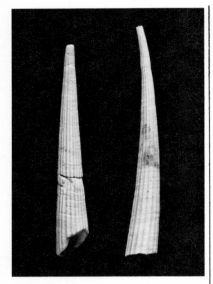

longitudinal ribs. Round in cross section. 6·2–7·0cm. Indo-Pacific (Arabian Sea). Rare.

Dentalium vernedei Sowerby $\times$ 0·5

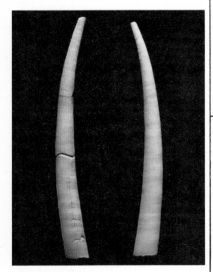

Probably largest tusk shell. Tube moderately arcuate, circular in cross section. Notched posterior end. Densely covered with fine, longitudinal threads. White, sometimes ringed with pale brown or yellow. 12–15cm. Japonic. Common.

Dentalium vulgare Da Costa
Thick, slightly arcuate. Posterior notched. Smooth, dull, white, cream or yellow. 2·7–2·9cm. Boreal. Common.

Dentalium zelandicum Sowerby
Thin, slightly arcuate. Longitudinal ribs, stronger near apex. White or cream. 5·2–6·0cm. Australian (New Zealand). Uncommon.

Class
GASTROPODA

Largest class of the Mollusca, with about 80,000 species. The term Gastropod signifies that the animal crawls on its stomach, which is not strictly true: in most species, the visceral mass containing the digestive organs is contained within the shell which is carried above the foot. Hallmark of gastropods is a one-piece shell which is usually coiled around the central axis and is therefore bilaterally asymmetrical. In limpet-like species, such as *Patella*, the shell is often symmetrical although the anatomy of the contained animals displays asymmetrical features. Coiling of shell may be right-handed (dextral), i.e. clockwise when viewed from apex, or left-handed (Sinistral), i.e. anti-clockwise when viewed from apex. Shells coiled in a direction contrary to the normal are rare and are usually highly prized by collectors. Most gastropods crawl on a large, flat, muscular foot and have tentacles with eyes at their bases or at their tips. Nearly all marine gastropods are equipped with gills, and many species have a well-developed siphon, which is often contained within a long or short tube or channel at the anterior end of the shell (the siphonal canal). Many gastropods possess a corneous or calcareous plate, known as the operculum, which is attached to the upper surface of the foot and partially or completely seals the aperture when the animal withdraws into its shell. The operculum is variously ornamented and is often important in classification and identification. Shape and ornamentation in gastropod shells varies enormously from group to group, and there is often a correlation between these features and the habits of the animals. In life, if the shell is glossy and smooth, it is usually enveloped in the fleshy folds of the animal's mantle, the organ which secretes the material composing the shell. Dull shells with spiny or tubercular processes are not enveloped by the mantle, and in these species there is often a thin or thick outer layer on the shell, known as the periostracum; this layer often masks the underlying colour and pattern of the shell. Gastropods are carnivorous, herbivorous, or omnivorous and their mode of feeding is usually reflected in the character of the radula, hence its importance in classification. The many marine gastropods without shells are not featured in this book, but it should be pointed out that they are very numerous in the sea, often very beautiful, and essentially similar in most other respects to shelled gastropods. The only other class with shell-less species is Cephalopoda.

Superfamily
Pleurotomariacea

Family HALIOTIDAE

The abalones or ormers. Nacreous, spiral shells with small spire and large, dish-shaped body whorl with a row of perforations above outer margin. Columellar margin produced into a flattened spiral. Horseshoe-shaped muscle impression with left branch inside columellar plate, right branch very large, rounded and central in aperture. No operculum. One genus. Australian province rich in species. Found mostly in shallow waters of warmer seas.

Genus HALIOTIS Linnaeus
Details as for Family Haliotidae. About 50 species which some authorities distribute among several genera.

Haliotis asinina Linnaeus $\times$ 0·5
Thin, elliptical shell with 6–7 open, ovate perforations. Apex near margin. Axial growth lines crossed by spaced ridges,

strongest near spire. Olive green with olive brown and cream markings, flecks and stripes. Nacreous interior with pink and green predominant. 8–10cm. Indo-Pacific. Common.

Haliotis conicopora Peron
vixlirata Cotton, *granti* Pritchard & Gatliff.
Large, thick shell, with moderately raised spire and rather flat dorsal surface. About six or seven open holes on conical tubercles.

Depression between holes and margin. Irregular and interrupted axial folds crossed by weak spiral striae. Green or reddish brown with greenish patches and broad, green, curved rays. c20cm. Australian (Australia). Uncommon.

Haliotis corrugata Wood × 0·25
Pink Abalone

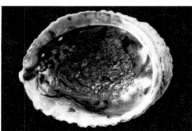

Subcircular shell is strongly convex. Nodulose ribs may be crossed by obliquely radiating corrugations. Ornamentation carinate at perforations and below these is a strong spiral channel. Elevated, tubular perforations, 2–4 of them open. Dull, olive brown shell with oblique, greenish streaks. Nacreous, dark red interior with large, rough muscle impression. c16cm. Californian. Frequent.

Haliotis cracherodii Leach × 0·3
Black Abalone

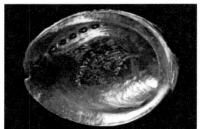

Ovate shell with depressed spire near margin. Convex body whorl with two sides equally curved. Not carinate at perforations, of which 5–9 are open. Smooth other than for spiral lirae. Dull, black shell with nacreous aperture iridescent red and green. 11–15cm. Californian. Common.

Haliotis cyclobates Peron
excavata Lamarck.
Shell almost circular in outline with relatively tall spire and rounded dorsal surface. About five or six open holes. Shallow depression below holes, then an oblique row of beaded ribs before margin. Weak, obliquely axial folds and strong, coarse spiral ribs. Brown and green, with irregular, cream rays. c6cm. Australian (Australia). Common.

Haliotis elegans Philippi
Very elongate shell with short spire situated near posterior margin. Up to eight or nine open, oval holes. Raised spiral ribs cover whole surface. Reddish brown or orange with spiral, creamy bands. c10cm. Australian (Western Australia). Uncommon.

Haliotis emmae Reeve
Ovate shell with short spire. About six or seven open holes on conical tubercles. Narrow groove between holes and several angular spiral ribs near margin. Rough spiral riblets and irregular, obliquely axial folds which are weaker near holes. Orange red with curved, irregular, cream axial rays. c10cm. Australian (Australia). Common.

Haliotis fulgens Philippi × 0·25
Green Abalone
splendens Reeve.
Ovate, convex shell with depressed spire. 30–40 spiral lirae on upper surface. Small,

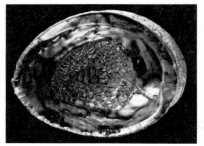

elevated perforations about five or six of which are open. Dull, reddish brown with dark, nacreous interior, mostly blue and green with coppery stains, pinkish within spire. Brilliant muscle impression. 15–25 cm. Californian. Common.

Haliotis iris Martyn × 0·4/0·3

Large, thick shell with 6–7 open, nearly circular perforations. Broad spiral ribs at lower margin and fine, axial growth ridges. Greenish. 10–17cm. Australian (New Zealand). Common.

Haliotis laevigata Donovan × 0·4
albicans Quoy & Gaimard, *excisa* Gray, *glabra* Swanson.
Thin shell with margins equally curved.

Convex body whorl not angulate at perforations. Apex a sixth to an eighth length of shell from margin. Wide, flattened columellar plate depressed and sloped inwards. About twelve perforations; small without raised borders. Smooth, dull with radiating scarlet and whitish bands. Aperture iridescent. 10–23cm. Australian. Frequent.

Haliotis midae Linnaeus   × 0·3

Large, thick, flat shell with nine open, circular and raised perforations. Conspicuous, raised, axial lamellae. Reddish or pinkish. 7–18cm. South African. Common.

Haliotis ovina Gmelin
latilabris Philippi.
Thin, ovate shell with short spire and low dorsal surface. About four open holes on conical tubercles. Shallow depression between holes and the several narrow ribs near margin. Weak spiral striae and low, rounded, axial folds sometimes forming rows of nodules. Greenish or brownish with broad, curved rays of yellow or white. *c*6cm. Indo-Pacific (West Pacific). Common.

Haliotis pustulata Reeve   × 1·1/0·8
pertusa Reeve, *alternata* Sowerby, *nebulata* Reeve, *revelata* Deshayes, *zealandica* Reeve, *strigata* Weinkauff.

Small, thick, elongate-oval shell with 5–6 open, nearly circular perforations. Strong spiral grooves and ridges crossed by fine, axial growth lines. Pinkish, mottled with reddish brown. 4–6cm. Indo-Pacific (Indian Ocean). Common.

Haliotis roei Gray   × 0·6

Thick, flattened shell with seven open, oval perforations. Strong, imbricate spiral cords with fine, axial growth lines. 5–8cm. Australian. Frequent.

Haliotis ruber Leach
clathrata Reeve, *improbulum* Iredale.
Thick, ovate shell, with short spire and rounded dorsal surface. Six or seven open holes on conical tubercles. Weak growth striae and broad axial folds crossed by fine, beaded spiral cords. Concave zone between holes and margin. Reddish brown with green, radiating rays. 18–30cm. Australian (Australia). Common.

Haliotis rufescens Swainson   × 0·25

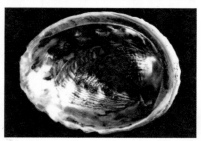

Very thick shell with four ovate, open perforations, elevated externally. Numerous narrow spiral ridges. Dull, pastel pink to rose shell. Nacreous interior with strong muscle impression; pink and green predominate. 25–30cm. Californian. Common.

Haliotis scalaris Leach
tricostalis Lamarck.
Thin, ovate shell with moderately raised spire. 4–6 open, nearly circular holes on high, conical tubercles. Broad, raised, central spiral rib ornamented with roughly scaled, spiral riblets and thin, axial lamellae. A deep smooth depression separates it from holes, and another deep, smooth depression separates holes from margin. Margin rough and warty. Orange red or brown with cream or light brown patches. *c*10cm. Australian (Australia). Uncommon.

Haliotis speciosa Reeve   × 0·8
alfredensis Bartsch.

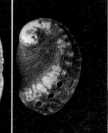

Fairly thick, flattened shell with 3–4 open, almost circular perforations. Fine spiral striae with irregular, axial growth lines. Brown and greenish white. 4–7cm. South African. Frequent.

Haliotis tuberculata Linnaeus
Thick, depressed shell with spire close to posterior margin. Three or four whorls, including body whorl. About 6 to 8 of the numerous rounded perforations are open. Ornamented with narrow, close set spiral grooves crossed by irregular growth lines. Reddish brown, often with a pale green cast, sometimes speckled with brown, pink or white. Light yellowish periostracum. Nacreous underside is dark towards margin. 8–10cm. Boreal. Mediterranean. Common.

Haliotis varia Linnaeus   × 0·8
viridis Reeve, *semistriata* Reeve, *concinna* Reeve, *astricta* Reeve, *rubiginosa* Reeve, *stomatiaeformis* Reeve.

Thick shell with warty or pustulose surface. 4–7 open, oval perforations. Extremely variable in ornament, colour and pattern. 3·5–8cm. Indo-Pacific (South West Pacific). Common.

Haliotis virginea Gmelin × 0·5

Thick, elliptical shell with apex at margin. Six open, oval perforations. Strong spiral ridges and weaker, axial growth lines. Brownish. 5–8cm. Indo-Pacific (New Zealand). Common.

Superfamily
Fissurellacea

Family FISSURELLIDAE

Conical, limpet-like shells with perforation, slit, notch or emargination. Muscle scar horseshoe-shaped, open anteriorly. Species attach themselves to rocky surfaces. Found in most seas usually in fairly shallow water. About 20 genera.

Genus EMARGINULA Lamarck

Small shells with a long or short marginal slit or notch at anterior end. Apex may be nearly central or situated posteriorly. Reticulate ornament usually on surface. Usually whitish. Numerous species in cold and warm seas.

Emarginula anassa Dean

Shell moderately large, thin and elevated with long slit. Strong axial ribs crossed in the interstices by finer, concentric lines giving reticulation. Apex small, pointed and downcurved. Dull, yellowish white. Interior greyish white. c2cm. Boreal (North West Europe). Rare.

Emarginula fissura Linnaeus × 2·0

Thin, moderately tall shell with central apex and relatively long notch. Strong radial ribs with weaker spiral ribs in interstices. Unicolorous white. c1cm. Boreal. Common.

Genus SCUTUS Montfort

Shield-shaped shells with flattened apex directed posteriorly, slightly incurved anterior end. Surface smooth or with weak, irregular ribs and prominent, concentric growth marks. White or creamy yellow, sometimes stained blackish on surface. Underside white or yellowish, occasionally with orange staining on muscle scar. Few species on rocks in shallow water in Indo-Pacific and Australian provinces.

Scutus anatinus Donovan × 0·35
longatus Blainville, *australis* Lamarck, *convexus* Quoy & Gaimard, *astrolabeus* Hedley.

Shell large, shield-shaped, flattened with parallel sides, slightly converging anteriorly. Anterior end slightly dented, posterior end rounded. Apex towards posterior end. Indistinct, elongated, horseshoe-shaped muscle impression on underside. Fine, irregular, spiral growth lines. Yellowish white. Underside white or yellowish white. 8–10cm. Australian. Common.

Scutus unguis Linnaeus

Shell smaller, thinner and relatively more elevated than *S. anatinus*. Apex also more raised and anterior end with more conspicuous indentation. Numerous fine, concentric growth ridges with indistinct ridges running to each side of anterior indentation. Some specimens with coarsely granular surface. Yellowish white. Underside nacreous white, darker towards apex. 2–4cm. Indo-Pacific, South African. Common.

Genus MEGATHURA Pilsbry

Shell and perforation large for the family. Faint muscle scar. Surface radially striate. Inner margin finely crenulate. Few species in Japonic and Californian provinces.

Megathura crenulata Sowerby × 0·6

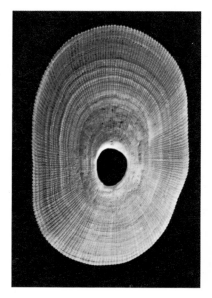

Large, radially and spirally striate shell with large, nearly central perforation. Mauve to brown, edge of perforation white. 7–15cm. Californian. Common.

Genus FISSURELLA Bruguière

Small to moderately large shells with a more or less central perforation. Inner margin of shell usually crenulate. Underside of perforation surrounded by a rounded callus. Many species in most seas; particularly numerous on West coast of South America.

Fissurella antillarum d'Orbigny × 0·9

Thick, tall shell with central, circular perforation. Strong, sharp-edged axial ridges crossed by numerous weaker spiral ribs forming points at intersections. Creamy white. Dark or pale green with

dark green rim round underside of perforation and whitish green blotches, white margin. 3–4cm. Caribbean. Common.

Fissurella lata Sowerby × 0·9

Thick, large, almost circular shell with central, oblong perforation. Low, irregular axial cords crossed by finer, concentric ribs. Yellowish green with broad, purplish or purple brown, interrupted rays. Pale or dark zone around perforation. Underside opaque white with purplish or greenish margin. 5–7cm. Peruvian (Chile). Common.

Fissurella listeri d'Orbigny × 0·7

Thick, solid, moderately raised shell with central, ovate perforation. Strong axial cords crossed by strong spiral ribs giving deeply cancellated surface. Underside radially grooved. Creamy white occasionally with greenish ridges and green blotches at margin. Rim of perforation dark green. Underside nacreous white. 3–4cm. Caribbean. Common.

Fissurella maxima Sowerby × 0·7 ▷
Large, thick, moderately elevated shell with lateral margins slightly raised. Relatively small, oblong, central perforation with sharp, raised, upper edge. Coarse, irregular axial ribs crossed by coarse spiral ribs. Roughly tuberculated at intersection

of ribs. Yellowish white with broad, brownish or purplish rays. Underside opaque white. 6–10cm. Peruvian (Chile). Frequent.

Fissurella natalensis Krauss
Thick, solid, moderately elevated shell, broader posteriorly than anteriorly with oblong perforation which is roughly keyhole-shaped. Strong, irregular axial cords crossed by finer, concentric growth ridges. Rim of perforation very sharp. Whitish or creamy with broad purplish or brownish rays and sometimes with reddish tinting round perforation. Rim of aperture white. Underside white. 3–4cm. South African. Common.

Fissurella nigra Lesson
Large, thick and heavy shell much broader anteriorly than posteriorly and with subcentral, oval perforation. Irregular, coarse axial ribs crossed by fine growth lines. Ornament more clearly defined on juvenile specimens. Greyish or blackish with lighter zones. Rim on perforation white. Underside opaque white with purple margin. Considerable variation in height. 7–10cm. Peruvian (Chile). Common.

Fissurella peruviana Lamarck × 0·8

Shell very thick, elevated, with central, circular perforation. Fine axial lines crossed by irregular, concentric growth lines. Green or pinkish with broad, axial, pinkish, reddish or brownish rays. Younger specimens dark purplish red. Underside opaque white. 3·0–4·5cm. Peruvian. Common.

Fissurella pulchra Sowerby
Similar to *F. maxima*, but smaller, much flatter and with perforation longer and constricted at centre. Margin sharp. Almost smooth or with rough axial ribs which become obsolete towards margin, and whole shell with very fine, concentric striae. Prominently impressed muscle scar. Reddish or greyish pink with darker reddish rays and irregular, dark and light mottling around perforation. Rim of perforation white. Underside yellowish white with brownish or reddish brown margin. 6–8cm. Peruvian (Chile). Common.

Fissurella virescens Sowerby × 0·7
Shell thick, ovate in outline with large, oblong, central perforation. Very broad, callused rim around underside of perfora-

tion. Strong axial ribs. Dark green around perforation then a lighter zone, with pale green around margin. Broad and narrow greenish rays. Rim of perforation dark green. Underside dark green at centre, becoming paler with darker green round margin. 4–5cm. Peruvian, Panamic. Common.

Genus FISSURELLIDEA d'Orbigny
Moderately large, thick shells with very large, oval perforation at centre. Rim of perforation thickened with callus on underside. Numerous species in shallow water of warm and cool seas.

Fissurellidea aperta Sowerby   × 1·2

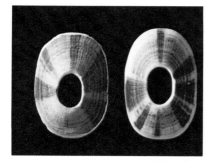

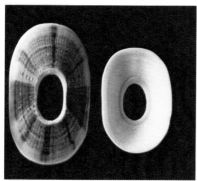

Shell thick, oval and moderately raised. Large, oval hole centrally placed. Fine axial lines crossed by more numerous finer spiral lines. Pinkish or greyish with broad or narrow axial rays which may be brownish, greyish or purplish and sometimes form interrupted, spotted lines. Occasional fine lines in same colours. Rim of aperture white. Underside opaque white. 2·5–3·5cm. South African. Common.

Genus AMBLYCHILEPAS Pilsbry
Moderately thick shells, almost rounded in outline with thickened margin and almost central, oblong, usually keyhole-shaped perforation. Posterior and anterior ends elevated, giving shell a saddle shape. Numerous species found on undersurface of stones in shallow water, tropical and warm seas.

Amblychilepas trapezina Sowerby   × 0·9

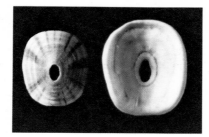

Moderately thick shell almost circular in outline, slightly compressed laterally so that anterior and posterior ends are arched. Aperture almost central, usually keel-shaped but sometimes irregular. Yellowish white with broad or narrow, purplish brown rays which vary considerably in number from specimen to specimen. Fine, concentric growth ridges. Underside opaque white. 2·5–3·0cm. Australian (Tasmania). Common.

Genus MACROCHISMA Sowerby
Moderately small, narrowly oblong shells with large, keyhole-shaped perforation. Wider end of perforation close to posterior margin of shell. Rim of perforation on underside surrounded by thick callus. Numerous species living on rocks in shallow water in Indo-Pacific province.

Macrochisma africana Tomlin
Like a smaller version of *M. sinensis*, but with relatively longer and narrower perforation and more straight-sided in outline. Numerous low axial ribs crossed by finer concentric lines. Creamy, with variegated blotches, lines and rays, which may be pinkish, reddish, purple brown or greenish. Occasional darker spots. Rim of perforation stained pinkish. Underside white with surface coloration showing through, rim of perforation pinkish. 1·5–2·2cm. South African. Frequent.

Macrochisma dilatata A. Adams
Much shorter than *M. producta* and *M. tasmaniae*, with broad, oblong perforation more nearly at centre of shell. Both ends rounded and few axial ribs at both ends, numerous fine spiral striae. Reddish, pinkish or greyish brown with broad, darker axial rays. Rim of perforation white. Underside whitish with surface colour showing through. c1·5cm. Japonic. Frequent.

Macrochisma producta A. Adams   × 1·6

Shell thin, very elongated; large, long, triangular perforation about one quarter length of shell situated close to posterior edge. Flat, rounded axial ribs are crossed by numerous irregular, concentric striae to give cancellated surface. Edge of perforation white. Underside opaque white. c2·5cm. Australian (Australia and Tasmania). Rare.

Macrochisma sinensis A. Adams   × 1·5

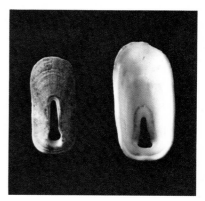

Shell moderately thick, elongate with anterior end more rounded than posterior. Aperture long and moderately broad, keyhole-shaped. Fine, irregular, concentric growth ridges crossed by numerous fine, axial lines. Greyish or reddish with broad rays of paler or darker colour and one or two dark, spotted rays. Edge of aperture white. Underside opaque white. c2cm. Japonic. Frequent.

Macrochisma tasmaniae Sowerby   × 0·9

Some resemblance to *M. producta*, but less elongate and has coarser radial ribs and a wider, shorter perforation which is less close to the posterior margin. Creamy white, yellow or brown, occasionally with zigzag, brownish markings and rarely purple rays. Underside white. 2·0–2·7cm. Australian (Australia). Common.

Superfamily
Patellacea

Family PATELLIDAE

Limpet-like, uncoiled shells sharing many features with members of Family Acmaeidae (q.v. for differentiating characteristics). Patellidae, or true limpets, occur on rocky coasts in all seas. Four genera.

Genus PATELLA Linnaeus

For details see Family Patellidae. Apex usually central or nearly so. Many species on rocky coasts in all seas.

Patella barbara Linnaeus   × 0·6

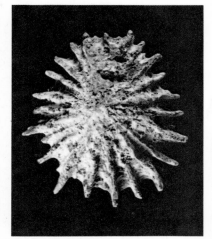

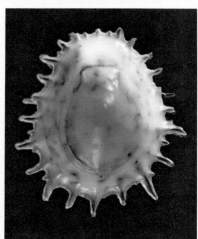

Thick, solid shell with broad, sharply ridged ribs radiating from central apex, extending as sharp spines beyond edge. Yellowish white. Inside nacreous white, with whitish muscle impression which may be tinged pink. c8·5cm. South African. Common.

Patella caerulea Linnaeus   △ × 0·7
Broad radial ribs alternate with weak ridges giving crenulate margin. Dull, dark brownish red. Interior reddish brown marginally then dark bluish grey, nacreous with whitish muscle impression, often stained yellow. 3·3–7·2cm. Mediterranean (Canary Islands).

Patella cochlear Born   × 0·5

Relatively large, thick shell, pear-shaped in outline, with coarse axial ridges. Muscle impression yellow, surrounded by blackish zone. c6cm. South African. Common.

Patella compressa Linnaeus
Thin, narrowly ovate shell. Apex posteriorly recurved. Axial ridges; faint spiral lirae. Dull, orange brown. Aperture greyish white, orange towards margin. c6·0cm. South African. Common.

Patella ferruginea Gmelin
Dull, greyish brown shell. Aperture off-white with yellowish muscle impression, white or grey within impression. 5–7cm. Mediterranean (North West Africa). Common.

Patella granatina Reeve   × 0·3
Large, thick and moderately tall shell, with broad ribs radiating from central apex. Ribs produced as broad, sharp points at edge. Whitish or greyish, but nearly always corroded and encrusted. Inside nacreous white, with edge stained reddish

or blackish, and muscle impression black. c8cm. South African. Common.

Patella granularis Linnaeus   × 1·0
morbida Reeve.

Radial imbricate cords. Dull, greyish brown to black. Interior grey, with black margin and bluish white band. Reddish brown to dark brown within muscle impression. 2·3–4·5cm. South African (South Angola to Natal).

Patella longicosta Lamarck   × 0·6
Shell thick and solid, with heavy, broad axial ribs which are produced as star-shaped points at margin. Muscle impression brownish; rest of underside nacreous white. c8cm. South African. Common.

                                    × 0·3
Patella mexicana Broderip & Sowerby
Shell large, very thick and ovate in outline. Nucleus central with thick ribs radiating to edge with finer ribs between. Dull white, generally eroded outside. Inside pinkish orange with broad, translucent, white,

Patella oculus Born   × 0·6
Strong radial ribs produced to star-like points. Outside dull, green to greyish black. Inside dark brown graduating to grey near muscle impression, light brown within impression. 4–9cm. South African. Common.

Patella plumbea Lamarck
Fine radial ridges crossed by spiral growth lines. Dull, grey shell. Inside grey, black marginally, dark grey or greyish cream within muscle attatchment. 3·2–3·9cm. West African (St Helena).

Patella safiana Lamarck   × 0·6

Radial ridges crossed by axial growth lines. Dull, buff shell. Blue inside with white muscle impression. Cream and brown lines alternate marginally. 5·0–7·0cm. Mediterranean (North Africa), West African. Common.

Above: Patella longicosta; below: Patella mexicana; bottom: Patella oculus.

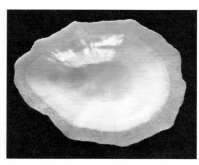

Patella vulgata Linnaeus   × 0·8
Common Limpet

marginal band and whitish, horseshoe-shaped muscle impression. The largest living limpet. 15–35cm. Panamic. Common.

Patella miniata Born
Moderately thick shell with numerous, regularly spaced ribs radiating from nearly central apex, produced as sharp points at edge. Purplish brown. Inside nacreous, with external colour showing through. Muscle impression opaque white, with orange blotches at edge. c7·5cm. South African. Common.

Shell thick, tall or short, with central apex. Coarse ribs radiate to edge. May be nearly smooth. Dirty white or greenish. Inside nacreous, with outside pattern showing through, muscle impression whitish. Extremely variable in size, shape, ornament and colour. 2–5cm. Boreal (Western Europe). Common.

Genus CELLANA H. Adams
Helcioniscus Dall.
Fairly solid shells with subcentral apex. Strong radial ribs. Brilliantly glazed interior. Numerous specimens in Indo-Pacific.

Cellana grata Gould
stearnsi Pilsbry.
Radial, nodulose cords. Dull, dark brown and green, axial mottling, may be white on ridges. External pattern shows through to interior as dark and light brown. 3–4cm. Japonic. Common.

Cellana livescens Reeve
Weak radial ribs crossed by axial growth lines. Dull. Nine or ten dark brown, radial bands alternate with cream or olive bands. Interior same colour and pattern as exterior, or may be grey. White muscle impression may have yellow stain. 3·0–4·5cm. Indo-Pacific (Mauritius). Uncommon.

Cellana mazatlandica Sowerby
nigrisquamata Reeve.
Large, relatively thin. Radial, nodulose cords. Faint, spiral growth lines marginally. Dull, creamy pink marginally; cords white, pale and dark grey with light brown or green interstices. Interior silvery with spiral rows of dark brown marks. Light to dark brown muscle impression; cream apically. 4·5–5·0cm. Indo-Pacific (Bouin Islands, Pacific). Uncommon.

Cellana ornata Dillwyn   × 0·7

Strong ribs alternate with weaker granulose ribs, crossed by axial growth lines. Dark brown dotted with white, ribs grey. Interior with dark brown and silvery white rays. Dark brown muscle impression with caramel apex. 1·5–3·5cm. Australian (New Zealand). Frequent.

Cellana radians Gmelin   × 0·8
Thick, almost circular shell with eccentric

nucleus. Regularly spaced, coarse ribs radiate to edge. Apex usually eroded. Greyish white, ribs darker. Underside nacreous, greyish white with darker grey muscle impression. c4·5cm. Australian (New Zealand). Common.

Cellana stellifera Gmelin
Wide and narrow, weak radial ridges alternating. Dull, reddish to purple brown outside. Inside grey with orange stained muscle impression. c2·5cm. Australian (New Zealand). Frequent.

Cellana toreuma Reeve   × 1·0
amussitata Reeve, *affinis* Reeve.

Shell flattened. Fine, unequal ribs. Pale blue spotted with variable dark colours. 4·5–7·0cm. Japonic, Indo-Pacific (Pacific). Common.

Family ACMAEIDAE

Limpet-like, uncoiled shells which are not coated inside with a silvery white layer (as they are in Patellidae). They have distinct, dark-coloured, peripheral zone around the outer margin of inner surface (lacking, or less clearly defined in Patellidae). Both families have muscle scar, usually horseshoe-shaped, at centre of inner surface. Externally both families have similar shells which may be circular, oval or irregular in outline, and may be smooth, or ornamented with radial ribs and cords. Acmaeidae occur on rocky coasts in all seas. Five genera.

Below: Acmaea pallida

Genus ACMAEA Eschscholtz
For details see Family Acmaeidae. Shells smooth or radially ribbed, circular or oval in outline. Subcentral nucleus. Muscle impressions joined by a thin line anteriorly. Many species in all seas.

Acmaea costata Sowerby   × 1·6

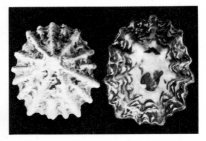

Thickish shell. External colour obscured by dark brown, opaque periostracum. Inside black and cream marginally, white or grey with dark brown muscle impression. 1·5–2·5cm. Australian. Common.

Acmaea pallida Gould   × 1·0
Broad radial ridges alternate with narrow ridges and are crossed by axial growth lines. Dull, chalky white outside, white inside sometimes with olive patches. 4·0–5·5cm. Japonic, Indo-Pacific. Common.

Acmaea saccharina Linnaeus   × 1·0
Seven large radial costae with narrow radial ridges between. Dull, dark grey. White interior, black marginal zone, brown within muscle impression. 1·5–3·5cm. Indo-Pacific. Common.

Acmaea stellaris Quoy & Gaimard   × 1·4

Shell small, thin but solid. Nearly central nucleus with eight strong ribs radiating to edge like points of a star. Fine axial striations between. Whitish, pinkish or reddish with dark reddish purple lines along tops of ridges. Inside white, occasionally with external colour showing through. Muscle impression sometimes stained golden. 2·0–2·5cm. Australian. Common.

Genus LOTTIA Gray

Like *Acmaea* but has large, low apex situated near margin. Muscle impressions joined by curved line. One species.

Lottia gigantea Gray   × 0·7

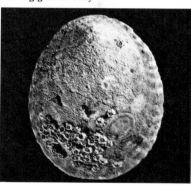

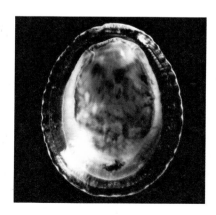

Thick shell with fine radial ridges. Dirty brown externally, usually stained green. Interior glossy with broad, dark brown margin. 5·0–7·5cm. Californian. Common.

Superfamily
Trochacea

Family TROCHIDAE

Large family of conical shells with flat base and discontinuous peristome. Popular name, top shells, suggested by their resemblance to a child's spinning top. Most have a nacreous interior and open umbilicus. Thin, corneous or calcareous operculum with central nucleus separates them from related Family Turbinidae (q.v. for details of operculum). About 60 genera mostly found in temperate and tropical waters.

Genus LISCHKEIA Fischer

Relatively large, thick shells with tall spire and flattened base. Ornamented with numerous fine, beaded spiral cords. Usually with one or two broader spiral ribs bearing pointed nodules. Few species from deep water around Japan and Taiwan.

Lischkeia alwinae Lischke   × 1·0

Relatively thick shell with tall, conical spire, flat base and slightly impressed suture. Covered with numerous fine, beaded cords. Each whorl has two broader spiral ridges with pointed tubercles. Small, deep umbilicus. Dull white, aperture and columella pearly. *c*4·5cm. Japonic, Indo-Pacific (Taiwan). Common.

Genus MONODONTA Lamarck

Thick, turbiniform, small or medium-sized shells. Smooth or spirally ornamented. Conspicuous columellar tooth. Many species have denticulate outer lip. Numerous species in all seas.

Monodonta colubrina Gould   × 1·0
Thick, turbinate shell with simple suture. Grey with dark grey, oblique lines. 2–3cm.

Mediterranean (Madeira, South West France). Common.

Monodonta concamerata Wood
striolata Philippi.
Thick, depressed-turbinate shell with convex, keeled whorls. Black with narrow, cream or yellow, axial, wavy bands. White aperture with creamy rim within dark margin. Small tooth on columella. *c*4cm. Australian. Frequent.

Mondonta lineata Da Costa
Thick, solid and heavy shell with well rounded whorls and impressed suture. Strong, blunt tooth on columella. Rough surface texture. Umbilicus absent or a mere chink. Dull, reddish brown with yellowish white flecks. Apex usually eroded. Aperture, columella and umbilical area whitish. 2–3cm. Boreal, Mediterranean. Common.

Monodonta neritoides Philippi
Smooth, globose, shell with large columellar tooth. Greenish brown with fine, reddish spots. 2·0–2·5cm. Indo-Pacific (Pacific only). Frequent.

Monodonta turbinata Born
Thick, strong shell with a conical spire of six convex whorls. Round aperture and weak median nodule on columella. Ash grey, yellowish or greenish with comma-shaped, reddish brown, black or deep red spots in spiral bands. *c*3·6cm. Mediterranean. Common.

Genus BANKIVIA Krauss
Small, very elongate, pointed shells with sinuous columella. Apparently smooth but microscopically striate. Outer lip thin. Aperture smooth. Highly polished surface. Extremely variable colour and pattern. Few species in Australian province and in South Pacific.

Bankivia fasciata Menke   × 2·0/1·3
varians Beck, *undatella* Menke,
nitida Adams, *purpurescens* Adams,
major Adams.

Thin, very elongate shell with pointed spire and twisted columella. Spire whorls straight-sided or moderately rounded and body whorl well rounded. Smooth and glossy. Bewildering range of colour and pattern variation. Ground colour white, pink, yellow, dark or light brown. Typical variants have broad, brown or white spiral bands, brown axial, zigzag lines and combinations of these features. 1·5–3·5cm. Australian (Australia and Tasmania). Common.

Genus BATHYBEMBIX Crosse
Thin, moderately large and fairly inflated shells. Spirally nodose or almost smooth. No umbilicus. Usually colourless or greenish. Thin operculum. Only in deep water off Japan and in North Atlantic Ocean. About ten species.

Bathybembix crumpi Pilsbry   × 1·1

Tall-spired, convex-based shell with spiral rows of spiny tubercles. Basal part of body whorl with widely spaced, beaded cords. Silvery white all over. 3·5–5·0cm. Japonic. Rare.

Genus CANTHARIDUS Montfort
Small to medium-sized, tapering shells with nearly smooth surface. Columellar fold usually absent. Many species in tropical and warm seas.

Cantharidus bellulus Dunker   × 2·0

Shell small, moderately thick, elongate ovate with tall spire, pointed apex and rounded body whorl. Suture scarcely apparent. Aperture constricted at posterior margin, toothed and lirate inside. Columella with single prominent tooth. Greenish or reddish ground colour with thin, spiral, red lines and white bordered triangles, loops and lines between them. Apex iridescent dark green. Aperture iridescent greenish white. c1·3cm. Australian (Australia). Common.

Cantharidus eximius Perry
badius Wood, *lividus* Kiener, *carinatus* Perry, *splendidulus* Swainson.
Shell comparable in size to *C. opalus* but body whorl not angulated at periphery and colour quite different. Tall-spired with pointed apex and moderately rounded whorls. Columella smooth and nearly vertical. Aperture strongly lirate within. Colour very variable, usually light brown, darker brown, greenish or reddish, sometimes with spiral lines or stripes of lighter colour. Iridescent aperture. c4cm. Australian (Australia). Common.

Cantharidus leucostigma Menke   × 2·0
Small, elongate-ovate shell with tall, pointed spire and moderately rounded whorls. Body whorl not angulate at periphery. Outer lip thickened. Small tooth on columella. Smooth and glossy.

Colour and pattern very variable. Ground colour usually greenish, brownish or reddish with few fine spiral lines and broader, axial, zigzag streaks which are usually whitish. Aperture iridescent green. c1·2cm. Australian (New South Wales). Common.

Cantharidus opalus Martyn   × 1·2

Thin, high, almost straight-sided cone with simple suture. Smooth with faint, oblique growth lines. Glossy, purple body whorl, blue penultimate whorl, next whorl pink; greenish spire. Irregular, wavy, reddish, axial bands. Green, nacreous aperture. 4·0–4·5cm. Australian (New Zealand). Uncommon.

Cantharidus ramburi Crosse   × 2·0
lesueuri Fischer.

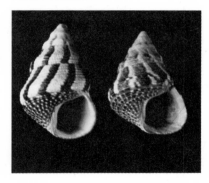

Thick, tall shell with spiral grooves and ridges. Colour variable. Cream with axial, dark brown lines; white with brown to yellow, axial lines; deep pink with wide, cream quadrants; or cream and reddish brown, alternating, axial bands. 1·0–1·5 cm. Australian. Frequent.

Genus DILOMA Philippi
Medium-sized shells with mostly short spire and oblique aperture. Smooth or ornamented. Columellar tooth weak or absent, rarely strong. Widespread in most seas. Numerous species.

Diloma nigerrima Gmelin   × 1·6

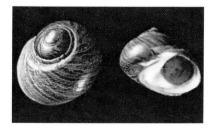

Thin, globose shell with short spire. Dull, smooth, blackish. White columella, nacreous aperture without ornament. 1·5–3·0 cm. Australian (New Zealand). Common.

Diloma odontis Wood
tesserula Tenison Woods.
Thick, turbinate shell, globose and conical but somewhat depressed. Umbilicus absent or very tiny. Apex usually eroded. Suture moderately shouldered. Numerous flattened spiral ridges crossed by irregular, axial growth lines. Columella with an obscure tooth near base. Greyish black covered with numerous evenly spaced, yellowish white dots. Dots vary in size and may be lozenge-shaped. Columella greenish. Aperture iridescent greenish and whitish. 1·5–2·0cm. Australian (South Australia). Common.

Diloma sinensis Gmelin   × 0·7

Thick, short-spired shell with rounded whorls. Fine, oblique growth lines. Reddish black; parietal area cream stained pink. Thick, dark brown, opaque periostracum. Greyish cream aperture. 1·5–3·5 cm. South African. Common.

Genus TEGULA Lesson
Medium-sized, thick, globose to conical shells. Smooth to strongly ribbed and always with a well marked columellar tooth. Most of the numerous species live in tropical and warm seas.

Tegula argyrostoma Gmelin
Thick, solid turbinate shell with well rounded whorls and impressed suture. Apex blunt. Periphery of body whorl moderately rounded. Numerous oblique axial ribs crossed by fine spiral grooves. Two teeth on columella. 4·0–4·5cm. Indo-Pacific (West Pacific). Common.

Tegula brunnea Philippi
Shell similar to *T. funebralis*, but spire rather shorter with whorls more shouldered and periphery of body whorl more angled. Tooth on columella less conspicuous. Surface roughly textured and often worn smooth on earlier whorls. Light or dark brown with glossy brownish white base. Aperture, columella and umbilical area white. 3·5–4·0cm. Californian. Common.

Tegula carpenteri Dunker
Shell very similar to *T. pfeifferi*, but usually much taller spire and much coarser axial ribs. Oblique, axial growth striae cross axial ribs. Spiral ribs on base more prominent than on *T. pfeifferi*. Umbilicus wide and very deep. Coloration similar to *T. pfeifferi*. Intermediate forms between the two species occur and suggest that at most they are only subspecifically distinct. 4–5cm. Japonic. Common.

Tegula funebralis A. Adams
Thick, solid, heavy, broadly conical shell with slightly impressed suture and usually worn apical whorls. Well rounded periphery of body whorl. Weak spiral cords crossed by weak, oblique, axial growth lines. Strong tooth at lower end of columella. Outer lip sharp-edged. Dark purplish black with white umbilical area and columella and aperture, except for thin, purplish black rim at inner edge of outer lip. 2·5–4·0cm. Californian. Common.

Tegula pellisserpentis Wood
elegans Lesson, *strigilatus* Anton.
Thick, solid, conical shell with tall spire and impressed suture. Flattened spiral cords on each whorl but worn smooth on base opposite aperture. Cords are axially ridged on spire whorls and above body whorl. Columella with large, blunt tooth. Yellowish green, oblique, axial, black stripes and blotches. Aperture, smooth part of base and columella nacreous white. 4·0–4·5cm. Panamic. Common.

Tegula pfeifferi Philippi
There is superficial resemblance to *T. regina* but immediately separable from it by a wide, deep umbilicus and less

numerous, broader axial ribs. Purplish black; base with axial, curved, black lines on a yellowish white ground. Area round umbilicus white. *c*4cm. Japonic. Common.

Tegula regina Stearns   × 0·8

Shell moderately large, thick with each whorl slightly overlapping suture. Strong, irregular axial ribs on each whorl. Strong lamellae on base. Greyish black with golden yellow ring around umbilical region and aperture stained yellow. 4·0–5·5cm. Californian. Rare.

Genus THALOTIA Gray
Small, thick shells with elevated, conical spire and spirally ribbed or granular ornament. Nearly always without umbilicus. The few species are nearly all from Australian waters.

Thalotia conica Gray   × 1·5
Thick, solid shell with tall spire, moderately sharp, basal angle and scarcely impressed

suture. Three short folds on columella, the lowest coinciding with columella tooth. Inner margin of outer lip toothed. Strong, spiral, beaded cords on each whorl, crossed by fine axial lines. Pale brown with dark brown axial streaks. Apex bright red. Aperture white. c1·5cm. Australian (Australia). Common.

Genus CITTARIUM Philippi
Livona Gray.
Large, turbinate. Inner lip with small callus. Multispiral, black, corneous operculum. One species.

Cittarium pica Linnaeus   × 0·6

Large, thick shell mottled with black and white markings. Large body whorl. Deep umbilicus. Callused umbilical region. 5–9 cm. Caribbean. Frequent.

Genus CALLIOSTOMA Swainson
Conical or turbinate shells with no umbilicus. Usually have strong spiral ridges. Many species and widely distributed.

Calliostoma africana Bartsch   × 1·5

Moderately thick, trochoidal shell with elevated spire and moderately rounded whorls. Body whorl well rounded at periphery. Suture moderately impressed. Whole shell covered with numerous spiral, beaded cords crossed by fine radial striae. Columella gently curved. Creamy yellow, pinkish or white with reddish brown blotches. Aperture white. 2·0–2·5cm. South African. Frequent.

Calliostoma annulatum Lightfoot   × 1·3

Thin, conical shell with slightly convex whorls and pointed spire. Simple suture. Spiral ridges are beaded. Dullish, cream interstices, beads alternate white and reddish brown. Two post-sutural rows are lilac with some white bands. 3–4 lilac rows on base. 1–3cm. Californian. Frequent.

Calliostoma antonii Koch   × 1·6

Thick, straight-sided cone. Simple suture. Spiral ridges carry minute beads. The three or four ridges below suture are strongest and give stepped outline to shell. Dull, flesh-coloured to cream. Creamy pink, nacreous aperture. 1·5–3·0cm. Australian. Frequent.

Calliostoma armillata Wood
Similar in shape and ornament to *C. annulatum*. Moderately thick, tall-spired shell with sharply angled periphery on body whorl. Strong, beaded spiral cords on all whorls with beads more numerous on sutural and peripheral cords. Beads largest on cords surrounding umbilical area. Yellowish with broad, pale brown axial streaks. Aperture and columella nacreous white. 3·0–3·5cm. Australian (Tasmania). Frequent.

Calliostoma australe Broderip
Thin, tall-spired shell with flat sides and base and sharply keeled basal margin. Height is greater than width. Narrow, beaded spiral cords on all whorls including

base, and thick spiral rib crossed by axial folds around basal keel and above suture of spire whorls. Cream, with broad, axial, brown streaks, reddish brown base, beads on ribs brown or mauve. c3cm. Australian (Australia). Uncommon.

Calliostoma canaliculatum Lightfoot ×1·4

Thin cone with straight sides and simple suture. Strong spiral ridges have canaliculate interstices. Dull with cream ridges, reddish brown or grey interstices. External colour shows through aperture which is nacreous. Grey, nacreous columella. 2·0–3·75cm. Californian. Frequent.

Calliostoma ciliaris Menke
Small shell with flat sides and base, sharply angulated basal margin and pointed apex. Width is equal to or slightly greater than height. Surface smooth and shiny with spiral rows of punctate striae and short, weak axial folds above and below suture. Outer lip and columella smooth. Pinkish brown with darker red brown blotches around basal margin and suture, and spiral lines of alternating brown and white dashes on base. c3·5cm. Australian (Western Australia). Uncommon.

Calliostoma consor Lischke   × 2·0
multilirata Sowerby.

Thin, trochoidal shell with moderately angulate shoulder on spire whorls and also angulated at periphery of body whorl. Numerous strong, beaded spiral cords on spire and upper portion of body whorl;

fine, flattened spiral threads on base of body whorl. Sharply curved columella. Outer lip thick. Yellowish white with broad, axial, dark brown streaks. 1·5–2·0 cm. Japonic. Frequent.

Calliostoma conulus Linnaeus   × 0·9

Moderately thick, tall-spired shell with straight sides and sharply keeled periphery on body whorl. Glossy, with very fine, axial growth striae. Early whorls with strong, beaded spiral cords. Pale brown with darker brown and yellowish blotches. Often has strong spiral ribs just above suture. 2·5–3·5cm. Mediterranean. Frequent.

Calliostoma cunninghami Griffith & Pidgeon   × 0·8

Thin cone with slightly convex whorls and simple suture. Spiral ridges are beaded. Glossy shell with alternating groups of reddish brown and white beads and cream interstices. White or pink, nacreous aperture. 3·5–5·0cm. Australian (New Zealand). Frequent.

Calliostoma eucosmia Bartsch   × 2·0
albolineata Turton, *convexa* Turton.

Thin, trochoidal shell with rounded base and tall, straight-side spire. Suture scarcely apparent. Body whorl sharply angled at periphery. Numerous fine, spiral, beaded cords crossed by fine, axial growth lines with brownish or pinkish blotches. Aperture pinkish white; columella pink or white. Apex often eroded. *c*2cm. South African. Frequent.

Calliostoma formosensis Smith   × 0·7

Shell thin and light, sharply keeled, acuminate. Much broader than high. Ornamented with evenly-spaced, spiral, beaded cords, those at the suture being much more pronounced and more elvated. Broad, false umbilicus. Spire iridescent golden, the beaded cords being reddish brown. Coloration on cords forms broad axial streaks. Aperture highly iridescent. 5–6 cm. Indo-Pacific (Taiwan). Common.

Calliostoma granulata Born   × 1·6

Thin, straight-sided cone with pointed spire and simple suture. Spiral ridges have minute beads, post-sutural rows strongest. Basal ridges unornamented. Glossy pink with reddish brown dashes in spiral lines on base. Pink, nacreous aperture. 2·5–3·0 cm. Mediterranean. Uncommon.

Calliostoma haliarchus Melvill
Large, thin shell with tall spire and sharp apex. Whorls moderately rounded, suture slightly impressed, periphery of body whorl sharply angled and base somewhat rounded. Numerous scarcely raised spiral ridges. Fine, axial growth striae. Columella curved, with blunt nodule at base. Creamy white, with large, irregular, pale brown, axial blotches on spire whorls and upper portion of body whorl. Base creamy white, whole shell beset with numerous spiral rows of interrupted, brown lines. Columella pearly, white towards basal portion. Aperture nacreous white. 4–5cm. Japonic. Uncommon.

Calliostoma hungerfordi Sowerby   × 1·5

Thin, trochoidal shell with a rounded base, tall spire with pointed apex and impressed suture. Whorls sharply angied at shoulder and body whorl also angled at periphery giving shell stepped outline. Fine spiral lines crossed by oblique, axial growth ridges. Silky sheen. Columella arched. Creamy yellow with pinkish or pale brown blotches and occasional spiral rows of alternate, whitish and reddish brown dashes. *c*2·5cm. Japonic. Frequent.

Calliostoma jujubinum Gmelin   × 1·4
Jujube Top Shell

Thick, straight-sided cone, with simple suture and narrow umbilicus. Spiral, beaded ridges. Shell dull, cream with axial, reddish brown blotches and white aperture. 2–3cm. Caribbean, Transatlantic. Common.

41

Calliostoma layardi Sowerby
Bears some resemblance in general outline to *C. consor* but spire whorls more straight-sided and suture much more impressed. Strong spiral cord just above suture and at periphery of body whorl and another strong spiral cord just below periphery of body whorl. Rest of shell encircled by spiral cords. Pinkish or pale brown with white or brownish spots on spiral cords. Columella white. Aperture whitish with external colour showing through. *c*1·5cm. South African. Frequent.

Calliostoma ligatum Gould   × 1·5
costatum Martyn.

Thick turbinate shell with simple suture. Spiral ridges have canaliculate interstices. Dullish with cream ridges, reddish brown interstices and occasional, axial, reddish brown markings. Greyish, nacreous aperture. 1·0–2·2cm. Californian, Aleutian (Alaska to San Diego). Common.

Calliostoma monile Reeve   × 1·3

Thick, conical, straight-sided shell with tall spire and weakly keeled, basal margin. Taller than wide. Whole shell covered with numerous fine spiral striae and finer axial striae. Cream with pale purple spots on a slightly raised, broad spiral ridge at suture and periphery. 2·0–2·5cm. Indo-Pacific (Australia). Frequent.

Calliostoma pellucida Valenciennes × 0·8
Thin, conical shell with convex whorls and pointed spire. Simple suture. Spiral ridges are beaded. Dullish, with reddish brown

and cream beads alternating on base, peripheral row of reddish brown quadrants and reddish brown, axially oriented blotches on spire. Nacreous, white or pink aperture. 3–4cm. Australian (New Zealand). Frequent.

Calliostoma perfragile Sowerby
Thin, conical shell with convex whorls and simple suture. Fine spiral ridges are beaded below suture. Shell is nacreous, white ridges separated by pink, nacreous interstices. White aperture. 1·75–2·0cm. South African. Rare.

Calliostoma punctulatum Martyn   × 1·3

Thick, conical shell with convex whorls bearing beaded spiral ridges. Glossy, brown with white and reddish brown marks alternating along ridges giving irregular axial lines. Greyish, nacreous interior. 1–4cm. Australian (New Zealand). Frequent.

Calliostoma speciosum A. Adams   × 1·5

Thick, straight-sided shell with pointed spire and simple suture. Spiral ridges crossed basally by strong, axial growth lines. Oblique axial growth lines. Ridges weakly beaded, stronger just below suture. Glossy, cream shell with reddish brown mottling, often faint and reduced to rows of spots on base. Creamy pink, nacreous aperture. 2·5–3·0cm. Indo-Pacific. Frequent.

Calliostoma tigris Martyn   × 0·7

Moderately thick cone with pointed spire and simple suture. Weak spiral ridges are faintly beaded. Glossy cream with reddish brown reticulate, axial stripes. Flesh-coloured, nacreous aperture. *c*5·5cm. Australian (New Zealand). Common.

Calliostoma zizyphinum Linnaeus   × 1·6

Thin, nearly straight-sided cone with simple suture and narrow umbilicus. Weak spiral ridges and weak, oblique growth lines. Glossy, deep pink or orange with reddish brown axial marks in spiral bands. Whitish aperture and white columella. 1·5–2·0cm. Mediterranean. Common.

Calliostoma zonamestum A. Adams
Moderately thick, tall-spired shell with flat sides, flat base and sharply keeled basal margin. False umbilicus deep and smooth-sided. Ten spiral, beaded threads on each whorl with a dark brown line between them. Fine, brown spiral lines on base. 2·0–2·5cm. Caribbean. Rare.

Genus ASTELE Swainson
Eutrochus A. Adams.
Shells resemble *Calliostoma* but have an umbilicus. Many species in tropical and warm seas.

Astele pulcherrimus Sowerby
Moderately thick, tall-spired shell with moderately stepped whorls. Three prominent spiral ridges on each whorl, with finer, granulated lines upon them. Six or seven granulated spiral ridges also on basal surface. Umbilicus fairly broad. Creamy white with red granules. Aperture and columella creamy white. *c*2cm. Indo-Pacific (West Pacific). Rare.

Astele subcarinatus Swainson   × 1·2
adamsi Pilsbry, *pespectivus* Adams.

Thin, almost straight-sided shell. Simple suture. Deep, narrow umbilicus. Spiral ridges are weakly beaded below suture. Dull, cream with greenish spire; reddish brown mottling. Flesh-coloured or white, nacreous aperture. 2·5–3·5cm. Australian. Uncommon.

Genus PHOTINULA H. & A. Adams
Depressed, nearly smooth, thin shells with rounded body whorl and umbilicus sealed by thick callus. Few species mostly limited to cold waters of southern South America.

Photinula coerulescens King & Broderip
   × 1·8

Thin, light, depressed shell with short spire, large body whorl and rounded periphery. Suture not impressed. Smooth all over. Umbilicus sealed with thick, white callus. Greyish white with densely crowded, fine, brownish black spiral lines. 1·5–2·0 cm. Magellanic. Common.

Photinula taeniata Wood   × 2·3

Shell similar in shape to *P. coerulescens*, but smaller and with slightly taller spire. Umbilical callus not so well developed. Shell smooth all over. Yellowish white with thin, pinkish or reddish, spiral bands and white area surrounding umbilicus. *c*1·2cm. Magellanic. Common.

Genus TROCHUS Linnaeus
Medium-sized to large shells with flat-sided whorls. Angular periphery, conspicuous umbilicus or 'false umbilicus' with callus coating. Columella toothed or almost smooth meeting basal lip at a well marked angle. Many species in tropical and warm seas.

Trochus concavus Gmelin   × 0·8
Thick, solid, almost limpet-shaped shell with convex base and straight-sided whorls. Outer lip forms continuous rim with sharply angled periphery of body whorl, so that both are almost on the same plane. Slightly impressed suture. Low, coarse, wavy axial folds and fine, axial growth lines. Occasional coarse spiral ridges. Base with strong, evenly spaced, smooth ridges. Deep umbilicus with curved columella

ascending into it. Bluish grey or pinkish red with lighter blotches near suture. Base greenish white. 3·5–5·0cm. Indo-Pacific. Common.

Trochus elegantulus Wood   × 1·3

Thick, straight-sided cone with simple suture and narrow umbilicus. Spiral, beaded ridges and wavy, axial folds. Deep pink with irregular, axial, white bands. White aperture and plicate interior. Columella ends in a tooth. 2–3cm. Indo-Pacific (Indian Ocean). Uncommon.

Trochus erythraeus Brocchi   × 1·4
Moderately thick shell which may be short- or tall-spired. Very broad, deep umbilicus. Suture moderately or deeply impressed. Periphery of body whorl sharp and encircled by large, warty tubercles. Rest of shell surface covered with numerous spiral, beaded cords and coarse axial ridges. Greenish, reddish brown or yellowish white with broad axial streaks of darker colour. Umbilicus nacreous white; aper-

Trochus erythraeus

ture nacreous. 3·0–3·5cm. Indo-Pacific (Indian Ocean). Frequent.

Trochus firmus Philippi
Thick, solid and heavy shell with tall spire and slightly impressed suture. Roundly angulated periphery on body whorl. Base moderately rounded. False umbilicus wide and deep. Columella almost straight. Irregular axial ribs on body whorl and spiral cords on all whorls. Shell often worn to give roughened texture. Base smooth. Umbilical area surrounded by smooth spiral ribs. *c*3cm. Indo-Pacific (North Arabian Sea). Common.

Trochus incarnatus Philippi
Thick, solid shell resembling *Tectus niloticus* in shape. Tall spire with slightly impressed suture. Body whorl sharply angled at periphery. Wide, deep umbilicus. Strong axial ribs on lower half of each whorl and at periphery of body whorl. Numerous beaded spiral cords on rest of shell. Umbilical area encircled by smooth spiral ridges. Columella with blunt teeth. Yellowish white with axial, brown streaks on spire whorls and spiral rows of brown and white dots on base. Umbilical area and aperture whitish. 2–3cm. Indo-Pacific (Indian Ocean). Common.

Trochus kochi Philippi ⠀⠀⠀⠀× 1·4

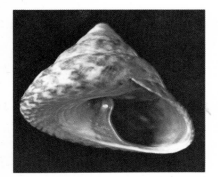

Thick, solid, trochoidal shell with moderately tall spire, slightly impressed suture and angulated periphery on body whorl. Coarse oblique, axial ridges on each whorl crossed by strong, axial, growth ridges. Base smooth but strong, smooth spiral ribs around broad, deep umbilicus. Columella strongly curved. Whitish with axial, zigzag, green streaks, white round umbilical area, aperture iridescent greenish. 3·0–3·5cm. Indo-Pacific (Indian Ocean). Frequent.

Trochus laciniatus Reeve ⠀⠀⠀⠀× 1·3

Shell very similar to *T. sacellum*. Trochoidal shell with moderately rounded whorls and moderately impressed suture. Strong axial cords at base of each whorl and one or two beaded spiral cords between them. Base has numerous beaded spiral cords. Wide, deep umbilicus. Aperture lirate within. Columella with one or two blunt teeth. Bluish grey mottled, streaked and spotted with reddish markings. Sometimes yellowish white with reddish markings. Aperture whitish. 2·0–2·5cm. Indo-Pacific. Frequent.

Trochus lineatus Lamarck ⠀⠀⠀⠀× 1·1
Large, thick, conical shell with flat sides and flat base. Sharply or moderately angulate periphery of body whorl. Approximately as tall as it is wide. Columella smooth or with weak teeth. Numerous spiral ribs with fine, regularly spaced

nodules. Early whorls have obscure axial ribs. Fine spiral cords on base. Greenish with reddish axial lines which are most conspicuous on base. Umbilical area whitish. Aperture brownish white. 4–5cm. Indo-Pacific (West Pacific). Common.

Trochus nigropunctatus Reeve
Moderately thick shell resembling *T. erythraeus* in shape. Spire relatively short and body whorl with sharply angled periphery. Wide, shallow, false umbilicus. Numerous spiral, beaded cords on all whorls. Ribs round umbilicus not beaded. Columella sinuous with strong folds projecting from it into false umbilicus. Aperture lirate within. Pinkish with broad, irregular, axial, dark brown streaks and spiral rows of dots and dashes on base. Aperture and umbilical area white or pinkish. 2·0–2·5cm. South African. Common.

Trochus radiatus Gmelin ⠀⠀⠀⠀× 1·4

Thick, solid, trochoidal shell with moderately elevated spire and sharply angled periphery on body whorl. Suture moderately impressed. Whole shell is encircled by spiral, beaded cords. Columella with blunt teeth. Aperture lirate within. Umbilicus wide and deep. Yellowish white with broad, interrupted, axial, reddish streaks. Aperture, columella and umbilical area nacreous white. 3·0–3·5cm. Indo-Pacific (Indian Ocean). Common.

Trochus sacellum Philippi   × 1·7

Like a larger version of *T. tricatenatus* but in *T. sacellum* there are four rows of beaded spiral cords instead of the three in *T. tricatenatus*. Also this species is larger than *T. tricatenatus* and lacks the prominent teeth at base of outer lip. Pinkish white with broad, axial, reddish streaks on spire whorls, base has thinner axial streaks which are also paler. 2–3cm. Indo-Pacific (Philippines). Frequent.

Trochus scabrosus Philippi
Thick, solid shell bearing some resemblance to a *Clanculus*. Moderately tall spired with impressed suture and angulate periphery on body whorl. Base moderately rounded. Large, coarse umbilicus which is spirally ribbed inside. Strong, beaded spiral cords with weaker spiral cords between. Pale yellowish brown with dark brown spots and blotches. Aperture and columella nacreous white. *c*1·5cm. Indo-Pacific (Indian Ocean). Common.

Trochus tiaratus Quoy & Gaimard
Thick, solid shell with elevated spire and impressed suture. Sharply angulated periphery and wide, deep umbilicus. Coarse spiral cords with fine spiral striae between them. Inside edge of umbilicus smooth. Columella sinuous. Yellowish white with axial, dark brown streaks and spiral rows of dark brown spots. *c*2cm. Australian (New Zealand). Common.

Trochus tricatenatus Reeve
Thick, solid shell with tall spire and sharply angled periphery on body whorl. Deep, wide umbilicus. Each whorl has a row of prominent, rounded nodules just above suture and three rows of spiral beads below. Base has numerous beaded spiral cords. Aperture strongly lirate within. Columella and base of outer lip strongly toothed. Yellowish white with broad, reddish axial stripes, earlier whorls being almost unicolorous reddish. Aperture yellowish white. 2·0–2·5cm. Indo-Pacific. Uncommon.

Trochus tubiferus Kiener   × 1·3
concinnus Philippi.
Thick, solid, trochoidal shell with

moderately tall spire and slightly impressed suture. Just above suture on each whorl is a spiral row of thick, fluted tubercles. Above and below these are spiral rows of beads. Base has numerous spiral, beaded cords. Aperture strongly lirate, lirae also extending onto parietal wall. Columella large and deep. Basal portion of outer lip strongly toothed. Yellowish white or greenish with dark red axial streaks. Aperture yellowish white. 2·5–3·0cm. Indo-Pacific (Pacific). Frequent.

Trochus venetus Reeve   × 1·4

Thick, solid, trochoidal shell with tall spire and moderately rounded whorls. Base flattened. Numerous spiral, beaded cords, those on base being less coarsely beaded. Wide, deep umbilicus. Aperture lirate within. One or two blunt teeth on columella. Whitish with broad, axial, reddish and greenish bands. Base with inner, brownish bands and lines. Aperture, columella and umbilicus yellowish white. *c*3cm. Indo-Pacific (Indian Ocean). Common.

Trochus virgatus Gmelin   × 0·9
Thick, heavy, very tall-spired shell with almost flat base. Suture wavy and slightly impressed. Strong, nodulous spiral cords crossed by axial growth ridges. Numerous flattened spiral ribs on base. Columella thickened and ending in blunt tooth.

Whitish with broad, axial, interrupted, red or purplish streaks. Interrupted, pinkish red spiral bands on base. Umbilical area and aperture white. Ground colour often pinkish. 4·5–6·5cm. Indo-Pacific. Common.

Trochus viridis Gmelin
Thick, solid shell with tall spire and pointed apex. Early whorls have concave sides, later whorls being rounded. Sharp basal keel. Suture slightly impressed. Umbilicus small and umbilical area widely and deeply excavated. Coarse, beaded spiral cords on all whorls, base being finely spirally ridged. Columella sinuous and toothed. Mature specimens greenish or brownish, apex usually eroded. Juvenile specimens bright red. Base fawn with darker spiral lines. Aperture nacreous reddish brown. 2·0–2·5cm. Australian (New Zealand). Common.

Genus CLANCULUS Montfort
Small to medium-sized shells, rounded-conical. Surface beaded. Columella with large tooth, and umbilical pit bordered with crenulate ridge. About 50 very similar species in tropical and warm seas.

Clanculus flagellatus Philippi
Low-spired shell with convex whorls bearing spiral, beaded cords. White or cream with irregular, brown spiral bands. White aperture, deep umbilicus. Plicate parietal lip and parietal region. Recurved columellar lip beaded. *c*2cm. Australian (South Australia). Uncommon.

Clanculus limbatus Quoy & Gaimard
mallacoota Iredale.
Depressed, conical shell with convex whorls and narrow umbilicus. Dull, white to cream, sometimes pink, with irregular, spiral, brown bands. White aperture and umbilicus; plicate parietal lip; everted, beaded columellar lip. 1·5–2·0cm. Indo-Pacific (Australia).

Clanculus maugeri Wood
Shell similar to *C. undatus* but with sharply angled periphery on body whorl. Spire also taller and with blunter apex. More

45

numerous and less well defined teeth on columella. Coarse, beaded spiral cords and broad parietal callus. Ground colour brownish but apex is bright green which is chief distinguishing feature. *c*2·5cm. Australian (East Australia). Frequent.

Clanculus pharaonius Linnaeus × 1·3
Strawberry Top

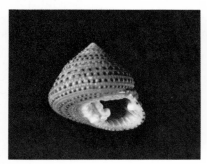

Glossy red shell with thick, granulose, spiral cords. In each spire whorl are three cords with alternating black and white granules. Columellar lip with inner columellar fold. Outer lip has two marginal denticles. Aperture lirate. *c*2cm. Indo-Pacific. Common.

Clanculus puniceus Philippi × 1·8

Arrangement of colouration on varices distinguishes this species from *C. pharaonis* which it otherwise resembles. Each spiral whorl has a rib on which three red granules alternate with a single black granule. Four such ribs on body whorl. Rest of surface red. Deep umbilicus. *c*2cm. South African. Frequent.

Clanculus stigmatarius A. Adams × 2·0

Small, thick shell with large, swollen body whorl and short spire. Columella and parietal teeth thick and strong. Moderately large, deep umbilicus. Numerous spiral, beaded cords. Dull, brown shell. Every fourth row of beads has a single red bead alternating with three pinkish beads. *c*1·0cm. Indo-Pacific. Common.

Clanculus undatus Lamarck × 1·4

Shell solid, thick, widely umbilicate, with short depressed spire. Whorls rounded and subangulate at base. Inner margin of outer lip toothed. Strong, tooth-like folds on columella. Rough, beaded spiral cords. Dark brown with numerous very dark, reddish brown spots evenly distributed. 3–4cm. Australian (Australia). Uncommon.

Genus TECTUS Montfort
Trochus of many authors.
Medium-sized to large shells. Taller than wide, base nearly smooth. No umbilicus. Columella with strong or weak spiral fold. Many species in tropical and warm seas.

Tectus conus Gmelin × 0·6
hirasei Pilsbry.

Moderately large, solid shell with tall, pointed spire. Columella strongly curved. Large, false umbilicus. Coarse, nodulous spiral ridges which are strongest at periphery of body whorl and just above suture. Pinkish white with darker red blotches and irregular, whitish axial streaks. Base with numerous interrupted, spiral, red bands. Aperture pinkish white. 5–8cm. Indo-Pacific. Frequent.

Tectus crenulatus Lamarck
Moderately thick, tall-spired shell with slightly impressed suture. Spire whorls almost straight-sided. Sharply angled periphery on body whorl. Relatively weak fold on columella. Early whorls with strong axial ribs which are pointed at lower extremity. Later whorls with coarse spiral cords. Base finely spirally ribbed. Whitish with pale brownish streaks and blotches. Aperture and umbilical area whitish. *c*3cm. Indo-Pacific (Pacific). Frequent.

Tectus dentatus Forsskal
Thick, heavy shell with very tall spire and flat base. At suture of each whorl and at periphery of body whorl is a row of widely spaced, large, blunt tubercles. Coarse, wavy axial ridges over whole of upper surface. Base polished and smooth. Surface orange brown, yellowish or whitish; base white towards margin with spiral rows of bright green lines towards centre. Aperture nacreous yellow. 5–8cm. Indo-Pacific (Indian Ocean). Common.

Tectus fenestratus Gmelin × 1·5

Thick, solid, tall-spired shell with flat base and deeply impressed suture. Strong, axial ribs on lower half of each whorl crossed by numerous finer, spiral, nodulous cords. Fine, smooth spiral ridges on base which are worn away opposite aperture. Aperture lirate within. Strong, hooked columella. White, with greenish blotches between axial ribs, white base and aperture. 2·5–4·5cm. Indo-Pacific. Common.

Tectus niloticus Linnaeus × 0·8

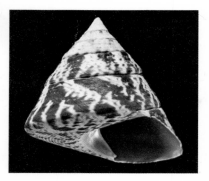

Large, thick and heavy shell. May be nearly smooth or axially tuberculated. Pinkish with dark reddish brown, axial blotches. 5–13cm. Indo-Pacific. Common.

Tectus pyramis Born   × 0·8
Pyramid Top

Large, thick, tall-spired shell with straight sides and flat base. Spiral row of coarse, irregular tubercles and spiral rows of smaller, irregular tubercles on all whorls. Base with flattened spiral ribs. Dark green with paler green and brownish blotches, early whorls usually whitish. Base bright green near margin, white at centre and yellowish between. Aperture nacreous green. 5–7cm. Indo-Pacific. Common.

Genus UMBONIUM Link
Rotella Lamarck.
Medium-sized to small shells, lenticular in shape with umbilicus partly or entirely filled by a callus pad. Mostly smooth and glossy but a few species with a beaded ridge round callus pad. Numerous species in Indo-Pacific and Japonic provinces.

Umbonium conicum Adams & Reeve
Small, thick shell with moderately elevated spire and roundly angulated periphery. Callus pad usually indented. Unicolorous dark brown, sometimes with single, spiral, white band. Conical shape distinguishes this species from *U. vestiarium*. c0·7cm. Indo-Pacific (West Pacific). Frequent.

Umbonium giganteum Lesson   × 1·1 ▽

Like a large version of *U. vestiarium*. Shell taller and less angulated at periphery than *U. vestiarium*. Suture slightly impressed. Faint spiral grooves round periphery. Large, irregular callus plug seals umbilicus. Colour and pattern very variable. Usually greyish with dextral streaks and blotches of white and dark purplish brown. Lower half of body whorl often pinkish and yellowish. 2·5–3·5cm. Indo-Pacific (Pacific), Japonic. Common.

Umbonium moniliferum Lamarck
Resembles *U. vestiarium* in shape but differs in ornament, having moderately strong spiral ridges with grooves between and a strong, spiral, beaded cord round suture. Umbilicus covered by an irregular, warty callus plug. Very variable in colour and pattern. Ground colour creamy white with axial, black or brownish streaks, sometimes unicolorous yellowish brown flushed with pink. Callus plug pinkish violet. c1·5cm. Japonic. Common.

Umbonium superbum Gould
Shell almost as large as *U. giganteum* but rather more conical and with strong spiral grooves on all whorls. Large, irregular callus plug conceals umbilicus. Very variable in colour and pattern. Ground colour yellowish white with crowded, axial, purplish brown streaks, sometimes flushed pink on early whorls, streaked and dotted with pale purplish brown, or combinations of these. Callus plug pinkish violet. 1·5–2·0cm. Japonic. Frequent.

Umbonium thomasi Crosse
Shell intermediate in size between *U. vestiarium* and *U. giganteum*. Moderately elevated spire with whorls slightly keeled at suture. Almost flat base with callus plug only slightly raised. Whitish or greyish white with broad or narrow, brownish or purplish brown axial streaks. c1·3cm. Japonic. Uncommon.

Umbonium vestiarium Linnaeus   × 1·0
Small, flattened shell with roundly angulated body whorl. Umbilicus covered by a large, flattened callus plug. Smooth and glossy. Extremely variable colour and pattern. Ground colour grey, pinkish, brownish, white, yellow or combinations

of these, banded, streaked, spotted and flammulated with markings of same colours. 1·0–1·5cm. Indo-Pacific. Common.

Family ANGARIIDAE

Small to moderately large shells. Short-spired or moderately conical. Rows of nodules or branching spines. Wide umbilicus with pronounced rim. Apertural rim usually not attached to penultimate whorl. Aperture nacreous within. Operculum thin, corneous and multispiral. One genus living on coral reefs in Indo-Pacific.

Genus ANGARIA Röding
Delphinula Lamarck.
For details see Family Angariidae. Numerous species described, most of which seem to be forms of the variable *A. delphinus*.

Angaria delphinus Linnaeus
distorta Linnaeus, *nodulosus* Gmelin, *laciniatus* Lamarck, *aculeata* Reeve, *formosa* Reeve, *incisa* Reeve, *atrata* Reeve, *melanacantha* Reeve, *nodosa* Reeve.   × 1·2/0·8/0·8
Depressed, thick shell with flat apex. Body whorl with angulate shoulder bearing spiny nodules. Spiral ridges of body whorl with lamellate spines. Three rows of nodules on body whorl. Deep red markings

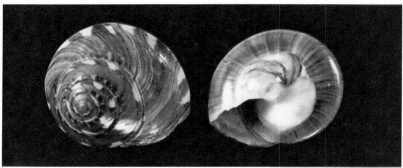

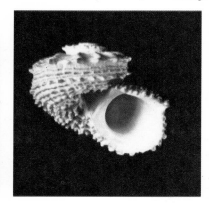

on cream or pinkish shell. Cream aperture. Operculum dark brown. Extremely variable in colour, pattern and form. 4–7cm. Indo-Pacific. Common.

Angaria sphaerula Kiener   × 1·4

Similar to *A. delphinus*, but upper surface of body whorl has strong, rounded axial ribs and uppermost row of peripheral spines are curved and peculiarly flattened. This too may prove to be merely a form of *A. delphinus*. 3–4cm. Indo-Pacific (West Pacific). Rare.

Family TURBINIDAE

Large family of strong, solid, turbinate or trochoidal shells. Globose and few whorled, or depressed and few-whorled. Usually well developed ornament. Nacreous interior. Entire peristome in most genera, rounded and lying in one plane, in others sharply angled at periphery. Operculum calcareous, spiral, with central or eccentric nucleus; often thick, heavy and granulose, or with concave ribs exteriorly (these features immediately separating species from those in Family Trochidae). About 20 genera in tropical and warm seas.

Genus ASTRAEA Röding
Imperator Montfort.
Medium-sized to large shells. Conical, usually short spire. Periphery ornamented with spines. Base flattened. Calcareous operculum usually oval, thick and ribbed. Many species in tropical and warm seas.

Astraea americana Gmelin
Thick, tall-spired shell with slightly concave-sided whorls. Sharply angled basal margin. Suture moderately impressed. Strong, oblique axial ribs on all whorls. Fine spiral cords on base. White or cream. Thick, convex, circular operculum with an off-centred dimple. 3–4cm. Caribbean. Common.

Astraea caelata Gmelin
Thick, solid, trochoidal shell with tall spire and moderately impressed suture. Upper side of each whorl with coarse axial ribs. Lower half of each whorl with coarse spiral cords bearing long, fluted scales. Base of body whorl with three or four spiral cords bearing numerous fluted scales and very fine axial ribs between. Operculum thick and finely .granulose. Yellowish white, blotched and streaked with dark and light green and pinkish orange. Aperture nacreous white. Operculum white. 5–6cm. Caribbean. Common.

Astraea gibberosa Dillwyn
Thick, heavy, medium-sized shell with short spire, moderately impressed suture. Sharply angled basal margin. Strong, wavy spiral cord at basal margin of body whorl and at suture on spire whorls. Six strong spiral cords on base. Spire whorls with oblique axial ribs on upper half and two or three spiral, beaded cords below. Red to reddish brown, columella white. Operculum oval, convex, smooth and white. 5–6cm. Californian. Frequent.

Astraea girgyllus Reeve
Similar to *A. modesta* in shape and ornament but differs from it by having two spiral rows of strong, tubular peripheral spines which are expanded at their ends, and by a groove which borders the

columella callus. Covered with spiral, granulated cords and fine, axial growth lines. Greenish to orange brown in colour with a bright orange yellow outer edge to the otherwise white columella. The thick convex operculum is white. *c*4cm. Japonic. Rare.

Astraea heliotropium Martyn   × 0·6/0·5

Large, thick shell with moderately tall spire, well rounded whorls and very large, deep umbilicus. Angulated base of body whorl has large, triangular, fluted scales which are continued around spire whorls and suture. Spiral rows of strong tubercles on whole shell, those on base being scaly. Dull, greyish white with umbilicus yellowish. Aperture whitish. Thick, almost smooth, creamy white operculum. 8–10cm. Australian (New Zealand). Common.

Astraea japonica Dunker   × 0·5
Large, thick, heavy shell with moderately tall spire and flat base. At basal margin of body whorl is a row of strong, evenly spaced, large, outward-pointing, open spines which are continued around spire whorls at suture. Strong, oblique axial ribs on all whorls. Strong, axial growth ridges. Numerous flattened spiral cords on base which are crossed by strong axial ridges. Umbilicus gently curved. Yellowish white with uneven, reddish brown blotching. Base with blotching. Columella and umbilical area opaque white, aperture and parietal wall pearly. 9–11cm. Japonic. Rare.

Astraea kesteveni Iredale   × 1·2

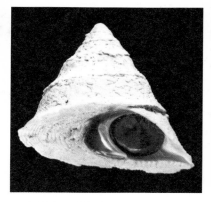

Shell thick, solid, trochoidal with sharp, basal keel. Thick, curved columella. Thin outer lip. Numerous scaly spiral ribs. Whitish or greyish. Columella and oval operculum bright purple. Aperture white. 3–4cm. Australian. Frequent.

Astraea modesta Reeve
Solid, heavy, trochoidal shell with almost flat base and conical spire with deeply impressed suture. Each whorl has moderately long, fluted spines at periphery, two on each spire whorl and three on body whorl. Short, axial corrugations below suture and irregular, spiral rows of nodules. Numerous scaly spiral ribs on base. Large parietal callus extends over half base. Entire shell surface reddish purple. Aperture creamy white with vermilion tinge to parietal callus. Thick, white, obscurely granulose operculum. 5–6cm. Japonic. Common.

Astraea olivacea Wood
brevispinosa Valenciennes,
erythrophthalma Philippi.
Large, thick, trochoidal shell with rounded whorls and sharp, downturned lip at periphery of body whorl. Coarse, wavy, axial ribs on each whorl with the thick, wavy cord at suture. Two strong spiral ridges on base. Smooth, curved columella. Olive green surface, paler green on base with brilliant blotch of reddish orange around umbilical area. Aperture whitish. Thick, greenish periostracum. 5·0–6·5cm. Panamic. Frequent.

Astraea phoebia Röding   × 0·8
longispina Lamarck.
Thick, solid shell with short spire and flat apex. Body whorl sharply keeled with single spiral row of moderately long, open, fluted spines. Spines usually worn away from earlier whorls. Also ornamented with strong, scaly spiral cords which are crossed by axial growth ridges and lamellae. Small umbilicus, sometimes closed by callus. Yellowish with pale brown mottlings. Often pinkish around umbilicus. 4–6cm. Caribbean. Common.

Above: Astraea phoebia
Below: Astraea pileola

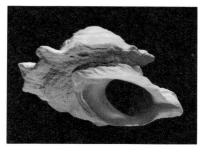

Astraea pileola Reeve   × 1·0
Thick, solid shell with moderately raised, blunt spire and depressed body whorl. Fluted flange runs round basal margin and above suture. Scaly spiral ribs on base. Sides of spire whorls mostly smooth. Columella smooth. Light brown, greyish or white. Aperture white with greenish tinge on columella. Operculum purple brown. 4·5–6·5cm. Australian. Common.

Astraea rotularia Lamarck   × 1·2

Solid, depressed shell with keeled basal margin. Whorls ornamented with oblique ridges and imbricated nodules around basal margin and suture. Scaly spiral ribs on base. Fawn or grey. Aperture white. Operculum oval; dark green or purple brown. Surface layer of shell often worn away to reveal nacreous layer below. 3·5–4·5cm. Australian. Common.

Astraea rugosa Linnaeus
Thick, squat shell, angular at periphery. Each whorl with peripheral row of spines and broad axial ridges. Body whorl has basal row of spines. Reddish yellow. Thick, limy, ovate operculum glossy, cream or orange with whorls on outer surface. Nacreous, grey aperture and yellow parietal area. *c*4cm. Mediterranean.

Astraea stellaris Gmelin
Thick, solid shell with each whorl slightly overhanging suture. Broad, eave-like projections at lower edge of whorl. Coarse axial ribbing on spire, scaly spiral ribbing on base. Greyish white with bright blue staining on columella and bright blue, oval operculum. 2·5–4·0cm. Indo-Pacific (Australia). Uncommon.

Astraea sulcata Martyn   × 0·8

Thick, solid shell with rounded whorls and moderately tall spire with blunt apex. Strong, curved axial ridges on body whorl and spire, crossed by weaker spiral cords. Base has spiral cords only. Whitish, flushed with reddish or brownish markings. Aperture and columella pearly, base whitish. Thick, reddish brown periostracum. Operculum with single thick rib. 5–9cm. Australian (New Zealand). Common.

Astraea tuber Linnaeus   × 0·7

Thick, trochoidal shell with rounded base and moderately tall spire. Upper half of spire whorl and body whorl with strong nodulous axial ridges with blunt ends. Another row of more numerous, more pointed tubercles at suture of spire whorls and at periphery of body whorl. Base and tubercles white, rest of shell dark green or yellowish brown. Spire whorls usually worn down to nacreous lower layer. Aperture and columella nacreous white. 3–4cm. Caribbean. Common.

Astraea undosa Wood   × 1·1

Thick, solid shell with thick, wavy, lower edge of whorls overhanging suture. Coarse, widely spaced axial ribs. Spire with thick, nodulous spiral ribs. Operculum ornamented with spiny ribs. Light brown flushed with pink. Base pale brown. Aperture and columella white. Operculum white. 4–8cm. Californian. Common.

Genus GUILDFORDIA Gray
Thin, very depressed shells with few long or short spines at periphery. No umbilicus. About six species in deep water in Indo-Pacific.

Guildfordia triumphans Philippi   × 0·45
Flattened shell with convex whorls carrying spiral rows of beading. Body whorl carries peripheral row of nine spines. Pink or greyish pink with an off-white, nacreous

Above: Guildfordia triumphans   *Below: Guildfordia yoka*

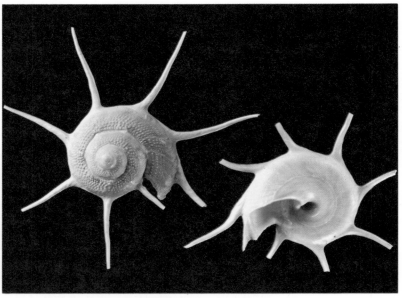

base and white undersides to the spines of body whorl. Pink band around umbilical zone. Aperture nacreous and silvery pink. 4–7cm. Japonic. Frequent.

Guildfordia yoka Jousseaume   × 0·7
Resembles *G. triumphans* in general appearance, but is distinguished from it by the long, crooked spines. Mature shells have 8–9 spines. Upper surface ornamented with spiral rows of rounded granules. Base smooth with a well-defined callus around umbilical area. Iridescent pink on upper surface, creamy white or yellowish on base. Aperture pearly. 7–10cm. Japonic. Frequent.

Genus LIOTIA Gray
Small, turbinate or discoidal shells with well developed axial and spiral ribs forming

a latticed surface. Umbilicus funnel-shaped and bounded by beaded cord. Peristome continuous and very thick. Inside edge of operculum corneous, outer surface calcareous, often hairy or bristly. The two species described here placed in the one genus although numerous genera have been proposed for the many species known from the tropical and warm seas of the world.

Liotia cidaris Kiener
Small, thick, depressed shell with short, few-whorled spire. Strong axial cords crossed by strong spiral cords, the two strongest being at periphery. Weaker spiral cords between large spiral cords. Umbilicus large and deep. Unicolorous white. c1·2cm. Indo-Pacific. Common,

Liotia depressa Reeve

Shell large for the genus, thick and solid. Short spire with few whorls and impressed suture. Very large body whorl with few widely spaced axial ribs and three strong spiral ribs crossing them. Very thick cord around the large umbilicus. Axial ribs form prominent upturned points at periphery. Aperture with flared outer lip. Unicolorous white, sometimes with underlying pearly layer revealed. *c*2cm. Indo-Pacific (Philippines). Rare.

Liotia varicosa Reeve   × 1·7

Very thick, depressed shell with large body whorl, short spire and moderately wide umbilicus. Thick varices crossed by strong spiral ridges. Dull pinkish cream with white aperture and nacreous pink interior. 1·5–2·0cm. Indo-Pacific. Frequent.

Genus TURBO Linnaeus

Mostly large, thick shells. Few whorls, smooth, nodulose, grooved or spiny. Callused inner lip. Operculum thick, heavy and often granulose or ribbed exteriorly. Many species in most seas.

Turbo argyrostomus Linnaeus   ▽ × 0·9
Silver-mouthed Turban

Very thick, tubinate shell with relatively tall spire. Strong spiral cords. Cords on periphery and shoulder of body whorl have lamellate folds. Outer lip imbricate. Dull, grey to cream with some reddish brown markings. Creamy, nacreous aperture. Thick operculum granulose, whith white, green and orange staining. 6–10cm. Indo-Pacific: Common.

Turbo canaliculatus Hermann   × 0·7
Channelled Turban
spenglerianus Gmelin.

Thick, globose shell with moderately tall spire, rounded whorls and deeply channelled suture. Numerous smooth, strong spiral cords with narrow interstices crossed by fine, axial growth lines. Yellowish white, flushed pinkish brown on upper whorls and blotched and spotted with darker brown markings. Aperture and columella white. 5–7cm. Caribbean. Uncommon.

Turbo chrysostomus Linnaeus
Gold-mouthed Turban

Thick, solid, heavy shell with large, inflated body whorl and short spire. Whorls angulated at shoulder and body whorl well rounded at periphery, giving shell a

square-sided appearance. Suture moderately impressed. Surface covered with spiral, sometimes scaly cords, those at base and around umbilicus being much stronger than others. Axial lamellae between spiral cords. Outer lip crenulate. Whitish or yellowish with broad, irregular, axial, brownish streaks and spiral dashes. Aperture golden and white edged. Thick operculum is whitish blotched with brown and green. 5–8cm. Indo-Pacific. Common.

Turbo cidaris Gmelin   × 1·1

Thick, turbinate shell with low, blunt spire and heavily callused columella. Outer lip thickened. Three or four strong spiral cords at periphery of each whorl. Fine, axial growth lines. Glossy and smooth. Very variable colouring. Chocolate brown with paler brown mottlings and spiral rows of brown and whitish flecks; pale brown with two spiral, yellowish bands at periphery of body whorl; pinkish orange with two spiral, purple-brown bands bearing broad, white spots at periphery and numerous spiral, brown and white lines near base. Columella stained greenish or brownish. Aperture white or greenish white. 3–4cm. South African. Common.

Turbo circularis Reeve   × 1·2

Thick, turbinate shell with moderately tall spire, deeply impressed suture and callused columella which ends in a lump at the base. Strong, flattened spiral cords with weaker, beaded spiral cords in the interstices. Beaded cords absent on base. Yellowish or creamy with axial, light or dark brown stripes which are interrupted on body whorl. Aperture yellowish, columella white. 3·0–3·5cm. Australian (Australia). Uncommon.

Turbo cornutus Lightfoot × 0·6
Horned Turban

Large, thick, turbinate shell with strong spiral cords crossed by growth ridges and raised as lamellate horns on shoulder, periphery and base of body whorl. Sometimes without horns. Punctate interstices of spire cords. Glossy, reddish brown, green and cream oblique mottling. Operculum granulose and spirally ribbed. 7–10cm. Japonic. Uncommon.

Turbo coronatus Gmelin
Thick, heavy, globose shell with depressed spire. Very thick columella, produced at base. Body whorl has two rows of large, evenly spaced, blunt tubercles on either side of periphery, with a row of smaller more numerous tubercles between. At suture is a row of upturned, fluted, scale-like tubercles which are adpressed to penultimate whorl, giving coronate appearance. Rest of shell ornamented with coarse, spiral, beaded cords. Spire whorls usually worn smooth. Greenish, mottled and flecked with purplish brown markings. Thick, greenish brown periostracum. 3·5–4·0cm. South African, Indo-Pacific. Common.

Turbo excellens Sowerby
Thick, small, turbinate shell with well rounded whorls, tall spire and impressed suture. Two to three spiral, granulated cords just below suture. Rest of shell with smooth cords. Dull pinkish brown. Very similar to *T. stenogyrus* but the white operculum is not granulated and has a spiral ridge. *c*2cm. Japonic. Frequent.

Turbo fluctuosus Wood × 0·9

Moderately large, thick shell with short spire, large body whorl and columella thickened and broad at base. Strong spiral cords give shell squarish sides. Finer spiral ribs between strong cords. Light and dark brown with flecks, zigzag markings and chevrons in white and darker brown. Aperture greenish white. Operculum with large, central, granulose knob surrounded by several rows of raised, needle-like points, innermost row resembling fine-toothed comb. 4–5cm. Panamic. Common.

Turbo foliaceus Philippi × 0·6

Thick, turbinate shell with narrow umbilicus. Evenly spaced axial lamellae and spiral cords. Dull, green with dark brown, axial markings. White aperture. 3·5–4·5cm. Australian. Frequent.

Turbo granosus Martyn
Thin but strong shell with convex whorls. Spiral bands of beads are crossed by striae and there may be faint, irregular, white, axial bands. Dull, pink to reddish. Oval, thick, dull, white or cream operculum granulose with smooth margin. *c*6·5cm. Australian (New Zealand). Rare.

Turbo jourdani Kiener
Very large, solid, turbinate shell with moderately tall spire, impressed suture and rounded whorls. Thick columella and broad parietal callus. Irregular, axial growth lines, otherwise smooth. Reddish brown except for some cream patches on early whorls. Aperture, columella and parietal wall white. The thick, heavy operculum has a smooth, white, outer surface. *c*20cm. Australian (Australia). Uncommon.

Turbo lajonkairii Deshayes
Very thick, turbinate shell with strong spiral cords. Cords at shoulder, periphery and base of body whorl have lamellate horns. Dull, greenish shell with creamy, nacreous aperture. Calcareous, dull operculum has orange staining. 5–10cm. Indo-Pacific (Indian Ocean only). Uncommon.

Turbo mamoratus Linnaeus × 0·3/0·6
Green Snail

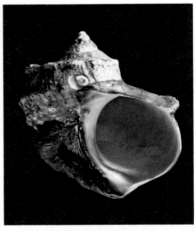

Largest representative of family. Heavy, dull green shell with angular shoulder on body whorl. Massive body wall and large aperture. Greyish green with spiral bands of alternating reddish brown and greyish cream quadrants. Golden, nacreous aperture is slightly extended and recurved at base. Thick, circular operculum, whitish. Shell commercially important. 15–20cm. Indo-Pacific. Common.

Turbo petholatus Linnaeus   × 1·1
Tapestry Turban
Strong, heavy, smooth, glossy shell with convex whorls. Body whorl often concave below suture. Colour variable but lips usually have yellow or greenish yellow stain. Variations include: ochre ground colour with spiral, greyish blue bands on body whorl, irregular near suture; greenish yellow shell with no pattern; flesh-coloured, cream or pink with wide, irregular, axial bands alternating with similar wide brown bands and dark greenish brown, spiral bands with flesh-coloured marks. Large, round operculum with glossy, deep green centre, brown granules near parietal lip, white next to the columellar lip; commonly known as 'cat's eye'. 4–8cm. Indo-Pacific. Common.

Turbo pulcher Sowerby   × 1·0
Thick, turbinate shell with short spire. Strong spiral cords alternate with fewer, weak axial ridges. Dull, buff to yellowish green shell; may have irregular, axial, brown to grey lines. Large, pink, nacreous aperture with everted columellar lip. Operculum with large granules. 5–9cm. Australian. Uncommon.

Turbo reevei Philippi
Closely resembles *T. petholatus* but has a less constricted suture which gives whorls a rounder appearance. Colour and pattern similar but green is less evident. Thick, calcareous operculum similar to that of *T. petholatus*. c4cm. Japonic. Common.

Above: Turbo petholatus
Below: Turbo pulcher

Turbo sarmaticus Linnaeus
Large, thick and heavy shell with short, few-whorled spire and very large body whorl with inflated aperture. Three or four spiral rows of large, evenly spaced tubercles which are often worn down to reveal the nacreous layer underneath. Columella greatly thickened. Dark reddish brown with whitish axial streaks. Large, blackish patch on parietal wall. Columella white. Inner margin of outer lip brown or blackish brown, aperture pearly. Operculum studded with large and small, white granules. 8–11cm. South African. Common.

Turbo saxosus Wood
Thick, solid, turbinate shell with moderately tall spire and deeply impressed suture. Each whorl is coronated with thick, raised tubercles and angled periphery has slightly smaller tubercles. Lower portion of body whorl also with spiral rows of tubercles. Strong, oblique, axial growth ridges over whole shell. Columella gently curved. Whitish with broad, axial, green

streaks, sometimes a white spiral band on body whorl. Operculum similar to that of *T. fluctuosus*, but central pit is not entered by a spiral rib. c4·5cm. Panamic. Frequent.

Turbo setosus Gmelin
Thick, solid, heavy, globose shell with moderately tall spire and deeply impressed suture. Columella lip produced basally. Outer lip thin and crenulate. Whole shell encircled by numerous strong, broad, flattened ribs with finer spiral cords in the interstices. Strongest spiral rib just below suture. Fine, axial growth lines. Dark brown or greenish, mottled with whitish or yellowish blotches and dots. Aperture nacreous white. 5–7cm. Indo-Pacific. Common.

Turbo splendidulus Sowerby   × 0·7

Thick, turbinate shell with strong spiral ridges and spiral striae. Dull, buff with alternating dark and light brown to cream spots on ridges. Nacreous, white aperture. Operculum thick, irregularly ovate, cream to greenish. 7–9cm. South African. Rare.

Turbo squamiger Reeve
Small, globose, short-spired shell with almost circular aperture. Spiral ribs have large, triangular, scale-like nodules, rows of large nodules alternating with rows of smaller ones. Greenish, dotted with reddish brown. c2·7cm. Panamic, Peruvian. Frequent.

Turbo stenogyrus Fischer
Thick, small shell with tall spire and rounded whorls. Prominent, smooth spiral cords on all whorls. Fine axial riblets between cords. Yellowish white with broad axial stripes on all whorls but absent on body whorl. Spiral rows of brownish blotches on base. White operculum is finely granulated. c2cm. Japonic. Common.

Turbo torquatus Gmelin   × 0·5/1·1

Large, thick, solid, turbinate shell with short spire. Large body whorl and deeply impressed suture. Large, very deep umbilicus. Numerous strong spiral cords on all whorls with those above periphery nodulous. Crossed by numerous strong, axial, growth ridges. Pale brown mottled, in juvenile specimens, with green or orange. Columella, umbilical area and aperture white. Covered with thick, greenish periostracum. Operculum thick, circular, outer side with fine prickles and spiral ridges; white outside and pale yellowish brown inside. 6–11cm. Australian (Australia). Common.

Turbo tricarinulatus Euthyme   × 2·0

Thin, but strong, smooth shell with convex whorls and flattened spire. Spiral cords at periphery. Pink or orangey pink sometimes with alternating brown and cream markings. Greenish grey, nacreous interior. Umbilical groove. 2·5–3·0cm. South African. Uncommon.

Turbo undulatus Lightfoot
Thick, turbinate shell with short spire and rounded whorls. Strong, smooth spiral ribs. Umbilicus very deep. Pale green with wavy, axial, dark green streaks. Thick, circular operculum has a smooth, convex, outer surface. c7cm. Australian (Australia). Common.

Family PHASIANELLIDAE

Cylindrically ovate to globose, few-whorled shells lacking periostracum. Usually smooth but occasionally finely spirally ornamented. Only small species are occasionally umbilicate. Often very colourful and great variation in colour and pattern is exhibited by several species. Calcareous operculum either externally convex or flat and spirally ridged. Three genera widely distributed over globe.

Genus PHASIANELLA Lamarck
Small to moderately large, elongate-ovate shells. Whorls rounded and smooth. No umbilicus. Parietal callus. Suture not deeply impressed. Apex pointed. Thick, convex white operculum. Few species in Indo-Pacific.

Phasianella aethiopica Philippi   × 1·2
Like a small version of *P. australis*, but much smaller. Whorls well rounded and suture moderately impressed. Apex blunt.

Extremely variable in colour and pattern. Ground colour often creamy white but may be pinkish. Mottled, flecked, spotted with pink, red, purple, green, dark brown; sometimes with broad, axial blotches which may be orange brown or purplish. Apex pink or white. Aperture and columella white. 1·5–2·5cm. Indo-Pacific (Indian Ocean). Frequent.

Phasianella australis Gmelin   × 1·0
Painted Lady.
Shell moderately large, thick and tall-spired. Whorls rounded. Thick, white parietal callus. Numerous distinct colour forms are known. Ground colour may be greyish, brownish, yellowish white, pinkish red. Pattern consists of axial bands, spiral lines, blotches, dots and crescent-like markings arranged in numerous different combinations and colours. 5–8cm. Australian (Australia). Common.

Phasianella kochii Philippi   × 2·3

Below: Phasianella australis

Thin, conical shell with convex whorls, large aperture and short spire. Smooth, glossy, red with oblique or spiral bands of red and ochre flecks, and cream or ochre marks along borders of bands. White aperture. 0·3–1·3cm. South African. Common.

Phasianella venosa Reeve
Like a smaller version of *P. australis*, but with more globose whorls and shorter spire. Colour and pattern extremely variable. Whitish, yellowish or pinkish, variegated with axial streaks, blotches, lines and dots of various colours. Often with a single row of squarish, brown dots at periphery of body whorl and above suture on spire whorls. *c*4cm. Australian (Australia). Frequent.

Phasianella ventricosa Swainson
perdix Wood.
Similar to *P. australis*, but smaller, more ventricose and with relatively larger aperture. Several distinct colour patterns are found. The commonest is rose pink with irregular, wavy, brown axial bands, yellow flecks and numerous thin spiral lines of brown and yellow dashes. Another form has brown axial bands broader and more regular, giving shell an axially striped appearance. Unicolorous red-brown form occurs. Operculum thick and white. *c*4cm. Australian (Australia). Common.

Superfamily
Neritacea

Family NERITIDAE

Short-spired, globose or patelliform shells. Outer lip may be thickened and denticulate, while the columella may be denticulate and may have a callus. No umbilicus. The calcareous operculum has a hooked appendage (or apophysis) and is often granulate. Tropical family inhabiting rocky areas of the shore. Some species in estuaries or freshwater habitat. Ten recent genera, widely distributed.

Genus NERITA Linnaeus
Thick, solid shells with short or flattened spire and strong spiral ribbing. Columella with small or large teeth; outer lip smooth or denticulate. Very variable in colour. Operculum has an appendage known as the apophysis. About a hundred species in tropical and warm seas.

Nerita albicilla Linnaeus   × 1·0
Thick, flat-topped shell, white or yellowish with black spiral bands expanding towards parietal lip. Yellow or white granulose, parietal region. Pinkish grey, granulose

operculum. 2·0–3·5cm. South African. Indo-Pacific. Common.

Nerita antiquata Récluz   × 1·0

Thick, axially striate and spirally ridged. Variously coloured bands in greyish green and cream, occasionally white. Yellow or cream outer lip. Orange parietal lip. May be a population variant of *N. polita*. 2–3 cm. Indo-Pacific. Common.

Nerita exuvia Linnaeus
Snake-skin Nerite
Solid shell with short spire and thickened, denticulate outer lip. Parietal region pustulose. Strong spiral ridges with deep grooves between. Black, with white spotting on ribs. *c*3cm. Indo-Pacific. Common.

Nerita fulgurans Gmelin
Antillean Nerite
Thick, globose, flat-topped shell with obscure suture. Spiral ridges with narrow interstices. Dull, black with irregular, yellow, axial lines. White or cream aperture with 2–3 parietal denticles. Operculum bluish white. 2·0–2·5cm. Caribbean. Common.

Nerita granulata Reeve
Solid, dark grey shell with spiral ridges crossed by striae. White aperture with weakly denticulate parietal lip. Expanded parietal region may be yellowish. Columellar lip has two median denticles. *c*2cm. Indo-Pacific (Pacific). Common.

Nerita lineata Gmelin   × 1·2
Thick, globose, flat-topped shell with simple suture. Spiral ridges separated by narrow grooves; faint, axial growth lines.

Dull, dark grey ridges, greyish cream interstices. Pale yellow aperture. 3–5 median denticles on columella, smooth parietal shield. 2·5–3·0cm. Indo-Pacific (Malaysia). Common.

Nerita maura Récluz
Very thick, globose, flat-topped shell with simple, obscure suture. Spiral striae crossed by axial growth lines. Dull, black with axial, yellowish grey markings occasionally forming irregular bands. White aperture, columella may be yellow and has two median denticles. Weak beading on parietal shield near denticles, finely plicate outer lip. 3·5–4·0cm. Indo-Pacific. Common.

Nerita morio Sowerby
haneti Récluz, *carbonaria* Philippi, *neritinoides* Reeve.
Thick, globose, flat-topped shell with simple, obscure suture. Axial growth lines. Glossy, dark slate grey to black. Cream aperture with smooth parietal shield and two median denticles on columella. 1·75–2cm. Indo-Pacific. Frequent.

Nerita peloronta Linnaeus   × 0·7
Bleeding Tooth
Shell large and thick. Short spire. Smooth

or spirally ridged. Conspicuous orange mark around white parietal denticles. Shell may be pinkish white with dark reddish brown, zigzag, spiral lines; yellow with broad, black, zigzag bands; or flesh-coloured with alternating black and red, mottled bands. Black, granulose operculum. 2–4cm. Caribbean. Common.

Nerita plicata Linnaeus   × 1·0

Shell thick, globose, short-spired. Strong spiral cords. Plicate parietal region and 3–4 denticles on columellar lip. Outer lip has two large denticles enclosing five smaller ones. Creamy grey or creamy pink, cords sometimes spotted with black. Shiny, brown operculum. 2–3cm. South African, Indo-Pacific. Common.

Nerita polita Linnaeus   × 0·8

Shell thick and heavy, nearly flat-topped. Axial striae. Broad parietal shield. Columella grooved. Creamy grey or creamy pink sometimes banded rose pink and mottled with white or black. Shiny, brown operculum. 2·0–3·5cm. Indo-Pacific. Common.

Nerita pupa Linnaeus
Zebra Nerite
Shell small and solid. Smooth, white with axial black stripes. Yellow aperture. Smooth, cream operculum. 1·0–1·5cm. Caribbean. Common.

Nerita scabricosta Lamarck   × 1·2
ornata Sowerby.

Thick, globose shell with prominent spiral cords. Grey with cream or brown bands on body whorl. Parietal lip has small denticles. Columellar lip has 2–4 denticles. Grey, granulose operculum. 2–5cm. Panamic. Common.

Nerita tessellata Gmelin   × 1·4
Tessellate Nerite

Shell thick, globose, with depressed spire and simple suture. Spiral cords are separated by narrow grooves. Dull, white or yellowish grey with black, quadrangular marks on cords. White aperture with beaded, bluish white parietal shield, plicate parietal lip with two denticles. Operculum black. 1·0–2·5cm. Caribbean. Common.

Nerita textilis Gmelin   × 0·9
plexa Dillwyn.

Thick, heavy shell with depressed spire. Broad spiral cords. White with black spots widely spaced on cords. Granulose, yellow or white, parietal region with two columellar denticles. Outer lip thick and denticulate. Bluish grey, thick, granulose operculum. 3·5–5·0cm. Indo-Pacific. Frequent.

Nerita undata Linnaeus   × 1·4
undulata Gmelin, *quadricolor* Gmelin.
Shell thick, short-spired. Ornamented with spiral cords. Parietal wall irregularly ribbed. Strongly toothed columella. Outer lip toothed. Cords maculated with alternate black and yellow markings. Granulose

operculum. 2·5–3·5cm. Indo-Pacific. Common.

Nerita versicolor Gmelin   × 1·0

Thick, short-spired shell. Ornamented with spiral cords. 2–4 denticles on columellar lip. Dirty white with red, pink, black or grey marks on cords. White or flesh-coloured aperture. Plicate parietal region. Operculum finely granular, brownish grey. 2·0–2·5cm. Caribbean. Common.

Genus NERITINA Lamarck
Usually smaller and thinner shelled than *Nerita*. Outer lip thin, inner lip smooth or finely dentate. Many species in tropical and warm seas; also in brackish or freshwater.

Neritina communis Quoy & Gaimard
Thin but strong shell. Short-spired and smooth. Columella denticulate. Extremely variable in colour and pattern. Colours range from unicolorous black, red or yellow to combinations of these colours arranged in axial or spiral bands and streaks, often variegated with white. *c*2cm. Indo-Pacific (Philippines). Common.

Neritina gagates Lamarck   × 1·2
zigzag Férussac, *caffra* Gray, *strigilata* Deshayes, *lineolata* Liénard.
Smooth, black shell with axial striae. Strikingly patterned with axial, zigzag streaks. Columellar lip and aperture white or cream. 2·0–3·5cm. Indo-Pacific (Pacific only). Common.

Nerita gagates

Neritina turrita Gmelin
Shell thick, ovate, short-spired, smooth. Variable in colour through brown, olive and grey. Black axial bands may be zigzag. Creamy or white aperture and lips. Outer lip smooth, columellar lip denticulate. Grey, violet or yellow operculum has apical nucleus and striae. 2·0–2·5cm. Indo-Pacific (Philippines). Common.

Genus SMARAGDIA Issel
Small, obliquely ovate shells with short spire and large aperture. Operculum ribbed. Few species widespread in warm seas.

Smaragdia viridis Linnaeus   × 2·0

Thin but strong shell with large, narrow aperture. Smooth, pea green often with white flecks, rarely with purplish brown, narrow, zigzag markings. 0·25–0·75cm. Mediterranean, Caribbean. Common.

Superfamily
Littorinacea

Family LITTORINIDAE
Shells small, thick or fairly thin. Short and squat, or tall and conical spire, rounded or nearly straight-sided whorls, suture usually slightly impressed. No umbilicus. Peristome discontinuous. Smooth, or ornamented with spiral ridges or rows of strong or weak nodules. Columella without processes. Corneous operculum. Commonly known as winkles or periwinkles. About 20 genera. Widely distributed inhabitants of shore between tide marks. Also in mangrove swamps.

Genus LITTORINA Férussac
For details see Family Littorinidae. Mostly smooth-shelled species many of them resembling each other closely and making identification difficult. Probably less than 100 species.

Littorina angulifera Lamarck
Thin, high cone with large body whorl. Simple suture. Spiral grooves and ridges; columellar lip slightly thickened. Dull, yellow to cream body whorl and grey spire with axial, wavy, brown lines. Some specimens orange or yellow with lines reduced to dots. Greenish cream specimens have reddish brown dots on brown spiral bands. Yellow parietal lip; purplish columellar lip. 0·5–2·5cm. Caribbean. Frequent.

Littorina carinifera Menke
perdix King & Broderip, *conica* Philippi. Thin, high cone with simple suture. 3–5 strong keels on body whorl or well marked spiral striae. Spire usually decollate. Dull, yellowish brown with straight, zigzag or oblique, axial, reddish brown lines. Grey-

ish cream aperture with dark brown lines on parietal lip. 2·0–2·3cm. Indo-Pacific. Common.

Littorina coccinea Gmelin   × 1·7
obesa Sowerby, *limax* Gray.

Thick, conic-turbinate shell with short spire and simple suture. Fine spiral striae and axial growth lines. Dull, grey with cream bands and axial brown lines. Violet columella, outer lip cream, brown or violet. 0·7–2·6cm. Indo-Pacific. Common.

Littorina fasciata Philippi   × 1·1

Globose, conical shell with simple suture. Weak spiral striae crossed by oblique, axial growth lines. Dull, cream around aperture, grey body whorl, purplish to dark red spire. Aperture is white marginally, interior cream, yellow or with external markings showing through. 2·5–2·8cm. Panamic, Peruvian. Common.

Littorina irrorata Say   × 1·3
Marsh Periwinkle
Thick, turbinate shell with simple suture. Spiral striae separated by stepped ridges. Faint, axial growth lines on body whorl.

Dull, white to cream or grey. May have spiral bands of reddish brown spots. White aperture, brown columella. 1–2cm. Caribbean, Transatlantic. Common.

Littorina littoralis Linnaeus   × 1·8

Thick, globose shell with depressed spire and simple suture. Faint spiral striae and faint, axial growth lines. Dull, orange, yellow or yellowish green spiral bands alternating with dark brown or orange brown bands. White or cream columella, outer lip brown and orange or brown. 0·75–1·25cm. Boreal (North West Europe). Common.

Littorina littorea Linnaeus   × 1·0
Common Winkle

Thick, globose cone with simple suture. Faint spiral striae and fine ridges. Faint, axial growth lines. Dull, cream, yellow or grey with dark brown or reddish brown spiral bands and lines. Dull white columella, external colour and marking show through outer lip. 1·5–3·5cm. Boreal. Also North East Coast of USA (apparently introduced). Common.

Littorina mandchurika Schrenck
Shell solid, short-spired, with large body whorl and shallow suture. Columella thick. Three strong spiral cords on body whorl. Blackish brown. c1·3cm. Japonic. Common.

Littorina melanostoma Gray   × 1·7
Black-mouth Littorine
Thickish, slim, conical shell with pointed spire and simple suture. Spiral striae and

faint, axial growth lines. Dull, yellowish white with brown quadrants on ridges giving axial stripes, oblique or zigzag. Apex often grey. Dark brown columella. Aperture cream and brown. 2·0–2·8cm. Indo-Pacific. Common.

Littorina obtusata Linnaeus   × 2·0
palliata Say.

Thin, globose shell with simple suture. Smooth with axial growth lines. Dull, variable yellow, orange or purplish brown. White, nacreous columella; external colour shows through inner lip. 1·0–1·5cm. Boreal (Labrador to Cape May, Scandinavia). Common.

Littorina pintado Wood   × 2·0

Conic-turbinate shell with short spire and simple suture. Fine spiral striae, faint axial growth lines. Reddish brown streaks or spots all over. Dark brown aperture with external pattern showing through. 1·0–2·5cm. Indo-Pacific (Pacific). Common.

Littorina pulchra Sowerby   × 0·8

Thick, turbinate shell, depressed, with simple suture. Dull and rough with alternating spiral bands of brown and cream, sometimes reduced to flecks on spire. Brown aperture with evenly spaced, dark brown dots on lip. 2–3cm. Panamic. Common.

Littorina scabra Linnaeus   × 2·0
Rough Periwinkle
luteola Quoy & Gaimard, *intermedia* Philippi.

Thin shell with conical spire and simple suture. Weak spiral ridges crossed by axial growth lines. Dullish and very variable in colour and pattern. Mosaic of irregular, axial, brown lines separated by cream or yellow; pattern may be lacking, lines may be zigzag. Large, pale aperture with external markings showing through. 1·5–2·0cm. Indo-Pacific. South African. Common.

Littorina undulata Gray   × 2·1
tenuis Philippi, *acuminata* Gould.

Thick, high, turbinate shell with pointed spire and simple suture. Faint spiral striae, faint axial growth lines. Dull, cream to greenish grey with variable, brown, axial lines. Violet or purplish brown columella, brown or purplish brown parietal lip.

Mottled yellowish grey to banded dark brown forms also occur. 2·0–2·4cm. Indo-Pacific. Common.

Littorina unifasciata Gray
Thickish, conical shell with simple suture. Spiral striae mark weak ridges crossed by oblique, axial growth lines. Dull, cream with grey spiral band above suture and above periphery of body whorl. Brown aperture with white patch towards upper margin of parietal lip. 1–3cm. Australian (Australia). Frequent.

Littorina varia Sowerby   × 1·1

Very thick, turbinate shell with impressed suture. Strong spiral ridges and axial growth lines. Dull, greyish yellow with dark brown, axial bands made irregular by ornamentation. White aperture. 2–3cm. Peruvian. Common.

Littorina ziczac Gmelin   × 2·1

Conical shell with simple suture and short, pointed spire. Weak spiral striae and axial growth lines. Glossy, grey with axial band of yellow and grey, brown and white, or cream and brown stripes. Brown aperture. 0·5–1·0cm. Indo-Pacific. Common.

Genus ECHININUS Clench & Abbott
Similar to *Tectarius* but has multispiral operculum. Few species. Caribbean.

Echininus nodulosus Pfeiffer   × 1·6

Thick shell with spiral cords around base and spiral rows of large nodules on whorls. Dull, dark olive. Aperture with narrow, white margin and brown interior. 2·0–2·5cm. Caribbean. Frequent.

Genus TECTARIUS Valenciennes
Turbinate, solid shells ornamented with tubercles, spines and nodulose cords. Ovate aperture not nacreous within. No umbilicus. Operculum paucispiral with a broad, membranous edge. Few species in warm or tropical seas.

Tectarius grandinatus Gmelin   × 1·0

Thick, tall-spired shell with straight sides. Simple, obscure suture. Spiral rows of nodules. Base of body whorl flattened, with spiral, beaded cords. Nodules discontinuously linked by axial ridges. Median denticle on columella; outer lip plicate, lirate. Body whorl with dark brown band, rest of whorl orange or cream. Spire whorls often with dark brown band on cream, olive or yellow. Cream base. 3–4cm. Indo-Pacific. (Pacific only). Common.

Tectarius pagodus Linnaeus   × 1·0

Thick, heavy, turbinate shell. Base of body whorl papillate with peripheral ring of blunt spines and ring of nodules. Rough, spiral cords. Columella with median denticle; outer lip plicate, lirate. Dull, greenish cream shell or cream with spiral grey bands. Cream aperture. 1·5–3·0cm. Indo-Pacific. Common.

Superfamily
Rissoacea

Family RISSOIDAE
Small or minute shells, smooth, finely striated or ribbed. Ovate aperture. Corneous operculum Numerous genera and hundreds of species in all seas. Only a few species are large enough to attract the collector's attention.

Genus RISSOINA d'Orbigny
For details, see Family Rissoidae. Shells large for the family, many-whorled and usually strongly ribbed or cancellated. Many species in tropical and warm seas.

Rissoina caelata A. Adams   × 2·0

Thick shell with reticulate ornamentation of axial and spiral ridges. Dull, cream with white aperture. 1·75–2·0cm. Indo-Pacific. Frequent.

Rissoina cumingii Kiener   × 2·0

Shell relatively large, thick, elongate-fusiform with tall spire and impressed suture. Axial ribs and spiral lines produce cancellation on early whorls, later worls smooth. Unicolorous white. *c*2·5cm. Indo-Pacific (Pacific). Common.

Rissoina scolopax Souverbie
Solid, elongate-fusiform shell with impressed suture. Thick spiral cord round umbilical area. Strong, oblique axial ribs on each whorl. Apex usually worn away. Outer lip thickened. Unicolorous white. c1·2cm. Indo-Pacific (Central Pacific). Uncommon.

Superfamily
Cerithiacea

Family TURRITELLIDAE

With the possible exception of the Terebridae, this family includes the longest and most slender-spired of all gastropod shells. Apart from spiral ornament which differs from species to species, the members of this family all show a close resemblance to each other. Corneous operculum is flexible. Most species are found below low-tide line. Numerous genera have been proposed, but it is convenient to treat the following species under the single genus *Turritella*. Family represented in almost all seas.

Genus TURRITELLA Lamarck
For details, see Family Turritellidae.

Turritella bacillum Kiener   × 0·8

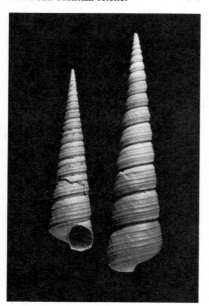

Large, thick, very long shell, reminiscent of *T. terebra* but with less strongly marked spiral ornament. Suture deeply impressed, but whorls are flat-sided. Weak to strong spiral cords which tend to become obsolete on later whorls. Yellowish brown to dark brown. Spiral cords occasionally of lighter colour. 6–13cm. Indo-Pacific. Frequent.

Turritella bicingulata Lamarck   × 1·0

Thick, stout shell with almost straight-sided whorls and deeply impressed suture. Mature specimens average about 16 whorls. Usually two strong, beaded or smooth spiral cords with finer spiral ribs above and below. Yellowish white with broad and narrow, axial, purplish brown streaks. Columella white. 4–7cm. West African. Common.

Turritella broderipiana D'Orbigny
Thick, heavy, very tall shell with flat sides and impressed suture. Fine spiral striae on each whorl. Creamy white with axial, brown streaks and blotches. Some specimens have lower whorls concave at periphery. 15–17cm. Peruvian. Frequent.

Turritella carinifera Lamarck
Thick, broad-based, elongate-conical shell with sharp ridge at periphery of each whorl and sharply angulated basal margin. Fine spiral lines encircle all whorls. Creamy, with underlying purplish coloration showing through; blotched or spotted with pale brown. c5cm. South African. Common.

Turritella cingulata Sowerby
Solid shell, broad relative to height. Deeply impressed suture. Whorl has three strong, beaded spiral cords with a fine spiral ridge between them. Yellowish white with spiral cords and ridges dark brown. 5–7cm. Peruvian. Common.

Turritella communis Risso   × 1·5
Moderately thin, light shell with rounded whorls and impressed suture. Strong, coarse spiral ribs, crossed by fine, axial

growth lines. Reddish brown. Columella white. 4–6cm. Boreal, Mediterranean. Common.

Turritella duplicata Linnaeus   × 0·45

Shell very thick and heavy, with numerous relatively broad, concave or almost straight-sided whorls and deeply impressed suture. Usually there are two or three thick, strongly keeled spiral ribs which tend to become obsolete towards aperture. Numerous finer spiral ribs crossed by fine, axial growth striae. Aperture round; columella curved. Yellowish white with upper whorls flushed pinkish brown. 12–15cm. Indo-Pacific (Indian Ocean). Common.

Turritella fortilirata Sowerby
Thick, solid shell with almost straight sides

and moderately impressed suture. Broad and narrow, flattened spiral cords on each whorl, peripheral cords the strongest. Pinkish brown fading to yellowish white. Aperture purplish brown. c6·5cm. Japonic. Common.

Turritella gonostoma Valenciennes × 0·7
punctata Kiener, *marmorata* Kiener.

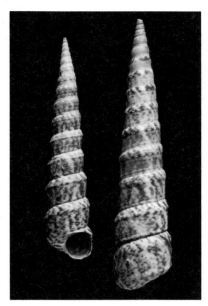

Thick, very tall shell with straight sides and acutely pointed apex. Outline of whorls and suture vary according to ornament. Specimens with several spiral cords to each whorl have impressed suture, while other specimens have almost smooth, flat-sided whorls. Early whorls always have single strong spiral cord. Grey to dark purplish brown with white mottling. Aperture same colour as surface. 9–12cm. Panamic. Common.

Turritella gunnii Reeve × 1·2

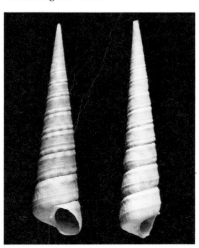

Tall, narrowly elongate shell with acutely pointed apex and deeply impressed suture. Whorls straight-sided. Basal margin roundly angulate. Three or four strong spiral cords with finer spiral lines between. Creamy white, with irregular, axial brownish streaks. 4–5cm. Australian (Australia and Tasmania). Common.

Turritella leucostoma Valenciennes × 0·8
tigrina Kiener, *cumingii* Reeve.

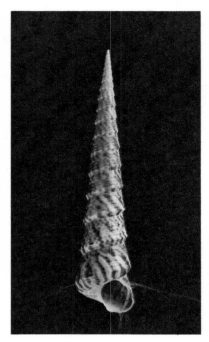

Thin, very slender shell with base of each whorl expanded and keeled just above suture. Numerous fine spiral threads crossed by finer, axial growth lines. Columella curved. Whitish with irregular, axial, brown streaks and dots. 8–10cm. Panamic. Uncommon.

Turritella ligar Deshayes
flammulata Kiener.
Heavy, very tall shell with well rounded whorls and deeply impressed suture. 7–8 spiral cords on each whorl and about 14 spiral cords on body whorl. Whitish, tinged with pale purple, blotched, streaked and spotted with darker brown. Aperture purple. 8–12cm. East African. Frequent.

Turritella maculata Reeve × 1·1
Thick, solid, tall shell with deeply impressed suture and moderately angled basal margin. Two strong spiral cords on each whorl with finer spiral lines between, sometimes a third spiral cord on each whorl. Creamy white with irregular, axial, brown or purplish brown streaks and blotches. Fine, spiral, brown lines on all whorls. Considerable variation in shape, ornament and pattern. Sometimes, as in

specimens illustrated, shells are almost colourless. 6–10cm. Indo-Pacific (North Arabian Sea). Common.

Turritella nodulosa King & Broderip
papillosa Kiener. × 1·2

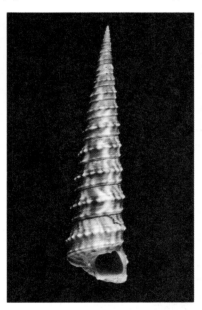

Tall, almost straight-sided shell with sharply angled base and impressed suture. Spiral row of large beads at periphery of each whorl; two or three rows of smaller beads on each whorl. Fine spiral lines between rows of beads. Grey to pale brown with irregular, axial, reddish brown stripes. 3–5cm. Panamic. Uncommon.

Turritella terebra Linnaeus × 0·6
Shell thick, extremely long and tapering with about 25 or more rounded whorls and deep suture. Each whorl has about six

61

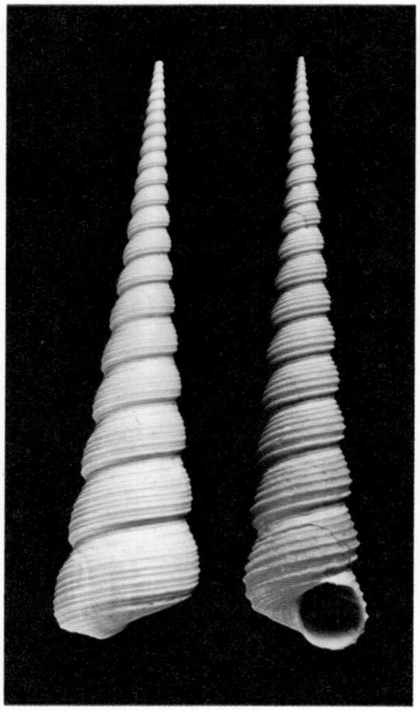

strongly-keeled spiral ribs with fine spiral lines between them crossed by fine, axial growth lines. Aperture rounded, columella almost straight. Unicolorous dark or pale brown. 11–18cm. Indo-Pacific. Uncommon.

Turritella torulosa Kiener × 0·9

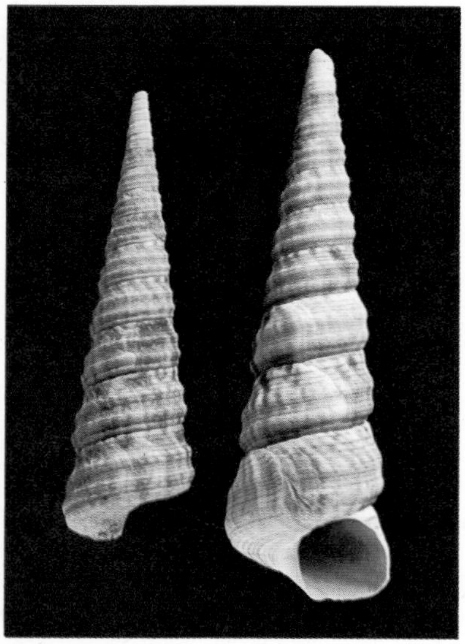

Shell thick, tall, with relatively broad base and acutely pointed spire. Suture deeply impressed. Two broad spiral cords and fine spiral striae on each whorl. Aperture squarish, columella thin. Pinkish white with light and dark brown mottlings and fine, spiral, brown lines. 5–7cm. Indo-Pacific. Frequent.

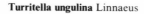

Turritella ungulina Linnaeus × 0·8

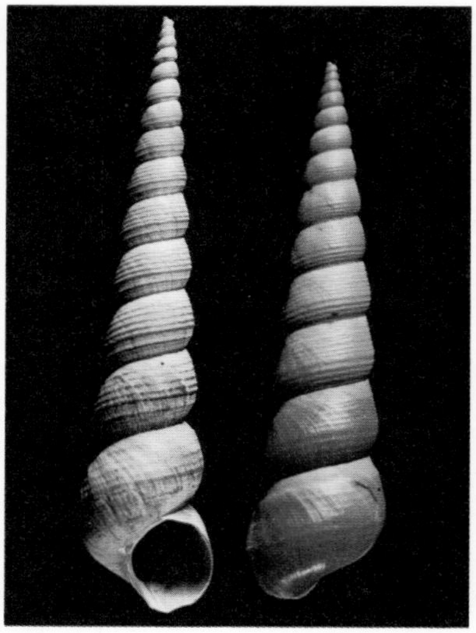

Large, moderately thick shell with well rounded whorls and deeply impressed suture. Numerous strong, regular spiral cords on all whorls. Aperture oval. White, pale brown or purplish brown. 5–8cm. West African. Common.

Turritella vittata Hutton
Thin shell, relatively broad in relation to height. Almost straight-sided with moderately impressed suture. Fine spiral lines on each whorl. Yellowish white with axial, brown streaks and thin, spiral, pale brown lines. 6–7cm. Australian (New Zealand). Common.

Family ARCHITECTONICIDAE

Small to large shells, usually many-whorled. Moderate to very large, wide and deep umbilicus which is open up to apex and reveals structure of inner side of each whorl. Radially and axially ribbed; ribbing on inside edge of whorls usually corrugated. Some species show very close resemblance to each other and the differences between them are often difficult to see, particularly in juveniles. Operculum usually corneous but in a few species it is calcareous. About six genera in warm and tropical seas.

Genus ARCHITECTONICA Röding

Solarium Lamarck.
Medium-sized to large shells with many tightly coiled whorls, sharp, peripheral keel and large, wide umbilicus open to apex. Inner surface of whorls corrugated. Few species in warm and tropical seas.

Architectonica maxima Philippi × 0·5
Closely resembles *A. trochlearis*, but has shorter spire and three instead of two spiral grooves on dorsal surface of whorls. Also, spiral ribs on inside wall of umbilicus

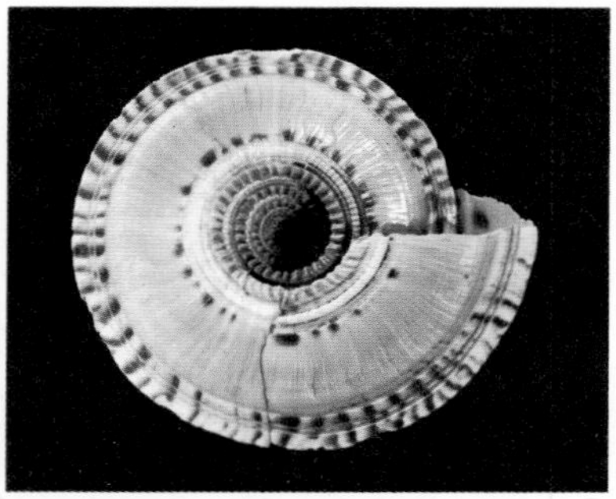

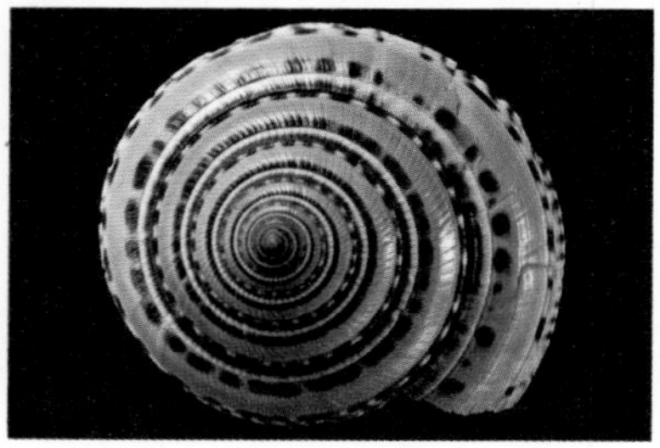

are not dark-coloured. 5–8cm. Indo-Pacific (Pacific). Uncommon.

Architectonica nobilis Röding
granulata Lamarck.
Thick, solid, low-spired shell with relatively small umbilicus. Numerous broad spiral ribs with deep grooves between. Grooves on base beaded. Heavily beaded spiral cord round umbilicus. Cream, with reddish brown spots which are most conspicuous just below suture. 2·5–5·0cm. Caribbean. Common.

Architectonica perdix Hinds
Some resemblance to *A. perspectiva*, but more conical with more tumid whorls and less conspicuous axial ribs. Flesh-coloured with spiral rows of brown spots on each side of suture and on peripheral keel. Marginal crenulations around umbilicus white. *c*3·5cm. Indo-Pacific (Pacific). Common.

Architectonica perspectiva Linnaeus
Closely resembles juvenile specimens of *A. trochlearis* in shape and colour. Deeply incised groove below suture, below periphery, and two others on lower surface around umbilicus. Numerous equidistant axial grooves cross whole shell. Umbilicus wide and deep. Bluish brown with white and black spiral bands below suture and blackish brown band at periphery on upper surface, two brown bands on peripheral area and two others on base around umbilicus. 3–4cm. Indo-Pacific. Common.

Architectonica reevei Hanley
offlexa Iredale.
Resembles *A. perdix*, but smaller, more conical and has fine, incised spiral lines between sutural and peripheral grooves. Colour and pattern similar to *A. perdix*,

but umbilical crenulations have a few brown spots. c2·5cm. Australian (Australia, New South Wales). Common.

Architectonica trochlearis Hinds   × 0·7

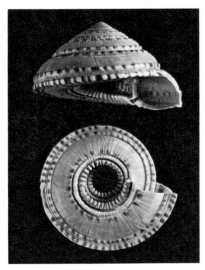

Shell large, thick and relatively tall-spired. Beaded spiral rib on each whorl just above suture. Spiral groove just above rib and another one below suture. Axial striae on all whorls becoming obsolete on body whorl. Two spiral grooves round umbilicus. Umbilicus very wide and deep with prominent corrugations on inside of each whorl. Light brown with broken spiral bands of dark brown along suture line and on spire ribs. 5·0–7·5cm. Indo-Pacific (Pacific). Uncommon.

Genus TORINIA Gray
Heliacus d'Orbigny.
Small, tightly coiled, usually depressed shells with very wide umbilicus and rounded or angular body whorl. Usually with strong spiral cords. The corneous operculum is thick and top-shaped in profile view. Numerous species in shallow water of tropical and warm seas.

Torinia variegata Gmelin   × 1·6

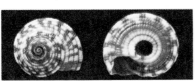

Shell small, with slightly raised, obtuse spire. Large, deep umbilicus. Two strong spiral cords at periphery with weaker spiral cords above and below. Cords crossed by strong axial grooves. Dark brown with white blotches. Umbilicus white with brown spiral line. 1·0–1·5cm. Indo-Pacific (Indian Ocean). Common.

Family SILIQUARIIDAE
Shells of this small family are remarkable for the loose, irregular coiling of their later whorls. Early whorls are tightly coiled and sometimes resemble *Turritella*. At some stage in the life of the animal, the shell is attached to the substrate, but it does not necessarily remain so. Some species have tiny holes arranged in a line along the upper surface of the tube. Operculum corneous, circular and multispiral, with a thickened edge. Several genera inhabiting shallow water of warm and tropical seas.

Genus VERMICULARIA Lamarck
Thin, twisted, tube-like shells with apical portion tightly coiled and resembling a young *Turritella*; the later whorls become progressively more uncoiled and distorted so that no two specimens of the same species look alike. Smooth, or ornamented with rough spiral ribs. Not attached to rocks or other objects. Few species in warm seas.

Vermicularia fargoi Olsson
Shell thin, with earlier, tightly coiled stage about 2·0–2·5cm. in length. Subsequent whorls progressively more uncoiled and worm-like. Two or three spiral cords on early whorls with subsequent whorls ornamented with three thicker cords. Early whorls dark brown, subsequent whorls dark brown variegated with paler brown. c8cm. Caribbean. Common.

Vermicularia lumbricalis Linnaeus
Thin, loosely and irregularly coiled shell. For less than a centimetre, the shell is tightly coiled like a *Turritella*, then it quickly unwinds and becomes haphazard in the direction of its growth. Three strong spiral cords which become obsolete towards later growth stage. Purplish brown with paler yellow on inside edge of coils. 4–6cm. West African. Frequent.

Vermicularia spirata Philippi   × 0·7

Closely coiled for about 1cm. or less, then the whorls become drawn out and worm-like. Moderately thin-shelled with one or occasionally two smooth spiral cords on middle of whorl. Two cords on loose coils, which soon become almost obsolete. Orange brown, amber or yellowish with early whorls darker. 7–9cm. Caribbean. Common.

Family PLANAXIDAE
Small to medium-sized shells, thin to solid, elongate ovate. Columella truncate at base. Aperture usually lirate internally. Operculum corneous, thin and paucispiral. Although the shells bear some resemblance to members of the Littorinidae, the distinct notch below the truncated columella immediately distinguishes them. About six genera in tropical and warm seas.

Genus PLANAXIS Lamarck
Thick, solid, ovately conical shells with acuminate spire and large body whorl. Columella smooth and truncate at base. Thick parietal callus within posterior angle of aperture. Aperture lirate within. Usually strong spiral cords. Animals crawl on stones near margins of pools left by receding tide. Some species in mangrove swamps. Numerous species in tropical and warm seas.

Planaxis lineatus da Costa
Thick, strong, ovate shell with spire about the same length as aperture. Apex sharply pointed. Short, truncated columella. Glossy and smooth. Few small spiral cords on spire becoming obsolete on body whorl. Creamy white with brown spiral bands. Smooth, translucent periostracum. Small size, smooth glossy surface and neat spiral bands distinguish the species from others. c0·6cm. Caribbean. Common.

Planaxis nucleus Bruguière
Thick, highly polished, ovate shell with rounded whorls and strong cords which are developed only below suture and, on the body whorl, only at base and just behind outer lip. Small parietal pimple. Strongly crenulate on inside of outer lip. Unicolorous dark brown. Cannot be confused with any other species. c1·2cm. Caribbean. Common.

Planaxis savignyi Deshayes   × 2·0

Similar to *P. sulcatus*, but smaller and with much less prominent spiral cords with narrower interstices. Parietal callus flushed reddish brown. Columella more curved. Similar to *P. sulcatus* in most other respects. 1·5–2·0cm. Indo-Pacific. Common.

Planaxis sulcatus Born   × 1·2

Thick, solid shell with large body whorl, moderately short spire, usually with worn apex. Suture roughly crenulate. Outer lip crenulate, aperture lirate within. Thick parietal callus. Truncate columella with deep notch below. Numerous broad, flat spiral cords with slightly narrower interstices. Fine, axial growth lines. Purplish brown with few whitish spots on cords. Aperture, columella and parietal callus whitish, inner margin of outer lip purplish brown. 2–3cm. Indo-Pacific. Common.

Family MODULIDAE

Small, solid, globose shells with short spire and large, inflated body whorl. Aperture large and wide. Tooth on columella and deep notch below it. Operculum corneous and thin, circular and multispiral. Small family with one genus. Found in shallow waters of warm and tropical seas.

Genus MODULUS Gray

For details, see Family Modulidae.

Modulus carchedonius Lamarck

Resembles *M. modulus*, but differs from it by having the periphery of the shell strongly angulated and in lacking axial ribs. Spiral cords smaller. *c*1·5cm. Caribbean. Common.

Modulus modulus Linnaeus   × 1·6

Thick, solid shell with short spire, large-angled body whorl and suture deeply impressed. Penultimate whorl overhangs suture. Thick spiral ribs on early whorls and upper side of body whorl. Strong, beaded spiral cords cross axial ribs. Aperture lirate within. Strong downward pointing tooth on columella with deep notch below it. Umbilicus small. Yellowish with spiral bands of purple brown dots. 1·2–1·6 cm. Caribbean. Common.

Modulus tectus Gmelin

Similar to *M. modulus*, but larger, with wider aperture and less strongly developed spiral cords on base of body whorl. Light yellow with only occasional brown spots. *c*2·5cm. Indo-Pacific. Common.

Family POTAMIDIDAE

Members of this family are closely related to those of Family Cerithiidae which they resemble in shell form and in habitat. Differences are mainly anatomical, though there are some differences in the shells. Outer lip usually flared and columella often twisted and complex; short anterior canal is not upturned as in the ceriths. Shells usually thick and very strong. Nearly all species are drab in colour and show considerable variation in shape and ornament. Unlike the sand-living ceriths, members of this family live on muddy shores near high-tide level and are often found living out of water. About twelve genera in warm and tropical seas.

Genus TELESCOPIUM Montfort

Thick, elongate-conical shells with pointed spire, flat base and narrow aperture. Suture scarcely discernible. Strong spiral ribs alternate with strong spiral grooves. Columella twisted in corkscrew fashion. Aperture uneven with basal projection. One species.

Telescopium telescopium Linnaeus   × 0·8

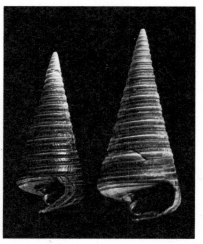

For description, see genus *Telescopium*. Shell very dark brown, with spiral, white or dark grey lines. 5–8cm. Indo-Pacific. Common.

Genus TEREBRALIA Swainson

Thick, elongate-fusiform shells with tall spire and wide, flaring lip. Strong axial cords on all whorls, crossed by deep spiral grooves. Outer lip projects in front of siphonal canal. All species are greenish brown to dark brown. Few species in Indo-Pacific.

Terebralia palustris Linnaeus   × 0·5

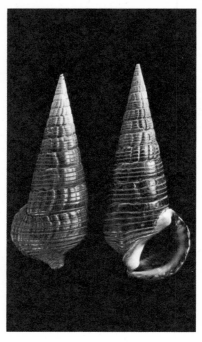

Thick, heavy, conical shell with long, pointed spire. Base of outer lip somewhat produced. Columella curved. Almost straight-sided with crenulate suture. Each whorl with strong axial ribs becoming obsolete on later whorls, crossed by deeply incised spiral grooves. Aperture crenulate. Unicolorous dark brown, aperture darker brown. 8–12cm. Indo-Pacific. Common.

Terebralia sulcata Born

Shell smaller than *T. palustris*, but otherwise similar. Thick and heavy with tall spire, moderately rounded whorls, impressed suture and flattened varix above siphonal canal on body whorl. Outer lip thickened and slightly flaring. Strong, flattened axial cords on all whorls but strongest on penultimate whorl. Cords bisected by deep spiral grooves. Coarse, axial growth ridges over whole shell. Dull, dirty brown. Inner margin of outer lip paler brown. 4–6cm. Indo-Pacific (Pacific). Common.

Genus TYMPANOTONOS Schumacher

Thick, elongate shells with many whorls, each of which bears strong tubercles, spines or nodes. Narrow, deep, posterior canal and broad siphonal notch. The few species live in the mud of West African coastal swamps and show enormous variation in ornament, the same species being almost spineless to very spiny.

Tympanotonos radula Linnaeus × 1·0

Thick, solid, elongate-conical shell with tall, pointed spire. Base of aperture juts forward and is slightly flared. Columella short and curved. Spiral row of thick, conical tubercles on shoulder of each whorl with two coarsely beaded spiral cords at suture. Five or six spiral ribs on base. Olive green to dark brown. Aperture whitish with pinkish brown blotches at margin. c4·5cm. West African. Common.

Family CERITHIIDAE

Thick, strong, elongate shells with many whorls. Smooth, or ornamented with strong axial ribs or tubercles and spiral cords or smooth ridges. Siphonal canal usually short and recurved, but sometimes moderately long. Extended to form a hook-like process passing in front of siphonal canal. Operculum corneous with an eccentric nucleus. Most species live in weed or on sand or among coral debris in shallow water. Mostly scavenge for food. Some species vary enormously in size, ornament and pattern. Numerous genera have been proposed, most of them having a strong family likeness. Although the genus *Cerithium* has been divided into many genera and sub-genera, the species described here are all placed in *Cerithium*.

Genus CERITHIUM Bruguière

Thick, fusiform to elongate, elliptical shells usually with nodules and raised ribs. Outer lip often projects forward at base.

Aperture relatively small, rounded to elliptical. Often a long, twisted siphonal canal. Operculum corneous, subcircular and with an eccentric nucleus. About 200 species in tropical and warm seas.

Cerithium adustum Kiener

Thick, solid, broadly ovate-fusiform shell with moderately impressed suture. Body whorl very convex with thin outer lip which is indented opposite the thick parietal callus. Light spiral cords with fine grooves between. Cords with widely spaced, low pustules on lower half of body whorl. Purplish brown with paler spiral lines, early whorls much lighter. Aperture white with purple staining on lower end of columella. c5cm. Panamic. Common.

Cerithium alternatum Sowerby

Solid, ovate-fusiform shell with slightly impressed suture and thick varix on body whorl above siphonal canal. Spiral cords on all whorls, about four on each spire whorl and 6–8 on body whorl. Cords either beaded or with sharp, raised, short spines which are strongest at suture. Aperture thickened and crenulate. Aperture lirate within. Thin parietal fold. Yellowish white, reddish brown or whitish with dark brown lines between cords. Most specimens have conspicuous varices on all whorls. 3–4cm. Indo-Pacific. Common.

Cerithium aluco Linnaeus × 0·9

Thick, elongate shell with swollen whorls which overlap slightly at suture. Each whorl has one spiral row of pointed nodules which are connected up by a thin spiral ridge. Outer lip thickened. Siphonal canal recurved. Parietal knob. Creamy white with axial, brown blotches and dashes. 5–7cm. Indo-Pacific. Common.

Cerithium armatum Philippi

Moderately thick, elongate-fusiform shell with impressed suture and strong varix on body whorl above siphonal canal. Early whorls with strong axial ribs. Later whorls with spiral rows of tubercles, those at shoulder being strong and upturned. Yellowish white with brown spots on lesser tubercles and axial, brown streaks on body whorl. c2·5cm. Indo-Pacific (Pacific). Common.

Cerithium articulatum Adams & Reeve × 1·1

Solid, thick shell with almost straight-sided spire and body whorl with prominent swelling just above columella. Flattened on ventral side of lower whorls. Outer lip thickened but sharp at edge. Broad spiral ribs which are flattened on ventral side and slightly nodulous on dorsal side. Slight axial ribs which are most pronounced at suture, becoming obsolete on body whorl. Creamy, with irregular, pale brown blotches and spots. Aperture white. 3·5–4·5cm. Indo-Pacific (Indian Ocean). Frequent.

Cerithium asper Linnaeus × 1·2

Thick, slender, elongate-fusiform shell with impressed suture. Siphonal canal short and recurved. Inner lip well separated from body whorl. Small parietal callus and two columella folds. Strong axial ribs crossed by three or four spiral ribs which are produced as upturned points where they cross axial ribs. Interspaces are characteristically squarish. Two spiral, beaded cords at base. White with brown spiral lines. 5–6cm. Indo-Pacific. Common.

Cerithium attenuatum Philippi
Shell long, narrow and tapering, with very long, sharply recurved, straight siphonal canal. Outer lip thickened and crenulate. Inner lip detached from body whorl. Thick varix on body whorl above siphonal canal. Numerous spiral, beaded cords, most prominent at suture. Yellowish or brownish with lighter, axial streaks. Aperture white with external pattern showing through; parietal lip and columella white. c5cm. Indo-Pacific. Common.

Cerithium bifasciatum Sowerby   × 1·7

Thick, ovate-fusiform shell with rounded whorls and pointed spire. Suture moderately impressed. Aperture thickened. Body whorl has thick varix. Strong fold on parietal wall. Numerous regularly beaded spiral cords with finer spiral lines between them. Whitish with broad, yellowish brown, spiral bands and darker brown lines corresponding with beaded cords. Aperture white flushed violet. Parietal wall pinkish white. Closely resembles *C. chemnitzianum* in all but coloration. 2–3cm. Indo-Pacific (Pacific). Frequent.

Cerithium carbonarium Philippi   × 1·4
Thick, solid, ovate-fusiform shell with slightly impressed suture. Outer lip thickened. Spiral rows of strong, blunt tubercles, two rows on each spire whorl and five rows on body whorl. Tubercles vary

considerably in size and in some specimens are turned upwards. Fine spiral lines between rows of tubercles. Apical whorls often eroded. Yellowish or greyish with tubercles stained light or dark brown. Aperture greyish white. 2·5–3·5cm. Indo-Pacific. Common.

Cerithium chemnitzianum Pilsbry   × 1·4

Shell thick, ovate-fusiform with moderately rounded whorls and pointed apex. Suture moderately impressed. Fold on parietal wall. Small fold at base of columella. Outer lip thickened. Numerous irregularly beaded spiral cords and fine axial riblets. Creamy yellow with spiral lines of brown dots on beads and axial, brown streaks. Aperture white. c3cm. Indo-Pacific (North West Pacific). Frequent.

Cerithium citrinum Sowerby
Shell moderately thick, elongate-fusiform with slightly impressed suture and pointed apex. Large varix on body whorl above the long, bent siphonal canal. Strong, regular, widely spaced axial ribs crossed by numerous fine spiral ridges. Outer lip crenulate, thick fold on parietal wall. Unicolorous light yellow or yellowish white. Edge

of aperture yellow but aperture white deep inside. 3·0–3·5cm. Indo-Pacific (North West Pacific), Japonic. Frequent.

Cerithium columna Sowerby
Similar to *C. echinatum*, but more elongate and has less prickly surface. Spiral cords broad and flat with no groove between and broad, lumpy axial ribs which are bluntly pointed at periphery. Spiral cords more conspicuously nodulous on base of body whorl. Outer lip strongly crenulate. Strong fold on parietal wall which almost touches crenulation on outer lip opposite. Creamy white with sparsely distributed, purplish brown axial streaks. c5·5cm. Indo-Pacific (Pacific). Common.

Cerithium cumingi A. Adams   × 0·8

Very similar to *C. aluco*, but longer and with only the early whorls spirally ribbed and nodulose. Colour similar but darker brown overall. 6–10cm. Indo-Pacific (Pacific). Common.

Cerithium dorsuosum A. Adams
Thick, stout shell with straight-sided whorls, varix on each whorl. Ventral side flattened. Occasionally one or two axial ribs on lower whorls. Faint spiral striae. Outer lip thickened. Whitish, with irregular, purplish brown axial streaks and blotches, sometimes dark brown with one or two fine, spiral, whitish lines. Aperture white or brown. c2cm. Indo-Pacific (Philippines). Common.

Cerithium eburneum Bruguière
Shell small, thick, solid, elongate-fusiform with obscure suture. Two varices to each whorl. Spiral, beaded cords on each whorl. White or creamy with occasional, reddish brown blotches. Aperture white. c2·2cm. Caribbean. Common.

Cerithium echinatum Lamarck

Shell thick, stout, oblong-ovate. Convex whorls are encircled by numerous spiral cords and have indistinct axial ribs. Thick varix on body whorl above siphonal canal. Spiral cords have short, upturned, pointed spines which are longest where they cross axial ribs and varix. Whole shell spiny in appearance. Outer lip thickened and crenulate. Thick fold on parietal wall with canal above. Unicolorous yellowish white. Aperture, parietal wall and callus white. *c*4cm. Indo-Pacific. Common.

Cerithium fasciatum Bruguière   × 1·6

Shell thick, solid, elongate with tall, pointed spire and sharply recurved siphonal canal. Columella thickly callused and with broad, spiral fold at centre. Outer lip slightly thickened. Early whorls moderately crenulate and coarsely axially ribbed. Later whorls with fine axial striae only. Opaque white with spiral, brown bands which have darker brown, crescent-shaped markings within them. Callus and aperture white. Colour and pattern very variable. 5–9cm. Indo-Pacific. Common.

Cerithium floridanum Mörch

Like a smaller version of *C. vulgatum*. Ovate-fusiform shell with pointed spire and two or three varices on each whorl. Moderately long, recurved siphonal canal. Several spiral rows of beads on each whorl with fine spiral threads between. Axial ribs on earlier whorls. Whitish with reddish brown mottling and speckles. 2·5–3·0cm. Caribbean. Common.

Cerithium gemmatum Hinds

Thick shell with broad body whorl and tall, tapering spire. Thick varix on body whorl

above siphonal canal. Beaded spiral ribs which are strongest at suture. Lower part of body whorl has smooth, flat ribs. Small fold at base of columella. Yellowish white, spotted and blotched with brown. Aperture whitish with external pattern showing through. *c*3·5cm. Panamic. Frequent.

Cerithium gourmyi Crosse   × 1·1

Shell thick and heavy with tall, pointed spire. Base of outer lip curves round columella but does not touch it. Thick fold on parietal wall. Smooth, with very fine spiral lines. Yellowish with axial, brown streaks and lines which may be almost obsolete. Aperture white. 5·5–6·0cm. Indo-Pacific (Pacific). Uncommon.

Cerithium guinaicum Philippi

Thick, solid ovate-fusiform shell with strong, broad axial ribs crossed by numerous fine spiral striae. Fine, axial growth lines. Aperture thickened. Yellowish white, often with broad and narrow, spiral, light brown bands and axial, brown streaks. *c*3·5cm. West African. Frequent.

Cerithium hanleyi Sowerby   × 2·0

Shell small, ovate-fusiform with straight-sided spire and pointed apex. Suture well impressed. Varix on body whorl above siphonal canal. Axial ribs on all whorls crossed by spiral ridges which produce points at intersections. Basal portion of body whorl with strong, spiral, beaded cords. Outer lip thickened. White with a broad, purplish brown, spiral band on each whorl. *c*1·5cm. Indo-Pacific. Common.

Cerithium kochi Philippi

Moderately thick, elongate-fusiform shell with a low varix on each whorl. Early whorls axially ribbed, later whorls with spiral, beaded cords. Cords on dorsal surface of body whorl are occasionally smooth. Outer lip sharp. Whitish, with spiral zones of greyish brown and spiral lines of darker brown, occasionally unicolorous pale brown. *c*3·5cm. Indo-Pacific, South African. Common.

Cerithium litteratum Born   × 1·7

Thick shell with moderately rounded whorls and tall spire. Coarse spiral ribs. Row of pointed nodules just below suture. White speckled with reddish brown. Aperture whitish. 2–3cm. Caribbean. Common.

Cerithium maculosum Kiener

Thick, stout shell with impressed suture and relatively short spire. Body whorl very broad and squarish. Single row of large, pointed nodules on each whorl with several nodulous spiral cords below. Outer lip not thickened and with curious indentation at its upper part opposite a thick parietal callus, producing a canal above. Short, recurved siphonal canal. Bluish grey or

yellowish with numerous dark brown spots and blotches and white tips to tubercles and spiral beads. Aperture whitish. 9–13cm. Panamic. Common.

Cerithium morus Lamarck   × 1·5

Thick, solid, ovate-fusiform shell with slightly impressed suture. Varix on body whorl. Thick parietal callus. Outer lip thickened. Numerous spiral rows of nodules with beaded cords between. Fine, axial growth ridges. Greyish white with black nodules and sometimes spiral, brown bands. Aperture white with brown spots at lip. 1·5–2·5cm. Indo-Pacific. Common.

Cerithium muscarum Say
Thin, elongate-ovate shell with strong axial ribs and fine spiral threads between them. Spiral ridge round base of body whorl. Whitish or yellowish with numerous fine, interrupted, spiral, brown lines. Aperture white with external pattern showing through. c2·5cm. Caribbean. Common.

Cerithium nassoides Sowerby
Small, moderately thick, elongate-ovate shell with obscure suture. Spiral row of strong, evenly spaced tubercles on each whorl, becoming obsolete on body whorl. One varix on body whorl above siphonal canal. Outer lip thickened. Yellowish white with dark brown blotch at top of aperture. Occasionally blotched and speckled with

brown on rest of shell. c1·3cm. Indo-Pacific (Pacific), Japonic. Frequent.

Cerithium nesioticum Pilsbry & Vanatta
Thick, moderately slender shell with sharp apex. Bulbous varix on body whorl above siphonal canal. Fine spiral lines with occasionally fine axial ridges giving cancellated appearance to early whorls. Yellowish white with pale yellowish brown blotches below suture on each whorl. 1·5–2·0cm. Indo-Pacific, Japonic. Common.

Cerithium nobilis Reeve   × 0·5

Shell very large for genus, thick and heavy. Suture slightly impressed, giving whorls straight-sided appearance. Heavily callused columella and parietal wall and thickened outer lip. Thick spiral cord with channels on either side around umbilical area. Spiral cords on early whorls and axial ribs on later whorls, obsolete on middle whorls. Coarse spiral ribs on body whorl and penultimate whorl. Pale yellowish brown with whitish squares and blotches. Aperture white. 10–13cm. Indo-Pacific (Pacific). Uncommon.

Cerithium nodulosum Bruguière   × 0·5

Large, thick, heavy shell with stout tubercles encircling each whorl, very conspicuous at periphery of body whorl. Large, warty varix above siphonal canal. Broad, flattened or nodulous spiral cords with strong grooves between. Outer lip strongly crenulate with sharp projection in front of the short, broad siphonal canal. Yellowish white with irregular, brown, axial spots, streaks and blotches. Aperture white. One of the largest known ceriths. c12cm. Indo-Pacific. Common.

Cerithium obeliscus Bruguière   × 1·0

Thick, heavy shell with tall spire and slightly impressed suture. Outer lip produced at base. Siphonal canal short and strongly recurved. Two folds on columella. Spiral row of large, pointed nodules just below suture. Smaller, spiral, beaded cords below. Cream with black to violet dots and dashes on spiral ornament. Aperture white. 3·5–6·5cm. Indo-Pacific. Common.

Cerithium patulum Sowerby
Thick, stout, elongate-fusiform shell with attenuated, pointed spire and impressed suture. Strong axial ribs crossed by strong spiral ribs which produce blunt tubercles at intersection. Varices on body whorl strong, almost wing-like. Outer lip thickened and crenulate. Dark brown with paler, spiral zones. c2·5cm. Indo-Pacific (Philippines). Common.

Cerithium piperitum Sowerby   × 1·6

Shell small, with large body whorl and tall spire. Two or three lumpy nodules on each whorl crossed by fine spiral ribs. Outer lip thickened. White or yellowish white with numerous small, brown spots arranged spirally. c1·5cm. Indo-Pacific (Pacific). Common.

Cerithium pulchrum A. Adams × 1·2

Thick, heavy shell with impressed suture and flattened, ventral side. Thick swelling on body whorl of columella. Each whorl coronated with thick, blunt ridges which are half length of each spire whorl. Excavated hollows between each pair of ridges. Numerous flat spiral ribs with fine spiral grooves between. Outer lip thickened. Columella with one fold. Creamy yellow with purple brown blotches on one side of each axial ridge. Few small, brown dashes on rest of each whorl. Aperture white. 4–5cm. Indo-Pacific (Pacific). Uncommon.

Cerithium ruppellii Philippi
Moderately thick, fusiform shell with moderately impressed suture and attenuate spire. One varix on each whorl. Strong axial ribs crossed by thin but strong spiral ridges producing points at intersections. Axial ribs absent from body whorl. Outer lip thickened and crenulate. Yellowish white with few brown spots just below suture. Spiral cords on body whorl also have few brown spots. Aperture white. c5cm. Indo-Pacific (Indian Ocean). Common.

Cerithium sowerbyi Kiener
Resembles *C. aluco* but lacks the prominent, upturned tubercles on middle whorls. Tubercles on body whorl and penultimate whorl blunt. Colour and pattern similar to *C. aluco*. 7–9cm. Indo-Pacific. Common.

Cerithium stercus muscarum Valenciennes
ocellata Bruguière, *irroratum* Gould, *exaggeratum* Pilsbry & Lowe.
Thick, solid, ovate-fusiform shell with obscure suture and acutely pointed apex.

Single row of large, pointed tubercles at periphery of each whorl. Outer lip greatly thickened. Thick parietal callus. Bluish grey to brownish with fine, white speckles arranged spirally. Occasionally white speckles are so numerous as to give shell greyish appearance. Tubercles usually brown. Aperture purplish with white rim to aperture. c3·5cm. Panamic. Common.

Cerithium torulosum Linnaeus
Thick, stout shell with early whorls attenuate and sharply pointed, later whorls stepped. Thick varix on body whorl above recurved siphonal canal. Early whorls axially ribbed with one spiral rib between each pair of axial ribs. Later whorls have a broad, rounded, sub-sutural cord which may itself be axially ribbed. Below spiral cords may be smooth or ornamented with few spiral and axial ribs. Unicolorous yellowish white. 2·5–3·0cm. Indo-Pacific. Frequent.

Cerithium trailli Sowerby
Relatively thin, ovate-fusiform shell with slightly rounded whorls and obscure suture. One low varix on each whorl. Spiral rows of evenly spaced, round pustules and thin, spiral beaded cords. Outer lip thickened and crenulate. Yellowish white with dark brown pustules, varices white. Aperture white. 2·5–4·5cm. Indo-Pacific. Frequent.

Cerithium variabile C. B. Adams × 2·0

Small, elongate-ovate shell with slightly impressed suture. Aperture slightly thickened. Slight fold on parietal wall. Spire whorls with three rows of tuberculated ribs, about ten rows on body whorl. Whitish, with irregular, brown spots at suture and few spots on lower portion of body whorl. Aperture whitish with spots showing through. Columella and parietal wall purple. 1·0–1·3cm. Caribbean. Common.

Cerithium vertagus Linnaeus × 0·9
Shell thick, cylindrically fusiform with tall spire and moderately impressed suture. Thick callus on parietal wall and two folds on columella. Inner lip thickened. Outer lip thin and curved. Fine spiral striae and axial folds at suture becoming obsolete on

body whorl. Yellowish white or chestnut brown. Aperture white. 5–6cm. Indo-Pacific. Common.

Cerithium vulgatum Linnaeus × 0·9

Shell large, thick and heavy with large body whorl and tapering spire. Outer lip crenulate. Each whorl has two rows of pointed tubercles and body whorl has four or five rows of smaller, blunt tubercles below. Fine spiral grooves between tubercles. Fine, axial growth lines. Cream with irregular, closely packed, axial, dark brown streaks. Whitish between tubercles. Aperture whitish with external pattern showing through. Extremely variable in size, pattern and ornament. 4–8cm. Mediterranean. Common.

Superfamily
Pyramidellacea

Family EULIMIDAE
Small or minute shells, which are usually thin but strong, narrowly elongate and have sharply .pointed apex. Spire often needle-like. Surface glossy and. smooth. Whorls straight sided or only slightly convex. Spire straight or curved. Umbilicus absent in some genera. Rarely colourful. Animals parasitic on molluscs and other invertebrates. Numerous genera and many species in all seas.

Genus BALCIS Leach
Thin, narrowly elongate shells with tapering, many whorled spire. Whorls straight-sided or only slightly convex. Spire sometimes curved or inclined to one side. Occasionally a fine axial groove on each whorl. Aperture ovate, sharply narrowed posteriorly. No umbilicus. Outer lip thickened on inside. Many species in all seas, but very few attain a size comparable to that illustrated here.

Balcis martinii A. Adams   × 1·8

Shell large for the genus with tall, pointed, sometimes curved, spire. Axial groove curves up from top of aperture to tip of spire. Very glossy. Unicolorous opaque white. 2·5–3·0cm. Indo-Pacific. Uncommon.

Superfamily
Epitoniacea

Family EPITONIIDAE
Large family of small to moderately large thin shells, which may be either elongate and narrow or moderately globose and short. The prinicipal feature which distinguishes wentletraps from other molluscs is the series of thin, regularly spaced varices which decorate the whorls of most species. Varices assume variety of shapes; they may be either almost non-existent or produced into wing-like extensions of remarkable delicacy. Suture usually very deeply impressed; sometimes whorls are completely separated from each other and only joined by varices. Aperture circular. Many genera, subgenera and smaller divisions have been proposed for this family, but it is convenient to place the few species described here under the one genus *Epitonium*. Widely distributed in most seas.

Genus EPITONIUM Röding
Scalaria Lamarck.
For details, see Family Epitoniidae. Commonly known as wentletraps.

Epitonium acuminatum Sowerby   × 2·0
Thin, tapering shell with sharp, pointed

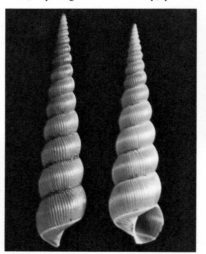

apex and rounded whorls. Covered with close-set, weak, axial riblets. Pale brown with spiral, white band in centre of each whorl. Body whorl has a second spiral, white band near base. Columella white. Some populations occur with narrow and broad-shelled forms. *c*3cm. Indo-Pacific (Pacific), Japonic. Frequent.

Epitonium alatum Sowerby   × 2·3

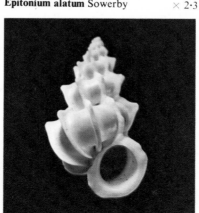

Thin, light, tall-spired shell with disconnected whorls. Thick, well developed varices on each whorl developed into upturned points on shoulder. Umbilicus concealed by ends of varices. Aperture has recurved, thickened lip. Whitish, with median, broad, brownish spiral band on each whorl. Varices and aperture white. *c*2cm. Indo-Pacific. Frequent.

Epitonium communis Lamarck   × 1·4

Moderately thick, tall-spired shell with disconnected whorls. Numerous flattened varices with small points at suture. Varices continuous, curving around spire. No umbilicus. Creamy, with spiral rows of irregular, purple brown blotches which extend onto varices. 2–4cm. Mediterranean, Boreal. Common.

Epitonium commutatum Monterosato
Thin, elongate-fusiform shell with deeply impressed suture and tall spire with pointed apex. Numerous evenly spaced, thin varices which form continuous, slightly curved lines up spire. Single spiral cord between varices on lower portion of body whorl. Bluish grey, lighter on earlier whorls. Aperture white. 2·5–3·5cm. Mediterranean. Frequent.

Epitonium diadema Sowerby
Thick, solid, squat shell with scalariform whorls. Strong axial ribs on each whorl, becoming obsolete on body whorl. Body whorl encircled by thick spiral ribs. Unicolorous white. *c*1·5cm. Panamic. Frequent.

Epitonium imperialis Sowerby
Fragile shell with tall spire and very rounded whorls. Suture deep. Numerous thin, fine varices, about 30 on each whorl. Umbilicus low and deep. Purple brown or pale brown with white varices and white umbilical area. *c*4cm. Indo-Pacific (Pacific). Frequent.

Epitonium kieneri Tapparone-Canefri
Very tall-spired shell with rounded whorls and deep suture. No umbilicus. Numerous fine axial ribs crossed by equally fine spiral ridges producing cancelled texture. Unicolorous white. c8cm. Indo-Pacific (Pacific). Uncommon.

Epitonium magnificum Sowerby × 1·0

Shell thin, light, very tall-spired with rounded whorls and impressed suture. Cancellated with moderately strong axial and spiral ribs with an occasional rib standing out from the rest. No umbilicus. Whitish with broad, spiral, pale brown bands on earlier whorls. Later whorls white. 7–10cm. Japonic. Rare.

Epitonium pallasi Kiener × 2·0

Like *E. scalare*, but much smaller. Whorls separated so that only varices are joined. Varices strong and widely spaced, about ten on each whorl. Umbilicus narrow and very deep. White, with pale brown zone between varices. 2–3cm. Indo-Pacific (Pacific). Frequent.

Epitonium scalare Linnaeus × 1·1
Precious Wentletrap
pretiosum Lamarck.

Large, thin, loosely coiled shell with rounded whorls. Narrow, deep umbilicus; regular, thin varices which are joined together and form the only points of connection between one whorl and the next. Pinkish, fading to white. 3·5–6·0cm. Indo-Pacific. Uncommon.

Epitonium turtonis Risso
Moderately thick, tall-spired shell with pointed apex. Suture deeply impressed. Numerous flattened varices which form continuous, curved line up spire. Some varices much broader than others. Pale brown with one or two reddish spiral bands on each whorl. Sometimes much darker brown. Aperture brown. 3–4cm. Mediterranean, Boreal. Frequent.

Epitonium zelebori Dunker × 2·0

Shell moderately thick, tall-spired with deeply impressed suture. Numerous slightly recurved varices on each whorl. Strong spiral cords between varices and thick spiral cord at base. Unicolorous white. 2·0–2·5cm. Australian (New Zealand). Common.

Family JANTHINIDAE

Small family of fragile-shelled molluscs comprising two genera and few species. Shells are thin, globose and almost entirely without surface ornament. Most shells violet but a few are brown. No operculum. All species are pelagic and are only occasionally washed ashore.

Genus JANTHINA Röding

Fragile, globose shells, smooth or axially striate. Long, twisted or straight columella. Popularly known as violet snails in allusion to their predominant colour. Few species in all seas. Pelagic animals which may drift for thousands of miles over open oceans and belonging to no particular faunal provinces. Their eggs are carried in bubble-like rafts to which the shells attach themselves. Few species.

Janthina exigua Lamarck
Much smaller than *J. janthina* and with a prominent, broad notch in outer lip. Pale violet with paler band at suture. 0·5–1·0cm. Worldwide in warm seas. Common.

Janthina globosa Swainson
About same size as *J. janthina* but whorls more rounded, suture more pronounced and aperture longer. Long, straight columella. Unicolorous violet. 2·5–3·5cm. Worldwide in warm seas. Common.

Janthina janthina Linnaeus × 1·5

Globose, short-spired shell with long, twisted columella. Lower half of shell violet; upper half whitish violet. 3–4cm. Atlantic Ocean. Common.

Superfamily
Calyptraeacea

Family CAPULIDAE

Thin, flattened or elevated, limpet-like shells with apex usually near posterior margin. Surface usually roughly ornamented. No operculum. Animals attach themselves permanently to shells or other hard objects. About three genera, widespread in most seas.

Genus CAPULUS Montfort
Pileopsis Lamarck.
Thin, cap-shaped shells with very large aperture and tightly coiled apex near posterior end. Interior marked with horseshoe-shaped muscle impression. Species live attached to shells or other hard objects and do not move about. Shape of shell influenced by nature of substrate. Numerous species in most seas.

Capulus capensis Tomlin
Very thin, patelliform shell with eccentric, pointed spire. Smooth, dull, white, flesh-coloured or lilac, and semi-transparent. Thin, irregular, inner shelf is colour of shell. 0·8–2·0cm. South African. Uncommon.

Capulus ungaricus Linnaeus   × 0·8

High, patelliform shell with recurved spire overhanging shell margin. Axial striae and ridges; strong, imbricate growth lines. Glossy, white shell with white aperture. Thick, brown, opaque periostracum. 4–5cm. Boreal. Frequent.

Family CALYPTRAEIDAE

Thin, flatly conical, patelliform shells with central or posterior apex. Surface usually ornamented with ridges and spines but sometimes smooth. Characterised by a cup-shaped or shelf-like appendage on inner side. No operculum. Animals attach themselves to hard substrates but move about at will. Few genera, widely distributed in most seas.

Genus CALYPTRAEA Lamarck
Trochita Schumacher.
Rounded or elongate, short-spired, limpet-like shells with strong, shelly platform attached inside. Apex usually at posterior margin, smooth, ribbed or spiny. Shape varies with nature of substrate. Often congregate in masses one on top of another. Numerous species in most seas.

Calyptraea chinensis Linnaeus
Thin, round shell forming short, flattened cone in profile view. Central apex. Thin, twisted shelf projects across posterior part of shell. Smooth or rough. Unicolorous white or yellowish. *c*1·5cm. Boreal, Mediterranean, West African. Common.

Genus CRUCIBULUM Schumacher
Rounded and flattened or elevated, limpet-like shells with a cup-shaped or spoon-shaped appendage on inside. Apex central or near posterior margin. Coarsely ribbed or spiny. Numerous species in warm seas.

Crucibulum scutellatum Gray   × 0·6
imbricata Sowerby, *rugosa* Lesson, *corrugatum* Gould & Carpenter.

Thick, patelliform shell with strong radial ribs which may be nodulose or scaly. Spiral ridges crossed by ribs giving rough

reticulation. Dull, pink or pinkish brown. Interior whitish pink. Inner cup white or same as rest of shell. 1·5–6·5cm. Panamic, Peruvian. Common.

Crucibulum spinosum Sowerby   × 0·6
peziza Wood, *tubifera* Lesson, *maculata* Broderip, *hispida* Broderip.

Thin or thick, depressed, patelliform shell with axial rows of hollow spines except on smooth, recurved spire. Dull, grey, pinkish grey or reddish brown. Grey specimens may have brown axial bands. Interior similar colour to outside. Thin, white cup is crescent-shaped. A very variable species in colour and spines may be absent. 1–4cm. Panamic. Common.

Crucibulum umbrella Deshayes   × 1·1
rudis Broderip.
Shell more or less circular in outline, with central apex. Not strongly ribbed like *C. scutellatum*, from which it also differs in having internal cup attached only at its apex and not, as in that species, along one side as well. Rough texture externally. Deep chocolate brown internally with white zone round lower part of cup. 3·5–5·0cm. Panamic. Uncommon.

Genus CREPIDULA Lamarck
Flattish or rounded shells which are irregularly ovate in outline and have a posteriorly-directed apex. Commonly known as slipper limpets in allusion to appearance of underside which has a thin, shelf-like plate towards posterior. Rarely move from the spot to which they first attach themselves, and their shape often varies according to the contours of objects to which they are attached. Numerous species on coasts of warm and temperate seas.

Crepidula aculeata Gmelin
Thin, ovate, patelliform shell with eccentric spire and varying degree of depression. Axial rows of hollow spines or fine axial ridges which may be nodulose. Dull, white or flesh-coloured. Shelf is striated and has a central ridge. 0·5–2·5cm. Caribbean, Transatlantic. Common.

Crucibulum umbrella

Crepidula costata Sowerby × 0·6
Thick, ovate, patelliform shell with apex overhanging margin. Strong, irregular

ridges radiate from apex. Dull, pink with white varices, flesh-coloured, or brown variegated with white. Interior white with external colour showing through. White shelf. Specimens show variation in height. 1–5cm. Australian (New Zealand). Common.

Crepidula fornicata Linnaeus × 1·3
Atlantic Slipper Limpet

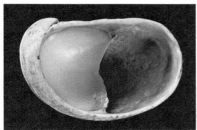

Ovate, patelliform shell of varying height. Dull, brown with cream to dark brown interior and white, silky shelf. Yellowish brown, opaque periostracum. 2–5cm. Transatlantic, Boreal (introduced to Western Europe). Common.

Crepidula plana Say
Ovate, extremely depressed, even concave, shell. Rough, concentric ridges. Dull, white with white interior and shelf which may be semi-transparent. Yellow, dull, semi-transparent periostracum. 3·0–3·5 cm. Transatlantic, Caribbean. Common.

Family TRICHOTROPIDAE

Small family of thick, turbinate or trochoidal shells. Base often strongly keeled. Umbilicus wide and deep. Body whorl large and spire tall, short or depressed. Columella lacks folds. Smooth or strongly ornamented. Epidermis often thick, fibrous and hairy. Operculum corneous and multispiral. Widely distributed in northern seas and Antarctic Ocean, but some species in deeper water in warmer parts of globe. About twelve genera.

Genus TRICHOTROPIS Broderip & Sowerby

Thin, usually tall-spired shells but some species with short spires. Smooth or strongly ornamented. Umbilicus wide and deep, shallow or non-existent. Some species have one or two very pronounced spiral keels. Few species in cold waters and often from great depths.

Trichotropis bicarinata Sowerby
Shell large for the genus, thin with large body whorl and short spire. Umbilicus slit-like. Two strong spiral keels on body whorl and one on each spire whorl. Yellowish white. Thin, brown periostracum which is produced into hairy spicules on spiral keels. 3–4cm. Arctic, Aleutian. Uncommon.

Trichotropis borealis Broderip & Sowerby
Shell thin, with large body whorl, short spire and chink-like umbilicus. Large spiral cord round umbilicus. Three spiral cords on body whorl. Numerous axial threads. White. Thick, brown periostracum which is produced to hairy points on spiral cords. *c*1·5cm. Arctic, Californian. Common.

Trichotropis cancellata Hinds × 2·3

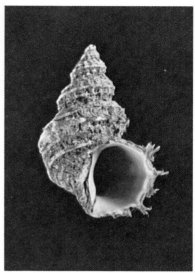

Thin, tall-spired shell with impressed suture. Umbilicus a tiny slit. Strong spiral cords on each whorl with finer spiral ribs between. Sometimes small axial ribs which produce cancellate ornament. Whitish. Thin, brown periostracum which is produced to bristle-like points on spiral cords. 2·0–2·5cm. Aleutian, Californian. Common.

Trichotropis unicarinata Broderip & Sowerby × 2·0

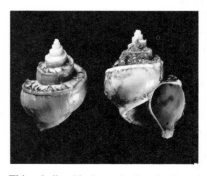

Thin shell with large body whorl and moderately tall spire. Umbilicus wide and deep, surrounded by a prominent spiral keel. Each whorl has strong keel at shoulder. Smooth, with faint spiral and axial striae. Yellowish white. Covered with thin, brown periostracum which is very hairy at shoulders. 1·5–2·0cm. Indo-Pacific, Japonic. Frequent.

Superfamily
Strombacea

Family XENOPHORIDAE

Medium-sized, trochoidal or moderately flattened shells, with or without umbilicus. Characteristically covered by fragments of other shells which may be a form of camouflage. Shells dull and coarsely ornamented. Found in shallow or relatively deep water in tropical and warm seas. Three genera.

Genus XENOPHORA Fischer von Waldheim
Phorus Montfort.
For details, see Family Xenophoridae. Umbilicus small, or absent. Usually more or less concealed by fragments of shells and stones. Operculum thin. About twelve species.

Xenophora conchyliophora Born
Atlantic Carrier Shell
Squat, conical shell with all sorts of debris, including heavy pebbles, and shell fragments attached. Umbilicus absent. *c*5cm. (excluding debris). Caribbean, Transatlantic. Uncommon.

Xenophora konoi Habe   × 0·55

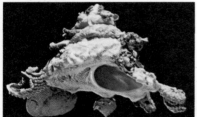

Conical shell with strong, wavy, beaded ridges. Umbilicus narrow. Shell covered with many pieces of gravel and shell fragments. Aperture white. *c*6cm. (excluding debris). Japonic, Indo-Pacific. Frequent.

Xenophora pallidula Reeve   × 0·6

Squat, conical shell with broken shells and debris arranged regularly around whorls. Aperture white, nacreous. *c*6cm. (excluding debris). Japonic. Frequent.

Genus TUGURIUM
Similar to *Xenophora*, but more depressed and with wide and deep umbilicus. Operculum subquadrate with elevated elements on the upper surface at regular intervals forming continuous ridges radiating from a lateral nucleus. About ten species.

Tugurium exutum Reeve   × 1·1
Squat, conical shell with last whorl extended to form an irregular flange around

whole of base. Irregular, wavy ridges over entire shell. Umbilicus wide. Shell glossy, cream to pale brownish yellow. Does not attach shells and debris to its surface. Aperture white, nacreous. 4–9cm. Indo-Pacific. Frequent.

Genus STELLARIA
Distinguished from *Xenophora* and *Tugurium* by having numerous, long, radiating spines around periphery. Does not attach shells or debris to surface. One species.

Stellaria solaris Linnaeus   × 0·4

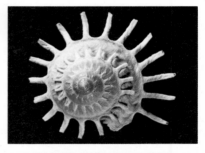

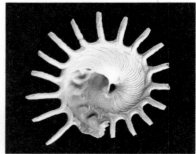

Squat, conical shell, whorls bearing long, slender projections spread out like spokes of a wheel. Umbilicus wide. Aperture white shell creamy. 6–11cm. (including spines). Indo-Pacific. Frequent.

Family APORRHAIDAE

Thick shells with conical spire and a well developed, flattened lip often ending in flat, finger-like projections (resembling a bird's foot). Small operculum. Two genera in temperate and cool waters.

Genus APORRHAIS Da Costa
Details as for Family Aporrhaidae. Four species.

Aporrhais pespelecani Linnaeus   × 1·1
Pelican's Foot Shell

Thick shell with long, conical spire bearing blunt tubercles. Flattened lip strongly ridged with four finger-like projections (like pelican's foot). Shell yellowish or brownish. Narrow aperture and lip cream. c5cm. Mediterranean, Boreal. Frequent.

Aporrhais senegalensis Gray
Shell smaller than *A. pespelecani*, with four less massive, pointed digitations. One digitation joined to length of spire, two are opposite aperture and widely divergent, and one envelops siphonal canal. Spire with spiral rows of small tubercles. Unicolorous pale brown. 2·0–2·5cm. West African. Uncommon.

Family STRUTHIOLARIIDAE
Thick, ovate shells with large aperture and stout, usually nodulous whorls. Short siphonal canal. Columella and lips thickened and callused. About six species in Australian province and one in Indian Ocean.

Genus STRUTHIOLARIA Lamarck
For details, see Family Struthiolariidae.

Struthiolaria papulosa Martyn   × 0·8
Shell thick, solid, heavy and tall-spired. Outer lip strongly curved and thickened. Columella and parietal wall thickly callused. Parietal callus extends above aperture. Single spiral row of pointed nodules on all whorls. Rest of shell covered with

thin, spiral ridges. Whitish, with fine, axial, pale and darker brown lines. 7–8cm. Australian (New Zealand). Common.

Struthiolaria scutulata Martyn   × 0·8

Shell thick, solid, heavy and tall-spired. Whorls markedly stepped, with callus deposit extending on to penultimate whorl. Early whorls with median spiral band of blunt tubercles. Later whorls smooth. White, with irregular, axial, darker brown streaks; two faint spiral bands on body whorl. Aperture and parietal wall whitish. 4–5cm. Australian (Australia). Uncommon.

Struthiolaria vermis Martyn   × 0·9
crenulata Lamarck.

Shell small, solid and high-spired, with impressed suture. Outer lip curved. Parietal callus continuous with columella. Body whorl straight-sided below shoulder. Coarse spiral ridges crossed by fine, axial lines. Dull, reddish brown. Aperture, columella and parietal wall whitish. 3·0–4·5cm. Australian (New Zealand). Common.

Family STROMBIDAE
Thick, heavy shells, often large, with conical spire which may be ornamented. Usually a thick lip often broad and wing-like, typically with a notch near the anterior (the 'stromboid notch') and occasionally bearing long projections. Long, rather narrow aperture and usually a long, strong, curved operculum which helps locomotion. Herbivorous. Widely distributed in tropical waters. Four genera.

Genus TEREBELLUM Lamarck
Smooth, elongate shell without 'stromboid notch' at base of outer lip. Shell thin and light. Can shoot rapidly through water. One species.

Terebellum terebellum Linnaeus   × 1·0
subulatum Lamarck.

Smooth, torpedo-shaped shell with truncate lip. Glossy shell, cream with many spiral, brownish yellow lines. Very variable colour pattern. 4–5·5cm. Indo-Pacific. Common.

Genus TIBIA Röding
Rostellaria Lamarck.
Smooth, elongate shells. Long, conical spire. Long siphonal canal and finger-like projections on outer lip around elliptical aperture. About six species in tropical seas, mostly in fairly shallow water.

Tibia delicatula Nevill △ × 0·9
Shell moderately thick, ovate-fusiform
with moderately pointed apex and gently
rounded whorls. Siphonal canal moderately short for the genus; outer lip with 3–5
prominent, slightly curved digitations.
Early whorls with faint spiral lines; rest
of shell smooth. Yellowish or brownish
with indistinct, pale purplish bands on
earlier whorls and three or four narrow,
pale, whitish spiral bands on body whorl.
Aperture nacreous white. 5·0–7·5cm. Indo-
Pacific (North West Indian Ocean). Rare.

Tibia fusus Linnaeus ▷ × 1·3
Spindle or Shinbone Tibia
rectirostris Lamarck, *melanocheilus* A.
Adams.
Long, slender spire. First few whorls bear
axial ribbing, anterior of last whorl with
fine, transverse ridges. Outer lip cream,
becoming purple and middle whorls
smooth. Stout lip bears several long
projections. Straight siphonal canal which
points in line with columella may be
almost as long as rest of shell. Shell coffee
to brown, lips and aperture cream to lilac.
One form (*T. melanocheilus*) with purple
black aperture. 16–30cm. Indo-Pacific.
Uncommon.

Tibia insulaechorab Röding × 0·8
Arabian Tibia
curvirostris Lamarck, *brevirostris*, Schumacher, *magna* Schröter, *luteostoma*
Angas.
Heavy shell with long, even spire bearing
axial ribs near apex. Stout lip with several
blunt projections and stout siphonal canal

Shell small for genus, elongate, with pointed apex and relatively short, straight, pointed siphonal canal. Whorls rounded; suture deeply impressed. Outer lip thickened, with five strong digitations. Strong spiral ribs with fine axial lines between them giving reticulation. Pale brown with darker brown blotches and large part of body whorl whitish. Aperture pale brown, columella and outer lip white. 4–5cm. Indo-Pacific (South West Pacific), Japonic. Uncommon.

Genus VARICOSPIRA Iredale

Small, thick, tall-spired and compressed shells. Two or three varices on spire whorls. Outer lip thickened and curved, denticulate and lirate. A thick, white callus extends from base of columella up to top of penultimate whorl. Contiguous with upper part of callus is a long, narrow channel. Whole shell strongly axially ribbed and cancellated with fine spiral striae. Pinkish white with pinkish brown spiral bands. One species.

Varicospira cancellata Linnaeus   × 1·8

brown and white. 10–12cm. Indo-Pacific (Philippines). Rare.

Tibia powisi Petit   × 2·0

Above: Tibia insulae chorab

up to half as long as rest of shell. Narrow projection of lip applied closely to spire and covering part of last two whorls. Shell coffee to brown, aperture white. Rare form (*T. luteostoma*) with yellow aperture. Not as slender as *T. fusus*. 14–20cm. Indo-Pacific (North Indian Ocean). Common.

Tibia martinii Marrat   × 0·7

Shell thin, light, fusiform, ovate. Tall-spired with rounded whorls and large, moderately inflated body whorl. Siphonal canal long and straight. Outer lip with five or six short digitations. Columella with single, blunt tooth. Shell smooth with very fine axial and spiral lines. Pale brown with purplish brown blotching on spire. Outer edge of outer lip blotched with

For details, see genus *Varicospira*. The only living species comes from Indo-Pacific (Philippines). 2·5–3·5cm. Uncommon.

Genus LAMBIS Röding

Pterocera Lamarck.

Thick shells with conical spire but with characteristic, long, finger-like projections of well developed lip masking basic shape. Slender, curved, corneous operculum. Often called spider conchs. Nine species in tropical seas.

Lambis chiragra Linnaeus   × 0·35
Chiragra Spider
Thick, heavy shell with blunt tubercles and coarse, spiral ridges on spire and body whorl. Thick, heavy lip with six long, stout, curved projections, the two from the columellar lip directed away from the aperture and extending under and well past the rest of the shell. Shell creamy with brownish orange, axial markings. Pink, ridged lips which are much more pro-

Below: Lambis chiragra

nounced in the uncommon subspecies *L. chiragra arthritica* Röding, which has a smaller and heavier shell with very coarse, transverse ridges. 12–23cm. Indo-Pacific. Common.

Lambis crocata Link   ▷ × 0·5
Orange Spider
aurantia Lamarck, *aurantiacum* Sowerby.
Thick, heavy shell with tubercles and transverse ridges. Heavy lip with seven long, stout, curved projections similar to *L. scorpius* but without tubercles. Shell

mushroom overlaid with many dark brown patches. Smooth orange lips. 7–15cm. Indo-Pacific. Uncommon.

Lambis digitata Perry   × 0·5
Elongate Spider Conch
crocea Reeve, *elongata* Swainson.
Thick, heavy shell with coarse, transverse ridges and blunt tubercles. Heavy lip with 7–9 short projections, longer towards spire, as well as anterior and posterior

projections. Shell cream with brownish yellow axial lines. Lips cream, brown and dark brown between ridges. 11–14cm. Indo-Pacific. Rare.

Lambis millepeda Linnaeus   × 0·6
Millepede Spider Conch

*Above and above right: Lambis digitata
Below: Lambis lambis*

Lambis lambis Linnaeus   × 0·5
Common Spider Conch
Shell with coarse, transverse ridges and large tubercles. Heavy lip with seven more or less straight projections the most anterior of which are short. Shell coffee with brown patches in axial rows. Smooth, cream to mushroom lips and aperture. 10–15cm. Indo-Pacific. Common.

Thick, heavy shell with blunt tubercles and transverse ridges. Thick, heavy lip with eleven short, stout projections. Shell yellow orange with dark brown, axial markings, lips cream with dark violet aperture bearing many cream ridges. 10–13cm. Indo-Pacific (South West Pacific). Common.

Lambis scorpius Linnaeus   × 0·6
nodosa Lamarck.
Thick, heavy shell with blunt tubercles on spire and body whorl. Heavy lip and seven

long, stout, curved projections bearing blunt tubercles; posterior projection passing under and past apex more or less in line with columella, anterior projection continuing same line forwards before curving gently towards the lip. Shell coffee marked with brownish patches. Outer lip cream, becoming purple between white ridges in aperture. 10–15cm. Indo-Pacific. Uncommon.

Lambis truncata Lightfoot   × 0·25
Giant Spider Conch
bryonia Gmelin
Thick, heavy shell with blunt tubercles. Thick, heavy lip with seven stout, almost straight projections (occasionally more than seven as in illustrated specimen). Shell basically brown with smooth lips,

bluish white at edges becoming lilac near aperture. Nacre covering underside of shell. 25–33cm. Indo-Pacific. Common.

Lambis violacea Swainson
Violet Spider Conch
purpurea Swainson.
Distantly similar to *L. millepeda*. Thick, ovate shell with flared outer lip bearing about 17 short or moderately long digitations. Long, recurved siphonal canal. Strong, nodulous spiral cords. Aperture lirate. White, flecked, mottled and spirally banded with reddish brown, fading to pale brown. Aperture white near edge of outer lip, violet inside. 7–10cm. Indo-Pacific (Indian Ocean). Rare.

Genus STROMBUS Linnaeus
Heavy shells usually with squat, conical spire and large, extended lip. Conspicuous 'stromboid notch'. Corneous, sickle-shaped operculum which helps locomotion. Feed on seaweeds in shallow, tropical or warm seas. About 50 species.

Strombus alatus Gmelin
Florida Fighting Conch
Extended apex on stepped spire. Blunt tubercles on spire and posterior end of body whorl. Thick, flattened lip that does not extend full length of body whorl. Shell cream, almost covered with brownish yellow to lilac axial lines and broad transverse bands. Lips and ridged aperture marked with blue, pink and lilac. 5–10cm. Caribbean. Common.

Strombus aurisdianae Linnaeus   × 1·1
Diana Conch
lamarcki Sowerby.
Almost elliptical shell with sharp spire often ornamented with small tubercles. Thick, rolled lip with posterior projection extending length of body whorl and almost

lines, sometimes broad zigzags. Aperture white. Occasional albino shells. 3·0–7·5cm. Indo-Pacific. Common.

Strombus costatus Gmelin   × 0·5
Milk Conch
accipitrinus Lamarck.

deep pink inside, white at margin. 5–6cm. Indo-Pacific (South West Pacific). Uncommon.

Strombus campbelli Griffith & Pidgeon
× 1·0

parallel to axis. Shell creamy with few brown, transverse markings. Large, heavily callused, columellar lip creamy to orange, sometimes brown, aperture usually orange. Outside of lip often with transverse, coffee bands. 5–7cm. Indo-Pacific. Common.

Strombus bulla Röding   × 1·1
Shell thick, heavy, with elevated, pointed spire. Siphonal canal sharply bent backwards. Short, broad spine projecting upwards from outer lip parallel with axis. Parietal wall and most of spire heavily callused. Single spiral row of broad tubercles at shoulder. Narrow spiral ribs over rest of shell. Creamy, mottled with brown; purple staining at edge of callus. Aperture

Similar to *S. vittatus* but smaller and more vividly coloured. Solid, thick shell with flared outer lip. Strong axial ribs on spire whorls. White with spiral bands of dark brown blotches, flecks and zigzag lines. Aperture white. *c*7cm. Indo-Pacific (North Australia). Uncommon.

Strombus canarium Linnaeus   × 0·5
Yellow or Dog Conch
isabella Lamarck.
Spire very small compared with globose, pear-shaped body whorl. Thick, wide, incurved lip extending length of body whorl. Colours variable, often creamy yellowish to coffee with brownish axial

Conical spire with blunt tubercles extending to posterior of swollen body whorl. Large, thick, flat lip slightly longer than body whorl. Shell with mushroom to brown transverse and axial markings. Lips creamy pink and pale violet. 10–13cm. Caribbean. Common.

Strombus decorus Röding   × 0·7
Mauritian Conch
mauritianus Lamarck, *coniformis* Sowerby,
flammeus Link.

Squat spire with extended apex and rounded, triangular body whorl with hook-like anterior. Thick, incurved lip extending most of length of body whorl. Shell with wavy axial striae. White often with brownish orange markings in transverse rows, usually overlaid with a thin periostracum. Lips white, aperture pinkish to violet. Immature shells resemble *Conus* in shape. 4–8cm. Indo-Pacific (Indian Ocean). Common.

Strombus dentatus Linnaeus   × 1·8

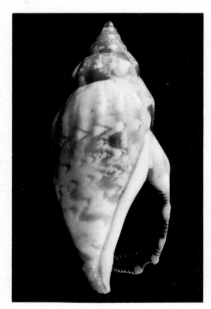

Shell solid, thick, elongate-fusiform. Fairly short-spired; tall body whorl with aperture more than half its height. Broad, widely spaced axial ribs with nodes at shoulder. Columella smooth except for few plications at base. Outer lip lirate. Yellowish white with brown or yellowish brown, zigzag markings or blotches. Aperture orange with lirae whitish against dark brown background. 2·5–5·0cm. Indo-Pacific (Pacific). Common.

Strombus dilatatus Swainson
swainsoni Reeve, *orosminus* Duclos.
Resembles *S.variabilis* but has relatively narrower spire and larger body whorl. Outer lip slopes down at shoulder and is more rounded. Posterior canal curves up and across ventral side of spire. Body whorl almost smooth. Creamy white with pale brown blotches and spiral bands. Aperture white with purple brown blotch deep inside. 3·5–6·0cm. Indo-Pacific (South West Pacific). Uncommon.

Strombus epidromis Linnaeus   × 0·8
Swan Conch
Long spire with axial ribs and tubercles. Nearly smooth body whorl with almost ovate shape and wide, curved lip extending onto lower whorls. Shell white with

brownish yellow axial markings which may merge. Lips and smooth aperture white and nacreous. 5–9cm. Indo-Pacific (South West Pacific). Common.

Strombus fasciatus Born   × 1·0
lineatus Lamarck, *polyfasciatus* Dillwyn.

Short spire with small tubercles. Body whorl triangular with tubercles at posterior end; thick, incurved lip almost extending length of body whorl. Shell white with fine, brown, transverse bands or patches. Lips and smooth aperture white, pink or yellow. 3–5cm. Indo-Pacific (Red Sea). Common.

Strombus galeatus Swainson
Large, very heavy, ovate shell with short spire, inflated body whorl and flaring aperture. Broad, smooth, spiral ridges on body whorl. Wide, shallow stromboid notch. Outer lip corrugated. Parietal wall and columella smooth. White, with a darker spire. Juvenile shells are brown and white, banded or blotched with orange yellow. Aperture white, brown or orange. 15–22cm. Panamic. Common.

Strombus gallus Linnaeus   × 0·5
Rooster-tail Conch
Shell light in weight compared with other

strombs of similar size. 3–5 prominent tubercles on body whorl. Large, thick lip reflected to cover part of last whorl with long projection extending well beyond the apex, and with curved siphonal canal. Shell with mushroom and brown spiral markings, lips creamy to pink. 10–13cm. Caribbean. Uncommon.

Strombus gibberulus Linnaeus   × 1·1
Humped Conch

Angular spire, often with last whorl swollen, and swollen, pear-shaped body whorl. Thick lip which does not extend whole length of body whorl. Shell cream to mushroom with variable orange to brown patches in transverse and axial rows. Lips cream becoming violet in ridged aperture. One form with white shell and pink to lilac aperture. 4–7cm. Indo-Pacific. Common.

Strombus gigas Linnaeus
Queen Conch
Conical, stepped spire with large tubercles extending to posterior of body whorl. Tubercles sometimes long and spine-like. Body whorl triangular with large, thick, flattened lip extending whole length of shell. Shell creamy with a few brownish yellow patches. Aperture and lips pink to violet. 15–30cm. Caribbean. Common.

Strombus goliath Schröter
Very large, thick and heavy shell with ovate body whorl, short spire and greatly expanded, flaring outer lip. Widely spaced, large, low nodules at shoulder of body whorl. Widely spaced, deep, spiral channels on outside of outer lip. Broad, shallow stromboid notch. Columella greatly thickened; thick parietal callus spreading on to upper portion of body whorl. Yellowish brown, with darker brown axial band and spiral streaks. Aperture, columella and

parietal callus yellowish pink. 30–35cm. Caribbean (Brazil). Rare.

Strombus gracilor Sowerby
Panama Fighting Conch
Conical spire with tubercles extending to posterior of swollen body whorl. Thick lip extending most of length of body whorl, and slightly curved siphonal canal. Shell cream with broad, transverse, mushroom bands often overlaid with tough, brownish yellow periostracum. Smooth, white lips and aperture. 6–8cm. Californian. Common.

Strombus granulatus Swainson   × 0·6

Thick shell with elongated, conical spire bearing strong tubercles which extend to posterior of triangular body whorl. Lips extend whole length of body whorl. Curved siphonal canal. Shell white with brownish yellow periostracum. 6–10cm. Panamic. Common.

Strombus labiatus Röding
plicatus Lamarck.
Thick shell, spire with angular whorls bearing axial ribs. Most of body whorl with axial ribs and some transverse ridges. Thick lip with very shallow 'stromboid notch'. Cream with brownish yellow, brown or violet, spiral bands. Lips and ridged aperture orange to brown. 2–5cm. Indo-Pacific. Common.

Strombus labiosus Wood
Stepped spire with axial ribs. Blunt tubercles on posterior of body whorl often running into axial ribs which become folds on thick lip. Shell cream with brownish yellow markings. Lips and aperture usually pale, sometimes with small, purple patch in aperture. 2–5cm. Indo-Pacific. Uncommon.

Strombus latissimus Linnaeus   × 0·35
picta Röding, *alata* Schumacher.
Large, thick, heavy shell with moderately tall spire which is almost covered by the broadly expanded outer lip. Low, rounded knobs on body whorl, that opposite outer lip being largest. Single row of large knobs on spire whorl. Outer lip very broadly expanded, with incurved edge. Stromboid

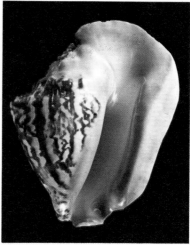

notch wide and shallow. Callus extending from base of columella to edge of aperture. Body whorl almost smooth; spire whorls with fine spiral striae. Dark or light brown with irregular, axial, white blotches. Aperture and parietal and columellar callus white. 13–21cm. Indo-Pacific (South West Pacific). Uncommon.

Strombus latus Gmelin
bubonius Lamarck.
Conical spire with blunt tubercles extending to form two or three transverse rows on body whorl. Thick, rounded lip as long as body whorl and short, curved siphonal canal. Shell brownish yellow, sometimes violet between tubercles, often overlaid with tough, brownish periostracum. Lips brownish yellow becoming creamy in aperture. 10–13cm. West African. Common.

Strombus lentiginosus Linnaeus   × 0·45
Silver Conch
Stepped spire and body whorl covered with small, blunt tubercles. Thick, rolled lip extending along spire almost to apex. Shell

white with brown markings often forming incomplete transverse bands. Creamy, nacreous columellar lip and orange aperture. Rolled part of lip creamy with coffee axial bands. 5–10cm. Indo-Pacific. Common.

Strombus listeri T. Gray   × 0·8
Shell thin, but solid, elongate-fusiform, with large body whorl and tall, tapering spire with angulate whorls. Outer lip large and flaring, almost straight-sided with long, upward pointing digitation parallel with spire and wide, moderately deep stromboid notch. Upper whorls with strong axial ribs crossed by finer spiral riblets. Body whorl mostly smooth with fine spiral lines crossed by finer, axial growth striae. Yellowish white with axial, zigzag, brown lines which are fused together on outer lip. Callused columella

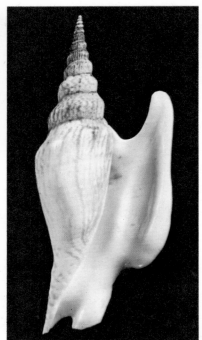

and aperture white. 10–13cm. Indo-Pacific (Indian Ocean). Rare.

Strombus luhuanus Linnaeus   × 1·2
Strawberry or Blood-mouth Conch

Small, conical spire and ovate body whorl often with fine spiral ridges on anterior third. Almost rectangular, curved lip extending for most of body whorl. Shell cream sometimes with coffee axial markings and sometimes with several brown, spiral bands. Columellar lip dark brown and aperture orange. Operculum serrated. 2–7cm. Indo-Pacific. Common.

Strombus marginatus Linnaeus
Marginate Conch
carinata Röding, *robustus* Sowerby, *succinctus* Linnaeus.
Long spire with axially ribbed apex. Lower whorls and body whorl with fine spiral ridges, and lip with wavy margin which extends onto spire whorls. Shell white with fine, coffee, herring-bone markings which merge to form broad spiral bands. Lips and aperture white. 4–5cm. Indo-Pacific. Common.

Strombus minimus Linnaeus
Minute Conch
troglodytes Lamarck.
Long, stepped spire with tubercles, one large tubercle on posterior of body whorl and spiral ridges near anterior. Thick lip extending onto last whorl. Shell cream with orange brown, axial markings which may merge. Lips white, aperture yellowish. *c*2·5cm. Indo-Pacific (South West Pacific). Common.

Strombus mutabilis Swainson   × 1·9
floridus Lamarck.

Conical spire and swollen, ovate to pear-shaped body whorl. Thick, flattened lip extending part way along body whorl. Variable shape and shell colours, usually yellowish to orange with broad, darker, transverse bands and often with irregular, dark, axial lines. Lips and ridged aperture usually pale. 2–4cm. Indo-Pacific. Common.

Strombus peruvianus Swainson   × 0·5
Large, thick, heavy shell with short spire, ovate body whorl, wide, shallow stromboid notch and columella which is curved at base. The thickened outer lip is produced upwards at an angle of about 45° to axis and is moderately pointed. Spiral row of

large nodules at shoulder of body whorl and coarse spiral ridges on rest of whorl. Upper part of columella has series of folds. Strong folds also along outer lip. Pale brown with spire brown and white. Aperture bright orange. Thick, dark brown periostracum. 10–15cm. Panamic. Peruvian. Frequent.

Strombus pipus Röding   × 1·0
Butterfly Conch
papilio Dillwyn.

Conical spire and ovate body whorl bearing spiral rows of tubercles. Incurved lip extending length of body whorl. Shell white with orange brown and lilac, wavy, axial markings. Lips and aperture, which occasionally has wavy ridges, cream and lilac, but aperture sometimes brown. 4–7 cm. Indo-Pacific. Uncommon.

Strombus plicatus Röding
Pigeon Conch
columba Lamarck, *sibbaldi* Sowerby, *pulchellus* Reeve.
Long, stepped spire with axial ribs. Swollen body whorl with blunt tubercles at posterior end and spiral ridges extending onto the lip which bears a fold. Shell cream with brownish yellow patches which may fuse. Lips and ridged aperture white, often with brown patches. 5–6cm. Indo-Pacific. Uncommon.

Strombus pugilis Linnaeus   × 0·7
West-Indian Fighting Conch

Short spire with tubercles extending to posterior of body whorl. Tubercles often spine-like. Very thick, curved lip, with slight posterior hook, extends whole length of body whorl. Shell mushroom, coffee and brownish orange with dark, nacreous lips, often pinkish in smooth aperture. 5–9cm. Caribbean. Common.

Strombus raninus Gmelin   × 0·8
Hawk-wing Conch
lobatus Swainson, *bituberculatus* Lamarck.
Conical, slightly concave, spire with very blunt tubercles. Two large tubercles on

swollen body whorl with thick, irregular lip extending beyond body whorl and past apex. Shell mushroom with coffee to brown patches, nacreous lips mushroom with violet and lilac tinges. 5–10cm. Caribbean. Common.

Strombus sinuatus Lightfoot   × 0·7
cristatus Lamarck, *laciniatus* Dillwyn.

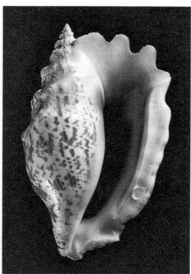

Conical, stepped spire and swollen body whorl with anterior, spiral ridges. Large, thick outer lip extends beyond and partly covers apex to form broad, spoon-like projections. If lip is ignored shell has an almost elliptical outline. Shell creamy with olive brown, wavy axial bands. Lips creamy at edges and purple in smooth aperture. 9–12cm. Indo-Pacific. Uncommon.

Strombus terebellatus Sowerby
Tall, thin, elongate-ovate shell with moderately tall spire and large body whorl. Whorls somewhat rounded and suture slightly impressed. Aperture moderately sharp-edged. Creamy, mottled with yellowish brown. Shows a striking resemblance to *Terebellum terebellum*, hence specific name. 2·5–5·0cm. Indo-Pacific. Frequent.

Strombus thersites Swainson
ponderosa Philippi.
Thick, ovate-fusiform shell with tall spire and large body whorl with flaring outer lip. Prominent knobs at shoulder of body whorl which are continued as much smaller knobs at suture of spire whorls. Broad, shallow stromboid notch. Margin of outer lip thickened and incurved. White with pale brown blotches. Aperture whitish flushed with pink and yellow. Parietal wall pinkish with underlying shell pattern showing through. Shows some resemblance to *S. latissimus*, but smaller and with proportionately taller spire. 10–15cm. Indo-Pacific (South West Pacific). Rare.

Strombus tricornis Lightfoot   × 0·6
Three-knobbed Conch
pertinax Duclos.

Shell thick and heavy, with three tubercles on posterior of body whorl. Large lip with angular posterior projection often extending well past apex. Shell cream with brown axial markings, often overlaid with a thin, coffee layer of periostracum. Lips and smooth aperture white. 6·0–13cm. Indo-Pacific (Red Sea). Common.

Strombus urceus Linnaeus   × 1·1
Little Bear Conch
ustulatus Schumacher.
Pointed spire with axial ribs or tubercles and swollen body whorl with transverse ridges on anterior half and thick lip sometimes with a high shoulder. Shell cream or orange yellow to coffee, sometimes with faint, darker, spiral bands. Lip colour variable, usually light, except for black-

lipped and white-mouthed forms. Aperture ridged. 2–5cm. Indo-Pacific. Common.

Strombus variabilis Swainson
Variable Conch
Conical, stepped spire with regular tubercles, also on posterior of body whorl. Thick lip extending beyond length of body whorl. Shell creamy with fine, brown, axial, zigzag markings and often broad, spiral bands. One form black-banded. Often a columellar colour patch nearer anterior. Lips and smooth aperture white. 2–5cm. Indo-Pacific (South West Pacific). Common.

Strombus vittatus Linnaeus   × 0·6
turritus Lamarck, *japonicus* Reeve.

Long spire with a sutural band and axial ribs usually extending onto body whorl. Anterior with spiral ridges. Thin lips extending most of length of body whorl, outer lip incurved. Shell white with coffee spiral markings. Lips and aperture, which is usually lirate, white. Colours variable.

4–9cm. Indo-Pacific (South West Pacific). Common.

Strombus vomer Röding
pacificus Swainson.
Long, stepped spire with small, blunt tubercles and spiral ridges. Body whorl with bulge and transverse ridges near anterior. Thick lip with a hook passing back nearly as far as apex. Large columellar lip extending onto penultimate whorl and anterior of body whorl. Prominent, curved siphonal canal. Shell white with pale violet to brown axial markings. Lips white, sometimes with a brown columellar patch. Aperture brownish yellow between white ridges. Occasional albinos. 5–9cm. Indo-Pacific (South West Pacific). Uncommon.

Superfamily
Lamellariacea

Family LAMELLARIIDAE

Small family of thin, fragile shells, which are globosely ear-shaped, smooth and polished, but usually covered with a thick periostracum. Spire is small and short, but body whorl is very large and aperture is usually widely expanded. No operculum. The mantle of most species almost or completely covers the shell. Few genera. Widely distributed in most seas.

Genus VELUTINA Fleming
For details, see Lamellariidae. Few species, mostly from shallow water; equally distributed in warm and cool seas.

Velutina cryptospira Middendorff
Thin, fragile, ear-shaped shell with very small spire at posterior end and very large body whorl with wide aperture. Reddish brown, but usually covered by a thick, brown periostracum which has spiral ridges. c2·5cm. Japonic. Common.

Velutina velutina Müller   × 1·4
laevigata Pennant.

Thin, globose shell with very short spire and deeply impressed suture. Body whorl very large and aperture expanding outwards. Whitish brown, sometimes tinged pink. Aperture pinkish white, columella white. 1·5–2·0cm. Boreal (North West Europe). Frequent.

Superfamily
Cypraeacea

Family TRIVIIDAE

Small, globose and humped shells with concealed spire. Teeth produced as spiral ribs which encircle dorsum and sides and extend on to columella. Narrow, straight aperture. Unicolorous or blotched but never banded. Sometimes known as false cowries. About six genera comprising about 70 species living in most seas.

Genus TRIVIA Broderip
For details see Family Triviidae.

Trivia californiana Gray
Inflated, globular shell with coarse, transverse ridges over entire shell, 15 crossing outer lip. Slight dorsal groove. Shell mauve. c1cm. Californian. Common.

Trivia maugeriae Gray ×2·0

Shell small, thin, with teeth produced as fine ribs covering the entire shell except for distinct, dorsal axial groove. Apex covered but visible underneath external layer. Pale pink with large, dorsal, reddish blotch and reddish extremities. c1·3cm. Indo-Pacific (Galapagos Islands). Frequent.

Trivia monacha Da Costa ×2·0

Inflated almost globular shell with transverse ridges covering entire shell. Very fine, pointed teeth and ridged aperture. Shell glossy, coffee with three purple brown spots on dorsum. Base white. c1cm. Mediterranean, Boreal. Common.

Trivia pediculus Linnaeus
Thick, globular shell with 16–19 ribs on outer lip. Shell brown to pink with three pairs of large, dark brown spots on dorsum, centre pair largest. c1cm. Caribbean. Common.

Trivia radians Lamarck ×1·3

Shell large for the genus, thick and solid. Encircled by strong, widely spaced ridges, some of which are produced as pustules on dorsum. Distinct axial groove down centre of dorsum. Pinkish, with obscure brownish spots on dorsum. c2cm. Panamic. Common.

Trivia solandri Sowerby ×1·6

Resembles *T. radians*, but shell smaller with fewer spiral ribs. Dorsal groove wider. Browner than *T. radians* with whitish dorsal groove. c1·7cm. Panamic. Common.

Trivia suffusa Gray
Inflated, globular shell. Dorsum covered with beaded ribs and obvious dorsal groove. 18–23 ribs cross outer lip. Shell pink with brown speckles. Brownish blotch on each side of siphonal canal. c1cm. Caribbean. Common.

Genus ERATO Risso
Small, biconical or globose shells. Smooth, with margined and reflexed outer lip. Narrow aperture. Both lips dentate. Numerous species in most seas.

Erato columbella Menke
Smooth, pear-shaped shell with elevated, conical spire and thickened, shouldered outer lip with about twelve very small teeth. Shell glossy blue grey with white lip and brown to purple siphonal canal. c1cm. Californian, Panamic. Frequent.

Erato lachryma Sowerby ×2·0

Shell very small, thick, inflated, with short, blunt spire. Outer lip minutely denticulate. Yellowish white with large, brownish violet blotches. Aperture, columella and parietal wall white. c0·6cm. Japonic.

Erato vitellina Hinds
Thick, smooth, pear-shaped shell with small, conical spire and thickened lip. Teeth on columella and outer lip about equal in size. Shell glossy cream to brown with purple area on body whorl. c1cm. Californian. Frequent.

Genus PEDICULARIA Swainson
Small, thin shells with irregular, large aperture. Number of fine reticulations or decussations. Often brightly coloured and sometimes assuming the coloration of the corals to which they are attached in life. Few species in tropical and warm seas.

Pedicularia californica Newcomb ×2·0

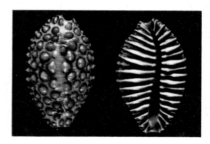

Shell small, thin but solid. Irregular in shape. Aperture very enlarged and flaring. Apex hidden by expanded lip. Minutely decussate early whorls; rest of shell with fine spiral threads. Aperture glossy. Rosy with whitish stripes on outer lip. 1·0–1·5cm. Californian. Uncommon.

Genus JENNERIA Jousseaume
Small, solid shells with finely striate surface markings and with dorsum studded with very conspicuous nodes. One living species.

Jenneria pustulata Lightfoot ×2·0

Shell and ornament as described for *Jenneria*. The bright orange nodules stand out starkly from the purplish brown ground colour. Apertural teeth extend to margins as white ridges against the ground colour. 1·5–2·0cm. Panamic. Common.

Family CYPRAEIDAE

The most popular and best known of all shell groups. The cowries all have tortoise-like or globular shells most being smooth, glossy and usually colourful. Aperture generally narrow, the two lips denticulate in nearly all species. Small anterior and posterior canals. Spire overlaid with enamel in adult. Lip margins often thickened. The glossy surface is caused by the mantle which envelops shell completely when animal is active. Operculum absent. Cowries are nocturnal herbivores. Females incubate their eggs. About 185 species, the majority living in tropical waters where they favour coral reefs. According to some authorities there are many genera in this family. Others admit only one genus, *Cypraea*, this simpler alternative being followed here.

Genus CYPRAEA Linnaeus
Details as for Family Cypraeidae. Specific distinctions often difficult to describe as many species are fundamentally similar in size, shape and dentition. Considerable variation occurs within a given species when shells from different populations are compared.

Cypraea albuginosa Gray   × 1·2
nariaeformis Schilder.

Inflated, elliptical shell with poorly marked teeth. Dorsum mushroom, irregularly covered with small, brownish orange or brownish lilac rings. Margins, base and teeth white. *c*2·5cm. Californian. Frequent.

Cypraea angustata Gmelin
alba Coen, *coronata* Schilder, *fuscodentata* Gray.
Thin, inflated, ovate shell with sharp, weak teeth. Dorsum uniformly mushroom, brownish yellow or brownish violet. Slightly callused, cream margins with brown spots. Base and teeth cream. Often brown, terminal patches. 3·5–4·5cm. Australian. Frequent.

Cypraea annettae Dall   × 1·0
sowerbyi Kiener.

Elliptical to ovate shell. Dorsum white overlaid with many brownish yellow and brown blotches forming indistinct bands. Margins coffee with brown spots and violet tinges. Base coffee, teeth cream. 2·5–4·5cm. Californian, Panamic. Frequent.

Cypraea annulus Linnaeus   × 1·2
Gold Ringer

Ovate, humped shell with coarse teeth. Dorsum creamy bluish with clear, golden yellow ring where dorsum meets marginal calluses. Margins, base and teeth mushroom. *c*2·5cm. Indo-Pacific. Common.

Cypraea arabica Linnaeus   × 0·4
Arabian Cowry

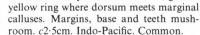

Elliptical, humped shell with coarse teeth. Dorsum cream with large, mushroom blotches overlaid with short, fine, brown axial lines which merge leaving occasional spots and give appearance of arabic script. Callused margins cream with blurred brown and lilac spots. Base mushroom with brownish orange teeth. 3·5–8·0cm. Indo-Pacific. Common.

Cypraea arabicula Lamarck   × 1·3
Little Arabian Cowry

Elliptical, humped shell with plate-like teeth. Dorsum creamy overlaid with many brownish yellow markings. Callused margins mushroom with lilac and brownish spots. Base mushroom to coffee, teeth paler. Lilac to brown terminal markings. 2–3cm. Californian, Panamic. Frequent.

Cypraea asellus Linnaeus   × 1·5
Asellus Cowry

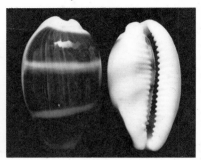

bitaeniata Geret, *vespacea* Melvill.
Elliptical shell. Dorsum white with three broad, jet black, dorsal bands (which fade to chocolate). Base, lips and teeth white. 1·5–2·5cm. Indo-Pacific. Frequent.

Cypraea aurantium Gmelin   × 0·7
Golden Cowry
Inflated, ovate shell. Dorsum uniformly magenta (fading to a golden orange with time). Slight creamy marginal calluses. Base cream. Lips deep orange between lighter teeth. 6–11cm. Indo-Pacific (Pacific). Rare.

Cypraea bistrinotata Schilder & Schilder
                                      × 1·6

Thin, inflated, globular shell with extended anterior and posterior canals and fine teeth. Dorsum brownish orange with three pairs of large, brown spots near centre, and many smaller spots towards margins. Four well defined spots on base. Margins, base and teeth yellowish. 1·5–2·0cm. Indo-Pacific Uncommon.

Cypraea boivinii Kiener   × 1·1
amoena Schilder.

Thin, elliptical shell with blunt, widely-spaced teeth. Dorsum mushroom with few brownish yellow spots and occasionally grey blue tinges. Labial margin white, columellar margin continues dorsum colour to base. Teeth and labial base white. Spire visible. *c*2·5cm. Indo-Pacific. Frequent.

Cypraea capensis Gray
Cape Cowry
elizabethensis Rous.
Inflated, ovate shell covered with fine transverse ridges except for labial lip which bears teeth. Dorsum dirty mushroom with occasional brown markings. Base dirty cream on columellar side, white with mushroom teeth on labial side.

Cypraea aurantium

Sunken spire. *c*2·5cm. South African. Frequent.

Cypraea caputdraconis Melvill   × 1·0
Dragon's Head Cowry

Shell similar to *C. caputserpentis* but higher and more humped, teeth wider spaced, aperture broader. Dark brown between teeth. 1·5–4·5cm. Indo-Pacific (Easter Island). Frequent.

Cypraea caputserpentis Linnaeus   × 0·9
Snake's Head Cowry
reticulum Gmelin, *caputanguis* Philippi, *caputcolubri* Kenyon.
Elliptical, humped shell with coarse teeth. Dorsum chocolate with cream mottling. Margins chocolate. Slightly convex base,

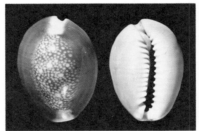

brown near margins becoming pale towards cream lips and teeth. Prominent, light, anterior and posterior, terminal blotches. 1·5–4·0cm. Indo-Pacific. Common.

Cypraea carneola Linnaeus   × 0·8
Carnelian Cowry

Elliptical, almost cylindrical shell with fine teeth. Dorsum mushroom overlaid with light brown and with several brownish orange bands. Margins coffee with indistinct mushroom spots, base mushroom and teeth lilac. 2·5–9·0cm. Indo-Pacific. Common.

Cypraea caurica Linnaeus   × 1·0

Elliptical, almost cylindrical shell with coarse teeth. Dorsum bluish cream with light brown spots and blotches occasionally forming poorly marked bands. Marginal calluses mushroom with a few brown spots. Base mushroom, orange between white teeth. Two faint dark, anterior, terminal blotches and a spire blotch. 2·5–5·0cm. Indo-Pacific. Common.

Cypraea cervinetta Kiener   × 0·4
Little Deer Cowry

Almost cylindrical shell. Dorsum mushroom with brownish orange markings, often with bands, leaving spots of mushroom showing, especially near margins. Base mushroom, teeth brown. 5·0–8·5cm. Californian, Panamic. Frequent.

Cypraea cervus Linnaeus × 0·6
cervina Lamarck.

Thick, inflated, elliptical shell with wide aperture and coarse, blunt teeth. Dorsum light brown to chocolate with white spots. Margins paler and base mushroom to cream with brownish orange teeth. 9–15cm. Caribbean. Uncommon.

Cypraea chinensis Gmelin × 0·9
variolaria Lamarck, *cruenta* Dillwyn, *tortirostris* Sowerby.

Elliptical shell. Dorsum mottled orange yellow on cream. Cream marginal calluses with lilac spots. Base cream, orange between white teeth. 1·5–5·0cm. Indo-Pacific. Frequent.

Cypraea cicercula Linnaeus × 1·4
Chick-pea Cowry
purissima Coen.

Thin, globular shell with fine teeth and elongated anterior and posterior canals. Dorsum white to coffee with brownish spots and patches. White to coffee base and teeth. Dark brown depression near posterior end. 1·5–2·0cm. Indo-Pacific. Frequent.

Cypraea cinerea Gmelin × 1·8
Atlantic Grey Cowry
sordida Lamarck, *fragiliodes* Hidalgo.

Inflated, elliptical shell with blunt teeth. Dorsum mushroom to yellowish, with faint, darker bands. Base and teeth white. 2–3cm. Caribbean. Frequent.

Cypraea clandestina Linnaeus × 2·1

Ovate shell with fine teeth. Dorsum mushroom becoming white nearer margins. Fine, orange brown, zigzag lines from margin to margin. Base and teeth white. Small, dark spot on spire. *c*1·5cm. Indo-Pacific. Frequent.

Cypraea coloba Melvill
Thick, irregularly elliptical shell with large marginal calluses and well developed, large teeth. Dorsum creamy with very small, brownish yellow spots. Margins cream to white with lilac spots. Base coffee, becoming darker between creamy teeth. *c*3·5cm. Indo-Pacific. Frequent.

Cypraea cribraria Linnaeus × 1·0
Sieve Cowry
zadela Iredale.

Elliptical shell. Dorsum orange brown with large, circular, white spots. Margins, base and teeth white. 2·0–3·5cm. Indo-Pacific. Frequent.

Cypraea cylindrica Born × 1·4

Cylindrical Cowry
emaculata Coen.
Almost cylindrical shell with widely spaced teeth. Dorsum bluish grey to mushroom with very small, brownish orange spots and usually a large, brownish orange patch at centre. Margins, base and teeth white. Two anterior and two posterior, dark brown, terminal blotches. Sunken spire. 2·5–3·0cm. Indo-Pacific. Frequent.

Cypraea declivis Sowerby   × 1·4

Almost ovate shell with fine, widely spaced, teeth. Dorsum white with brown spots. Margins and base white. *c*2·5cm. Australian. Uncommon.

Cypraea depressa Gray   × 0·8
Depressed Cowry
intermedia Redfield, *gillei* Jousseaume.

Dorsum brown with close, white spots and wide, slightly darker band at centre. Thick calluses and margins with smudged, brown spots on lilac and white. Base and lips white with distinct, brown teeth. 2·5–5·6cm. Indo-Pacific. Common.

Cypraea diluculum Reeve   × 0·9

Shell very similar in most respects to *C. ziczac* (q.v.), but zigzag pattern much darker brown. *c*3·0cm. Indo-Pacific (Indian Ocean). Frequent.

Cypraea edentula Gray   × 1·1
Toothless Cowry

Thin, globose to ovate shell with slight terminal projections. No teeth and a wide aperture. Dorsum coffee occasionally with darker banding. Brown spots on callused labial margin and a few on the columellar side. Often brown, terminal and spire blotches. 2–3cm. South African. Frequent.

Cypraea eglantina Duclos   × 0·7
Eglantine Cowry
niger Roberts, *couturieri* Vayssière, *perconfusa* Iredale.

Elliptical, slightly humped shell. Dorsum with thin, brown, axial stripes on cream interrupted by cream spots. One complete cream, axial, dorsal stripe. Slight marginal calluses with brown spots on mushroom. Base mushroom with distinct brown teeth. Two dark, anterior blotches and three dark, posterior blotches. 3·8–6·9cm. Indo-Pacific. Common.

Cypraea erosa Linnaeus   × 1·0
Eroded Cowry

Ovate shell with coarse teeth extending to callused labial margin and giving serrated outline. Dorsum coffee with fine, mushroom spots and sometimes a grey blue axial line. One large, faint, bluish to coffee

patch midway along each margin. Margins, base and teeth mushroom to cream. 2–5cm. Indo-Pacific. Common.

Cypraea errones Linnaeus   × 1·4
Wandering Cowry
cruenta Gmelin, *olivacea* Lamarck.

Elliptical shell with poorly marked, coarse teeth. Dorsum grey blue with brown spots which may merge to almost cover other colours. Usually darkest at centre of dorsum. Margins, base and teeth white, but occasionally with dark blotch continuing from dorsum midway along columellar lip. Dark spot on spire. 2–4cm. Indo-Pacific. Common.

Cypraea felina Gmelin   × 1·3
Kitten Cowry

Elliptical shell with poorly developed teeth. Dorsum olive brown to grey blue with many fine, brown blotches and rows of large, brown patches which may merge to form four bands. Base and teeth cream to mushroom. Two brown, anterior, and two posterior, terminal blotches. 2·0–2·5 cm. Indo-Pacific. Frequent.

Cypraea fimbriata Gmelin   × 1·6

Small ovate shell with fine teeth. Dorsum bluish to lilac with very small, brownish orange blotches and a band of regular, brownish orange axial lines running across middle. Colours continue around margin to base on columella side, fading to white teeth. On labial side, margin, base and teeth white. Two anterior and two posterior, brownish, terminal blotches. 1·3–2·0cm. Indo-Pacific (East Africa). Common.

Cypraea fuscodentata Gray × 1·2

Long, elliptical to ovate shell with coarse, widely spaced teeth and ridges over base. Dorsum creamy to mushroom with brownish patches. Margins and base creamy to mushroom, teeth and ridges brownish orange. 3·0–4·5cm. South African. Frequent.

Cypraea gangranosa Dillwyn × 2·0
reentsii Dunker.
Elliptical shell with coarse teeth. Dorsum greyish mushroom to coffee with creamy to bluish spots. Callused margins, base and teeth white. Two anterior, and two posterior, terminal patches. 1·0–2·5cm. Indo-Pacific. Uncommon.

Cypraea globulus Linnaeus × 2·0
Globular Cowry
affinis Gmelin.

Thin, globular shell with extended anterior and posterior canals and fine teeth. Shell uniformly cream, yellowish or brownish yellow, occasionally bearing a few darker spots. Sometimes small, warty tubercles. Base and teeth paler than dorsum. 1·5–2·0cm. Indo-Pacific. Frequent.

Cypraea gracilis Gaskoin × 2·3
Graceful Cowry
hilda Iredale, *irescens* Sowerby.

Inflated, elliptical shell with poorly developed teeth. Dorsum mushroom to blue grey with very small, brownish orange spots and often a large, brown patch in centre. Slightly callused margins cream with small, dark brown spots. Base and teeth cream. Two anterior and two posterior, lilac, terminal patches. 0·5–2·5cm. Indo-Pacific. Common.

Cypraea granulata Pease × 1·0
honoluluensis Melvill.

Thick, elliptical shell with fine teeth and ridges covering base. Dorsum with ridges and warty tubercles. Colours variable, pink to red or brown, but never glossy in adult except for indented dorsal line. c3·5 cm. Indo-Pacific (Hawaii only). Uncommon.

Cypraea grayana Schilder
Elliptical, humped shell with small teeth and almost flat base. Dorsum creamy with brownish orange axial lines and patches leaving some creamy spots. Margins mushroom with blurred, brown spots, base mushroom with orange teeth. 2·5–4·0cm. Indo-Pacific (Red Sea, Persian Gulf, Gulf of Oman). Common.

Cypraea helvola Linnaeus × 1·2
Honey Cowry

Elliptical to ovate shell with well developed teeth. Dorsum mushroom to grey blue with small, white spots and larger, brown patches merging to form brown areas above margins. Terminal areas lilac. Margins mushroom deepening towards brownish orange teeth. 2·0–2·5cm. Indo-Pacific. Common.

Cypraea hirundo Linnaeus
cameroni Iredale, *peropima* Iredale, *neglecta* Sowerby.
Elliptical, almost cylindrical shell. Dorsum blue grey with creamy patches and very small, brownish orange spots. Creamy margins with few small, brownish orange spots. Base and teeth white. Two anterior and two posterior, dark brown, terminal spots. 1–2cm. Indo-Pacific. Frequent.

Cypraea histrio Gmelin
westralis Iredale, *duploreticulata* Coen.
Thick, humped shell, almost triangular in side-view. Dorsum cream with faint mushroom to violet patches completely overlaid with fine, brownish orange reticulations leaving almost circular spots, and with finer reticulations between these spots. Heavily callused margins cream with large, dark brown spots and lilac tinges. Cream base and brown teeth. Brown, anterior, posterior and spire blotches. 5–6cm. Indo-Pacific. Frequent.

Cypraea irrorata Gray × 2·0

Elliptical, almost cylindrical, shell with sharp and prominent anterior teeth. Dorsum white with small, regular, brownish yellow spots extending to margins. Base and teeth white. 1–2cm. Indo-Pacific. Frequent.

Cypraea isabella Linnaeus × 1·2
controversa Gray.

Almost cylindrical shell with fine teeth. Dorsum mushroom to coffee with several fine, dark brown axial lines composed of long, narrow blotches. Margins, base and teeth white. Two anterior and two posterior, orange brown, terminal blotches. 2·0–4·5cm. Indo-Pacific. Common.

Cypraea kieneri Hidalgo   × 2·0

Elliptical, almost cylindrical, shell with well marked teeth. Dorsum with extensive, greyish blue blotches on cream, stippled with fine, brownish orange spots, clearer near margins. Base and teeth cream. Two large anterior and two posterior, brown, terminal blotches. c2cm. Indo-Pacific. Frequent.

Cypraea labrolineata Gaskoin   × 2·3

Elliptical shell. Columellar teeth fine. Dorsum pale olive brown with well marked pale grey blue spots. Margins with a ring of brown spots just above the slight callus. Base and teeth white. c1·5cm. Indo-Pacific. Frequent.

Cypraea lamarcki Gray   × 1·0
Lamarck's Cowry
inocellata Coen.

Ovate shell. Dorsum coffee with white spots of various sizes. Margins creamy with smudged, brownish orange spots often becoming short, axial stripes at anterior and posterior. Base and teeth white. 3–5cm. Indo-Pacific (Indian Ocean). Frequent.

Cypraea lentiginosa Gray   × 1·4
Freckled Cowry

Elliptical, slightly humped shell. Dorsum creamy with brownish orange and coffee smudges. Slightly callused, white margins with small, brown spots. Base and teeth white. 2·5–4·0cm. Indo-Pacific. Uncommon.

Cypraea limacina Lamarck   × 1·3
nitens Coen, *interstincta* Wood.

Elliptical shell with ridge-like teeth. Anterior canal often pitted above. Dorsum mushroom, sometimes with a violet tinge, and with few white spots of various sizes. Margins white, teeth cream to coffee. 2·5–3·2cm. Indo-Pacific. Frequent.

Cypraea lurida Linnaeus   × 0·6
badia Coen, *incrassata* Coen.

Elliptical to almost cylindrical shell with poorly developed, blunt teeth. Dorsum coffee to brownish sometimes with three faint, broad bands. Margins, base and teeth creamy. Two anterior and two posterior, dark brown, terminal patches. 4–5cm. Mediterranean. Frequent.

Cypraea lutea Gmelin   × 1·6
bizonata Iredale.

Almost ovate shell with regular teeth. Dorsum usually greenish and poorly marked with brownish spots. Two white, transverse bands running across dorsum and dividing it into three equal parts. Margins and base orange with black spots on margins. White teeth. 1–2cm. Indo-Pacific. Frequent.

Cypraea lynx Linnaeus   × 0·8
Lynx Cowry
vanelli Linnaeus, *caledonica* Crosse, *michaelis* Melvill.

Inflated, elliptical shell. Dorsum with a few distinct brown spots over many smaller, lilac and grey blue spots which may merge; occasionally narrow, axial, dorsal stripes of lighter brown markings. Slight marginal calluses cream with brown spots. Base has two distinct axial ridges midway between aperture and margins peculiar to this species. Base white with orange between white teeth. Markings variable. 1·9–6·5cm. Indo-Pacific. Common.

Cypraea maculifera Schilder
Reticulated Cowry
reticulata Martyn.
Heavy, ovate, humped shell with coarse teeth. Dorsum mushroom overlaid with brownish orange reticulations leaving spots and axial lines of mushroom visible.

93

Heavily callused margins mushroom with lilac tinges and orange brown and lilac spots. Base dirty cream, teeth orange brown. Often dark, terminal patches. 5–9cm. Indo-Pacific. Frequent.

Cypraea mappa Linnaeus   × 0·4
Map Cowry
rosea Gray, *alga* Perry.

Thick, humped shell with coarse, blunt teeth. Dorsum creamy with brownish orange reticulations often giving a map-like appearance. Callused margins mushroom with smudged brownish spots. Base creamy, teeth orange. 6–9cm. Indo-Pacific. Frequent.

Cypraea mauritiana Linnaeus   × 0·6
Hump-back Cowry

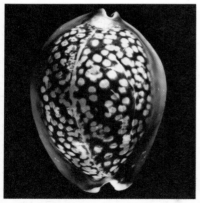

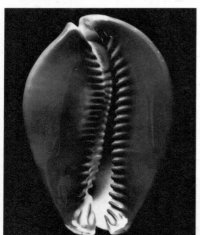

Ovate, humped shell with slightly convex base and coarse teeth. Flat, spade-like projections pointing downwards around anterior siphonal aperture. Dorsum cream overlaid with brownish, lilac, then chocolate, leaving striking, light spots. Margins uniformly dark brown to black. Base dark brown to black and mushroom to white between dark brown teeth. 7–11cm. Indo-Pacific. Common.

Cypraea microdon Gray   × 2·1
katha Iredale.

Small, thin shell with fine teeth. Dorsum coffee to lilac with faint, brownish yellow to brown patches. Columellar margin continues dorsum colours. Lilac blotches at extremities. Labial margin, lip and teeth creamy. *c*1cm. Indo-Pacific. Frequent.

Cypraea miliaris Gmelin   × 1·0
differens Schilder, *effossa* Schilder.

Inflated, ovate shell with coarse teeth. Anterior and posterior canals often pitted above. Dorsum coffee with cream spots. Margins, base and teeth creamy. 2·5–3·5cm. Indo-Pacific. Frequent.

Cypraea moneta Linnaeus   × 1·3
Money Cowry
icterina Lamarck, *barthelemyi* Bernardi.

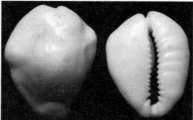

Shell greatly thickened at margins, ovate to deltoidal or pentagonal in outline. Short, coarse teeth. Dorsum creamy to orange yellow, sometimes three darker bands. Base creamy, teeth and margins whitish. Extremely variable in size, shape and colour. 1·2–3·6cm. Indo-Pacific. Common.

Cypraea mus Linnaeus   × 0·8
Mouse Cowry
bicornis Sowerby, *suta* Coen, *tuberculata* Gray.

Thick, humped, ovate shell with poorly developed teeth and flat projections around anterior canal. Dorsum creamy covered with smudged, mushroom spots. Two axial rows of brown spots at centre, leaving creamy axial line. At margins the mushroom spots may extend to form transverse stripes. Base mushroom, teeth brown. 2·5–4·5cm. Caribbean (North Columbia and West Venezuela). Uncommon.

Cypraea nebrites Melvill   × 1·0

Thick, ovate shell with coarse teeth and well developed marginal calluses. Dorsum brown with creamy spots. A well defined, large, brown patch extending from dorsal part of each marginal callus towards dorsum on each side. Base white with brown spots. 2·5–4·5cm. Indo-Pacific. Frequent.

Cypraea nigropunctata Gray
Elliptical to cylindrical shell with coarse teeth. Dorsum brownish yellow with small, creamy patches. Margins with small, black spots. Base and teeth creamy to mushroom. 2·5–4·0cm. Indo-Pacific (Galapagos Islands). Uncommon.

Cypraea nucleus Linnaeus   × 1·4
Nucleus Cowry
madagascariensis Gmelin.

Globose, solid shell with extended anterior and posterior canals and fine, well marked teeth. Base markedly convex. Entire shell white to mushroom with many warty nodules and some transverse ridges. Often an axial groove along middle of dorsum. Teeth extend over whole of base. 2·0–3·2cm. Indo-Pacific. Frequent.

Cypraea obvelata Lamarck   × 1·5
Tahiti Gold Ringer
perrieri Rochebrune.

Irregularly ovate shell with prominent teeth. Dorsum normally creamy, sometimes bluish. Distinct depression marked with thin, orange line between extremely well developed marginal calluses and dorsum. Base, lips and teeth cream. 4–5cm. Indo-Pacific (East Polynesia). Common.

Cypraea ocellata Linnaeus   × 1·1
fasciomaculata Coen.
Inflated, ovate shell. Dorsum coffee to brownish yellow with many white spots,

some of which have a smaller brown spot inside them giving an 'eyed' appearance. Margins creamy with smudged, brownish spots. Base and strong teeth creamy. 1–3cm. Indo-Pacific. Frequent.

Cypraea onyx Linnaeus   × 0·8
Onyx Cowry
succincta Linnaeus.

Inflated, ovate shell with wide aperture and poorly developed teeth. Dorsum creamy with three pale brown bands tinged with lilac, occasionally uniformly brown. Margins, base and teeth dark chocolate to black. 2·5–3·5cm. Indo-Pacific. Frequent.

Cypraea ovum Gmelin   × 1·4
sophiae Brazier.

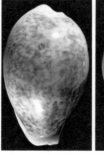

Shell pyriform; dorsum bluish white spotted with greenish brown and with two or three poorly defined, transverse bands. Creamy white, unspotted sides. Teeth short, with orange interstices. 2–4cm. Indo-Pacific (Pacific only). Common.

Cypraea pallida Gray   × 1·4

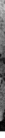

Ovate shell with blunt teeth. Dorsum bluish with brownish yellow patches and small spots, with larger, darker patches at centre. Base and teeth white. 2·5–3·0cm. Indo-Pacific. Uncommon.

Cypraea pallidula Gaskoin   × 2·1

Elliptical almost cylindrical shell with fine teeth. Dorsum creamy to greenish with brownish yellow patches and mottling. Four dark transverse bands. Base and teeth usually white. 1·5–2·5cm. Indo-Pacific. Frequent.

Cypraea pantherina Lightfoot   × 0·4
Panther Cowry
obtusa Perry, *tigrina* Lamarck, *vinosa* Gmelin.

Inflated shell with flat, narrow base and coarse teeth. Dorsum usually whitish or bluish mottled with small, brown spots. Base and teeth white. Colours variable, one variety chocolate brown all over. Usually similar to *C. tigris* but relatively longer and narrower, and so shaped and weighted that shell quickly rights itself if placed upside down. 5–8cm. Indo-Pacific (Red Sea, East Africa). Frequent.

Cypraea piperita Gray   × 1·4
dissecta Iredale.

Ovate shell with thin teeth. Dorsum creamy to yellow with faint, darker bands and sometimes spots. Margins usually creamy with smudged, brown spots. Base and teeth creamy. Colours variable. 2–3cm. Australian. Frequent.

Cypraea poraria Linnaeus   × 1·2

Porous Cowry
theoreta Iredale.
Inflated, ovate shell. Dorsum cream to coffee with creamy spots, many having brownish yellow rings around them. Margins and base lilac, teeth cream. 2·0–3·5cm. Indo-Pacific. Common.

Cypraea pulicaria Reeve
Thin almost cylindrical shell with spire clearly visible. Blunt teeth. Dorsum white with four bands of brownish yellow patches. Margins white with brown spots. Base and teeth white. *c*2·5cm. Australian. Frequent.

Cypraea punctata Linnaeus   × 1·7
Punctate Cowry
berinii Dautzenberg.

Ovate shell with fine teeth. Dorsum mushroom with a few small, brownish yellow spots extending to margins. Base creamy, teeth slightly darker. 1–3cm. Indo-Pacific. Frequent.

Cypraea pyriformis Gray   × 1·9
smithi Sowerby.
Almost pear-shaped shell. Dorsum creamy mottled with small, brownish yellow patches and often a large, brown patch towards centre. Margins and base creamy,

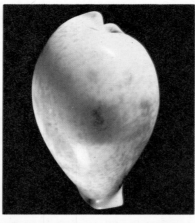

teeth black or dark brown. *c*2·5cm. Indo-Pacific. Uncommon.

Cypraea pyrum Gmelin   × 0·9
Pear Cowry
maculosa Gmelin, *insularum* Schilder.

Inflated, pear-shaped shell. Dorsum creamy overlaid with brownish yellow to brown, patchy markings. Margins and base salmon pink to brownish orange. Teeth usually slightly paler. 4–5cm. West African, Mediterranean. Frequent.

Cypraea quadrimaculata Gray   × 1·3
Four-spotted Cowry
Almost cylindrical shell with widely spaced

teeth. Dorsum creamy to grey blue often with pale brownish orange speckles. Margins, base and teeth creamy. Two anterior and two posterior, dark brown, terminal patches. 2–4cm. Indo-Pacific. Frequent.

Cypraea robertsi Hidalgo   × 1·5
punctulata Gray.

Ovate, humped shell with marginal calluses. Dorsum blue grey with brown speckles and patches. Margins cream to mushroom with lilac spots. Base and teeth white. 2–3cm. Californian, Panamic. Frequent.

Cypraea scurra Gmelin   × 0·7
Jester Cowry
antelia Iredale, *indica* Gmelin.

Almost cylindrical shell with narrow teeth. Dorsum creamy to bluish with brownish yellow reticulations leaving circular patches and an axial stripe at middle. Margins mushroom with violet to brown spots. Base mushroom, teeth brownish orange. 3–5cm. Indo-Pacific. Uncommon.

Cypraea spadicea Swainson   × 0·7
Chestnut Cowry
Inflated, ovate shell. Dorsum brownish yellow at centre becoming progressively

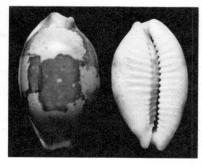

darker towards dark brown, wavy band above margins. Margins creamy to lilac, base and teeth white. *c*4cm. Californian. Frequent.

Cypraea spurca Linnaeus   × 1.3
European Yellow Cowry
flaveola Linnaeus, *acicularis* Gmelin, *lunata* Fischer, *atlantica* Monterosato.

creamy. 2·5–3·5cm. Indo-Pacific. Uncommon.

Cypraea subviridis Reeve   × 1.0
Greenish Cowry
vaticina Iredale.

pale between teeth. 5–8cm. Indo-Pacific. Frequent.

Cypraea teres Gmelin   × 1.0
hermani Iredale, *pentella* Iredale.

Dorsum cream with yellow to brown mottling or spots. Margins, base and lips white to yellow. Occasionally a labial callus and marginal, brown spots. 1·5–3·5cm. Mediterranean, West African, Caribbean. Common.

Cypraea staphylaea Linnaeus   × 2.0

Ovate shell with poorly developed teeth and wide aperture. Dorsum creamy to bluish, sometimes mushroom, with brownish orange patches often large at centre. Margins creamy, base and teeth white. 2–4cm. Indo-Pacific. Frequent.

Cypraea talpa Linnaeus   × 0.9
Mole Cowry

Almost cylindrical shell. Dorsum creamy to mushroom with three broad bands of brownish, herring-bone markings. Margins, base and teeth white. 2–4cm. Indo-Pacific. Frequent.

Cypraea tigris Linnaeus   × 0.6

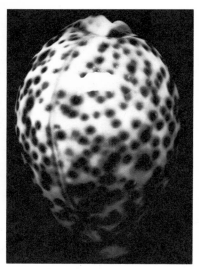

Inflated, elliptical shell with fine teeth, extending as ribs to cover base. Dorsum bluish to brown with paler, warty tubercles. Margins white, base and teeth usually coffee. 1–2cm. Indo-Pacific. Frequent.

Cypraea stolida Linnaeus   × 1.5
brevidentata Sowerby
Inflated, ovate shell with coarse teeth. Dorsum bluish with few brownish orange spots and patches, usually one large one at centre. Margins, base and teeth usually

Almost cylindrical shell with fine teeth. Dorsum cream to coffee with four wide, darker bands usually brownish orange. Brown or chocolate margins and base,

Tiger Cowry
pardalis Shaw, *schilderiana* Cate.
Thick, heavy, inflated shell with coarse, short teeth. Dorsum usually whitish or bluish mottled with brown spots. Base and teeth white. Extremely variable in size, shape and colour. 4–14cm. Indo-Pacific. Common.

Cypraea turdus Lamarck × 0.7
Thrush Cowry
pardalina Dunker, *ovata* Perry.

Ovate, humped shell with coarse teeth. Dorsum pale grey blue to pale lilac stippled with small, brownish orange spots. Margins, base and teeth white. 3–5cm. Indo-Pacific. Frequent.

Cypraea ventriculus Lamarck × 0.6
achatina Perry.

Thick, elliptical, humped shell with coarse teeth. Dorsum cream to mushroom becoming darker until chocolate above margins. Margins and base mushroom, becoming paler towards white teeth. 4·5–5·5cm. Indo-Pacific. Uncommon.

Cypraea vitellus Linnaeus × 0.7
Pacific Deer Cowry
orcina Iredale, *sarcodes* Melvill, *dama* Perry.

Inflated, elliptical to ovate shell with coarse teeth. Dorsum creamy overlaid with different shades of creamy brown often forming faint, broad bands and with cream spots. Usually thin, pale, transverse stripes near margins. Margins and base mushroom, teeth white. 4–9cm. Indo-Pacific. Common.

Cypraea walkeri Sowerby × 1.3
amabilis Jousseaume.

Dorsum with one broad, brown band bordered by two narrower, light brown bands on a greyish background mottled with brown. A few brown spots on margins. Teeth and lips lilac. Sunken spire. Lilac, terminal blotches. 1·8–3·7cm. Indo-Pacific. Frequent.

Cypraea xanthodon Sowerby × 1.1

Ovate shell with coarse teeth. Dorsum creamy to bluish with many small, brownish orange patches often forming broad bands. Margins mushroom to pinkish with small, dark brown spots. Base and teeth pinkish. One variety violet with brown bands on dorsum, and white base and teeth. 2–4cm. Indo-Pacific. Frequent.

Cypraea zebra Linnaeus
Zebra Cowry
Cylindrical shell with fine teeth. Dorsum light brown with broad, dark brown, transverse bands, all covered by large, whitish spots. Margins with ocellated spots. Base mushroom, teeth brown. 5–9cm. Caribbean. Frequent.

Cypraea ziczac Linnaeus × 2.0
Zigzag Cowry
signata Iredale.

Inflated, ovate shell with fine teeth. Dorsum cream with faint, brownish yellow, zigzag, herring-bone markings in bands. Creamy margins with small, brown spots. Base and teeth creamy. 1–3cm. Indo-Pacific. Frequent.

Cypraea zonaria Gmelin × 1.1
zonata Lamarck.

Thick, ovate shell with coarse, blunt teeth. Dorsum olive brown, often with broad, blurred, brown, zigzag markings running across centre. Base and teeth creamy to pale orange. 2–3cm. West African. Uncommon.

Family AMPHIPERATIDAE

Small to medium-sized shells, pear-shaped to spindle-shaped. Generally white, sometimes with central, spiral band, or spotted, or blotched. Outer lip thickened and denticulate or almost smooth. Columellar teeth often obsolete. About six genera comprising about 100 species living in warm and temperate seas.

Genus OVULA Bruguière
Medium-sized, inflated shells with smooth dorsum. No columella teeth. Produced canals. White outside and brown or rosy inside. Two species living in Indo-Pacific.

Ovula ovum Linnaeus × 0.7

Elliptical to pear-shaped, smooth, inflated shell with thick lip bearing folds. Outside of shell glossy, white, inside dark brown. 6–10cm. Indo-Pacific. Common.

Genus VOLVA Röding
Spindle-shaped shells with long extremities and bulbous body whorl. Outer lip slightly grooved, columella striate. Numerous species living in Indo-Pacific.

Volva sowerbyana Weinkauff × 2.3
Shells small, thin, elongated and inflated in the middle. Aperture wide with outer lip thickened and smooth. On upper parietal wall is a distinct nodule. Pale pinkish brown with two reddish spiral bands.

2–3cm. Indo-Pacific (Pacific), Japonic. Uncommon.

Volva volva Linnaeus × 0.6
striata Lamarck.

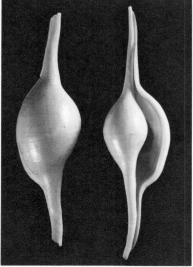

Inflated, elliptical shell with extremely long, thin, gently curved anterior and posterior canals. Shallow transverse grooves. Shell pinkish brown. 7–12cm. Indo-Pacific. Frequent.

Genus CALPURNUS Montfort
Small, elongate-ovate shells. Yellowish or white with rosy, nodulous processes at extremities. Two species living in Indo-Pacific.

Calpurnus verrucosus Linnaeus × 1.5
Almost rhomboidal, inflated shell with high, angular hump and a rounded, rosy

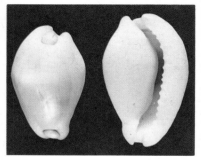

wart at each extremity above anterior and posterior canal. Teeth on outer lip. Shell white, canals pink-tinged. c2·5cm. Indo-Pacific.

Genus CYPHOMA Röding
Ovate, smooth shells. Aperture length of shell. Obtuse, dorsal spiral ridge. Extremities rounded. Margin right around sides of shell. Vividly coloured animal envelops shell in life. Three or four species living in Caribbean.

Cyphoma gibbosum Linnaeus × 1.7
Flamingo Tongue

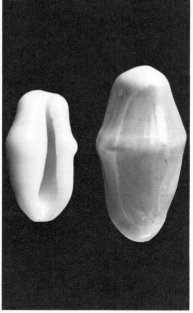

Elliptical to fusiform shell with thick, transverse ridge just below centre of shell. No teeth. Creamy orange to pink with white, rectangular patch on dorsum. 2–3cm. Caribbean. Common.

Cyphoma intermedia Sowerby
Elliptical to fusiform shell with thickened lip and slight, transverse ridge in middle of shell. Columella twisted. Shell glossy, creamy to yellowish. c4cm. Caribbean. Rare.

Superfamily
Naticacea

Family NATICIDAE

Small to medium-sized shells. Thick, globular or flattened, smooth and glossy. Small, few-whorled spire and large aperture. Umbilicus open and usually with a large, thick callus occupying most of it. Some species colourful. Operculum corneous or calcareous. Eggs laid in ribbon of sand. Animals which are carnivorous bore neat round holes in other shells. Numerous genera and hundreds of species in all seas.

Genus NATICA Scopoli

For details, see Family Naticidae. Spire rather elevated, shell usually globose. Columella adheres to and is spirally contorted in the umbilicus. Operculum corneous with a calcareous outer layer. Many species in all seas.

Natica canrena Linnaeus   × 1.1

Thick, globose shell with raised, convex spire. Narrow umbilicus partly occluded by callus. Glossy, cream, with spiral rows of axial, reddish brown spots and axial streaks. Three brown, spiral bands on body whorl. White aperture with limy operculum with about ten concentric grooves. 3–4cm. Transatlantic, Caribbean. Frequent.

Natica catena Da Costa   × 1.4

Thick, solid shell with globose body whorl, short spire, rounded whorls and impressed suture. Large, deep umbilicus. Smooth. White, flushed pale brown. Spiral row of indistinct brownish spots on early whorls. Aperture and columella white. c3·5cm. Boreal (North West Europe). Common.

Natica chinensis Lamarck   × 1.0

Thick, globose shell with narrow aperture partly obscured by columellar callus. Smooth with thick columella. Large callus in umbilicus. Glossy, white to cream with spiral rows of reddish brown or brown dots or quadrants. White aperture and columella; interior may be violet. Conspicuously grooved operculum. 2·0–2·5cm. Indo-Pacific. Common.

Natica clausa Broderip & Sowerby

Thin, globose shell with umbilicus sealed over by small callus. Glossy, yellowish white with white aperture and white callus. Operculum thin, slightly concave. Brown periostracum. 2·0–2·5cm. Boreal (East Coast of North America), Arctic, Transatlantic, Californian. Common.

Natica kraussi Smith

Thickish shell with wide umbilicus and small callus within. Smooth. Dull, pale flesh-colour to white basally. White aperture. 1·3–1·9cm. South African.

Natica lineozona Récluz
gaidei Souverbie, *notata* Sowerby.

Small, globular shell with very short spire. Semi-ovate aperture, with thin parietal callus partially covering the large umbilicus. White, with four dark brown spiral lines. Irregular, straight or wavy axial streaks are contained within bands demarcated by spiral lines, leaving a central, white spiral zone and another white zone at base. Calcareous white operculum. 5–10cm. Indo-Pacific. Common.

Natica livida Pfeiffer

Thick, globose shell with narrow umbilicus almost occluded by callus. Glossy, grey to orange brown shell with brown aperture and columellar callus. Base white. Light brown operculum. 0·8–1·6cm. Caribbean. Frequent.

Natica paucimaculata Sowerby   × 1.3
Thick, globose shell with very large callus pad covering narrow umbilicus and

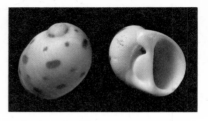

parietal wall. Glossy, white shell with widely spaced, reddish brown spots arranged in spiral rows. White aperture. 0·5–2·3cm. Indo-Pacific (Pacific). Rare.

Natica undulata Röding   × 1.6
zebra Lamarck.

Thin, globose shell with small callus in umbilicus. Glossy, lilac to white basally with brown axial stripes, wavy or zigzag. Stripes may be thin and discontinuous in spiral bands. White aperture. Operculum grooved. 0·8–3·2cm. Indo-Pacific, Japonic. Common.

Natica vitellus Linnaeus
rufa Born, *spadicea* Gmelin, *helvacea* Lamarck.

Thick, globose, short-spired shell with deep umbilicus. Aperture slightly thickened parietally. Glossy, white shell with orange, irregular spiral bands and axial streaks. White aperture. Columellar edge of white operculum serrated. 2·8–4·2cm. Indo-Pacific. Frequent.

Natica violacea Sowerby
glabra Wood, *rhodostoma* Philippi.

Small, solid, globose shell, with short spire and impressed suture. Parietal callus almost completely covers umbilicus. White, with five spiral rows of irregular, orange brown spots or wavy lines on body whorl and one spiral row of spots on penultimate whorl. Callus and base of shell rosy violet. 1·5–2·0cm. Indo-Pacific. Frequent.

Natica zonalis Récluz

Shell small, globular, with short spire and raised apex. Parietal callus narrow, not obscuring the deep umbilicus. White or brown, with two darker, spiral brown bands on body whorl and a similar band at suture of penultimate whorl. Bands on body whorl sometimes joined. Calcareous white operculum. 1–2cm. Indo-Pacific (Pacific). Frequent.

Genus POLINICES Montfort

For details, see Family Naticidae. Ovate or nearly ovate solid shells. Lip oblique, thickened and callused. Operculum entirely corneous. Otherwise similar to *Natica*. Numerous species in warm and tropical seas.

Polinices aurantius Röding   × 0.9
aurantia Lamarck, *straminea* Récluz, *Sulphurea* Récluz, *mellosum* Hedley.

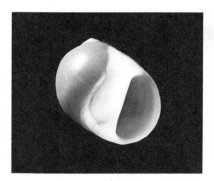

Thick, plano-globose shell with depressed spire and narrow umbilicus. Axial growth lines. Glossy, orange yellow to orange with white apex and umbilical area. Aperture white. 2·5–3·5cm. Indo-Pacific. Frequent.

Polinices duplicatus Say
Atlantic Moon Snail
Globose, depressed shell but may have tall spire. Deep, narrow umbilicus. Axial growth lines. Glossy, grey to orange brown with pale base. White to grey aperture with purplish brown umbilical callus. 3·2–7·5cm. Transatlantic, Caribbean. Common.

Polinices flemingiana Récluz   × 1.4
virginea Philippi, *jukesi* Reeve.

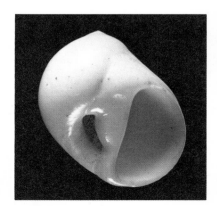

Thick, globose shell with narrow umbilicus partly occluded by massive columellar callus. Callus deposit extends to spire. Axial growth lines. Glossy, white to cream, sometimes grey along growth lines. White aperture. 1·5–4·5cm. Indo-Pacific (Pacific). Australian. Common.

Polinices glauca Humboldt
Thick, depressed shell with concave base and narrow umbilicus almost occluded by callus. Glossy, pinkish grey shell, often pale basally; callus brown. Brown, glossy aperture. c5cm. Panamic. Uncommon.

Polinices hepaticus Röding   × 0.6
mamillaris Lamarck, *brunnea* Link.
Thick, globose shell with wide umbilicus.

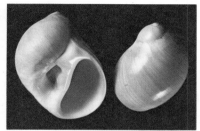

Smooth except for axial growth lines. Columella lip with callus on umbilical margin. Glossy, flesh-coloured shell with dark and light banding due to growth lines. Flesh-coloured outer lip; white columella and callus. 2·5–4·5cm. Panamic, Californian, Caribbean.

Polinices incei Philippi   × 0.9

Thick, globose shell with umbilicus sealed by callus. Glossy, pinkish grey or cream; fleshy brown with pink, cream or yellow band. White aperture with pink to brown callus. 1·0–3·5cm. Australian. Frequent.

Polinices josephinae Risso   × 1.1
Thin, globose, depressed shell with narrow umbilicus which may be occluded by

button-like callus. Glossy, white to pinkish grey shell with flesh-coloured to pinkish grey spiral bands. Flesh to pink callus; pink, flesh-coloured or brown aperture. 2·0–3·5cm. Mediterranean. Common.

Polinices maurus Lamarck   × 0.8

Shell moderately thick, ovate. Large body whorl and tiny, few-whorled spire. Large, semi-ovate aperture. Thick parietal callus almost conceals umbilicus. Smooth satin sheen. Light brown, with darker brown axial streaks. Callus and edge of outer lip dark brown. Apex white. Aperture white. 2–5cm. Indo-Pacific (Pacific). Common.

Polinices plumbea Lamarck   × 1.1

Thick, ovate shell with narrow umbilicus. Glossy, brown to grey or flesh-coloured, colour strongest on axial growth lines. Brown aperture with orange or red columella and callus. c5cm. Australian. Common.

Polinices reclusianus Deshayes   × 0.5
Récluz's Moon Snail

Thick, globose shell with narrow umbilicus which may be quite occluded by callus. Callus with small scar; shell smooth. Dull, grey with reddish brown mottling. White to grey aperture. 3·8–6·2cm. Californian, Panamic. Common.

Polinices simiae Deshayes   × 1.3

Shell similar to *P. maurus* but thinner and lighter. Apex slightly larger. Umbilicus less covered by parietal callus. Smooth, with silky sheen. White or cream, with broad, central spiral band on body whorl, and brownish axial streaks, the darker zones above and below being demarcated by thin, spiral, brown lines. Callus and umbilical zone dark brown. Aperture whitish, with external pattern showing through. 1–4cm. Indo-Pacific. Common.

Genus SINUM Röding
Sigaretus Lamarck.
Small to moderately large, thin shells which are flattened and ear-shaped. Few species in warm and tropical seas.

Sinum perspectivum Say   × 1.2

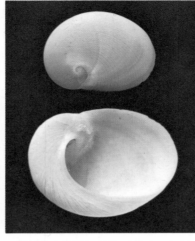

Shell thin, very flat with very large aperture and thick, curved columella. Crowded, fine spiral threads crossed by occasional, fine, axial growth ridges. Unicolorous white. Thin, light brown periostracum. 2·5–3·5cm. Transatlantic, Caribbean. Common.

Sinum scopulosum Gould
Similar to *S. perspectivum*, but more elevated and with correspondingly more capacious body whorl. Many shallow spiral grooves at top of last whorl. Unicolorous white. Thin, yellowish periostracum. 2·5–3·5cm. Californian, Panamic. Common.

Genus LUNATIA Gray
For details, see Family Naticidae. Shells very large, rounded and heavy. Umbilicus deep, occasionally almost closed. Operculum corneous. About six species mostly restricted to cooler waters off East and West coasts of North America.

Lunatia heros Say   × 0.5
Common Northern Moon Snail

Thick, globose shell with deep, narrow umbilicus. Smooth, glossy, grey to brownish grey with pale cream aperture. Thin, yellow brown periostracum. 6–10cm. Boreal (East coast of North America). Common.

Lunatia pallida Broderip & Sowerby
Thin, ovate, taller than wide, globose shell with narrow umbilicus almost occluded by callus. Smooth, with thickened columella. Glossy, white or grey. White aperture. 2·8–3·5cm. Arctic, Aleutian, Boreal (East coast of North America). Common.

Superfamily
Tonnacea

Family CASSIDIDAE
Small to very large, moderately thin, but occasionally very thick, shells. Elongate-ovate to globose, with large body whorl and conical spire. Whorls smooth or ornamented with spiral and axial cords. Varices commonly present. Aperture narrow, outer lip thickened and denticulate. Operculum corneous. About seven genera and about 80 species in all seas, most abundant in the tropics, feeding mostly on sea urchins. Popularly known as helmet shells.

Genus CASSIDARIA Lamarck
Moderately thick, globose shells with short or moderately produced spire and shallow suture. Siphonal canal short and recurved. Large, deep umbilicus. Aperture entire with outer lip not very thickened; no varices. One or two species in Atlantic and Mediterranean.

Cassidaria echinophora Linnaeus   × 0.7

Shell fairly thin, globose, with moderately tall or short spire. Aperture entire with few nodules or teeth on outer lip and some indistinct nodules on columella. Body whorl has five or six nodulous spiral ribs, largest nodes being on whorl at shoulder. One or two spiral ribs on spire whorls, with finer ribs crossed by fine axial lines on all whorls. Nodulous tips of spiral ridges white with brown interspaces. Rest of shell pale brown. Aperture white. 6–8cm. Mediterranean. Frequent.

Cassidaria rugosa Linnaeus
tyrrhena Lamarck.
Shell similar to *C. echinophora* but larger, with more numerous spiral ribs lacking nodes. Aperture relatively longer and narrower. Spire more produced with suture more deeply impressed. Unicolorous yellowish brown. Edge of thickened outer lip dark brown. *c*10cm. Mediterranean, West African. Uncommon.

Genus MORUM Röding
Oniscia Sowerby, *Lambidium* Link.
Small to medium-sized ovate shells with short spire and large body whorl. Ornamented with axial and spiral ribs which may form sharp, upturned points at intersections. Outer lip with irregular, strong or weak, folds. Large parietal shield with small pustules. Parietal shield often brightly coloured. About 20 species, widely distributed in warm and tropical seas.

Morum cancellatum Sowerby   × 1.3

Shell thick, ovate and short-spired. Outer lip thickened and coarsely denticulate. Columella and parietal wall with rough pustules. Strong, ridged axial ribs crossed by numerous strong, ridged spiral ribs which produce sharp, upturned points at

intersections. Reflected edge of outer lip crenulate. Yellowish white with pale brown spiral bands. Aperture white. *c*4cm. Indo-Pacific (Pacific). Uncommon.

Morum grande A. Adams
Medium-sized, thick, ovate, fusiform shell with moderately tall spire and short, broad siphonal canal. Strong axial ribs crossed by stronger spiral cords producing sharp, sometimes scaly, knobs at intersections. Strong, scaly, axial growth ridges between axial ribs. Outer lip thickened, broad, somewhat recurved and with strong teeth on inner margin. Broad parietal shield laid on rather thinly so that underlying surface ornament stands out in relief; also covered with warty pustules. Creamy white with irregular dark and light mottlings. Outer lip with darker brown spots and blotches. Resembles a large form of *M. cancellatum* and is sometimes mistaken for that species. 5–7cm. Indo-Pacific (West Pacific), Japonic. Rare.

Morum macandrewi Sowerby
Medium-sized, solid, ovate shell with short spire and pointed apex. Strong axial ridges on later whorls crossed by low spiral cords. Ribs nodulous or scaly at shoulder. Coarse axial lamellae cover whorl. Outer lip thickened and recurved, inner margin strongly toothed. Thick parietal shield with coarse, irregular, wavy folds and pustules. Whitish with brown and blackish brown blotches and streaks which may form two or three broad spiral bands. Aperture and parietal wall white. More squat than *M. cancellatum* and with fewer and stronger axial ribs. 3·0–4·5cm. Indo-Pacific (West Pacific), Japonic. Rare.

Morum oniscus Linnaeus
Shell much smaller than *M. cancellatum,* and with smoother ornament. Ovate, with short spire and thickened, denticulate outer lip. Body whorl has three rows of blunt tubercles. Parietal wall and columella glazed and minutely pustulose. Apex sharply pointed in fresh specimens but often worn smooth. White, with brown speckling; darker brown, irregular axial stripes. Aperture and parietal wall white. 2·0–2·5cm. Caribbean. Frequent.

Morum ponderosum Hanley
Compared with *M. cancellatum* this is a much thicker and more coarsely ornamented shell and spire is much flatter. Medium-sized, thick, trigonal, with very short spire, broadly inflated body whorl and short, broad, recurved siphonal canal. Strong spiral cords are tuberculated at regular intervals to form spiral rows, tubercles at shoulder much larger than others and rounded. Course and fine spiral grooves cover whole shell. Fine, axial growth lines. Outer lip thickened and toothed. Parietal wall thickly callused and has indistinct, irregular folds down colu-

mella side. Creamy white with irregular blotches and spots of brown and reddish brown. Parietal callus with pale reddish brown dots, blotches and streaks. Broad and narrow bands of reddish brown spots on outer lip. 3·5–4·5cm. Japonic. Rare.

Morum tuberculosum Reeve   × 1.0

Thick, solid, elongate-ovate shell with flattened spire. Aperture length of shell with outer lip thickened and denticulate in its middle portion. Thin parietal callus has a few low pustules on its upper portion. Five or six spiral rows of large nodules with finer spiral riblets between. Yellowish white, heavily mottled and streaked with dark brown, there being two interrupted, spiral, brown bands. Aperture yellowish. 3–4cm. Panamic. Frequent.

Genus PHALIUM Link
Small to large shells, thin to moderately thick with large, globose body whorl and short spire. Outer lip thickened. Some species have prominent varices. Ornament consists of axial ridges, spiral tubercles and ridges. Many species almost smooth. Outer lip often dentate. Some species have digitations at lower end of outer lip. Columella often crossed by numerous strong, wavy folds. Deep umbilicus but usually sealed up by columella shield. Numerous species in tropical and warm seas.

Phalium angasi Iredale   × 1.3

Shell thin and light with globose, large body whorl and fairly tall, conical, pointed spire. Reticulate ornament on spire whorls and upper portion of body whorl. Few spiral grooves around umbilicus. Outer lip thickened and toothed. Columella with few thin, coarse folds. Parietal callus with small, warty folds. Small, deep umbilicus. White, fawn or pale pink, occasionally with small, brown blotches near suture. 4–6cm. Australian. Uncommon.

Phalium areola Linnaeus   × 1.1

Shell resembling *P. decussata,* but smaller and has smooth body whorl. Short acuminate spire with decussate ornament and a few varices. Thickened outer lip with varix on opposite side of body whorl. Other varices on spire. Numerous strong teeth on outer lip. Columella with numerous coarse folds. Parietal area highly glazed. Dull, white with spiral bands of rectangular, dark brown blotches which are also present on outer lip and varices. 5–10cm. Indo-Pacific. Common.

Phalium bandatum Perry   × 0.45

Shell similar to *P. glaucum,* but more elongate and with taller spire. Spiral row of sharp, pointed nodules at shoulders of whorls which do not become obsolete on body whorl. Outer lip thickened and with numerous teeth. Columella with many long, thin ridges and folds. Deep um-

bilicus. Columella shield not conspicuously glazed. Rest of body whorl smooth with fine, axial growth striae. Varix on body whorl opposite thickened outer lip not always present. Greyish white with broad, interrupted, yellowish brown spiral bands on body whorl. 7–12cm. Indo-Pacific (Pacific). Common.

Phalium bisulcatum Schubert & Wagner
pila Reeve, *japonica* Reeve, *nucleus* Küster, *pfeifferi* Hidalgo.
Similar in shape and general appearance to *P. saburon,* but shows several points of difference. Medium-sized, moderately thick, globose-ovate shell with short spire and large, inflated body whorl. Large, thin parietal shield. Strongly recurved, broad and short siphonal canal, above which is a small umbilicus. Smooth or covered with numerous fine, clearly incised lines or, sometimes, with coarse, weakly beaded or smooth spiral cords. May have no varices or, rarely, may have up to five. Outer lip with numerous strong teeth. Parietal shield covering columella area has numerous strong, irregular, wavy folds. Whitish, cream or greyish and may or may not have five or six spiral rows of small or large, yellowish or reddish brown blotches. Aperture and columella white. An extremely variable species in size, ornament, colour and pattern. 2–7cm. Indo-Pacific, South African. Common.

Phalium canaliculatum Bruguière
Shell small, thin, light, with short spire and deeply channelled suture. Outer lip thickened and denticulate. Parietal wall thickly callused, with numerous long folds. Flat, spiral ridges with fine grooves between. Pinkish white with irregular, light brown blotches. 4–5cm. Indo-Pacific. Common.

Phalium craticulatum Euthyme
Very similar to *P. saburon,* but differs slightly in shape and in columellar details. Instead of being globosely rounded and moderately short-spired, it is relatively tall-spired and has a more elongate body whorl which is narrowed at the anterior end. The inner part of the columella has a raised axial ridge which is toothed. Ornamented with strong, closely spaced, irregular spiral threads; some specimens are smooth at the middle portion of body whorl. White or grey, with or without irregular, brownish red spots. 3–8cm South African. Rare.

Phalium decussata Linnaeus   × 1.0
Shell thick, globose, with short, conical spire. Fine reticulated ornament all over and a stout varix on side of body whorl opposite thickened outer lip. Other varices on spire. Outer lip strongly denticulate. Columella with numerous coarse folds. Parietal wall grey with underlying pattern showing through. Greyish with spiral rows

of large, squarish, brown spots. Varices and recurved portion of outer lip with alternate white and dark brown, square blotches. Aperture brownish white. 6–7cm. Pacific. Common.

Phalium faurotis Jousseaume
Very similar to *P. bisulcatum,* but distinguished from that species by its bluish black or purple brown apex and by the large, rounded knobs on left border of columella shield. Numerous spiral, incised lines on body whorl; the early whorls are often also weakly axially ribbed. Cream to yellowish brown with five spiral rows of square, reddish brown spots. Aperture, columella and parietal shield white. The only species of the genus with a dark coloured apex. 3·5–6·0cm. Indo-Pacific (West Indian Ocean), South African. Uncommon.

Phalium fimbria Gmelin
rugosa Röding, *plicaria* Lamarck,
plicatum Linnaeus (of authors).
Large, solid, heavy, elongate-ovate shell with short, pointed spire and very large body whorl. Three or four varices on spire and body whorl; broad, thick parietal shield. Well developed, obliquely axial ridges on body whorl which are strong and pointed at shoulder and become obsolete towards base; axial ridges weaker on spire whorls. Two or three broad, flat spiral ridges round recurved siphonal canal. Outer lip thick, recurved and with sharply pointed denticles on inner margin with short folds entering aperture behind each of them. Three or four folds on columella. Yellowish white with wavy, axial, yellowish brown bands. 5–7 dark brown, squarish blotches on varices. Aperture and parietal wall white. 6–11cm. Indo-Pacific (Indian Ocean, West Pacific). Rare.

Phalium glaucum Linnaeus   × 0.5
Shell moderately large, ovate to globular, with short, pointed spire. Spiral row of

blunt or sharp tubercles on spire becoming obsolete on body whorl. Surface of body whorl malleated and obscurely ribbed. Outer lip thickened, with sharp teeth along inner edge and three or four sharp spines projecting basally from outer edge. Broad columella shield flared and crossed by numerous strong and irregular ridges. Light to dark grey with orange or brownish blotches on varices. Aperture dark brown, pinkish on outer lip. 9–12cm. Indo-Pacific. Common.

Phalium iredalei Bayer   × 0.8
Shell thick, solid and heavy with short spire and large, globose body whorl; thickened outer lip. Thick, large parietal callus

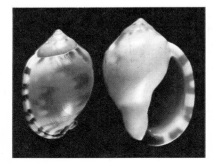

extending above aperture. Spiral row of low, smooth nodules at shoulder of body whorl. Rest of shell smooth. Brownish white flecked with darker brown blotches and indistinct, white dots arranged in spiral rows. Edge of outer lip with dark brown blotches. Columella and parietal callus white flushed with yellow. Outer lip white with pale brown streaks. 4·0–7·5cm. South African. Uncommon.

Phalium pauciruge Menke
Globose, ovate shell with moderately tall spire and inflated body whorl. Fine spiral striae with axial ribs on early whorls, later spire whorls being weakly nodulose at shoulders. Body whorl smooth except for nodules at shoulder which become obsolete towards outer lip. Parietal shield thick and smooth, but there are short folds along inner margin. Moderately deep umbilicus. Outer lip thickened and denticulate along inner margin. Yellowish or white with brownish or yellowish brown blotches at suture and four spiral bands of small, widely spaced, yellowish brown spots. Outer lip and columella and parietal shield white. Interior of aperture yellowish brown. 3·5–7·0cm. Australian (Western Australia). Common.

Phalium pyrum Lamarck
tumida Petterd, *nivea* Brazier,
finlayi Iredale, *hamiltoni* Powell,
powelli Finlay, *hedleyi* Iredale.
Globose to ovate shell with moderately tall spire and inflated body whorl. One or two spiral cords below suture on body whorl which may be deeply nodulose at shoulder. Rest of shell smooth. Outer lip narrow with a smooth inner margin. Columella and parietal shield smooth. Deep umbilicus. Whitish, brownish or pinkish brown with spiral bands of pale brown spots or blotches; siphonal canal with a brown patch at its base. Columella, parietal wall and inner edge of outer lip white. Interior of aperture brownish. Extremely variable species which has received many names. 6–9cm. Australian, South African. Common.

Phalium saburon Bruguière   ▷ × 0.8
Shell thick, globose, with short spire and shallow suture. Outer lip thickened and denticulate. Broad callus on parietal wall and columella. Numerous spiral, flattened ribs with narrower grooves between. Fine radial striae which are more conspicuous on spire whorls. Small, deep umbilicus. Yellowish brown with numerous small, darker brown blobs arranged in spiral rows.   4·5–7·0cm.   Mediterranean. Common.

Phalium semigranosum Lamarck
Thick, elongate-ovate shell with inflated body whorl and moderately tall spire with smooth, rounded apex. 3–4 spiral rows of pointed or rounded beads below suture.

Body whorl below shoulder ornamented with weak, irregular axial ribs. Fine spiral striae towards base of body whorl. Columella strongly reflected and with numerous long, revolving folds. A callus knob on parietal wall. Outer lip strongly reflected. Yellowish brown to brown. Outer lip, columella and parietal callus white, brownish in interior of aperture. 3–6cm. Australian (South Australia, Tasmania). Common.

Phalium strigatum Gmelin   × 0.4
Striped Bonnet

Shell thick, solid, elongate with long aperture and short, pointed spire. Outer lip thickened and denticulate. Columella with numerous folds and warts. Parietal wall glazed, with few warty folds. Few varices on spire whorls; varix on body whorl opposite outer lip. Body whorl smooth in median area with irregular

spiral grooves above and below. Greyish white with axial, brown stripes. Outer lip and varices with orange and white blobs. 6–9cm. Indo-Pacific. Common.

Phalium thomsoni Brazier
Similar to some forms of *P. pyrum*. Medium-sized, ovate shell with tall spire and inflated body whorl. Usually strongly shouldered body whorl with 1–3 spiral rows of rounded or axially elongated nodules, fine spiral striae and some stronger, incised lines towards base. Umbilicus deep. Outer lip thick and with teeth on inner margin. Cream, whitish or pale brown, with 3–5 spiral rows of large, reddish brown spots. Outer lip and columella white. *c*9cm. Australian (South Australia and Tasmania). Frequent.

Genus CASMARIA H. & A. Adams
Medium-sized, ovate shell with short spire, smooth and poorly developed columella shield and one or two rows of sharp denticles on outer lip. Two species in tropical seas.

Casmaria erinaceus Linnaeus × 1.2
vibex Linnaeus.

Medium-sized, ovate shell with short spire and large, moderately inflated body whorl. Shoulder of body whorl smooth and steeply sloping, occasionally with heavy nodules. 5–6 small, sharp spines on lower portion of outer lip. Deep, broad siphonal notch. Outer lip thickened and reflected. Creamy white, with wavy, axial, pale brown streaks. Reflected part of outer lip has dark brown, rectangular blotches. Aperture pale brown. 4·0–7·5cm. Indo-Pacific. Frequent.

Casmaria ponderosa Gmelin
Very similar to some forms of *C. erinaceus* and sometimes difficult to distinguish from that species. Thick, ovate-elongate, glossy shell with tall spire and well rounded whorls. Smooth, or with axial nodules at shoulder. Rarely, a varix is present. Outer lip thick to very thick and parietal shield may be thin or very thick also. One or two rows of prickly tubercles on outer lip which are usually present along its entire length. Spire is relatively higher and whorls more globose in this species than in *C. erinaceus*. White, bluish white or cream with spiral row of squarish, brown spots just below suture and at base of body whorl. These spots are not present in *C. erinaceus*. Reflected portion of outer lip has numerous large, rectangular, dark brown blotches. Aperture, columella and parietal shield whitish. 2·0–5·5cm. Indo-Pacific, Australian (East Coast of Australia), South African, Japonic. Common.

Genus CASSIS Scopoli
Large, massive shells with large, blunt spines and prominent varices. Columellar area heavily and broadly callused concealing most of ventral side of shell. About seven species, mostly in Indo-Pacific and Caribbean.

Cassis cornuta Linnaeus × 0.25
hamata, Röding, *labiata* Dillwyn.
Very large, heavy and solid. Short spire with slightly produced, usually worn apex. Three or four spiral rows of large tubercles, those at shoulder being much longer and

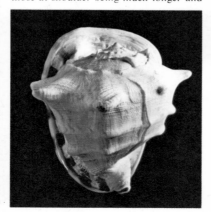

stouter than the others. Varices on spire at right angles to each other. Very large, thick parietal shield obscures bulk of shell completely. Outer lip very thick, confluent with parietal shield and bearing few large teeth at middle. Columella with few strong, wavy folds. Outer surface entirely covered with spiral rows of small pits. Whitish with few brown markings on spiral ribs. Parietal shield and outer lip white or pinkish; orange on columella and between wide columella folds. 18–35cm. Indo-Pacific. Common.

Cassis fimbriata Quoy & Gaimard × 0.6
decresensis Hedley, *bicarinata* Jonas.

Thick, globose shell with imbricate suture and narrow umbilicus. Coronate shoulder and weak coronation below shoulder. Axial ridges. Columella lip everted and expansive. Parietal lip everted and thick. Narrow siphonal canal. Dull, cream to light brown with spiral rows of brown dashes and weak, spiral, brown bands becoming dark at parietal lip. White aperture. 7–13cm. Australian (Victoria to West Australia).

Cassis flammea Linnaeus   ×0.7

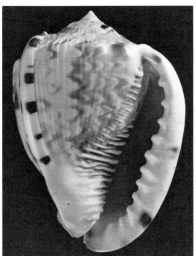

Shell similar to *C. tuberosa* but smaller. Ornament consists of axial growth lines only and there are no brown markings between teeth on outer lip. In mature specimens, corners of parietal shield are rounded. Specimen illustrated is immature and lacks thick parietal shield. 8–13cm. Caribbean. Common.

Cassis madagascariensis Lamarck
Emperor Helmet
cameo Stimpson, *rotundata* Perry, *spinella* Clench.
Shell very large, massive with three spiral rows of large, blunt spines, largest spine being on the uppermost row. In the form or subspecies *spinella*, the spines are much smaller and more numerous. Varices at right angles to each other, one varix to each whorl. Very broad parietal shield with thin rim. Outer lip with few widely spaced, strong teeth; the teeth are strongest at the constricted centre portion of lip. Series of

long, irregular folds from base of columella to top of parietal wall. Pale cream, with axial streaks on spire. Parietal shield and outer lip pinkish orange with brownish black staining between folds and teeth; teeth whitish. 10–30cm. Caribbean. Common.

Cassis tessellata Gmelin
maculosum Gmelin, *fasciata* Bruguière, *coronata* Röding.
Shell large but thin and surprisingly light for its size. Ovate with very large body whorl and short spire. Outer lip greatly thickened and with several large, broad and blunt teeth. One varix on each whorl. Varix on body whorl flattened and joined to parietal callus. Siphonal canal broad and strongly recurved. Three or four spiral rows of pointed nodules between suture and shoulders. Row of blunt nodules at centre of body whorl. Whitish and pinkish brown mottled with darker brown crescents and streaks. c15cm. West African. Uncommon.

Cassis tuberosa Linnaeus   ×0.45
Shell very large, thick, heavy and solid. Broad, thick, parietal shield obscuring rest of shell in apertural view. Outer lip very thick with broad, prominent teeth. Columella and parietal wall with strong, long, wavy folds. Whole surface of shell finely reticulated. Prominent varices at right angles to each other. Brownish cream

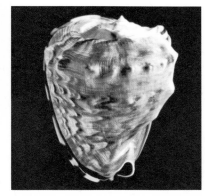

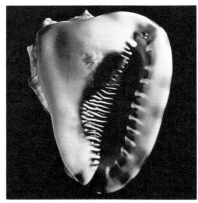

mottled and blotched with dark brown, crescent-like marks. Parietal shield pale brown, darker brown near aperture and dark brown between white folds. Outer lip pale brown with darker brown blotches; teeth on outer lip white with dark brown blob each side. 10–23cm. Caribbean. Common.

Genus CYPRAECASSIS Stutchbury
Moderately large, heavy shells with narrow, long aperture, strongly dentate or plicate columella and outer lip. Distant resemblance to cowry aperture, hence scientific name. Operculum usually absent. Four species.

Cypraecassis coarctata Sowerby   ×1.1
Shell smaller and more solid than *C. tenuis*. Spire more produced. Parietal callus covering less of the body whorl. Regular,

strong teeth on outer lip. Numerous fine folds on columella and parietal wall with a groove separating the columella folds from parietal folds. Pale brown, mottled with darker brown spots, occasionally a large part of body whorl dark brown. 5·5–7·0cm. Panamic. Uncommon.

Cypraecassis rufa Linnaeus   ×0.4
Bull's-mouth Helmet

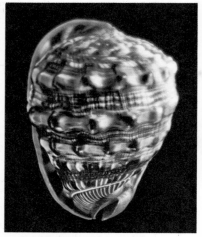

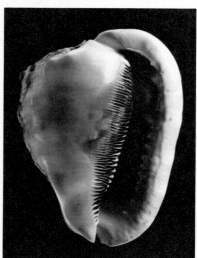

Shell large, thick and heavy with very large aperture, greatly thickened outer lip being produced above spire. Aperture long and narrow. Parietal callus very large and thick. Spire short with moderately shallow suture. Three or four broad spiral bands with large, rounded nodules. Spiral nodules replaced by more numerous coarse axial ribs towards base. Reddish mottled and blotched with dark and light brown and grey. Parietal callus blood red; outer lip and aperture dark red or pink. Columella and parietal folds whitish, dark brown between. 10–15cm. Indo-Pacific. Common.

Cypraecassis tenuis Wood   ×0.6

Very thick, biconical shell with imbricate suture and narrow umbilicus. Nodulose shoulder and occasional nodules on spiral costae which have distinct interstitial bands. Parietal and columella lips wide and plicate. Parietal lip thick. Brown with cream axial streaks near parietal lip. Columella lip dark brown between white plicae. Salmon markings on parietal lip. 10–13cm. Panamic (Mexico to Galapagos Islands). Uncommon.

Cypraecassis testiculus Linnaeus   ×1.0

Thick, solid with very short spire and long, narrow aperture. Crowded axial ribs cut by more widely spaced spiral grooves. Outer lip denticulate; inner lip with more numerous and finer teeth. Light orange brown with purplish brown and grey blotches. Edge of reflected aperture with

dark brown blotches. 3–8cm. Caribbean. Common.

Family CYMATIIDAE

Shells moderately small to very large, solid, ovate and ventricose, occasionally flatly compressed. Prominent, discontinuous, rarely continuous, varices. Whorls ornamented with spiral cords, axial ridges, nodules and tubercles, or comparatively smooth. No anal canal. Siphonal canal short or long, sometimes twisted or recurved. Periostracum often thick and covered with fibrous hairs. Worldwide in distribution. Many genera proposed; about six generally used.

Genus APOLLON Montfort
Gyrineum Link.
Shells small and flatly compressed. Varices continuous and vertical. Ornamented with spiral rows of nodules. About twelve species in the Indo-Pacific province.

Apollon bitubercularis Lamarck   ×1.7
chemnitzii Kobelt.

Shell thick, solid, compressed with large body whorl and tall spire. Long, broad, recurved siphonal canal. Outer lip denticulate. Columella with irregular folds. Callus with folds on parietal wall. Strong varices, somewhat compressed. Two large tubercles between varices. Irregular spiral threads and cords. Yellowish white with brown tubercles. Aperture white. 3·5–5·0cm. Indo-Pacific. Uncommon.

Apollon gyrinus Linnaeus   ×2.3
raninus Lamarck.

Thick shell with broad body whorl and simple suture. Spiral rows of tubercles on ridges. White with two spiral, reddish brown bands on body whorl, reddish brown base and one band on each spire whorl. White aperture. 2–4cm. Indo-Pacific (Pacific only). Frequent.

Apollon perca Perry   ×0.8
jucunda A. Adams, *pulchra* Sowerby,
pulchella Forbes, *microstoma* Fulton.

Moderately thick, solid shell with tall spire and remarkable development of wing-like

varices on opposite sides of each whorl. Very compressed in same plane as varices, giving whole shell a squashed appearance. Long, recurved siphonal canal. Very impressed suture. Spiral and axial ribs of equal strength, beaded at intersections. Varices resemble webbed feet of a duck. Pale brownish yellow or whitish with darker brown markings and white beads on whorls. Aperture white. 5–8cm. Japonic, Indo-Pacific (West Pacific). Frequent.

Apollon pusillus Broderip   ×1.4
lacunatum Mighels, *laciniatum* Pease

Thick shell, with small aperture and simple suture. Axial and spiral ridges give reticulation with beads at intersections. Six parietal denticles. Cream or brown with median, light band on each whorl. A white form may have brown spiral streaks. Lilac to dark violet aperture. 1·0–2·4cm. Indo-Pacific. Rare.

Apollon roseus Reeve   ×1.4

Thick shell, with small aperture and simple suture. Spiral rows of beads cross varices as ridges. Seven parietal denticles. Rose, with white, cream or yellow beads and varices. Rose aperture. 1–3cm. Indo-Pacific. Rare.

Genus ARGOBUCCINUM Herrmannsen
Small to moderately large, thin or thick, ovate to ovate-fusiform shells. Usually two strong, flattened varices per whorl. Body whorl usually large and inflated. Spire whorls usually well rounded. Suture well impressed. Few blunt teeth on inner margin of outer lip and usually a parietal tubercle. Coarsely ornamented with axial and spiral ribs sometimes producing cancellate pattern. Subdued colour. Thin or thick periostracum. About 20 species widely distributed in temperate waters. Often from deep water.

Argobuccinum argus Gmelin   ×0.9
polyzonalis Lamarck.

Thick, solid, ovate shell with moderately tall spire and rounded apex. Body whorl swollen, siphonal canal short and broad. Oblique axial ribs and low spiral ribs which are nodulous at intersections. Two flattish, broad varices on body whorl. Outer lip thickened, tooth on inner margin. Columella smooth, parietal wall with blunt tubercle at posterior end. Fawn or yellowish brown with darker brown spiral bands. Aperture and columella white. 6–10cm. South African. Frequent.

Argobuccinum australasium Perry   ×0.7

Shell thick, fusiform, with moderately tall spire and large, inflated body whorl. Siphonal canal short and broad. Outer lip with 7–10 short teeth. Thick nodule on parietal wall. Columella with a few weak folds. Light to very dark brown. Varices banded brown and white. Aperture and columella white. Thick periostracum. 8–10cm. Australian (Australia). Common.

Argobuccinum tumidum Dunker   ×0.7

Thick, globose shell with moderately tall spire and large body whorl. Outer lip thickened, with small teeth on inner edge. Siphonal canal short and broad. Columella with small nodules. Parietal wall with one moderately large fold. Weak varices on spire whorls. Numerous fine spiral ridges and ribs. Axial rows of nodules becoming obsolete on lower part of body whorl. Pale brown with darker brown spiral bands. Aperture white. 8–10cm. Australian (New Zealand). Frequent.

Genus RANELLA Lamarck
Gyrina Schumacher, *Eugyrina* Dall.
Moderately large, thick, ovate-fusiform shells with well rounded whorls bearing two varices on each and with strong axial and spiral ribbing. Outer lip thickened and toothed on inner margin. Siphonal canal moderately long and broad. One species.

Ranella olearium Linnaeus   ×0.5
gigantea Lamarck, *reticularis* Gmelin, *multinodosa* Bucknill, *ostenfeldi* Iredale.
Thick, ovate-fusiform shell with tall spire and moderately long, slightly recurved siphonal canal. Whorls well rounded and suture deeply impressed. Two varices per whorl. Strong axial ribs crossed by numerous weaker spiral riblets producing a cancelled ornament, intersections of ribs and riblets being produced as prominent nodules. Outer lip thick, flattened and toothed. Columella with few nodules towards base. Distinct posterior canal. Creamy white with irregular, darker brown blotches. Aperture and columella white. Yellowish brown periostracum. Very variable in size and strength of ornament. 10–18cm. Boreal, Mediterranean, West African, South African, Australian. Frequent.

Genus CHARONIA Gistel
Moderately large to very large, ovate-fusiform, thin or thick shells. Varices usually present but sometimes scarcely apparent. Ornamented with strong, flattened spiral ribs and axial ridges, or more strongly ornamented with coarse axial and spiral ribs. Columella usually ornamented with strong, long folds; outer lip usually with strong teeth on inner margin and these are often paired. Apex of mature specimens frequently missing. Very extensive distribution of some species has led to multiplication of species names and the nomenclature of the numerous forms or species is still confused. About 15–20 species are now accepted. Very widely distributed in temperate and tropical seas.

Charonia rubicunda Perry   × 0·45

Large, moderately thick, ovate shell with tall, pointed spire. Outer lip somewhat flaring with reflected edge bearing small, tooth-like projections on inner side. Columella with an indentation in its middle portion and two or three weak folds basally. Thick fold on parietal wall. One weak varix on each whorl. Two or three nodulous ribs on body whorl and one row on spire whorls. Numerous finer spiral ribs cover whole shell. Yellowish brown or reddish with darker reddish brown blotches. Apex pink; aperture white. Brown, quadrangular markings on outer lip. 12–15cm. Australian. Common.

Charonia tritonis Linnaeus   ×0.35
marmoratum Link.

Very large, ovate-fusiform shell with inflated body whorl, tall spire with narrow, rounded whorls and elevated apex which is usually missing in mature specimens. Usually two thin varices per whorl. Broad, flattened spiral cords with deep grooves between, spiral cord at suture puckered. Broad, short siphonal canal. Outer lip has large teeth on inner margin. Numerous folds along entire length of columella and parietal wall. Creamy white or yellowish with dark brown, crescent-shaped markings on each spiral cord. Columella and parietal teeth white with dark brown interstices. Aperture brownish with white channels between teeth on outer lip. One of the largest gastropod shells in the world. 15–45cm. Indo-Pacific, Japonic, Australian (New Zealand). Common.

Charonia variegata Lamarck ×0.35
nobilis Conrad, *seguenzae* Aradas & Benoit.

Like a smaller more squat version of *C. tritonis*, of which some authors consider it to be merely a form or at most a subspecies. Body whorl relatively stouter and spire relatively shorter in *C. variegata*. Teeth on columella thinner and those on inner margin of outer lip usually paired. Tends to be bluntly tuberculated at shoulder. Colour and pattern similar in the two species but in *C. variegata* the dark brown zone between folds and teeth are broader. *C. variegata* also tends to have a more pinkish cast. 20–40cm. Caribbean, Mediterranean. Frequent.

Genus CYMATIUM Röding
Shells moderately small to large, thick and heavy, ovate and ventricose. Siphonal canal short or long, often recurved or twisted. Ornamented with knobs, spiral cords and axial ridges. Thick periostracum with hair-like structures usually most prominent on varices. Free-swimming veligers of some species may drift thousands of miles before settling; this explains wide distribution of species. Most live in vicinity of coral reefs and in sandy habitats.

Cymatium australasiae Perry ×0.6
Thick, solid shell with moderately tall spire, large body whorl and impressed suture. Usually one strong varix on body whorl. Outer lip thickened and denticulate, the teeth being paired. Columella and parietal wall with numerous wavy folds. Strong spiral cords on spire and body whorl with finer spiral lirae between, crossed by fine axial lirae. Pale brown with

darker brown axial streaks. Columella folds and teeth on outer lip white, dark brown between. Periostracum thick. 10–14cm. Australian (Australia). Common.

Cymatium dunkeri Lischke ×0.7

Resembles *C. pyrum* in shape and ornament but differs in colour. Light brown and whitish with blotches of blackish brown on varices. Aperture white. 6–8cm. Japonic. Uncommon.

Cymatium exaratum Reeve ×1.0
Shell small for genus, with moderately tall spire, strong varices and impressed suture. Outer lip thickened. Siphonal canal long and slightly recurved. Whorls ornamented with heavy nodules between varices, crossed by strong, granulose spiral ribs. Bluish grey or yellowish grey

blotched with brown. Aperture whitish with purplish brown streaks deep inside. Ornament varies considerably and siphonal canal varies in length. 5–7cm. Australian, Japonic, Indo-Pacific (Australia). Common.

Cymatium femorale Linnaeus ×0.6

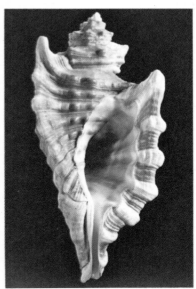

Shell large, fairly thick with short spire and very large body whorl. Varices very pronounced and wing-like. Strong, nodulous spiral cords with weaker spiral ribs between. Outer lip crenulate. Siphonal canal long and recurved. Reddish brown, but white where thick spiral cords cross varices. Aperture and columella white. 7–18cm. Caribbean. Frequent.

Cymatium hepaticum Röding
Very similar to *C. rubeculum*, but somewhat larger and stouter. Reddish brown

with 6–8 blackish spiral bands in the interspaces between spiral ribs. Reddish orange between teeth on inner margin of outer lip. 4–6cm. Indo-Pacific (Pacific). Uncommon.

Cymatium lotorium Linnaeus   ×0.6
distortum Lamarck,
grandimaculatum Reeve.

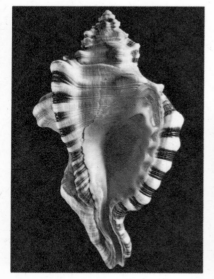

Thick, heavy, ovate shell with moderately tall spire and large, inflated body whorl. Siphonal canal moderately long, broad and sinuous. 4–5 well developed varices with 2–4 axial ridges which are most pronounced at shoulder of body whorl where they form prominent tubercles. Fine spiral grooves cross axial ribs and varices. Fine, axial growth lines. Outer lip thickened and bluntly toothed on inner margin. Columella smooth. Yellowish brown with dark brown and white varices. Columella whitish stained dark brown at base; dark brown patch on parietal wall. 10–16cm. Indo-Pacific, Japonic. Common.

Cymatium muricinum Röding   ×1.0
tuberosum Lamarck, *crispus* Reeve,
pyriformis Conrad, *nodulus* Link,
productum Gould,
albocingulatum Deshayes.

Thick, solid shell with moderately tall spire and large, inflated body whorl. Siphonal canal moderately long and recurved. Two varices per whorl. 3–5 tubercles between varices. Coarse spiral cords. Parietal wall and columella shield very thick and covering most of ventral side of body whorl. A few teeth on inner margin of outer lip. Greyish white with occasional light and dark zones on body whorl. Aperture creamy white, but purplish brown deep within. 3·0–7·5cm. Indo-Pacific, Japonic, Caribbean. Common.

Cymatium pileare Linnaeus   ×0.6
aquatilis Reeve, *vestitus* Hinds,
effusa C. B. Adams.

Thick, solid, ovate-fusiform shell with tall spire, blunt apex, well-rounded whorls and moderately impressed suture. Siphonal canal short, moderately broad and slightly recurved at extremity. Two varices per whorl. Spiral row of 5–10 tubercles between each varix, most prominent at shoulder of body whorl. Many spiral cords which are crossed by thin axial ridges. Numerous irregular, narrow folds on columella and parietal wall. Inner margin of outer lip strongly curved. Creamy white with light and darker brown spiral bands and axial streaks. Aperture reddish. Columella and parietal folds white. Thick, brown periostracum. 4–11cm. Indo-Pacific, South African, Australian, Californian, Panamic, Caribbean. Common.

Below: *Cymatium hepaticum* (left and centre) *and Cymatium rubeculum* (right). ×0.6.

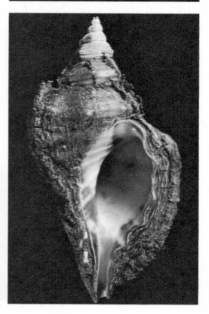

Cymatium pyrum Linnaeus   ×0.9
Solid, thick shell with short spire and relatively long siphonal canal. Inner margin of outer lip has about seven thick, divided teeth. Thick varices with about five axial rows of nodules between them. Spiral ribs become thick and heavy where they cross varices. Columella with strong folds. Orange brown or orange red, occasionally with white on varices. Columella and margin of outer lip orange with teeth white. Interior of aperture white. Periostracum thin but forms long rows of bristles on nodules. 7–10cm. Indo-Pacific. Common.

Cymatium rubeculum Linnaeus
Small but very thick, solid shell with moderately tall spire and large body whorl. Varices broad and strong. Siphonal canal short. Outer lip thickened, with strong teeth on inner margin. Beaded spiral cords cover entire shell. Bright red or pinkish with occasional white patches on varices and outer lip. Interior of aperture white. 3·5–5·0cm. Indo-Pacific. Common.

Cymatium spengleri Perry   ×0.6
Shell very thick and heavy, fusiform with tall spire. Thick varices. Strong, nodulous spiral cords at centre of each whorl with flattened spiral cords above and below. Outer lip thickened and crenulate. Small umbilicus. Yellow brown with dark brown spiral lines between spiral cords and ribs. Aperture white. 9–15cm. Australian (Australia). Common.

Cymatium tigrinum Broderip   ×0.5
Large, thick, solid shell with very large body whorl, expanded aperture and short, pointed spire. Outer lip very thick and crenulate. Columella almost smooth. Numerous flat spiral cords with narrower grooves between. Yellowish brown with darker brown blotches. Covered with thick, dark brown, hairy periostracum. 13–16cm. Panamic. Uncommon.

Genus LINATELLA Gray
Medium-sized, light and inflated shells with large body whorl and no varices. Whorls convex or angulated and ornamented with strong, flattish or rounded, spiral cords. Aperture large with reflected and denticulate outer lip. Columella callused and denticulate. Broad, moderately short siphonal canal. Four widely distributed species.

Linatella cingulata Lamarck   ×1.0
voigtii Anton, *neptunia* Garrard.
Thick, ovate shell with moderately tall spire and inflated body whorl moderately angulate at shoulders. Siphonal canal short and broad. Outer lip slightly reflected and denticulate. Numerous flat or rounded

Left (top to bottom): *Cymatium pyrum, C. spengleri* and *C. tigrinum*

spiral cords on all whorls. 8–11 denticles on columella. Creamy white, with two pale brown spiral bands on body whorl. Occasionally unicolorous pale fawn. Aperture whitish. 4–7cm. Indo-Pacific. Uncommon.

Linatella clandestina Lamarck   ×0.8

Moderately thick, globose shell with rounded whorls and short spire. Siphonal canal moderately long and slightly recurved. Outer lip thickened and denticulate on its inner margin. Large tooth on parietal wall. Columella with short but strong folds. Whole shell covered with strong spiral ribs with wider interstices. Fine, axial growth lines. Light brown with spiral cords dark brown. Brown denticles on outer lip. 2·5–4·5cm. Indo-Pacific (Pacific). Uncommon.

Genus COLUBRARIA Schumacher
Epidromus Mörch.
Thick, solid, tall-spired shells with thick varices on each whorl. Callused and reflected columella and parietal shield often extend up to penultimate whorl. Siphonal canal short and upturned. Suture shallow. Outer lip thickened and denticulate. Ornamented with rough, nodulous axial and spiral ribs. Operculum corneous with a terminal nucleus. Some authors now place members of this genus in a separate family, Colubrariidae.

Numerous species living in shallow water in warm and tropical seas.

Colubraria maculosa Gmelin   ×1.1

Thick, solid shell with large varices on each whorl. Wavy, shallow suture. Parietal callus reaches to penultimate whorl. Strong axial ribs with sharp points where they are intersected by finer spiral ribs. Whitish, blotched and speckled with dark and light brown. Columella white. Aperture white. 6–9cm. Indo-Pacific. Frequent.

Colubraria testacea Mörch   ×1.3

Thick, solid shell, with tall, slightly curved spire and large body whorl. Outer lip thickened, with inner margin denticulate. Flattened varix on each whorl. Strong axial ribs crossed by fine spiral lines. Parietal wall callused almost to penultimate whorl. Columella smooth. Siphonal canal short and recurved. Pale brown with dark brown blotch on each varix. Paler brown spiral bands on lower whorls. c5cm. Indo-Pacific. Uncommon.

Colubraria tortuosa Reeve   × 1.5

Shell smaller than *C. maculosa* and has curiously twisted spire. Numerous whorls are ornamented with spiral rows of nodules. Yellowish or orange brown, with wavy, brown bands sometimes arranged in one or two bands on whorl. Columella and parietal wall callused. Not so vividly coloured as *C. maculosa*. 4·5–6·0cm. Indo-Pacific (Pacific). Uncommon.

Genus DISTORSIO Röding
Curiously distorted shells of moderate size. Whorls irregular, varices discontinuous. Aperture irregular and constricted. Very hairy periostracum. Columella and parietal wall heavily and broadly callused, almost concealing ventral side of shells. Seven species. Under coral blocks.

Distorsio anus Linnaeus   × 0.6
rugosa Schumacher.
Ovate-fusiform shell with moderately tall spire, large body whorl and very short,

recurved siphonal canal. Varices prominent. Equally strong axial and spiral ribs. Outer lip flat and expanded, continuous with large parietal and columellar shield which has a thin, plate-like extension all round. Prominent folds on columella and parietal wall. Outer lip with few, strong pointed teeth. Aperture very irregular and constricted by teeth and folds. Whole shell has a much more distorted appearance than *D. reticulata*. Whitish, with brown bands and blotches. Parietal callus, columella and outer lip whitish streaked with brown. 4–8cm. Indo-Pacific. Common.

Distorsio clathrata Lamarck
smithi von Maltzan.
Similar to *D. reticulata*, but with more inflated spire whorls and stronger varices. Siphonal canal broader and slightly shorter. Axial and spiral ribs produce cancellate ornament which is coarser than in *D. reticulata*. Parietal shield glossy. Yellowish brown to brown with white teeth and folds. Brown, hairy periostracum. 5–9cm. Caribbean, West African. Uncommon.

Distorsio reticulata Röding   × 1.4
ridens Reeve, *perdistorta* Fulton, *acuta* Perry, *decipiens* Reeve.

Shell smaller than *D. anus*. Spire moderately tall, body whorl large and siphonal canal moderately long and slightly recurved. Varices weak. Fine spiral and axial ribs with a small nodule at each intersection. Outer lip flat and expanded, crossed by strong teeth. Two prominent folds on parietal wall. Columella with strong teeth. Cream or yellow with yellowish brown spiral bands. Occasionally unicolorous light brown. Periostracum brown with single, long bristle from each nodule on dorsal surface. 4–9cm. Indo-Pacific (Pacific). Uncommon.

Family BURSIDAE

Shells heavy, coarsely ornamented, ovate or flatly compressed, with prominent varices. Outer lip and columella are prominently denticulate or plicate. Siphonal canal usually produced and partially closed. Operculum corneous, yellowish brown or brown, with lateral or terminal nucleus. Widespread in tropical and warm seas. Most species live on or near coral reefs, generally under coral rocks, on sand or coral rubble. Few genera and numerous species.

Genus BURSA Röding
Details as for Family Bursidae.

Bursa bubo Linaeus   × 0.35

Shell large, heavy and inflated, with tall spire and large body whorl. Varices on each whorl and 6–8 blunt nodes between varices. Prominent spiral cords and smaller nodulous ribs on body whorl. Edge of outer lip with 20–25 rounded denticles. Columella white, with few small folds. Parietal wall glazed. Creamy white or yellowish brown flecked with brown spots. Very variable in size. 19–25cm. Indo-Pacific. Common.

Bursa bufo Röding
Large, thick, heavy, ovate-fusiform shell bearing a strong resemblance to *B. bubo*, but differing from that species in several respects, particularly in the parietal shield which is smooth and not, as in *B. bubo*, ornamented with weak folds. Outer lip with 5–6 pairs of teeth. White, cream or pink with a conspicuous dark red rim round inside of columella and just inside aperture. c14cm. Indo-Pacific (West Pacific), Australian (Australia). Frequent.

Bursa bufonia Gmelin   × 0.7
Shell thick, squat. Two varices on each whorl. Spiral rows of nodules and beads

cross the varices. Ten denticles on parietal lip; plicate columella. Granulose around siphonal canal. Glossy, pinkish grey or cream with reddish brown on varices and occasionally as spiral lines. Cream or yellow aperture, occasionally brown. 6–8cm. Indo-Pacific. Uncommon.

Bursa californica Hinds
Large, thick shell with large body whorl and short spire. Posterior canal and siphonal canal about equal breadth. Columella with indistinct folds. One parietal fold below posterior canal. Thick varices. Spiral rows of strong, pointed tubercles which are most developed on varices. Numerous coarse spiral ridges. Yellowish white with brown lines crossing tubercles. c9cm. Panamic. Frequent.

Bursa candisata Lamarck   ×0.8
Thick, elongate-fusiform shell with large body whorl and tall spire. Elongate aperture. Short, broad siphonal canal.

Broad posterior canal. Aperture lirate within. Two varices on each whorl. Close-set, spiral, beaded cords. Yellowish white with brown dots on spiral cords and brown varices. Aperture yellowish white. 8–10cm. Indo-Pacific. Uncommon.

Bursa cruentata Sowerby   ×1.3

Shell like a large version of *B. thomae*. Strong varices are crossed by strong spiral cords. Strong, axial rows of thick tubercles. Whitish yellow with spots and blotches of dark brown. Aperture white, columella stained with series of black blotches. 2–4cm. Indo-Pacific, South African. Uncommon.

Bursa crumena Lamarck
Thin shell with two varices per whorl. Fine, spiral, beaded ridges and one spiral row of tubercles per whorl, three on body whorl. Everted, plicate columella lip, dentate parietal lip. Creamy brown with pale tubercles, often dark brown streaks between tubercles. Yellow or white aperture. 5·1–8·9cm. Indo-Pacific. Uncommon.

Bursa echinata Link   ×0.9
spinosa Lamarck.

Thick, ovate, compressed shell with large body whorl, moderately tall spire and impressed suture. Outer lip irregularly crenulate. Siphonal canal short and broad. Varices on opposite sides of each whorl bear long, straight spines. Spine at top of aperture bent downwards. Few shorter spines on each whorl between varices. Whitish, flushed and streaked with light and dark brown. Aperture whitish. 4–6cm. Indo-Pacific. Frequent.

Bursa foliata Broderip   ▽ ×0.7
Shell moderately large, thick with large body whorl and short spire. Outer and inner lip widely expanded and thin. Outer lip strongly denticulate. Columella with long folds. Strong folds on parietal wall. Posterior canal deep and produced upwards. Varices thick with foliate edges. Numerous strong spiral cords. Three spiral rows of pointed nodules on body whorl. One row on spire whorls. Yellowish white spotted with pale brown. Aperture bright yellow. Lips bright reddish orange. 6–9cm. Indo-Pacific. Frequent.

Bursa granularis Röding × 0.7
elegans Perry, *granifera* Lamarck,
livida Reeve, *semigranosa* Lamarck.

Small specimens thin; larger specimens
thick. Spiral ridges with beads or nodules
cross varices. Granulose around siphonal
canal. Three denticles on parietal lip;
plicate columella lip. Cream to purplish
grey with creamy grey aperture. Brown,
opaque periostracum. 2–6cm. Indo-Pacific,
Caribbean. Common.

Bursa margaritula Deshayes
Thick, almost biconical shell with simple
suture. Beaded spiral ridges and a single
ridge with nodules, sometimes spinose, per
whorl. Dull, light brown with darker
tubercles and irregular axial bands. White
aperture. 3·0–5·5cm. Indo-Pacific (Pacific).
Uncommon.

Bursa marginata Gmelin × 1.0
laevigata Lamarck.

Thick, almost pear-shaped shell with
depressed spire. Smooth with weak spiral
ridges basally. Dentate parietal lip, plicate
columella lip. Cream to flesh-coloured
with narrow white or yellow aperture.
Thin, olive, opaque periostracum. 2–4cm.
West African. Rare.

Bursa nobilis Reeve
Medium-sized, solid, ovate shell with large
body whorl and moderately tall spire with
pointed apex. Bears some resemblance to
B. bufonia with which it has occasionally
been confused. Varices are aligned vertically. Flat or triangular tubercles between
varices. Most nodulose spiral ridges on
body whorl and on penultimate whorl.
Outer lip with numerous, often elongate

teeth. Numerous teeth and folds on
columella. Siphonal canal short, posterior
canal longer. Creamy white with brownish
blotches or interrupted spiral lines. Outer
lip yellow or orange with white teeth.
Columella yellow or orange, also with
white teeth and folds. Aperture white.
2·5–5·5cm. Indo-Pacific (Pacific). Uncommon.

Bursa rana Linnaeus × 0.5

Thick, flattened shell with short spire and
large body whorl. Strong varices placed on
opposite sides of each whorl. Outer lip
thickened and denticulate. Siphonal canal
upturned. Posterior canal deep and
bordered with nodules on parietal side.
Whole shell covered with spiral ribs which
may be granulose, nodulose or beaded.
Pale brown or whitish with darker brown
spots and spiral bands on ribs. Outer lip,
columella callus and aperture white or
yellowish brown. 6–8cm. Indo-Pacific
(Pacific). Common.

Bursa ranelloides Reeve × 0.7

Thick, stout shell with large body whorl
and relatively short spire. Short, broad
siphonal canal. Outer lip thickened and
denticulate. Columella with small folds.
One thick varix. Two or three spiral rows
of nodules on body whorl and one or two
rows on spire whorls. Whitish flushed with
yellowish brown and darker brown, broken
spiral bands between nodules. Aperture
white. Columella white with brown
mottling. 4–6cm. Japonic. Frequent.

Bursa rhodostoma Sowerby × 1.3
Shell thick, squat. Spiral, nodulose ridges
alternate with spiral rows of beads and
cross varices. Dull, creamy white, may

have reddish brown markings between
spiral ridges. Rose aperture. 1·5–2·5cm.
Indo-Pacific. Uncommon.

Bursa rosa Perry × 1.1
siphonata Reeve.

Shell thick, with one varix on each whorl.
Heavy, punctate and granulose ornamentation. Double row of denticles on parietal
lip. Siphonal appendages on three or four
varices. Grey or creamy yellow. Cream
aperture, interior often violet, dentition
white. 2·0–5·5cm. Indo-Pacific. Uncommon.

Bursa rubeta Linnaeus × 0.45

Shell moderately large, very thick and
heavy, with moderately tall spire, large
body whorl and strong varices. Outer lip
thickened, with small teeth on inner
margin. Siphonal canal short and recurved.
Posterior canal moderately long and
recurved, about the same size as siphonal

canal. Columella and parietal wall glazed and bearing fine folds. Coarse spiral ribs which may be warty, beaded or rough. Pale brown and whitish with spirally arranged, darker brown blobs. Aperture pinkish with broad, reddish brown band deep inside and reddish brown on columella and parietal wall. *c*8cm. Pacific. Common.

Bursa scrobiculator Linnaeus   ×1.0

Stout, thick shell with large body whorl and short, tapering spire. Whorls with almost flat shoulders and a strong varix on each. Outer lip thickened behind reflected aperture. Inside of outer lip with a few coarse teeth. Coarse folds on columella. Varices tuberculate and with deep pits on each side. Fine spiral threads and cords. Yellowish blotched with brown. *c*7cm. Mediterranean, West African. Common.

Bursa siphonata Reeve
Thick, heavy shell with large body whorl, short spire and short, recurved siphonal canal. Previous posterior canals stand out prominently on strong varices. Strong, nodulous spiral cords on all whorls. Aperture thickened and strongly denticulate. Columella with small pustules. Yellowish white mottled with brown on spiral cords. Aperture violet. *c*5cm. Indo-Pacific. Frequent.

Bursa subgranosa Beck   ×0.45
Moderately large, thick shell somewhat compressed with large body whorl, tall spire and short, broad siphonal canal.

Outer lip reflected and denticulate. Columella with small folds. Varices strong but not very thick. Numerous irregular, nodulous spiral cords. Whitish mottled with light and dark brown spiral lines. Aperture brownish. 6–8cm. Indo-Pacific. Frequent.

Bursa thomae D'Orbigny.   ×0.9

Small, thick, squat shell with large body whorl and short spire. Aperture relatively small with siphonal canal short and broad. Outer lip dentate. Columella with folds. Two varices on each whorl. Coarse spiral cords and large, blunt tubercles on each whorl. Spiral cords beaded and strongest where they cross the tubercles. Whitish, flushed with yellow. Spiral cords with small, brown dots. Aperture yellow or violet. *c*3cm. Caribbean. Uncommon.

Bursa ventricosa Broderip   ×0.6

Thick, solid shell with large body whorl and short spire. Columella curved and lacking folds on pustules. Outer lip crenulate. Broad posterior canal and broad siphonal canal. Large, widely spaced tubercles on shoulder of each whorl. Another row of tubercles on body whorl.

Yellowish, with dark brown blotches and dark brown spiral bands. 4–5cm. Panamic. Frequent.

Bursa venustula Reeve   ×1·4

Shell closely resembles *B. rhodostoma* but is slightly larger and posterior canal is generally longer. Outer lip not expanded and flattened beyond denticles. 3·5–4·0cm. Indo-Pacific, Japonic. Frequent.

Bursa verrucosa Sowerby   ×1.7·
papilla Wood.

Thick, solid shell with large body whorl and short spire. Outer lip thickened and denticulate. Columella with strong folds. Thick varices with deep pits on each side. Body whorl has three spiral rows of large tubercles. One row of tubercles on spire whorl. Yellowish with dark spots on tubercles. Aperture white. Columella white with thin, brown lines. 3–5cm. Indo-Pacific. Uncommon.

Family TONNIDAE

Shells usually thin, large and globose. Short spire, deep suture. No varices, no thickening of outer lip (with exception of genus *Malea*). Operculum absent. Popular name of tun shells in allusion to barrel-like shape. Three genera widely distributed in tropical and temperate seas.

Genus TONNA Brünnich

Dolium Lamarck.
For details see Family Tonnidae. Approximately 26 species, all thin-shelled, several very large, all with thin outer lip.

Tonna allium Dillwyn   × 0.5
costata Menke, *picta* Hanley,
lactescens Mörch.

Thin, globose shell with narrow umbilicus. Spiral costae and faint axial striae, latter strong on columellar pleat. Parietal lip crenulate. Glossy, white, with cream costae. White aperture. 7–13cm. Indo-Pacific. Frequent.

Tonna canaliculata Linnaeus   △ × 1.0
cepa Röding, *olearium* Linnaeus.
Shell thin, light with moderately raised spire and deeply channelled suture. Outer lip crenulate. Broad, smooth spiral ribs with narrow grooves between. Creamy brown variegated with darker brown and white blotches. 6–12cm. Indo-Pacific. Frequent.

Tonna cerevisina Hedley   × 0.25

Shell very large, thin, globose with deep, canaliculate suture. Broad, widely spaced spiral ribs with finer riblets between. Yellow, cream or light brown with some of the intervals between ribs white. Columella and upper part of parietal wall white. Early whorls pinkish; upper part of remaining whorls blotched with dark brown, irregular streaks and blobs. c21cm. Australian. Uncommon.

Tonna chinensis Dillwyn
australis Mörch, *variegata* Philippi,
magnificum Sowerby.
Medium-sized, thin shell with shallow suture. Strong, rounded spiral ribs separat-

ed by slightly narrower grooves. Light yellow, brown or cream, with white streaks and brown spots on ribs. Interior yellowish brown, whiter near margin. c6cm. Indo-Pacific (Pacific), Japonic. Frequent.

Tonna dolium Linnaeus   × 1.0
Spotted Tun
maculata Lamarck *albus* Röding.

Very thin, globose shell with narrow umbilicus. Spiral ribs have weak ridges in interstices. Pleated columella and very thin parietal lip. Glossy, semi-transparent, white shell. Ribs opaque with brown spotting. White aperture. 4·5–8·5cm. Indo-Pacific. Common.

Tonna galea Linnaeus   × 0.5
tenuis Menke, *tenebrosa* Hanley,
antillarum Mörch.

Shell large, thin, light with short spire and channelled suture. Outer lip crenulate. Fairly narrow spiral ribs with interspaces the same width as ribs. Brownish white, darker brown at edge of aperture. 10–20cm. Transatlantic, Caribbean, West African, Indo-Pacific. Frequent.

Tonna luteostoma Küster   ×0.4
japonica Dunker, *tankervillei* Hanley.

Large, globular shell with flat or slightly raised spire and deeply channelled suture. Broad, flattened ribs with narrower, channelled interspaces which appear in aperture as ribs. Whitish with irregular, light brown blotches and darker brown axial streaks which are interrupted at the interspaces. A thinner-shelled form occurs with flatter ribs and wider interspaces less prominently blotched with brown. 10–18 cm. Japonic. Frequent.

Tonna maculosa Dillwyn
sulphurea C. B. Adams, *pennata* Mörch, *alba* Conrad, *occidentalis* Mörch.
Thin, strong, globular, but moderately elongate shell with impressed suture. Umbilicus chink-like, with broad spiral rib surrounding it. Fine spiral grooves on all whorls. Apical whorls shiny and smooth. Yellowish brown, with irregular darker brown blotches. Early whorls golden brown. Thin periostracum which flakes off. 5–13cm. Caribbean. Common.

Tonna melanostoma Jay
Shell very large, thin, short-spired with deeply channelled suture. Broad, flat spiral cords with narrower interspaces. Pale yellowish brown or whitish with columella and parietal region stained deep brown. Spiral grooves stained above and below with two thin, deep brown lines which become much more conspicuous towards outer lip. 20–23cm. Indo-Pacific (Pacific). Rare.

Tonna perdix Linnaeus   ×0.5
Partridge Tun
coturnix Röding, *rufa* Blainville.
reticulata Montfort, *ventricosior* Menke.
Thin, globose shell with narrow umbilicus. Spiral costae, thin reflected columella and crenulate parietal lip. Pinkish buff with irregular, cream, axial markings. White

aperture with brown parietal margin and siphonal notch. 7–13cm. Indo-Pacific. Common.

Tonna sulcosa Born   ×0.9
fasciata Bruguière, *fasciata* Röding, *varicosa* Preston.

Shell fairly small for the genus; elongate globose with short spire and channelled suture. Aperture thickened and reflected, with well marked teeth. Evenly spaced, rounded spiral ribs. Four or five dark brown spiral bands alternating on body whorl with white spiral bands of same width. Apex black and spire whorls creamy white with brown ribs. Aperture whitish with brown bands showing through. 5–11cm. Indo-Pacific (Pacific), Japonic. Frequent.

Tonna tessellata Lamarck   ×0.8
fimbriata Sowerby, *minjac* Deshayes.
Shell large, thin with moderately raised spire and channelled suture. Broad, widely spaced spiral ribs with broader interspaces. Whitish with axial rows of light brown spots on ribs. Aperture pale brown, whiter

near margin. 6–13cm. Indo-Pacific (South West Pacific), Japonic. Common.

Tonna tetracotula Hedley
Similar to *T. cerevisina* and *T. variegata*. Usually uniform white to pale orange but sometimes with light brown spiral bands. Spire higher than that of *T. cerevisina* and has riblets between ribs on shoulder. 15–20cm. Indo-Pacific (Pacific). Rare.

Tonna variegata Lamarck
Shell very similar to *T. cerevisina* of which it may be a form. Unlike *T. cerevisina* it lacks the fine ribs between the broad ribs. 8–15cm. Indo-Pacific (Pacific). Frequent.

Genus MALEA Valenciennes
Globose, thick shells with thickened, reflected and denticulate outer lip. Ornamented with wide, smooth and flat spiral ribs. Inner lip with heavy callus. Columella deeply notched and callused. Two species.

Malea pomum Linnaeus   ×0.7
labrosa Gray.
Smaller and less massive than *M. ringens*. Short spire and weakly impressed suture. Broad, rounded, spiral cords separated by wide, shallow grooves. Thickened outer lip

has about ten strong teeth on inner margin. Columella deeply notched and callused. Creamy orange or light brown with large, white spots on cords. Aperture yellow with outer lip white or cream. 5–8cm. Indo-Pacific. Common.

Malea ringens Swainson   ×0.35
Grinning Tun
latilabris Valenciennes, *crassilabris* Valenciennes.

Large, thick, short-spired shell. Greatly thickened outer lip with large teeth protruding inwards, outer edge crenulate. Columella very deeply notched below mid-line with warty calluses above and below. Regularly spaced, broad, flat spiral cords with smooth interspaces. White except for early whorls which are yellowish brown. Aperture dark brown. Callused parietal area flushed yellowish brown. Teeth on outer lip whitish with yellowish brown spaces between. 12–17cm. Panamic. Common.

Family FICIDAE

Medium to large, light, fig-shaped or pear-shaped shells. Short-spired and ventricose, with many fine spiral ribs, sometimes reticulated with axial ridges. Aperture long and wide, with long or short siphonal canal. Operculum absent. Mostly Indo-Pacific distribution. One genus, about 15 species.

Genus FICUS Röding
Details as for Family Ficidae.

Ficus communis Röding   ×0.7
reticulata Lamarck, *papyratia* Say.
Thin, pyriform shell. Spiral ridges crossed by weak axial ridges giving reticulate ornamentation. Dull, pinkish white with white aperture and reddish brown interior. 8–11cm. Caribbean. Common.

Ficus ficus Linnaeus
Shell similar to *F. subintermedius* in shape but is more swollen and surface is finely reticulated all over. Aperture deep purple. 5–7cm. Indo-Pacific. Common.

Ficus filosa Sowerby
Medium-sized shell with short spire and slightly impressed suture. Strong, evenly-spaced spiral ribs with fine axial lines giving reticulation. Orange yellow, with spiral ribs orange brown. Aperture pale brown, whiter towards margin. *c*7cm. Indo-Pacific (China Sea), Japonic. Rare.

Ficus gracilis Sowerby   ×0.4

Shell large, thin and light. Whole shell covered with spiral and axial threads, spiral threads being thicker. Light brown with axial striping of darker brown.

Aperture same colour becoming whiter near margin. 10–15cm. Indo-Pacific (Pacific), Japonic. Frequent.

Ficus subintermedius d'Orbigny   ×0.5

Medium-sized shell with almost flat spire. Finely reticulate ornament. Shell brown with few spiral, lighter bands containing darker brown spots. Aperture whitish. 5–7cm. Japonic. Common.

Ficus tessellatus Kobelt
Small, nearly flat-topped shell with slightly impressed suture. Whorls cancellated with strong spiral ribs and weaker axial ribs. Cream or white with 6–10 spiral rows of large, squarish, brown spots. *c*5cm. Indo-Pacific (Australia). Common.

Superfamily
Muricacea

Family MURICIDAE

Large family of predominantly spiny shells. Basic shape varies from squat and short-spired to long and tall-spired. Siphonal canal may be short or very long. Aperture smooth, denticulate or crenulate. Columella folds rarely present. Ornament varies from almost smooth or coarsely nodulous and tuberculated to very spiny. Spines, when present, are usually developed on strong varices. Large, corneous operculum. Members of this family are carnivorous and attack other molluscs by drilling holes in their shells. Many genera have been proposed for this very extensive group which is represented in all tropical and warm seas. Many species live among rocks or in muddy and sandy places. Some are found under rocks or on coral reefs.

Genus MUREX Linnaeus
Thin or fairly thick shells with very long siphonal canal. Strong varices ornamented with short spines. Body whorl large and spire usually short. Numerous species in tropical seas.

Murex brandaris Linnaeus   ×0.5
Moderately thick shell with long siphonal canal, large body whorl and short spire. Spiral row of fluted spines on shoulder of

whorls and at periphery and base of body whorl. Recurved columellar lip. Dull, buff or creamy yellow shell with glossy yellow, brown or cream aperture. Operculum dull, reddish brown with apical nucleus. 6–11 cm. Mediterranean. Common.

Murex chrysostoma Sowerby   ×0.9
Golden-mouthed Murex
bellus Reeve.

Stout shell with large, convex body whorl, short spire and long siphonal canal. Three strong axial varices, two or three axial ribs between varices. Numerous spiral ridges which are very prominent on varices. Recurved columella lip weakly plicate. Outer lip denticulate. Grey with pink varices which may have brown markings. Yellow columella lip. 5–8cm. Caribbean. Frequent.

Murex hirasei Hirase
Thin shell with large body whorl and long, narrow siphonal canal. Resembles *M. chrysostoma* in shape. Varices nodulose, spines absent or reduced. Thin columella and parietal lip. Dull, pinkish cream with fine, brown spiral lines. Creamy aperture. Reddish brown operculum. 5–8cm. Japonic. Rare.

Murex nigrospinosus Reeve   ×0.8

Thick, stout shell with short spire and long, broad siphonal canal. Long, mostly straight spines on three thick varices. Axial ribs between varices. Whitish with spines greyish increasing in intensity towards their tips. 5·5–8·0cm. Indo-Pacific (Pacific). Frequent.

Murex pecten Lightfoot   ◁   ×0.6
Thorny Woodcock or Venus Comb
triremis Perry.
Fairly thin, but solid, shell with long siphonal canal and numerous, long, slightly curved spines which are well developed down length of siphonal canal. Spines more numerous and closer together than in *M. ternispina* and *M. troscheli*. Yellowish white without spiral, brown bands. 10–15 cm. Indo-Pacific. Frequent.

Murex pliciferoides Kuroda   ×0.7
pliciferus Sowerby.

Shell moderately thick, elongate-fusiform with tall spire and long, recurved siphonal canal. Moderately strong varices with sharp spines on each, the spine at shoulder being considerably longer than the others. Spines continue about half-way down siphonal canal. Between each pair of varices on each whorl there are two low axial folds. Low spiral ridges cover shell surface. Columella lip smooth and reflected. White with indistinct, brown spiral bands. Aperture and columella white. *c*10cm. Japonic. Uncommon.

Murex rectirostris Sowerby   ×1.0
Shell fairly thin but strong with short spire, large body whorl and very long siphonal canal. Spines on varices small and weak. Siphonal canal usually spineless. Yellowish white, banded with light and

121

dark brown. 5·0–7·5cm. Indo-Pacific
(Pacific). Common.

Murex scolopax Dillwyn   ×0.6

Thick, solid shell with inflated body whorl,
short spire and long, straight siphonal
canal. Varices strong with long and short,
slightly curved or occasionally straight,
open, sharp spines. Spines stronger but
less numerous than those of *M. pecten*. A
few flattened, smooth spiral ridges on each
whorl. Lower half of outer lip has a strong,
flat tooth. Creamy white with yellowish
brown blotches at base of spines on outer
lip. Columella white. 8–18cm. Indo-
Pacific. Uncommon.

Murex trapa Röding   ×0.7
martinianus Reeve.
Thin shell with tall spire and very long
siphonal canal. Each whorl has three

varices, each bearing short, sharp spines.
Three or four axial ribs between varices
which become nearly obsolete on body
whorl. Siphonal canal has spines for only
the anterior half of its length. Greyish
white becoming brownish towards posterior end of siphonal canal. Aperture dark
brown, columella white. 5–10cm. Indo-
Pacific (Pacific), Japonic. Uncommon.

Murex tribulus Linnaeus
ternispina Lamarck, *crassispina* Lamarck,
forskahlii Röding.
Resembles *M. troscheli*, but is smaller and
lacks the darker brown spiral bands. *c*10cm.
Indo-Pacific. Common.

Murex troscheli Lischke   ×0.5
Shell large with very long siphonal canal.
Whorls rounded, suture deep. Very long,
curved spines which are developed nearly

to the base of the siphonal canal. Yellowish
brown with thin spiral bands of darker
brown extending onto the spines. *c*15cm.
Japonic. Frequent.

Genus HAUSTELLUM Bruguière
Medium-sized shells with very long siphonal canal, strong varices and relatively
short, hollow spines. Columella smooth.
Aperture entire, almost circular. Few
species in tropical seas.

Haustellum haustellum Linnaeus   ×0.6

Thick shell with short spire and very short
spines on varices. Three or four axial ribs
between varices. Round aperture with
slightly reflected lips. Bluish brown with
spiral, brown bands. Aperture pinkish.
6–10cm. Indo-Pacific. Common.

Haustellum tweedianum Macpherson ×1.2

Solid shell with large aperture and moderately tall spire. Moderately long to long, narrow and straight siphonal canal. Three strong varices. Beaded spiral ribs and cords which often have short spines where they cross varices. Few spines also at base of anterior canal. Two axial rows of nodules between varices. Outer lip dentate, columella smooth. Pinkish with brown patches and spots. Apex reddish pink. Aperture white flushed pink. 6–8cm. Australian (Australia). Uncommon.

Genus CHICOREUS Montfort
Medium-sized or large shells with short or tall spire and characterised by long, curved or straight spines. Spines, which are not flattened, are developed on thick, prominent varices. Many species in tropical seas.

Chicoreus asianus Kuroda   ×0.8

Relatively thin but strong shell with fairly tall spire and deep suture. Three axial rows of spines which are not pointed or flattened, open throughout their length. Sharp, fang-like process sometimes occurs between third and fourth spine on outer lip. Whitish mottled with light and dark brown. Aperture white. 6–9cm. Japonic. Frequent.

Chicoreus brevifrons Lamarck
purpuratus Reeve, *alabastrum* A. Adams, *crassivaricosa* Reeve, *adamsi* Kobelt, *approximatus* Sowerby, *pudoricolor* Reeve. Thick, ovate shell with moderately long, broad siphonal canal and moderately long spire. Three varices with numerous frond-like spines alternate with axial rows of nodules. Open siphonal canal has spiral ridging. Dull, cream with reddish brown and brown interstices or many brown

bands. White aperture. 8–15cm. Caribbean. Common.

Chicoreus brunneus Link   ×0.7
adustus Lamarck, *rubicundus* Perry, *australiensis* A. Adams.

Very thick, broad, ovate-fusiform shell with simple suture. Moderately long, broad siphonal canal. Varices expanded at intervals forming stout, finely scaled fronds. Nodulose between varices. Columella smooth. Outer lip dentate. Dark brown to black, with some white or cream. Small aperture. Columella lip pink or creamy yellow. Aperture white. 5–8cm. Indo-Pacific. Common.

Chicoreus cervicornis Lamarck   ×0.9

Relatively thin shell with very long, recurved and sometimes bifurcate spines. Shorter spines on siphonal canal. Creamy white mottled and banded with pale brown. Aperture white, translucent. 5–7 cm. Indo-Pacific, Australian. Uncommon.

Chicoreus cornucervi Röding   ×0.6
monodon Sowerby.

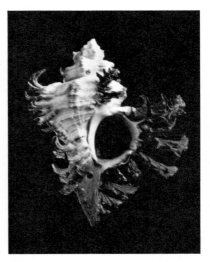

Moderately thick shell with inflated body whorl, moderately tall spire and moderately long, broad siphonal canal. The strong varices bear very long, strongly recurved spines which are hollow and have very small side ramifications. One or two axial folds present between varices. Coarse spiral ribs. Columella smooth and reflected. In some specimens spines are recurved so considerably that their points almost touch shell's surface. Several small teeth on outer lip. Dark or light brown, with darker brown varices and spines. Aperture yellowish, sometimes with pink edge. 8–11cm. Indo-Pacific (North Australia). Uncommon.

Chicoreus dilectus A. Adams   ×1.3
Shell solid with short, pointed spire, long siphonal canal and three strong varices on each whorl. Spines mostly connected together by leafy processes on the varices. Longest and largest spine is at shoulder and is curved upwards. Light brown with

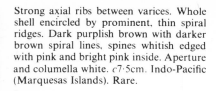

Strong axial ribs between varices. Whole shell encircled by prominent, thin spiral ridges. Dark purplish brown with darker brown spiral lines, spines whitish edged with pink and bright pink inside. Aperture and columella white. $c7.5$cm. Indo-Pacific (Marquesas Islands). Rare.

Chicoreus torrefactus Sowerby   ▷ ✕0.8
Thick, ovate-fusiform shell with tall spire and moderately long and broad siphonal canal. Thick, rounded varices bearing short, open, frondose spines which are present down to the end of siphonal canal. One or two blunt axial ridges between varices. Strong spiral ribs and fine, rough striae. Outer lip denticulate. Columella smooth. Dark or paler brown with dark brown spiral lines and dark brown tips to

axial, darker brown markings. Aperture white. 4.5–5.5cm. Indo-Pacific (Pacific), Japonic. Uncommon.

Chicoreus foliatus Perry   ✕0.6
Rose Branch Murex
palmarosae Lamarck.

Shell thick, tall-spired, with long siphonal canal and relatively small aperture. Spines long, open-ended and frondose, curving in three lines down length of spire, becoming very long on body whorl. Spiral ridges sometimes produced as nodules at periphery. Colour brownish red becoming pinkish or violet towards end of spines. Margin of outer lip dark brown. Inside of aperture white. 7–12cm. Indo-Pacific. Uncommon.

Chicoreus ramosus Linnaeus   ✕0.7
Shell very large, thick and heavy. Body whorl inflated, spire moderately short and siphonal canal moderately long, broad and

slightly curved. Thick varices have short, upturned spines, the longest of which is on shoulder of body whorl at edge of aperture. This spine sometimes very long and straight. One or two axial ribs between varices. Weak spiral ribs and fine spiral cords. Whitish, with brown patches which extend to spines. Aperture white, margin of aperture and columella pinkish. 9–25 cm. Indo-Pacific. Common.

Chicoreus sauliae Reeve   ✕0.8
Shell similar to *C. foliatus*. Spines shorter and more numerous especially on body whorl. Aperture relatively larger. Margin of outer lip pink. 8–10cm. Indo-Pacific (Pacific). Rare.

Chicoreus steeriae Reeve   ▽ ✕0.7
Thick, solid, ovate-fusiform shell with tall spire and long, moderately broad siphonal canal. The strong varices have moderately long and short, open-ended and foliate spines, reminiscent of those on *C. sauliae*.

124

spines. Aperture and columella white, orange or yellowish brown. 7–10cm. Indo-Pacific (Pacific), Japonic. Common.

Chicoreus triqueter Born   × 1.1

Relatively thick shell with strong, thick varices not conspicuously frondose. Three or four strong axial ribs between varices. Pale brown with darker brown bands on varices. Early whorls purplish. *c*7cm. Indo-Pacific. Common.

Genus HEXAPLEX Perry
Moderately large shells with more than four varices to each whorl. Varices spinose at shoulder and not attached to previous whorl at suture. Few species in tropical seas, well represented off west coast of Central and South America.

Hexaplex brassica Lamarck   × 0.4
Cabbage Murex
ducalis Broderip.

Thick, globose-ovate shell with short spire and simple suture. Thick varices with stout spines which are strongest at shoulders. Occasionally a node between varices. Siphonal canal short and broad. Columella lip smooth. Parietal lip strongly dentate. Dull, white with three brown spiral bands. Margins of varices rose pink. Margin of outer lip pink, aperture white within. 12–18cm. Panamic, Peruvian. Common.

Hexaplex cichoreus Gmelin   × 0.6
foliacea Perry, *endivia* Lamarck.

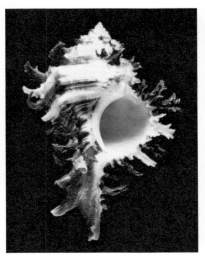

Thick, broadly ovate shell with simple suture and moderately long siphonal canal. Foliate spines on varices are strongly recurved. Coarse spiral cords and fine striae between. Occasional node between varices. Columella lip smooth and well curved. Outer lip plicate. Dull, with alternating white and reddish brown spiral bands. Aperture white. 6–11cm. Indo-Pacific. Uncommon.

Hexaplex erythrostoma Swainson   × 0.45
Pink-mouthed Murex
bicolor Valenciennes, *rhodocheilus* King.

Thick, globose-ovate shell with short spire. Thick varices with alternate rows of closed and open spines. Inside of open spines glossy. Siphonal canal short and broad. Thin columella lip. Outer lip crenulate. Siphonal canal broad. Creamy pink with inner surface of spines pink. Pink aperture. 7–15cm. Panamic, Peruvian. Common.

Hexaplex hoplites P. Fischer   × 0.7

Shell moderately large, thick, heavy, with globose body whorl, short spire and short, broad siphonal canal. Outer lip crenulate. Columella smooth. Numerous thick varices on each whorl crossed by strong, spiral, scaly ribs. Varices have sharp, upturned points at shoulder. Pale brown with one or two darker brown spiral bands becoming blackish brown on varices. Columella and outer lip bright, pinkish red, aperture white. 8–10cm. West African. Uncommon.

Hexaplex pomum Gmelin
Apple Murex
asperrimus Lamarck, *mexicanus* Petit, *oculatus* Reeve, *pomiformis* Mörch.
Thick, globose ovate shell with moderately tall spire and simple suture. Thick varices with short, blunt or occasionally foliated spines. Columella lip thin. Outer lip crenulate. Short, broad siphonal canal. Siphonal canal broad. Resembles *H. regius* in shape, but is smaller and relatively heavier. Purplish brown and white. Parietal wall yellow, light brown or orange with a dark brown blotch at anterior end. Aperture brownish. 5–10cm. Transatlantic, Caribbean. Common.

Hexaplex regius Swainson   ×0.45
Regal Murex

Similar in shape to *H. erythrostoma*, but distinguished from it by the more numerous and frilly spines on varices. Also conspicuous differences in colour. Aperture and lower half of columella wall is pink as in *H. erythrostoma*, but parietal wall has a broad, dark chocolate brown band and there are traces of same colour on inside of siphonal canal. Varices and suture of spire whorls also have dark brown patches. 9–12cm. Panamic, Peruvian. Common.

Hexaplex stainforthi Reeve   ×1.6
Thick, stout shell with numerous strong, broad varices with short, fluted spines along their length. Prominent spiral ribs run over and between varices. Short, thick siphonal canal. Wide, deep umbilicus. White, pink, orange or yellow spiral ribs; dark brown fronds; pink, orange or yellow

aperture. 4·5–7·0cm. Indo-Pacific (Australia). Uncommon.

Genus MURICANTHUS Swainson
Large, solid shells with inflated body whorl, varices 5–14 per whorl and broad, open spines which may be simple or foliated. Numerous species, mostly off west coast of Central and South America.

Muricanthus callidinus Perry   ×1.3
nitidus Reeve.

Similar to *M. nigritus*, but axial spines are more numerous, curved and more foliated. Shell is also smaller. Outer lip denticulate. White, with purplish brown spiral bands extending onto spines. Aperture and columella white. 4–10cm. Panamic. Frequent.

Muricanthus fulvescens Sowerby
Giant Eastern Murex
spinicostatus Reeve, *spinicosta* Kiener, *turbinatus* Sowerby.
Thick, solid shell with broadly expanded

body whorl, moderately tall spire and long, broad siphonal canal. Strong varices ornamented with stout, straight, moderately long and open spines. Spines white or greyish white with thin, spiral, brownish lines. Aperture and columella white. 12–17 cm. Transatlantic, Caribbean. Common.

Muricanthus nigritus Philippi   ×0.4
melanoleucus Mörch.

Large, very thick, globose shell with short spire and short, broad siphonal canal. About ten axial rows of short and long, pointed and open spines. Weak spiral ridges. Dull white with dark brown spiral bands extending onto spines. Columella and aperture white. 12–15cm. Panamic. Common.

Muricanthus princeps Broderip   ×0.8
norrisii Reeve.

Thick, tall-spired shell with relatively long siphonal canal. 5–8 varices with spines longest and thickest at shoulder. Spines and ribs tinged with brown, much darker brown between varices. 6–12cm. Panamic. Common.

Muricanthus radix Gmelin ×0.6

Large, heavy, pear-shaped shell with moderately short spire and short, broad siphonal canal. Varices with short and long, sharply pointed spines which are largest at shoulder of body whorl. Spines tend to overlap each other. Smaller and thicker than *M. nigritus*. White with purplish black spines and spiral bands. Aperture and columella white. *c*9cm. Panamic. Frequent.

Genus PHYLLONOTUS Swainson
Moderately large to large shells with globose body whorl, broad and short siphonal canal and 3–6 varices with short spines. Numerous species, mostly from warm and tropical seas.

Phyllonotus trunculus Linnaeus ×0.8

Shell thick, ovate with large body whorl, moderately tall spire and short, recurved siphonal canal. Numerous strong varices on each whorl with one fluted and pointed spine on each at shoulder. Fine spiral threads. Umbilicus deep. Yellowish white with broad, brown spiral bands. Columella

white, aperture white with external, brown bands showing through. *c*7cm. Mediterranean. Common.

Genus POIRIERIA Jousseaume
Small, thin shells with long siphonal canal; smooth surface with few prominent spines at shoulder; axial rows of smaller spines below, not continuing onto siphonal canal. Columella smooth. Few species in Pacific and Australasian waters.

Poirieria zelandica Quoy & Gaimard ×1.5

Thin, ovate-fusiform shell with tall spire and long, curved siphonal canal. Varices have few short spines except for spines at shoulder which are moderately long and open. Shell otherwise nearly smooth. Unicolorous yellowish white. Spines are usually much more developed than in specimen illustrated. 4·5–5·5cm. Australian (New Zealand). Frequent.

Genus PTERYNOTUS Swainson
Thick or thin, tall-spired shells with three varices per whorl each flaring to form wide, usually thin and fluted fronds. Numerous species.

Pterynotus acanthopterus Lamarck
Similar to *P. triformis*, but adult specimens larger and top of varices more prominent and strongly curved. *c*10cm. Indo-Pacific (North West Australia). Frequent.

Pterynotus alatus Röding ×0.8
pinnatus Swainson.
Shell thick, solid, tall-spired with long, curved siphonal canal with an adjacent canal curved in the opposite direction. Three strong varices with flaring lamellae which are twisted in a clockwise direction. Single strong, axial tubercle between varices on each whorl. Shell covered with

numerous spiral, scaly ribs which extend onto lamellae. Outer lip crenulate and with a row of blunt teeth just inside. Columella smooth. Unicolorous white. *c*6cm. Indo-Pacific. Rare.

Pterynotus angasi Crosse
Small, thin shell having some resemblance to *P. uncinarius*. Tall-spired and with a broad, moderately long and reflected siphonal canal. Varices are produced upwards to form projecting, recurved and almost closed tubercles. Fine spiral striae and nodules between each pair of varices. Outer lip smooth. Usually unicolorous orange, brown or yellowish, but some specimens are banded with dark brown. *c*2cm. Australian (Australia). Frequent.

Pterynotus elongatus Lightfoot ×2.0
clavus Lamarck.

127

Very elongate shell with tall spire and obscure suture. Aperture small, siphonal canal long. Varices on all whorls have thin, upturned, foliated processes, those on body whorl being expanded to form wing-like extensions. Fine spiral striae usually visible on varices and well seen on the body whorl wings. Processes on spire whorls often worn away. Outer lip denticulate. Aperture sometimes lirate within. Unicolorous white but aperture may sometimes be pinkish. 4–7cm. Indo-Pacific (Pacific), Japonic. Rare.

Pterynotus triformis Reeve
Moderately thick shell with tall spire and long, almost straight, siphonal canal. Three well developed, fin-like varices on each whorl. Posterior canal well developed. Irregular spiral cords and one prominent nodule between each pair of varices. Outer lip sometimes toothed. Brown, yellow or creamy white with brown patches. Aperture white. c6cm. Australian (Australia). Common.

Pterynotus uncinarius Lamarck   × 2.0

Small, thin but strong shell with moderately tall spire, deep suture and broad, short siphonal canal. Thick varices with upturned, claw-like spine on each and numerous smaller spines below. Pale brown with whitish apex and white columella. Nearly always found in a more or less worn condition. 1·5–2·0cm. South African. Common.

Genus CERATOSTOMA Fischer
Medium-sized, thin shells with foliaceous, wing-like varices which are particularly well developed around aperture. Moderately long siphonal canal. Numerous species in cool and warm seas.

Ceratostoma burnetti A. Adams   × 0.6
Shell large for the genus, thick and strong with large body whorl, relatively short spire and short, broad siphonal canal. Strong, large tooth at lower part of outer lip. Strong varices with widely expanded recurved and foliate lamellae. Pale brown with darker brown axial streaks. Under-

side of each lamella pale whitish brown. 6–8cm. Japonic. Uncommon.

Ceratostoma fournieri Crosse   × 1.3

Moderately thin, light shell with small, acute spire, large body whorl and moderately long siphonal canal. Three twisted, axial rows of varices bearing irregularly crooked, wing-like processes. Large tubercle at shoulder between varices. Inner margin of outer lip with teeth, sharp spine at anterior end. Whitish or pale brown with darker brown blotches. Aperture white. 4–5cm. Japonic. Frequent.

Genus MAXWELLIA Baily
Small, solid shells with globose spire, moderately short canal and 6–7 reflected varices. Deep pits behind varices at suture. Few species in American waters.

Maxwellia gemma Sowerby   × 2.3
Moderately tall-spired shell with six varices per whorl. Varices swollen, rounded and smooth connecting with each other in middle area of whorl. Varices thin, elevated, curled back and may be spiny. Deep

pits between curled over ends at tops of varices. White, with dark brown spiral streaks which are most conspicuous at upper part of varices and on thickened outer lip. 2·5–3·0cm. Californian. Common.

Genus PTEROPURPURA Jousseaume
Small, thin shells usually with lamellate varices with scaly surfaces and fluted, but not spiny, edges. Siphonal canal moderately curved. Numerous species in Atlantic and Eastern Pacific.

Pteropurpura macroptera Deshayes   × 1.4

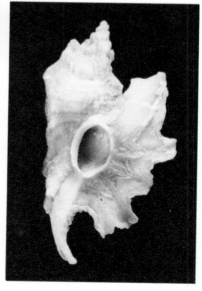

Moderately thick, elongate-fusiform shell with tall spire and long, curved siphonal canal. Suture crossed by three axial varices which have broadly expanded, wing-like extensions. Nodule between varices on spire whorls. Aperture relatively small. Dull, pinkish cream. White aperture. 4–5 cm. Aleutian. Uncommon.

Pteropurpura plorator A. Adams ×0.9

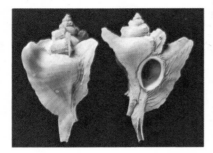

Shell moderately thin, solid, with large body whorl and moderately tall spire and long siphonal canal. Three strong varices with broad, recurved, wing-like lamellae. Whorls humped between varices. Fine, axial growth striae. Pale yellowish brown with light brown spiral bands which extend onto lamellae. Aperture white. 3·5–4·0cm. Japonic. Frequent.

Pteropurpura trialata Sowerby ×1.7

Small, thick shell with three large, wing-like varices on each whorl. Siphonal canal long and almost completely closed. Low, rounded tubercles between varices. Weak spiral threads. Dark or light brown with white spiral bands. 4·5–7·5cm. Californian. Common.

Genus SHASKYUS Burch & Campbell
Small shells resembling *Ceratostoma* but lacking a tooth on outer lip and with three varices which are strongly recurved. One species.

Shaskyus festivus Hinds ×0.8

Small, moderatly thick, elongate-fusiform shell with large body whorl, tall, acuminate spire and moderately long, broad siphonal canal. Each varix has thin, recurved lamellae which are continuous from one whorl to the next. Surface of lamellae scaly and whole shell encircled by spiral ribs. Large, axial nodule between varices. Brownish white with darker brown, fine spiral lines. Aperture white, columella white. 4–5cm. Californian. Common.

Genus COLUMBARIUM von Martens
Thin, spindle-shaped shells with tall spire and very long siphonal canal. Triangular or needle-like spines which may be upturned or projected at right angles to axis. Apex smooth and blunt. Operculum corneous. About twenty species, all from deep water in tropical and warm seas.

Columbarium eastwoodi Kilburn ×1.2

Shell thin, light with tall spire and siphonal canal longer than spire. Each whorl has a median keel with strong tubercles. Columella regularly spirally ribbed. Unicolorous white. Siphonal canal occasionally bent. 4–5cm. South African. Rare.

Columbarium pagoda Lesson ×0.8
diadema Sowerby.
Thin, spindle-shaped shell with tall spire and long siphonal canal. Spines at shoulder

are flattened, triangular in shape and sharply upturned. Base of body whorl has sharp spiral ridge with small scales or spines. Scaly spiral ribs on siphonal canal. Whole shell covered with fine, axial growth lines. Smooth, bulbous apex. Unicolorous dull brown. Aperture paler brown. 5–8cm. Japonic. Common.

Columbarium spinicinctum von Martens
Similar in shape to *C. pagoda* but differently ornamented. Tall spire has rounded whorls which are strongly keeled at periphery, and spines on keels are pointed outwards and not upwards as in *C. pagoda*. Strong spiral cord at base of body whorl. Very long siphonal canal with short spines. Columella smooth. Cream or pale brown. *c*8cm. Australian (Queensland). Uncommon.

Genus MACULOTRITON Dall
Small, elongate-fusiform shells with short siphonal canal and thickened outer lip, denticulate on its inner margin. Axially ribbed and usually ornamented with axial stripes and spiral, whitish bands. Sometimes with spire decollate. Few species in Indo-Pacific.

Maculotriton bracteata Hinds ×2.0

Thick, solid, fusiform shell with tall spire and blunt apex. Suture slightly impressed. Three or four spiral rows of beads on each whorl, beads situated on strong axial ribs. Outer lip thickened with inner margin denticulate. Low, warty pustules on basal portion of columella. Yellowish white with dark brown beads. Aperture white. 1·5–2·0cm. Indo-Pacific. Common.

Maculotriton decapitata Reeve   ×1.6

Thick, elongate-fusiform shell with moderately rounded whorls and slightly impressed suture. Top quarter of spire is always broken off, as indicated by the scientific name. Slight axial ribs crossed by numerous fine spiral lines. Outer lip thickened and denticulate on its inner margin. Columella smooth. Yellowish white with axial, brown or yellowish brown streaks, interrupted on each whorl by thin, spiral, white lines, one line on each spire whorl and two lines on body whorl. *c*1·6cm. Indo-Pacific (Indian Ocean). Frequent.

Genus PHYLLOCOMA Tapparone-Canefri
Elongate-fusiform shells with two broad, frilled varices on each whorl. Varix forms edge of outer lip. Prominent posterior canal. Moderately long, broad, recurved siphonal canal. Inner lip thin, mostly separated from body whorl. One or two species in Indo-Pacific.

Phyllocoma convolutum Broderip   ×1·2

For details, see genus *Phyllocoma*. Shell is unicolorous white. 2·5–3·5cm. Indo-Pacific. Rare.

Genus HOMALOCANTHA Mörch
Small shell with long siphonal canal and short spire. 4–8 varices with long, flattened spines which are expanded and somewhat spade-shaped at ends. Few species, mostly from Pacific waters.

Homalocantha scorpio Linnaeus   ×1.0

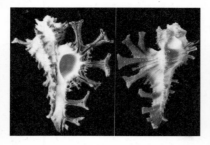

Small, thick shell with moderately tall spire which seems to be out of alignment with rest of shell. Long, moderately broad siphonal canal. Aperture round. Each varix has open, fluted spines, but only on apertural varix are they long and expanded with bifurated ends. Smaller spines between large ones. Creamy yellow with dark or lighter brown, axial markings on varices extending to tips of spines. Aperture whitish. Usually smothered by coral growths. 2·5–6·0cm. Indo-Pacific (Central Pacific). Common.

Homalocantha secunda Lamarck
Thick, rather flattened shell with short spire and broad, flat, moderately long siphonal canal. Six varices on each whorl, the last one broad and having 8–10 flat and broad, scaly fronds which dilate at their ends. Coarse spiral ribs between varices. Distinguished from other species of genus by much less produced spines. Pale brown with dark brown fronds. Aperture white. *c*4·5cm. Indo-Pacific (Pacific). Uncommon.

Homalocantha zamboi Burch & Burch
   ×0.6

Thick, solid shell with short spire, long, broad siphonal canal and small aperture. The long digitations are recurved at their tips. Apart from some small scales and very short spines near aperture, the shell is without finer ornament. Has a very corroded appearance. 5–6cm. Indo-Pacific (Philippines to New Britain). Uncommon.

Genus TROPHON Montfort
Relatively thin shells, small or medium-sized and with well developed, long or short, narrow and open, siphonal canal. Regular varices not present, but usually there are numerous laminar axial ridges. Aperture is smooth within. All species dull coloured or whitish. Many species in all seas, often from deep water.

Trophon geversianus Pallas   ×0.6

Large, thick shell with rounded whorls, deeply impressed suture, deep umbilicus and short, broad, recurved siphonal canal. Whole shell covered with thick, axial lamellae. Strong spiral cords between lamellae. Unicolorous white. 5–8cm. Magellanic. Common.

Genus DRUPA Röding
Canrena Link, *Sistrum* Montfort, *Ricinula* Lamarck, *Pentadactylus* Mörch. Medium-sized, solid shells with short spire, large body whorl and aperture with large teeth on outer lip. Outer lip may be sinuate at edge or digitated with frilled spines, and may or may not be contracted at centre. Siphonal canal always short. Numerous species, mostly in Indo-Pacific.

Drupa clathrata Lamarck   ×1.5

Thick, solid shell with short spire, large body whorl and relatively large aperture. About five rows of spiral ribs on body whorl, which have thick, short and sharp spines at regular intervals. Spines open ventrally. Inner margin of outer lip with large, paired teeth. Three or four folds on columella. Orange brown between spines. Margin of outer lip orange brown, teeth white. Interior of aperture purple. c3cm. Indo-Pacific (Pacific). Uncommon.

Drupa elegans Broderip   ×2.0

Thick, small shell with short spire, large body whorl and long, narrow aperture. Numerous spiral rows of short, pointed spines which become moderately long and open at edge of outer lip. Two blocks of fused teeth on inner margin of outer lip and two isolated teeth basally. Three or four strong folds on columella. White, with a thin, orange band encircling aperture. 2–2·5cm. Indo-Pacific (Central Pacific). Rare.

Drupa grossularia Röding   ×0.8

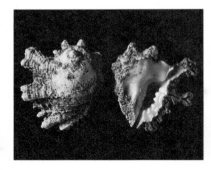

Thick, squat shell with spire almost concealed by body whorl. Outer lip with two long, flat, bifurcating digitations on posterior part, and three shorter, more pointed digitations on anterior half. Rest of shell with irregular, nodulous projections and rough spiral cords. Inner margin of outer lip with five or six teeth. Columella with two or three small teeth. Parietal lip broadly callused. Greyish white. Aperture and columella yellow. 3–5cm. Indo-Pacific. Common.

Drupa iodostoma Lesson   ×0.7

Very thick, globose shell, roughly quadrate in outline. Very large body whorl with flaring aperture. Five very weak spiral ribs. 5–6 teeth on two inwardly directed ridges on inside edge of outer lip. Four small folds on columella. Thick, bulbous callus on parietal wall. Dull, white with spiral, reddish brown stripes. Lilac aperture. 2·5–4·5cm. Indo-Pacific. Frequent.

Drupa lobata Blainville   ×1.4

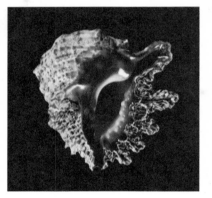

Similar in almost all respects to *D. grossularia*, but aperture whitish inside and stained dark chocolate brown around margin, columella and parietal callus. c3cm. Indo-Pacific. Common.

Drupa morum Röding   ×1.3
neritoidea Gmelin, *horrida* Lamarck, *violacea* Schumacher.

Thick, globose shell with low spire and large body whorl with flat base. Four spiral rows of large, conical nodes on body whorl, but produced as broad, open, flat spines on edge of outer lip. Scaly spiral cords between nodes. Inner margin of outer lip with two fused pairs of denticles and two isolated ones basally. Columella with three or four strong folds. White, with brown or blackish nodes. Aperture dark violet. 3·5–4·5cm. Indo-Pacific (Pacific). Common.

Drupa ricinus Linnaeus   ×1.0
tribulus Röding, *album* Montfort, *arachnoides* Lamarck, *hystrix* Linnaeus.

Thick, ovate shell with depressed spire and obscure suture. Five spiral rows of short, sharp or blunt spines which are longest on apertural edge. Scaly spiral ridges in interstices. Two raised blocks of fused teeth on inner margin of outer lip. 2–4 folds on columella. White, with dark brown or black spines. White aperture may have orange to yellow line around margin. 1·5–3·5cm. Indo-Pacific. Common.

Drupa rubusidaeus Röding   ×0.9
hystrix Linnaeus.

Very thick, globose-ovate shell with short, acuminate spire (which is often eroded). Five rows of short spines on body whorl with fine, scaly, spiral ridges in interstices. 7–12 teeth on outer lip, 3–4 folds on columella. Dull, white or buff. Aperture and columella purple, fading to pink (as in illustrated specimen). 2·5–5·5cm. Indo-Pacific. Frequent.

Drupa speciosa Dunker   ×2.0

Very thick, globose-ovate shell with short spire and simple suture. Nine axial ribs on body whorl crossed by five spiral cords which are developed as short, stout spines where they cross axial ribs. Outer lip crenulate with inner margin denticulate. Columella lip with three folds. One fold on parietal wall. Dull, creamy white shell with pinkish lilac aperture and white teeth. 2–3cm. Indo-Pacific (Polynesia). Uncommon.

Genus MORULA Schumacher
Small, thick shells with elevated spire, usually with nodose axial and spiral ornament, and relatively inconspicuous, apertural teeth. Rarely spinose. Numerous species in warm and tropical seas.

Morula cavernosa Reeve   ×2.0

Thick, ovate-fusiform shell with moderately tall spire and slightly impressed suture. Strong axial ribs crossed by strong spiral ribs. Creamy, with occasional pinkish blotches. Aperture cream or yellow. 1·5–2·2cm. Indo-Pacific. Common.

Morula fragum Blainville   ×2.0
Thick, fusiform, almost biconical, shell with slightly impressed suture. Six or seven spiral rows of nodules which are also

arranged axially. Spiral cords between nodules. 4–6 teeth on inner margin of outer lip; buff or greenish brown colour with reddish brown or orange nodules. Aperture white. 1·5–2·5cm. Indo-Pacific (Indian Ocean). Frequent.

Morula tuberculata Blainville   ×1.4

Thick, ovate shell with moderately tall spire, slightly impressed suture and moderately rounded whorls. Spiral rows of large, squarish nodules which are aligned axially. Spiral grooves between nodules. Four teeth on inner margin of outer lip. Dark olive brown with black nodules. Purplish grey aperture. 2–3cm. Indo-Pacific. Common.

Morula uva Röding   ×2.0
Thick, ovate shell with moderately tall spire and relatively small aperture. Spiral rows of stout, pointed tubercles, about five rows on body whorl and two on spire whorls. Scaly spiral grooves between

tubercles. Inner margin of outer lip with two large teeth near centre and about three smaller teeth above. Three or four folds on columella. White, with black tubercles. Aperture and columella violet. 1·5–2·0cm. Indo-Pacific. Common.

Genus THAIS Röding
Purpura of some authors.
Small to large, solid shells with relatively large aperture, a crenulate or dentate outer lip and broad columella. Spiral ornament usually nodose. Corneous operculum with lateral nucleus. Nearly all species live among rocks or corals in inter-tidal zone. Like other members of the Muricidae they are carnivorous. Many species in tropical and warm seas.

Thais armigera Link
Thick, heavy shell with moderately tall, blunt-topped spire and large, broadly ovate body whorl. Spire usually well worn. Three spiral rows of large, blunt spines, those at shoulder of body whorl being much the strongest. Weak spiral striae. Inner margin of outer lip with small teeth. Three or four weak folds on columella. Whitish with orange brown spiral bands between spines. Aperture white within, becoming yellow near margin of outer lip. Parietal wall and columella brown or orange. 6–8cm. Indo-Pacific (Pacific). Common.

Thais bufo Lamarck
Thick, broadly ovate shell with short spire and large, inflated body whorl. Four spiral rows of low nodules and prominent spiral ridge round base. Columella very thick and smooth. Outer lip denticulate. Dark brown with thin, whitish spiral lines and white blotches between nodules. Margin of outer lip dark brown. Aperture cream. Parietal wall and columella yellowish. 2·5–4·0cm. Indo-Pacific, Japonic. Common.

Thais carinifera Lamarck   ×1.3

Thick, almost biconical shell with simple suture and peristome almost free from body whorl. No umbilicus but large, thick ridge around its area. Each whorl with a strong, coronate spiral ridge. Rest of shell covered with crowded, irregular spiral cords. Cream, with dark brown, quadrangular mottlings. Aperture cream, flesh-coloured deep inside. 1–4cm. Indo-Pacific. Common.

Thais cingulata Linnaeus
Thick, tall-spired shell with deeply impressed suture and slightly curved columella. The few whorls are encircled by thick, flat spiral cords, each having a turned rim above and below, two cords on spire whorls and three on body whorls. Fine spiral ribs crossed by finer axial growth lines between spiral cords. Aperture with grooves corresponding to spiral cords. Greyish with whiter spiral cords and white columella. 2·5–4·0cm. South African. Common.

Thais echinata Blainville   ×1.0

Thick, solid shell with large body whorl, short, pointed spire and slightly impressed suture. Shallow, false umbilicus encircled by thick spiral ridge. Whole shell covered by spiral rows of large, pointed nodules with fine spiral ridges between them. Pale brown or pinkish brown. Aperture white. 3–5cm. Indo-Pacific. Common.

Thais haemastoma Linnaeus
Thick, solid shell with large, inflated body whorl and short, blunt spire. Two spiral rows of tubercles on body whorl and single spiral row on spire whorls. Spiral and axial striae give reticulated ornament. Inner margin of outer lip plicate. Creamy orange or greyish cream. Aperture orange. 3–10 cm. Mediterranean, West African. Common.

Thais hippocastanum Linnaeus   ▷ ×1.1
Thick, solid shell resembling T. echinata but larger and with stouter tubercles. Outer lip strongly crenulated and bearing folds and teeth. Whitish, blotched and streaked with greenish brown. Inner edge of outer lip dark brown, aperture and columella white. 4–5cm. Indo-Pacific. Common.

Thais kiosquiformis Duclos   ×1.2

Thick, solid, ovately fusiform shell with tall spire, deeply impressed suture and large body whorl. Chink-like umbilicus encircled by broad spiral ridge. Spiral row of strong, rounded spines on each whorl at periphery. Another weaker row below. Numerous spiral cords crossed by axial ribs which are lamellose at suture. Margin of outer lip crenulate. Columella almost straight. Chocolate brown with whitish spiral bands on spines and more prominent spiral cords. Aperture white, dark brown at inner margin of outer lip. 5–6cm. Panamic. Common.

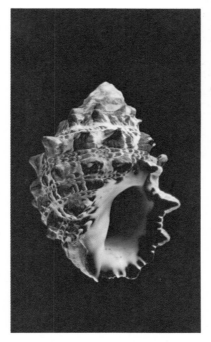

Thais planospira Lamarck   ×0.8

Thick, globose shell, depressed spire and very large aperture. Strong spiral ribs at shoulder, periphery and base of body whorl. Deep excavation by columella corresponding roughly to position of umbilicus. Columella with strong folds. Aperture strongly lirate. Pale yellowish brown with pale brown folds on parietal lip and basal portion of columella. Centre of columella crossed by single blackish rib. 3·5–5·5cm. Panamic. Common.

Thais sacellum Born   ×1.1

Thick solid, almost biconical shell with deeply impressed suture and long, straight columella. Spiral rib at periphery of each whorl with strong, pointed, fluted spines. Body whorl has two more similarly ornamented ribs and numerous scaly spiral ribs cover rest of shell. Outer lip crenulate. Dull white with pink and pinkish grey ridges. Aperture white. 2–4cm. Indo-Pacific. Common.

Thais tuberosa Röding
Thick, solid, squarish shell with large body

133

whorl and short, blunt spire. Three spiral rows of solid tubercles, those at shoulder being conical and larger than the others. Aperture lirate within. Two weak folds on columella. Purple brown with white patches between tubercles. Aperture white or cream with yellow or pale orange lirae. Columella and parietal wall cream with purple or brown blotches. c5cm. Indo-Pacific (Pacific). Common.

Thais undata Lamarck   ×1.4

Thick, solid, ovate shell with large body whorl and short, pointed spire. Thick, low axial ridges crossed by numerous flattened spiral cords with narrow grooves between. Ridges tubercular at shoulders of whorls. Thick ridge round umbilical area. Outer lip crenulate. Aperture lirate within. Columella with one or two indistinct folds. Parietal tooth. Whitish with chocolate brown, irregular axial streaks and blotches. Columella and inner margin of outer lip orange, whitish deep inside aperture. 4–5 cm. Indo-Pacific. Common.

Genus ACANTHINA Fischer
Solid, short or tall-spired shells with an outer lip bearing stout tooth at anterior end. Surface scaly, nodose or smooth, sometimes with strong spiral ribs. Aperture sometimes denticulate within. Numerous species off west coast of North, Central and South America.

Acanthina angelica Oldroyd
Moderately thick, ovate-fusiform shell with whorls angulated at suture. Coarse spiral ribs which are tuberculated at shoulder. Columella smooth and gently curved. Inner margin of outer lip with few small denticles and moderately long tooth towards base. Yellowish, with irregular, axial, brown blotches. Aperture whitish or brownish. c4cm. Panamic. Common.

Acanthina grandis Gray
Large, thick and heavy shell with short

spire, large body whorl and slightly flared aperture. Suture very deep. Thick, coarse spiral ridges which are flattened and reflected towards shell above and below. Deep grooves between. Ridges are very scaly especially towards aperture. Deep grooves within aperture corresponding to position of spiral ridges. Long, curved tooth at base of outer lip. Pale brown, fawn or pinkish brown. Aperture white, columella white or flushed with orange and pink. 7–8cm. Panamic (Galapagos Islands). Uncommon.

Acanthina lugubris Sowerby   ×1.3
cymatum Sowerby, *armatum* Wood, *denticulatum* Wood.

Similar to *A. angelica* but larger, thicker, stouter and with much longer tooth on outer lip. Coarse spiral cords on all whorls, the cord at shoulder being especially well developed. About seven teeth on inside of outer lip. Sometimes another row further into interior. Shell is very often eroded. Pinkish brown with irregular, axial dark brown streaks and blotches. Aperture creamy brown. 2·5–7·0cm. Panamic. Common.

Acanthina muricata Broderip   ×0.8

Thick, solid, broadly ovate shell with short spire. Aperture large with crenulate outer lip. Columella without folds. Whole shell covered with axial lamellae which are most pronounced where they cross the three· or four strong spiral ribs. Yellowish brown. Aperture white flushed pink. c6cm. Panamic. Frequent.

Genus CONCHOLEPAS Lamarck
Large, thick shells with short spire, large body whorl and widely flaring aperture. Smooth, very thick columella. Siphonal canal very narrow. Shell sits on rocks rather like a limpet. One species.

Concholepas peruvianus Lamarck   ×0.7

Thick, patelliform shell with strongly recurved spire, apex near margin. Strong groove from apex to anterior margin; one or two denticles on margin near groove. Spiral lamellae cross strong axial ridges. Dull, pinkish brown. Aperture cream, brown marginally. 2·5–7·0cm. Peruvian. Common.

Genus NUCELLA Röding
Thick, ovate shells with ornament consisting of fine spiral ribs which may be nodose or scaly. Inner margin of outer lip dentate within. Shells vary greatly in shape and ornament. Few species, mostly from cooler waters.

Nucella lamellosa Gmelin   ×1.0
Thick, short or tall-spired shell with impressed suture. Columella vertical and straight. Outer lip thickened, with about

three thick teeth on inner margin. Smoothish or ornamented with strongly or weakly developed, foliated axial ribs. Occasionally spiny. Weak or strong spiral cords. Very variable in colour. Unicolorous white, grey, cream or orange, and sometimes with brown and yellowish spiral bands. The great variability in size, shape, ornament and colour has led to a multiplication of scientific names for this shell. 4–13cm. Aleutian, Californian. Common.

Nucella lapillus Linnaeus
Similar to *N. lamellosa* and equally variable. Shell thick, broadly ovate to elongate ovate, with thickened outer lip. Ornamented with smooth or rough spiral ribs crossed by fine, axial growth lines. Rarely specimens occur with foliaceous axial lamellae. White, yellow, purple brown or intermediate between these colours, often with broad, spiral, brown or orange brown bands. Great variation in size, colour and ornament even within a small area. 4–10cm. Boreal. Common.

Genus PURPURA Bruguière
Haustrum Perry.
Moderately large shells with smooth or nodose surface, large aperture with somewhat flaring outer lip. Large siphonal notch. Few species in tropical seas.

Purpura persicum Lamarck

Large, thick, ovate shell with large body whorl, widely expanded aperture and short, blunt spire. Spiral, widely beaded cords with plain spiral cords between. Inner margin of outer lip plicate, aperture lirate within. Columella almost straight. Chocolate brown with white spaces between beads on beaded cords. Inner margin of outer lip chocolate brown. Aperture whitish with brown lirae. Columella and parietal callus white. 8–10cm. Indo-Pacific. Common.

Purpura rudolphi Lamarck
Very similar to *P. persicum*, but body whorl has four or five spiral rows of moderately large, low tubercies and whole shell encircled by fine grooves. Siphonal canal narrower than that of *P. persicum*. Dark brown with nodules darker brown and large, creamy white blotches between. Aperture and columella white. 4–5cm. Indo-Pacific, Japonic. Common.

Genus VEXILLA Swainson
Resembles *Purpura* but is smaller and has a dentate outer lip. Few species in Indo-Pacific.

Vexilla vexillum Gmelin ×1.5

Shell small, thin, roundly ovate with short, blunt spire. Outer lip with numerous teeth on inner margin. Columella gently curved. Small parietal denticle. Finely spirally striate. Yellowish white, suffused with pinkish brown and with 6–8 broad, reddish brown spiral bands. Aperture white. 2·0–2·5cm. Indo-Pacific. Common.

Genus RAPANA Schumacher
Large, moderately thick to very thick shells with short spire, inflated body whorl and

flaring aperture. Relatively weak ornament and large fasciole. Columella smooth. Edge of outer lip crenulate. Operculum very large with lateral nucleus. Some species are pests of oyster beds. Few species in Indo-Pacific and Japonic provinces.

Rapana bezoar Linnaeus
Thicker and usually larger than *R. rapiformis*. Coarse spiral cords are crossed by axial lamellae which are most strongly developed near base. Light yellowish brown. Aperture and columella white. c5cm. Indo-Pacific (West Pacific), Japonic. Common.

Rapana rapiformis Born ×0.8
Thin, light very globose shell with short, pointed spire. Wide, deep umbilicus with scaly rim surrounding it. Siphonal canal broad, short and recurved. Aperture very wide. Spiral row of thick, fluted scales at whorl shoulders and another two or three weaker rows of scaly nodules on body whorl. Whole shell with coarse spiral riblets crossed by fine, axial growth lines. Yellowish brown with darker brown axial streaks. Aperture and columella creamy brown flushed with white. 6–8cm. Indo-Pacific. Common.

Rapana venosa Valenciennes
thomasiana Crosse.
Usually much larger and thicker than *R. bezoar* and *R. rapiformis*. Spire short, body whorl very large with flaring lip. Three spiral ridges with tubercles on shoulder, periphery and base of body whorl. Fine spiral threads all over shell. Thick, scaly ribs over fasciole. Reddish brown. Aperture and columella red. May lack tubercles and other ornament and

Rapana rupiformis.

may be white externally. 10–12cm. Japonic (and introduced into Black Sea). Common.

Genus FORRERIA Jousseaume

Moderately large, ovate or fusiform shells with axial ridges bearing long, upturned, foliaceous spines at shoulder. Siphonal canal long and broad. Single spiral furrow at base which ends in large, apertural tooth. Chink-like umbilicus. Two or three species off coast of California.

Forreria belcheri Hinds   ×0.8

Rapa rapa.

Solid, broadly ovate shell with large body whorl, short spire and moderately long, broad siphonal canal. Each whorl has about ten prominent, sharp, upturned, fluted spines. Spines are continued downwards as varices on body whorl. Body whorl sharply narrowed at middle. Upper surface of whorls yellowish. Rest of shell has broad, darker brown bands. Aperture yellowish white. 7–15cm. Californian. Common.

Family CORALLIOPHILIDAE

Small family containing some of the world's most exquisite shells. Mostly small to medium-sized shells with strong or fragile shells which are usually globular and frequently spiny. The very dissimilar shells of the few genera belonging to this family all contain animals which lack a radula. Most of the species live on or inside hard and soft corals and sea-fans. The many species are all from tropical and warm seas. About six genera are in general use.

Genus RAPA Bruguière

Thin, globose shells with short spire and pointed apex. Very large body whorl and large aperture. Short, broad siphonal canal and tiny umbilicus. Translucent whitish. Few species living in soft coral.

Rapa incurva Dunker

Smaller than *R. rapa* but with similar ornament. Siphonal canal narrow and short. Body whorl slightly more angled towards base. Yellowish brown. *c*3·5cm. Indo-Pacific (Pacific). Uncommon.

Rapa rapa Linnaeus   ×0.6
Shell encircled by strong spiral ridges crossed by fine axial lines giving the whole shell a roughish appearance. 7–9cm. Indo-Pacific. Common.

Genus LATIAXIS Swainson

Thick or thin shells with short or moderately tall spire. Umbilicus usually present and may be broad and deep. Usually ornamented with spines, lamellae and scales. Confined to the Indo-Pacific province, the shells of this genus are most abundantly represented in Japanese waters. Numerous species mostly in deep water.

Latiaxis deburghiae Reeve   ×1.6

Small, thin, light shell with moderately tall spire, large, inflated body whorl and broad, deep umbilicus with sides flared at base and ornamented with four open, fluted canals. Each whorl has long, broad, upturned and open-sided spines. Between rows of spines are crowded spiral cords which are ornamented with fine fluted scales. Aperture obscurely lirate within. Columella smooth and almost straight. Unicolorous white. *c*3cm. Indo-Pacific (Taiwan), Japonic. Uncommon.

Latiaxis dunkeri Kuroda & Habe   ×1.0

Thick, solid shell with relatively short spire, large body whorl and deep umbilicus. Single row of large, triangular, upturned scales on angulated shoulder of whorls. Rest of shell covered with numerous, slightly scaly spiral ribs. Interior of aperture lirate. Unicolorous white. *c*4cm. Japonic, Indo-Pacific (Taiwan). Rare.

Latiaxis echinatus Azuma   ×1.6
Small, thin, light shell with basic shape obscured by a profusion of thin, long, upturned spines. Small, pointed apex; narrow, deep umbilicus. Shell whitish with

spines yellowish white. 2·0–2·5cm. Japonic. Rare.

Latiaxis gyratus Hinds × 1.5

Shell thick, solid, tall-spired with deeply impressed suture. Large, deep umbilicus. Strong, scaly spiral cord at shoulder of each whorl with finer, scaly spiral ribs above and below. Ridge around umbilicus with long scales. Whitish with aperture flushed pale violet. c4·5cm. Pacific (South West Pacific), Japonic. Frequent.

Latiaxis idoleum Jonas × 0.8
eugeniae Bernardi, *exfoliatus* Sowerby.

Thick, solid shell with tall spire and deeply impressed suture. Large, deep umbilicus. Shell covered with crowded, rough spiral ridges with narrower grooves between. Shell pinkish white becoming whiter towards aperture. Aperture and columella white. 3·5–4·5cm. Indo-Pacific (Taiwan), Japonic. Frequent.

Latiaxis japonicus Dunker × 1.3

Shell thick, solid, tall-spired with long siphonal canal and deep umbilicus. Upper half of whorls ornamented with two rows of triangular, upturned scales; beneath these rows are numerous coarse spiral ridges. Outer lip crenulate. Unicolorous white. c5cm. Japonic. Rare.

Latiaxis kinoshitai Fulton × 1.4
Shell relatively thick, tall-spired with long, recurved siphonal canal and deep umbilicus. Single row of large, broad-based, upcurved spines on each whorl with four or five rows of smaller spines on lower half of body whorl. Dull, white with row of large, indistinct, pinkish blobs on upper

Latiaxis mawae.

part of each whorl. c3·5cm. Japonic, Indo-Pacific (Taiwan). Rare.

Latiaxis lischkeanus Dunker × 1.4

Shell thin, tall-spired, with long, broad siphonal canal. Long, upturned and curving spines radiate from shoulder of whorl. Rest of shell covered with numerous spiral, scaly ribs which are strongest towards base and near to the row of long spines. Unicolorous white. 3·5–4·0cm. Japonic, Indo-Pacific (Taiwan), Australian. Rare.

Latiaxis mawae Griffith & Pidgeon × 1.2

Thick, flat-topped shell with thick, curled-up lamellae around shoulder. Very deep, wide umbilicus. Siphonal canal recurved. Unicolorous yellowish white. 4–6cm. Japonic. Frequent.

Latiaxis pagodus A. Adams   × 1.2

Shell very thin and light with tall, pointed spire. Wide, deep umbilicus. Long, upturned spines on each whorl which are broad at their base. Yellowish white, flushed pink. c3cm. Japonic, Indo-Pacific (Taiwan). Rare.

Latiaxis tosanus Hirase
Resembles *L. kinoshitai* and *L. pagodus* but has longer siphonal canal and spines are less well developed. Coarse spiral ribs with short, fluted spines where they cross the broad axial ridges. Whitish with yellowish ribs and spines. c3·5cm. Japonic. Uncommon.

Genus MAGILUS Montfort
Solid, irregularly formed shells which grow within meandrine corals. Coiled, turbinate shell at early stage; subsequent growth is tube-like and irregular. As mollusc grows, it fills up the early growth stage with solid, shelly matter. No operculum. One species.

Magilus antiquus Montfort   × 1.1
As for genus *Magilus*. Coarse spiral ribs crossed by rough, axial growth ridges.

Magilus antiquus in brain coral.   × 0.6

Strong basal keel on uncoiled portion. 4–12cm. Indo-Pacific. Frequent.

Genus CORALLIOPHILA H. & A. Adams
Small shells with inflated body whorl and large aperture. Surface rough and sometimes scaly, aperture is usually lirate within. Majority of species with deep purple aperture and columella. Considerable variation in shape has led to unnecessary multiplication of species names. Probably less than 100 species. Found in tropical seas in association with corals and sea-fans. Usually incrusted with coral growth.

Coralliophila abbreviata Lamarck   × 1.3

Thick, ovate shell with large, globose or squarish body whorl and large umbilicus. Rounded axial ridges crossed by numerous fine, sharp spiral ribs which are thicker and more scaly towards base. Aperture lirate within. Greyish white, sometimes yellowish orange. Aperture whitish or yellowish. 3·0–4·5cm. Caribbean. Common.

Coralliophila bulbiformis Conrad   × 1.0

Thick, ovate shell with moderately tall spire and impressed, wavy suture. Aperture lirate inside. Small umbilicus present. Broad axial ridges crossed by numerous, fine, scaly spiral ribs. Scales very pronounced and sometimes spiny on outer lip. Yellowish white. Aperture purple. c2·5cm. Indo-Pacific (Pacific), Japonic. Common.

Coralliophila caribaea Abbott
Distinguished from most other species of the genus by its triangular outline. Whorls sharply angled at shoulder. Slit-like umbilicus. Rounded axial ridges are crossed by numerous spiral cords. Rounded nodules at periphery. Aperture purple. 1·5–2·5cm. Caribbean. Common.

Coralliophila costularis Lamarck   × 1.1

Thick, fusiform shell with tall spire and moderately long, straight siphonal canal. Broad axial ribs crossed by numerous, fine, scaly spiral ribs; spiral ribs often worn smooth. White or greyish white. Aperture deep purple. 2·5–6·0cm. Indo-Pacific, Japonic. Common.

Coralliophila neritoidea Lamarck × 2.0
diversiformis Kiener, *violacea* Kiener,
squamulosa Reeve.

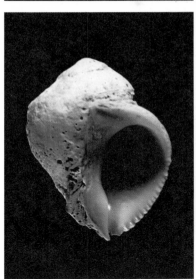

Thick, globose or narrowly ovate shell
with short or moderately tall spire. Aperture lirate within. Siphonal canal narrow
and curved. Covered with numerous fine,
scaly spiral ribs. Smooth columella obscures umbilicus. White. Aperture deep
purple. 2·5–4·0cm. Indo-Pacific, Japonic.
Common.

Coralliophila pyriformis Kira
Similar to *L. neritoidea* but broader at
shoulder and with aperture more elongated
and tapered at base. Short spire. Aperture
lirate inside. Covered by numerous fine
spiral ribs. Greyish white. Aperture purple.
*c*3·5cm. Indo-Pacific (Pacific), Japonic.
Common.

Superfamily
Buccinacea

Family BUCCINIDAE
Ovate, pyriform, globular or elongate
shells, usually thick but some very fragile.
No folds on columella. Variously ornamented or smooth. Includes large and
medium-sized shells. Corneous operculum
with lateral or terminal nucleus. Many
species and dozens of genera. Mostly living
in cooler waters and often at great depths.

Genus NEPTUNEA Röding
Medium-sized to large shells, fusiform,
ventricose. Spire elevated, whorls rounded,
aperture oval. Short siphonal canal.
Smooth or spirally ribbed. Numerous
species in cooler waters.

Neptunea antiqua Linnaeus   × 0.45

Shell thick, fusiform, swollen. Moderately
tall spire, apex pointed. Convex whorls.
Coarse, dense lattice of axial and spiral
striae, some irregular, low axial ribbing.
Short, stout siphonal canal. Unicolorous
whitish. *c*13cm. Boreal. Frequent.

Neptunea decemcostata Say
Brown Corded Neptune
Shell thick, heavy, fairly tall-spired with
pointed apex. Smooth, with strong spiral
cords. Greyish, with reddish brown spiral
cords, brown band below suture. 7–
11cm. Transatlantic. Common.

Neptunea tabulata Baird   × 1·45
Thick, elongate-ovate shell with flat-
topped whorls. Whorls rounded and
edged with a raised spiral ridge. Siphonal
canal broad and recurved. Deep umbilicus.
Coarse, spiral ridges crossed by fine, axial

growth lines. White or yellowish. 10–17cm.
Californian. Rare.

Neptunea ventricosa Gmelin
Fat Neptune
Shell thick, heavy, ventricose. Low, coarse
axial ribs, sometimes faint nodules on
shoulder. Brownish white. Aperture white
or flushed brownish violet. 7–10cm.
Arctic, Aleutian. Frequent.

Genus SIPHONALIA A. Adams
Medium-sized, ovate to ovate-fusiform
shells with large, inflated body whorl and
moderately long, broad and recurved
siphonal canal. Aperture lirate within.
Smooth or spirally ribbed. Ovate, corneous operculum with terminal nucleus.
Numerous species in warm and tropical
seas.

Siphonalia cassidariaeformis Reeve × 1.3

Shell ovate, with moderately tall spire and pointed apex. Axial ribbing fading towards anterior, nodules at shoulder. Shallow axial striae and pronounced spiral grooves. Whitish, with a few wavy, brown streaks. Aperture white. 4–5cm. Japonic. Common.

Siphonalia filosa A. Adams
Thick, fusiform shell with tall spire, moderately rounded whorls and slightly impressed suture. Siphonal canal broad, moderately long and strongly recurved. Numerous strong spiral riblets crossed by fine, axial growth lines. Outer lip thickened. Small callus on outer part of parietal wall. Columella smooth and strongly curved. Creamy yellow with pale brown spiral lines and paler yellowish brown blotches. 3·0–3·5cm. Japonic. Common.

Siphonalia fusoides Reeve
Thick, solid, ovate-fusiform shell with moderately tall spire and pointed apex. Whorls well rounded with occasional low tubercles below shoulder on later whorls. Siphonal canal moderately long, broad and strongly recurved. Numerous strong spiral riblets and occasionally low axial nodules on later whorls. Aperture lirate within. Yellowish white with sparsely scattered, small, brown dots and paler brown blotches. Aperture creamy white. 5–6cm. Japonic. Common.

Siphonalia mikado Melvill
Thick, ovate-fusiform shell with angulate whorls and deep suture. Siphonal canal moderately broad, long and strongly recurved. Small, deep umbilicus. Strong axial ribs at periphery of each whorl crossed by moderately strong spiral cords. Earlier whorls have cancellate appearance. Strong, callused tubercle on parietal wall. Outer lip thickened. Aperture obscurely lirate within. Creamy with irregular, light and dark brown blotches and lines. Aperture and columella whitish. 4–5cm. Japonic. Common.

Siphonalia modificata Reeve
Similar to S. fusoides and S. filosa, but with body whorl more swollen and siphonal canal longer and more strongly recurved. Strong spiral riblets on all whorls and shoulder of later whorls with low axial tubercles. Aperture lirate within. Creamy white, blotched and spotted with pale and darker brown. Aperture creamy white. 4–5cm. Japonic. Frequent.

Siphonalia pfeifferi Sowerby   ×1.1
Shell ovate, extended apex, convex whorls. Axial ribs on early whorls, only spiral threads and grooves on last two. Outer lip lirate. Distinct columella lip. Recurved siphonal canal. Whitish, with small, brown dots on spiral threads. Aperture and colu-

mella lip coffee. c4·5cm. Japonic. Frequent.

Siphonalia signum Reeve   ×0.9

Shell ovate, small spire, apex pointed. Nodules at shoulder, fine axial striae. Siphonal canal recurved. Pale brown to cream, with thin, brown spiral lines and patches. Wide aperture cream. 3·5–4·5cm. Japonic. Common.

Siphonalia trochulus Reeve
Thick, ovate, fusiform shell with moderately tall spire, roundly inflated whorls and impressed suture. Siphonal canal long, moderately broad and strongly recurved. Moderately strong, widely spaced riblets with weaker riblets between. Fine, axial growth lines. Spire whorls have strong axial cords. Outer lip thickened. Aperture lirate within. Thick callus on parietal wall. Beige with larger spiral riblets whitish. Aperture creamy brown. 3–4cm. Japonic. Common.

Siphonalia vanattai Pilsbry
Small, thick, ovate-fusiform shell with large body whorl, moderately tall spire and impressed suture. Siphonal canal broad, moderately long and recurved. Strong axial ribs crossed by numerous

spiral riblets. Axial ribs tuberculated at shoulder of body whorl. Outer lip thickened. Aperture lirate within. Creamy white, blotched, streaked and lined with pale and darker brown. Aperture creamy white. 2–3cm. Japonic. Frequent.

Genus PENION Fischer
Verconella Iredale.
Large, ovate, oblong or pear-shaped shells with moderately long or short siphonal canal. Ornamented with strong, spiral threads. Columella has no folds. Few species in Australian province.

Penion adusta Philippi   ×0.35

Shell thick, fusiform, swollen. Tall spire, apex pointed. Axial ribbing on early whorls. Spiral row of large, raised nodules low on early whorls, central on last. Whitish, with brown spiral cords. Siphonal canal slightly recurved. 9–12cm. Australian (New Zealand).

Penion grandis Gray
Large, ovate-fusiform shell with moderately tall spire and well rounded whorls. Siphonal canal moderately broad. Numerous broad axial ribs which are most pronounced at whorl shoulders. Numerous fine spiral cords over whole shell. Outer lip denticulate. Aperture lirate. Pale brown, with dark brown spiral cords. Aperture and columella white. c13cm. Australian (Australia, Tasmania). Frequent.

Penion mandarina Duclos
Large, thick, fusiform shell with well rounded whorls and moderately impressed suture. Long, broad, slightly recurved siphonal canal. Umbilicus a mere chink. Numerous broad, flattened spiral cords crossed by fine, axial growth lines. Lip corrugated. Greyish white. Aperture and columella whitish. 10–13cm. Australian (New Zealand). Frequent.

Penion maxima Tryon
Large, thick, fusiform shell with tall spire and sharp apex. Siphonal canal open, long and slightly curved. A spiral row of strong tubercles at periphery of each whorl and numerous strong spiral cords. Irregular

axial growth striae. Outer lip denticulate. Aperture lirate within. Columella smooth. Yellowish brown with darker brown spiral band at periphery and two broader, interrupted spiral bands below periphery on body whorl. Aperture white. *c*25cm. Australian (Australia, Tasmania). Frequent.

Penion oligostira Tate
Medium-sized, fusiform shell with gently rounded whorls and tall spire with sharp apex. Siphonal canal short and broad. Early whorls with nodulous ornament, later whorls with numerous spiral cords. Outer lip with fine teeth on inner margin. Aperture lirate. White, pale brown or greyish with dark brown spiral cords. Aperture white. *c*10cm. Australian (South Australia). Frequent.

Genus PHOS Montfort
Turreted, elongate shells with pointed spire. Whorls ornamented with prominent, sharp-pointed ribs. Outer lip lirate within. About 20 species in tropical seas.

Phos articulatus Hinds
turritus A. Adams.
Thin, elongate-fusiform shell with pointed apex, moderately rounded whorls and impressed suture. Strong, rounded axial ribs crossed by much weaker spiral riblets producing small points at intersection. Outer lip sinuous and slightly flared. Aperture lirate within. Yellowish white with pale brown blotching. 2·5–4·5cm. Panamic. Uncommon.

Phos crassus Hinds
clarki M. Smith.
Shell large for the genus, thick, heavy, elongate-fusiform. Whorls moderately rounded and suture moderately impressed. Strong axial ribs crossed by weaker spiral riblets forming weak nodes at intersections. Spiral cords at base of body whorl beaded. Outer lip thickened and denticulate. Aperture lirate within. Columella with strong fold at base. Pale yellowish brown with darker brown mottlings. 4–5cm. Panamic. Frequent.

Phos grateloupianus Petit
ligatus A. Adams.
Somewhat similar in shape and ornament to *P. roseatus,* but less slender with less rounded whorls and thinner axial ribs. Aperture also not so narrow and outer lip not so thick. Aperture more strongly lirate within. Pale brown mid sections of axial and spiral ribs white. Aperture violet in fresh specimens, fading to yellowish brown. 2–3cm. West African. Frequent.

Phos hirasei Sowerby
Moderately thick, stout, ovate-fusiform shell with well rounded whorls and deeply impressed suture. 2–3 low varices on each whorl with numerous less prominent axial ribs between. Fine, regular spiral riblets cross varices and axial ribs. Two strong folds at base of columella. Small pimple on parietal wall. Aperture lirate within. Whitish, with yellowish brown and darker brown blotches and spiral bands. Apex dark brown. Aperture and columella white. 2·5–3·0cm. Japonic. Common.

Phos muriculatus Gould
Superficially like *P. senticosus,* but usually smaller and with much less strongly developed spiral ribs. Whorls less rounded and suture less impressed. Axial ribs strong and more regular than in *P. senticosus.* Aperture lirate within. Creamy white, with dark brown blotches above and below suture and on axial ribs. Apex mostly dark brown. Aperture and columella white. 2·5–3·5cm. Indo-Pacific (Philippines). Uncommon.

Phos roseatus Hinds   × 1.2

Shell thick, fusiform, with tall spire and pointed apex. Slight shoulder. Numerous axial ribs, an occasional varix. Spiral striations. Outer lip finely dentate, lirate. White to brown, sometimes banded. 3–4cm. Indo-Pacific. Uncommon.

Phos senticosus Linnaeus   × 1.6

Shell thick, ovate with tall, pointed spire. Convex whorls. Twelve axial ribs, sharp spiral ridges forming sharp nodules at intersection. Outer lip crenulate, lirate. Whitish or cream, with spiral, violet bands. Violet aperture. 3–4cm. Indo-Pacific. Common.

Phos textum Gmelin
rhodostoma von Martens.
Small, solid, ovate-fusiform shell with large body whorl and moderately tall spire with slightly impressed suture. Numerous strong axial ribs crossed by finer spiral riblets. Strong fasciole at umbilical area. 2–3 folds at base of columella. Small dimple on parietal wall. Axial ribs sometimes strongly shouldered and coronate. Yellowish white. Aperture and columella bright orange (purplish in the form *P. rhodostoma*). *c*2cm. Indo-Pacific (Indian Ocean). Uncommon.

Phos varians Sowerby
Thick, solid, elongate-fusiform shell with large body whorl and moderately tall spire with gently rounded whorls. Prominent fasciole around umbilicus which is a minute chink. Numerous low axial ribs crossed by fine spiral riblets producing sharp points at intersections. Smooth spiral band above fasciole. Two folds on columella. Aperture lirate within. Yellowish white. Orange brown or dark brown blotch at upper part of parietal wall and at base of columella, also deep within aperture. 1.5–2·0cm. Indo-Pacific (Pacific). Uncommon.

Phos virgatus Hinds
Moderately thick, elongate-fusiform shell with tall spire and slightly impressed suture. Strong axial ribs and one or two varices on each whorl. Deep spiral grooves on whorls bisect axial ribs and give them a beaded appearance. Two folds on columella. Outer lip thickened. Aperture lirate within. Early whorls whitish, later whorls yellowish with spiral grooves light and dark brown. Aperture and columella white. 3·5–4·0cm. Indo-Pacific (Sri Lanka). Rare.

Genus ENGINA Gray
Resembles *Cantharus* but usually smaller, aperture relatively narrower, siphonal canal shorter, columella callused and denticulate along its entire length. Also an angular projection towards base of columella. Numerous species in warm seas.

Engina alveolata Kiener   × 2.0
lauta Reeve.
Shell thick, fusiform, swollen. Conical spire, apex pointed. Beading of axial ribs cut by spiral channels. Alternating spiral rows of dark brown and orange, colour being restricted to the axial ribs, the inter-

stices of the ribs being white. Outer lip dentate. Concavity in columella. c1·5cm. Indo-Pacific. Uncommon.

Engina bonasia von Martens
In shape, this species is very similar to *E. phasinola* and *E. alveolata* but ornament and colour pattern differ from both. The axial ribs are crossed by strong spiral cords ornamented with stout, pointed tubercles which have the effect of breaking up the ribs so that they are not easily seen. Two or three strong folds on columella which is deeply incurved above. Outer lip thickened and denticulate. Purplish brown with white tubercles. Aperture yellowish white. 1·2–1·6cm. Indo-Pacific (Indian Ocean). Uncommon.

Engina elegans Dunker   ×1.7

Shell fusiform, swollen. Conical spire, apex pointed. Broad axial ribs bearing nodules. Thick outer lip, dentate. Two folds on columella. Cream, with pale brown, spiral lines, or white, with brown bands. 2·0–3·5cm. Indo-Pacific. Uncommon.

Engina incarnata Deshayes
astricta Reeve,
paulucciae Tapparone-Canefri.
Small, almost biconical shell with rounded shoulder to body whorl and almost straight-sided spire whorls. Suture impressed. Low axial ribs crossed by distinct fine spiral cords which are closer together at shoulder than elsewhere. Aperture narrow. Outer lip with small teeth. Colu-

mella finely denticulate. Off-white or creamy yellow with dark reddish brown spiral cords. Columella white. 1·5–2·0cm. Indo-Pacific.

Engina lineata Reeve
Very similar to *E. zonalis* but smaller and with different colour and pattern. Narrow, spiral, blackish bands are not interrupted. Between bands there are often large, roundish or comma-shaped, blackish spots. Aperture white and not purplish brown as in *E. zonalis*. c1cm. Indo-Pacific (Pacific). Frequent.

Engina mendicaria Linnaeus   ×2.0

Shell very thick, ovate. Conical spire, apex pointed. Weak axial ribbing, slightly nodulose shoulder, callus on parietal region. Thickened outer lip with large teeth. Small notch in columella. Black and yellow spiral bands on body whorl. Spire whorls white. 1·2–1·5cm. Indo-Pacific. Common.

Engina phasinola Duclos
zatricium Melvill.
Small, thick, squat, biconical shell with spire approximately as tall as body whorl. Suture moderately impressed. Numerous spiral rows of squarish, smooth beads on all whorls which are also arranged in axial rows. Aperture very narrow. Deeply incurved columella which has two folds at lower end. Outer lip thickened and denticulate. Blackish brown with beads standing out white. Aperture white. Broader outline and absence of spiral colour bands distinguish this species from *E. zonalis*. 1·0–1·5cm. Indo-Pacific (Pacific). Uncommon.

Engina turbinella Kiener
zonata Gray.
Small, thick, biconic shell with sharply angled shoulder on body whorl and nearly straight-sided spire. Short axial ribs at shoulders bearing two or three prominent, thin tubercles. Several spiral rows of tubercles below shoulder on body whorl. Outer lip thickened and toothed on inner margin. Columella pustulose. Dark brown, with white spots and spiral

bands on axial ribs. Aperture brownish, teeth on inner margin of outer lip white. c1·5cm. Caribbean. Common.

Engina zea Melvill
Very similar to some forms of *E. alveolata* and may be conspecific. Small, thick, biconical shell with slightly rounded whorls and angulate periphery on body whorl. Strong axial ribs have beaded ornament. Broad and narrow spiral cords between axial ribs. Outer lip thickened and strongly denticulate on inner margin. Columella with few irregular folds. Yellowish white, blotched and spotted with dark brown, orange and white markings. Unlike *E. alveolata*, the aperture of the species is white and does not have a coloured margin. 1·2–1·7cm. Indo-Pacific (Indian Ocean). Uncommon.

Engina zonalis Lamarck   ×2.0
zonata Reeve.

Shell thick, fusiform, swollen. Suture slightly impressed. Beading of axial ribs and spiral striae. Thick outer lip, dentate. White, with dark brown spiral bands. Aperture and columella brown. c1cm. Indo-Pacific (Pacific). Frequent.

Genus NORTHIA Gray
Tall-spired, smooth shells. Short, broad siphonal canal. Incurved columella, serrated outer lip. One or two species.

Northia northiae Gray   ×0.9

Shell thick or thin, fusiform, with turret-like spire and pointed apex. Convex whorls shouldered. Smooth, axial ribbing on early whorls. Dentate and thickened outer lip, lirate. Slightly glossy. Pale or dark brown. 6–8cm. Panamic. Common.

Genus SEARLESIA Harmer
Shells small to moderate in size. Columella curved, siphonal canal short and twisted slightly to left. Coarse axial ribs and fine spiral striae and threads. One species.

Searlesia dira Reeve   ×1.4

Shell fusiform, tall spire, apex pointed, whorls convex. Axial ribbing on spire whorls often fading or absent on last whorl. Numerous coarse spiral threads. Short, slightly recurved siphonal canal. Outer lip crenate, lirate. Brownish. Columella coffee. 1·5–3·5cm. Californian, Aleutian. Common.

Genus BABYLONIA Schlüter
Eburna Lamarck, *Latrunculus* Gray.
Shells small to medium-sized. Thick, ovate, deeply umbilicated. Spire pointed, whorls convex, suture channelled, columella curved. Inner lip spreading and often covering umbilicus. Ten species living in tropical seas.

Babylonia areolata Link   ×0.8
Shell relatively thin, ovate, light. Spire tall, apex pointed, whorls rounded. Suture channelled. Edge rounded at shoulder. Wide umbilicus. Thin inner lip. Spiral bands of rectangular or irregular, brown

patches on white. 4–7cm. Indo-Pacific (South East Asia). Common.

Babylonia ambulacrum Sowerby
Similar to *B. pallida* and *B. spirata* but differs from both by having a narrower sutural groove. Its colour pattern, though similar, is also less pronounced. The wide umbilicus has a pronounced fasciole around it which is not knobbed on its interior edge. Covered by a thin, yellowish green periostracum. 4·0–7·5cm. Indo-Pacific (Indian Ocean and West Pacific). Uncommon.

Babylonia japonica Reeve
Shell ovate, short spire, apex pointed. Smooth, slightly glossy. Whitish, with spiral bands of crescent-shaped, brown patches alternating with bands of brown spots. Covered with thick, dark brown periostracum. 6·0–7·5cm. Japonic. Common.

Babylonia pallida Perry   ×1.4
borneensis Sowerby.

Shell relatively thin, ovate, squat. Spire moderately tall, apex pointed. Channelled suture. Shoulder with prominent edge, not sharp. Wide umbilicus. White, with irregular, brown spots. 2·0–4·5cm. Indo-Pacific (South East Asia, Indonesia). Common.

Babylonia spirata Linnaeus   ×1.0

Shell ovate, heavy. Spire moderately raised, apex pointed. Suture widely and deeply channelled. Faint, diagonal striae. White, with irregular, orange brown spots generally larger below suture. Umbilicus bounded by a thick ridge. 3·5–4·5cm. Indo-Pacific. Common.

Babylonia valentiana Swainson   ×1.1

Shell ovate, squat. Spire short, apex raised. Body whorl very large. Channelled suture. Blunt edge at shoulder. Shallow depression at umbilicus. White, with orange brown to coffee spots, patches or streaks. 4–8cm. Indo-Pacific (Indian Ocean). Common.

Babylonia zeylandica Bruguière   × 1.0

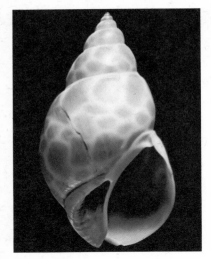

Shell relatively thin, light, ovate. Tall spire, apex pointed. Whorls convex. Slight shoulder. Wide umbilicus surrounded by denticles and thick ridge. White, with orange brown spots generally larger below suture. Apex bluish, flush of violet near umbilicus. 4·5–6·5cm. Indo-Pacific. Common.

Genus EUTHRIA Gray
Resembles *Pisania* but has a recurved siphonal canal. Thick, fusiform shells with simple inner lip. Outer lip with a posterior sinus. Few species in warm seas.

Euthria cornea Linnaeus   × 1.0

Shell thick, fusiform to ovate. High spire, apex pointed. Convex whorls, rounded shoulder, overlapping suture. Axial ribs on early whorls, fine axial striae. Small posterior sinus. Recurved siphonal canal. Creamy, with brown mottling and spots. Elliptical aperture white, denticulate. 4·5–5·5cm. Mediterranean. Common.

Euthria ponsonbyi Sowerby
Similar in several respects to *E. queketti*, but ornament on spire whorls and other features distinguish it from that species. Thick, ovate-fusiform shell with concave-sided whorls, spiral row of sharp nodules at shoulder of body whorl, and blunter nodules above suture on spire whorls. Fine spiral lines on early whorls. Fine, axial growth lines cover whole shell. Siphonal canal moderately short and recurved. Aperture lirate within. Thick, parietal callus. Smaller and more pointed apex than in *E. queketti*. Dull, yellowish white. Aperture and columella creamy white. 3·0–4·5cm. South African. Rare.

Euthria queketti Smith
Medium-sized, thick shell with tall spire and very long, narrow, recurved siphonal canal. Spiral row of large, rounded nodules at shoulder of body whorl and at periphery of spire whorls. Fine, axial growth lines over whole shell. Tooth-like parietal callus. Angular ridge at base of columella. Creamy white, blotched with brown, with paler nodules. Aperture and columella white. *c*5cm. South African. Frequent.

Genus BUCCINULUM Deshayes
Small to medium-sized shells with slender, moderately produced siphonal canal. Outer lip plain or ornamented with teeth or serrations. Parietal wall has single denticle. Columella denticulate or smooth. Few species in warm or cool seas.

Buccinulum heteromorphum Powell
Similar in shape to *B. littorinoides*, but with different colour and pattern. Spire whorls have moderately elevated axial ribs but body whorl is smooth. Inner margin of outer lip lirate. Columella smooth. Yellowish, with underlying purplish hue showing through. Aperture yellowish white, purplish brown deep inside. Colour varies considerably in intensity. *c*2cm. Australian (New Zealand). Common.

Buccinulum lineum Martyn   ▷ × 1.8
Shell fusiform, swollen. Conical spire, apex pointed, convex whorls. Fine, axial striations. Short siphonal canal slightly recurved. Whitish or cream, with brown spiral lines. Faint gloss. Aperture white. 2–4cm. Australian (New Zealand). Common.

Buccinulum littorinoides Reeve
Similar in shape and general appearance to *B. lineum*, but smaller, shorter-spired and with thickened outer lip which is lirate within. Shell is also more slender. Greenish yellow with fine, brown spiral lines which are more numerous and closer together than in *B. lineum*. Aperture and columella white. 2–3cm. Australian (New Zealand). Common.

Genus COMINELLA Gray
Thick, ovate shells with shallow suture, the last whorl being pinched in below suture to form small groove posteriorly. Outer lip thin. Usually ornamented with spiral ribs. Few species, mostly in Australian waters.

Cominella adspersa Bruguière   × 1.2

Thick, solid shell with large body whorl and short, acuminate spire. Outer lip strongly curved. Broad, short siphonal canal. Thick parietal callus. Chink-like umbilicus surrounded with large fasciole. Early whorls with broad axial ribs becoming obsolete towards body whorl. Indistinct spiral cords. Creamy yellow with spiral rows of dark brown dots and some axial, brown streaks. Aperture orange. 5–6cm. Australian (New Zealand). Common.

Cominella iredalei Finlay
Thick, broadly ovate shell with moderately tall spire and inflated body whorl. Coarse axial ribs crossed by fine spiral lines. Below suture are two spiral rows of nodules on axial ribs. Columella smooth. Inner margin of outer lip lirate. Unicolorous yellowish white. 4·5–5·5cm. Australian (New Zealand, Chatham Islands). Common.

Cominella maculosa Martyn
Similar in several respects to *C. adspersa*, but thinner, lighter and relatively taller. Body whorl well rounded, spire whorls gently rounded, suture shallow. Except for thin axial ribbing on early whorls, shell lacks ornament. Colour and pattern similar to *C. adspersa*. Very variable in density of dark brown coloration. Aperture purplish brown. 4·5–5·5cm. Australian (New Zealand). Common.

Cominella nassoides Reeve
Medium-sized, thick, ovate-fusiform shell with moderately tall spire. Weak axial ribs crossed by spiral cords which are nodulous on spire whorls at upper portion of body whorl and smooth on lower part of body whorl. Outer lip thickened, indistinctly lirate within. Columella smooth. Unicolorous yellowish orange. 4–5cm. Australian (New Zealand). Common.

Cominella virgata H. & A. Adams
Thick, solid, ovate-fusiform shell with gently rounded whorls and simple suture. Early whorls with coarse axial ribs, later whorls smooth except for fine, axial growth lines. Broad fasciole round umbilical region. Aperture yellowish white with thin, spiral, blackish lines and axial streaks of same colour. Inner margin of outer lip and columella orange, lirae white with brown interstices. *c*3·5cm. Australian (New Zealand). Common.

Genus PISANIA Bivona
Small to medium-sized shells. Fusiformly ovate to elongate. Smooth or ornamented with spiral threads, cords, axial striae or granules. Outer lip thickened. Parietal wall with or without denticle. Lower part of columella sometimes with angular projection. Corneous operculum. About 30 species in tropical and warm seas.

Pisania crocata Reeve
◁ × 2.0
Shell fusiform, tall spire, apex pointed, slightly convex whorls. Axial ribs spiral crossed by fine riblets, raised nodules at periphery of whorls. Outer lip lirate. Whitish, with orange brown blotches. Aperture white. May be a form of *P. gracilis*. 2–3cm. Indo-Pacific. Common.

Pisania decollata Sowerby
strigata Pease.
Medium-sized, elongate-fusiform shell which looks as though it has lost its earlier whorls but these are merely compressed and immersed in third and fourth spire whorls. Moderately rounded whorls with impressed suture. Strong, flattened spiral cords which are granulose in fresh specimens. Outer lip thickened. Two or three denticles on columella. One fold on parietal wall. Spiral cords reddish orange; interstices are blackish brown. White spots and blotches scattered over whorls. Apical whorls in worn specimens bright purple. Aperture and columella whitish. 2·5–3·0cm. Indo-Pacific (Central Pacific). Uncommon.

Pisania fasciculata Reeve
Small, elongate-fusiform shell with gently sloping whorls and pointed apex. Aperture slightly impressed. Fine, smooth spiral cords with finer spiral striae between them. Crossed by fine, axial growth lines. Outer lip thickened and inner margin lirate. Columella with strong fold towards base. One fold on parietal wall. Creamy yellow or white with reddish brown spiral cords and paler brown blotches; dotted with white spots. Aperture yellowish brown. *c*2·5cm. Indo-Pacific (Pacific). Frequent.

Pisania gracilis Reeve   × 2.0
billeheusti Petit.
Shell fusiform, tall spire, apex pointed. Numerous axial ribs beaded with small granulose nodules. Outer lip lirate. Whitish, mottled pale brown, spire sometimes flushed violet. Aperture white. 1·7–3·2cm. Indo-Pacific. Common.

Pisania ignea Gmelin   × 1.4
Shell fusiform, tall spire, slightly convex whorls. Fine axial striae, spiral threads round broad anterior canal. Outer lip dentate. Coffee, with dark brown patches and axial streaks. Aperture whitish. 3–4cm. Indo-Pacific. Common.

Above: *Pisania gracilis*.
Below: *Pisania ignea*.

Pisania maculosa Lamarck   × 1.3

Shell thick, fusiform. Conical spire, apex pointed. Slightly convex whorls. Fine spiral striae. Outer lip crenate, lirate. 2–3 small columellar folds. Denticle at posterior notch. Olive, with variegated, brown streaks and brown and white flecks. Aperture brownish orange, with white band. 2–3cm. Mediterranean. Common.

Pisania pusio Linnaeus   × 0.9
Miniature Triton Trumpet
Shell thick, fusiform. Smooth. Outer lip finely dentate. Prominent parietal tooth. Glossy, violet to brown, with spiral bands

145

of irregular, dark and pale spots. 3·5–5·5cm. Caribbean. Frequent.

Pisania townsendi Melvill
Small, elongate-fusiform shell with large body whorl and tall spire. Whorls angulated at periphery and suture well impressed. Strong axial cords crossed by numerous fine spiral riblets. Outer lip thickened. Aperture lirate within. Columella with one or two indistinct folds. Siphonal canal moderately long and broad. Yellowish, with occasional dark and light brown blotches. Aperture and columella white. c2cm. Indo-Pacific (Indian Ocean). Rare.

Pisania tritonoides Reeve ×1.4

Shell fusiform, swollen. Conical spire, apex pointed. Convex whorls. Very faint axial and spiral ornament; anterior spiral threads. Outer lip crenate, lirate. Variegated brown and white; irregular, whitish spiral band. Aperture whitish. c2·7cm. Indo-Pacific. Frequent.

Genus METULA H. & A. Adams
Small to medium-sized, elongate, oval shells which are usually very thin and have a finely cancellate ornament and smooth aperture and columella. Usually not colourful. Few species in tropical seas, often from deep water.

Metula amosi Vanatta ×1.8
Shell thin, light, cylindrically ovate with

large body whorl and tall spire. Outer lip thickened; columella almost straight. Short, broad siphonal canal. Whorls cancellated with numerous axial and spiral ribs. Early whorls smooth. Yellowish white with three orange brown spiral bands on body whorl. Aperture yellowish white flushed with pink and with darker band just inside outer lip. c4cm. Panamic. Rare.

Genus OPEATOSTOMA Berry
Short-spired, with large and shouldered body whorl. Long tooth on outer lip near siphonal canal. One species.

Opeatostoma pseudodon Burrow ×1.1
Shell thick, ovate. Conical spire, apex often worn. Angular shoulder. Suture callused. Long, white, curved tusk at

anterior. 3–5 folds on columella. Outer lip crenate. Whitish or pale brown, with dark brown spiral bands. Wide aperture white. 2·5–6·5cm. Panamic. Common.

Genus CANTHARUS Röding
Small to medium-sized, solid shells, often biconical, usually with rounded whorls and with strong axial and spiral ornament. Several species have bold colouring around margin of aperture and columella. Numerous species in tropical and warm seas and particularly well represented in the Panamic province.

Cantharus auritulus Link
Gaudy Cantharus
Shell thick, ovate with shouldered whorls. Axial ribs, spiral threads on last whorl. Yellow, brown or bluish grey, sometimes mottled white. Outer lip incurved. 1·5–3·0cm. Caribbean. Common.

Cantharus bicolor Cantraine ×2.0

Shell small, fusiform, apex pointed, convex whorls. Raised axial ribs, spiral ridges. Outer lip lirate. Brownish, with whitish spiral band. c1cm. Mediterranean. Common.

Cantharus cancellarius Conrad
Cancellate Cantharus
Shell rhombic. Tall, conical spire. Narrow axial ribs, sharp spiral threads forming cancellate beading. Yellowish brown to bluish grey. Resembles *C. tinctus*. 1·5–3·0cm. Caribbean. Frequent.

Cantharus coromandelicus Lamarck ×1.6
Small, thick, ovate shell with moderately tall, straight-sided spire and short, broad siphonal canal. Strong axial ribs crossed by weaker spiral ribs which are produced

as blunt nodules at intersections. Outer lip thickened and corrugated. Aperture lirate within. Numerous irregular folds on columella, strong fold on parietal wall. Dark or light brown, mottled and banded with white. Aperture and columella white. 2–3cm. Caribbean. Frequent.

Cantharus distortus Wood   × 0.8

Shell thick, ovate. Small, conical spire, apex pointed. Thickly callused and elevated shoulder on last whorl. Axial ribs on spire only. Thin spiral channels. Outer lip plicate. Whitish, with brown axial streaks. Aperture white. Thick, brown periostracum. c4cm. Panamic. Common.

Cantharus dorbignyi Payreaudeau   × 1.4

Small, thick, ovate-fusiform, almost biconic shell with large body whorl, moderately tall spire and slightly impressed suture. Strong axial ribs crossed by numerous strong spiral cords producing a tuberculated shoulder. Two or three folds on columella. A fold on each side of posterior canal. Outer lip thickened and denticulate on inner margin. Dark brown, with median spiral white band on body whorl and thinner band at suture on spire whorls. Aperture and columella yellowish. 1·5–2·0cm. Mediterranean. Common.

Cantharus elegans Griffith & Pidgeon × 1.3
insignis Reeve, *aequilirata* Carpenter.
Medium-sized, thick, ovate-fusiform, almost biconic shell with moderately rounded whorls and pointed apex. Siphonal canal moderately long and broad. Strong, sharp spiral ridges on all whorls. Some specimens have spiral ridges nodulous. Fine, axial growth lines between spiral ridges. Columella and parietal wall

with long folds. Aperture lirate within. Dark brown variegated with whitish blotches. Aperture and columella white or yellowish white. 4–5cm. Panamic, Peruvian. Frequent.

Cantharus erythrostomus Reeve   × 1.9

Shell ovate with moderately tall spire, pointed apex and convex whorls. Axial ribs and numerous spiral threads. Outer lip plicate. Whitish, with broken brown bands on axial ribs. Aperture white, margin orange. 3–4cm. Indo-Pacific. Uncommon.

Cantharus exaratus Dunker   × 2.0
Shell fusiform, slightly swollen. Convex whorls. Axial ribs and numerous spiral

ridges. Small posterior notch. Outer lip lirate. Pale brown, with indistinct, white spiral band. c1·5cm. West African. Frequent.

Cantharus fumosus Dillwyn   × 1.6
proteus Reeve.

Shell thick, fusiform, with convex whorls. Axial ribs and numerous strong spiral ridges. Outer lip crenate, lirate. Posterior notch with denticle either side. Yellowish white, brown on ribs. Aperture white, margin yellow or orange. Closely related to *C. undosus*. 2·5–3·2cm. Indo-Pacific. Common.

Cantharus fusiformis Blainville   × 1.1
Shell fusiform, last whorl swollen, flattened above, sharply shouldered. Axial ribs on early whorls. low nodules at shoulder, raised spiral ridges. Outer lip plicate. Whitish. Aperture white. Dark,

147

thick periostracum. *c*5·5cm. Panamic. Frequent.

Cantharus melanostomus Sowerby × 1.2

Shell thick, swollen, fusiform. Apex pointed. Convex whorls with strong shoulder. Coarse axial ribbing, pronounced spiral cords. Outer lip dentate, lirate. Brownish yellow. Aperture white, margin brownish. Dark brown gloss on parietal wall and columella. 5–7cm. Indo-Pacific. Uncommon.

Cantharus picta Scacchi × 2.0

Shell fusiform, apex pointed. Convex whorls. Low axial ribs and spiral threads. Outer lip lirate. White, with cluster of brown, spiral dashes on ribs. *c*1cm. Mediterranean. Common.

Cantharus rubiginosus Reeve × 1.1

Shell fusiform, swollen. Conical spire, apex pointed. Convex whorls. Wavy axial ribs crossed by raised spiral threads, and striae. Thick outer lip crenate, lirate. Whitish, with brown axial bands and often a whitish spiral streak. Aperture whitish, sometimes orange at margin. Closely related to, if not a form of, *C. fumosus*. 2–3cm. Indo-Pacific. Common.

Cantharus sowerbyana Melvill
Medium-sized, thick, broadly ovate shell with moderately tall spire and deeply impressed suture. Siphonal canal moderately long and broad. Columella sharply incurved towards base. Strong axial ribs on all whorls crossed by fine spiral lines. Aperture lirate within. White with broad, pale brown spiral band below suture and fine, brown spiral lines near base of body whorl. Aperture and columella white. Thick, greenish brown periostracum. 2·5–3·0cm. Indo-Pacific (Persian Gulf). Uncommon.

Cantharus spiralis Gray × 1.4
Shell thick, ovate. Moderately tall spire,

apex pointed. Prominent shoulder on whorls. Raised spiral ridges, weak axial ribbing. Outer lip crenulate. Brownish yellow. Aperture white. *c*4cm. Indo-Pacific. Frequent.

Cantharus tinctus Conrad × 1.2
Tinted Cantharus

Shell thick, rhombic. Conical spire, convex whorls. Low axial ribs, spiral striae, indistinct beading. Outer lip dentate. Yellowish brown to bluish grey, often mottled white. 2–3cm. Caribbean. Common.

Cantharus tranquebaricus Gmelin × 0.6

Shell ovate, short spire, apex pointed. Shouldered whorls, low axial ribs, numerous spiral threads. Outer lip plicate, lirate. White to yellowish. Aperture white. 3·3–4·0cm. Indo-Pacific. Uncommon.

Cantharus undosus Linnaeus × 0.9
affine Gmelin.
Shell very thick, swollen, fusiform. Tall, conical spire, apex pointed, slightly convex whorls. Sometimes broad, low axial ribs. Numerous brown spiral cords on whitish ground. Very thick outer lip dentate, lirate. Small posterior notch. Columella sometimes with ridge. Aperture white,

margin yellow. 2·0–4·2cm. Indo-Pacific. Common.

Genus BURNUPENA Iredale

Similar to *Cominella* but differs anatomically. Few species, all South African.

Burnupena cincta Röding × 1.5

Shell fusiform to ovate. Spire variable, usually tall. Coarse spiral ridges. Pale brown, with darker flecks. Curved columella and parietal gloss white. Elliptical aperture white. Brown periostracum. 3·0–4·5cm. South African. Common.

Burnupena delalandii Kiener

Thin, ovate-fusiform shell with rounded whorls and simple suture. Fine spiral striae crossed by fine, axial growth lines. Aperture lirate within. Dark brown or grey, often with darker brown axial streaks. Aperture pale brown. Columella whitish. 3–4cm. South African. Common.

Burnupena lagenaria Lamarck × 1.5

Shell ovate. Short, conical spire, apex worn. Spiral ridge at suture and concave slope to shoulder. White, with broken, irregular, axial, brown lines. Wide aperture. Columella white. 2·0–3·5cm. South African. Common.

Burnupena limbosa Lamarck × 1.2

Shell very thick, ovate. Spire stout, short, apex often worn. Convex whorls. Axial striae. Slightly flared outer lip, lirate. Dull, with enamelled inner lip. Brown, with paler spiral lines. Dark periostracum. 4·0–5·5cm. South African. Common.

Genus BUCCINUM Linnaeus

Medium-sized to large shells. Rounded to elongate-ovate, with elevated spire and pointed apex. Aperture large. Wide siphonal canal. Columella smooth, curved and truncate. Outer lip thin, without internal ornament. Shells of males generally smaller and less inflated than those of females. Numerous species chiefly in cool or very cold waters and often at considerable depth.

Buccinum humphreysianum Bennett

Medium-sized, thin, ovate-fusiform shell with moderately rounded whorls and slightly impressed suture. Apex blunt, siphonal canal broad and short. Columella moderately long and straight. Very fine spiral striae over all whorls. Yellowish white, irregularly blotched and streaked with pale brown. Parietal wall, columella and aperture white. 4–6cm. Boreal (North West Europe), Mediterranean. Uncommon.

Buccinum plectrum Stimpson

Similar to *B. undatum*. Thin, ovate shell with well rounded whorls, impressed suture and sinuous outer lip. Numerous strong, oblique axial ribs which become obsolete from periphery of body whorl downwards. Fine, coarse spiral lines on all whorls crossing axial ribs. Greyish white often covered with darker deposit. Aperture, columella and parietal wall, white. 5–7cm. Arctic. Common.

Buccinum striatissimum Sowerby

Large, moderately thick shell with inflated whorls, deep suture and tall spire. Broad, short siphonal canal. Outer lip thickened and sinuous. All whorls covered with numerous fine spiral striae which are crossed by irregular, fine, axial growth lines. Thick, smooth parietal callus. Yellowish white with a thick, greyish periostracum. Aperture creamy white but yellowish around margin of outer lip and parietal callus. 10–12cm. Japonic. Common.

Buccinum tenue Gray

Small, moderately thick shell with rounded whorls, impressed suture and broad, short, slightly recurved siphonal canal. Strong, irregular axial folds crossed by microscopically fine spiral striae. Columella and parietal wall smooth. Pale brown. Aperture, columella and parietal wall yellowish white. Resembles some forms of *B. undatum* but spiral striae are distinctive. 4–6cm. Arctic, Aleutian, Boreal. Common.

Buccinum totteni Stimpson

Moderately thick, ovate shell with tall spire and small, blunt apex. Whorls well rounded, suture deep. Broad, short, slightly recurved siphonal canal. Columella straight. Numerous coarse, axial folds crossed by finer spiral riblets and striae. Whitish with yellowish brown periostracum. 5–6cm. Arctic, Boreal. Uncommon.

Buccinum undatum Linnaeus × 0.9
Common Northern Whelk

Shell ovate; tall, pointed spire; convex whorls. Low axial ribs sometimes take form of irregular folds. Axial and spiral striae. Outer lip slightly flared. Short anterior canal. Whitish, chalky grey or yellowish. Parietal region enamelled white. Grey periostracum. 5–10cm. Boreal. Common.

Family PYRENIDAE

Shells small and thick, mostly spindle-shaped. Short spire, narrow aperture with denticulate and often incurved outer lip. Operculum corneous, minute. Widely distributed in warm seas. About 10 genera of which five are generally used. Many species, usually in sandy places.

Genus COLUMBELLA Lamarck
For details see Family Pyrenidae. Thick, spirally ribbed and shorter spired than *Pyrene*.

Columbella mercatoria Linnaeus   × 1.6
Common Dove Shell

Shell ovate, small, with conical spire. Shouldered body whorl. Numerous spiral cords. Thickened outer lip dentate, with central callus. Columella with two folds, row of denticles and semicircular concavity. Whitish or olive, sometimes with brown and yellow spots and patches, or white, with brown axial streaks. 1·0–1·8cm. Caribbean. Common.

Genus PYRENE Röding
For details see Family Pyrenidae. Relatively tall-spired and smooth, or apparently smooth.

Pyrene alizonae Melvill & Standen
Thick, solid, ovate-fusiform shell with acuminate spire. Smooth and shiny. Very variable in colour and pattern. Brown or chestnut coloured with white spiral bands. Occasionally unicolorous brown or chestnut. Occasionally with tessellate pattern. 1·0–1·5cm. Indo-Pacific (Persian Gulf). Common.

Pyrene bidentata Menke   × 2.0
Shell fusiform, slightly swollen. Conical spire. Whorls shouldered. Outer lip dent-

ate. Two folds on columella. White, with zigzag, axial, brown lines, apex sometimes dark blue. 1·0–1·5cm. Australia (Western Australia). Common.

Pyrene blanda Sowerby
Shell fusiform, tall spire, apex pointed. Glossy, smooth. Whitish or grey, with thin, wavy, brown, axial lines. c1·0cm. Indo-Pacific. Common.

Pyrene coronata Sowerby   × 2.0

Small, thick, elongate-fusiform shell with tall spire and moderately stepped whorls. Few evenly spaced axial ribs on each whorl which have a pointed tubercle at upper end. Fine spiral grooves at base of body whorl. Outer lip thickened and denticulate. Whitish, with dark brown mottling and zigzag streaks. Aperture white. c1·4cm. Panamic. Frequent.

Pyrene discors Gmelin   × 1.3

Shell thick, ovate. Short spire, raised apex. Suture impressed. Smooth. Thick outer lip with inner denticles. Brown, with white patches and spots. Violet lip. 1·5–2·0cm. Indo-Pacific. Common.

Pyrene epamella Duclos   × 1.2
philippinarum Reeve.

Thick, solid, ovate shell with a large body whorl and moderately tall spire. Bears slight resemblance to a small *Conus*. Spire whorls and upper portion of body whorl smooth, lower portion of body whorl with low spiral ribs and narrow grooves between. Outer lip thickened and denticulate within. Columella smooth. Creamy white with brown and yellowish brown, zigzag or axial, streaks and blotches. 2·0–2·5cm. Indo-Pacific. Uncommon.

Pyrene flava Bruguière   × 1.5
flavida Lamarck, *punctata* Sowerby, *lugubris* Kiener.

Shell fusiform, swollen. Tall spire, apex pointed. Suture impressed. Smooth, with anterior spiral threads. Dentate outer lip and columella usually violet. Brown, with irregular, white spots. 1·5–2·5cm. Indo-Pacific. Common.

Pyrene floccata Reeve   × 2.0
Shell thin, fusiform, apex pointed. Suture slightly impressed. Smooth. One fold on

columella. Glossy. White, yellow, orange, pink or white mottled with brown. Aperture white. 1·0–1·5cm. S African. Common.

Pyrene fulgurans Lamarck   ×2.0

Shell thick, fusiform, swollen. Conical spire, apex extended, point often worn. Whorls shouldered. Smooth, with anterior spiral threads. Outer lip dentate, with central callus inside. Indentation on columella. Black or brown, with wavy, axial, white lines. Aperture flushed violet on margin. 1·5–2·0cm. Indo-Pacific. Common.

Pyrene guttata Sowerby   ×1.6

Shell fusiform, tall spire, apex pointed. Suture impressed. Dentate outer lip, slightly flared. Dark brown, with white spots. Aperture whitish. 3·0–3·5cm. Indo-Pacific (Indonesia).

Pyrene haemastoma Sowerby   ×1.6

Shell very thick, swollen fusiform. Tall spire, apex pointed often worn. Smooth, with fine, spiral threads anteriorly. Thick outer lip dentate. Columella and outer lip with concave curve. Variegated brown and white, with orange around aperture. 1·5–2·2cm. Indo-Pacific (Galapagos Islands). Frequent.

Pyrene harpaeformis Sowerby   ×1.6

Shell thick, ovate. Conical spire. Callused posterior canal obliquely extended. Outer lip thickened, finely dentate. Axial ribs fading towards anterior. Brown, with white or olive spots. 1·5–1·8cm. Panamic. Frequent.

Pyrene labiosa Sowerby   ×1.3

Thick, solid shell with large body whorl and short, blunt-topped spire. Outer lip greatly thickened and incurved with inner margin denticulate. Columella thickened and with few teeth. Grey to bluish grey with numerous brown spiral lines and few whitish spots. Aperture white. 2·0–2·5cm. Panamic. Frequent.

Pyrene laevigata Linnaeus
Shell moderately thick, ovate, with moderately tall spire and blunt apex. Whorls shouldered. Two folds at base of columella. Smooth, glossy. Whitish, with pale or darker brown mottlings and axial streaks. White band at centre of body whorl with dark brown blotches. Similar band at suture on early whorls. 1·0–1·5cm. Caribbean. Common.

Pyrene major Sowerby   ×2.0

Shell very thick, ovate with conical spire, apex pointed. Smooth. Columella with two folds and denticles. Outer lip dentate, centrally callused. Reddish brown, with white spots on anterior half of whorl. White patch on shoulder near outer lip. Aperture white. 2–3cm. Californian. Common.

Pyrene misera Sowerby   ×2.0

Shell fusiform. Tall spire, apex pointed. Axial ribs, anterior spiral striae. Whitish, with spiral bands of dark brown lines and narrow, wavy, brown, axial lines. c1·5cm. Indo-Pacific. Frequent.

Pyrene pardalina Lamarck   × 2.0
Shell ovate. Conical spire, apex pointed.

Anterior spiral threads. Outer lip plicate. Smooth, slightly glossy, dark or light brown with white, variegated patches and spots. Aperture white. 1·5–1·8cm. Indo-Pacific (Indian Ocean). Common.

Pyrene paytensis Lesson   ×1.3

spire, apex pointed. Anterior spiral threads. Outer lip plicate. Mottled brown and white. 1·5–1·8cm. Indo-Pacific (Persian Gulf). Uncommon.

Pyrene rugosa Sowerby   ×1.6
bicolor Kiener.

Shell thick, resembling a miniature *Strombus*. Spire conical, pointed apex often worn down. Whorls with distinct angular shoulder. White callus on posterior notch. One fold and row of denticles on columella. Outer lip thick, dentate. Brown, with wavy, axial, white stripes. Olive periostracum. 1·5–2·3cm. Panamic. Common.

Pyrene tankervillei Montrouzier   ×2.1
tringa Lamarck.

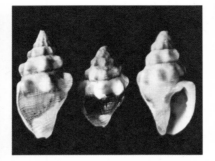

Thick, ovate shell with swollen body whorl and short spire with blunt apex. Spiral groove below suture. Whorls moderately stepped. Smooth except for fine spiral striae on early whorls and spiral grooves at base of body whorl. Outer lip thickened and denticulate. Columella with two or three teeth and two folds. Smooth and dull. Yellowish white or brownish peppered with small, whitish spots. Aperture white, tinged with violet. Thick, greenish brown periostracum. *c*2·5cm. Peruvian. Common.

Pyrene plicaria Montrouzier
Thin, ovate-fusiform shell with moderately rounded whorls and slightly impressed suture. Numerous strong, evenly spaced axial folds on each whorl. Fine spiral ribs at base of body whorl reaching around columella. Outer lip moderately thickened. Fawn, with darker brown spiral lines and blotches. Early whorls purplish. Aperture whitish. *c*1·3cm. Indo-Pacific (Pacific). Common.

Pyrene propinqua Smith   ×2.0
Shell thick, fusiform, swollen. Conical

Shell fusiform, swollen. Conical spire, apex pointed. Partial axial ribbing, with spiral row of prominent nodules. Spiral striae. Outer lip finely dentate. Whitish, with irregular, broken, green band on last whorl. Aperture white. 1·2–1·7cm. Panamic. Common.

Pyrene rustica Linnaeus   ×1.6

Shell ovate, conical spire, apex pointed. Smooth, with anterior spiral threads. Outer lip dentate, central callus. Columella with 1–3 folds and row of denticles. Slightly glossy; brown, irregularly spotted white. *c*2cm. Mediterranean. Common.

Shell fusiform, swollen. Tall spire, extended apex, point often worn. Anterior spiral threads. Denticles in outer lip. Smooth, slightly glossy. White, with axial, brown variegations or broken lines. 1·5–2·5cm. Indo-Pacific. Uncommon.

Pyrene terpsichore Lamarck   ×2.0
Shell fusiform. Tall spire, apex pointed. Axial ribs sometimes fading towards anterior. Whitish, brown on ribs, spiral

band of broken, wavy, brown lines. 1·5–1·8cm. Indo-Pacific. Common.

Pyrene turturina Lamarck
Very thick, globose shell with short spire. Large body whorl has rounded shoulder. Whole shell smooth except for dorsal side of body whorl which has broad spiral ribs, and early spire whorls which are spirally tuberculated. Outer lip thickened and denticulate in middle portion. Columella with two or three deep-seated folds and about five or six teeth in front. Yellowish white with axial, brown streaks and white patches. Aperture white; parietal wall and columella tinged pinkish violet. 1·0–1·5cm. Indo-Pacific. Frequent.

Pyrene varia Sowerby   ×1.6
veleda Duclos.

Thick, ovate-fusiform shell with tall spire and pointed apex. Regularly spaced, prominent axial ribs on each whorl, becoming obsolete towards base of body whorl. Numerous spiral grooves between ribs. Whitish or yellowish white with irregular, light and dark brown mottling, sometimes arranged in broad spiral bands. Thick, light brown periostracum. 2·0–2·5cm. Panamic. Frequent.

Pyrene versicolor Sowerby   ×1.8

Shell fusiform, swollen. Moderately tall spire, apex pointed, Suture impressed. Fine spiral channels. Outer lip and columella dentate. Slight gloss. Whitish to pale olive, with brown spots; wavy, axial lines below suture or all over. Aperture white. 1·0–1·5cm. Indo-Pacific. Common.

Genus STROMBINA Mörch
Slender shells with elongate spire. Thickened edge to aperture. Heavy ridge, sometimes toothed, in outer lip. Fine to coarse axial ornament, often nodulose at whorl shoulders. Siphonal canal long, well developed, sometimes recurved. Numerous species in Panamic and Californian provinces. Two species in Caribbean.

Strombina elegans Sowerby
Closely resembles *S. maculosa*, but body whorl more rounded and has long axial ribs. Outer lip more thickened and toothed. Whitish, with brown mottling and zigzag lines which tend to form spiral bands. *c*3·5cm. Panamic. Frequent.

Strombina fusinoidea Dall
fusiformis Hinds.
Superficially resembles a much elongated *S. lanceolata*. Fusiform, almost biconic shell with long, straight columella and thickened outer lip without teeth. Body whorl has two large tubercles at periphery. Early whorls axially ribbed; rest of shell almost smooth except for strong spiral ribs on lower half of body whorl. Yellowish white with pale brown blotches. Aperture white. 4–5cm. Panamic. Rare.

Strombina lanceolata Sowerby   ×1.4

Thick, fusiform, almost biconic shell with tall spire and pointed apex. Early whorls with single row of large, axially lengthened tubercles. Two or three large, oblique, blunt tubercles at shoulder of body whorl. Outer lip thickened and denticulate in its middle portion. Columella straight. Early whorls axially ribbed. Lower portion of body whorl strongly spirally grooved. Fine,

axial growth lines. Yellowish white with thin, brown periostracum. 3·0–3·5cm. Panamic. Frequent.

Strombina maculosa Sowerby   ×2.3

Shell fusiform, slender. Very tall spire, extended apex. Last two or three whorls with spiral row of nodules just below suture. Creamy with fine, brown reticulations. White gloss on parietal region and aperture. 3·0–3·5cm. Panamic. Frequent.

Strombina recurva Sowerby
Similar in shape to *S. fusinoidea*, but shorter and with spiral row of tubercles on each whorl. Lower half of body whorl with strong spiral ribs. Siphonal canal also more recurved than *S. fusinoidea*. Outer lip thickened, with notch in upper portion. Yellowish white with darker brown markings round tubercles. Aperture white. 2·5–3·0cm. Panamic. Uncommon.

Strombina turrita Sowerby   ×1.8

Shell fusiform, slender. Spire tall, apex extended, slightly convex whorls. Smooth, outer lip thickened. Dotted with violet brown markings on cream. 2–3cm. Panamic. Frequent.

Family MELONGENIDAE

Medium-sized to large shells with capacious body whorl, relatively short spire and long siphonal canal. Several genera in warm and tropical seas.

Genus MELONGENA Schumacher

Thick, heavy shells, nearly smooth or rough and spiny. Several species. Great variation within species.

Melongena corona Gmelin   × 1.0
American Crown Conch   × 0.6

Shell thick, ovate, with raised spire. Suture densely plicate. Shouldered whorls, with spiral row of sharp, upturned tubercles which become hollow spines on body whorl. Weak axial ribbing, spiral threads. Short, broad anterior canal. White, with dark brown spiral bands. Pale brown periostracum. Numerous distinct forms occur. Shells may be tall- or short-spired, and may be multi-spined or spineless. 3·0–9·5cm. Caribbean (South East United States). Common.

Melongena melongena Linnaeus
West Indian Crown Conch
Resembles *M. corona*, but is larger, heavier and with rounded shoulders. Spines more solid and usually shorter. Suture channelled. Columella with thick callus and outer lip thickened, especially posteriorly. Usually two rows of spines on body whorl. Broad, chocolate brown spiral bands alternating with narrower, creamy brown spiral bands. 10–13cm. Caribbean. Common.

Melongena patula Broderip & Sowerby
  × 1.0

Like a larger version of *M. melongena*, but with much more flared outer lip and single row of blunt spines at shoulder. Very thick and heavy. Columella thickened and gently curved. Body whorl compressed posteriorly. Broad, chocolate brown spiral bands with narrower bands between and a broad creamy spiral band at shoulder. Aperture orange brown. 7–13cm. Panamic. Common.

Genus BUSYCON Röding

Fulgur Montfort.
Medium-sized to large shells with short spire and long siphonal canal. Usually heavy and inflated, sometimes very thick and bearing tubercles or blunt spines at shoulder of body whorl. Includes sinistral and dextral species. About six species in East American waters.

Busycon canaliculata Linnaeus   × 0.4
Shell large, thin, with globose body whorl, moderately tall spire and deeply and broadly channelled suture. Siphonal canal moderately long, broad and curved. Shoulders strongly keeled with spire whorls almost straight-sided below keel and with

body whorl globosely rounded below keel. Coarse spiral cords with axial growth lines and ridges. Unicolorous pinkish or whitish brown. Thick, pale brown periostracum. 15–18cm. Transatlantic. Common.

Busycon carica Gmelin
Knobbed Whelk
eliceans Montfort.
Shell very large, thick, ovate-fusiform with moderately tall spire and large, inflated body whorl. Moderately long, broad siphonal canal which is somewhat recurved. Spiral row of large, blunt tubercles on body whorl continued at suture of spire whorls. Greyish white often stained green. Aperture creamy red. The form or subspecies *B. eliceans* is almost a mirror image of the sinistral *B. perversum*, and is by some authorities considered to be more closely related to that species. 13–20cm. Transatlantic. Common.

Busycon contrarium Conrad   × 0.45

Shell sinistral, pyriform. Short, broad spire, apex slightly extended. Coronet of upturned nodules on shoulder. Coarse axial folds, axial striae and spiral threads. Long, sometimes twisted, siphonal canal. Cream and greyish to orange, with lighter spiral band and brown axial streaks. Aperture whitish to orange, brown margin. 5–16cm. Caribbean (Florida). Common.

Busycon coarctatum Sowerby
Similar in shape and size to *B. spiratum*. Has well rounded whorls, flattened spire without channelled suture and smaller aperture which is strongly lirate within. Spiral row of small, sharp spines at shoulder of body whorl and suture of spire whorls. Siphonal canal long and narrow. Yellowish white with thin, axial, dark brown streaks. Aperture yellow. *c*12cm. Caribbean. Uncommon.

Busycon perversum Linnaeus
Perverse Whelk
kieneri Philippi.
Large, heavy shell which is always sinistral (but see *B. carica*). Low spire and broad, flaring outer lip which is sinuous. Large, pointed spines at shoulder of body whorl, and these are continued at suture on spire whorls. Round middle of body whorl is a large, swollen ridge. Strong spiral cords which are most conspicuous on swollen ridge and on spire whorls. 10–23cm. Caribbean. Uncommon.

Busycon spiratum Lamarck   × 0.7

Shell pear shaped; short, broad spire; slightly extended apex. Body whorl with low, rounded shoulder, spiral whorls with angular shoulders. Fine axial and spiral striae, spiral threads anteriorly. Whitish, with broken, spiral, brown bands, and

streaks. Wide aperture coffee to dark brown, margin white. 7–10cm. Caribbean. Frequent.

Genus PUGILINA Schumacher
Large, ovate-fusiform shells with strong nodes at shoulders and lirate aperture. Few species in tropical and warm seas.

Pugilina colosseus Lamarck
Giant Stair Shell
Shell large, fairly thick, fusiform; tall, pointed spire. Occasionally with raised nodules at shoulder, coarse spiral threads, fine axial threads. Outer lip plicate. Long anterior canal. Glossy, white parietal callus. Dull, creamy white. Aperture cream. Hairy periostracum. *c*26cm. Japonic.

Pugilina morio Linnaeus   × 0.4

Shell large, fusiform; moderately tall spire, apex pointed. Shouldered whorls, weak axial ribbing with raised nodules. Spiral ribs. Coffee to dark brown, with white to cream spiral band below thin, orange line. Columella creamy brown. 4–12cm. West African. Uncommon.

Syrinx aruanus.

Genus SYRINX Röding
Megalatractus Lamarck.
Very large, thick, heavy shells with very strongly angulated whorls, long, broad siphonal canal and very tall spire. One species in the Indo-Pacific.

Syrinx aruanus Linnaeus   × 0.16
proboscidiferus Lamarck.
For details, see genus *Syrinx*. Unicolorous apricot, fading to pale yellow. Long, cylindrical apex present only on immature specimens. One of the largest gastropod shells in the world. 35–50cm. Indo-Pacific (Pacific). Frequent.

Family NASSARIIDAE
Small to medium-sized shells. Thin or solid, globose to elongate oval. Spire tall or short, aperture relatively small and narrow. Surface usually reticulated, axially ribbed or spirally striate, sometimes nodulose, rarely smooth. Some species have heavy callus on parietal wall. Aperture often denticulate and usually lirate, anterior notch conspicuous. Operculum corneous with apical nucleus and serrated margin. The animals are carnivorous. About twelve genera, in most seas.

Genus NASSARIUS Duméril
Nassa Lamarck.
For details see Family Nassariidae. Many subdivisions of this genus have been proposed to accommodate the many species. Great variation within single species makes identification difficult.

Nassarius arcularius Linnaeus   × 1.0

Shell very thick, ovate. Spire variable. Axial ribs, fading on last whorl. Large nodules, sometimes double, at broad shoulder. Narrow spiral grooves. Outer lip with internal channels. Heavily callused parietal wall extending over body whorl. Whitish, pale brown to bluish grey. Brown spiral line at shoulder, paler lines on last whorl. 1·8–2·8cm. Indo-Pacific. Common.

Nassarius californianus Conrad
Shell ovate. Numerous slanting axial ribs cut by spiral striae forming beads. Outer lip thin. White. Yellow to grey periostracum. *c*2·5cm. Californian. Frequent.

Nassarius coronatus Bruguière   × 1.2
Shell ovate, spire extended, apex pointed.

Spiral coronet of tubercles below suture. Outer lip dentate. Parietal tooth. Thick parietal callus. Olive to dark brown. *c*2·5 cm. Indo-Pacific. Common.

Nassarius echinatus Quoy & Gaimard × 2.1

Shell ovate, apex pointed. Slanting axial ribs with short spines, four rows on last whorl. Glossy parietal callus. Whitish. *c*1·3cms. Indo-Pacific. Uncommon.

Nassarius fossatus Gould
Giant Western Nassa
Shell ovate. Conical spire, apex pointed. Early whorls coarsely beaded, last whorl with incomplete axial ribs. Spiral cords. Outer lip rough-edged, posterior constriction. Brownish white to orange brown. 3·5–5·0cm. Californian, Aleutian (North West America). Common.

Nassarius gemmulatus Lamarck × 2.3

Shell ovate, conical spire, apex pointed. Suture channelled. Raised axial ribs, narrow spiral grooves forming beaded lattice, and coronet of nodules at suture. White parietal callus. Outer lip dentate. Whitish to pale brown. 2·5–3·0cm. Japonic, Indo-Pacific (Pacific). Common.

Nassarius gemmulifer A. Adams × 1.6

Shell ovate, slightly convex whorls. Conical spire, apex pointed. Numerous axial ribs, spiral striae. Outer lip with internal channels. White parietal callus. Whitish to pale yellow, faint brown spiral banding. 1·5–2·0cm. South African. Common.

Nassarius gibbosula Linnaeus × 1.6

Shell very thick, ovate. Spire often callused. Last whorl sometimes with 1–3 large tubercles. Parietal wall heavily callused. Olive, or mottled brown, white, with brown spiral line. Dark brown or orange line on callus margin. 1·5–2·0cm. Mediterranean. Common.

Nassarius glans Linnaeus × 1.3

Shell thin, fusiform, swollen. Tall spire, apex pointed. Axial ribs on early whorls, later whorls smooth. Outer lip dentate. Thin, transparent parietal callus. Glossy, white, with pale brown patches and thin, spiral, brown lines. Rounded aperture white. 4–5cm. Indo-Pacific. Common.

Nassarius hirtus Kiener × 1.6

Shell ovate, slightly fusiform. Conical spire, apex pointed. Axial ribbing, with coronet of nodules at suture. Parietal tooth. Broad anterior canal. Smooth, glossy, pale brown, lighter spiral bands. Apex tinged violet pink. 2·0–2·5cm. Indo-Pacific. Common.

Nassarius insculptus Carpenter
Smooth Western Nassa
Shell ovate. Numerous fine spiral striae. Axial ribs on early whorls only. Thick outer lip. White to yellowish white. Parietal shield white. *c*1·8cm. Panamic. Common.

Nassarius kieneri Deshayes × 2.3

Shell ovate, tall spire, apex pointed. Slight suture deeply impressed. Lattice of curved axial ribs and spiral striae. Channelled outer lip. Large parietal callus, with tooth. Glossy, whitish. Violet aperture. 2·5–3·0cm. Indo-Pacific. Frequent.

Nassarius livescens Philippi   ×1.6

Shell fusiform, swollen. Numerous curved axial ribs cut by spiral striae forming row of prominent nodules below suture. Parietal callus with tooth. Greyish with darker bands. c2·5cm. Indo-Pacific. Frequent.

Nassarius margaritifer Dunker   ×2.3

Shell fusiform, swollen. Spire slightly raised, apex pointed. Nodulose axial ribbing, separate row below suture, smooth spiral band. Parietal tooth. White, with broken, brown bands. 1·4–2·2cm. Indo-Pacific. Common.

Nassarius mendicus Gould
Shell ovate, slightly elongate. Broad, low axial ribs, crossed by thin spiral cords. Outer lip thin. Greyish yellow. 1·2–1·8cm. Californian, Aleutian (Alaska). Common.

Nassarius monilis Kiener   ×1.6
Shell fusiform, swollen. Apex pointed. 15 axial ribs, slightly curved. Spiral row of nodules just below suture with channel below. Outer lip internally channelled. White parietal callus. Whitish or pale

olive, with pale brown or green spiral bands. 1·5–2·3cm. Indo-Pacific. Frequent.

Nassarius mutabilis Linnaeus   ×1.6

Shell ovate, spire extended, apex pointed. Suture impressed, slight shoulder. Narrow spiral grooves, fine axial striae. Outer lip with internal channels. Parietal callus. Creamy or pale brown, with darker spots below suture. 1·7–2·5cm. Mediterranean. Common.

Nassarius papillosus.

Nassarius obsoletus Say
Eastern Mud Nassa
Shell ovate, apex worn. Numerous faint beads. Brown and grey parietal wall. One fold on columella. Dark brown to blackish. Usually covered with mud and algae. 1·8–2·5cm. Boreal (North America only), Transatlantic. Common.

Nassarius papillosus Linnaeus   ×1.5
Shell very thick, fusiform, swollen. Conical spire, apex pointed. 3–4 spiral rows of small, raised nodules, 7–8 on last whorl. Columella and parietal region glossy, callused. Outer lip dentate. White or creamy, with brown blotches. 4–5cm. Indo-Pacific. Common.

Nassarius plicosus Dunker   ×1.2

Shell fusiform, swollen, tall-spired. Broadly spaced axial ribs, with low nodules at shoulder, fading at anterior. Spiral striae. White parietal callus. Whitish to pale brown. 1·8–2·5cm. South African. Common.

Nassarius pyrrhus Menke   ×2.1

Shell fusiform, swollen. Broken axial ribs, with numerous small nodules. Denticles in outer lip. White or olive, with brown spiral ring above suture and two others on body whorl. 1·0–1·8cm. Australian (Australia). Frequent.

157

Nassarius reticulatus Linnaeus   ×2.1

Shell thick, raised spire, apex pointed. Slightly convex whorls. Beading of numerous axial ribs cut by spiral channels. 6–10 denticles in outer lip. Glossy, callused, white parietal region. Shades of pale brown, darker spiral band below suture. Occasionally pale green on spire. *c*2·5cm. Mediterranean, Boreal. Common.

Nassarius subspinosus Lamarck   ×2.1

Shell ovate, pointed apex. Axial ribs, spiral row of sharp upturned nodules mid-whorl, three rows on last. Whitish brown spiral lines, and bands at nodules. *c*1·5cm. Indo-Pacific. Common.

Nassarius tegula Reeve
Western Mud Nassa
Shell ovate. Thick, conical spire, apex pointed. Broad, low nodules below suture. Thick outer lip. Parietal callus. Olive grey to brown, often with paler spiral band. *c*1·8cm. Californian. Common.

Nassarius trivittatus Say
New England Nassa
Shell thin, ovate. Tall spire. Suture channelled. Numerous axial ribs cut by spiral striae to form beading. Outer lip thin, sharp-edged. Grey to yellowish grey. *c*1·8cm. Transatlantic, Boreal (Nova Scotia). Common.

Nassarius venustus Dunker   ×1.6

Shell thick, ovate. Tall, conical spire. Lattice of axial ribs and spiral threads. Spiral row of small nodules just below suture. One fold on columella. Ventral surface of shell callused. Thickened teeth in outer lip. Whitish, some yellow with dark brown rings or bands. *c*1·8cm. Indo-Pacific (Pacific). Common.

Nassarius vibex Say
Eastern Nassa
Shell thick, ovate. Conical spire, apex pointed. Low axial ribs, spiral ridges. Parietal shield sometimes yellowish. Whitish or greyish brown, often with dark brown patches and bands. *c*1·3cm. Caribbean, Transatlantic. Common.

Genus DEMOULIA Gray
Globular, short-spired shells with spiral costae or lirae and well defined suture. Few species in South African and West African waters.

Demoulia abbreviata Wood   ×1.6

Shell thick, spherical. Short spire, apex slightly extended, often worn. Suture impressed. Strong spiral threads. Dentate outer lip slightly thickened. Mottled white to yellowish. White enamelled parietal region. 2·0–2·8cm. South African. Common.

Demoulia pinguis Lamarck   ×1.2

Shell thin, spherical. Short spire, apex slightly extended. Suture deeply impressed. Lattice of faint axial and spiral striae. Outer lip finely dentate. Cream to olive, spiral ring of alternate white and brown spots just below suture. 1·5–2·0cm. West African. Frequent.

Demoulia retusa Lamarck   ×1.1

Shell thin, ovate, slight shoulder at impressed suture. Apex usually worn. Fine spiral striae. Prominent fold on posterior of columella. Fasciolar ridge. Outer lip dentate. Whitish, flecked or mottled pale brown, early whorls pale lilac, orange or pink. 2·0–2·5cm. South African. Common.

Genus BULLIA Griffith
Thin or thick, elongate or elongate-ovate shells, with pointed spire and broad siphonal notch. Smooth or ornamented with spiral cords. A large, thick parietal callus is often present. Numerous species in shallow water of warm and tropical seas.

Bullia callosa Wood   ×1.1

Fusiform, swollen shell with large body whorl and small, pointed spire. Thick parietal callus. Axial striae. Whitish or brown to brownish blue. Brown encircling wide aperture. 3·5–4·0cm. South African. Common.

Bullia gradata Deshayes $\times 1.2$

Shell ovate with callused ridge on shoulder. Thick parietal callus. Cream, with pale brown axial streaks. 4·5–5·5cm. Patagonian. Common.

Bullia kurrachensis Angas $\times 1.3$

Shell fusiform, turret-like. Convex whorls with angular shoulder bearing beaded ridge. Axial and spiral channelling forms beaded lattice on earlier whorls. Strong spiral ridges on body whorl. Whitish or pale brown. Blue-grey on spire. 2·5–3·5cm. Indo-Pacific (Indian Ocean). Uncommon.

Bullia livida Reeve $\times 1.1$
Very similar to *B. vittata*, of which it may

be a population variant. Usually larger and darker coloured. Often with prominent varix on body whorl. 2·5–5·0cm. Indo-Pacific (Indian Ocean). Common.

Bullia mauritiana Gray $\times 1.3$

Shell fusiform, with large body whorl and acuminate spire. Narrow, angular shoulder. Spiral grooves sometimes faint. Axial striae. Aperture flared anteriorly, broad siphonal canal. Whitish to greyish lilac. Aperture brown. 4·5–5·5cm. Indo-Pacific (Indian Ocean). Common.

Bullia natalensis Krauss $\times 1.3$
Shell fusiform, almost straight-sided. Coronet of small axial ribs below suture. Axial striae. Outer lip slightly flared anteriorly. Whitish, with faint bands of

yellow and brown. Aperture orange brown. 4·0–5·5cm. South African. Frequent.

Bullia persica Smith $\times 1.6$

Shell fusiform, with slightly shouldered whorls and thick ridge above suture. Lattice of axial and spiral striae. Outer lip slightly flared anteriorly. White with broad, blue spiral band. Aperture brown, white margin. Columella white. *c*3·0cm. Indo-Pacific (North Arabian Sea). Frequent.

Bullia taheitensis Gray $\times 1.2$
Shell solid with tall spire and convex whorls. Numerous raised spiral ridges. Distinct platform below suture. Creamy

white, or with brown mottling, spire sometimes flushed violet. Aperture coffee. 4·5–5·5cm. Indo-Pacific. Common.

Bullia vittata Linnaeus ×1.3

Shell fusiform, with gradually tapering spire. Thin band of numerous axial ribs just below suture, narrow spiral groove sometimes bisecting ribs. Axial striae. Outer lip with thick margin. Whitish to bluish grey. Aperture coffee. 3·5–4·5cm. Indo-Pacific (Indian Ocean). Common.

Family FASCIOLARIIDAE

Spindle-shaped shells without varices. Columella straight with few folds. Outer lip not thickened. Strong, corneous operculum pointed at posterior end. Several genera in tropical and warm seas.

Genus FASCIOLARIA Lamarck

Fusiform, light-weight shells with pointed spire and rounded whorls. Elongate-ovate aperture as long as spire. Outer lip crenate.

A few oblique folds on columella. Widely distributed in tropical and warm seas. About 20 species.

Fasciolaria heynemanni Dunker ×0.5

Medium-sized shell with moderately tall spire and long siphonal canal. Outer lip thin. Spiral row of strong, broad tubercles at whorl shoulders. Irregular, broad spiral ribs below row of tubercles on body whorl. Greenish white with tubercles flushed pale brown. Aperture and columella greenish white. 12–15cm. South African. Uncommon.

Fasciolaria hunteria Perry ×1.1
Banded Tulip

Shell fusiform, swollen. Apex pointed, whorls convex. Smooth. Spiral threads on fasciole. Short, stout anterior canal. Slightly glossy, white axial streaks, grey and mushroom patches; thin, brown spiral lines. 6–7cm. Caribbean. Common.

Fasciolaria ocelliferus A. Adams ×0.5

Above: *Fasciolaria ocelliferus*.
Below: *Fasciolaria salmo*.

160

Medium-sized, moderately thick shell with tall spire, long siphonal canal and impressed suture. Deep umbilicus. Moderately sharp spiral keel and numerous broad spiral ribs on each whorl. Axial growth striae cross spiral ribs. Columella and parietal wall with obscure long folds. Yellowish with brown spots irregularly placed on keel. Spiral ribs. 13–15cm. South African. Uncommon.

Above and below: *Fasciolaria tulipa*.
Right: *Pleuroploca filamentosa*.

Fasciolaria salmo Wood   ×0.5
Thick, solid, ovate shell with large body whorl and short spire. Spire whorls rounded, body whorl with spiral row of blunt tubercles at shoulder. Long, broad, gently curved siphonal canal. Large aperture with outer lip crenulate and pinched in at posterior end next to posterior canal. Strong and weak spiral cords with irregular, axial growth ridges. Columella callused and with three folds. Yellowish brown. Aperture pinkish brown. Thick, dark brown periostracum. 10–14cm. Panamic. Frequent.

Fasciolaria tulipa Linnaeus   ×0.25
Tulip Shell
Shell fusiform, slightly swollen. Tall pointed spire, convex whorls. Irregular, axial striations. Outer lip dentate, lirate within. Long anterior canal. Pinkish and cream, or whitish with brown blotches in broad spiral band, darker spiral lines. Elliptical aperture brownish or pinkish. 10–23cm. Caribbean. Common.

Genus PLEUROPLOCA Fischer
Shells moderately large to very large, thick, fusiform. Usually strong knobs at shoulder. Folds on columella. Thick, strong operculum fitting snugly into aperture. About 20 species living in warm and tropical seas.

Pleuroploca australasia Perry
Thick, broadly fusiform shell with moderately long, broad siphonal canal. Whorls moderately rounded with a spiral row of low rounded nodules at periphery of each whorl, giving angulated appearance.

Numerous coarse, rounded spiral cords. Aperture weakly lirate. Columella smooth with two or three folds on siphonal canal. Well developed parietal ridge. Light brown with darker brown spiral lines. Aperture pale brown. Thin, olive brown periostracum. c15cm. Australian (Australia). Common.

Pleuroploca filamentosa Röding   ×0.5
Shell fusiform, tall spire, apex pointed. Axial ribs swollen at mid-whorl, fading towards anterior. Numerous spiral cords. Long, straight siphonal canal. Outer lip dentate, lirate within. Coffee or cream, with broken spiral lines and bands. Aperture coffee or cream. 9–15cm. Indo-Pacific. Common.

Pleuroploca gigantea Kiener
Shell very large, thick, heavy, elongate-fusiform. Large, tubercular axial ribs on each whorl crossed by strong, coarse spiral cords. Moderately long, broad siphonal canal. Columella curved with moderately sharp angle at siphonal canal. Aperture lirate within. Greyish white to pinkish brown. Thick, brown periostracum which flakes off when dry. Juvenile shells are bright orange red with thinner periostracum. One of the largest gastropod shells in the world. 40–60cm. Transatlantic, Caribbean (Florida). Common.

Pleuroploca trapezium Linnaeus
Shell fusiform, swollen. Conical spire, apex pointed. Spiral row of large, raised nodules. Narrow spiral channels, axial striae. Outer lip slightly flared at shoulder, lirate. Stout anterior canal. Three folds on columella. Shades of brown. Aperture cream. 9–10cm. Indo-Pacific. Common.

Genus LATIRUS Montfort
Shells turreted, fusiform with produced spire and nodulous whorls. Aperture oblong with thin outer lip. Umbilicus present. Straight columella with two or three small, oblique folds. Many species in tropical and warm seas.

Latirus bairstowi Sowerby
Thick, elongate-fusiform shell with broad, short, recurved siphonal canal. Apex blunt and suture impressed. Whorls moderately rounded. Long spiral ribs on median portion of each whorl. Whole shell encircled by strong spiral ribs. One strong columellar fold just visible within narrow aperture. Aperture lirate within. Yellowish brown with fine, spiral, white lines. c3cm. South African. Frequent.

Latirus barclayi Reeve
Similar in shape and general appearance to *L. polygonus*, but with larger tubercles and different colour pattern. Tubercles form thick axial ribs on upper portion of body whorl. Yellowish brown with white

tubercles. 4·5–6·5cm. Indo-Pacific (Indian Ocean). Rare.

Latirus belcheri Reeve
Thick, solid, fusiform shell with shorter siphonal canal than *L. polygonus*. Strong axial ribs most strongly developed at periphery of each whorl where they are crossed by spiral cord. Body whorl has a second spiral cord below. Fine spiral striae cover entire shell. Three folds on columella. Aperture squarish. Yellowish white with interrupted, axial, dark brown streaks and blotches and the spiral cord has a median, interrupted, spiral, dark brown band. Aperture and columella white. 3·5–5·0cm. Indo-Pacific (West Pacific). Frequent.

Latirus cinguliferus Lamarck   ×0.7

Shell ovate, conical spire, apex pointed. Spiral row of large, pointed nodules at periphery, weak axial ridges, fine spiral striae. 3–4 folds on columella. Long siphonal canal, slightly recurved. Small posterior canal. Mottled yellow and dark brown. 4·0–6·5cm. Caribbean.

Latirus craticulatus Linnaeus   ×0.9
Shell fusiform; spire swollen, turret-like. Broad, low axial ridges, raised spiral ridges. Outer lip crenulate. Siphonal canal slightly recurved. Pale yellow to brown, reddish brown on ribs. Small, creamy white aperture. *c*5·0cm. Indo-Pacific. Frequent.

Latirus filosus Schubert & Wagner
Thick, elongate-fusiform shell with acutely pointed apex and broad, moderately long siphonal canal. Whorls moderately rounded and suture impressed. Strong axial ribs crossed by numerous fine spiral riblets. Outer lip dentate. Columella with numerous irregular folds. Whitish with fine,

Latirus craticulatus.

spiral, brown lines. Aperture and columella white. 4·5–5·0cm. West African. Common.

Latirus infundibulum Gmelin   ×0.6

Shell very thick, fusiform. Tall spire, pointed apex. Raised axial nodules cut by sharp spiral ridges. Stout, trunk-like siphonal canal, long and hollow. Pale brown to coffee, darker on ridges, spiral band below suture. 2–4 folds on columella. 4–8cm. Caribbean. Frequent.

Latirus iris Lightfoot
prismaticus Martyn.
Thick, solid, ovate-fusiform shell with short, broad siphonal canal and acuminate spire. Suture moderately impressed. Broad axial ribs each bearing elongate spiral nodes. Whole shell encircled by fine spiral ridges. 3–4 short folds on columella. Yellowish with dark brown nodes. Aperture yellowish orange. Periostracum strikingly iridiscent when placed in water. 3·0–3·5cm. Indo-Pacific (Central Pacific). Uncommon.

Latirus maximus Sowerby
Shell large, ponderous and ovate. The inflated whorls each have large, axial knobs just below suture, median portion of body whorl is smooth and lower portion strongly spirally ribbed. Broad, short siphonal canal with moderate umbilicus. Columella pustulose along its entire length. Aperture lirate within. In appearance it could be considered a *Fasciolaria* or even a *Fusinus*, but its ponderosity suggests a closer relationship to the genus *Latirus*. *c*9cm. West African (Cape Verde Islands). Rare.

Latirus mediamericanus Hertlein & Strong
castanea Reeve.
Thick, heavy, fusiform shell with tall spire and wavy suture. Broad, rounded axial ribs on all whorls crossed by fine spiral riblets which are stronger towards base. Thick, broad siphonal canal. 3–4 folds on columella. Aperture lirate within, the lirae being beaded. Usually covered with a thick, dark brown periostracum which is sometimes worn away to reveal a yellowish brown shell underneath. Aperture and columella white. 5·5–7·0cm. Panamic. Uncommon.

Latirus mosselensis Tomlin
Moderately thick, elongate-fusiform shell with tall, acuminate spire and long, broad, slightly curved siphonal canal. Broad axial ribs crossed by obscure spiral lines. Tuberculated spiral cords around siphonal canal. Fine, axial growth lines. Pinkish white covered by thin, yellowish brown periostracum. Aperture pinkish white. 5–6cm. South African. Rare.

Latirus nodatus Gmelin   ×0.7
Shell moderately large, thick, solid and tall-spired. Siphonal canal very broad and moderately long. Umbilicus a small chink. Aperture lirate within. Each whorl has several very broad, strong axial ribs. 3–4 strong spiral cords on siphonal canal. About five small folds on columella. Yellowish, flushed pink. Aperture and columella pink. 6–9cm. Indo-Pacific. Frequent.

Latirus ocellatus Gmelin   ×2.3
Shell fusiform, swollen, with conical spire. Axial ribs with sharp nodules at shoulder.

Above: *Latirus nodatus.*

Below: *Latirus ocellatus.*

Low spiral ridges with beading on last whorl. 3–4 folds on columella. Outer lip dentate, slightly flared. White, with brown axial bands and spiral lines. 1·5–2·7cm. Caribbean. Frequent.

Latirus polygonus Gmelin   ×1.1
Thick, heavy, fusiform, almost biconic shell with tall spire and large body whorl. Suture impressed. Siphonal canal broad and long. Strong tubercles at periphery of each whorl and a second lower row of tubercles on body whorl. Irregular spiral cords on each whorl. Outer lip thin. 2–4 small folds on columella. Yellowish with interrupted, dark brown, axial

markings. Aperture and columella yellowish white. 5–7cm. Indo-Pacific, South African. Common.

Latirus recurvirostris Schubert & Wagner
Bears some resemblance to *L. polygonus*, but is more slender, has a taller spire, broader siphonal canal and wide, deep umbilicus. Strong axial ribs are crossed by strong spiral cords which produce sharp-edged nodules where they cross. Siphonal canal encircled by strong spiral cords. Aperture weakly lirate. Columella slightly bent towards base of siphonal canal. Pinkish brown with cream spiral lines and axial rows of dark brown markings between nodules. Interrupted, spiral, brown lines round siphonal canal. Aperture and columella orange brown. *c*8cm. Indo-Pacific (Pacific). Frequent.

Latirus turritus Gmelin
taeniatus Deshayes.
Shell fusiform with turret-like spire. Swollen axial ribs crossed by spiral cords. Four folds on columella. Brownish orange, cords brown. Aperture cream. *c*5·5cm. Indo-Pacific. Frequent.

Genus LATIROLAGENA Harris
Globose, thick, smooth shells with large aperture and strongly incurved, slightly toothed, columella. Outer lip thin. One species.

Latirolagena smaragdula Linnaeus
rustica Lamarck.
Shell ovate; short, conical spire; deeply incurvèd columella. Thin spiral ridges, axial striae. 3–4 small folds on columella. Glossy. Numerous narrow, chocolate and white, spiral lines. Aperture white. *c*3·5cm. Indo-Pacific. Common.

Genus PERISTERNIA Mörch
Shells resembling *Latirus* but not umbilicated. Whorls axially ribbed, aperture oval. Canal fairly short and recurved. Outer lip thin and crenulated. Columella incurved and with one or two small teeth. Numerous species in tropical and warm seas.

Peristernia australiensis Reeve
Thick, solid, biconic shell with moderately tall spire, broad body whorl and short siphonal canal. About eight broad axial ribs crossed by numerous sharp spiral cords. Aperture lirate within. Whitish with brown blotches between ribs at suture and two further spiral rows of blotches on lower half of body whorl. Aperture reddish brown. *c*3·5cm. Indo-Pacific (Pacific). Common.

Peristernia caledonicus Petit
Thick, solid, elongate-fusiform shell with moderately tall spire and blunt apex. Broad, short siphonal canal. Impressed suture. Columella with two or three tiny folds. No umbilicus. Yellowish white with dark brown blotch at base and dark brown apex. Aperture yellowish white. 2·5–3·0 cm. Indo-Pacific (Central Pacific). Uncommon.

Peristernia kobeltiana Tapparone-Canefri
Thick, solid, elongate-fusiform, almost biconic shell with impressed suture and moderately broad, straight siphonal canal. Broad, low axial ribs crossed by numerous strong, thin, spiral cords. Cord at suture crenulate. Two tiny folds on columella. Pinkish white with spiral, dark brown bands between spiral cords. Aperture and columella pinkish white. 2·5–3·0cm. Indo-Pacific (Indian Ocean). Rare.

Peristernia nassatula Lamarck   ×1.1

Shell thick, rhombic, fusiform. Conical spire, apex pointed. Coarse axial ribs crossed by spiral threads forming nodules. Outer lip plicate. Siphonal canal moderately long. Whitish, brown between ribs, pale brown spiral bands. Aperture pink or violet. 2·0–3·5cm. Indo-Pacific. Common.

Peristernia philberti Récluz   ×1.6
Shell thick, fusiform, swollen. Conical

spire, apex pointed. Axial ribs crossed by small spiral channels forming spiral row of large nodules mid-whorl. Outer lip slightly flared, anterior canal slightly re-curved. White, with brown spiral bands and lines. Aperture white, sometimes flushed violet. 2·0–2·5cm. Indo-Pacific. Uncommon.

Genus FUSINUS Rafinesque
Fusus of most authors.
Elongate, spindle-shaped shells with long, many-whorled spire and long siphonal canal. Ornamented with spiral ribs and axial threads. Many species in tropical and warm seas.

Fusinus colus Linnaeus   ×0.6
Distaff Spindle

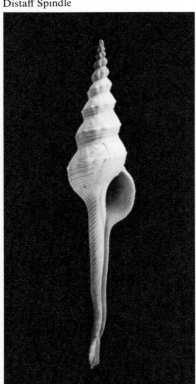

Shell fusiform, spire turret-like. Angular, nodulous keel mid-whorl. Numerous spiral threads. Outer lip plicate, lirate. Long siphonal canal. Whitish, flushed brown on early spire whorls, between nodules on later whorls, and on canal. 12–17cm. Indo-Pacific. Common.

Fusinus crassiplicatus Kira   ×1.0

Tall-spired shell with well rounded whorls and long, tapered siphonal canal. Strong, rounded axial ribs, not aligned from whorl to whorl, interstices slightly wider than ribs. Crowded, well defined spiral riblets are strongest where they cross axial ribs. Yellowish white. Aperture and columella white. 7–10cm. Indo-Pacific (West Pacific), Japonic. Uncommon.

Fusinus distans Lamarck
Shell fusiform, spire pointed. Slight shoulder. Axial ribs crossed by numerous spiral ridges. Outer lip plicate. Long anterior canal. Brownish. Aperture white. *c*9cm. Indo-Pacific. Frequent.

Fusinus dupetitthouarsi Kiener
Shell very large, heavy and elongate-fusiform. Siphonal canal very broad and only moderately long. Whorls moderately rounded and suture well impressed. Strong, smooth spiral cords on all whorls, earlier whorls being also broadly axially ribbed. Outer lip crenulate. Aperture lirate within. Yellowish white. Thick, greenish yellow periostracum. 15–25cm. Panamic. Frequent.

Fusinus forceps Perry   ×0.45
turricula Kiener
Shell thick, very long, with rounded whorls and deeply impressed suture. Broad axial ridges are crossed by strong spiral ribs. Siphonal canal long and thick. Outer lip

crenulate. Unicolorous white. 12–22cm. Indo-Pacific, Japonic. Frequent.

Fusinus nicobaricus Lamarck   ×0.5
Nicobar Spindle

Thick, solid shell with tall spire and long, broad siphonal canal. Suture moderately impressed. Outer lip lirate within. Columella and parietal wall with irregular folds. Strong spiral cords with nodules on strongest cord at periphery. Fine axial striae. Whitish with axial, light and dark brown, streaks. Aperture white. 12–14cm. Indo-Pacific. Common.

Fusinus nipponicus Smith ×1.2

Thin, slender shell with rounded whorls, impressed suture and long, broad siphonal canal. Strong, broadly spaced axial ribs have elongated granules on their surface arranged in spiral rows. Fine spiral riblets crossed by finer, axial growth lines. Yellowish brown with darker brown blotches above and below each granule. Aperture white. 5–6cm. Japonic. Uncommon.

Fusinus oblitus Reeve
Shell fusiform with turret-like spire. Raised nodules. Coarse spiral channels. Outer lip plicate, spaced denticles on lip. Long anterior canal. White to creamy, with brown streaks. Aperture white. 12–16cm. Indo-Pacific. Frequent.

Fusinus perplexus A. Adams
Thin, slenderly fusiform shell with tall spire and very long siphonal canal. Coarse spiral ribs on all whorls becoming obsolete on body whorl on some specimens. Strong, spiral cords which are tuberculated at periphery. Outer lip crenulate. Aperture lirate within. Whitish with a few brownish spots between tubercles. Thick, yellowish periostracum. 10–13cm. Indo-Pacific (Pacific), Japonic. Common.

Fusinus salisburyi Fulton
Very large, elongate-fusiform shell with long, straight siphonal canal and tall, pointed spire with well rounded whorls. Strongly ornamented with broad axial ribs which are crossed by thick, sharp spiral ridges. Spiral ridges well developed at periphery. Outer lip crenulate. Aperture lirate within. Unicolorous white. Thick, yellowish periostracum. 17–20cm. Japonic, Indo-Pacific (Queensland). Uncommon.

Fusinus similis Baird
Moderately thick shell with tall, tapering spire and long, wavy siphonal canal. Each whorl has a spiral row of thick, moderately pointed tubercles. Whole shell encircled by spiral ridges. These are strongest where they cross tubercles. Outer lip denticulate. Aperture lirate within. Columella with fine, irregular ridges. Yellowish white. Thick, yellow periostracum. c16cm. Indo-Pacific (Pacific), Japonic. Uncommon.

Fusinus tuberculatus Lamarck ×0.8

Shell fusiform. Tall, pointed spire. Long siphonal canal displaced to right. Spiral row of nodules mid-whorl, and spiral threads. Outer lip plicate. White, brown spots between nodules. Aperture white. 10–13cm. Indo-Pacific. Common.

Fusinus turricula Kiener
Shell fusiform, slender. Spire turret-like. Whorls convex. Axial ribs crossed by spiral ridges. Outer lip plicate, lirate. Long siphonal canal. Whitish. Aperture white. c11cm. Indo-Pacific. Frequent.

Superfamily
Volutacea

Family OLIVIDAE

Generally known as olives because of the usually cylindrical, squat shape of most of its members. Shells are thick, very glossy and have elongate aperture, obliquely plicate columella terminating in a callus, short spire and distinct, often channelled, suture. Glossy surface caused by animal's mantle which envelops shell almost completely. Brilliant, often highly variable, coloration. Operculum absent (except in *Olivella*). Olives are carnivorous and most active at night or at turn of tide, moving just below sand surface. About 150 species belonging to four genera. All are tropical or warm water species.

Genus ANCILLA Lamarck
Shells small to large, ovate, with pointed spire. Whorls and suture usually callused. Operculum present. About 30 species in tropical and warm seas.

Ancilla albocallosa Lischke ×0.6

Shell ovate, with heavily callused spire. Pink to pale violet, banded brown at both ends. 5–7cm. Japonic. Frequent.

Ancilla elongata Gray
Shell small, cylindrical, thin and translucent. Spire small and extended. White, brown towards posterior. c3cm. Indo-Pacific. Uncommon.

Ancilla glabrata Linnaeus ×0.8

Shell ovate, with shouldered whorls. Spire large, broad suture partially callused. Glossy. Cream to rich golden yellow. 3–7cm. Caribbean. Frequent.

Ancilla lienardi Bernardi   ×2.0

Shell thick, strong, with large body whorl, short spire and slightly impressed suture. Two deep fasciolar grooves. Deep umbilicus. Thick callus not reaching penultimate whorl. Bright orange, flushed pinkish red, with white fasciolar groove. Aperture, columella and callus white. c3cm. Caribbean (Brazil). Uncommon.

Ancilla velesiana Iredale   ×0.8

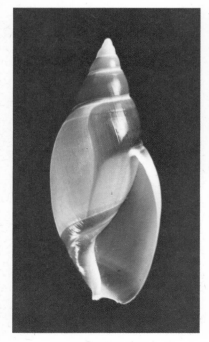

Shell ovate, thin and glossy. Spire raised, with convex whorls, suture callused. Brown, banded at ends darker brown, with creamy white area diffused over much of last whorl. c9·5cm. Australian. Uncommon.

Genus OLIVANCILLARIA d'Orbigny
Thick, solid shells with heavily callused body whorl and spire. Body whorl large, with aperture wide and almost as tall as spire. Thick folds on columella. Fasciole broad and well developed. Few species, mostly in Brazilian waters.

Olivancillaria brasiliana Lamarck   ×0.7

Shell massive, broadly ovate, heavily callused above aperture. Spire flat, callused, apex slightly raised. Mushroom and cream, streaked and mottled with brown. 4–5cm. Caribbean (Brazil). Frequent.

Olivancillaria gibbosa Born   ×0.9

Shell thick and heavy, bulbose ovate. Spire short, whorls heavily callused, particularly last whorl. Mottled brown, spire and columella white. Several distinctive colour forms. 5–7cm. Caribbean (Brazil). Common.

Genus OLIVELLA Swainson
Generally smaller than *Oliva*, elliptically elongate. Outer lip turned outwards anteriorly. Usually white or yellow in colour. Unlike *Oliva*, members of this genus pos-

sess an operculum. Widely distributed in tropical and warm seas. About 50 species.

Olivella biplicata Sowerby   ×1.6
Purple Dwarf Olive

Shell small, thick, elliptical. Spire callused, convex. Obliquely incised lines from columella. Callus on posterior of columella. Colour variable, bluish grey, or white to light brown with violet axial lines. 2–3cm. Californian. Common.

Olivella volutella Lamarck   ×1.2

Shell small, elliptical. Spire raised, apex pointed. Colour varieties are white, lilac, violet and brown, and colours may be mixed. 2·5cm. Panamic.

Genus OLIVA Bruguière
Details as for Family Olividae. About 60 species ranging in size from 1–13cm. Some species abundant in places but some are exceedingly rare. Advisable to have several shells from a single population to establish identity because of great colour variations.

Oliva australis Duclos   ×1.3

Shell small, narrow, cylindrical. Spire extended to sharp cone. Usually whitish violet, sometimes with light brown spots or reticulations. White columella with 5-7 folds. Aperture white. 2·5-3·0cm. Indo-Pacific (Australia). Common.

Oliva caerulea Röding   ×0.6
episcopalis Lamarck.

Thick, ovate shell, with short spire and channelled suture. Coarse folds on columella. Creamy white or yellow, with numerous blotchy, zigzag, axial lines and fainter blackish spiral bands. Columella whitish, stained pale orange. Aperture dark violet. 3-5cm. Indo-Pacific. Common.

Oliva carneola Gmelin   ×1.9

Shell cylindrical or slightly ovate. Spire callused, all but last spiral suture concealed. Colour, form and size variable. Usually white or pale yellow with pale violet reticulations, often banded yellow or orange, sometimes all white. Aperture white. 1·4-2·4cm. Indo-Pacific (Pacific). Common.

Oliva elegans Lamarck   ×1.0
flava Marrat, *keeni* Marrat.
Shell cylindrically ovate. Spire short, suture channelled, callus on end of last spire whorl. Interrupted zigzag lines of brown, olive and yellow on white. Columella with 4-5 folds, white flushed with orange. Aperture bluish white. Also all-

white variety. 3·5-4·5cm. Indo-Pacific. Common.

Oliva episcopalis Lamarck
Shell very thick, elliptical. Spire elevated, apex raised. Deeply channelled suture. Outer lip very thick. Lilac spots on cream, sometimes with light bands. Varieties with darker pattern. Aperture usually violet, occasionally orange. 3·8-5·8cm. Indo-Pacific. Common.

Oliva julieta Duclos   ×0.8
timorea Duclos, *pantherina* Philippi, *porcea* Marrat, *graphica* Marrat.

Shell thick, ovate. Spire raised, apex extended, slight callus on end of last spire whorl. Suture distinct. Brown spots on white, spire flushed with violet. Aperture white. 2-3 folds on columella. *c*5cm. Panamic, Peruvian. Rare.

Oliva miniacea Röding   ×1.1
Red-mouthed Olive
erythrostoma Lamarck, *magnifica* Ducros, *porphyritica* Marrat.
Shell very thick, cylindrical, thick-lipped, short-spired. Often has fine axial threads on last whorl near lip. Extremely variable colour pattern generally yellowish white, streaked and banded with blue, green, purple and brown. Usually two transverse

bands. Aperture always reddish orange. 4·5-9·0cm. Indo-Pacific. Common.

Oliva oliva Linnaeus   ×1.1
algida Vanatta, *candida* Lamarck, *hispidula* Blainville, *ispida* Röding, *longispira* Bridgman, *taeniata* Link.

Shell narrowly cylindrical with low, conic spire. Usually has dark brown aperture but external colour pattern extremely variable. Typical form dull white with a few black blotches. About eleven named forms have their own distinctive colour pattern. 2-4cm. Indo-Pacific. Common.

Oliva peruviana Lamarck   ×0.9
Peruvian Olive
senegalensis Lamarck.
Shell thick, ovate, sometimes angulated at the shoulder. Spire short, suture deeply channelled. Striking, longitudinal, wavy, brown lines on white; flesh-coloured with many chestnut spots; or unicolorous chestnut. Many varieties. Columella white, two

prominent folds. Aperture white. 4·5–5·5cm. Peruvian. Frequent.

Oliva polpasta Duclos   ×1.0

Shell thick, elliptical. Spire raised, conical. Suture distinct. Dark brown spots. or reticulations on olive brown. White triangles border suture. Columella and aperture white. 3·6–4·2cm. Panamic. Common.

Oliva ponderosa Duclos   ×0.6

Thick, ovate shell, with large body whorl, short spire and channelled suture. Columella with numerous thick folds; small callus projects above. Whitish, blotched greyish purple. Aperture pale pink. 5–7cm. Indo-Pacific (Indian Ocean). Frequent.

Oliva porphyria Linnaeus   ×0.6
Tent Olive
Shell large, solid, cylindrically ovate, spire

short, depressed. In profile view margin of outer lip slightly concave in middle section, unique among olives. Violet flesh colour angularly reticulated with red lines resembling tents. Base violet. Largest, most handsome species of genus. *c*10cm. Panamic. Uncommon.

Oliva reticularis Lamarck   ×1.1
Netted Olive

Shell resembles *O. sayana* but smaller and ovate. Spire raised, apical whorls slightly convex, suture shallow. Orange or brown reticulations on white, may form two darker bands on body whorl, one on lower spire whorls. Very variable in colour pattern. 3·5–5·8cm. Caribbean. Common.

Oliva reticulata Röding   ×1.1
Blood Olive
sanguinolenta Lamarck, *variabilis* Röding, *variegata* Röding.
Shell cylindrical or slightly ovate. Spire short, apex slightly extended. Posterior end of last whorl ends in a callus. Yellow-

ish with fine reddish brown reticulations. Columella blood red, may fade to orange. Two darker bands encircle last whorl. Aperture whitish. 4–5cm. Indo-Pacific. Uncommon.

Oliva sayana Ravenel
Lettered Olive
litterata Lamarck, *circinata* Marrat.
Shell cylindrical, spire slightly extended, or depressed, with callus on last spire whorl. Numerous violet brown reticulations on cream. Zigzag lines may darken to form two distinct, dark bands on last whorl. Rarely all-yellow shells occur. 4–8cm. Caribbean. Common.

Oliva scripta Lamarck   ×0.8

Shell narrow, cylindrical. Spire depressed, apex pointed. Suture deeply channelled. Pale brown reticulations on mushroom, sometimes two darker interrupted bands. Columella white. Aperture flushed violet. 3–5cm. Indo-Pacific. Frequent.

Oliva sericea Röding   ×0.6
textilina Lamarck.
Shell thick, narrowly ovate, with short spire and channelled suture. Columella with strong folds; small callus projects

above. Creamy white, reticulated with white spots, fine wavy brown lines and two broad, dark brown spiral bands. Columella and aperture yellow. 8–9cm. Indo-Pacific. Uncommon.

Oliva tigrina Lamarck   ×0.9
holoserica Marrat.

Shell thick, ovate, inflated in the middle. Spire depressed, apex slightly extended. Callus on last spire whorl. Brown, triangular spots on cream. Aperture white. 3–4 folds on columella. Also a dark brown variety. 3·5–6·0cm. Indo-Pacific. Common.

Oliva tremulina Lamarck   ×0.6
nobilis Reeve, *concinna* Marrat, *fumosa* Marrat.

Shell thick, cylindrical. Spire elevated, conical. Channelled sutures. Slight callosity on end of last spire whorl. Irregular, brown to lilac, axial stripes on cream, two darker brown, transverse bands on last whorl. Aperture white. 4·5–9·0cm. Indo-Pacific. Frequent.

Oliva tricolor Lamarck   ×0.8
guttula Marrat.

Shell thick, cylindrical. Spire depressed, callus on end of last spire whorl. Mottled with blue and yellow spots. Black and yellow streaks on spire. Columella with three prominent folds. Aperture white. 4·5–6·0cm. Indo-Pacific. Common.

Family MITRIDAE

Known popularly as mitres from the fancied resemblance of some of them to the headgear of bishops. Mostly slim, elongated and colourful shells. Few exceed 15cm. in length. Columella has prominent folds. Many species have strong axial or spiral ridges. Outer lip smooth or crenulate. Most of the 500 or more species live in sand, on coral reefs or under coral blocks in the tropics, those from temperate waters being less colourful. Mitres live on flesh of other animals. Numerous genera have been proposed of which eight are generally in use.

Genus PUSIA Swainson

Shells generally small compared to other mitrids. Elongate-ovate or ovate, solid, mostly short-spired. Whorls ornamented with axial nodes or ribs, rarely smooth, spirally striate. Aperture constricted basally. Perhaps 30 species or less.

Pusia bernhardina Röding
muriculata Lamarck.
Shell small for the genus, thick, ovate and short-spired. Body whorl large and coronate, with spire whorls stepped. Strong spiral ribs with axial ribs descending to base from coronations. 3–4 folds on columella. Greenish brown fading to brownish yellow. 1·5–2·0cm. Indo-Pacific. Uncommon.

Pusia corallina Reeve
glabra Schepman.
Shell narrowly fusiform, smooth, with broad axial and fine spiral striae. 4–5 folds on columella. Unicolorous red or orange. c5·5cm. Indo-Pacific (Pacific). Rare.

Pusia crocata Lamarck   ×1.6
concinna Reeve, *pyramidalis* Reeve.

Shell fusiform-ovate. Strong axial ribs crossed by elevated spiral cords. 4–5 folds on columella. Outer lip crimpled. Variegated yellow and orange with white spiral band on all but earliest whorls. Aperture pale orange. 1·5–4·0cm. Indo-Pacific. Frequent.

Pusia pardalis Kuster
Shell small, elongate–ovate, solid, with large body whorl and moderately tall spire with impressed suture. Whorls convex, rounded at suture. Four folds on columella. Broad, low axial ribs which become obsolete on lower half of body whorl. Spiral striae between axial ribs. Dark reddish brown with spiral row of irregular, white blotches on body whorl and triangular, white blotches at suture of early whorls. c1·5cm. Indo-Pacific. Uncommon.

Pusia patriarchalis Gmelin
Thick, short-spired shell with strongly shouldered whorls and thick nodules on shoulders. Punctate spiral grooves. Four folds on columella. White or cream with a broad, reddish brown or orange spiral band at centre of body whorl. More inflated than *P. bernhardina*, with stronger folds on columella and differently coloured. 2·5–3·0cm. Indo-Pacific. Uncommon.

Genus VEXILLUM Röding

Similar to *Mitra* but shells have strong axial ribs or striae, and generally transverse grooves or ridges. Outer lip thick and smooth, constricted at base. Anterior canal narrow and produced. Many species in tropical seas.

Vexillum cadaverosum Reeve   ×2.0
mutica Dautzenberg & Bouge,
rubrozonata Dautzenberg & Bouge.

Thick, cylindrical-ovate shell with moderately tall spire and narrow aperture. Spiral ridges sharply nodulose on shoulders. Weaker axial lines and spiral ridges. Columella with three strong folds. Dull, cream with reddish brown spiral band below row of nodules. c2·0cm. Indo-Pacific. Common.

Vexillum caffrum Linnaeus   ×1.1
bifasciata Swainson, *zonalis* Quoy & Gaimard.

Shell solid, fusiform, glossy. Small axial ridges and fine spiral striae. 3–4 folds on columella. Outer lip smooth. Dark brown, with yellow spiral bands. Light brown around columella. Aperture white, with brown margin. 3·5–5·0cm. Indo-Pacific (Pacific). Rare.

Vexillum costatum Gmelin
subulata Lamarck, *terebralis* Broderip, *vitellina* Gould, *lanceolata* Hervier.
Shell narrowly fusiform. Fine lattice of axial and spiral striae. 4–5 folds on columella. Outer lip crenate. Variegated patches of pale orange on white. Aperture pale orange. 2·1–4·5cm. Indo-Pacific (Pacific). Uncommon.

Vexillum costellaris Lamarck   ×1.4
nigrina Lamarck.

Thick, solid, tall-spired shell with nearly straight-sided whorls which are stepped just below suture. Strong axial ribs on all whorls, with weaker spiral ribs between them. 4–5 folds on columella. Dark brown with narrow, spiral white band below suture. A second white band on body whorl. Aperture and columella white. Margin of outer lip dark brown. 3·5–5·0cm. Indo-Pacific (West Pacific). Uncommon.

Vexillum crebriliratum Reeve
Shell elongate-fusiform. Fine lattice of axial and spiral striae. Suture deeply impressed. 4–5 folds on columella. Outer lip smooth. Uniformly brown or cream ornamented with a narrow, whitish or orange spiral band on each whorl. 3–4cm. Indo-Pacific. Rare.

Vexillum deshayesi Reeve   ×1.6
Shell fairly solid, with strongly shouldered whorls. Prominent axial ribs with spiral grooves between. 3–5 folds on columella. Whitish, bluish white or purple with 2–3 interrupted bands of reddish brown. Aperture brownish violet with white spiral band. Colour of bands sometimes pale orange

instead of reddish brown. 1·0–2·4cm. Indo-Pacific. Common.

Vexillum exasperatum Gmelin   ×2.0
torulosa Lamarck.

Shell narrow and pointed, turreted. Axial ribs, which are coarse or fine, crossed by spiral threads. Four folds on columella. White, with two dark brown spiral bands. Aperture white. Colour bands sometimes scarcely visible. 1·3–2·6cm. Indo-Pacific. Common.

Vexillum formosense Sowerby

Thick, solid, almost biconic shell with spire as tall as body whorl. Rounded whorls and impressed suture. Earlier whorls axially ribbed; later whorls smooth except for spiral ribs on lower portion of body whorl. Four folds on columella. Purplish brown with spiral, whitish band on each whorl. Columella white. External colour shows through aperture. c4cm. Indo-Pacific (West Pacific). Frequent.

Vexillum melongena Lamarck
simplicata Swainson.
Shell fusiform. Broad axial ridges, fine spiral striae. 3–4 folds on columella. Outer lip dentate. Spiral bands of brown on white, with a thin, paler, brown ring between. Aperture coffee or pale violet. 3·5–5·3cm. Indo-Pacific (Pacific). Rare.

Vexillum ornatum Link   × 0.9

Thick, tall-spired shell with moderately rounded whorls, impressed wavy suture and short, recurved siphonal canal. Outer lip thickened and smooth, lirate within. Columella with five folds. Numerous punctate spiral grooves crossed by coarse ribs and fine, axial growth striae. Deep reddish or orange pink with a median, yellow, brown or white, spiral band. Outer lip red; aperture whitish orange. 7–8cm. Indo-Pacific (Pacific). Uncommon.

Vexillum plicarium Linnaeus   × 1.1
plicatum Röding, *lividum* Reeve.
Shell thick with coarse axial ribs. 4–5 folds on columella. White, with broad, brown band and 1–2 thinner, interrupted bands.

Aperture bluish white. Outer lip with dark brown flecks. 3–5cm. Indo-Pacific (Eastern Indian Ocean to Samoa). Uncommon.

Vexillum regina Sowerby   × 1.1

Thick, tall-spired, slender shell with angular whorls, impressed suture and recurved siphonal canal. Outer lip straight-sided, thickened and smooth on inside edge. Five folds on columella. Numerous broad, sharply ridged ribs with V-shaped grooves between them and crossed by numerous spiral riblets. Whitish with broad, yellowish spiral band below each suture, below which is a thin, brown spiral band. Body whorl has median, yellowish spiral band bordered above and below by a thin, brown spiral band. Basal portion brown, banded with thin, white spiral lines. Aperture yellowish white. 5–7cm. Indo-Pacific. Uncommon.

Vexillum rugosum Gmelin   × 1.1
corrugata Lamarck.

Shell heavy, elongate-fusiform. Axial ribs elevated, sometimes obscure on last half of body whorl. Faint spiral striae. 4–5 folds on columella. Outer lip smooth. Black spiral bands on white. Aperture white, brown at margin. 3·0–4·5cm. Indo-Pacific. Rare.

Vexillum sanguisugum Linnaeus   × 1.3
stigmataria Lamarck, *caerulescens* Dautzenberg & Bouge, *castaneosticta* Dautzenberg & Bouge.

Shell thick, solid with moderately rounded whorls and impressed suture. 3–5 folds on columella. Strong, broad, wavy axial ribs crossed by numerous spiral grooves. Early whorls dark brown; later whorls whitish yellow with single reddish brown band on each whorl interrupted by spiral grooves, two bands on body whorl. Base same colour as apex. Aperture whitish with brown blotches. 2·5–5·0cm. Indo-Pacific. Common.

Vexillum subdivisum Gmelin ×1.5
lyrata Lamarck.

Shell fairly light, fusiform. Broad, smooth axial ribs, spiral striae. Light brown, grey or olive green, with two or three dark brown spiral bands. 4–5 bluish white or violet folds on columella. Aperture bluish white flushed with brown. 3·5–5·0cm. Indo-Pacific. Uncommon.

Vexillum taeniatum Lamarck ×1.3
vittata Swainson.

Shell similar to *V. regina*, but shorter and relatively broader. Axial ribs broad but smooth. Spiral grooves in interstices and all around base of body whorl. Banded with alternate orange, blackish brown and white zones. White zone with orange brown, spiral flecks. Aperture creamy yellow. 4–7cm. Indo-Pacific. Uncommon.

Vexillum transpositum Dautzenberg & Bouge ×1.8

Thick, tapering shell with pointed apex and impressed suture. Four folds on columella. Numerous slender, slightly curved axial ribs bisected by fine spiral grooves. Greyish white with bright red or reddish brown axial ribs and two faint, broad, white spiral lines on body whorl. Aperture white with columella and most of outer lip stained dark brown. 3–4cm. Indo-Pacific (Pacific). Rare.

Vexillum vulpecula Linnaeus ×1.1
superbum Röding, *variabilis* Link.

Shell thick, elongate, turreted. Coarse axial ribs and moderately deep spiral striae. 3–5 folds on columella. Orange with brown, occasionally with white and black spiral bands. Aperture white, usually with purplish brown patch on posterior end. 4·0–5·5cm. Indo-Pacific. Common.

Genus MITRA Röding
Shells usually thick and strong, elongate-ovate or fusiform. Spire pointed. Suture plain or coronate. Whorls smooth or spirally ridged and striate. Columella with prominent folds. Many species in tropical seas.

Mitra ambigua Swainson ×1.1
brevis Dautzenberg.

Shell elongate-ovate. Fine spiral ridges. 6–7 folds on columella. Outer lip dentate. Yellowish brown merging into whitish spiral bands. Aperture mushroom. 3·5–7·0cm. Japonic, Indo-Pacific. Uncommon.

Mitra annulata Reeve ×2.3

Fusiform shell. Convex whorls. Narrow spiral ridges, and double row of small punctures. 4–6 folds on columella. Outer lip dentate. Broken, brown bands on white. Aperture white flushed with brown. 2·3–3·3cm. Indo-Pacific. Frequent.

Mitra cardinalis Gmelin   × 1.0
Cardinal Mitre
monachialis Röding.

Shell thick, fusiform to slightly ovate. Fine axial and spiral punctures. Outer lip dentate. 5–6 folds on columena. Glossy. Brown blobs in spiral rows on white. Aperture white. 2–7cm. Indo-Pacific. Uncommon.

Mitra chinensis Gray
Shell thick, elongate-ovate, whorls convex. Apex blunt. Faint axial striae crossing stronger spiral grooves. 4–5 folds on columella. Outer lip smooth. Greyish white. Aperture bluish grey. 4–6cm. Indo-Pacific. Uncommon.

Mitra chrysalis Reeve
caledonica Récluz, *fraga* Dautzenberg & Bouge.
Resembles *M. cucumerina* but less globose and with longer aperture. Differs also in ornament. In *M. cucumerina* spiral ridges are angulate, elevated and with moderately broad V-shaped interstices; in *M. chrysalis* interstices are narrow, rounded grooves, ridges are broad and rounded or flat. *M. cucumerina* is a darker brown shade. 1·0–2·2cm. Indo-Pacific. Common.

Mitra chrysostoma Broderip
contracta Kiener.
Shell thick, heavy, body whorl inflated, spire conical. Spiral ridges and finer axial ridges. 5–6 folds on columella. Outer lip constricted, thickened, crenate towards base. Variegated brown patches on white or cream. Aperture pale brown or golden orange. 3·0–4·5cm. Indo-Pacific. Rare.

Mitra clathrus Gmelin
maculosa Gmelin, *crenifera* Lamarck, *pretiosa* Reeve.
Shell fusiform. Dense lattice of axial and spiral striae. 4–5 folds on columella. Outer lip crenate. Interrupted, brown spiral bands on white and cream. Aperture white or cream. 1·7–4·3cm. Indo-Pacific. Uncommon.

Mitra coffea Schubert & Wagner
fulva Swainson, *attenuata* Reeve.
Shell solid, heavy, elliptical. Fine axial striae, spiral rows of small punctures. 5–6 folds on columella. Outer lip dentate. Coffee spotted with minute white dots. 3·5–5·0cm. Indo-Pacific. Rare.

Mitra coronata Lamarck   × 1.8
tiarella A. Adams, *deleta* Dautzenberg & Bouge.

Shell solid, elongate-ovate. Fine axial striae, spiral rows of small punctures. Suture moderately impressed, coronate. 4–6 folds on columella. Outer lip crenate. Brown, mottled with white spots, white band below suture. Aperture white. 1·5–4·0cm. Indo-Pacific (Pacific). Uncommon.

Mitra cucumerina Lamarck   × 2.0
ferrugata Dillwyn, *globosa* Mörch.
Thick, solid, short-spired, squat shell with lightly impressed suture. Aperture longer than spire. Strong, spiral ribs with V-shaped grooves between them. Grooves finely, axially striate. 3–4 folds on columella. Dark reddish brown with interrupted, white band on body whorl and another, less well defined band near base.

1·5–2·5cm. Indo-Pacific (Pacific). Common.

Mitra ebenus Lamarck
Small, thick, elongate-fusiform shell with well-defined suture. Indistinct and irregular axial ribs. Three strong folds on columella. Glossy and smooth. Dark brown with one spiral, yellow band on each whorl. Aperture purplish. Folds white. 1·5–2·0cm. Mediterranean. Common.

Mitra eremitarum Röding   × 0.8
adusta Lamarck, *ruffina* Dillwyn.

Shell heavy, solid, fusiform. Spiral ridges and axial striae. Outer lip thick and crenate. Suture shallow, with small coronations. 5–6 folds on columella. Brown and dark brown axial streaks on white. Paler zone in middle of body whorl. Aperture white. 5·5–8·5cm. Indo-Pacific (Pacific).

Mitra ferruginea Lamarck × 1.2
clara Sowerby, *vitulina* Dillwyn.

Shell thick, fusiform. Thickened nodules on lip. Columella folds extended to form plaits. Distinct spiral ridges over entire shell. Interrupted bands of brownish orange on white. 3·0–4·5cm. Indo-Pacific. Rare.

Mitra filaris Linnaeus × 1.2
filosa Born, *nexilis* Lamarck,
bornii Philippi, *bernardiana* Philippi.

Shell elongate-ovate. Latticed with axial and spiral striae. 3–5 folds on columella. Outer lip dentate. Brown, spiral, equidistant lines on white. Aperture white 3·0–4·5cm. Indo-Pacific. Uncommon.

Mitra flammea Quoy & Gaimard
Shell small, ovate, moderately solid with weakly impressed suture. Numerous regularly spaced spiral ridges. Interstices cancellated with moderately broad axial riblets. 4–5 folds on columella. Whitish or creamy with fairly regular, chestnut

brown axial streaks. 2·0–2·5cm. Indo-Pacific. Uncommon.

Mitra glabra Swainson
Large, moderately thick, elongate shell with slightly convex whorls and slightly impressed suture. Fine, widely spaced spiral grooves and fine axial striae. Five folds on columella. Light brown with darker brown spiral grooves; fades to creamy white. Dark brown periostracum, paler brown below level of apertural suture. 6–9cm. Indo-Pacific (Australia), Australian (Australia). Frequent.

Mitra imperialis Röding
digitalis Dillwyn, *millepora* Lamarck,
cribum Dillwyn.
Shell elongate-ovate, with fine axial striae, spiral rows of small punctures. Suture coronate. 4–6 folds on columella. Outer lip thick, sharply dentate. Mottled brown and white. Aperture yellow to orange. 4–6cm. Indo-Pacific. Uncommon.

Mitra isabella Swainson × 0.8

Thick, heavy, tall-spired shell. Strong spiral ribs crossed by finer axial lines. 4–5 folds on columella. Whitish banded with axial, brown lines and blotches. Aperture yellowish white. 7–9cm. Indo-Pacific (Pacific). Uncommon.

Mitra mitra Linnaeus × 0.7
Episcopal Mitre
episcopalis Linnaeus, *carmelita* Röding.
Shell thick, smooth, fusiform. Outer lip dentate, 4–5 folds on columella. Spiral

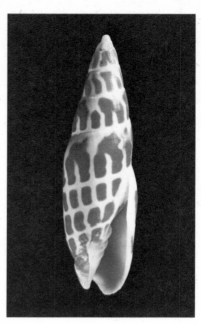

rows of variegated, orange blobs on white. Aperture white to creamy yellow. 3–17cm. Indo-Pacific. Frequent.

Mitra nubila Gmelin × 1.3
versicolor Lamarck.

Shell elongate-ovate, with spiral rows of punctures. Outer lip crenate, five folds on columella. White, with reddish brown axial streaks and spots, and two narrow spiral bands. Aperture white. Sometimes uniformly reddish brown with orange aperture. 3·8–6·4cm. Indo-Pacific. Uncommon.

Mitra papalis Linnaeus   ×0.6
Papal Mitre

Shell thick, heavy, fusiform. Coronate suture. A few spiral striae towards base. Densely variegated with reddish brown blobs of various sizes on white. Aperture white. 5–6 folds on columella. 6–12cm. Indo-Pacific. Uncommon.

Mitra papilio Link
sphaerulata Reeve, *scabriuscula* Lamarck. Shell fusiform. Elevated spiral cords, fine axial striae. 4–5 folds on orange columella. Outer lip dentate. Small, brown dots on white. Aperture equal to or longer than spire, creamy orange. 1·5–5·5cm. Indo-Pacific. Rare.

Mitra praestantissima Röding   ×1.5
Shell thick, elongate-fusiform, narrow, with moderately impressed suture and thin

outer lip. 10–12 chestnut brown spiral ridges on body whorl, fewer on spire whorls; interstices cancellated with equally strong spiral and axial lines. 3–5 strong folds on columella. Whitish with brown spiral ridges. Aperture and columella white. 3·5–4·5cm. Indo-Pacific. Uncommon.

Mitra puncticulata Lamarck   ×1.4
diadema Swainson, *serpentina* Wood.

Shell fairly solid, elongate-ovate. Suture coronate, with distinctive short nodules pointing slightly outwards. Axial ridges and spiral rows of small punctures. 4–5 folds on columella. Outer lip crenate. Broken axial bands of black on yellow and orange. Aperture pale yellow. 2·8–5·0cm. Indo-Pacific. Uncommon.

Mitra scabricula Linnaeus   ×1.4
texturata Lamarck, *radiatum* Wood.

Shell ovate and broad. Elevated and rounded spiral cords interspersed with fine striae and cut by thin axial grooves. 4–5 folds on columella. Outer lip dentate. Cords pale orange brown and white. Rest of shell whitish with orange brown axial bands. Aperture cream. 3·0–5·5cm. Indo-Pacific. Rare.

Mitra stictica Link   ×1.0
Pontifical Mitre
pontificalis Lamarck.

Shell elongate-ovate, thick, smooth except for rows of spiral punctures, glossy. Suture coronate. Fine axial striae. Outer lip dentate. 4–5 folds on columella from which extend spiral ridges. Spiral bands of orange or vermilion patches on creamy white 2·8–6·5cm. Indo-Pacific. Uncommon.

Mitra terebralis Lamarck   ×0.8

Large, thick, elongate-fusiform shell with almost straight-sided whorls and crenulate suture. Broad spiral cords at centre of whorls, finer lirae near suture; axial ribs

175

give cancellate ornament on early whorls. Outer lip crenulate. Six folds on columella. Creamy, tinged with orange brown; dark brown axial streaks. Broad, whitish spiral band on lower half of body whorl. Aperture pinkish yellow. 6–12cm. Indo-Pacific. Common.

Mitra zaca Hertlein & Hanna   ×0.7

Above: *Swainsonia casta*.
Below: *Swainsonia fissurata*.

Shell large, thick, slender with almost straight-sided whorls, sloping shoulders and scarcely impressed suture. Siphonal canal broad and recurved. Columella with three folds. Faint spiral striae at base of body whorl and on early whorls. Fine, axial growth lines which become coarser on body whorl. Yellowish white. Brownish black periostracum. 9–10cm. Panamic. Uncommon.

Genus SWAINSONIA H. & A. Adams
Shells fairly small, resembling *Oliva* in shape and smooth, shiny surface. Short spire, long, narrow aperture. Outer lip thick and smooth. About 10 species.

Swainsonia casta Gmelin   ×1.6
Shell smooth, whorls slightly convex. Aperture longer than spire. Glossy. 5–6 folds on columella. Broad, black or dark brown spiral bands on white. Aperture white. Outer lip smooth. 2–5cm. Indo-Pacific. Uncommon.

Swainsonia fissurata Lamarck   ×1.6
Shell narrowly fusiform, smooth, glossy. 4–5 folds on columella. Outer lip smooth. Oblique, white reticulations on orange white and pale brown. Aperture pale brown. 3·5–4·0cm. Indo-Pacific (Indian Ocean). Uncommon.

Swainsonia olivaeformis Swainson
Superficially resembles *S. casta* but much smaller and has relatively much shorter spire. Apex sharply pointed. Axially ribbed on early whorls of some specimens. Body whorl smooth or ornamented with 1–6 spiral, punctate grooves. Five strong folds on columella. Yellow; purple at apex and base. 1–2cm. Indo-Pacific (Pacific). Common.

Swainsonia variegata Gmelin   ×1.8
Thick, solid shell with tall spire and large body whorl. Whorls shouldered and not very rounded. Ornamented with widely spaced and deeply punctate spiral grooves, the punctures becoming obsolete towards

base. Outer lip sometimes crenulate. Columella with 5–6 folds. Whitish, with dark brown, axial, curved streaks and one or two broad bands of lighter brown with white blotches arranged spirally on them. 2–4cm. Indo-Pacific (Pacific). Rare.

Genus STRIGATELLA Swainson
Shells ovate to elongate-ovate, solid and heavy. Pointed spire, smooth whorls, narrow aperture. Outer lip thick, smooth or crenulate. Perhaps 30 species or less.

Strigatella litterata Lamarck
Shell intermediate in size between *S. paupercula* and *S. scutulata* but bearing a closer resemblance to *S. paupercula* in shape and colour. Thick, solid, with moderately tall spire and impressed suture. Outer lip incurved and thickened in middle portion. Fine spiral grooves which become more conspicuous towards base. 4–5 folds on columella. Creamy white with broad, axial, wavy streaks arranged, on body whorl, in three spiral bands. 1·5–3·0cm. Indo-Pacific. Common.

Strigatella paupercula Linnaeus   ×1.6
venosa Röding, *zebra* Lamarck, *lineata* Swainson, *obtusata* Dautzenberg & Bouge.

Shell solid, elongate-ovate. Outer lip crenate. 3–4 folds on columella. Broad, axial, white stripes on dark brown. 1·4–3·2cm. Indo-Pacific. Frequent.

Strigatella pellisserpentis Reeve
granata Reeve, *cretacea* Sowerby, *brumalis* Reeve, *nassoides* Sowerby.
Shell small, thick, elongate-ovate with pointed spire and deeply impressed suture. Slightly convex whorls. Numerous irregular spiral grooves bisected by equally numerous axial grooves. Outer lip thickened and incurved at posterior end, denticulate. Four folds on columella. Yellow or yellowish brown. Aperture paler yellow or white. 2–3cm. Indo-Pacific. Uncommon.

Strigatella retusa Lamarck
Resembles *S. paupercula* but differs in having a crenulate outer lip. Orange brown, reddish brown or dark brown, with wavy, axial, white lines. Narrow, whitish spiral band on body whorl also differentiates this species from *S. paupercula*. 1·5–3·0cm. Indo-Pacific. Uncommon.

Strigatella scutulata Gmelin   × 2.1
discolor Röding, *amphorella* Lamarck, *sertum* Duval.

Shell solid, elongate-ovate,. with slightly convex whorls. Fine spiral ridges becoming rounded cords near base. 4–5 folds on columella. Outer lip thick, smooth. Olive brown with axial white or cream streaks and patches. Aperture white, flushed brown at margin. 2·5–4·5cm. Indo-Pacific. Frequent.

Genus PTERYGIA Röding
Shells cylindrically-ovate, solid and thick. Short, conical spire. Smooth or spirally ridged whorls. Columella usually callused. Perhaps 20 species or less.

Pterygia conus Gmelin
conulus Lamarck.
Shell conical-ovate. Spire short, apex pointed. Callus on whorl shoulder and columella. Lattice of thin, dark spiral lines on grey to olive brown. Aperture white. 5–6 folds on columella. 3·0–3·6cm. Indo-Pacific (Pacific). Rare.

Pterygia crenulata Gmelin   × 1.6
coronata Schumacher, *toleranda* Iredale, *fastidiosa* Iredale.

Shell thick, cylindrical and short-spired. Long, narrow, denticulate aperture. 7–9 folds on columella. Numerous punctate spiral grooves crossed by fine, axial growth striae. Whorls crenulate at suture. Whitish with irregular, light or darker brown, spiral and axial bands. *c*3cm. Indo-Pacific. Uncommon.

Pterygia dactylus Linnaeus   × 1.3
nucella Röding, *obesa* Reeve.

Shell solid, cylindrically ovate. Spire short, pointed at apex. Lattice of axial and more conspicuous spiral striae. Suture shallow. 6–7 folds on columella. Outer lip very thick, smooth. Mottled brown bands on white. Aperture white. 2·5–5·2cm. Indo-Pacific. Uncommon.

Pterygia fenestrata Lamarck   × 1.6

Shell thick, cylindrically ovate, with short spire. Shell encircled by elevated spiral ridges bisected by weak, broad, irregular axial ridges. Outer lip thick and crenulate. 8–9 oblique folds on columella. White with dark brown spiral ridges. 2·0–2·5cm. Indo-Pacific. Uncommon.

Pterygia nucea Gmelin   × 1.0
spuria Gmelin, *olivaria* Lamarck.

Thick, solid shell with very large, inflated body whorl and short, blunt spire. Suture impressed. 5–6 strong folds on columella. Creamy white with one or two dark brown bands and spiral rows of small, brown dots. Aperture white. May be pinkish instead of white. 3·5–5·5cm. Indo-Pacific (Pacific). Uncommon.

Pterygia sinensis Reeve   × 1.6
Thick, strong shell with spire relatively taller than that of *P. crenulata*. Prominently ornamented with close-set spiral ridges which are bisected by axial grooves giving

a rough texture to surface. Suture coronate and impressed. Nine folds on columella. Light brown with irregular, darker axial streaks. *c*4cm. Indo-Pacific. Uncommon.

Pterygia solida Reeve
Shell much less solid and more slender than most species of this genus. Tall spire with convex whorls. Outer lip sharp. Glossy and ornamented with punctate spiral grooves. Four folds on columella. Fawn with spiral bands or irregular, white spots and blotches. Aperture and columella white. 3·0–4·5cm. Indo-Pacific (Pacific). Uncommon.

Genus IMBRICARIA Schumacher
Conoelix Swainson, *Conohelix* Sowerby.
Small, short-spired, conical shells with smooth or striate whorls and straight, narrow aperture. Outer lip thickened. Columella plicate. Thin periostracum. Few species in Indo-Pacific.

Imbricaria conularis Lamarck   ×2.0
conica Schumacher, *marmoratus* Swainson, *lineatus* Swainson.

Thick, fusiform shell with short spire and acutely pointed apex. 6–8 folds on columella. Smooth and glossy. Grey with spiral, orange lines and irregular, axial cream bands. Aperture brownish violet. 1·5–2·5cm. Indo-Pacific. Common.

Family VASIDAE
Thick to very thick, heavy shells. Short- or tall-spired with moderately long, or long siphonal canal. Usually three or four folds on columella. Weakly or strongly tuberculated and sometimes spiny. The 20 or more living species are all carnivorous and belong to about six genera. Widely distributed in tropical and warm seas.

Genus VASUM Röding
Cynodonta Schumacher,
Scolymus Swainson.
Very thick, heavy shells usually with short spire and large, inflated body whorl. Oranamented with large nodules, spines or rough ridges. About twelve species all of them carnivorous which live in sand among rocks in shallow and deep water in tropical seas.

Vasum ceramicum Linnaeus   ×0.6
Shell large, very solid and heavy. Elongate-fusiform with tall spire and attenuate siphonal canal. Spiral row of large, conical spines on shoulders; body whorl has 3–5 low spiral ribs bearing smaller tubercles or spines. Columella with three strong folds. Small or closed umbilicus. Whitish with blackish brown blobs sometimes arranged in axial and spiral bands. Tips of spines always black. Aperture white; columella white with blackish brown patches at centre and base. 8–13cm. Indo-Pacific. Common.

Right: *Vasum ceramicum*.

Below: *Vasum muricatum*.

Vasum muricatum Born   ×0.6
caestus Broderip.
Shell large, thick and heavy with moderately raised spire and large body whorl. Spines at shoulder and near base. Sometimes with heavy spiral cords (on Panamic form *V. caestus*). Columella with five strong folds. White, obscured by thick, dark brown periostracum. Aperture white tinged with purple. 7–11cm. Panamic, Caribbean. Common.

Vasum tubiferum Anton   ×0.9
Thick, heavy, broadly ovate shell with large body whorl and moderately tall, acuminate spire. Small but deep umbilicus. Moderately long and broad siphonal canal. Puckered outer lip. Five or six folds on columella. Stout axial ribs with short and long, fluted spines. Body whorl

Below: *Vasum turbinellum*.   Above: *Vasum tubiferum*.

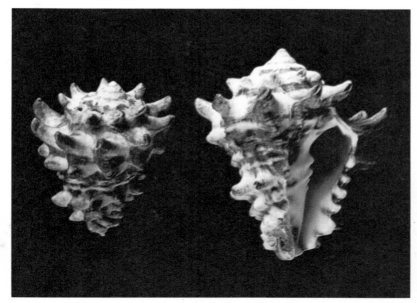

has spines longest at shoulder and another shorter row is developed below mid-line. Creamy, with dark and light brown, axial mottling and streaks. Aperture white, columella pinkish brown and white. 6–11cm. Indo-Pacific (Philippines). Uncommon.

Vasum turbinellum Linnaeus   ×0.8
cornigerum Lamarck.
Very thick, ovate shell with short, blunt spire. Outer lip crenulate. Columella with five or six folds. Apart from the usually worn apex, whole shell bears spiral rows of large, thick, slightly curved tubercles which may be lengthened to form spines. Whitish, blotched and spirally banded with dark brown. Aperture creamy yellow

with brown bars on inside of outer lip. Very variable in size and ornament. 3–8cm. Indo-Pacific. Common.

Genus TUDICLA Röding
Thick, solid shells with large, inflated body whorl and long siphonal canal. Spire very short, apex papillary. Columella smooth with fold at anterior end. One species.

Tudicla spirillus Linnaeus   ×0.8
For details, see genus *Tudicla*. Body whorl has sharp spiral ridge at shoulder. Numerous low spiral cords and a single spiral row of large tubercles at lower part of body whorl becoming obsolete towards aperture. Suture wavy. Aperture lirate

within. Siphonal canal may be curved. 5–8cm. Indo-Pacific (Indian Ocean). Uncommon.

Genus TUDICULA H. & A. Adams
Fairly thick, pear-shaped shells with broad, squat apex and long siphonal canal. Spiral ribs with short or long, hollow spines between shoulders and suture. Outer lip thickened. Three or four folds on columella. Four species, all from Australian waters.

Tudicula armigera A. Adams   ×0.9

Shell fairly thick, pear-shaped with long, straight siphonal canal. Spiral row of long, hollow spines on shoulders and fine spiral ribs with short spines. Aperture smooth but outer lip may be weakly crenulated. Columella with three or four strong folds. Cream or white sometimes spotted with brown. Aperture white. 6–8cm. Indo-Pacific (Australia). Uncommon.

Tudicula inermis Angas
Differs from *T. armigera* by its smaller size and spineless shell. The globose body whorl has a very long, straight anterior canal. Ornament consists only of fine spiral threads with finer axial striae between them. Aperture strongly lirate within. Well developed parietal shield. White, cream or pale brown with dark brown axial streaks and blotches. Aperture, parietal wall and columella white. *c*5cm. Indo-Pacific (North Australia). Uncommon.

Genus AFER Conrad
Thick, ovate-fusiform shells with inflated body whorl, moderately tall spire and long siphonal canal. Usually ornamented with spiral ribs or cords. One or two folds on columella. Few species in Atlantic, West African and Indo-Pacific waters.

Afer cumingii Reeve   × 0.9

Thick, globose shell with large body whorl, moderately long spire and long siphonal canal. Blunt tooth at beginning of siphonal canal. Thin parietal callus. Outer lip lirate within. Shoulder of each whorl has spiral row of nodules. Above and below each whorl are numerous irregular spiral cords. Yellowish brown, mottled and spotted with darker brown. Aperture white. *c*7cm Indo-Pacific (Taiwan and South China Sea). Uncommon.

Family XANCIDAE

Small family of large, thick and very heavy shells. Elongate-fusiform or globose and short-spired with moderately long and thick siphonal canal. Three or four folds on columella. One species in Indian Ocean and two in Caribbean.

Genus XANCUS Röding
Turbinella Lamarck.
For details, see Family Xancidae.

Xancus angulatus Lightfoot
scolymus Gmelin.
Much larger than *X. pyrum* and *X. laevigatus*, ornamented with prominent axial ribs which are coronated at shoulder. Moderately long, very broad siphonal canal. Narrow, chink-like umbilicus. Spiral grooves and ridges on spire, and on upper and lower portions of body whorl. Three or four widely spaced folds on columella. Whitish orange. Thick, dark brown periostracum. 17–34cm. Caribbean. Uncommon.

Xancus laevigatus Anton
Compared with *X. pyrum* this species is more elongate, has a longer, straighter siphonal canal, taller spire with rounded whorls and a small papillary apex. Body whorl less inflated with well rounded sides. Three strong folds on columella. Thick and solid but not so thick or as heavy as *X. pyrum*. Numerous fine spiral ridges. Unicolorous pinkish white. Thick, brown periostracum. 10–13cm. Caribbean (North East Brazil). Uncommon.

Xancus pyrum Linnaeus   × 0.35
Indian Chank
fusus Sowerby.
Shell large, thick and heavy with moderately raised spire and slightly impressed suture. Very large body whorl with long aperture. Four strong folds on columella; broad thick callus on parietal wall and columella. White with few small, scattered, brown spots on body whorl and on early whorls. Parietal wall, columella folds and edge of outer lip flushed pink. Rest of aperture white. Covered with thick, dark brown, fibrous periostracum.

Below: *Harpa amouretta*.

10–15cm. Indo-Pacific (Indian Ocean). Common.

Family HARPIDAE

Harp shells are easily distinguished by their well defined axial ribs and usually bright colour patterns. Shells are ovate with large body whorl and small, conical spire. Points which terminate the ribs form a coronet around spire. Aperture is wide, adjacent labial region usually smooth and glossy. Operculum lacking. Harps are carnivorous. Twelve species known, all members of genus *Harpa*. They occur in Indo-Pacific, Panamic, West African and Japonic provinces.

Genus HARPA Walch
Details as for Family Harpidae. Callus extends over spire.

Harpa amouretta Röding   ×1.5
minor Lamarck.
Small, elongate, with slightly folded ribs.
Spire slightly elevated. White, with cream
and pale brown bands. Aperture white,
sometimes flushed brown. 4–6cm. Indo-
Pacific (South West Pacific). Common.

Harpa articularis Lamarck   ×0.7

Ribs few and narrow, blend into whorl.
White, pink and light brown, with brown,
crescent-shaped markings between ribs.
Aperture light brown, white towards lip.
5–9cm. Indo-Pacific (South West Pacific).
Frequent.

Harpa costata Linnaeus
Imperial Harp
imperialis Lamarck.
Many densely folded ribs (normally up to
35), overlapping towards spire. about
a dozen ending abruptly at columella.
Banded white, cream and brown. Columella may be orange. Aperture cream. 6–
8cm. Indo-Pacific (Mauritius). Rare.

Harpa crenata Swainson   ×0.8
testudinalis Lamarck.
Ribs narrow and low, each bearing three

or four callused points. Outer lip may be
dentate. Usually pale, violet and brown,
with fine, brown line on ribs. Variable
blotches near aperture. 6–9cm. Panamic
(Mexican West Coast). Uncommon.

Above: *Harpa costata.*
Below left: *Harpa crenata.*

Harpa davidis Röding   ▽ ×0.8
conoidalis Lamarck.
Ribs less thickly folded than those of *H.*

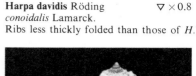

major, thin, sharp-edged, with dark bands. Light brown and cream, with occasional flushes of violet. Columella with one large patch of brown. 6·5–9·0cm. Indo-Pacific. Common.

Harpa doris Röding   × 1.2
rosea Lamarck.

Above: *Harpa harpa*.
Below: *Harpa major*.

Shell thin. Narrow, low ribs with small coronate points. Rose pink, pale violet and white, with light brown bands and crescent-shaped markings. Brown patches on labial lip. Aperture white, with some external colour showing through. 3·5–6·5 cm. West African. Rare.

Harpa harpa Linnaeus
Common Harp
nobilis Röding.
Ribs blend smoothly into whorl, produced towards spire. White, cream, brown and violet. Groups of thin, dark brown bands on ribs. Crescent-shaped markings between ribs. Columella cream, with dark brown patches. Aperture white flushed orange, with brown markings at margin. 5–7cm. Indo-Pacific (South West Pacific). Frequent.

Harpa major Röding   × 0.8
ventricosa Lamarck.
Ribs wide, strongly folded. Spire short, apex raised. Ribs with clear banding of white, pink and brown. Brown tooth-like markings on cream in between. Two dark brown patches near aperture. 6–9cm. Indo-Pacific. Common.

Family VOLUTIDAE

Large family containing 43 genera. Shells mostly thick, heavy and colourful, but some deeper-water species have fragile, colourless shells. About 30 of the 200 or more known living species have an operculum. Great variation in size, sculpture and colour has given rise to description of excessive number of so-called species. Volutes are among most popular, most beautiful and most expensive of all shells coveted by collectors. Most species feed on other molluscs or scavenge for food. The majority live in tropical waters and are often found in relatively deep water.

Genus VOLUTA Linnaeus
Shells solid, moderately large to very large. Ovate to elongate. Smooth or axially ribbed, with strong or weak shoulder nodules. Spiral sculpture sometimes present. Strong folds on columella. Operculum present. Three species in Caribbean province.

182

Voluta ebraea Linnaeus   ×0.5
Hebrew Volute

Shell thick, massive, ovate. Sutures irregular and impressed. Five shouldered whorls with blunt spines. Irregular, brown reticulations on cream. Slightly glossy. 4–6 raised folds on columella. c15cm. Caribbean (Brazil). Uncommon.

Voluta musica Linnaeus   ×0.8
Music Volute

Shell thick, especially outer lip. Ovate. Axial ribs with tubercles at shoulder. Fine axial striae. Alternating bands of very thin, brown lines and small, brown dots on cream making pattern resembling sheet music. Aperture cream, flushed violet. Approximately ten folds on columella. Extremely variable. 4·5–9·5cm. Caribbean. Frequent.

Genus TERNIVOLUTA von Martens
Elongate-fusiform, light shells with moderately tall spire and blunt apex. Shoulders coronated with small nodules. Whorls angled just below suture. Siphonal notch poorly developed. Few folds on columella. One species.

Ternivoluta studeri von Martens   ×0.9

For details see genus *Ternivoluta*. Narrow axial ribs on spire whorls becoming obsolete towards body whorl. Shoulders sloping to sharp-edged ridge. Spiral lirae on body whorl. Four folds on columella. Creamy brown with crowded, axial, wavy, brown lines. Three bands of creamy brown blotches on body whorl. 4–5cm. Indo-Pacific (North East Australia). Frequent.

Genus LYRIA Gray
Elongate to fusiform shells varying greatly in size. Axial ribs sometimes present. One or more folds on columella. Siphonal notch and fasciole distinct. 22 species inhabiting the continental shelves of tropical and subtropical seas.

Lyria mitraeformis Lamarck   ×1.4
multicostata Broderip.

Shell fusiform. Spire moderately high. Numerous, narrow axial ribs. Outer lip thick, elliptical. Three folds on columella. Brown spots and patches tending to form bands on cream or yellow. Aperture creamy white. 3·0–5·5cm. Australian. Common.

Genus FULGORARIA Schumacher
Shells medium to large. Ovate to fusiform. Heavy or light. Spire short or tall. One or more folds on columella. Siphonal notch absent or shallow. Operculum lacking. Species vary from glossy to dull, colourful to plain. 21 uncommon and rare species from Japonic province.

Fulgoraria concinna Broderip
Shell fusiform, with shouldered whorls. Spire raised, with axial ribs. 4–5 folds on columella. Siphonal notch and fasciole absent. Dull. Spiral bands of dark and pale brown. 9–19cm. Japonic. Frequent.

Fulgoraria daviesi Fulton   × 0·7

Large, fusiform, fairly solid shell with tall, slender spire. Few low axial ribs becoming weak on body whorl. Fine, closely spaced spiral lines. Axial growth lines on body whorl. No siphonal notch. Four or five folds on columella. Greyish brown with indistinct, brown, zigzag markings arranged spirally. 7–17cm. Japonic. Frequent.

Fulgoraria hamillei Crosse
Shell fusiform. Spire extended, with rounded apex. Sculpture and colour variable. Typically with shouldered whorls, axial ribs, axial and spiral striae. Dull, except near aperture. Creamy brown, with some dark brown, zigzag reticulations. 10–16cm. Japonic. Uncommon.

Fulgoraria mentiens Fulton

Mainly resembles *F. daviesi*, but can be distinguished from that species by having more numerous axial ribs and an almost smooth body whorl. Early whorls with strong spiral striae which become obsolete on body whorl. Outer lip thickened and slightly reflected. Indistinct siphonal notch. 4–5 folds on columella. Light reddish brown with spiral bands of dark brown, interrupted, axial markings. 7–21cm. Japonic. Frequent.

Fulgoraria prevostiana Crosse   ×0.8

Moderately large to large, fusiform shell. Spire almost as tall as aperture. The moderately inflated whorls have strong axial ribs crossed by weak spiral striae. Outer lip thick. No siphonal notch. Three or four folds on slightly concave columella. Yellowish brown to reddish brown, sometimes with three broad bands of dark brown, zigzag markings. Very variable in size and ornament. 10–22cm. Japonic. Common.

Fulgoraria rupestris Gmelin   ×0.5

Medium-sized, fusiform, solid shell with moderately short, blunt spire. Apex large and papillary. Outer lip thickened and smooth. Columella with 7–9 short folds. Coarse axial ribs which become obsolete on body whorl crossed by numerous strong lirae. Creamy white or greenish white with axial, brownish, zigzag lines.

Aperture pale brown, whiter towards margin. 7–12cm. Indo-Pacific (Taiwan). Uncommon.

Genus ERICUSA H. & A. Adams

Shells medium to large, solid. Elongate to ovate-fusiform. Apex large and bulbous, or small and papillary. Siphonal notch present. Three or more folds on columella. Operculum absent. Six species living in Australian waters.

Ericusa papillosa Swainson
kenyoniana Brazier.

Shell thick, oblong-ovate. Fine axial striae. Slight gloss. Coffee with broken, brown bands. Aperture mushroom. Derives name from apex which is extended and papillate. 4–5 folds on columella. 7–14cm. Indo-Pacific (East Australia). Frequent.

Ericusa sericata Thornley   ×0.7

Medium-sized, narrowly ovate, solid shell with short spire and rounded apex. Suture slightly impressed. Whole shell smooth. Siphonal notch wide and shallow. Four folds on columella. Creamy brown with paler, irregular, triangular markings arranged in two broad spiral bands. Aperture orange. 7–12cm. Australian (East Australia). Uncommon.

Ericusa sowerbyi Kiener   ×0.35

Sowerby's Volute

Shell ovate-fusiform. Spire extended. Fine, longitudinal striae. Slight gloss. Brown, zigzag reticulations on cream, or light brown. Aperture cream flushed with orange. Four folds on columella. 9–26cm. Indo-Pacific (East Australia). Uncommon.

Genus CYMBIUM Röding   ×0.5

Shells medium to very large. Cylindrically or globosely ovate. Spire short or sunken, occasionally callused and surrounded by a sharp or rounded ridge formed at shoulder of body whorl. Strong folds on columella. Operculum absent. Eight species from western end of Mediterranean to coast of Central West Africa.

Cymbium cucumis Röding

Shell moderately large for the genus and heavy. Cylindrically ovate with short spire and blunt apex. Spire is sometimes higher than shoulder ridge which is usually slightly curved inwards towards apex. Deep channel separates spire from shoulder ridge. Three folds on columella. Siphonal notch deep. Body whorl usually heavily glazed and smooth except for occasional warty pustules. Shell without surface ornament. Unicolorous pale brown. Thin, pale brown periostracum. 10–18cm. West African. Uncommon.

Above: *Cymbium cucumis.*
Below: *Cymbium glans.*

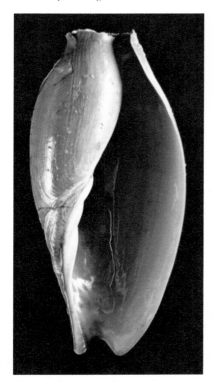

Cymbium cymbium Linnaeus
Elephant's Snout Volute
scafa Lightfoot, *unicolor* Link, *porcina* Lamarck.
Shell fairly thick, cylindrically ovate. Outer lip extends convexly to form very large aperture. Spire sunken, suture callused. Faint gloss. Cream to olive brown. 2–3 folds on columella. 10–16cm. West African. Rare.

Cymbium glans Gmelin   × 0.3
proboscidalis Lamarck.
Shell very large, light, cylindrically ovate, swollen at centre. Spire sunken and not visible over the sharp shoulder of body whorl. Surface ornament absent except for warty pustules on some specimens. Siphonal notch deep and moderately broad. Four folds on columella. Unicolorous deep creamy brown, becoming a dark chocolate brown at the raised, posterior rim of body whorl. 25–32cm. West African. Frequent.

Cymbium olla Linnaeus   × 0.5

Shell relatively small for the genus, thin but solid. Broadly inflated with exposed and rounded apex. Very deep channel at suture of body whorl. Siphonal notch wide and moderately deep. Two oblique folds on columella. Parietal area heavily and coarsely glazed. Reddish to yellowish brown. Thin, pale brown periostracum. 9–12cm. Mediterranean, West African (Dakar). Uncommon.

Genus MELO Broderip
Large to very large shells, narrowly ovate to globosely ovate with exposed or hidden spire. Apex smooth, large and dome-shaped. Spire whorls smooth or coronated. Suture may be channelled. Columella with several strong folds. Does not differ in shell characters from *Cymbium*; there are differences in the nervous system and incubation specialisations of the two genera.

Melo amphora Lightfoot   × 0.2

Shell very large and heavy. Ovate, with short, blunt spire and very large, inflated body whorl. Early whorls coronated with short, sharp spines which become obsolete on most of body whorl. Columella arched, with three strong, oblique folds. Siphonal notch wide and somewhat shallow. White or creamy orange with axial, chocolate brown lines which are often interrupted to form two spiral bands on body whorl. Suture creamy orange, whiter at margin. Thin, brown periostracum. 30–47cm. Indo-Pacific (Australia and New Guinea). Common.

Melo aethiopica Linnaeus   × 0.2
tesselata Lamarck, *nautica* Lamarck.
Shell moderately large, heavy, very inflated, with spire not visible above shoulder. Apex large, dome-shaped. Suture deeply channelled near aperture.

Numerous closely-spaced, sharp spines on later whorls which tend to curve inwards towards apex. Body whorl with fine, axial growth lines. Broad parietal callus. Three strong folds on the concave columella. Siphonal notch wide and deep. Yellowish or reddish yellow with two broad, lighter spiral bands. Thin, brown periostracum. 20–25cm. Indo-Pacific (Indonesia). Uncommon.

Genus CYMBIOLA Swainson

Shells small to very large and mostly heavy. Short, blunt-topped spire. Mostly smooth shells but some of the 16 living species have blunt or pointed spines on whorl shoulders. Strong folds on columella. Operculum absent. Found in tropical and subtropical waters of Eastern Indian Ocean and Western Pacific Ocean.

Cymbiola flavicans Gmelin   ×0.9
volvacea Lamarck.

Shell thick, ovate. Spire short, apex blunt. Blunt, widely spaced tubercles on shoulder, sometimes absent. Fine axial striae. Four folds on columella. Creamy white, with brown to dark violet streaks. Two spiral bands on last whorl. Aperture pale to dark violet, cream margin. 6–10cm. Indo-Pacific (Australia, New Guinea). Frequent.

Cymbiola imperialis Lightfoot   ×0.4

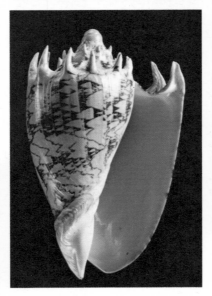

Shell thick, heavy, ovate, oblong with tall spire. Apex blunt, papillary. Body whorl very large with almost straight-sided edge to aperture. Siphonal notch narrow and deep. Four strong folds on columella. Single spiral row of large, upturned and open spines on shoulder. Pinkish with numerous axial, zigzag lines and tent-like, brownish markings which sometimes form two broad bands on body whorl. 15–25cm. Indo-Pacific (Philippines). Common.

Cymbiola magnifica Gebauer   ×0.4

Shell large, heavy, ovate with short spire and large body whorl. Blunt, papillary apex. Blunt, broad tubercles on shoulder of body whorl. Four oblique folds on columella. Columella and parietal wall glazed. Siphonal notch wide and deep. Pinkish white with three or four spiral, chocolate brown bands on body whorl. Few lines of large and small, whitish triangles. 18–30cm. Australian. Uncommon.

Cymbiola nivosa Lamarck   ×0.8
Shell thin, oblong-ovate, with short, blunt spire. Tubercles on whorl shoulder, some-

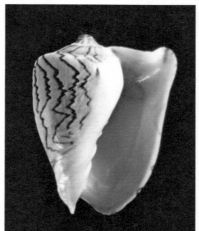

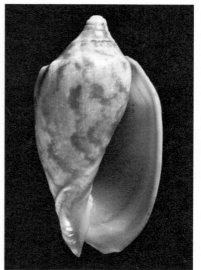

times absent. Glossy. Flecked white; spiral bands of thin, brown lines on mushroom or orange red. Aperture creamy brown. Very variable in colour and ornament. 6·0–9·5cm. Indo-Pacific (Northern Australia). Frequent.

Cymbiola nobilis Lightfoot   ×0.45
scapha Gmelin, *fasciata* Schubert & Wagner.
Large, very heavy, broadly ovate shell with short spire and blunt apex. Widely spaced, low, flattened tubercles on whorl shoulders, particularly on shoulder of body whorl. Outer lip thickened and, in mature specimens, with a wing-like extension at posterior end. Siphonal notch narrow and deep. Four folds on columella. Yellowish cream with axial, zigzag, dark brown lines and blotches which sometimes form two indistinct spiral bands on body whorl. Very variable in size and pattern. 10–18cm. Indo-Pacific (Pacific). Common.

Cymbiola rutila Broderip   ×0.7
norrisii Gray, *piperita* Sowerby.
Shell thick, ovate. Spire short, apex blunt. Axial ribs with nodules on shoulders, sometimes absent. Four oblique folds on columella. Fasciolar ridge well defined. Glossy. Greyish, with brown or blackish dots, reticulations and streaks forming three obscure bands on last whorl. Aperture creamy orange, expanding anteriorly. 6–13cm. Indo-Pacific (Pacific only). Frequent.

Cymbiola vespertilio Linnaeus   ×0.7
Bat Volute
Shell heavy, ovate to elongate. Spire short. Apex blunt. Axial ribs, with tubercles on shoulders. Fine axial striae. Four raised, oblique folds on columella. Glossy. Cream to olive, with network of brown reticulations. Aperture greyish cream. Very variable in shape and colour. 4–12cm. Indo-Pacific (Pacific). Frequent.

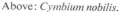

Above: *Cymbium nobilis.*

Right (top and centre): *Cymbium rutila;* (bottom): *Cymbium vespertilio.*

187

Genus CYMBIOLACCA Iredale

Medium-sized to moderately large, elongate or ovate shells with shouldered and noduled whorls. Short spire and small, blunt apex. No operculum. Seven species, all living along East coast of Australia and eastwards to New Caledonia.

Cymbiolacca peristicta McMichael × 0.9

Shell very similar to *C. pulchra* and may prove to be conspecific. Differs from *C. pulchra* by being relatively broader and having sharper, more pronounced shoulder tubercles. Pinkish white with numerous dark brown spots of varying sizes. Large, pinkish brown blotches form spiral band at middle of body whorl. Illustrated specimen is of a tall form closely resembling *C. pulchra*. 5·5–7·5cm. Indo-Pacific (Queensland, Australia). Rare.

Cymbiolacca pulchra Sowerby × 1.0
perryi Ostergaard & Summers, *woolacottae* McMichael, *nielseni* McMichael.

Medium-sized, narrowly ovate, solid shell with short spire and blunt apex. Sharp, pointed and upturned nodules at whorl shoulders. Spiral ribs on apical whorls. Siphonal notch narrow and deep. Four folds on columella. Very variable colour and pattern. Typically orange brown with triangular, white markings and dark brown spots and dashes. Two or three darker brown spiral bands on body whorl. 5·5–9·0cm. Indo-Pacific (North East Australia). Frequent.

Genus ZIDONA H. & A. Adams
Contains a single species, described below.

Zidona dufresnei Donovan
angulata Swainson.
Shell large and heavy. Basically fusiform, modified by shouldered whorls and large, oblong aperture. Entire shell covered by glaze. Callused spire very narrow, pointed, apex extended. Suture indented. 2–4 folds on columella. Operculum absent. Smooth and glossy. Cream, with wavy axial streaks of brown and violet. Orange on apex, outer lip and columella. 15cm. Patagonian. Frequent.

Genus ADELOMELON Dall
Shells medium to very large. Elongate or inflated with depressed or elevated spire. Columella without folds. Operculum absent. Seven species off Eastern South America and Falkland Islands. Most are rare deep-water forms.

Adelomelon beckii Broderip
fusiformis Kiener, *festiva* d'Orbigny.
Shell thick, fusiform. Spire tall, apex papillate. Nodules on whorl shoulders sometimes missing in adult. 2–4 folds on almost straight columella. Outer lip slightly thickened. Siphonal notch broad, deep. Cream to pale brown, with axial, brown, zigzag lines. Aperture cream. 35–45cm. Caribbean, Patagonian (Southern Brazil to Argentina). Uncommon.

Genus ALCITHOE H. & A. Adams
Shells small to large and light or heavy. Fusiform with bulbous apex. Outer lip thickened. Columella with four or more folds. Siphonal notch present. Operculum absent. All seven species live in New Zealand waters. Most are rare deep-water species.

Alcithoe arabica Gmelin
pacifica Perry.
Shell solid, fusiform, with elliptical outer lip. Spire narrow and pointed. Axial ribbing on shoulders of early whorls. Last whorl smooth with low tubercles on shoulder. 3–4 folds on columella. Cream to pale brown, with scattered, small, dark brown or blackish lines and patches. Aperture white. 8–20cm. Australian (New Zealand). Frequent.

Alcithoe swainsoni Marwick × 0.5
elongata Swainson, *calva* Powell, *ostenfeldi* Iredale.

Shell thick, elongate-ovate with short, acuminate spire and blunt apex. Low, wide axial ribs on early whorls. Body whorl smooth. Outer lip thickened, slightly reflected. Siphonal notch wide and deep. 4–6 folds on columella. Pale brown with widely spaced, zigzag, axial, brown lines which are more conspicuous on dorsal side of body whorl. Extremely variable in size, shape, colour pattern and presence or absence of shoulder tubercles and axial ribs. 9–22cm. Australian (New Zealand). Uncommon.

Genus HARPULINA Dall
Moderately large, oblong-ovate shells with short spire and pointed apex. Early whorls axially ribbed, tubercles on shoulders of later whorls. Numerous folds on columella. Siphonal notch present. No operculum. Two species in Indian Ocean.

Harpulina arausiaca Lightfoot
vexillum Gmelin.
Distantly similar to *H. lapponica* but spire taller and narrower and whorls more strongly shouldered. Also very different colour and pattern. Early whorls axially ribbed; low, blunt shoulder tubercles on later whorls including body whorl. 6–8 folds on columella. Pinkish white with narrow, bright orange, spiral bands and a few bright orange axial streaks. 7–11cm. Indo-Pacific (Sri Lanka). Rare.

Harpulina lapponica Linnaeus   ×0.7
indica Sowerby, *interpuncta* Reeve,
loroisi Valenciennes.

Thick, ovate shell with short spire and
small, pointed apex. Narrow axial ribs on
early whorls, low shoulder tubercles on
later whorls becoming obsolete on body
whorl. Outer lip thin. 7–8 folds on columella. Colour very variable. Typically with
cream ground colour and numerous fine,
brown spiral lines broken up into series of
short dashes. Two broad, interrupted
spiral bands of darker brown on body
whorl. Aperture creamy brown. 6–10cm.
Indo-Pacific (Sri Lanka and South India).
Uncommon.

Genus SCAPHELLA Swainson
Small to medium-sized, fusiform and solid
shells. Early whorls convex and finely
ornamented. Siphonal notch absent. Fasciole absent or indistinct. Columella with
several folds. Thin periostracum. Four
species in Caribbean.

Scaphella junonia Lamarck   ×0.7
Juno's Volute, The Junonia

Shell fusiform and solid with large body
whorl and short spire. Apex smooth and
rounded. First true whorl with axial ribs
crossed by fine spiral lines. Rest of shell
smooth. Columella almost straight and
with four strong folds. Yellowish white or
creamy with spiral rows of dark brown,
circular or squarish blotches. Aperture
creamy white. 8–13cm. Caribbean. Uncommon.

Genus AMORIA Gray
Shells small to moderately large. Elongate
or ovate, with elevated spire. Unicolorous
or strikingly patterned with bold, darker
colour. Strong or weak folds on columella.
Operculum absent. 19 species living
around Australia.

Amoria canaliculata McCoy   ×1.4
harfordi Cox.

Thick, rather small, elongate-ovate shell
with short, blunt spire. Large, smooth
apex. Suture channelled at body whorl.
Narrow siphonal notch. Four folds on
columella. Two colour forms occur.
Shallow-water form white with axial,
brown lines and widely spaced, orange
brown blotches arranged in spiral rows;
deep-water form pink with deep red, axial
lines and close-set, red blotches arranged
in spiral rows. 4–7cm. Indo-Pacific (East
Australia). Rare.

Amoria damonii Gray   ×0.6
reticulata Reeve, *reevei* Sowerby,
gatliffi Sowerby, *hedleyi* Iredale,
keatsiana Ludbrook.
Moderately large, solid, elongate-ovate
shell with short or moderately tall spire
and impressed suture. Apex rounded.
Aperture widens towards base. Broad
siphonal notch. Whole shell smooth and
glossy. Four folds on columella. Very
variable colour and pattern. Frequently
cream with two or three broad spiral bands
of brown reticulations. Paler brown, axial,

wavy streaks between bands. Sometimes
no spiral bands (form *A. keatsiana*). Spire
often has deep red callus deposit. 7–14cm.
Indo-Pacific (Australia). Common.

Amoria ellioti Sowerby   ×0.9
Elliot's Volute

Shell solid, elongate-ovate. Fine axial
striae. Thin, unbroken axial lines of brown
on cream. Aperture coffee, flushed with
violet at margin. Four prominent folds on
columella. 7–11cm. Indo-Pacific, Australian (Western Australia). Uncommon.

Amoria grayi Ludbrook
Shell solid, fusiform. Suture shallow, callused. Smooth, faint axial striae sometimes
visible. Four oblique folds on straight
columella. Creamy grey, usually with
brown ring encircling body whorl. Sometimes with pale brown reticulations on last
whorl. Aperture pale orange. 4–10cm.
Indo-Pacific, Australian (West Australia).

Amoria maculata Swainson   ×0.6
caroli Iredale.
Moderate-sized, elongate shell with short

spire, shallow suture and rounded apex. Aperture widens towards base. Siphonal notch wide and shallow. Smooth all over. 4–6 folds on columella. Colour variable. Usually creamy white with four spiral bands of axial, brown lines. On deep-water specimens axial lines coalesce into dark orange-red bands. Occasional narrow, pale yellow spiral band just above body whorl suture. 5·0–7·5cm. Indo-Pacific (East Australia). Common.

Amoria molleri Iredale   ×0.8

columella. Well defined fasciolar ridge. Creamy, with thin, golden, tent-like reticulations and bands of widely spaced, brown lines. Aperture coffee. 4·0–6·5cm. Indo-Pacific (North West Australia). Rare.

Amoria turneri Griffith & Pidgeon
Shell ovate. Spire conical, apex blunt. Very fine axial striae. Four oblique folds on columella. Glossy. Thin, brown axial lines on cream, light brown mottling forming two bands on last whorl. Aperture white. 4–5cm. Australian. Uncommon.

Amoria undulata Lamarck   ×0.7
Wavy Volute

broadly conical spire and small, raised apex. May be axial ribs on first spire whorl. Shell otherwise smooth. Siphonal notch narrow and deep. Four folds on columella. Yellowish white with orange brown axial stripes. Stripes may be numerous or few. Unicolorous golden and black forms have been found. 3·5–5·5cm. Indo-Pacific (North East Australia). Common.

Genus CYMBIOLISTA Iredale
Moderately large, light shells with short spire and large, conical, smooth apex. Prickly spines at whorl shoulders. Aperture flares outwards slightly towards posterior. Columella with strong folds. Siphonal notch conspicuous. One species.

Cymbiolista hunteri Iredale   ×0.6

Moderately large, light, elongate shell with short, sharply pointed spire. Suture slightly impressed. Aperture long, narrow with outer lip thickened in middle. Siphonal notch deep and wide. Whole shell smooth except for slight spiral ridge below suture. Five folds on columella. Creamy orange brown, paler at suture. 7–12cm. Australian (New South Wales). Frequent.

Amoria praetexta Reeve   ×0.9
Shell fairly light, slightly ovate. Spire short, blunt. Four folds on almost straight

Shell thick, fusiform to ovate, blunt apex. Suture indistinct. Thin, wavy, brown axial lines on cream. Glossy. Aperture creamy or apricot. 4–5 folds on columella. 8–13cm. Australian. Frequent.

Amoria zebra Leach   ×0.9
lineata Leach, *lineatiana* Weaver & duPont.
Shell small, solid, oblong-ovate with

For details see *Cymbiolista*. Colour varies according to habitat. Typically shell is creamy with sparsely distributed, chestnut brown, zigzag lines and four or five spiral bands of bluish grey blotches. A much deeper pink ground colour with axial, orange markings and three spiral bands of reddish brown blotches characterises some deep-water specimens. 10–17cm. Indo-Pacific (East Australia), Australian (South East Australia). Uncommon.

Family CANCELLARIIDAE

Globose or fusiform shells usually with strongly cancellate ornament on all or part of surface. Strong folds on columella. Aperture large, lirate within. Often deeply excavated suture. Most species live off-shore. About six genera and numerous subgenera. Found in all warm and tropical seas.

Genus CANCELLARIA Lamarck

For details see Family Cancellariidae. Many species.

Cancellaria bocageana Crosse & Debeaux
× 1.9

Thick, solid shell with very strong axial ribs and deeply impressed suture. Outer lip lirate. Columella with three prominent folds. Smooth between axial ribs. Purplish brown with a median, white stripe on body whorl and another around the tiny umbilicus. White above and below suture. 3·0–3·5cm. Indo-Pacific (Pacific), Japonic. Frequent.

Cancellaria bulbulus Sowerby

Similar to *C. solida*, but less globose and with taller spire. Spire whorls strongly axially ribbed, body whorl weakly axially ribbed, whole shell with weak spiral striae. No umbilicus. Thickened outer lip, slightly sinuous towards base. Aperture lirate within. 3–4 strong folds on columella. Unicolorous pinkish orange. Aperture orange white. 3·0–3·5cm. Panamic. Un-common.

Cancellaria cancellata Linnaeus × 1.1

Thick, solid shell with large body whorl, short spire and impressed suture. Siphonal canal short and slightly recurved. Um-bilicus deep. Outer lip thickened and lirate within. Columella with three folds. Strong, wavy axial ribs crossed by finer spiral ribs to give distinctive cancellate appearance.

White with pale and dark brown spiral bands. 3·0–4·5cm. Mediterranean. Fre-quent.

Cancellaria cassidiformis Sowerby × 0.9

Shell thick and solid with short, acuminate spire, large body whorl and impressed suture. Aperture lirate, columella with two or three prominent folds. Broad parietal callus. Single row of sharp, pointed tubercles at shoulder of each whorl produced as broad axial ribs towards base. Few moderately strong spiral ribs crossed by fine axial striae. Orange brown with a white band on lower part of body whorl. Aperture whitish. 3–4cm. Panamic. Frequent.

Cancellaria chrysostoma Sowerby

Thick, globose shell with short, acuminate spire and impressed suture. Outer lip thickened. White, dotted and lined with brown; row of dots around umbilicus. Margin of outer lip orange. c2·5cm. Panamic. Rare.

Cancellaria clavatula Sowerby

Thin, elongate-fusiform shell with rounded whorls and impressed suture. Axial ribs resembling varices, with fine spiral lines crossing them. Outer lip thickened. No umbilicus. Columella with two strong folds. Pale brown with two spiral, white bands on body whorl. Aperture whitish or pale brown. 2·0–2·5cm. Panamic. Un-common.

Cancellaria cooperi Gabb

Shell large for the genus, thick and heavy, elongate-fusiform. Strong axial ribs on each whorl which are produced as sharp points at periphery of spire whorls and

shoulder of body whorl. Fine spiral grooves on upper portion of whorls and more numerous spiral whorls towards base of body whorl. No umbilicus. Aperture lirate within. Yellowish brown with darker brown spiral lines. Aperture white. 5–6cm. Panamic. Frequent.

Cancellaria crenifera Sowerby

Thick, solid ovate shell with large body whorl and moderately tall, pointed spire. Suture deeply channelled. Outer lip thick-ened. Aperture lirate within. Deep, wide umbilicus. Strong, sharp, axial, wavy ribs have sharp points at suture. Spiral lirae have sharp points where they cross ribs. Whitish, with patchy, spiral, brown bands. Aperture white with brown banding. c2cm. Indo-Pacific (Pacific), Japonic. Common.

Cancellaria foveolata Sowerby × 1.1

Thin but strong shell with large body whorl and relatively short spire. Whorls very rounded, with keeled shoulder. Moderately large umbilicus. Columella with three strong folds. Few irregular, coarse axial ribs. Whitish with pale brown spiral streaks and bands; dark brown on sutural plat-form. Aperture, columella and umbilicus white. Unicolorous pale brown, white and pale pink forms also occur. 2–3cm. South African. Common.

Cancellaria hystrix Reeve

Compared with *C. cancellata*, this shell is smaller, less globose and has a deeply channelled suture. Axial ribs are sharper and more numerous and are crossed by numerous fine spiral riblets which are produced as sharp points at intersections. Small umbilicus with thick ridge surround-ing it. Aperture lirate within. Three strong folds on columella. Whitish with pale purplish brown spiral bands. 2·0–2·5cm. South African, Indo-Pacific (Indian Ocean). Uncommon.

Cancellaria pulchra Sowerby

Similar to *C. cancellata*, but smaller, more globose, and with scalariform whorls. Strong axial ribs crossed by equally strong spiral ribs producing deeply excavated rectangles all over shell. Small umbilicus with thick ridge surrounding it. Three strong folds on columella. Aperture lirate within. Whitish, with spiral, dark brown bands and lines. 3·0–3·5cm. Panamic. Rare.

191

Cancellaria reticulata Linnaeus ×2.0

Thick, solid shell with large body whorl, moderately tall spire and imbricate suture. 2–3 folds on columella. Spiral and axial ribs give reticulate ornamentation. Outer lip thickened and denticulate. White with orange brown or reddish brown stains arranged 2–3 interrupted in spiral bands. Aperture white. 3·5–4·5cm. Caribbean. Frequent.

Cancellaria scalata Sowerby
Shell similar in most respects to *C. textilis,* and is probably conspecific. Principal difference is in coloration which in *C. scalata* is pale brown to yellowish white with white aperture. 2·5–3·0cm. Indo-Pacific. Frequent.

Cancellaria semidisjuncta Sowerby ×1.2

Relatively thick but solid shell with very rounded whorls. Deep and widely channelled suture, last part of body whorl separated from penultimate whorl. Large, deep umbilicus. Numerous strong spiral cords, each of which has a punctate groove along it. Fine axial lines between spiral cords. Creamy, with reddish brown mottling and axial streaks. Aperture white. 1·5–2·2cm. South African. Frequent.

Cancellaria solida Sowerby
Thick, heavy, bulbous shell with very short spire. Easily distinguished from other species of the genus by being almost devoid of prominent ornament. Apart from axial ribs on early whorls and faint spiral striae on all whorls, shell is smooth. Thickened outer lip sinuous towards base. No umbilicus. Four strong folds on columella. Aperture obscurely lirate within. Unicolorous pinkish orange. Aperture white. 2·5–4·0cm. Panamic. Uncommon.

Cancellaria spengleriana Deshayes
Large, thick and heavy shell, ovately fusiform with moderately shouldered whorls and impressed suture. Strong, irregular axial ribs crossed by numerous rounded spiral cords. Cord at shoulder produced to nodulous points where it crosses axial ribs. Umbilicus a minute chink surrounded by broad spiral cord. Outer lip thickened. Aperture lirate within. Columella with three strong folds and numerous irregular pustules. Yellowish pink with few irregular, dark brown blotches which occasionally form spiral band. Aperture yellowish white. 5–6cm. Indo-Pacific (Indonesia and Philippines). Frequent.

Cancellaria textilis Kiener
Thick, tall-spired shell with large body whorl and elongate, relatively narrow spire. Whorls with keeled shoulder. Strong, curved, evenly spaced axial ribs which are produced as nodules at suture. Fine, widely spaced spiral riblets which are nodulous where they cross axial ribs. Umbilicus moderately large and deep. Aperture lirate within. Three strong folds on columella. Dark chocolate brown with tops of axial ribs and nodes on axial ribs whitish. Aperture paler brown. 2·5–3·0cm. Indo-Pacific. Uncommon.

Family MARGINELLIDAE

Shells usually small, ovate to fusiform. Spire small, extended or sunken. Gloss of thickly enamelled shell protected in life by animal's mantle. Thick outer lip with callus which may encircle shell base and may cover spire. Usually 3–5 folds on columella. Outer lip smooth or finely dentate. Marginellids have a large foot and most have no operculum. Found on coral reefs and on sand or mud, mostly in tropical waters. Abundant in West African province. As there is still no satisfactory classification of marginellids the numerous generic names in use by some specialists are ignored here in favour of the one genus *Marginella*. About 550 species.

Genus MARGINELLA Lamarck
Details as for Marginellidae.

Marginella adansoni Kiener ×1.7
bifasciata Sowerby.

Shell fusiform, slightly ovate. Spire raised, apex pointed. Nodules on whorl shoulder. Dentate outer lip with callus extending to base of spire. Four folds on columella. Creamy or grey, with thin, wavy, axial lines, sometimes dark, broken bands. Aperture white. 2·4–3·4cm. West African. Uncommon.

Marginella amygdala Kiener ×2.0

Shell small, thick, moderately inflated, with short, pointed spire. Three small folds on columella. Outer lip thickened. Pale yellowish brown with white suture. Columella and outer lip whitish. Aperture yellowish brown. *c*1·5cm. West African. Common.

Marginella angustata Sowerby ×2.3

Shell elongate, slightly ovate. Spire completely sunken and callused. Outer lip callused. Four folds on columella. Axial white lines and spiral bands form a lattice on a variety of pale colours, with a pattern resembling a tartan plaid. Aperture white. 1·3–2·5cm. Indo-Pacific. Uncommon.

Marginella aurantia Lamarck × 2.3

Shell fusiform, slightly ovate. Spire with small, blunt, convex whorls, partially callused. Callused outer lip dentate. Four folds on columella. Coffee or mottled pale brown with irregular, white markings. 1·8–2·2cm. West African. Uncommon.

Marginella avena Kiener × 2.0
livida Reeve, *vermiculata* Jousseaume, *southwicki* Davis, *beyerleana* Bernardi.

Shell thin, narrowly cylindrical, almost straight-sided, with short, blunt spire. Three small folds on columella. Outer lip thickened. Reddish with two faint, paler bands on body whorl, occasionally crossed by thinner, axial, white stripes. Apex yellowish. *c*1cm. Caribbean. Common.

Marginella bullata Born × 0.8
Shell large with depressed, sunken spire, inflated and with thickened outer lip. Four strong columella folds. Beige, with faint, lighter, spiral bands. Outer lip white;

aperture beige inside. Dorsal side of thickened outer lip orange. 5·0–7·5cm. Caribbean (Brazil). Uncommon.

Marginella carnea Storer × 2.0

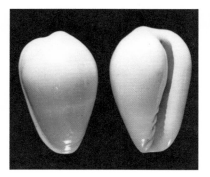

Solid, ovate shell with thickened outer lip and parietal callus which covers most of spire. Four strong folds on columella. Bright orange with faint, whitish band on middle of whorl and another just below suture. 1·5–2·0cm. Caribbean, Uncommon.

Marginella cincta Kiener
saulcyana Reeve.
Shell elongate, ovate. Spire small, pointed, may be enveloped in callus. Yellow callused margin encircles base. Cream or grey. Aperture white flushed with yellow. 2·0–2·5cm. Caribbean. Rare.

Marginella cingulata Dillwyn × 2.0
lineata Lamarck.

Shell thick, very inflated. Spire depressed and covered with callus. 4–5 folds on columella which run at right angles to axis. Outer lip thickened and finely denticulate. Yellowish with well defined, widely spaced, orange brown, spiral lines, one or two of which bifurcate. 1·5–2·2cm. West African. Uncommon.

Marginella cornea Lamarck × 1.6
azona Menke.

Moderately thick, cylindrically ovate shell with outer lip thickened, denticulate and produced above level of spire. Six or more folds on columella. Thick, lumpy parietal callus near spire. Whitish yellow with thin, brown line around reflected margin of outer lip. *c*2·5cm. West African. Uncommon.

Marginella desjardini Marche-Marchad × 1.0

Shell large, short-spired with outer lip thickened and denticulate in the middle. 3–4 thick folds on columella. Yellowish white suffused with orange and with three broad, spiral bands flecked with white. Spire whitish with brown band flecked with white below suture. Outer lip white; aperture orange brown inside. 4–5cm. West African. Uncommon.

Marginella diadochus Adams & Reeve × 2.1
Shell fusiform, slightly ovate. Spire conical,

apex blunt. Suture callused. Outer lip lightly callused. Four folds on columella. Greyish cream, with many, unbroken, thin, spiral lines. 1·8–2·3cm. South African. Rare.

Marginella elegans Gmelin × 1.1
sibilla Dillwyn.

Shell fairly large, thick, with small, obtuse spire. Thickened, slightly denticulate outer lip. Five prominent, thick folds on columella. Greyish white banded with darker grey and crossed by axial, white lines. Columellar area, lower folds and outer lip orange brown. 2·5–3·0cm. Indo-Pacific. Uncommon.

Marginella eumorpha Melvill × 2.3

Shell thin, narrowly cylindrical, with short spire. Three prominent folds on columella. Outer lip thickened. Body whorl light to dark grey with five purplish bands showing through. Apex pale purple with white streaks and white suture. Thickened outer lip, white with large, brown blotches. Aperture dark brown. 1·0–1·7cm. Indo-Pacific (North Arabian Sea). Rare.

Marginella goodalli Sowerby × 1.2

Shell ovate. Spire small, with rounded apex. Suture partially callused. Callused outer lip dentate. Four raised folds on columella. Cream to coffee, with pale spots. 2·5–3·0cm. West African (Senegal). Uncommon.

Marginella guttata Dillwyn × 1.6
longivaricosa Lamarck.

Shell very thick, ovate. Spire small, partially or completely callused. Outer lip callused. Four folds on columella. Faintly banded coffee, mushroom or creamy, with small, white spots. 1·3–2·3cm. Caribbean. Common.

Marginella helmatina Rang × 1.7
cumingiana Petit.
Shell thick, inflated; small, raised spire with obtuse apex. Outer lip thickened. Three prominent, thick folds on columella. Whitish mottled with pinkish violet and with two indistinct, broken, spiral bands of darker violet on body whorl. Outer lip

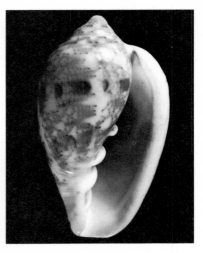

and aperture whitish. 2·5–3·5cm. West African. Rare.

Marginella interruptolineata Mühlfeld
× 2.1

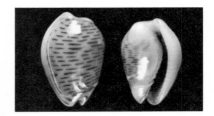

Shell small, thick and very inflated. Depressed spire covered with thick callus which extends down length of columella. Three small folds on columella. Outer lip thickened and slightly reflexed. Greyish with many fine, brown dashes arranged spirally around body whorl. Reflected edge of outer lip bordered by two or three thin, bluish brown lines. Callused portion of body whorl and outer lip grey. Aperture grey. *c*1·2cm. Caribbean. Uncommon.

Marginella irrorata Menke × 2.0

Shell ovate. Spire conical, apex pointed. Suture callused. Outer lip callused. Four folds on columella, end fold forming ridge around siphonal notch. Small, white spots on mushroom, grey or pink. Aperture white flushed pale orange. 2·5–3·0cm. West African. Uncommon.

Marginella labiata Kiener   × 1.7
Royal Margin Shell

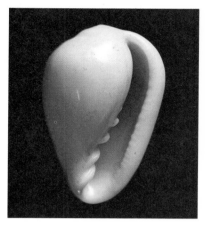

Shell ovate, thick. Spire sunken, short. Apex flat. Suture callused. Dentate outer lip, with callus extended to apex. Four folds on columella. High gloss. White, or flushed pale brown, pink or violet. Margin yellowish brown. 2·0–3·0cm. Caribbean. Uncommon.

Marginella largillieri Kiener   × 2.1
ovum Reeve, *paros* Jousseaume.

Large, ovate shell with sunken spire and thickened, denticulate outer lip. Four folds on columella the lowest being thicker and longer than the others. Broad parietal callus which reaches spire. Creamy to pale brown. Aperture, columella and outer lip white. 2·0–2·5cm. Caribbean (Brazil). Rare.

Marginella loebbeckeana Weinkauff × 2.0
glauca Jousseaume.

Shell ovate. Spire small, low. Callused margin extends to spire. Outer lip smooth or dentate. Five folds on columella. High gloss. White to bluish grey. 1·3–3·2cm. Indo-Pacific (South East Asia). Rare.

Marginella marginata Born   × 2.1
bivaricosa Lamarck, *crassa* Röding, *lactea* Swainson.

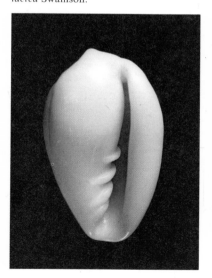

Shell ovate, very thick. Spire small, apex extended. Callused margin completely encircles shell, with two folds on outer lip side. Four folds on columella. White or brownish grey, with brown on outer lip. Aperture white to brown. 1·4–2·7cm. West African. Common.

Marginella mosaica Sowerby   × 1.7
Shell ovate. Spire low, apex blunt, suture lightly callused. Outer lip thickly callused. Four folds on columella. Spiral rows of

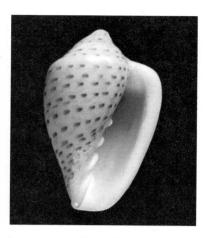

brown, blue and grey hyphens on white. Paler, broad, zigzag reticulations. Aperture white. 1·5–3·0cm. South African. Frequent.

Marginella musica Hinds
Shell ovate. Spire conical. Outer lip lightly callused. Four folds on columella. Greenish grey with thin, dark, spiral lines. 1·7cm. West African. Rare.

Marginella nebulosa Röding   × 1.9
flammea Link, *nubeculata* Lamarck.

Shell ovate, slightly fusiform. Spire conical, apex pointed. Suture partially callused. Outer lip lightly callused. Shoulder on body whorl. Four folds on columella. Whitish with pale brown, broken axial lines and patches. 3·2–4·0cm. South African. Uncommon.

Marginella ornata Redfield   × 1.6
intermedia Sowerby, *vittata* Reeve.
Shell ovate. Spire small, suture lightly callused. Slight callus on shoulder, thickly callused outer lip. Four raised folds on columella. Colour variable, white, mushroom, violet, brown. One broad spiral

Marginella prunum Gmelin   × 1.6
caerulescens Lamarck, *plumbea* Dillwyn, *glans* Menke.

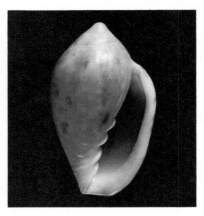

band with brown reticulations, flanked by two spiral lines. Aperture white or pale violet. 2·2–3·0cm. South African. Common.

Marginella persicula Linnaeus   × 1.6
avellana Lamarck, *guttata* Link, *maculata* Swainson.

Shell ovate. Spire flat, sunken, callused. Outer lip callused, dentate. Nodule on anterior of body whorl. 6–9 folds on columella. White, pale brown or pale yellow, with many small, brown spots, sometimes brown spiral streaks. Aperture white. 1·5–2·5cm. West African. Uncommon.

Marginella pruinosa Hinds   × 2.1

Shell thick, moderately inflated, with short, callused spire. Three prominent folds on columella. Thickened outer lip. Yellowish with faint axial lines of whitish spots. Parietal area, columella and outer lip white. *c*1·5cm. Caribbean. Frequent.

Shell ovate. Spire small, conical, partially callused. Callused outer lip angular posteriorly. Four folds on columella. Pale olive or cream, sometimes streaked white or pale brown, also yellow on outer lip. Aperture brown. 2·0–2·5cm. Caribbean. Common.

Marginella pseudofaba Sowerby   × 1.7
bifasciata Sowerby.

Shell fusiform. Spire raised, apex pointed. Suture callused. Outer lip callused and dentate. Mottled pale brown and white, with bands of widely spaced black and dark brown spots. Aperture white. 2·5–4·0cm. West African. Uncommon.

Marginella rosea Lamarck   × 2.3
Shell fusiform, slightly ovate. Spire extended. Outer lip callused. Four folds on columella. Pink, with darker, wavy axial lines or small, pale, blotches giving chequered

effect. Aperture white. 2·0–2·8cm. South African. Uncommon.

Marginella rostrata Redfield   × 2.0
oblonga Sowerby.

Shell oblong. Spire small, completely callused. Outer lip callused. Four folds on columella. High gloss. White, sometimes flushed coffee. Aperture white flushed with pale brown. *c*2cm. Caribbean. Rare.

Marginella sapotilla Hinds   × 2.0
xanthostoma Mörch, *burchardi* Dunker.

Shell elongate. Spire short, apex pointed. Suture partially callused. Outer lip callused. Four folds on columella. Greyish white. Aperture pale brown. 1·7–2·5cm. Panamic. Uncommon.

Marginella strigata Dillwyn   ×1.4
undulata Deshayes, *burchardi* Reeve,
praecallosa Higgins.

Shell ovate. Spire sunken, and completely
callused. Outer lip callused. Five folds on
columella, of which anterior three are
oblique. Well defined fasciole. Creamy,
with broken axial streaks of olive. Aperture
creamy white. *c*3·5cm. West African. Rare.

Marginella ventricosa G. Fischer   ×1.3
hainesii Petit, *quinqueplicata* Lamarck,
vermiculata Redfield.

Shell thick, inflated, with depressed spire.
Five very prominent folds which run at
right angles to axis. Unicolorous grey
with whiter outer lip. 2·0–2·5cm. Indo-
Pacific (South East Asia, Indonesia). Frequent.

Superfamily
Conacea

Family TURRIDAE
Very large family of small to medium-
sized shells which contains species having
a bewildering variety of shapes and
ornamental features. The majority of
species are fusiform and have a tall spire
and long siphonal canal. Many others
resemble species in other families such as
Buccinidae, Muricidae, Columbellidae,
Mitridae and Conidae. The only shell
feature common to all members of this
family is a slit or sinus on the outer lip,
located between the suture and periphery
of the body whorl. Many different kinds
of ornament are encountered, although
spines are never present, at least not in a
well developed state. With many hundreds
of species distributed amongst innumerable genera, this is the largest family of
marine gastropods in the world, and
species are found in all seas from the inter-
tidal zone down to abyssal depths. The
identification of the majority of turrids
poses many problems and the identification of most of them is a matter for the
specialist. The few species described here
include some of the largest and most
attractive, the great majority of species
being small and not likely to come into the
possession of most collectors.

Genus TURRIS Röding
Pleurotoma Lamarck,
Pleurotomus Montfort.
Moderately large, elongate-fusiform shells
with tall spire and long siphonal canal.
Sinus deep and narrow, situated usually on
a special rim above periphery of body
whorl. Usually ornamented with strong,
smooth spiral cords. Apex blunt and
smooth. Operculum leaf-shaped with an
apical nucleus. About ten species in the
Indo-Pacific.

Turris babylonia Linnaeus   ×0.8

Thick, tall-spired shell with strong, smooth
spiral cords and finer spiral lines between.
Long, narrow posterior canal. Creamy
white with spiral rows of widely-spaced,
dark brown blotches. Aperture white.
7–10cm. Indo-Pacific (Pacific). Common.

Turris cingulifera Lamarck
High-spired, almost straight-sided shell
with simple suture. Spiral cords of differing
thickness. Short siphonal canal. Dull, off-
white with reddish brown spots on pre-
sutural ridge of lower whorls. White
aperture. 2·5–8·0cm. Indo-Pacific. Frequent.

Turris crispa Lamarck   ×0.6

Shell thick, very tall with long spire and
long, broad siphonal canal. Whorls
slightly convex with numerous strong,
sharp spiral ridges with fine axial lines
between them. Outer lip with deep, narrow
posterior sinus. Dull, creamy white with
brown spots. 12–14cm. Indo-Pacific
(Pacific). Rare.

Turris cryptorrhaphe Sowerby
Moderately thick, very elongate shell with
very tall spire and relatively short, broad
siphonal canal. Sinus narrow and
moderately deep. Each whorl strongly
keeled at periphery, and above and below
are strong smooth and sharp spiral ridges.
Spiral ridges crowded towards base of
body whorl. Spire whorls have striking
resemblance to a species of *Turritella*.
Unicolorous brown, sometimes with
slightly darker brown lines on spiral ridges
and peripheral keel. Aperture and columella white. 5·5–8·0cm. Indo-Pacific
(Pacific). Rare.

Turris spectabilis Reeve   ×1.2
Shell superficially similar to *T. babylonia*.
Thick and solid, with tall spire and
angulated whorls. Deep, narrow posterior
sinus. Short, broad siphonal canal. Three
strong spiral ribs at middle of each whorl;
central rib the thickest. Body whorl has a
fourth strong spiral rib and weaker spiral
ribs below. Thin spiral threads below

suture. Whitish with spiral, light brown bands below suture and opposite posterior sinus on body whorl. Thick spiral ribs blotched and dotted with dark brown or orange red markings. Aperture white. *c*6cm. Indo-Pacific (Pacific). Uncommon.

Turris undosa Lamarck

Thick, very elongate shell with very tall spire and moderately long, broad, slightly curved siphonal canal. Strong, smooth spiral cords on each whorl, peripheral cord being strongest. Short posterior sinus. Apart from taller spire it has a close resemblance to *T. babylonia* in shape and ornament. Broad and narrow, interrupted, axial, dark brown streaks on all whorls. Aperture and interior of siphonal canal mauve or violet. *c*7·5cm. Indo-Pacific (Central Pacific). Uncommon.

Genus NIHONIA MacNeil

Narrowly fusiform shells with tall spire and long, straight siphonal canal. Numerous rounded, spiral cords with finer threads between. Fine, axial growth lines which may produce a decussate pattern in conjunction with the fine, axial growth lines. Sinus deep. Operculum leaf-shaped with terminal nucleus. Four species in Indo-Pacific and Japanese waters.

Nihonia australis Roissy   ×0.7

Shell large, elongate-fusiform with rounded whorls, tall spire and long, straight siphonal canal. Numerous sharp raised spiral cords on all whorls below the smooth globular apex. Sinus deep and narrow, its lower edge parallel to suture. Pale orange buff with stronger spiral cords

orange brown. 7·5–10·0cm. Indo-Pacific (South China Sea). Uncommon.

Nihonia mirabilis Sowerby

Large, narrowly fusiform shell with tall spire and long, straight siphonal canal. Prominent, widely spaced and rounded, smooth spiral cords with finer spiral threads between. Body whorl has about 12 spiral cords with 5–6 spiral threads between each pair of cords. Axial growth lines. Sinus broad and rounded. Buff with axial, reddish brown streaks. 7–10cm. Japonic. Uncommon.

Fusiturris undatiruga

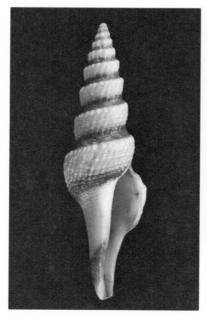

Genus FUSITURRIS Thiele

Elongate-fusiform shells with tall spire and long, straight siphonal canal. Spire turreted. Ornamented with wavy, thin axial ribs thickened at the rounded periphery. Sinus moderately deep and U-shaped. Operculum leaf-shaped with an apical nucleus. Few species in Mediterranean and West African provinces.

Fusiturris undatiruga Bivona   ×1.3

Thick, solid shell with tall spire and long broad, slightly curved siphonal canal. Posterior sinus broad and deep. Whorls greatly constricted at suture. Wavy axial ribs are crossed by weaker spiral lines. Orange yellow with broad, chocolate brown spiral band at suture and a similar band at centre of body whorl. Basal portion of siphonal canal also chocolate brown. Aperture whitish. 5–6cm. Mediterranean. Rare.

Genus TURRICULA Schumacher

Elongate-fusiform shells with tall spire, long, straight or slightly curved siphonal canal. Moderate to deep sinus with broadly to narrowly rounded apical terminations. In profile, sinus is broadly crescent-shaped. Almost smooth, or ornamented with strong spiral cords and ribs crossed by axial ribs which give a nodulous appearance to spiral ornament. Apex smooth and conical. Operculum ovate, pointed at upper and lower ends, with a lateral nucleus. About 20 species in deep water in Indo-Pacific province.

Turricula javana Linnaeus   ×1.0

turris Gmelin, *contorta* Perry, *nodifera* Lamarck.

Moderately large, fusiform, biconical shell with tall, turreted spire and moderately long, slightly curved siphonal canal. All whorls below the smooth, conical apex are strongly carinate and nodose. Numerous closely-spaced spiral cords crossed, on the peripheral cord only, by numerous strong, oblique nodules. Two strong cords below suture. Sinus deeply cut. Creamy buff to dull purplish brown, with peripheral nodules paler. 6·0–7·5cm. Indo-Pacific (Indian Ocean, West Pacific), Japonic. Uncommon.

Turricula tornata Dillwyn
flammea Schumacher,
fulminata Kiener.
Moderately large, elongate-fusiform shell with rounded whorls. Surface smooth except for weak spiral lirae on lower half of base. Siphonal canal long and slightly twisted. Sinus broad. White, sometimes with broad, axial reddish brown streaks. 2·5–8·5cm. Indo-Pacific (Indian Ocean). Uncommon.

Genus POLYSTIRA Woodring
Moderately large, thick, elongate-fusiform shells with numerous smooth spiral keels. Sinus shallow and broadly V-shaped. Operculum V-shaped with apical nucleus. Few species in deep water in Caribbean and Panamic provinces.

Polystira albida Perry   ×0.9
virgo Wood.

Shell thick, heavy, elongate, very tall-spired with pointed apex, long, broad siphonal canal and small posterior sinus. Strong spiral keels have weaker spiral ridges between them. Unicolorous white with early whorls pale brown. 7–10cm. Caribbean. Frequent.

Genus CLATHODRILLIA Dall
Medium sized, elongate-fusiform shells with well-rounded whorls, moderately broad siphonal canal and short, broad sinus. Broad axial ribs crossed by numerous coarse spiral cords. Small callus on parietal wall. Numerous species in tropical and warm seas.

Clathodrillia flavidula Lamarck   ×1.4

Medium-sized, thick shell with convex whorls and short, broad, slightly recurved siphonal canal. Strong, axial ribs are crossed by numerous spiral cords which develop nodules where they cross ribs. Creamy yellow, with light reddish brown spiral band at shoulder and spiral, white band on central part of whorl. Aperture and columella yellowish white. 4–6cm. Indo-Pacific, Japonic. Uncommon.

Genus PUSIONELLA Gray
Thick, heavy, ovate-fusiform shells with tall spire, short, broad siphonal canal and moderately shouldered whorls. Sinus scarcely apparent at middle portion of outer lip. Usually a thick parietal callus. Smooth, except for coarse spiral lirae towards base of body whorl. Ovately cylindrical operculum with lateral nucleus. Usually covered with a thin, dark brown periostracum. Few species in Atlantic and West African waters.

Pusionella nifat Bruguière   ×1.3

Thick, solid shell with large, broad body whorl and tall spire with slightly stepped whorls. Columella curved. Small but thick parietal callus. White with interrupted, brown spiral bands. Aperture white. Thin, dark brown periostracum. 3·5–4·5cm. West African. Common.

Pusionella rapulum Reeve
Thick, heavy, ovate-fusiform shell with well-rounded whorls and very broad, short siphonal canal. Distinct fasciole encircles siphonal canal. Coarse spiral lirae above fasciole. Green. Aperture white. Covered with thin, dark brown periostracum. 4–5cm. Indo-Pacific (Malaya). Uncommon.

Genus PERRONA Schumacher
Small, ovate-fusiform shells with large body whorl, tall spire with sharply pointed apex, long, broad siphonal canal and a broad, moderately deep sinus situated near periphery of body whorl. Smooth, except for weak lirae towards base of body whorl and sometimes one or two spiral keels. Few species in warm and tropical seas.

Perrona lineata Lamarck   ×2.0

Moderately thick, solid shell with inflated body whorl, acuminate spire and long siphonal canal. Posterior sinus deep. Large, thick parietal callus. Body whorl almost straight-sided, sloping sharply at base and at shoulder. Pinkish brown, with reddish brown, wavy axial lines. Parietal callus opaque white. Aperture pinkish violet. 2·0–2·5cm. West African, South African. Uncommon.

Genus COCHLESPIRA Conrad
Ancistrosyrinx Dall, *Coronasyrinx* Powell, *Pagodasyrinx* Shuto.
Small to medium-sized, elongate-fusiform shells with a tall, pagodiform spire and long body whorl which extends down to a long, siphonal canal. Whorls are encircled by a flange-like keel with pointed, serrated nodes or upcurved, short, spiny processes. Suture usually deeply impressed. Upper surface of whorls usually flattened. Sinus

moderately deep and very broad. Usually strong spiral ornament. The few known species are from deep water and are found in Indo-Pacific, Japanese and American waters.

Cochlespira pulcherrissima Kuroda ×2.3

Small, thin, elongate shell with tall spire and a siphonal canal of about equal length. Spire pagodiform. Each whorl has a strong keel with numerous small spines. Strong spiral cords on lower half of each whorl. Spiral cords granulose towards base. Upper portion of each whorl nearly smooth. Sinus deep and narrowly U-shaped. Orange or pale red fading to whitish. 2·5–3·5cm. Japonic. Rare.

Family THATCHERIIDAE

Large, thin shells with sharply angled whorls and broad, flat platform extending from suture to shoulder. Wide, broadly crescent-shaped sinus. Long, straight columella. No prominent surface ornament. One genus with one species.

Genus THATCHERIA Angas

For details see Family Thatcheriidae.

Thatcheria mirabilis Angas ×0.9

Japanese Wonder Shell

Shell large, very thin and light. Whorls flat-topped and acutely keeled. Aperture very large and open with wide, deep posterior sinus. Thin, narrow parietal callus. Fine spiral and axial striae. Dull yellowish. Aperture nacreous white. c7·5cm. Japonic. Rare.

Thatcheria mirabilis.

Family CONIDAE

Family of small to large shells, many thick and heavy. Flat-topped or conical spire, usually long and narrow aperture. Smooth, or ornamented with striae, ridges, beaded cords or grooves, many species coronated at suture. Colour and colour pattern very variable within species. Several have powerful poison apparatus and require careful handling as human fatalities are recorded. Small operculum usually presen Widely distributed in tropical seas. About 500 species living under coral, in coral reef crevices, in sand or in weed. Some authorities place species in several genera based on shell shape. The alternative of placing all species in the single genus *Conus* is followed here.

Genus CONUS Linnaeus

Details as for Family Conidae.

Conus abbreviatus Reeve ×1.1

Solid, bluish white or greenish grey shell with spiral rows of dark brown spots on body whorl. Short spire coronate. Thin parietal lip and brown or purplish, narrow aperture. Thin, semi-transparent peri-

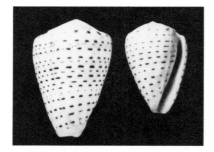

ostracum. 2·5–3·0cm. Indo-Pacific (Hawaii). Common.

Conus acuminatus Hwass ×0.8

insignis Sowerby.

Thin, tall cone with stepped spire. Smooth. White with irregular, reticulated spots, flesh-coloured to dark brown. Narrow, white aperture. 3·4–4·7cm. Indo-Pacific (Red Sea). Uncommon.

Conus amadis Gmelin ×0.45

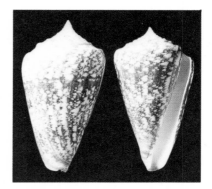

Shell fairly thick, solid. Spire short, apex sharply pointed. Broadly trigonal in outline, outer lip straight and thin. Brownish red with white triangles arranged axially and in indistinct, broad spiral bands. 7·5–10·5cm. Indo-Pacific (Indian Ocean). Common.

Conus ammiralis Linnaeus ×1.2

Very thick, broad shell. Faint, axial growth lines and faint spiral lirae. Dull, white shell with two reddish brown spiral bands on body whorl bearing white tents, separated by light brown tenting. White spire has faintly pink tip. White aperture. 6–7cm. Indo-Pacific. Uncommon.

Conus andamanensis Smith

Elongate-ovate shell with short, biconcave spire and pointed apex. Body whorl well rounded at shoulder and ornamented with widely spaced spiral grooves which are stronger towards base. Glossy, white with axial brown lines on spire, and with pale brown spots and blotches on body whorl. c3·5cm. Indo-Pacific (Indian Ocean, West Pacific). Uncommon.

bordered, triangles. Aperture white or pink. 4–8cm. Indo-Pacific. Rare.

Conus archon Broderip   ×1.8

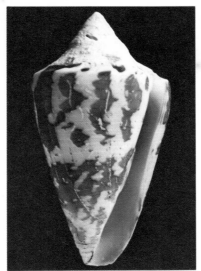

whorls. Spiral striae around base of body whorl. White, finely spotted with black. Two spiral bands and broad axial streaks. Thin, transparent periostracum. 2·5–7·0 cm. Indo-Pacific. Common.

Conus aulicus Linnaeus   ×0.35
Courtly Cone

Conus ammiralis.

Conus anemone Lamarck
ardisiaceus Kiener. *jukesii* Kiener.
White to bluish white with reddish brown mottling and streaks. In some specimens a white spiral band around body whorl which also carries spiral threads and axial striae. Bluish white aperture. 2·5–5·0cm. Australian. Common.

Conus araneosus Lightfoot   ×0.6
arachnoideus Gmelin.

Thick, conical shell with convex spire. Shoulders weakly coronate. Dull, white reticulated with fine, brown tenting. Two spiral bands of irregular, dark brown blotches. Cream aperture. Transparent, yellow periostracum. 2·6–8·0cm. Indo-Pacific (Philippines to Ceylon). Uncommon.

Conus archiepiscopus Hwass   ×0.9
Thick, solid shell with short spire. Yellowish with axial, brownish red streaks and spiral bands of white, reddish brown

Thick, broad cone with concave, pointed spire. Glossy, white shell with orange brown, axial markings, absent around median part of body whorl. Brown, spiral lines cross markings and bear white spots. 3·5–4·5cm. Panamic. Uncommon.

Conus arenatus Hwass   ×0.8
Sand-dusted Cone
arenosus Röding.
Conical shell with depressed, biconcave, pointed spire. Body whorl with coronate shoulder; weaker coronation on spire

Strong, thick, dullish shell, orange to reddish brown with white, irregular tenting. Globose body whorl and rounded shoulder. Smooth, pointed elevated spire. Background colour crossed by spiral striae in deeper shade. Cream or yellow aperture. Thin, brownish periostracum is almost opaque. 7–15cm. Indo-Pacific. Rare.

Conus aureus Hwass
Like a small version of *C. aulicus*, but with relatively longer spire and somewhat narrower aperture. Conspicuous spiral ribs on body whorl. Orange brown or dark brown, wavy axial lines and dark brown streaks and blotches, producing a tented effect. *c*5cm. Indo-Pacific. Rare.

Conus aurisiacus Linnaeus
Thick, solid, short-spired shell with last three whorls strongly canaliculate. Numerous fine spiral ridges over body whorl; shoulder smooth; few spiral threads on spire whorls. Pinkish white, or white with pink areas. Two or three broad, pale brown or yellowish brown spiral bands with small, dark spots and dashes arranged in spiral rows. Large, dark blotches at shoulder. Pattern very variable; dark markings sometimes almost entirely absent. 5–6cm. Indo-Pacific (Pacific). Rare.

Conus aurora Lamarck
secutor Crosse, *rosaceus* Dillwyn.
Thick shell, often worn. Weak spiral striae around base. Dull, flesh-coloured or pink, usually with orange mottling. May have spiral rows of brown spots on body whorl and white base. Pink aperture 2·5–5·0cm. South African. Common.

Conus australis Holten ×0.8
gracilis Sowerby.

Thick, tall cone with elevated, pointed spire. Spiral grooves crossed by axial growth lines and ridges. Dull, white shell with reddish brown, axial lines, expanded to form two irregular, spiral bands. Yellow basally. White aperture. 6·5–8·0cm. Indo-Pacific (China Sea), Japonic. Frequent.

Conus betulinus Linnaeus ×0.5

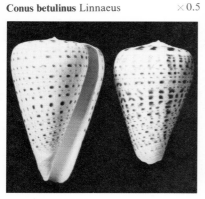

Thick, heavy shell with depressed spire and convex body whorl with heavy shoulder. Cream or yellow bands with small, dark brown spots alternate with narrow, whitish bands with larger spots. White aperture. 7–14cm. Indo-Pacific (South West Pacific). Common.

Conus boeticus Reeve
lachrymosus Reeve, *rivularius* Reeve.
Small, thick shell with short spire and rounded body whorl with low, rounded nodules at shoulder. Spiral cords with deep striae between them towards base of body whorl. Rest of shell smooth. Creamy white, with large, irregular blotches of reddish orange or dark brown and broken spiral band at shoulder, centre and at base. Aperture pinkish. *c*2·5cm. Indo-Pacific (Pacific), Japonic. Uncommon.

Conus bullatus Linnaeus
Thick, inflated, almost globose shell with well rounded sides, sloping shoulder and short, almost depressed spire. Aperture wide and flaring. Shape bears superficial resemblance to a species of *Oliva*. Glossy and smooth all over. Creamy white or pinkish, with irregular, light or darker brown blotches. Aperture whitish orange. 4·5–6·5cm. Indo-Pacific (West Pacific). Rare.

Conus cancellatus Hwass ×1.5
pagodus Kiener.
Thin, pyriform cone with biconcave, elevated, pointed spire. Axial growth lines and strong spiral ridges. Dull, white shell with median, brown band on body whorl as wide as two or three ridges and interstices. Brown, axial lines on spire. White aperture. *c*5·0cm. Indo-Pacific (Pacific). Uncommon.

Conus capitaneus Linnaeus ×1.2
classiarius Hwass.
Thick cone with depressed spire. Faint, axial growth lines and basal spiral ridges. White shell with two wide, olive brown,

Above: *Conus cancellatus.*
Below: *Conus capitaneus.*
Bottom: *Conus caracteristicus.*

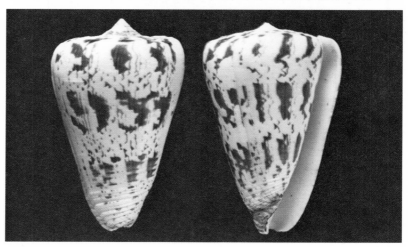

spiral bands on body whorl; white, median band with dark brown marks which may extend across bands as axial stripes. Violet aperture external colour and pattern showing through marginally. 4·5–5·0cm. Indo-Pacific. Frequent.

Conus caracteristicus Fischer   ×1.0
characteristicus Dillwyn.
Very thick, broad cone with depressed spire. Axial growth lines; spiral grooves on spire whorls. Orange brown to reddish brown, axial pattern concentrated in spiral bands. Pale yellow aperture. c6cm. Indo-Pacific. Uncommon.

Conus catus Hwass   ×0.8

Very thick, broad cone with spiral lirae and spiral ridges basally. Axial growth lines. Glossy, bluish white cone with extensive, brown mottling. Pink or lilac apex. White aperture and base. 3·5–4·0cm. Indo-Pacific. Common.

Conus chaldeus Röding   ×1.3
vermiculatus Lamarck.

Broad, thick cone with coronate shoulder on body whorl. Spiral ridges on spire and body whorl. Glossy, pinkish white shell with spiral, white band around shoulder of body whorl and two broad bands of alternating black and flesh-coloured axial stripes. 2–3cm. Indo-Pacific. Common.

Conus cinereus Hwass   ×1.0
bernardii Kiener, *gabrielii* Kiener.
Thin cone with short, concave, pointed spire. May have basal spiral striae. Glossy with variable coloration. Brown forms may have white mottling or fine, dark brown, spiral lines. Grey form has yellow mottling. Aperture white or same as

external colour. 4·2–6·5cm. Indo-Pacific. Common.

Conus circumcisus Born
affinis Gmelin, *laevis* Gmelin, *dux* Hwass, *purpuratus* Röding.
Solid, cylindrically ovate shell with short, blunt-topped spire. Shoulder rounded and smooth. Spire whorls have few spiral ridges, but body whorl has numerous crowded spiral ridges. Mauve, pale lavender or reddish, with three light brown bands bearing few widely spaced, reddish brown spots. Bands may be broken up into streaks and blotches. Spire has whitish blotches. Aperture pinkish white. 5–8cm. Indo-Pacific (Central Pacific). Rare.

Conus clarus Smith
Moderately thick, broadly trigonal shell with short, biconcave spire. Shoulders angulate, and sides of body whorl almost straight. Smooth except for a few spiral grooves towards base. Unicolorous white or yellow. Aperture white. c5cm. Australian (West Australia). Uncommon.

Conus cocceus Reeve
Moderately thick, ovate shell with short spire and tiny, papilliform apex. Body whorl has rounded shoulders and convex sides. Smooth and glossy with fine spiral cords towards base. Pinkish or yellowish, with white and orange blotches and spiral rows of white dashes. Aperture whitish or pinkish. c4cm. Australian (West Australia). Uncommon.

Conus coccineus Gmelin   ×0.9
solandri Broderip & Sowerby.
Thin cone with pointed spire. Weak spiral ridges which may be beaded. Glossy, reddish brown shell; dark brown patches on spire. Median, white spiral band on body whorl has dark brown marks and rows of spots. Cream apex. Greyish white aper-

ture. 4–5cm. Indo-Pacific (Philippines). Rare.

Conus coelinae Crosse
Elongate-ovate shell with short spire, sharply angled shoulder on body whorl, and straight sides tapering to a narrow base. Glossy and smooth. White to pinkish with closely spaced, fine spiral lines. Base is tinged with lavender. Aperture white. c5cm. Indo-Pacific (New Caledonia). Rare.

Conus collisus Reeve
Elongate ovate shell with short, biconcave spire and sharp apex. Body whorl has almost straight sides and is strongly shouldered. Widely spaced spiral grooves on body whorl become stronger towards base. Whitish, with interrupted, axial, dark brown streaks and blotches. Apex yellowish brown. c3cm. Indo-Pacific (Philippine Islands). Uncommon.

Conus consors Sowerby   ×0.9
Thick cone, swollen at shoulder. Axial growth lines; spire whorls with spiral

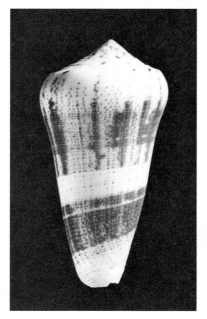

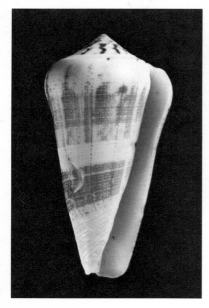

ridges. Dull, white shell with orange to brown markings in two irregular spiral bands bearing white spots, and orange to brown spots on white. Spire with dark brown, axial markings. White aperture. *c*7cm. Indo-Pacific. Common.

Conus coronatus Gmelin   ×1.4
minimus Born.

Small, thick, short-spired shell with inflated body whorl. Spiral, beaded ridges. Blue and white, mottled on spiral ridges with brown dots and blotches. Aperture dark brown and white with white margin. 1·5–2·5cm. Indo-Pacific. Common.

Conus daucus Hwass
mamillaris Green, *castus* Reeve, *archetypus* Crosse, *croceus* Sowerby.
Small, thick, broadly ovate, short-spired shell with apex often worn flat. Shoulder sharp. Fine spiral threads on spire. Fine spiral striae towards base of body whorl. Deep orange to lemon yellow, sometimes with a paler band centre of body whorl. Spiral rows of tiny, brown dots sometimes present on body whorl. Spire orange with large, white blotches. Aperture pinkish white. 0·5–5·0cm. Caribbean. Uncommon.

Conus dalli Stearns   ×0.7

Tall, thin shell. Faint, axial growth lines. Glossy, pinkish white tents outlined in reddish brown, and irregular, yellow patches bearing axial, reddish brown lines. White aperture. 4–6cm. Panamic. Uncommon.

Conus diadema Sowerby
Thick cone with tubercles on spire whorls and shoulder of body whorl. Glossy, dark brown, lighter on spire. Irregular, white spots form spiral, median band on body whorl. 4·0–4·5cm. Panamic. Frequent.

Conus distans Hwass   ×0.45

Very thick cone with coronate shoulders on all whorls. Axial growth lines become spiral basally. Outer lip thin. Bluish white with two orange brown, irregular spiral bands; dark brown marks on spire and dark brown basally. Lilac aperture, white marginally. 7·5–8·5cm. Indo-Pacific. Common.

Conus ebraeus Linnaeus   ×0.9
Hebrew Cone
Thick, stout cone with short, blunt spire. Spiral ridges with narrow grooves between. White banded with dark brown

chevrons and irregular quadrangles. 3·0–4·5cm. Indo-Pacific. Common.

Conus eburneus Hwass   ▷ ×1.1
polyglotta Weinkauff.   ▽ ×1.0

Thick, broad cone with flat spire and pointed apex. Axial growth lines; spiral grooves basally. Glossy, white shell with spiral rows of dark brown to black quadrants. May have faint, yellow bands on body whorl. White aperture. 3–7cm. Indo-Pacific. Common.

Conus eldredi Morrison
intermedius Reeve, *rosea* Sowerby.
Dull, ovate, pink shell with irregular bands of light brown mottling. Wide, pinkish white aperture. *c*7cm. Indo-Pacific. Uncommon.

Conus elegans Sowerby
Thin, white, fusiform shell with translucent appearance. Cream to yellow mottling. Spiral grooves around body whorl and delicate beading on spiral whorls. White aperture. *c*4cm. Indo-Pacific. Rare.

Conus elisae Kiener
Thick, short-spired shell. Fine axial striae. Glossy, dark brown with bluish white, trigonal spots. Bluish white aperture. 2·5–5·0cm. Indo-Pacific. Uncommon.

Conus encaustus Kiener
Thick, almost flat-topped, shell with coronate shoulder and 1–2 spiral ridges on spire whorls. Grey with white, spiral bars and small, orange brown spots. Dark brown between coronations. Bluish grey aperture with white parietal margin. 1·5–

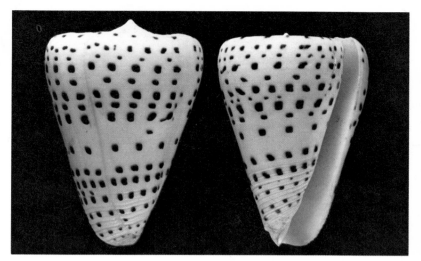

Conus eburneus.

2·5cm. Indo-Pacific (Marquesas Islands). Uncommon.

Conus episcopus Hwass   × 0.9

Thick, high cone, torpedo-shaped. Faint, axial growth lines. Glossy shell is .reddish brown with white tents concentrated in three axial and two spiral bands. White aperture. May be a form of *C. pennaceus.* c8cm. Indo-Pacific. Frequent.

Conus erythraeensis Reeve
Red Sea Cone
induratus Reeve, *adustus* Sowerby,
quadratomaculatus Sowerby.
Thick cone with depressed, pointed spire and simple suture. Spiral striae basally. Glossy, white with ochre or reddish brown quadrants forming spiral and axial rows. White aperture. 2·0–3·25cm. Indo-Pacific (Red Sea). Common.

Conus eximius Reeve
Smooth, dull, thick, whitish shell with two wide, spiral, orange brown bands on body whorl and radiating, brown lines on spire. Aperture light grey to white. 3·5–5·0cm. Indo-Pacific (South East Asia). Rare.

Conus figulinus Linnaeus   × 0.45

Thick, broad short-spired shell which is olive green, light brown or orange yellow. Pattern of spiral lines of deeper tone than ground colour. Fine axial striae. White aperture with thin outer lip. Brown, opaque periostracum. 4·0–7·5cm. Indo-Pacific. South African. Common.

Conus flavescens Sowerby   × 2.0
Bahama Cone
Thin, white, glossy shell with irregular, cream or yellow patches. Fine spiral

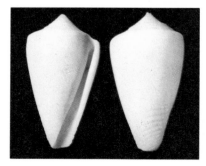

grooves around base of body whorl. White aperture. c2cm. Caribbean. Uncommon.

Conus flavidus Lamarck   × 1·4

Thick cone with depressed spire. Axial growth lines crossed by weak spiral ridges becoming stronger basally. Glossy, pinkish orange axial streaks overlying two light grey or brown bands. Violet basally. Aperture violet with median, white band. c4·5 cm. Indo-Pacific. Common.

Conus floridanus Gabb
Small, thick, almost biconical shell with slightly concave sides to body whorl and tall, stepped spire. Each spire whorl concave and with faint growth lines. Variable in colour. Usually white with wide, orange yellow to yellow, axial blotches. White spiral band round middle of body whorl; there may be small, yellowish brown dots within this. Very dark colour forms with spiral rows of reddish brown dots also occur. 3–4cm. Transatlantic, Caribbean. Common.

Conus frigidus Reeve
Thick, short-spired shell with spiral ridges around base of body whorl. Fawn to yellowish brown with pale shoulder and median bands. Violet basally, violet apex and dark violet aperture. 2·7–5·0cm. Indo-Pacific. Uncommon.

Conus fulgetrum Reeve
scaber Kiener.
Thick shell with broad, convex-sided body whorl and short, coronated spire. Spiral grooves more prominent towards base. Whitish with fine spiral threads and a fine network of pale brown lines. One or two broad, spiral, whitish bands usually visible on body whorl. Coronations whitish. c2·5cm. Indo-Pacific (Pacific), Japonic. Uncommon.

205

Conus furvus Reeve   ×1.1
aegrotus Reeve, *lignarius* Reeve.

Thick cone with depressed spire and pointed apex. Axial growth lines; spiral ridges basally. Dull, white shell with two brown bands on body whorl bearing spiral rows of minute, darker brown dashes. Ir-

regular, axial, brown bands. White aperture. *c*4cm. Indo-Pacific. Frequent.

Conus generalis Linnaeus   ×0.6
spirogloxus Deshayes.
Thick, short-spired shell with pointed apex. Smooth with variable pattern of brown axial streaks and broad spiral bands on white. Spiral bands occasionally yellowish, whole shell sometimes dark brown. 5–8cm. Indo-Pacific. Common.

Conus geographus Linnaeus   ×0.6
Thin shell with coronated spire and swollen body whorl. White, cream or yellow with irregular blotches flesh-coloured to brown. Translucent, white aperture.

Above and top right: *Conus geographus.*
Below: *Conus generalis.*

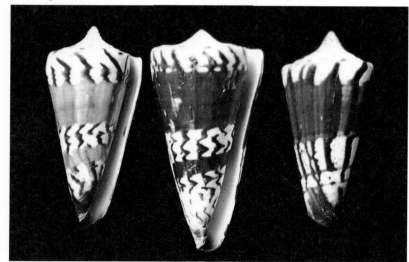

Periostracum sometimes has raised ridges. 6–11cm. Indo-Pacific, South African. Common.

Conus gilvus Reeve
Thick, broadly ovate shell with almost flat spire and tiny, sharply pointed apex. Sharply angled shoulder on body whorl. Shell smooth. Whitish to yellowish brown, with darker brown staining at base. Axial brown lines on spire. Aperture white. *c*4cm. Indo-Pacific. Uncommon.

Conus glans Hwass   ×1.1

Small, thick, fairly slender shell with rounded spire. Ornamented with conspicuously beaded spiral ridges. Whitish with broad areas of light or dark brown. *c*3cm. Indo-Pacific. Uncommon.

Conus glaucus Linnaeus   ×1.6
Thick, broad cone with depressed spire and pointed apex. Weak spiral ridges. Dull, light grey with spiral rows of dark to reddish brown dashes alternating with white on ridges. Axial, reddish brown markings on spire and shoulder. Grey aperture. *c*3·5cm. Japonic, Indo-Pacific. Frequent.

Conus gloriamaris Chemnitz   ×0.8
Shell very similar to some forms of *C. textile* but spire more raised and pointed, and body whorl more slender and relatively longer. Orange ground colour covered with innumerable, small, triangular markings. 4–5 irregular spiral bands often

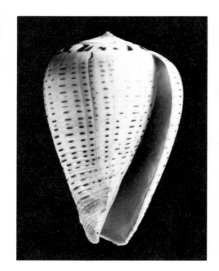

Above: *Conus glaucus.*
Below: *Conus gloriamaris.*

discernible. 7–14cm. Indo-Pacific (Indonesia, Philippines, Admiralty Islands). Rare.

Conus gradatulus Weinkauff
Stepped Cone
turritus Sowerby.
Thickish, dull shell, with stepped whorls and pointed apex. Pinkish white with light brown, irregular mottling. Pink aperture and yellow, smooth, transparent periostracum. 2–6cm. South African. Rare.

Conus granulatus Linnaeus
Glory of the Atlantic Cone
Thick, cylindrically ovate shell with rounded spire whorls and almost straight-

sided body whorl. Numerous coarse spiral threads and cords. Bright orange red to red, with blotches and flecks of brown and yellowish brown. Irregular spiral band of orange at centre of body whorl with darker blotches on its upper edge. Aperture rosy pink. *c*5cm. Caribbean. Rare.

Conus gubernator Hwass   ×0.6

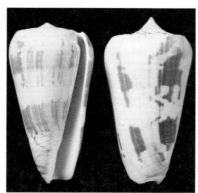

Thick, short-spired shell with pointed, concave apex. Glossy and smooth. Colour variable; commonly light brown or blue, wavy bands on cream. Lilac aperture. 7·0–8·5cm. Indo-Pacific. Common.

Conus guineensis Gmelin
aemulus Reeve.
Thick shell with simple suture. Spiral striae around base of body whorl. Dull, with white and orange brown, axial mottling. Aperture white marginally with flesh brown interior. 2·5–7·0cm. Indo-Pacific.

Conus imperialis Linnaeus   ×0.7
Imperial Cone
viridulus Lamarck.

Very thick cone with simple suture and depressed, coronate spire. Smooth. Dull, white with many bands of dark brown dots and dashes and two wide, brown bands also bearing dashes and dots. White aperture is grey or brown at base. Thick, yellow or brown, opaque periostracum. 6–10cm. Indo-Pacific. Frequent.

Conus jaspideus Gmelin
papillosus Kiener, *verrucosus* Hwass, *boubeeae* Sowerby, *pealii* Green.
Thick, inflated cone with simple suture. Spiral ridges may be beaded. White with irregular, brownish red patches. Lilac aperture white marginally. 2·5–3·25cm. Caribbean. Common.

Conus leopardus Röding   ×0.5

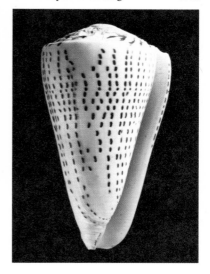

Thick, heavy cone with flattened spire. Axial growth lines. Dull, white with axial rows of dark brown dashes. White aperture becomes flesh-coloured basally. Thin, yellow, transparent periostracum. *c*14cm. Indo-Pacific. Common.

Conus lienardi Bernardi & Crosse
Slender, cylindrically ovate shell with tall spire and sharp apex. Smooth with well spaced, spiral grooves. Creamy white with brown, zigzag streaks and blotches. *c*4cm. Indo-Pacific (New Caledonia). Uncommon.

Conus litoglyphus Hwass   ×0.9
lithoglypus Lamarck.
Thick cone with depressed spire but pointed apex. 2–4 spiral ridges basally, weakly beaded. Glossy, brownish orange

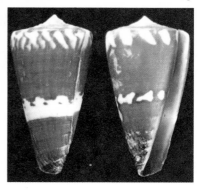

with shoulder and median, spiral rows of white, oblique marks on body whorl and white marking on spire. Dark brown base. White aperture. 4·5–5·0cm. Indo-Pacific (Red Sea). Frequent.

Conus litteratus Linnaeus   ×0.4

Thick, heavy cone with depressed spire and angulate shoulder. Smooth, white shell with two or three axial bands of yellow to orange stripes between spiral bands of black quadrants. Whole shell seems evenly spotted. 6–14cm. Indo-Pacific. Common.

Conus lividus Hwass
sanguinolentus Quoy & Gaimard, *plebeius* Tomlin.
Thick shell with coronate shoulder and granulose spiral striae around lower half of body whorl. Olive brown with white coronations having yellow brown interstices. Base purple. Purplish aperture. 2·5–5·0cm. Indo-Pacific. Common.

Conus magus Linnaeus   ×1.2
adansoni Sowerby, *bolneensis* Sowerby, *sipnifer* Crosse, *epistomium* Reeve, *raphanus* Hwass, *tasmaniae* Sowerby.

Thinnish cone with short spire and rounded shoulder. Fine spiral ridges. Glossy, white shell with two orange, spiral bands on body whorl; dark brown, axial markings on spire. White or bluish aperture. 3·5–4·5cm. Indo-Pacific. Common.

Above: *Conus malacanus*.   Below and bottom: *Conus marmoreus*.

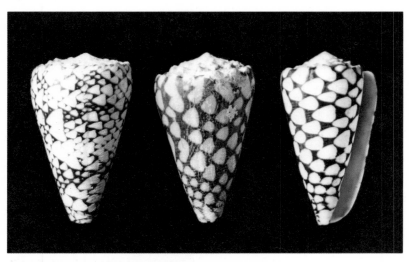

Conus malacanus Hwass   ×1·0
Thin shell with flattened spire and pointed apex. Axial growth lines. Pinkish brown, brown and grey, axial lines. Sometimes nearly all white. Bluish white aperture. Thin, transparent, brown periostracum. 6–7cm. Indo-Pacific. Rare.

Conus marmoreus Linnaeus   ×1.4 ×1.0
bandanus Hwass, *crosseanus* Bernardi, *vidua* Reeve, *nocturnus* Lightfoot.
Thick, broad cone with depressed spire. Smooth with coronate shoulders. Fairly glossy, dark brown with spiral, cream tenting; tents overlap. Often two spiral bands. Creamy white aperture. Very variable species. 8–10cm. Indo-Pacific. Uncommon.

Conus mediterraneus Hwass   ×0.9
Thin, dull shell with high, blunt spire. Sometimes very inflated body whorl. Colour is very variable, yellowish, brownish purple or greenish, sometimes mottled.

Dull, yellow, opaque periostracum. 3·0–6·5cm. Mediterranean. Common.

Conus mercator Linnaeus
Thin, fusiform shell with short spire. Dull, cream with two reticulate, dark brown bands on body whorl; bands often on yellow ground. Wide band near spire; narrow, median band. Thin, transparent periostracum. 1·5–3·7cm. West African. Frequent.

Conus miles Linnaeus   ×0.9
Soldier Cone
Thick shell with depressed spire. Axial growth lines. White with axial, orange marks and brown lines; median and basal, spiral, brown bands on body whorl. Aperture white with purplish brown bands. 6·5–7·0cm. Indo-Pacific. Frequent.

Conus moluccensis Küster
stainforthi Reeve, *pulcher* A. Adams, *proximus* Sowerby.
Small, thick shell with short, biconcave spire. Low coronations at suture and on spire whorls. Numerous prominent, raised spiral ridges. Creamy white, with dark brown, interrupted spiral lines. Two or three underlying spiral bands which are usually interrupted at intervals. Aperture white. 2·5–4·5cm. Indo-Pacific (Pacific). Rare.

Conus monachus Linnaeus   ×0.9
achatinus Hwass, *cinerarius* Röding, *nebulosus* Gmelin.

Thick shell with spiral striae on body whorl and two spiral cords on each spire whorl. Grey with small trigonal and elongate white spots on median and shoulder zones. Spiral, blackish brown lines. Aperture bluish white with dark brown spots on parietal lip. 3·5–6·0cm. Indo-Pacific. Frequent.

Conus monile Hwass   ×0.8
Thick, with depressed spire and raised apex. Dull, white, with several spiral rows of reddish brown spots. May have two flesh-coloured bands on body whorl. White aperture. 5·0–5·5cm. Indo-Pacific. Uncommon.

Conus moreleti Crosse
Similar in general appearance to *C. lividus,* but much more slender and with relatively taller spire. Apex blunter. Brown to purplish brown with pale bluish white band at shoulder and fainter spiral band at centre of body whorl similar to that on *C. lividus.* Spire white. Base of body whorl purple. Aperture purple. 3–4cm. Indo-Pacific (Pacific). Frequent.

Conus musicus Hwass
sponsalis Hwass.
Broad, solid white shell with longitudinal, pink or reddish brown, vermiculate lines. Depressed, coronate spire and beading on lower part of body whorl. Purple tip. Aperture white to purple. Very variable. Thin, transparent periostracum. 1·2–2·5cm. Indo-Pacific (Pacific). Common.

Conus mustelinus Hwass   ×1.1
Thick, short-spired shell with spiral ridges towards base. Greenish or yellowish, with central, broad, white spiral band bearing a row of irregular, blackish blotches above and below. Spire and shoulder whitish, with axial, bluish black streaks. Aperture violet, with median white spiral band. 5–8cm. Indo-Pacific. Common.

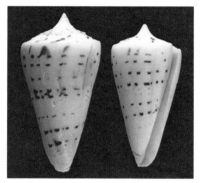

Above: *Conus monile.*
Below left: *Conus miles.*
Below right: *Conus mustelinus.*

Conus nicobaricus Hwass ×0.5
peplum Sowerby.

Thick shell with depressed, concave spire. Spire coronate with canaliculate whorls. Glossy, cream or pink with tenting. Two or three dark brown or black spiral bands with few tents. White aperture. Distinguished from *C. marmoreus* by stronger banding and smudging of tents near shoulder. 2·5–7·8cm. Indo-Pacific. Uncommon.

Conus nigropunctatus Sowerby
Thick cone with pointed spire. Spire whorls with spiral striae; fine spiral ridges around base. Glossy, with olive and white mottling and narrow, discontinuous, dark brown spiral lines. Spire with pink tip. White aperture. *c*4cm. Indo-Pacific. Frequent.

Conus nobilis Linnaeus ×1.7
cordigera Sowerby.

Thick shell with depressed spire and sharply shouldered body whorl. Axial growth lines; weak spiral ridges basally. Glossy, orange brown shell with white, triangular markings concentrated in three bands on body whorl. Orange brown and white on spire. White aperture. 2·5–5cm. Indo-Pacific. Rare

Conus nodulosus Sowerby
Very similar to *C. victoriae*, and may prove to be a form of that species. Mature specimens usually smaller, with slightly taller spire and a paler colour pattern. Tinted areas usually relatively larger; shell lacks bluish tints found on *C. victoriae*. Aperture pink. 4–5cm. Australian (West Australia), Indo-Pacific (North West Australia). Rare.

Conus nussatella Linnaeus ×1.1

Shell cylindrical, almost straight-sided at middle of body whorl. Body whorl covered by coarse spiral ribs. Diffuse brown areas on a whitish ground, the spiral ribs bearing alternate whitish and brown granules. 4–7cm. Indo-Pacific. Frequent.

Conus obscurus Sowerby
halitropus Bartsch & Rehder.
Thin, inflated cone with simple suture, resembling a juvenile *C. geographus*. Faint, axial growth lines. Dull, brown to light brown axial streaks on purple. Yellow form has white mottling. Grey aperture Thin, smooth periostracum. 2·5–7·0cm. Indo-Pacific. Uncommon.

Conus ochroleucus Gmelin
praefectus Hwass, *fasciatus* Sowerby.
Thick, elongate-ovate shell. Lower part of body whorl with broad, flat ridges and interstices cancellated with axial ribs. Orange brown to reddish brown, may have pale, narrow, median band. Cream parietal lip, deep orange interior. 4·0–6·5cm. Indo-Pacific (Pacific). Uncommon.

Conus orbignyi Audouin ×0.9
Thin, slender shell with long body whorl and elevated spire. Shoulders of spire and body whorls coronate. Spiral ridges have axial grooves in interstices. Dull, white, with reddish brown mottling arranged in irregular axial lines and spiral bands on

body whorl. 5·0–6·5cm. Japonic, Indo-Pacific (Taiwan). Uncommon.

Conus parvulus Link
roseus Lamarck, *imperator* Woolacott.
Thick shell with wavy suture. Coronate shoulders and weak spiral ridges. Strong, axial growth lines. Glossy, white with two pinkish grey to grey spiral bands on body whorl. Pink spire with white coronations. Purple to blue aperture. Brown, opaque periostracum. 2·0–3·5cm. Indo-Pacific (Northern Queensland). Frequent.

Conus patricius Hinds
pyriformis Reeve.
Solid, pale pink shell with biconcave spire. Light spiral striae on body whorl. White aperture. Thick, fibrous, opaque, greenish brown periostracum. 7–15cm. Panamic. Frequent.

Conus pennaceus Born ×1.0
magnificus Reeve, *omaria* Hwass, *rubiginosus* Hwass, *racemosus* Sowerby, *madagascariensis* Sowerby.

Thick shell with short, blunt spire. Faint, axial growth lines and faint axial lirae. Glossy, white, with dark or light brown tenting and irregular patches of minute tenting or reticulation. Pink or lilac spire.

White aperture. 4·5–5·5cm. Indo-Pacific (Hawaii). Japonic. Common.

Conus planorbis Born ×0.9 ×0.9

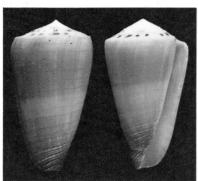

Thick shell with depressed spire and sharply angled shoulder. Axial growth lines; basal spiral ridges may have beads. White, dull with two wide, orange to dark brown, spiral bands on body whorl. White part of whorl crossed by axial, dark brown stripes. Axial, dark brown markings on white spire. White aperture. 4·0–7·5cm. Indo-Pacific. Common.

Conus princeps Linnaeus ×0.9
Prince Cone

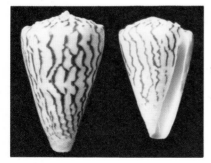

Thick shell, flesh-coloured with dark brown, axial, vermiculate lines. Sometimes all pink. Wide, pink aperture. Coronate shoulder and depressed spire. Thin periostracum, usually opaque. 4·5–8·0cm. Panamic. Frequent.

Conus prometheus Hwass
Thick, heavy, large shell with depressed spire. White with three bands of orange brown to brown mottling and spiral rows of brown spots or dashes. White aperture. Largest living cone shell. 20–30cm. West African. Uncommon.

Conus purpurascens Sowerby ×0.7
comptus Gould, *luzonicus* Sowerby.

Thick shell with stepped spire and pointed apex. Faint, axial growth lines are crossed by weak ridges near base. Spiral grooves on spire whorls. Lilac tinted, bluish grey with light to dark brown mottling and dashes in spiral rows. Blue or white aperture with violet margin. 4–5cm. Panamic. Frequent.

Conus radiatus Gmelin ×1.5

Thin, elongated shell with rounded shoulders and pointed spire. Glossy with basal spiral ridges. Orange or chestnut

brown; white base and aperture. c4·5cm. Indo-Pacific. Frequent.

Conus ranunculus Hwass
portoricanus Hwass, *flammeus* Röding.
Thick shell with spiral striae around base. Dull, cream with dark brown mottling in two irregular spiral bands on body whorl or with pink, grey and purple markings. Yellow, smooth periostracum. 4–5cm. Caribbean. Frequent.

Conus rattus Hwass ×1.0

Small, solid shell with short spire and fine spiral ridges. Whitish, blotched irregularly with olive green. Indistinct, median, spiral band on body whorl. Aperture purple. 3–4cm. Indo-Pacific. Common.

Conus regius Gmelin
nebulosus Hwass. ×1.2

Thick, broad cone with elevated, blunt spire and nodulose shoulder. Axial growth lines; irregular spiral beads on weak, narrow ridges. Glossy, brown shell with irregular, white patches; white beads on dark brown, spiral lines or ridges. White apex and aperture. 5–7cm. Caribbean. Common.

Conus regularis Sowerby   ×0.8
syriacus Sowerby, *angulatus* A. Adams,
monilifer Broderip.

Thick, elongate shell with concave spire.
Dull, whitish with reddish brown, irregular, spiral bands often alternating with
rows of dots. Thin, brown, semi-transparent periostracum. *c*5cm. Panamic.
Common.

Conus rufimaculosus Macpherson   ×1.1

Thin shell with very depressed spire and
raised apex. Glossy, white with brown
mottling, frequently pink around mottling
and may have pink streaks. Pink aperture.
3·5–4·0cm. Australian (Australia), extending into Indo-Pacific. Frequent.

Conus rutilus Menke
Thin, small shell with convex body whorl
and short, coronated spire. Spiral striae
towards base. Rest of shell smooth.
Pinkish or reddish brown, sometimes
yellow or violet, and usually with two or
more spiral bands of rectangular darker
spots on body whorl. Very variable in
colour. *c*1·5cm. Australian (Australia).
Common.

Conus scabriusculus Dillwyn   ×1.4
fabula Sowerby.
Thick shell with granulose spiral ridges on
body whorl. Spire whorls have fine striae.
White or lilac with large, brown patches.

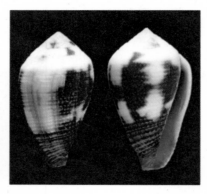

Aperture violet with white margin to
parietal lip. *c*2·6cm. Indo-Pacific (South
West Pacific). Uncommon.

Conus sieboldi Reeve   ×0.9

Thick, elongate with pointed spire having
canaliculate whorls and elevated ridge
below suture. Axial growth lines; weak
spiral grooves basally. Glossy, white with
occasional, orange brown markings in two
irregular bands on body whorl and towards apex on spire. White aperture.
*c*7·6cm. Japonic. Frequent.

Conus sowerbii Reeve
Small, biconical shell with spire almost as
tall as aperture. Spire biconcave, with
ridge above suture and sharply angled
shoulder on body whorl. Body whorl
tapers conspicuously towards base. Ornamented with deep spiral grooves. Creamy
white, with reddish brown spots on ridges
between spiral grooves, and three spiral
rows of larger, reddish brown blotches.
Some specimens have a more inflated body
whorl and have cords rather than ridges
between spiral grooves. *c*3cm. Indo-Pacific
(Pacific). Rare.

Conus spectrum Linnaeus
broderipii Reeve, *carota* Röding,
stillatus Reeve.
Solid shell with depressed spire and sharp
apex. Whitish with pattern of occasional,
yellow blobs or brown streaks. Spiral
grooves around base of body whorl and
spiral striae on spire whorls. Aperture
white. Thin, transparent periostracum.
2·5–5·0cm. Indo-Pacific, Australian. Frequent.

Conus stercusmuscarum Linnaeus   ×1.0

Thick, ovate cone with convex sides. Close,
spiral rows of dark brown or reddish
brown spots which may be arranged in
irregular axial bands. Occasional white
spots or dashes. White aperture. 3·5–
5·0cm. Indo-Pacific. Common.

Conus stramineus Lamarck
nisus Dillwyn.
Moderately thick, ovate shell with short or
moderately tall spire and sharply pointed
apex. Widely spaced spiral grooves on
body whorl. Very variable in colour and
pattern. Greyish marked with reddish
brown dots and blotches; greyish marked
with broad, dark brown axial streaks.
*c*4cm. Indo-Pacific (Pacific). Common.

Conus striatellus Link   ×0.9
pulchrelineatus Hopwood.
Thick shell with short spire. Weak spiral
ridges on spire whorls. Axial growth lines.
Narrow spiral ridges on lower half of body
whorl beaded. Glossy, white or creamy
orange shell with orange brown mottling;

reddish brown basally; reddish brown marks on spire. Bluish white aperture. 4–5cm. Indo-Pacific. Uncommon.

Conus striatus Linnaeus   ×0.5
floridus Sowerby.

Shell thick, cylindrical and short-spired. Suture channelled. Fine spiral threads all over body whorl. Ground colour white or pink mottled with purplish brown blotches composed of very fine lines. 7–10cm. Indo-Pacific. Frequent.

Conus sulcatus Hwass   ×0.8
asper Lamarck, *costatus* Dillwyn.

Shell thick, short-spired with pointed apex, ornamented with alternating narrow and wide spiral ribs. Whitish, sometimes covered with olivaceous periostracum. 5–6cm. Indo-Pacific (South East Asia). Uncommon.

Conus suturatus Reeve   ×1.8
turbinatus Sowerby.
Thick, broadly conical shell with flat spire and pointed apex. Axial growth lines and spiral grooves around base. Glossy, white with lilac staining on body whorl, strongest at base and shoulder. Median and basal band creamy orange. White aperture lilac basally and at shoulder. 3·0–3·5cm. Indo-Pacific (Pacific). Uncommon.

Conus taeniatus Hwass   ×1.0
Shell small, solid, broadly conical, short-

Above: *Conus suturatus*.
Below: *Conus taeniatus*.

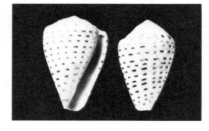

spired. White with numerous spiral rows of dots and lines of bluish black. 2–4cm Indo-Pacific (Indian Ocean). Common.

Conus telatus Reeve
Like a slender *C. textile*, but has coronated shoulder and coronations on spire. Body whorl also encircled with conspicuous spiral cords. Whitish, with broad, axial pale brown and darker brown streaks and fine lines enclosing large whitish tents. Aperture white. *c*6·5cm. Indo-Pacific (Philippines). Rare.

Conus tenellus Dillwyn
Moderately thick, cylindrically ovate shell with slightly convex sides. Short spire with concave sides. Moderately angulated shoulder on body whorl. Coarse spiral cords cover whole shell. Whitish with irregular, pale brown spiral bands and small, darker brown lines on spiral cords. Aperture white. 4–5cm. Indo-Pacific (Western Pacific). Uncommon.

Conus terebra Born   ×0.9
thomasi Sowerby.

Thick, tall but short-spired shell with bulbous apex. Dull spiral ridges crossed by weaker axial ridges. Unicolorous white. 5–8cm. Indo-Pacific. Frequent.

Conus tessulatus Born   ×1.3
tesselatus Born.
Thick with almost flat spire, slightly raised apex. Glossy, white with orange spots and

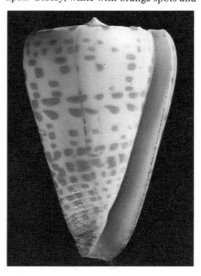

213

flammules, some in spiral rows. Lilac basally. 2·5–5·0cm. Indo-Pacific. Common.

Conus textile Linnaeus   ×0.4 ×1.1
tigrinus Sowerby, *verriculum* Reeve,
abbreviata Dautzenberg,
canonicus Hwass.

Below (left, centre and right): *Conus thalassiarchus*.

Thick, elongate or broadly ovate shell with short spire and pointed apex. White or yellowish, with many tent-like markings all over surface. 3–5 golden brown, spiral bands usually present. Extremely variable in size, outline, colour and pattern. 4–11 cm. Indo-Pacific. Common.

Conus thalassiarchus Sowerby   ×0.9
Thick or thin shell with depressed spire having moderately caniculate whorls. Glossy, creamy white shell with spiral bands of dark brown dots, lines and dashes. Dark brown basally. Pink aperture. 7–10cm. Indo-Pacific. Uncommon.

Conus tinianus Hwass   ×0.9
Thin, inflated cone with simple suture.

Smooth but may have spiral striae around base. Dull with pinkish lilac and ochre mottling or dark purplish brown with white mottling. Pinkish lilac aperture. May be a form of *C. aurora*. 3·5–4·0cm. South African. Uncommon.

Conus trigonus Reeve
Resembles *C. capitaneus*, but relatively narrower at shoulders. Sides of spire less concave. Spire sometimes flat. Pale brown or yellowish brown with darker spiral lines, a broad, interrupted, white band at centre and a narrower, interrupted, white band at shoulder. Spire has axial, brown and white, wavy streaks. *c*6·5cm. Indo-Pacific, (North West Australia). Uncommon.

Conus tulipa Linnaeus   ×0.6
borbonicus H. Adams, *purpureus* Röding.

Thin, cylindrical-ovate shell with short spire. Pinkish with brownish mottling. Numerous spiral rows of fine, brown dots and dashes. Aperture violet. 5–8cm. Indo-Pacific. Common.

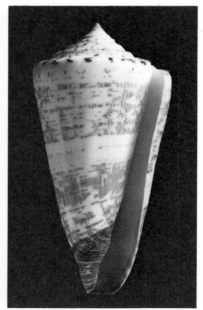

Conus venulatus Hwass
nivosus Lamarck, *nivifer* Sowerby.
Thick shell with simple suture and spiral striae around base. Dull, yellow or flesh-coloured with irregular, white blotches and white banding on spire. Aperture white or pink. 2·5–3·3cm. West African (Cape Verde Islands), Mediterranean (Canary Islands). Uncommon.

Conus vexillum Gmelin   × 1.0
sumatrensis Hwass.

Thick, broadly conical shell with depressed spire. Spire whorls with spiral ridges; body whorl has faint, axial growth lines. Glossy, orange brown with some white patches in median, pale spiral band of body whorl. White aperture. 6·5–8·0cm. Indo-Pacific. Common.

Conus victoriae Reeve   × 1.2
complanatus Sowerby.

Solid shell with pattern varying from yellow mottling on white to brown streaks on yellow, with white tents outlined by fine, brown lines. Thin parietal lip and white aperture. Thin, transparent peri-

ostracum. 3·5–6·0cm. Indo-Pacific (North West Australia). Common.

Conus virgatus Reeve
Thick, white shell with biconcave apex. Brown, axial, wavy stripes and spiral grooves around lower half of body whorl. Aperture is white marginally and then pale greyish brown. Thick, opaque periostracum. Banding varies with age and is stronger in younger specimens. 4–7cm. Californian, Panamic. Frequent.

Conus virgo Linnaeus   × 0.5
emaciatus Reeve.

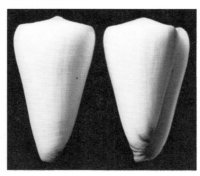

Thick, tapering, almost flat-topped cone. Faint spiral striae, stronger basally. Creamy white, violet basally. White aperture. Thick, black periostracum. 7–12cm. Indo-Pacific. Common.

Conus vitulinus Hwass
vulpinus Schubert & Wagner.
Thick shell with granulose spiral ridges on lower part of body whorl and spiral striae on spire whorls. Reddish brown with white shoulder and median bands. Brown basally. White aperture. 3–6cm. Indo-Pacific. Frequent.

Conus ximenes Gray   × 0.9

Thick shell with biconcave, pointed spire, and with spiral ridges basally. Spiral rows of small, reddish brown, quadrangular spots alternate with rows of short dashes. Irregular, brownish axial bands. Lilac

aperture white marginally. 4–5cm. Panamic. Common.

Conus zonatus Hwass   × 0.6
edwardi Preston.

Thick shell with simple suture. Depressed spire and coronate shoulders. Glossy, black with spiral bands of axial, white stripes and thin, brown, spiral lines. Purple aperture reflects external pattern marginally. Yellow periostracum. 4·8–7·8cm. Indo-Pacific (Indian Ocean). Rare.

Family TEREBRIDAE

Long, slender shells with numerous whorls and short aperture. Ornamented with axial ribs, spiral cords and beads. Ornament most pronounced at suture. Outer lip simple. Prominent fold on columella. Short, straight or recurved, siphonal canal. Operculum thin and variably shaped. Carnivorous and sand-dwelling. Hundreds of species in tropical and warm seas. Various genera in use but as principal differences are anatomical the single genus *Terebra* is used here.

Below: *Terebra affinis* (see over).

Genus TEREBRA Bruguière
For details, see Family Terebridae.

Terebra affinis Gray × 1.3
striata Quoy & Gaimard.
Shell thick, solid with slightly stepped whorls and impressed suture. Punctate spiral groove defines a pre-sutural band. Numerous curved axial ribs with spirally grooved interstices. Creamy white with brown blotches and brown spiral lines. Columella brown. 2·5–5·5cm. Indo-Pacific. Common.

Terebra albomarginata Deshayes
Thick, narrow shell with many whorls. Shoulder slopes gently just below suture and then whorls are almost straight-sided. Deeply incised pre-sutural groove with thick, rounded band above. Low ribs on pre-sutural band continued below as curved axial lirae, crossed by strong spiral ribs forming cancellation. Orange with pre-sutural zone white. Aperture orange. *c*7cm. Indo-Pacific (Pacific). Uncommon.

Terebra alveolata Hinds × 1.7
Sharp, pointed shell with axial ribs and spiral lines forming granulation at intersections of broad, beaded cord below suture. Yellowish brown with row of brown spots below suture on each whorl. two rows of spots on body whorl. Spots may fade on exposure to light. *c*5cm. Indo-Pacific. Frequent.

Left: *Terebra alveolata*.
Right: *Terebra areolata*.

Terebra areolata Link × 0.6
Large, thick, nearly straight-sided shell with axial ribs on early whorls. Shallow spiral groove on each whorl becoming obsolete towards base. Creamy with three rows of blackish brown, square blotches on whorls and four rows on body whorl. Early whorls lacking markings. 11–18cm. Indo-Pacific. Frequent.

Terebra babylonia Lamarck
acus Gmelin.
Narrow. tall and many whorled shell with straight sides and impressed suture. Incised, spiral pre-sutural groove and two weaker spiral grooves below. Curved axial grooves and growth striae. Flesh-coloured or pale brown with orange brown axial and spiral grooves; basal portion of body whorl orange brown. Aperture orange brown. *c*10cm. Indo-Pacific. Frequent.

Terebra bifrons Hinds × 1.7

Shell thick with acutely pointed apex. Whorls slightly constricted at suture; deep spiral groove below suture. Strong axial threads with fine spiral lines between them. Siphonal canal reflexed. Unicolorous dark brown. 4·5–5·5cm. Indo-Pacific (Pacific). Frequent.

Terebra caerulescens Lamarck × 1.4
Shell similar to *T. hectica* and by some authors considered to be conspecific. Thick, sharply pointed with almost straight sides and impressed suture. Coarse axial ribs crossed by a single broad spiral groove in middle of each whorl. Base of

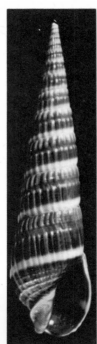

Left: *Terebra caerulescens*.
Right: *Terebra chlorata*.

body whorl with three or four spiral, nodulous cords. Whitish with broad, purple brown band below suture and another at base of body whorl. Aperture dark purple brown with white, central band. 4–6cm. Indo-Pacific (Pacific). Uncommon.

Terebra cerethina Lamarck
As its name implies, this species superficially resembles a cerithium. Solid and sharply pointed with relatively inflated lower whorls. Conspicuous groove in posterior corner of aperture. Thick callus on parietal wall. Strong, rounded axial ribs on early whorls becoming obsolete on later whorls. Weak pre-sutural groove becoming obsolete on body whorl. Greyish or whitish with orange yellow staining and four darker orange yellow spiral lines and irregular axial lines. *c*8cm. Indo-Pacific (Pacific). Frequent.

Terebra chlorata Lamarck × 1.0
Shell solid, almost straight-sided. Smooth, with a median spiral groove on each whorl, becoming obsolete on body whorl. Whitish with irregular, axial, violet brown blotches and wavy streaks. 5–9cm. Indo-Pacific. Frequent.

Terebra commaculata Gmelin
Very long, narrow shell with stepped whorls. Two thick, nodulose spiral ribs at suture separated by well incised spiral line. Also several spiral rows of fine nodules. White with brown streaks or rectangular

blotches and spiral row of round, brown markings on basal portion of body whorl. c8cm. Indo-Pacific. Uncommon.

Terebra conspersa Hinds
Thick, rather broad shell with impressed suture. Punctate spiral groove at suture. Numerous fine, curved axial ribs with 4–7 grooves in interstices. Cream to light brown with interrupted, brown spiral bands and axial streaks. Colour darker at suture. 2–5cm. Indo-Pacific (Pacific). Uncommon.

Terebra crenulata Linnaeus   ×0.9
varicosa Gmelin, *fimbriata* Deshayes, *interlineata* Deshayes.

Thick shell with widely spaced tubercles below suture. Brownish pink, with darker zones and two spiral rows of small, brown dots. These may be obsolete on later whorls. 3–12cm. Indo-Pacific. Frequent.

Terebra dimidiata Linnaeus   ×0.5
splendens Deshayes.
Shell thin, almost straight-sided. Prominent spiral groove below suture. Orange to orange red, ornamented with axial, Y-shaped, white lines and streaks. 3–13cm. Indo-Pacific. Common.

Left: *Terebra dislocata*. Right: *Terebra dussumieri;* Below: *Terebra duplicata.*

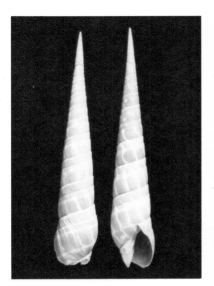

Below: *Terebra dimidiata.*

Terebra dislocata Say   ×1.3
Thick, slender shell. Spiral groove below suture. Each whorl with about 20–25 axial ribs. Spiral grooves between axial ribs. Two folds on columella. Orange red or pale grey, sometimes with darker bands of purplish grey and reddish brown. 4·0–5·5 cm. Transatlantic, Caribbean. Common.

Terebra duplicata Linnaeus   ×1.1
lamarckii Kiener, *reevei* Deshayes.
Thick, almost straight-sided shell. Deep spiral groove below suture and strong axial ridges. Cream, whitish or brown. 5–7cm. Indo-Pacific. Uncommon.

Terebra dussumieri Deshayes   ×0.9
Thick, almost straight-sided shell. Conspicuous, light band at suture. Strong axial ridges. Glossy, brown except for sutural band which is greyish white. Brown aperture. 8–10cm. Indo-Pacific (China Sea and Yellow Sea). Frequent.

Terebra evoluta Deshayes
Thick, solid shell, moderately slender with many whorls. Sides of whorls slightly convex. Prominent pre-sutural groove with a rounded zone above. Strong, narrow axial ribs. Cream, brown, greyish or almost black. Axial ribs are lighter. Single pale spiral line on lower part of body whorl. Very similar to *T. duplicata*, and sometimes mistaken for that species. c9cm. Indo-Pacific. Uncommon.

Terebra felina Dillwyn   ×1.3

Shell moderately thick, with straight-sided whorls, slightly impressed suture and median spiral groove on each whorl. Deep, broad siphonal notch. Early whorls with oblique axial ribs. Rest of shell smooth. Yellowish white with spiral rows of red-

217

dish brown spots above suture, two rows of spots on body whorl. Aperture and columella white. 5–9cm. Indo-Pacific (Pacific). Uncommon.

Terebra guttata Röding   × 0.6

Left: *Terebra inconstans*.
Right: *Terebra laevigata*.

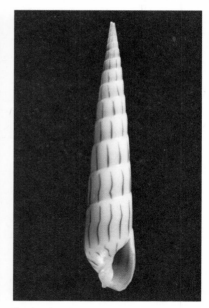

Terebra lanceata.

Shell large, very thick and heavy. Upper half of each whorl swollen. Fine, axial growth marks. Orange brown with a row of large, roundish, white spots with brown markings between; two spiral rows on body whorl. 11–14cm. Indo-Pacific. Uncommon.

Terebra hectica Linnaeus   × 1.7
Moderately thick shell with straight sides and sharp apex. Whorls smooth or oc-

casionally with fine growth striae. Thickened with a callus at suture. Creamy with purplish brown axial streaks and greyish brown, broad spiral bands. Sometimes unicolorous white. 4·5–7·5cm. Indo-Pacific. Frequent.

Terebra inconstans Hinds   × 1.7
Shell moderately thin with sharply pointed apex. Distinct spiral groove below suture and coarse, irregular axial ribs. Greyish blotched with brownish streaks; white, spiral band below suture and one spiral band on body whorl. External colour and pattern shows through aperture. 4–5cm. Indo-Pacific. Frequent.

Terebra laevigata Gray   × 1.7
Shell thin with acutely pointed apex and small aperture. Strong, axially ribbed spiral cord just below suture; whorls concave below spiral cord. Pale brown with darker brown early whorls and violet staining on columella. *c*5cm. Indo-Pacific (Pacific). Frequent.

Terebra lanceata Linnaeus   × 1.7
Shell very narrow with slightly stepped whorls. Early whorls with fine axial ribs. Widely spaced, thin, axial, reddish brown lines. 4–6cm. Indo-Pacific. Uncommon.

Terebra lima Deshayes
Thick, fairly narrow shell with almost rectangular aperture. Strong, spiral and axial ribs form cancellate pattern, with spiral rib just below suture much stronger than others. Groove below this rib wide

and deep. Unicolorous white or yellow. Aperture white. *c*10cm. Indo-Pacific (Pacific), Australian (Australia). Uncommon.

Terebra maculata Linnaeus   × 0.45

Large, thick and heavy shell, smooth and glossy. Creamy white with two spiral rows of axial, round blobs and streaks. 13–25cm. Indo-Pacific. Common.

Terebra nebulosa Sowerby
Thick, straight-sided shell with a punctate spiral groove at suture, and numerous broad and curved axial ribs with many spiral grooves in interstices. White, with large, irregular, orange red blotches on each whorl. 3–8cm. Indo-Pacific. Uncommon.

Terebra pertusa Born

undata Blainville, *bermonti* Lorois,
andamanica Melvill & Sykes.
Thick, narrow, pointed shell with straight
sides and slightly impressed suture. Deep
pre-sutural groove with short, straight
axial ribs above. Rest of each whorl with
curved axial ribs and spiral striae. Yellow
or pale orange with white spiral band
below middle of body whorl. Axial, brown
blotches and flecks on pre-sutural zone.
4–8cm. Indo-Pacific. Uncommon.

Terebra robusta Hinds   ×0.6

Thick, solid shell with inflated lower
whorls and narrow spire. Fine axial lines,
otherwise smooth. Yellowish white with
axial, brown stripes darker at suture.
9–13cm. Panamic. Uncommon.

Terebra strigata Sowerby   ×0.7
Shell thick and heavy with relatively
broad body whorl and nearly straight-
sided spire whorls with impressed suture.
Outer lip nearly straight; columella only
slightly curved. Shallow spiral groove on
each whorl. Coarse, wavy axial ribs becoming obsolete towards body whorl.
Yellowish white with widely spaced, broad,
axial, brown streaks. Aperture and columella yellowish white. 8–10cm. Panamic.
Uncommon.

Terebra strigilata Linnaeus   ×1.2
Straight-sided shell with pronounced axial
ribs. Dark grey or greenish grey with a
median, spiral, white band on body whorl.
Broad, white, spiral band below suture has
few large, blackish brown blobs. 3–6cm.
Indo-Pacific. Uncommon.

Terebra subulata Linnaeus   ×0.8
Rounded whorls with spiral groove at
suture. Dull, cream with reddish brown

Left: *Terebra strigata*.
Right: *Terebra subulata*.
Below: *Terebra strigilata*.

quadrants in two spiral rows on each
whorl; three rows on body whorl. Cream
aperture. 4–16cm. Indo-Pacific. Common.

Terebra succincta Gmelin
fissum Röding, *cancellata* Quoy &
Gaimard, *undatella* Deshayes.
Thick, solid shell with moderately rounded
whorls, impressed suture and deep spiral
groove at suture. Numerous curved axial

ribs with spiral ridges in interstices. Unicolorous dark brown or black. 2–4cm.
Indo-Pacific. Uncommon.

Terebra triseriata Gray   ×0.9

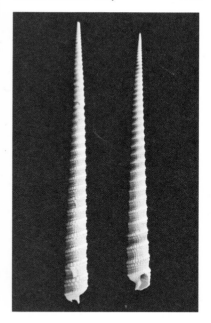

Very narrow shell with two rows of beads
at suture. Other spiral ridges more finely
beaded. Dull, orange or chestnut brown
shell with orange aperture. 7·0–8·5cm.
Indo-Pacific. Rare.

Terebra variegata Gray   ×1.2

Thick, solid shell with strong, noduled
spiral cord below suture. Four deeply incised spiral grooves below cord and others
towards base. Creamy, with dark brown
axial streaks in middle of whorl and
blotches on spiral cords. Aperture dark
brown with central, yellowish band. *c*5cm.
Panamic. Frequent.

Sub-Class
Opisthobranchia

Family ACTEONIDAE

Small, thin, ovate shells with inflated body whorl and short spire. One or two folds on columella. Ornament consists of weak or strong spiral ridges. Outer lip thin or thickened. Few genera in most seas.

Genus ACTEON Montfort

For details see Family Acteonidae.

Acteon tornatilis Linnaeus   ×1.8

Thin but strong shell. Cylindrically ovate with large body whorl and short spire. Large, curved fold on columella. Glossy, with fine spiral striae becoming coarser towards base of body whorl. Pinkish brown to yellowish orange with two broad, yellowish white spiral bands on body whorl. Aperture white. *c*2cm. Boreal, Mediterranean. Common.

Acteon virgatus Reeve
Shell larger, thicker and more ovate than *A. tornatilis*. Fine spiral striae on body whorl. Very strong, curved fold on columella. Whitish with few broad, axial, dark brown stripes on body whorl and penultimate whorl. *c*2·5cm. Indo-Pacific (West Pacific). Rare.

Family HYDATINIDAE

Small to medium-sized, ovate to globular, very thin, fragile shells with sunken spire and expanded outer lip. The large animals usually completely envelop shell, giving it a glossy smooth surface. Three genera in warm and tropical seas.

Genus HYDATINA Schumacher

For details see Family Hydatinidae.

Hydatina albocincta Hoeven   ×2.0
Shell extremely thin and fragile. Globular with sunken spire. White with spiral bands of greyish brown which are streaked axially with darker brown lines. 2·5–4·0cm. Indo-Pacific. Common.

Above: *Hydatina albocincta*
Right: *Hydatina physis*

Hydatina physis Linnaeus   ×1.6
Shell similar in shape to *H. albocincta*, differs principally in having a minute umbilicus. Whitish with many fine, spiral, brown lines, some stronger than others with occasional, axial, brown lines. Columella and parietal wall white. Aperture white with dark brown line near margin. 3·0–4·5cm. Indo-Pacific. Common.

Hydatina vesicaria Lightfoot
Large, fragile, globose shell very similar to *H. physis*, with which it was formerly confused. White or pale brown with numerous closely spaced, wavy, brown spiral lines. Thin, white parietal callus. Outer colour and pattern shows through aperture. 2–4cm. Caribbean. Frequent.

Hydatina zonata Lightfoot
Similar in size, shape and thickness to *H. albocincta*. Body whorl less inflated and colour and pattern very different. Glossy and smooth. Pale yellowish brown with densely crowded, axial, black lines. A zone around the sunken spire is free of axial bands. *c*3·5cm. Japonic. Frequent.

Family BULLIDAE

Thin but strong, globular or broadly ovate shells with spire inverted and completely surrounded by capacious body whorl so that it has the appearance of an umbilicus situated at apex instead of at base. Popularly known as bubble shells in allusion to their shape. One or two genera containing few species, which are widely distributed in warm and tropical seas.

Genus BULLA Linnaeus
For details see Family Bullidae.

Bulla ampulla Linnaeus   × 1.3

Moderately thick, solid, globular shell with intorted, deeply excavated spire. Upper edge of aperture taller than top of body whorl. Greyish brown, with creamy blotches all óver and four indistinct, spiral, brownish bands. Aperture white. *c*4·5cm. Indo-Pacific. Common.

Bulla gouldiana Pilsbry
Very similar to *B. ampulla* but with very different colour pattern. Large, fragile, smooth, globular shell with dark brownish, zigzag or angular streaks edged with white or cream. Dark brown, finely wrinkled periostracum. *c*4cm. Californian. Common.

Bulla occidentalis A. Adams
Fragile to moderately thick shell, much less inflated than *B. ampulla*. Deep and narrow perforation at apex. Outer lip almost straight-sided at centre. Whitish mottled with axial, brownish stripes and less conspicuous, spiral, brown bands. Colour very variable. 0·5–2·5cm. Transatlantic, Caribbean. Common.

Bulla orientalis Habe
A smaller, much narrower, species than *B. ampulla*. Outer lip almost straight-sided. Spire well-concealed under the body whorl. Glossy and smooth. Purplish brown with numerous triangular spots scattered over the shell. Four interrupted, dark brown bands encircle body whorl. *c*2cm. Indo-Pacific (West Pacific). Frequent.

Family SCAPHANDRIDAE

Small to moderately large, thin, ovate shells having the spire completely enclosed within the large, usually globular body whorl. Columella fold in some genera. Ornament usually restricted to fine spiral lines. Few genera, usually in cooler seas.

Genus SCAPHANDER Montfort
For details see Family Scaphandridae.

Scaphander lignarius Linnaeus   × 1.2
Thin, but fairly solid shell with widely expanded aperture, outer lip extending below and above spire. Most of inner whorls dissolved away. Fine spiral striae crossed by finer axial lines. Yellowish with brownish blotches. Aperture white. 5–6cm. Boreal. Common.

Scaphander punctostriatus Mighels
Similar to *S. lignarius* but smaller, more globose posteriorally and with posterior edge of outer lip not produced above apex. Thin but moderately strong. Smooth with rows of tiny dots. Periostracum thin and straw-coloured. 0·5–3·5cm. Arctic, Boreal (North America), Transatlantic, Caribbean. Frequent.

Above: Scaphander lignarius

Scaphander watsoni Dall
Very similar to *S. lignarius* but relatively narrower with outer lip slightly incurved and parietal wall somewhat straighter. Yellowish brown with darker brown, fine spiral lines. Aperture white. *c*5cm. Transatlantic, Caribbean (Florida). Uncommon.

Class BIVALVIA

Second largest class of molluscs, with about 20,000 species. The term Bivalvia refers to the possession, by each species, of a shell formed of two pieces or valves. Class also known as the Pelecypoda, meaning hatchet-footed ones, in allusion to shape of foot of most species when extruded through open valves. Lamellibranchia or Lamellibranchiata are other names applied to this class. Bivalves are essentially bilaterally symmetrical although many have valves of different sizes and shapes and in some the valves are partially or completely fused. Valves usually lie on each side of the fleshy body and are connected dorsally by an elastic ligament which forces them open when internal adductor muscles are relaxed. Valves usually strengthened dorsally by a thickened internal hinge which may have many or few teeth with corresponding sockets to facilitate interlocking. The opposite (or ventral) margin of valves, along which valves open most widely, is not strengthened internally but is sometimes crenulate, denticulate or fluted so

that valves fit tightly together. Externally, valves may be smooth or variously ornamented with ridges, scales, grooves, pits, spines or other processes. Some species have one valve cemented permanently to rocks, stones, coral or other hard objects. Some species, such as those of the mussel family, Mytilidae, anchor themselves to solid objects by a byssus, a bunch of tough threads excreted by the animal and extruded through a notch between the valves, or, as in the Anomiidae, through a hole in one valve. In some families, notably the Pholadidae and Teredinidae, there are accessory hard structures additional to the true shell. Internally, valves show the impressions of former muscle and tissue attachments, in particular those of posterior and anterior muscles which are used to close the valves, and of the mantle edge which produce a thin groove, known as the pallial line. The pallial line is parallel with valve margin except at posterior half of many species, where it loops inwards to form an embayment, known as the pallial sinus; the space

within the pallial sinus is where the retracted siphons are or were located. On each side of the animal is a lobe, the two lobes forming the mantle which secretes the shell. As the bivalve animal lacks a head, it follows that it must lack a radula, jaws, eyes, tentacles and other cephalic sensory organs found in other molluscs. In some bivalves, these organs are replaced by others with similar functions located mainly along periphery of mantle. The extensile foot is most commonly used for burrowing purposes. Most bivalves feed by straining off microorganisms from the water or from the mud and sand of the sea floor. The appearance of a bivalve shell often gives an indication of its mode of life. Laterally compressed, relatively smooth valves are obvious adaptations to a burrowing existence. Those molluscs which bore into hard substances are more irregular in shape. Those which are cemented in one position, e.g. Spondylidae and Chamidae, develop long, spiny or scaly processes. No bivalve is completely without a shell.

Superfamily
Nuculacea

Family NUCULIDAE

Small, triangular-elliptical shells formed of nacreous material. Ligament internal. Numerous small teeth arranged in a row on each side of ligament. No pallial sinus. Posterior half of shell shorter and less rounded than anterior half. Four genera widely distributed in most seas.

Genus NUCULA Lamarck
For details, see Family Nuculidae.

Nucula hanleyi Winckworth
Similar in shape to *N. nucleus*. Smooth and glossy. Olive or greyish with reddish brown or greyish brown rays emanating from umbones. *c*1·25cm. Boreal, Mediterranean. Frequent.

Nucula nitida Sowerby
Small, triangular to elliptical shell with fine crenulations at lower margin. Light brown, covered with smooth, yellowish green periostracum which imparts sheen. *c*1cm. Boreal.

Nucula nucleus Linnaeus   ×2.0
Small, triangular to elliptical shell with

delicate concentric ridges and fine crenulations at lower margin. Yellowish to brownish with a few dark rays. Green periostracum. *c*1.2cm. Mediterranean, Boreal, West African, South African. Common.

Nucula tenuis Montagu   ×2.0

Small, fragile, triangular to elliptical shell with irregular growth lines. Olive green with darker growth lines, covered with smooth, greenish yellow to brown periostracum which imparts sheen. *c*1cm. Japonic, Arctic, Boreal, Californian, Mediterranean. Common.

Superfamily
Nuculanacea

Family NUCULANIDAE

Broadly triangular or elongate-triangular shells with partially internal ligament and numerous teeth on each side of ligament. Pallial sinus usually present. Eight widely distributed genera.

Genus YOLDIA Möller
Small, thin, elongate-ovate shells with valves slightly gaping ventrally. Teeth more numerous on one side of ligament than the other. Pallial sinus wide and deep. Numerous species widely distributed in cooler waters.

Yoldia johanni Dall
Similar in shape to *Y. limatula,* but shorter from anterior to posterior end, and with umbones not centrally placed as in that species. Posterior end pointed and up-

turned, anterior end rounded. Posterior part of shell ornamented with concentric and oblique lines. Whitish, with yellowish brown periostracum. 3·0–4·5cm. Japonic. Frequent.

Yoldia limatula Say   × 1.3
File Yoldia

Narrowly elongate shell tapering towards posterior end. Umbones small, situated approximately at centre of hinge line. Fine, concentric growth lines. Glossy, greenish to light chestnut brown. Interior glossy, white. 2·5–6·0cm. Transatlantic, Aleutian, Boreal, (East coast North America), Arctic. Common.

Superfamily
Solemyacea

Family SOLEMYIDAE

Family of thin, fragile, oblong or oval shells which are moderately to strongly inequilateral. Umbones towards posterior end. Ligament entirely or mainly posterior to umbones. Hinge has no teeth. Pallial line usually obscure. Smooth or with weak radial ornament. Periostracum thick and projecting well beyond margins of calcareous part of valves. Animal buries itself in mud or sand. Two genera, with few widely distributed species.

Genus SOLEMYA Lamarck
Solenomya Children.
For details, see Family Solemyidae.

Solemya borealis Totten   × 0.9

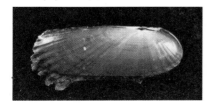

Thin, elongate-oval shell, well rounded at both ends and with long, straight, parallel sides. Thick, brownish periostracum which is paler towards umbones. Moderately pronounced radial ridges on periostracum. Interior bluish grey. 4·0–7·5cm. Transatlantic. Frequent.

Solemya togata Poli   × 0.7
mediterranea Lamarck.

Thin, fragile, elongate-oval shell with well rounded ends and straight, parallel sides. Thick, glossy, light or dark brown periostracum extends well beyond ventral and anterior margins. When dry, periostracum cracks around margins. 2·5–5·5cm. Mediterranean. Uncommon.

Solemya velum Say
Similar in most respects to *S. togata,* and even closer in appearance to *S. borealis* but smaller than both, relatively less elongate and often with light yellowish brown radial bands. 1·5–2·5cm. Transatlantic. Frequent.

Superfamily
Arcacea

Family ARCIDAE

Triangular, quadrangular or ovate shells which are usually equivalve, inequilateral and possess strong radial and concentric ornament. Hinge line more or less straight with many V-shaped or straight teeth. Umbones broad and inrolled. Several genera widely distributed in warm and tropical seas.

Genus ARCA Linnaeus
Medium-sized, strong shells with long, straight dorsal margin with many small teeth on hinge. Ventral border not crenulate but does have a shallow sinus or gap at margin for emergence of byssus. Broad, well raised umbones. Strong, radial and concentric ornament. Whole shell often appears boat-like. Numerous species in warm and tropical seas.

Arca imbricata Bruguière
Inflated almost elliptical shell with many fine radial ribs and concentric ridges. Valves strongly twisted at centre. Large byssal gape. White with dark brown, scaly periostracum especially near margins. 5·0–7·5cm. Transatlantic, Caribbean. Common.

Arca noae Linnaeus   × 0.6
Noah's Ark Shell
Elongate, rectangular shell with inflated,

radially ribbed valves and anterior, domed umbones. Light brown with darker concentric bands, covered with a brown periostracum bearing short hairs. 7–10cm. Mediterranean, Boreal. Common.

Arca tetragona Poli
Cornered Ark Shell
Thick, elongate, almost rectangular shell with inflated valves and anterior, domed umbones. White to yellow mottled with brown. Pale to dark brown periostracum. 4–6cm. Mediterranean, Boreal. Common.

Arca ventricosa Lamarck   × 0.8

Thick, very inflated, strong shell, narrowly rectangular but with large, rounded umbones and strong, broad ridge from umbones down to ventral margin. Coarse, radial ribs crossed by fine, concentric growth ridges. Posterior half of shell dark brown, anterior half creamy white with zebra-like, dark brown stripes. Resembles *A. noae* and *A. zebra,* but has strongly sloping dorsal margin posteriorly. 5·0–7·5cm. Indo-Pacific. Common.

Arca zebra Swainson
Turkey Wing
Thick, twisted, inflated, almost rectangular shell, heart-shaped from above. Some radial ribs towards posterior and fine concentric ridges. White with brownish orange to brown stripes and zigzags. Resembles *A. noae* but pattern stronger and more distinct. Similar pattern to *A. ventricosa* but in that species the posterior dorsal margin is curved and sloping. Large byssal gape. 5·5–7·5cm. Transatlantic, Caribbean. Common.

Genus BARBATIA Gray
Small to medium-sized, elongate, more or less rectangular shells which are generally equivalve but occasionally right valve is slightly the smaller. Fine radial and concentric ribbing give cancellate ornament.

223

Periostracum thick and beard-like. Numerous species in cool seas.

Barbatia barbata Linnaeus
Bearded Ark Shell ×0.7

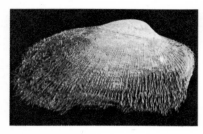

Elongate almost elliptical shell with inflated valves and slightly anterior, domed umbones. Fine decussate ornament. Pale brown with red brown rays and dark periostracum bearing stout, blackish hairs. 4·0–6·5cm. Mediterranean. Common.

Barbatia cancellaria Lamarck
Inflated, equivalve, inequilateral, elliptical to rectangular shell with low concentric and radial ridges. Somewhat compressed. Brownish purple. 3–4cm. Caribbean. Common.

Barbatia domingensis Lamarck
Inflated, equivalve, inequilateral, elliptical shell with coarse concentric ridges and radial ridges which are stronger near anterior and posterior ends. White. Thin, yellowish brown periostracum. 1–2cm. Transatlantic, Caribbean. Common.

Barbatia tenera C. B. Adams
balesi Pilsbry & McLean.
Thin, inflated, elliptical shell with narrow, finely beaded radial ribs and small byssal gape. White. 3–4cm. Caribbean. Frequent.

Genus TRISIDOS Röding
Parallelopipedum Mörch, *Epitrisis* Iredale. Resembles *Arca* in several respects, but is strikingly twisted around hinged axis. Two or three species in Indo-Pacific.

Trisidos semitorta Lamarck
Much less twisted than *T. tortuosa*, shorter from anterior to posterior and broader from ventral to dorsal side. Umbones also more rounded and more prominent. Fine radial riblets crossed by fine, irregular, concentric growth lines. Whitish, with pale yellowish periostracum. *c*8cm. Indo-Pacific (West Pacific). Uncommon.

Trisidos tortuosa Linnaeus ×0.5
Curiously twisted shell, elongate and laterally compressed anteriorly, dorso-ventrally compressed posteriorly. Inequivalve and inequilateral; right valve gently curved and left valve with a right-angle bend towards the posterior. Many

fine radial ribs and concentric growth lines. Dirty white with brown periostracum. 7–10cm. Indo-Pacific. Frequent.

Genus ANADARA Gray
Thick, heavy, rounded shells ornamented with strong radial ribs which match up with interlocking crenulations of shell margin. Furrows between ribs usually deep and narrower than rib width. Teeth numerous and of more or less equal size. Numerous species in warm and tropical seas.

Anadara brasiliana Lamarck
incongrua Say.
Thick, strong shell which is about as long as it is tall, with left valve slightly larger than right valve. About 26–28 ribs, posterior ribs being smooth and anterior ones strongly beaded. Whitish, with thin, pale brown periostracum. 5·5–6·0cm. Transatlantic, Caribbean. Common.

Anadara chemnitzi Philippi
Thick, very inflated, equivalve, equilateral and trigonal shell with strong, concentrically grooved radial ribs and concentric growth lines. White. *c*2cm. Caribbean. Uncommon.

Anadara ferruginea Reeve ×1.3

Similar to *A. granosa* but more elongate and with less produced umbones. Radial ribs less elevated and lacking tubercular ornament. Whitish, with dirty brown periostracum. *c*4cm. Indo-Pacific (West Pacific). Common.

Anadara granosa Linnaeus ×0.5
Thick, very inflated, elliptical shell, almost equilateral. About 20 elevated, straight-sided ribs bearing regular, rectangular nodules. White, covered with a tough,

brownish yellow to dark brown periostracum. 6–9cm. Indo-Pacific. Common.

Anadara multicostata Sowerby ×0.6

Inflated, almost rectangular, inequivalve shell with left valve slightly larger than right. 31–36 radial ribs. White with dark brown, hairy periostracum. 7–10cm. Panamic. Common.

Anadara nodifera von Martens
Similar in several respects to *A. granosa*, but considerably more elongated and with less pronounced umbones. Whitish, with pale brown periostracum. 3–4cm. Indo-Pacific (West Pacific). Frequent.

Anadara notabilis Röding
deshayesi Hanley.
Very inflated, equivalve, equilateral, elliptical shell with 25–30 radial ribs and concentric lines. White with thick, brown periostracum, eroded at umbones. 4–8cm. Caribbean. Common.

Anadara ovalis Bruguière
Inflated, elliptical shell with 25–35 radial ribs and concentric growth lines. Um-

bones almost touch each other. Shell white with dark brown periostracum. 3·5–5·0cm. Transatlantic, Caribbean. Common.

Anadara transversa Say
sulcosa Hyning.
Resembles *A. ferruginea* in shape, but is otherwise different. Small and moderately thick with left valve slightly larger and overlapping right valve. About 30–35 ribs on each valve, usually beaded on left valve only. Whitish, with greyish brown periostracum which wears off easily. 2·5–4·0cm. Transatlantic, Caribbean. Common.

Genus SENILIA Gray
Very thick, heavy, almost trigonal shells with well produced umbones and few broad radial ribs. Hinge short with relatively few teeth which are interrupted at centre. Few species in tropical seas.

Senilia senilis Linnaeus   ×0.7

Thick and heavy shell with inflated valves and domed, almost central umbones. About eight broad, flat, smooth radial ribs. White inside, covered outside with dark periostracum bearing short hairs. *c*8cm. West African. Frequent.

Family CUCULLAEIDAE

Medium-sized, smooth and heavy shells without a byssal gape and with almost central umbones. Anterior margin forms sharp angle with dorsal margin. Posterior margin well rounded. Hinge teeth horizontal at both ends with smaller, transverse denticles between. Umbones broad and tall. One genus.

Genus CUCULLAEA Lamarck
For details, see Family Cucullaeidae. Few species in Indo-Pacific.

Cucullaea concamera Bruguière   ×0.9
Large, ovate-quadrate, thick, very inflated shell with broad, tall umbones nearly centrally placed above hinge line. Anterior side straight and meeting dorsal and ventral margins at a sharp angle. Posterior side rounded. Numerous fine radial riblets

Strong, thin, plate-like process inside shell anteriorly descending from under dorsal margin. Brownish, paler towards margins. Inside purple with white margins. 8–11cm. Indo-Pacific (West Pacific). Uncommon.

Family NOETIIDAE

Thick, ovate or trigonal shells which are usually inequilateral and have a well developed, posterior umbonal ridge. Ornamented with strong radial ribs. Inner margin crenulated posteriorly. Hinge massive, often with chevron-shaped teeth. Four genera, widely distributed in warm and tropical seas.

Genus NOETIA Gray
For details, see Family Noetiidae. Shells are rhomboidal to trigonal in shape, usually heavy and with very tall umbones. Species frequent sandy places in shallow water of warm seas.

Noetia ponderosa Say   ×0.8

Thick, solid, trigonal shell, with strong, elevated radial ribs, each of which is grooved along its length. Each whorl has 27–31 ribs. Margin crenulate on inner edge. White, with thick, black periostracum. 5·0–6·5cm. Transatlantic, Caribbean. Common.

Superfamily
Limopsacea

Family GLYCYMERIDIDAE

Thick, nearly circular and equivalve shells which are more or less equilateral. Umbones approximately at centre of dorsal margin. The broad hinge plate is strongly arched and has numerous strong teeth which diminish in size towards the middle and towards extremities. Teeth transverse or chevron-shaped. Four genera, widely distributed in most seas.

Genus GLYCYMERIS Da Costa
Thick, almost circular and nearly equilateral shells with small umbones. Teeth short and transverse. Outer surface smooth or strongly ribbed, often with thick periostracum. Numerous species in most seas.

Glycymeris albolineata Lischke
Large, thick, heavy, elongate-ovate shell. Relatively small but prominent umbones situated midway along dorsal surface. Ornamented with radial ribs, each of which consists of smaller radial lines. Immature specimens have radial lines and small punctures. Yellowish, or pinkish yellow with thick periostracum. Pale brown internally. *c*6cm. Japonic. Frequent.

Glycymeris decussata Linnaeus
Thick, almost circular, inflated, inequilateral shell with smooth radial ribs and scratches. Creamy or white, blotched with dark brown. Larger and more inflated than *G. pectinata*. *c*5cm. Caribbean. Frequent.

Glycymeris glycymeris Linnaeus   ×1.0
Dog Cockle
orbicularis Da Costa.

Almost circular, equivalve, equilateral, moderately inflated shell with transverse and concentric grooves. White to orange brown flecked with brown and covered with a soft, dark brown periostracum. Inside white. 4·5–8·0cm. Mediterranean, Boreal. Common.

Glycymeris pectinata Gmelin
Inflated, circular, equilateral and equivalve shell with 25–40 elevated, medial ribs. White with fine, brownish yellow zigzags on ribs and occasional grey brown patches. Internal colour white, often with brown patches. 1·5–2·5cm. Caribbean. Common.

Glycymeris scripta Born
Circular, equivalve, equilateral shell. Pinkish with thin, brown, wavy or zigzag, concentric lines. c5cm. West African. Frequent.

Glycymeris violascens Lamarck   ×1.0

Circular, equivalve, equilateral and moderately inflated shell with fine radial grooves and concentric striae. Shell violet with lighter stripes and a soft, dark brown periostracum. 4–7cm. Mediterranean. Frequent.

Superfamily
Mytilacea

Family MYTILIDAE
Wedge-shaped, equivalve, inequilateral shells. Nacreous inside. Adductor scars unequal. Teeth few or absent. Pallial line simple or with a shallow embayment posteriorly. Periostracum thick, strong and often hairy. Species mostly attach themselves by a byssus to hard surfaces. About 30 genera widely distributed in most seas in shallow water.

Genus MYTILUS Linnaeus
Thin but strong, wedge-shaped, elongate, equivalve and inequilateral shells. Umbones at anterior end. No lateral teeth. Surface usually smooth but sometimes radially ribbed. Many species in shallow water of most seas.

Mytilus californianus Conrad
Large, thick, inflated shell, resembling *M. edulis* in shape. Nearly straight ventral margin. A few coarse, broad, low radial ribs which are strongest at middle portion

of shell. Coarse, concentric growth lines. Brownish. 5–25cm. Aleutian, Californian, Panamic. Common.

Mytilus canaliculus Martyn

Ovate shell with pointed terminal umbones and concentric growth lines. Shell glossy, often eroded to white at umbones. Bright, green periostracum. Inside creamy with green periostracum at margin. c17cm. Australian (New Zealand, Tasmania—probably introduced). Common.

Mytilus corscum Gould
Very similar to *M. edulis* and difficult to separate especially in juvenile stages. Differs principally by being thick-shelled even in juvenile stages and is covered with a very thick periostracum. c7cm. Japonic. Common.

Mytilus edulis Linnaeus   ×0.9
European Edible Mussel

Wedge-shaped, elongate, inequilateral shell with rounded umbones. Well rounded posteriorly. Purple brown or blue to blue black, sometimes yellowish brown, often with orange brown rays. Thin, pale periostracum. Nacreous inside and blue towards margins. Very variable in size and colour. 5–16cm. Boreal, Mediterranean, Arctic, Aleutian, Californian, Transatlantic (and introduced into Japonic and Indo-Pacific). Common.

Mytilus galloprovincialis Lamarck   ×0.7
Mediterranean Mussel

Broadly triangular shell with pointed umbones. Well rounded posteriorly. Violet to black with brownish sheen and thin, pale periostracum. Violet and slightly nacreous inside. May be merely a form of *M. edulis*. 5–12cm. Mediterranean, Boreal. Frequent.

Mytilus grayanus Dunker
Thick, large shell, more or less triangular in shape with curving umbones. Differs from *M. edulis* and *M. corscum* by having a long series of small crenulations on the ventral margin towards anterior end. Muscle impressions also larger. Greenish black periostracum. c14cm. Japonic. Common.

Mytilus planulatus Lamarck   ×0.7

Moderately inflated, equivalve, ovate shell with long ligament, terminal pointed umbones and concentric growth lines. Glossy, blue black eroded to pale blue at umbones. Inside bluish, darker towards margins, overlaid with white nacreous layer within pallial line. c7cm. Australian. Common.

Genus BRACHIDONTES Swainson
Resembles *Mytilus,* but is ornamented with strong, radial, bifurcating, ribs and

has relatively short ligament. Numerous species in warm and tropical seas.

Brachidontes citrinus Röding
Inflated, equivalve, elliptical shell with raised postero-dorsal margin and terminal umbones. Fine, wavy, bifurcating radial ribs. Brownish yellow. Inside violet and white. *c*3cm. Caribbean.

Brachidontes exustus Linnaeus
Inflated, elliptical to triangular shell with terminal umbones and fine radial ribs. Shell brownish yellow to dark brown. Inside violet to white. Less elongated and darker coloured than *B. citrinus* and with two small, purple teeth at hinge. *c*2cm. Caribbean. Common.

Brachidontes minimus Poli
Dwarf Mussel
Small, thin, wedge-shaped shell eroded at umbones. Blue black, covered with thin, pale periostracum, but often eroded so that nacre shows through at umbones. Very small teeth. *c*1cm. Mediterranean, Boreal. Common.

Brachidontes striatulus Hanley × 1.4

Thin, fragile, elongated shell with fine radial ridges. Greenish brown. *c*3cm. Indo-Pacific. Common.

Genus ISCHADIUM Jukes-Brown
Resembles an elongate form of *Mytilus*, but has radial, bifurcate ornament covering whole surface. Ligament relatively short, margins crenulated, anterior adductor impression absent. Restricted to North East coast of North America and Caribbean.

Ischadium recurvus Rafinesque
Hooked Mussel
hamatus Say.
Moderately inflated shell with hooked terminal umbones and fine, wavy axial ridges. Dark grey to black. Inside brown to violet, blue at margins. 4–6cm. Caribbean, Transatlantic. Common.

Genus PERNA Retzius
Moderately large, thin but solid shells resembling *Mytilus*, but much more elongated and without anterior adductor impression except in juvenile specimens. Numerous species in warm and tropical seas.

Perna chorus Molina
Large shell with triangular anterior half and regularly elliptical posterior. Moderately compressed and with coarse, concentric growth lines. Blue black to black with glossy sheen, often eroded at umbones to white or violet. 6–15cm. Patagonian, Peruvian. Common.

Perna viridis Linnaeus × 0.7
Green Mussel

Rather compressed, elongate shell with bluntly pointed umbones and long, straight, ventral margin. Coarse, concentric growth lines. Glossy, bright green, occasionally with bluish edges. Bluish green periostracum. 4·0–6·5cm. Indo-Pacific. Common.

Genus SEPTIFER Récluz
Similar to *Brachidontes,* but anterior abductor is placed on internal septum beneath umbones. Strong or weak radial ornament. Margins with fine or strong crenulations. Numerous species in Indo-Pacific and Japonic provinces.

Septifer bilocularis Linnaeus × 1.0
wiegmanni Küster.

Thick, trigonal or elongate-oval shell with numerous fine, bifurcating ridges and coarse, irregular growth lines. Umbones

curved and moderately pointed. Greenish brown. Inside purplish or bluish brown. 4–5cm. Indo-Pacific. Common.

Septifer excisus Wiegmann
fuscus Récluz.
Thick, solid, elongate-oval shell which is strongly curved at anterior end. Numerous fine radial ribs crossed by regular, widely spaced, coarse growth ridges. Purplish white or pinkish brown. *c*3cm. Indo-Pacific. Common.

Septifer virgatus Wiegmann
Elongate-trigonal shell with spade-like posterior end. The few divaricating, broad radial ribs are usually eroded. Covered with purplish periostracum. *c*3cm. Indo-Pacific (Pacific), Japonic. Common.

Genus MUSCULUS Röding
Modiolaria Beck, *Modiolarca* Gray.
Small, thin shells with broadly rounded umbonal keel and a diagonal furrow separating postero-dorsal part from rest of shell. Central area of shell more or less smooth, bordered on each side by broad radial ribs with narrow furrows between. Umbones low and well rounded. Numerous species in most seas.

Musculus barbatus Reeve
Thin, oblong-ovate shell with low radial ribs on either side of smooth median area. Characterised by a long, thick periostracum which is fibrous posteriorly. *c*1cm. Australian. Common.

Musculus discors Linnaeus × 1.3

Thin, fragile, equivalve and inequilateral shell which is rhomboidal in outline and has beaks a short distance from anterior end. 9–12 radiating ribs at anterior and 30–35 finer radiating ribs at posterior. Fine, concentric lines over whole shell. Yellowish brown with pale green or brown periostracum. Interior nacreous with external ornament showing through. Margin crenulate where ribs end. Smooth elsewhere. 1·5–3·5cm. Boreal, Mediterranean, Transatlantic, Arctic, Indo-Pacific (North West Pacific), Japonic. Common.

Musculus impactus Hermann
Inflated, equivalve, elliptical to ovate shell with eccentric umbones and concentric

growth lines. Radial ridges towards anterior and posterior. Brown 3·0–4·5cm. Australian. Common.

Musculus laevigatus Gray

Thin, moderately inflated shell with dull upper half, glossy lower half. Very fine, concentric striations. Transverse ridge divides dull from glossy area. Yellowish brown. 2·5–4·0cm. Arctic, Japonic, Boreal (North Atlantic). Frequent.

Musculus nanus Dunker
Thin, inflated, oblong-oval shell with broad, low umbones and low, wide radial ribs on either side of smooth, median area. Brown or yellow, greenish in juvenile stage. Gloss on juvenile examples lost on older ones. c2·5cm. Australian (South Australia). Common.

Musculus niger Gray
Resembles *M. discors* but is much more compressed and has strongly developed axial, decussated ribs on posterior and anterior ends. Microscopic, concentric, wavy threads in middle. Inside colour may be pinkish. Grows much larger than *M. discors*. 5–7cm. Arctic, Boreal (East coast of North America), Transatlantic, Aleutian. Common.

Genus LITHOPHAGA Röding
Long, cylindrical shells resembling cigars. Umbones near anterior end. Smooth or ornamented with fine, vertical striae. Ligament deep-set. Margins smooth. Strong, dark or light brown periostracum. Animals bore into stone. Numerous species in warm and tropical seas.

Lithophaga bisulcata d'Orbigny
Thin, elongate, cylindrical shell, well rounded at anterior end but wedge-shaped posteriorly. Oblique, grooved line divides each valve into two roughly equal sections. Anterior half of each valve smooth. Posterior end with a grey porous incrustation which projects beyond edge of shell. Anterior half brownish. 2·5–4·0cm. Transatlantic, Caribbean. Frequent.

Lithophaga curta Lischke
Fragile, elongated, cylindrical shell with rounded ends. Surface smooth and covered by brownish periostracum. Usually a thin, calcareous incrustation on outside. Inside pearly and glossy. 4–5cm. Japonic. Common.

Lithophaga lithophaga Linnaeus ×0.6
Date Mussel

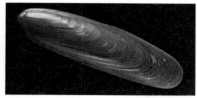

Long, thin, cylindrical, cigar-shaped shell, inflated anteriorly and rounded at both ends. Concentric growth lines and fine axial striae. Yellow to brown with a brown periostracum. No teeth. 6–9cm. Mediterranean. Common.

Lithophaga nigra d'Orbigny ×0.7

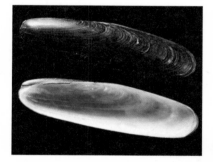

Similar in shape to *L. lithophaga* but has strong, vertical ridges at anterior part of each valve. Irregular, concentric growth lines. Very dark blackish brown. Inside iridescent. 2·5–7·0cm. Caribbean. Common.

Lithophaga truncata Gray
Bullet-shaped, inflated, equivalve shell with eccentric umbones and concentric growth lines. Dark brown. Grey blue inside. 3–4cm. Australian (New Zealand). Common.

Lithophaga zitteliana Dunker
Thin, inflated, cylindrical shell resembling *L. lithophaga*. Ornamented with numerous fine, divaricating radial ridges and strong, regular growth ridges. Pale yellowish brown periostracum. Inside glossy and pearly. 4–5cm. Japonic, Indo-Pacific (West Pacific). Frequent.

Genus MODIOLUS Lamarck
Modiola Lamarck.
Thin, inflated shells with rounded and low umbones placed just behind anterior end. Ligament fairly long. Periostracum often hairy. Numerous species in cool and warm seas.

Modiolus americanus Leach
tulipa Lamarck.
Thin, irregular, inflated, wedge-shaped equivalve shell with umbones near anterior. Dorsal margin slopes upwards. Concentric growth lines. Deep rose or pale purple rays. Light brown periostracum. Yellow byssus. c8cm. Caribbean. Common.

Modiolus barbatus Linnaeus
Bearded Horse-mussel
Thin, wedge-shaped, equivalve shell with almost terminal umbones. Fine, concentric lines and ridges. Shell violet to blue with orange brown periostracum bearing long, tough hairs. No hinge teeth. 5–7cm. Mediterranean, Boreal.

Modiolus capax Conrad
Very similar to *M. americanus* in shape but grows much larger, has coarse, concentric growth lines and develops a much thicker, hairy periostracum. Orange brown. Inside bluish white and purple. 5–13cm. Panamic. Frequent.

Modiolus hanleyi Dunker
Thin, large, oblong-ovate shell with broad, low umbones near anterior end. Ascending and curved dorsal margin which does not meet posterior margin at an angle as in *M. nitidus*. Ventral margin slightly concave. Glossy, blackish brown. c8cm. Japonic. Uncommon.

Modiolus modiolus Linnaeus ×0.6
Horse Mussel

Solid, inflated, wedge-shaped shell with broad, low, almost terminal umbones. Well defined, concentric growth ridges. Cream to violet or blue, covered with brown periostracum often bearing very short hairs. No hinge teeth. 18–22cm. Boreal, Transatlantic, Aleutian, Japonic. Common.

Modiolus nitidus Reeve ×0.6

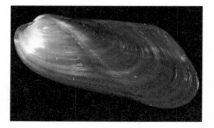

Elongate, almost elliptical shell with straight, fin-like, postero-dorsal margin. Posterior and dorsal margins meet at an angle. Umbones close to anterior end. Concentric growth lines. Glossy, brownish yellow to brown, darker posteriorly and often with dark, concentric bands. Thin, tough, brown periostracum. White internally. 7–9cm. Japonic. Common.

Genus GEUKENSIA Poel
Arcuatula Soot-Ryen.

Thin, very elongate, *Mytilus*-like shell with broad, rounded umbones nearly at anterior end. Strong radial ribs on posterior dorsal area, smoother on rest of shell. Margins crenulated, One or two species in North American and Caribbean waters.

Geukensia demissa Dillwyn   ×0.8
plicatulus Lamarck.

Thin, moderately inflated, elliptical shell with umbones close to anterior end. Numerous, strong, radiating and bifurcating ribs. Brown to black. White to bluish inside, often with brown tinges. 5–10cm. Boreal (East coast North America), Transatlantic (and introduced to San Francisco Bay, Californian province). Common.

Superfamily
Pinnacea

Family PINNIDAE

Thin, brittle, medium-sized to large shells which may be triangular, fan-shaped or paddleshaped. Nearly always compressed and sometimes with sharp scales. Umbones at anterior end which is always narrowed. Ventral margin with long, narrow gape for protrusion of long byssal threads. Posterior adductor muscle impression large, anterior adductor muscle impression relatively small. No teeth on hinge. Ligament extends length of hinge margin. Three genera in temperate warm and tropical seas.

Genus PINNA Linnaeus
For details, see Family Pinnidae. Shells usually keeled in middle portion, at least in earlier growth stages. Most species have radial ribs and sometimes these are orna-

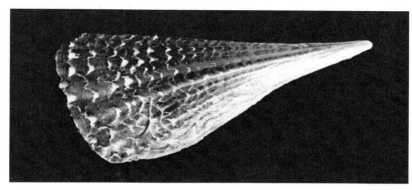

mented with scales. Numerous species worldwide in temperate, warm and tropical seas.

Pinna bicolor Gmelin   ×0.3

Thin, large, elongated shell which is semi-translucent. Long, straight hinge line. Weak radial ribs without scales. Greyish. 12–26cm. Indo-Pacific. Common.

Pinna carnea Gmelin
Resembles *P. fragilis* in shape and ornament but posterior end of shell is straighter, ventral margin less rounded and scales rather longer towards posterior end. About ten radial ridges which may be spiny or smooth. Pale orange to amber. 10–22cm. Caribbean. Common.

Pinna curva Gmelin
Thin, elongate, semi-translucent shell showing some resemblance to *P. bicolor*. Dorsal margin nearly straight and ventral margin also nearly straight forming between them a narrow, apical angle. Posterior margin gently arched. Weak radial ribs which are sometimes scaly. Pale yellow mottled with greyish black. *c*15cm. Indo-Pacific (Pacific), Japonic. Common.

Pinna fragilis Pennant   △ ×0.6
Shell thin, paddle-shaped in outline, with prominent anterior ventral and posterior gapes. Ornamented with concentric lines and low, radiating ribs, sometimes with fluted spines. Growth stages clear. Anterior adductor muscle impression small. Posterior adductor muscle impression large, in middle of shell. Margin often fragmented. Light brown or dark brown, occasionally with black patches. 15–30cm. Boreal, Mediterranean. Common.

Pinna muricata Linnaeus
Resembles *P. fragilis* in shape. Elongate-trigonal with few radial ribs which bear low scales. Towards umbones there is a ridge at the centre of each valve. Yellowish white blotched with greyish black especially towards posterior. *c*10cm. Indo-Pacific (Pacific), Japonic. Common.

Pinna nobilis Linnaeus
Rough Pen Shell
Large, paddle-shaped shell with strong or weak, overlapping scales. Yellowish brown to orange brown. Violet to blue grey nacre inside. 40–50cm. Mediterranean. Frequent.

Pinna rudis Linnaeus
Thin, paddle-shaped shell with about six radiating rows of large, strong, curled scales increasing in size towards posterior end. Olive brown. 20–45cm. Mediterranean, West African. Frequent.

Superfamily
Pteriacea

Family PTERIIDAE

Rounded or obliquely ovate shells usually with triangular, wing-like projection bordering each end of the straight hinge line. Left valve often more inflated than right valve. Inequilateral with umbones placed well towards anterior end. Anterior wing smaller than posterior wing. Byssal notch below anterior wing. Posterior adductor muscle impression large;

anterior adductor muscle impression absent or very small. Three genera in warm and tropical seas.

Genus PTERIA Scopoli

Avicula Bruguière, *Austropteria* Iredale, *Magnavicula* Iredale

For details, see Family Pteriidae. Moderately inflated, slightly inequivalve shells usually with an elongate posterior wing at end of straight hinge line. Two tooth-like processes on hinge below umbo. Usually smooth surface. Numerous species in warm and tropical seas.

Pteria cypsellus Dunker

Oblique shell with short, broad anterior and longer, broad, posterior wings. Posterior wing almost as large as main shell. Both wings more or less pointed at ends. Blackish, sometimes with thin, yellow, radial stripes. *c*6cm. Japonic. Frequent.

Pteria hirundo Linnaeus

crocea Lamarck.

Brittle, inequilateral shell with long, wing-like projections at each end of hinge line. Posterior wing the longer. Concentric growth lines and scales. Grey to greyish brown, with a violet sheen and brown periostracum. *c*10cm. Mediterranean, Boreal. Frequent.

Pteria loveni Dunker

Inflated, well rounded shell with short, pointed, anterior wing and much longer, blunt-ended, posterior wing. Fine growth lines. Greenish with a brownish periostracum. Very fragile margins. *c*5cm. Japonic. Frequent.

Pteria macroptera Lamarck

Compressed shell with one valve more convex than other. Straight, dorsal margin drawn out posteriorly to form a long, narrow wing; rest of shell elliptical. Dark brown often eroded at umbones to nacreous or white layer below. Tough, brownish yellow to dark brown periostracum with scaly, concentric lines. *c*18cm. Indo-Pacific. Common.

Pteria peasei Dunker   ×0.6

Straight hinge line extended to form short anterior and very long posterior wings. Rest of shell almost elliptical and inflated.

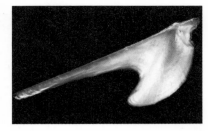

Purplish brown. *c*9·5cm. Indo-Pacific (Pacific). Uncommon.

Pteria penguin Röding   ×0.35

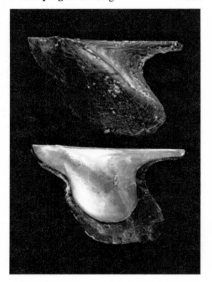

Compressed shell with straight hinge line extended to form short, wide, anterior and longer, narrow, posterior projection. Rest of shell elliptical. Dirty pinkish, mushroom or brown. Brilliantly nacreous inside, with black, marginal area. 10–25cm. Indo-Pacific. Frequent.

Genus PINCTADA Röding

Meleagrina Lamarck.

Thick, often heavy shells, which are less oblique than *Pteria* and lack a posterior wing. No hinge teeth. Surface usually lamellose. Numerous species in tropical seas.

Pinctada capensis Sowerby

Irregularly elliptical shell with eccentric umbones and scaly, concentric ridges. One valve concave, other almost flat. Shell glossy, greyish yellow with regular, brownish radial bands. Nacreous inside. *c*8cm. South African. Frequent.

Pinctada margaritifera Linnaeus

Thick, compressed, almost circular shell with one side squared. Concentric, scaly ridges; scales often projecting at margin. Shell dirty mushroom becoming greenish towards umbones and with several white radial lines on the green. Nacreous inside. *c*15cm. Indo-Pacific. Common.

Pinctada radiata Leach

Thick, elliptical to ovate shell with large, unequal ears and concentric, scaly ridges. Shell brownish yellow with radial rows of purple patches and occasionally some concentric rows. Inside nacreous. *c*6·5cm. Indo-Pacific. Common.

Family MALLEIDAE

Irregular, inequivalve shells with a triangular, ligamental area and usually with gaping valve margins. Two genera in tropical seas.

Genus MALLEUS Lamarck

Inequivalve, brittle shells which are elongated dorso-ventrally, are not oblique and which have a moderately long to very long posterior wing; anterior wing absent

Malleus malleus

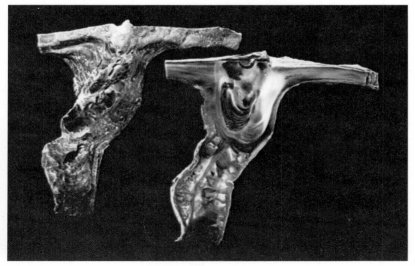

or, if present, not as long as posterior wing. Dorsal margin of right valve deeply notched on anterior side of ligament for protrusion of byssus. Single large adductor muscle impression. Few species in tropical and warm seas.

Malleus albus Lamarck ×0.3
White Hammer Shell

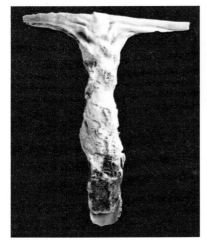

Thick, hammer-shaped shell with body of shell not oblique and straight hinge having long, thin, anterior and posterior projections of nearly equal length. Valves folded at margins. Shell dull, dirty white to creamy. Creamy internally, nacreous near ligament. 10–20cm. Indo-Pacific. Common.

Malleus malleus Linnaeus ×0.5
Black Hammer Shell
Thick, brittle shell with anterior and posterior wings long and nearly equal in length. Irregularly T-shaped appearance suggestive of a hammer. Blackish, often paler near umbones. Interior glossy and nacreous. 10–20cm. Indo-Pacific.

Superfamily
Pectinacea

Family PECTINIDAE

Equivalve or inequivalve, nearly circular or fan-shaped shells, usually ribbed and with equal or unequal auricles or ears. One valve usually more inflated than the other. Anterior ear usually has a distinct byssal notch or indentation below it. One adductor muscle impression. Attached to other objects by a byssus, or cemented to them by right valve, or both valves free. Upper (left) valve usually more brightly coloured than right valve. About twelve genera and many subgenera. Found in most seas of the world. Commonly known as scallops.

Amusium japonicum

Genus AMUSIUM Röding
Thin, almost circular shells with valves convex and gaping along margins below ears. Lirate within. Right valve strikingly different in colour from left valve. Few species in Indo-Pacific and Japonic provinces.

Amusium japonicum Gmelin ×0.4
Thin, circular shell with small, equal ears. Left valve convex, right valve flatter. Internal ribs in both valves, about 40 in left valve. Left valve reddish, right valve yellowish white. 10–12cm. Indo-Pacific (West Pacific), Japonic. Common.

Amusium pleuronectes Linnaeus ×0.5

Circular shell with similar, small ears. Fine, concentric striae. About 25 radial ribs on inside of each valve. Left valve pale reddish purple rayed with fine, bluish lines. Right valve white. c8cm. Indo-Pacific (West Pacific), Japonic. Common.

Genus CHLAMYS Röding
Medium-sized to moderately large shells with convex valves, left valve usually more convex than right valve. Large byssal notch below right anterior ear. Both ears well defined and usually moderately large. Radial and concentric ornament; small, scale-like spines where ribs and ridges cross. Some shells nearly smooth. Numerous subgenera and many species in most seas.

Chlamys asperrimus Lamarck
Prickly Scallop
Thin, circular shell with convex valves and unequal ears. About 30 scaly radial ribs and smaller ridge between each pair of ribs. Spiny scales on ribs and ridges. Colours variable: yellow, brown, red and purple with few creamy patches. c8cm. Australian (Australia). Common.

Chlamys australis Sowerby
Closely resembles *C. asperrimus* in size, shape and colour. It has more prominent, crowded scales on ribs and ears, the ribs being fewer in number. c6cm. Australian (Australia). Frequent.

Chlamys benedicti Verrill & Bush
Very small, narrowly fan-shaped shell closely resembling *C. sentis* but with slightly fewer radial ribs (about 45) and has its shorter ear more sharply angled and more spiny. Similar in colour to *C. sentis* but, unlike that species, may be pure yellow or mottled with white, zigzag stripes. c1cm. Caribbean. Frequent.

Chlamys bifrons Lamarck ×0.35
Well rounded shell with seven or eight radial ribs and many finer radial ridges; entire shell covered with microscopic

scales giving a matt effect. Ribs more pronounced on right valve. White with fine, reddish, radial markings on ribs and ridges especially near margins. Inside purplish. *c*8·5cm. Australian. Frequent.

Chlamys circularis Sowerby   ×0.8

Inflated shell with similar valves and ears. 15–20 broad and smooth radial ribs, scaly between ribs. Dull, drab white mottled with brown and violet. White and brown inside. *c*6cm. Californian. Frequent.

Chlamys convexus Quoy & Gaimard×0.4

Thin, unevenly triangular to elliptical, equivalve shell with five broad radial folds and radial ridges. Unequal ears. Both valves slightly concave. White to pink. White inside. 4–6cm. Australian. Rare.

Chlamys gibbus Linnaeus   △ ×0.7
Circular, equally convex valves with about 20 rounded ribs on each and unequal ears. Often smooth, sometimes with concentric grooves and occasionally with radial ridges between ribs. Colours variable. White, brownish yellow, brown or pink, often mottled. 3–6cm. Indo-Pacific. Common.

Chlamys glabra Linnaeus   ×0.5

Thin, compressed shell with similar valves bearing about six broad radial folds and many very fine radial ridges. Colours variable: white, brownish yellow, brown or brownish often mottled. 3·5–6·0cm. Mediterranean. Frequent.

Chlamys gloriosus Reeve   ×0.7

Fan-shaped shell with unequal ears. About 25 low, smooth radial ribs with broad interspaces containing fine radial riblets and concentric rows of small scales. Dark red, orange or pinkish, mottled with paler hues. *c*8cm. Indo-Pacific (West Pacific), Japonic. Uncommon.

Chlamys irradians Lamarck   ×0.35

Broadly circular shell with almost equal ears and very similar, convex valves. 12–21 radial ribs, wavy, scaly, concentric lines and prominent growth lines. Colours variable: white, brownish orange to dark brown, occasionally some yellow. 5–8cm. Transatlantic, Caribbean. Common.

Chlamys islandica Müller
Thin, moderately convex, fan-shaped shell with very unequal ears and numerous irregular, slightly scaly radial ribs. Creamy or greyish, yellow, reddish or purplish. 6–10cm. Arctic, Boreal (East coast of North America), Transatlantic, Aleutian, Californian. Common.

Chlamys lacteus Gould   ×0.45
Thin, fan-shaped shell with very unequal ears and about 11 strong radial ribs ornamented with fluted scales. Between ribs are finer scaly riblets. Ribs project beyond ventral shell margin. Deep

purplish red to pale pink variegated with white. 5–6cm. Japonic. Frequent.

Chlamys leopardus Reeve $\times 0.7$

Fan-shaped shell with slightly unequal ears; one valve slightly convex the other almost flat. Both valves with about 15–20 radial ribs bearing concentric, scaly ridges. Convex valve white, flatter valve pink, especially on ribs, with white patches and white ears. White inside. 5–7cm. Australian. Frequent.

Chlamys muscosus Wood $\times 0.8$
exasperatus Sowerby, *fuscopurpureus* Conrad.

Broadly fan-shaped, inflated shell with nearly equal ears. 18–20 rounded radial ribs bearing rows of small scales. Red, yellow, orange brown, or orange mottled with white and purple. 2·0–3·5cm. Transatlantic, Caribbean. Frequent.

Chlamys nobilis Reeve $\times 0.3$

Almost equally convex valves covered with coarse, rounded ribs bearing regularly spaced scales, especially near margins. Ears unequal. Ribs interlock at margins. Colours variable: cream with mushroom and orange, sometimes lilac in concentric bands, unicolorous yellow, purple, yellowish brown. 8–13cm. Japonic. Frequent.

Chlamys nodosus Linnaeus $\times 0.3$
Lion's Paw

Large, thick and heavy, broadly fan-shaped shell with unequal ears. 7–9 large, coarse radial ribs bearing large nodules. Whole surface beset by fine riblets. Dark red, bright red, orange or pinkish. 7–15cm. Transatlantic, Caribbean. Frequent.

Chlamys opercularis Linnaeus $\times 0.6$
Queen Scallop
Broadly circular shell with similar convex valves bearing 18–22 fine, grooved ribs and slightly unequal ears. Colours variable: white, yellow, grey or brown, sometimes spotted or striped, with right valve lighter. 5–8cm. Mediterranean, Boreal. Common.

Above: *Chlamys nodosus*
Below: *Chlamys opercularis*

Chlamys pallium Linnaeus   ×0.35

Thick, inflated, nearly circular shell with unequal ears and heavy, equally convex valves with 12–15 strong ribs bearing leafy scales and interlocking at margin. Colours very variable: white, orange and purple, often in striking concentric rings or patches. Inside glossy, golden to pinkish at margin. 4–9cm. Indo-Pacific. Common.

Chlamys purpuratus Lamarck   ×0.45

Thick, inflated shell with similar convex valves and almost equal ears. About 25 arched, scaly ribs with very narrow, scaly grooves between them. Ribs interlock at margins. Shell white with purple ribs mottled with white, sometimes uni-colorous yellow. Inside purplish red with white margin. 8–9cm. Peruvian. Frequent.

Chlamys sanguinolentus Gmelin   ×1.0

Fan-shaped shell with broad, unequal ears and both valves convex. About eight strong, large, rounded ribs with rows of scales between them. Ribs, which interlock at margin, have brownish orange to violet patches; rest of shell white or creamy. Inside white often with pink tinges. 4–6cm. Indo-Pacific (Indian Ocean). Frequent.

Chlamys senatorius Gmelin   ×0.8
miniaceus Reeve, *porphyreus* Gmelin, *aurantius* Lamarck, *crassicostatus* Sowerby, *florens* Lamarck.

Almost circular shell with both valves convex and unequal ears. 30–40 shallow ribs with grooves of equal width between. Denticles on dorsal margin. Brownish to red, often with creamy patches. 3–6cm. Indo-Pacific. Common.

Chlamys sentis Reeve   ×1.0
Thin, narrowly fan-shaped shell with un-equal ears, one being twice size of the

other, and almost equally convex valves. About 50 fine radial ribs. Colours variable: white, violet, orange, brownish, pink; colours strongest near umbones. 2–4cm. Transatlantic, Caribbean. Common.

Chlamys septemradiata Müller
Thin, brittle, almost equivalve, nearly circular shell with unequal ears. 3–10 smooth radial ribs, each rib broadening rapidly towards ventral margin. Numerous radial striae crossed by con-centric lines. Left valve red or purplish brown mottled with white: right valve white, or red around umbones and along ribs. 3–5cm. Boreal, Mediterranean. Frequent.

Chlamys squamatus Gmelin   ×1.4

Unequal ears. Thin, triangularly rounded shell with one valve flat, both with ribs of various sizes, the largest bearing scaly, leaf-like projections. Two or three radial cords between ribs. Colours variable: pinkish, brownish, pale orange, blotched and mottled with darker hue.

2·5–4·5cm. Japonic, Indo-Pacific (West Pacific). Frequent.

Chlamys subnodosus Sowerby   ×0.3

Large, thick, heavy, fan-shaped and inflated shell. Ten broad radial ribs on left valve and eleven on right. Interstices as wide as ribs. Coarse radial riblets over whole shell. Ribs have a series of small, coarse and sometimes hollow nodes or humps, best developed on left valve. Anterior ear larger and longer than posterior. Deep purplish red or red, sometimes mostly creamy with blotches of red. Inside of right valve usually white with purplish margins; left valve usually lighter shade. 8–12cm. Panamic, Peruvian. Frequent.

Chlamys swifti Bernardi   ×0.45

Thick, moderately inflated, narrowly fan-shaped shell with very unequal ears. About five broad, low radial ribs bearing moderately large nodules at widely spaced intervals. Numerous radial ridges cover whole shell. White or purplish red, usually with distinct concentric red lines. Inside glossy and white. 5–12cm. Japonic, Aleutian. Frequent.

Chlamys tigerina Müller

Thin but strong, almost equivalve, narrowly fan-shaped shell with very unequal ears. Variable ornament: may consist only of fine, radial and concentric lines or may have up to 30 or more radial ribs, some of which may be much broader than others. Colour and pattern also variable: reds, pinks, purples and browns predominate and white, cream, grey and yellow also may be present, all or some in combination, usually in streaks, spots and blotches. 1·5–2·5cm. Boreal, Mediterranean. Common.

Chlamys townsendi Sowerby   ×0.35

Thick, large and heavy, almost circular shell with equally convex valves and almost equal ears. About 20 low, rounded radial ribs with interspaces of same width. Light and dark brown, the pattern being concentric or zigzag rows of dark brown markings against a lighter ground colour. c16cm. Indo-Pacific (North Arabian Sea, Persian Gulf). Uncommon.

Chlamys varia Linnaeus   ×0.5
Variegated Scallop

Similar, convex valves with very unequal ears. 25–35 prominent radial ribs bearing spines. Colours variable: white, yellow, brown or violet, with concentric stripes or spots. 3–7cm. Mediterranean, Boreal. Common.

Chlamys ventricosus Sowerby   ×0.4
Thick, almost circular, very inflated shell with almost equal ears. About 22 smooth, low radial ribs with slightly narrower interspaces. Purplish black speckled with

Above: *Chlamys varia*
Below: *Chlamys ventricosus*

white on left valve; mostly white with irregular, concentric dark bands on right valve. c8cm. Panamic. Frequent.

Chlamys vexillum Reeve   ×0.5

Thick, almost circular shell with nearly equal ears. About ten broad, rounded ribs with fine riblets on and between them. Brown to black with irregular, white patches. Rarely orange with white patches. 4–5cm. Indo-Pacific (West Pacific). Uncommon.

Genus DECATOPECTEN Rüppel
Elongate, narrowly fan-shaped shells with right valve more convex than left valve and usually with few broad ribs. Ears short and unequal. Ribs radially striated. Short hinge. Few species in Indo-Pacific.

Decatopecten plica Linnaeus   ×0.5

For details, see genus *Decatopecten*. Five or six ribs. Colours variable but usually white variegated with pink or brown. 3·0–4·5cm. Indo-Pacific. Japonic. Frequent.

Decatopecten striatus Schumacher
Similar in most respects to *D. plica* but has fewer radial ribs. 3–4cm. Japonic. Frequent.

Genus PECTEN Müller
Medium-sized to large shells which are usually almost circular in outline, have equal or nearly equal ears and with the right valve very convex, the left valve gently convex, flat or even concave. Numerous species in most seas.

Pecten caurinus Gould
Almost circular shell with flat upper valve bearing about 17 radial ribs. Lower valve more convex with wider ribs. Similar ears, one with byssus groove. One valve white with brownish yellow ribs near margin, other brownish to violet. 15–20cm. Aleutian, Californian. Common.

Pecten excavatus Anton
Like a larger version of *P. sinensis,* being similar in shape and colour. Right valve less convex and left valve less concave. Left valve has 9–11 radial ribs. Inside glossy and white. 4–6cm. Japonic, Indo-Pacific (West Pacific). Frequent.

Pecten jacobaeus Linnaeus   ×0.5
Pilgrim Scallop

Concave left valve and convex right valve each with strong angular ribs producing deep emarginations. Left valve orange brown, right valve white to pink. White inside. 7–13cm. Mediterranean. Common.

Pecten maximus Linnaeus   ×0.3
Great Scallop

Thick, solid, large, almost circular shell with convex right valve slightly overlapping flat left valve. Ears occupy half width of shell. 15–17 broad radial ribs and numerous concentric lines. Left valve reddish brown; right valve white, cream, pinkish, yellow or red. Sometimes banded and spotted. Inside brownish with white central area. 7–16cm. Boreal, Mediterranean (Atlantic coasts). Common.

Pecten medius Lamarck   ×0.9.

Thin, almost circular, equilateral shell. Right valve convex with broad, rounded ribs and concentric, scaly ridges; left valve concave with narrow ribs and concentric grooves. White, pale brownish yellow, pink or brownish, concave valve sometimes with blotches or zigzag lines. 3–6cm. Australian (Australia). Frequent.

Pecten novaezelandiae Reeve
Thick, nearly circular shell with equal ears. Right valve deeply convex with broad, rounded ribs; left valve flat with narrow, square ribs. Right valve pink, other white. White inside. 11–14cm. Australian (New Zealand). Common.

Pecten sinensis Sowerby
puncticulatus Dunker.
Thin, almost equilateral, broadly circular shell with roundly convex right valve and concave left valve. Right valve has broad, flattened radial ribs with deep, narrow grooves one-third width of ribs. Left valve has square-edged radial ribs with broader interspaces which bear well defined growth lines. Reddish purple to orange spotted with white on right valve, and with dark reddish brown, zigzag lines on left valve. 3–4cm. Japonic. Frequent.

Pecten yessoensis Jay
Comparable in shape and ornament to *P. caurinus,* but larger and differently coloured. Right valve more convex than left valve and has low, smooth radial ribs. Left valve has narrow radial cords, and growth lines are prominent. Right valve yellowish white. Left valve reddish purple. Interior glossy and white. 12–16cm. Japonic. Common.

Pecten ziczac Linnaeus   ×0.3

Almost circular, equilateral shell with deeply convex right valve and flat left valve. Many flat ribs and fine concentric grooves on flat valve. Convex valve with broad, very low ribs and radial and concentric grooves. Colours variable: white, brown or orange brown on convex valve; brown to pink often with fine, zigzag markings on flat valve. 3–10cm. Caribbean, Transatlantic. Common.

Family SPONDYLIDAE

Small to medium-sized, usually thick shells with right valve usually more convex than left valve. Small ears. Two large cardinal teeth in right valve. Frequently ornamented with short or long spines. Single large adductor muscle impression. Species cement themselves by right valve to hard substrate. One genus in warm and tropical seas.

Genus SPONDYLUS Linnaeus
For details, see Family Spondylidae. Numerous species.

Spondylus americanus Hermann
Atlantic Thorny Oyster
echinatus Martyn, *dominicensis* Röding.
Moderately thick, inflated shell with long, flattened, stout spines arranged irregularly on valves and accompanied by

rows of smaller spines. White with yellow umbones, red, purple, rosy, cream or pinkish. 8–11cm. Caribbean. Frequent.

Spondylus crassisquamatus Lamarck
dubius Broderip, *pictorum* Sowerby, *basilicus* Reeve, *leucacantha* Broderip, *princeps* Broderip.   ×0.35

Above: *Spondylus crassisquamatus*
Below: *Spondylus gaederopus*
Bottom: *Spondylus lima*

Very heavy, thick shell with long, flattened spines curving towards ventral edge. Spines yellowish white, rest of shell red or yellowish red. Inner margin red, rest of inside white. Many different forms occur. *c*15cm. Panamic. Rare.

Spondylus gaederopus Linnaeus
Thick, massive shell with short spines. Usually inflated. Reddish or purplish, spines usually darker than rest of shell. Interior white, purple-edged, with brownish muscle impression. 5–8cm. Mediterranean. Frequent.

Spondylus ictericus Reeve   ×0.7

Small, relatively thin shell. Globose. Spines sometimes flat, sometimes curved towards ventral edge. Orange, yellow and purple zones, sometimes white on spines. Inner margin yellow, rest of inside white. *c*6cm. Indo-Pacific. Rare.

Spondylus lima Chenu   ▽×1.0
Thick, globose shell with very sharp, needle-like spines. Ventral edge curved, lower valve deep. Whitish rayed with pink or violet. White inside. *c*6cm. Japonic. Rare.

Spondylus monachus Chenu   ×0.6

Spondylus wrightianus Crosse   ×0.4

Relatively thin, broad shell with short, flattish spines. Yellowish at umbo turning violet towards ventral edge. Spines violet. Yellowish violet inside. c7cm. Indo-Pacific. Rare.

Spondylus regius Linnaeus   ×0.6

Thick, massive shell with long and short spines. Scaly ridges between rows of spines. Unicolorous purple, red or orange. Darker on spines and intermediate ridges. White inside with margin colour same as outside. Brownish green muscle impression. 8–12cm. Indo-Pacific (Pacific). Rare.

Spondylus sanguineus Dunker
Thick, elongate-oval shell completely devoid of spines but ornamented with finely scaled radial riblets. Orange, rosy or whitish rayed with vermilion. Distantly similar to *S. lima,* but the vermilion rays are sufficient to distinguish it. c3·5cm. Japonic. Uncommon.

Spondylus sinensis Schreibers
Large, thick, irregularly circular shell with relatively long hinge line and rather depressed valves. Ornamented with broad radial ribs each bearing three or four long, flattened spines which are expanded and fin-like at their ends. Fine striae between ribs. Purplish red, yellowish, the umbones being orange red and the spines whitish. c10cm. Japonic. Uncommon.

Relatively thin, light shell with long, straight spines. Two or three rows of small spines between rows of larger ones. Whitish with rays of brownish purple or pink between large spines. Large spines yellowish pink. Inside white. c12cm. Indo-Pacific, Australian (Australia). Frequent.

Superfamily
Anomiacea

Family ANOMIIDAE

Irregular, thin and fragile shells which are conspicuously inequivalve and have a byssus, at least in the juvenile stage. Byssus protrudes through a hole or an embayment in the lower (usually right) valve; older specimens have the hole plugged with corneous material. Three muscle impressions on central area of left valve. Impression of object to which it is attached shows in relief on upper valve. No hinge teeth. Five genera in most seas.

Genus ANOMIA Linnaeus
For details see Family Anomiidae. Numerous species in most seas.

Anomia walteri

Anomia ephippium Linnaeus
Thin, fragile, irregularly circular shell with lower (right) valve smaller and flatter than upper. Byssal hole irregularly pear-shaped. Surface scaly and frequently encrusted with marine organisms. White, purple or pale brown. 4–7cm. Boreal, Mediterranean, West African, Magellanic (Islands in Atlantic). Common.

Anomia peruviana d'Orbigny
Roughly circular shell which is thin, partly translucent, smooth or irregularly ornamented with coarse radial ridges. Orange or yellowish green. 2·5–5·0cm. Panamic. Common.

Anomia simplex d'Orbigny
Atlantic Jingle
Irregularly oval shell with small or large, pear-shaped byssal aperture which may be situated near dorsal margin or towards centre of lower (right) valve. Coarse, irregular, concentric growth lines. Translucent yellowish, orange or silvery black. 2·5–5·0cm. Transatlantic, Caribbean. Common.

Anomia walteri Hector   ×0.7
Thin but strong, irregularly circular to oval shell. Surface covered with coarse concentric ridges. Byssal aperture irregularly pear-shaped. Greenish white, but whiter inside around byssal aperture. 6·0–9·5cm. Australian (New Zealand). Frequent.

Genus PLACUNA Lightfoot
Placenta Philippson, *Ephippium* Röding.
Rounded or saddle-shaped shells with both valves very closely adpressed. Thin and usually translucent. Few species in Indo-Pacific.

Placuna placenta Linnaeus   ×0.35
Thin, brittle, almost circular, very compressed shell. Long cardinal teeth pointing towards the conspicuous, central adductor muscle impression. Fine, concentric scaly

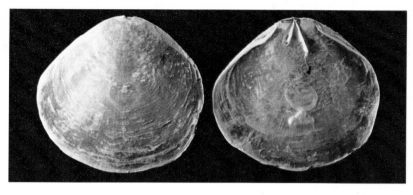

ridges. Translucent and almost colourless. 12–17cm. Indo-Pacific. Common.

Placuna sella Gmelin   ×0.3
Saddle Oyster

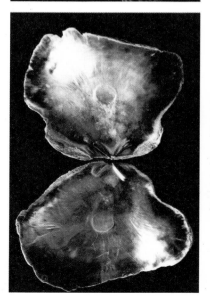

Placuna placenta

Large, thin, brittle shell easily distinguished from *P. placenta* by the curvature of the two valves giving a saddle shape. Juvenile specimens are quite flat. Surface scaly. Translucent whitish suffused with pale purple. 13–20cm. Indo-Pacific (West Pacific). Common.

Superfamily
Limacea

Family LIMIDAE

Equivalve shells, usually slightly or strongly oblique in orientation of valves. Two small ears on hinge line. Ligament internal and triangular. Anterior gape near to or far from hinge margin. Sometimes posterior gape. Hinge teeth weak or absent. Obscure adductor muscle impressions. Surface smooth or ornamented with radial, often scaly ribs. Usually colourless. Seven genera in most seas.

Genus LIMA Bruguière
Mantellum Röding.
For details see Family Limidae. Anterior ear smaller than posterior ear. Valve margins only slightly gaping. Scaly radial ribs. Numerous species in most seas.

Lima hians Gmelin   ×0.7

Thin, solid, obliquely ovate shell with almost straight, anterior and posterior dorsal slopes. Anterior ear slightly larger and more pointed than posterior ear. Wide dorsal gape anteriorly. Fine concentric

lines and clear growth stages crossing numerous coarse radial ribs. Unicolorous white. 2·5–3·5cm. Boreal, Mediterranean. Common.

Lima lima Linnaeus
Bears some resemblance in shape to *L. zealandica* but posterior dorsal margin is relatively shorter. Numerous strong, scaly radial ribs with narrower interspaces. Unicolorous white. 2·5–3·0cm. Caribbean. Common.

Lima orientalis Adams & Reeve
Small, thin, obliquely ovate shell with straight anterior side. Relatively well inflated and slightly gaping at margins. Finely radially ribbed with interspaces slightly broader than ribs. Unicolorous white. *c*2cm. Indo-Pacific (Pacific), Australian (Australia). Common.

Lima sowerbyi Deshayes
Thin, solid, medium-sized shell superficially resembling *L. zealandica* in outline but with anterior margin less straight and posterior ear slightly larger. About 21 strong, scaly ribs with narrower interspaces. Unicolorous white. *c*6cm. Indo-Pacific. Frequent.

Lima zealandica Sowerby   ×0.7

Moderately thick, elongate-ovate shell with long, straight posterior dorsal margin and small anterior ear. Strong, flat radial ribs with narrower interspaces. Ribs have sparsely scattered scales. Inner margins crenulate. Ribs pale brown, interspaces white. Inside white. 4–5cm. Australian (New Zealand). Rare.

Lima zushiensis Yokoyama
Medium-sized shell somewhat resembling *L. lima* in shape and ornament but with about 26 scaly radial ribs. Characterised by its reddish brown colour concentrically banded at regular intervals with darker brown. *c*5cm. Japonic. Uncommon.

Genus CTENOIDES Mörch
Similar in general appearance to *Lima* but with well developed byssal gape bordered by reflected margins. Also lacks ridges on umbones. Moderately strong lateral teeth on hinge. Rounded radial riblets, divaricating towards ventral margin and bearing fine scales. Numerous species in most seas.

Ctenoides annulata Lamarck   ×0.7

Thin but strong, compressed and not very elliptical shell with broad, smooth umbones and low, ill defined radial riblets bearing fine scales. Valve margins serrated posteriorly. Yellowish white. 3–5cm. Indo-Pacific. Common.

Ctenoides concentrica Sowerby
Medium-sized shell, egg-shaped in outline with unequal ears and umbones just protruding above dorsal hinge line. Numerous radial threads crossed by concentric growth lines produce cancellate ornament. *c*5cm. Japonic. Frequent.

Ctenoides scabra Born
Rough Lima
tenera Sowerby.
Larger and less elongate shell than *C. annulata*. Ornament usually stronger; radial ribs less numerous, except in the form *tenera* in which they are much more numerous and finer. Whitish, with persistent, dark or pale brown periostracum. 3–7cm. Caribbean. Common.

Superfamily
Ostreacea

Family OSTREIDAE
Thick or thin shell with unequal valves, the lower (left) valve being usually attached to other objects. Irregularly ornamented with radial ribs, sometimes resulting in a deeply crenulate ventral margin. Also ornamented with irregular, concentric shell layers. Broad adductor muscle impression more or less centrally placed on valves. Other important characteristics of this family relate to structures visible only in minute larval forms and to anatomical features. About six genera widely distributed over the globe.

Genus CRASSOSTREA Sacco
Small to large shells with variable outline but characteristically very much taller than wide. Surface roughened by irregular growth lamellae. Adductor muscle impression closer to ventral margin than to hinge. Numerous species in temperate and tropical seas.

Crassostrea angulata Lamarck
Portuguese Oyster
Thick, oblong, but usually irregularly distorted shell with deeply cupped left (lower) valve and flat or slightly convex right valve. Margins smooth near umbones but deeply and broadly folded elsewhere; the two valves interlock securely. Irregular concentric lines and ridges, and a few irregular radial ribs with deep grooves between. White, cream or pale brown, streaked or blotched with purple. Inside white, occasionally with purple margins; adductor muscle impression always purple or reddish brown. 3–18cm. Mediterranean (Atlantic coast), Boreal (introduced in British waters). Common.

Crassostrea virginica Gmelin
American Oyster, Eastern Oyster,
Blue Points
Thick, irregularly elongate shell with left (lower) valve convex and right valve usually flatter. No prominent undulating folds on margins. Thick internal ligament. Irregular concentric lines and ridges. Whitish with thin, dark brown periostracum. Inside white, but adductor muscle impression purple or reddish brown. 5–18cm. Transatlantic, Caribbean, Boreal (introduced in British waters). Common.

Genus OSTREA Linnaeus
Medium-sized to large shells with variable outline. Umbones never prominent, sometimes with auricles (or ears) on either side of them. Flattish with left valve sometimes more convex than right. Kidney-shaped adductor muscle impression. Typically large, flat and round, without crenulations along valve margins. This genus contains some, but not all, of the world's edible oysters. Many species in all seas except polar seas.

Ostrea edulis

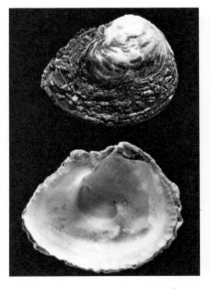

Ostrea denselamellosa Lischke
Large, thick, ovate, compressed shell with foliaceous growth lines and low radial ribs. Brownish. *c*6cm. Japonic. Common.

Ostrea edulis Linnaeus   ×0.4
Common European Oyster
Thick, heavy shell, more or less rounded in outline with left (lower) valve convex and right valve flat, its edges overlapped by left valve. Edges of valves very brittle and thinner than rest of shell. Relatively small internal ligament. Concentric ridges and grooves, often scaly near margins. Usually crenulate at margins. Greyish or brownish right valve; pale brown, greenish or yellowish left valve. Inside pearly white, sometimes blotched with external colours. 4–12cm. Boreal, Mediterranean. Common.

Ostrea equestris Say
Thick, oval shell, the lower valve with upturned, crenulated margin. Row of denticles on inside margin of upper valve. Pearly green to grey inside. *c*10cm. Transatlantic, Caribbean. Common.

Ostrea lurida Carpenter
Small, thick, irregularly oblong-ovate shell with coarse growth lamellae. Inside olive green. *c*5cm. Californian. Common.

Genus LOPHA Röding
Small to medium-sized shells; convex valves with few or many sharp-edged radial folds. Shells usually attached to other objects, affixed by recurved, clasping spines. Hollow, recurved spines sometimes arise from crests of radial folds but folds often without conspicuous ornament. Valves close tightly together. Few species in tropical waters.

Lopha cristagalli Linnaeus   ×0.6
Cock's-comb Oyster

Medium-sized, thick, strong shell. Few sharp-edged radial ribs with deeply cut hollows between giving zigzag margin ventrally. Attached by clasping spines to coral or other substrate. Dull brown to purple. 6–9cm. Indo-Pacific. Common.

Superfamily
Trigoneacea

Family TRIGONIIDAE

Small to medium-sized, thick shells markedly trigonal in outline. Usually taller than wide with strong radial ribs, either comparatively smooth or ornamented with scales or rounded tubercles. Moderately or well inflated and with tall, rounded or pointed umbones. Median tooth of left valve concave or deeply emarginate below, and strongly grooved above. Two teeth of right valve have strong transverse ridges. No pallial sinus. Many fossil genera but only one genus now living and restricted to Australasian waters.

Genus NEOTRIGONIA Cossmann
For details see Family Trigoniidae. Margin crenulate. Inside pearly and iridescent. About six species from South Australia and Tasmania.

Neotrigonia bednalli Verco
Small, trigonal, compressed shell with about 26 narrow ribs bearing closely spaced lamellae, each lamella broader at the free end than at the attached end. Colour varies from white, pale yellow or light orange to mauve, pink, red or purple. 2–3cm. Australian (South Australia). Uncommon.

Neotrigonia lamarcki Gray ×1.2

Small, trigonal, moderately compressed shell with about 24 strong radial ribs and interspaces of similar width. Each rib has numerous, short, regularly spaced lamellae. Strong concentric lines over whole surface. Purplish brown with whitish lamellae. Inside highly iridescent, margins deep purple. 2–3cm. Australian (East Australia). Frequent.

Superfamily
Lucinacea

Family LUCINIDAE

Nearly circular, ovate or trapezoidal shells, usually thick, strong and moderately compressed. Concentric ornament consists of irregular, strong ribs alternating with weaker ones. Radial ribs sometimes present. Two cardinal teeth. Inside of valves punctate or grooved. Elongated anterior adductor muscle impression. Posterior adductor muscle impression usually rounded. No pallial sinus. Margin usually finely crenulate internally. Usually a well marked groove extending from umbo to postero-ventral margin. About 30 genera in nearly all seas.

Genus LUCINA Bruguière
Medium-sized to large, more or less compressed shells with well marked grooves from umbones to postero-ventral margin. Evenly spaced concentric lamellae. Strongly or weakly crenulate margin. Numerous species in temperate and tropical seas.

Lucina floridana Conrad
Nearly circular, moderately compressed shell with small, deep lunule and small, pointed umbones directed anteriorly. Weak, irregular, concentric growth lines. White, with a dull white periostracum. Inside white. 2·5–4·0cm. Caribbean. Common.

Lucina muricata Spengler
Small, compressed shell, almost circular in outline and ornamented with numerous strong radial ribs and finer concentric riblets. Towards posterior and anterior ends, the radial ribs are scaly at intersections with concentric riblets. Unicolorous white. c1·5cm. Caribbean. Frequent.

Lucina pectinata Gmelin
jamaicensis Lamarck.
Differs from *L. pennsylvanica* by being somewhat larger, less circular in outline and by the less steeply sloping posterodorsal furrow. Concentric ridges unevenly spaced. Lunule prominently raised. Anterior muscle impression very long and narrow. White, or tinted bright orange. Inside whitish with orange staining. 3–6cm. Transatlantic, Caribbean. Frequent.

Lucina pennsylvanica Linnaeus ×0.9

Solid, inflated shell with pronounced and raised lunule. Deeply cut fold delineates posterior third of shell. Strong, irregular concentric ridges, unicolorous yellowish white inside and outside. 3·5–4·5cm. Transatlantic, Caribbean. Frequent.

Genus CODAKIA Scopoli
Codokia P. Fischer, *Pexacodakia* Iredale. Medium-sized to large, compressed and slightly inequilateral shells without a well defined groove on surface. Radial ornament may be stronger than concentric ornament. Ligament broad and sunken. Cardinal teeth and anterior lateral teeth well defined. Smooth shell margin. Few species in tropical seas.

Codakia orbicularis Linnaeus
Thick, compressed shell, nearly circular in outline; posterior margin straight. Umbones rather smooth; rest of shell with numerous coarse radial ribs crossed by finer concentric threads. Lunule small, deep and heart-shaped. White. Inside white to pale yellow, usually tinged pink on margins and hinge. 6–9cm. Caribbean. Common.

Codakia orbiculata Montagu
Like a small version of *C. orbicularis*, but more inflated and with less numerous, often divaricate ribs which extend on to umbones. Lunule large and elongate. White. Inside white or sometimes yellow, but lacks pink margins and hinge. 2–3cm. Transatlantic, Caribbean. Common.

Codakia punctata Linnaeus ×0.7
Moderately large, thick, solid, compressed shell, circular in outline and with small, moderately pointed umbones directed anteriorly. Broad, flattened, radial ribs

with narrow, deep grooves between. Fine concentric growth lines. Inside of valves have a few fine punctures. White outside; inside white near ventral margin. yellow centrally and purplish around margins and on hinge. 5–6cm. Indo-Pacific. Common.

Codakia tigerina Linnaeus
Larger than *C. punctata* and ornamented with strong concentric and radial ribs which give it a decussate appearance. Interior of valves not punctate. Coloration outside and inside similar to *C. punctata*. 5–12cm. Indo-Pacific. Common.

Genus DIVARICELLA von Martens
Rounded. small shells with well defined undulating, sometimes divaricating ornament. Shell margin smooth. but sometimes ends of ribs extend slightly over it. Umbones rounded. Cardinal teeth well defined. Lateral teeth obscure or absent. Numerous species in temperate and tropical seas.

Divaricella divaricata Linnaeus
Small, solid, almost circular and moderately inflated shell. Undulating lines across valves from anterior to posterior. Fine concentric lines. White outside and inside. 1–2cm. Boreal. Mediterranean. Frequent.

Family FIMBRIIDAE
Medium-sized. thick. elliptical or ovate shells with broad. rounded umbones. Strong concentric ribs crossed by strong radial ribs giving a decussate surface. External ligament. Hinge with two cardinal teeth in each valve. Anterior lateral teeth closer to cardinals than are the posterior laterals. Very small pallial sinus. One genus in Indo-Pacific and Australian provinces.

Genus FIMBRIA Megerle von Mühlfeld
Corbis Cuvier, *Idothea* Schumacher.
For details see Family Fimbriidae. Two species.

Fimbria fimbriata Linnaeus ×0.5

Moderately large. inflated. thick and heavy. broadly ovate shell with broad umbones. Fine axial riblets are crossed by strong concentric lamellae which produce a weakly decussate appearance. Ornament strongest at posterior and anterior ends. White. 6–8cm. Indo-Pacific. Common.

Fimbria soverbii Reeve
Very similar to *F. fimbriata* but more ovate, conspicuously wider than tall and more widely rounded posteriorly. Surface ornament similar but ribs more lamellate. White with rosy rays. Inside pale yellow with pale rosy margin. *c*5cm. Indo-Pacific (West Pacific). Rare.

Superfamily
Chamacea

Family CHAMIDAE
Small to medium-sized. thick. irregularly rounded shells permanently or temporarily cemented to substrate by one valve. Umbones usually strongly curved. Well developed concentric or radial ornament, sometimes both. At least one large cardinal

Below and right: *Chama lazarus*

tooth in either valve. Weak lateral teeth sometimes present. Two adductor muscle impressions. No pallial sinus. Three genera in tropical seas.

Genus CHAMA Linnaeus
For details see Family Chamidae. Attached to substrate by left valve permanently. Numerous species.

Chama isotoma Conrad
Small. thick shell with very irregular outline. lower valve much larger than upper. Concentric growth lamellae spiny towards margin. Deep purple colour of inner margin is most striking feature. 4–5cm. Indo-Pacific (Pacific). Frequent.

Chama lazarus Linnaeus ×0.6
Medium-sized. thick, irregularly rounded shell with both valves covered by numerous long, foliated spines and lamellae. Margins finely crenulate. Hinge thick. Very variable in colour, but usually has white ground colour variegated with yellow, brown, red, pink, or combinations of these. Inside white. 5–10cm. Indo-Pacific. Frequent.

Chama macerophylla Gmelin   ×0.7

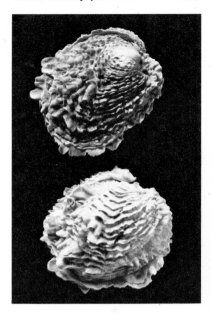

Shell thick, covered with many scaly ridges longer towards the ventral edge. Unicolorous yellow or pinkish red. Inside whitish flushed with external colour. c5cm. Caribbean. Frequent.

Chama reflexa Reeve
Small, solid, rounded shell with prominent umbone on lower valve. Smaller upper valve bears wavy rows of short scales. Whitish or reddish. 3–4cm. Indo-Pacific (West Pacific), Japonic. Common.

Chama sarda Reeve
Small, inflated shell with deeply excavated left valve. Irregular foliations. Sometimes worn smooth. Red inside and outside. c2·5cm. Caribbean. Common.

Chama sordida Broderip   ×1.0
digueti Rochebrune.

Small, irregularly rounded, thick shell with lower valve usually extremely produced dorsally. Upper valve ornamented with

short, flattened scales and spines as well as fine radial riblets. Deep red or pink. Inside translucent white. 3·5–4·5cm. Panamic. Uncommon.

Genus PSEUDOCHAMA Odhner
Like *Chama* but shell is fixed to substrate by its right valve, with umbones turned towards right. Few species in tropical waters.

Pseudochama corrugata Broderip   ×0.8

Oblong-ovate to semicircular shell. Right valve usually attached firmly to substrate by the larger part of its anterior side. Umbo of right valve large and inrolled, with deep umbonal cavity within. Left valve much flatter and smaller, not much larger than open dorsal margin of right valve. Posterior side of right valve finely ribbed. Close-set, short, fluted spines on left valve. Ornament of both valves usually worn down. Creamy with purplish brown blotches and lines. Inside whitish stained with purple. c5cm. Panamic, Peruvian. Common.

Superfamily
Carditacea

Family CARDITIDAE

Small to large shells, usually trapezoidal or rounded, with strong radial ribs and crenulate margins. External ligament. Anterior muscle impressions raised up. No pallial sinus. Shells usually thick and solid. 14 genera worldwide except in polar regions.

Genus CARDITA Bruguière
Elongated, inequilateral, trapezoidal shells with nodulose radial ribs. Trigonal, splayed-out cardinal teeth in left valve; weak anterior lateral teeth. Numerous species, almost worldwide in distribution.

Cardita crassicosta Lamarck   ×1.0

Elongate, quadrately oval shell with umbones at anterior end. Broad radial ribs with short and long, fluted scales which broaden out at extremities. Broad, deep furrows between ribs. Variable in colour: red, pink, yellow whitish, dark brown, or variegated. 2·5–6·5cm. Indo-Pacific (Pacific), Australian (South Australia). Frequent.

Cardita floridana Conrad   ×1.3

Shell thick, solid, with coarse, imbricated radial ribs. Off-white, irregularly mottled with dark brown. Inside whitish, occasionally flushed green anteriorly, brownish just above muscle impressions and on hinge. 3·5–4·0cm. Caribbean. Common.

Cardita gracilis Shuttleworth
Small, elongate, quadrate shell with straight, almost parallel dorsal and ventral

margins. Strong, broad radial ribs which are wrinkled in early stages and more spiny ventrally. Whitish with brownish markings. 2·5–4·0cm. Caribbean. Common.

Cardita gubernaculum Reeve   ×0.6

Shell fairly thick, solid. Coarse radial ribs, those on lower half of shell being imbricate. Reddish brown suffused with white posteriorly. Inside dark brown anteriorly, whitish posteriorly. 4·5–6·0cm. Indo-Pacific. Frequent.

Cardita laticostata Sowerby   ×1.2

Shell thick, solid with broad, widely imbricated radial ribs. Pale brown with irregular, darker brown transverse bands. Inside whitish, flushed with green towards margin. 3·5–4·0cm. Panamic. Common.

Cardita variegata Bruguière
Small, elongate-quadrate shell with um-

bones at anterior end. Rounded radial ribs with lamellate growth lines. Ribs broader towards dorsal margin. Yellowish white with widely spaced, blackish spots on ribs. 2–3cm. Indo-Pacific. Common.

Genus VENERICARDIA Lamarck
Rounded-trigonal, inequilateral and thickened shells with numerous regular radial ribs with narrow grooves between them. Curved cardinal teeth and poorly developed lateral teeth. Hinge very thick. Numerous species in warm and tropical seas.

Venericardia amabilis Deshayes
Moderately rounded, compressed shell with about 28 ribs bearing low scales, narrower grooves between. Yellowish white spotted with orange. Inside white, pinkish in umbonal cavities. c2cm. Australian (South Australia, Tasmania). Common.

Venericardia borealis Conrad
Rounded-trigonal thick, strong, moderately inflated shell. About 20 rounded radial ribs, beaded or merely roughened. Grooves about same width as ribs. White, covered by soft brown periostracum. Strong hinge with a large, central cardinal tooth. 2·5–4·0cm. Boreal (East coast North America), Transatlantic. Common.

Venericardia coreensis Deshayes
Thick, heavy, ovate-trigonal shell with tall, broad umbones. About 20 strong, rounded ribs with low, blunt lamellae. Yellowish white covered with dark brown periostracum. 4–6cm. Indo-Pacific (West Pacific). Japonic. Uncommon.

Venericardia ferruginosa Adams & Reeve
Solid, ovate-trigonal, moderately inflated shell with umbones nearer anterior end and slightly curved forwards. About 15 low, broad radial ribs with broad, shallow grooves between. Yellowish brown covered with thick, dark brown periostracum. 1·5–2·5cm. Japonic, Indo-Pacific (West Pacific). Common.

Venericardia purpurata Deshayes   ×1.5

Rounded-trigonal shell with strong radial ribs bearing large, smooth, regularly spaced tubercles. Grooves between ribs about half width of ribs. Margins crenulate. Yellowish brown. Inside margins purplish red. 3–5cm. Australian (New Zealand). Common.

Venericardia squamigera Deshayes   ×1.6

Shell small, fairly thick, with numerous imbricated radial ribs. Ribs much coarser posteriorly. Yellowish white with irregular, interrupted, brown bands. Inside white. c2·5cm. Australian. Uncommon.

Venericardia umbonata Sowerby   ×1.2

Shell thick, heavy with large, produced and inflated umbones. Ornamented with coarse, thick radial ribs. Yellowish orange occasionally with paler transverse bands. Inside white. c3·5cm. West African. Uncommon.

Genus CARDITES Link
Small to medium-sized, thick, trapezoidal to rounded shells. Broad, striate or tuberculated ribs. Umbones inflated and broad. Thick hinge with well marked cardinal

teeth. Margins crenulate. No pallial sinus. Numerous species in warm and tropical seas.

Cardites flammea Reeve   ×0.6

Shell very thick, trigonal, with produced umbones. Escutcheon broad and long. Edges of valves crenulate. Broad, coarse radial ribs. Whitish variegated with reddish, brownish or pale violet zigzag or flamelike markings. 4·0–5·5cm. Panamic. Uncommon.

Superfamily
Crassatellacea

Family ASTARTIDAE

Small, thick, rounded-trigonal to quadrangular shells which are smooth or concentrically ribbed. Ribs always present around umbones and always smooth. External ligament. No pallial sinus. Hinge often very thick. Six genera in cool or very cold seas.

Genus ASTARTE Sowerby
For details see Family Astartidae. Numerous species, most of them drab in colour.

Astarte borealis Schumacher   ×1.2

Solid, ovate-trigonal, moderately compressed shell with well produced umbones and large external ligament. Numerous concentric ridges, well developed only on umbones and disappearing altogether towards ventral margin. Inner margins smooth. Whitish but covered by a persistent dark brown periostracum. 2·5–4·0cm. Arctic. Boreal. Aleutian. Transatlantic. Common.

Astarte castanea Say
Thick, solid, rounded-trigonal, compressed shell which is as tall as it is wide and has well produced umbones. Inner margins crenulate. Hinge very broad. Apparently smooth, but has weak concentric lines. White, but covered by a persistent, pale brown periostracum. c2·5cm. Boreal (East coast of North America), Transatlantic. Common.

Astarte elliptica Brown
Thick, broadly oval, inequilateral shell with pointed umbones nearer anterior end. 25–30 broad concentric ridges and fine concentric lines. Margins smooth. Dark brown or reddish brown. 2–3cm. Boreal. Arctic. Frequent.

Astarte montagui Dillwyn
Small, solid, broadly oval to almost circular, moderately compressed shell with produced or low umbones. Ligament almost half as long as escutcheon. About 40 concentric ridges. Inner margins smooth. White, covered by a pale or dark brown periostracum. 1·2–1·8cm. Boreal, Arctic. Aleutian. Common.

Astarte sulcata da Costa   ×1.5

Small, thick, rounded-trigonal, compressed shell with moderately pointed umbones. Numerous broad concentric ridges from umbones to ventral margin. Prominent lunule and escutcheon. Inner margin usually crenulate. White, rarely pink. Pale or dark brown periostracum. 2·0–2·7cm. Boreal, Arctic, Mediterranean. Common.

Astarte undata Gould   ×1.3
Thick, solid, rounded-ovate, moderately compressed shell with pronounced, rounded umbones. About ten strong, equally spaced, concentric ridges with fine concentric lines overlying whole surface. Lunule and escutcheon large and well

defined. White, but covered by a brown periostracum which is darkest on ridges. 2–3cm. Boreal (East coast of North America), Transatlantic. Common.

Family CRASSATELLIDAE

Thick, often heavy, trigonal or elongated shells with straight-sided posterior margin in some species. Smooth or concentrically ribbed, ribs being smooth. Internal ligament. Thick hinge. Margins often very sharp and sometimes crenulate. No pallial sinus. Eight genera in warm seas.

Genus EUCRASSATELLA Iredale
Thick, broadly subtrigonal, inequilateral shells with rounded ventral margin and smooth or radially ribbed surface. Ribs become obsolete ventrally in many species. Strong cardinal teeth on thick hinge. Large lateral teeth. Smooth inner margin which may be very sharp. Numerous species widespread in cool and very cold seas.

Eucrassatella decipiens Reeve   ×0.8

Shell thick, solid. Strong concentric ridges. Unicolorous brown, sometimes paler on umbones. Inside creamy white; anterior muscle scar and anterior half of hinge dark brown. 7–8cm. Australian (Australia). Frequent.

Eucrassatella gibbosa Sowerby   ×1.2
Shell small, thick, solid, moderately in-

flated, with acutely produced anterior end. Umbonal area coarsely concentrically ridged. Rest of shell glossy, almost smooth. Light to dark brown. Inside whitish with brown staining on anterior half of shell. 3–6cm. Panamic. Frequent.

Eucrassatella kingicola Lamarck   ×0.6

Thick, solid, elongate-trigonal, compressed shell with moderately produced umbones and sharp-edged, rounded ventral margin. Numerous coarse concentric ridges, strongest at umbones becoming weaker ventrally. White, covered by a thick, dark brown periostracum. Inside white except for brown stained anterior adductor muscle impression. 5–6cm. Australian (South Australia). Common.

Eucrassatella speciosa A. Adams   ×1.3
floridana Dall, *gibbsi* Tuomey & Holmes.
Thick, solid, elongate-trigonal, compressed shell with distinct ridge from umbones to antero-dorsal margin. Numerous strong, concentric ridges cover whole surface. Whitish orange, but covered by a

thin, brown periostracum. Inside pale brown stained with orange. 3–6cm. Transatlantic, Caribbean. Frequent.

Eucrassatella verconis Iredale
Similar to *E. kingicola* but more elongate and with weaker ornament on umbones. Posterior side sometimes straight-edged. Umbones rose tinted. *c*9cm. Australian (South Australia). Common.

Superfamily
Cardiacea

Family CARDIIDAE

Large family of small to large shells which are mostly thin and light, more or less inflated and usually radially ribbed. Rounded-trigonal, elongated or oval. Umbones usually rounded and produced above dorsal line. Two cardinal teeth in either valve. One anterior tooth and one posterior lateral tooth in left valve; two anterior teeth and one posterior tooth in right valve. No pallial sinus. 17 genera mostly in shallow water in most seas.

Genus CARDIUM Linnaeus
Medium-sized to large shells, well inflated, with shell gaping posteriorly. Strongly ridged or spiny radial ribs. Few species in West African waters.

Cardium costatum Linnaeus   ×0.5

Large, thin but strong, well-inflated shell, slightly broader than tall. 16–17 well developed radial ridges, 9–10 of which are

set on broad, flat radial ribs. Edges of ridges of one valve correspond at ventral margin to the flat interspaces between ridges on the other valve. Valves gape posteriorly. Unicolorous white. 8–11cm. West African. Uncommon.

Cardium pseudolima Lamarck   ×0.5

Large, thick, heavy, quadrately rounded shell, inflated and with large, well-rounded umbones. Numerous low, squarish radial ribs bearing small, scaly spines which are almost obsolete at centre. Creamy with violet concentric bands and blotches becoming progressively darker towards ventral margin. Inside white. *c*11cm. West African. Uncommon.

Genus ACANTHOCARDIA Gray
Medium-sized, obliquely quadrate shells with spiny nodulous ribs. Numerous species in cooler seas.

Acanthocardia aculeata Linnaeus   ×1.0
Spiny Cockle

Medium-sized, solid, obliquely ovate, inflated shell with broad, moderately raised umbones. About 20 prominent radial ribs, each with a row of spines down centre; spines more strongly developed posteriorly. Concentric grooves over whole surface. Edges of ribs of one valve correspond at ventral margin to interspaces between ribs on other valve. Pale brown or yellow, sometimes blotched with dark brown. 6–11cm. Boreal, Mediterranean. Common.

Acanthocardia echinata Linnaeus ×0.8

Medium-sized, solid, broadly oval, inflated shell with almost central umbones. About 20 prominent radial ribs, each with a row of short, closely spaced spines down the centre, often connected to each other by a low ridge. Concentric grooves over whole shell. Edges of ribs of one valve correspond, at ventral margin, to interspaces between ribs on other valve. Pale brown, yellowish or white. 4–8cm. Boreal, Mediterranean. Common.

Acanthocardia tuberculata Linnaeus ×0.6

Solid, ovate-trigonal shell, very inflated and with large, broad umbones. About 20 broad ribs each bearing broad, blunt spines which are not connected to each other by a ridge. Fine concentric grooves and distinct concentric growth lines. 6–9 cm. Boreal, Mediterranean. Common.

Genus TRACHYCARDIUM Mörch
Thick, ovate but not oblique shells with short hinge, either straight or sharply bent. Umbones very prominent. Strong radial ribs sometimes smooth but usually scaly or spiny. Numerous species in American waters.

Trachycardium belcheri Broderip & Sowerby △ ×1.0
Shell thick, elongate, very inflated with produced umbones. Serrated radial ribs with deeply incised grooves between them. Yellowish white with two or three broad, orange or pinkish transverse bands. Inside yellowish flushed orange and pink. 3·5–4·5cm. Panamic. Uncommon.

Trachycardium egmontianum Shuttleworth
Thick, medium-sized, ovate, inflated shell with about 30 strong ribs, each bearing a row of tiny spines. Whitish or greyish, blotched with yellow, brown or purple. Inside white and shades of pink, red and purple. 5–6cm. Transatlantic, Caribbean. Common.

Trachycardium isocardia Linnaeus
Same size and approximately same shape as *T. magnum*, with broader umbones. About same number of ribs but ornamented with prominent, fluted scales. Yellowish with reddish blotches. Inside salmon pink grading into purple. 5–8cm. Caribbean. Common.

Trachycardium magnum Linnaeus ×0.8

Solid, elongate shell, conspicuously taller than wide, with protruding, narrowly rounded umbones. 30–35 radial ribs;

middle ones completely smooth and those at posterior end with small scales. Creamy blotched with reddish brown. 5–9cm. Caribbean. Common.

Trachycardium muricatum Linnaeus
Similar to *T. magnum*, but more nearly circular and with 30–40 radial ribs which are scaly rather than smooth. Also smaller. Creamy with brownish red patches or suffused with yellow. Inside white or, less commonly, yellowish. c5cm. Transatlantic. Caribbean. Common.

Trachycardium procerum Sowerby ×0.6

Shell large, thick, solid with inflated, produced umbones. Broad, arched ribs with much narrower grooves between. Whitish flushed with pale purple. Inside white, edged with purple. 8–10cm. Panamic. Frequent.

Trachycardium quadragenarium Conrad
Large, thick, strong and inflated shell somewhat taller than wide. About 40 strong, closely spaced, ridged spines, best developed towards margins and absent from umbones. Yellowish brown covered with a thin, brown periostracum. Inside white. 7–15cm. Californian. Frequent.

247

Genus ACROSTERIGMA Dall

Thick, ovate-elliptical and rather inflated shells with relatively small, rounded umbones. Hinge strongly bent. Numerous smooth or slightly ornamented, flattened radial ribs with deep, narrow grooves between. Numerous species in warm and tropical seas.

Acrosterigma alternatum Sowerby

Moderately large, solid, obliquely rounded shell with prominent, incurved umbones. About 27 strong, flat-topped radial ribs, scaly particularly at anterior side of shell. Deep, narrow grooves between ribs. Yellowish. c5cm. Indo-Pacific. Common.

Acrosterigma arenicola Reeve

Similar in shape and general appearance to *A. elongatum* but smaller, thinner and with about 45 low radial ribs. Yellowish brown, mottled with purplish red. c4cm. Japonic. Common.

Acrosterigma burchardi Dunker   ×0.6

Shell thick, solid, ovate-elliptical. Large, prominent external ligament. Numerous crowded, flat-topped, smooth ridges with narrower interspaces. Escutcheon sur-

rounded with few toothed ridges. Yellowish pink. Inside whitish yellow. 8–9cm. Japonic. Frequent.

Acrosterigma elongatum Bruguière   ×0.5
enode Sowerby.

Very similar to *A. burchardi* in shape and ornament, but ribs fewer and slightly scaly near umbones. White with faint reddish brown spots on umbones. 6–8cm. Indo-Pacific. Japonic. Common.

Acrosterigma flavum Linnaeus

Thick, inflated, elongated shell similar in shape to *A. elongatum* but with fewer and stronger ribs with scales towards margins. Glossy, cream, with mushroom, pink and yellow bands towards margins. 4–6cm. Indo-Pacific (Pacific), Australian (West Australia). Frequent.

Genus FRAGUM Röding

Quadrately triangular shells, usually very inflated and with produced umbones. Ornamented with numerous flattish ribs bearing crowded or sparsely scattered, lamellae. Margins strongly serrated. Few species in Indo-Pacific and Japonic provinces.

Fragum fragum Linnaeus

Similar in shape to *F. unedo*, but not so quadrate and with smaller, more pointed umbones. Ribs finer and ornamented with closer spaced nodulous scales. Yellowish white. 3–4cm. Indo-Pacific, Japonic. Common.

Fragum mundum Reeve

Small, solid, elongated, quadrangular shell, somewhat resembling a small *F. fragum*. Umbones very prominent and obliquely directed towards anterior. Strong keel from umbo to postero-ventral margin. About 28 flattened radial ribs with narrow grooves between. Yellow mottled with red on postero-dorsal region. c2cm. Indo-Pacific (West Pacific). Common.

Fragum unedo Linnaeus   ×1.3
Strawberry Cockle

Thick, solid, quadrately triangular, very inflated shell with broad, produced umbones and straight posterior margin. Numerous low, flat radial ribs with very narrow grooves between. Ribs ornamented with sparsely scattered, blunt lamellae which are more numerous ventrally. Posterior ribs end in sharp points. Ventral margin finely serrated. White, with pink or dark red lamellae on ribs. 3–4cm. Indo-Pacific. Common.

Genus CORCULUM Röding

Thin, heart-shaped shells which are compressed from anterior to posterior. Outline of shell heart-shaped, bounded by a strong keel. Numerous radial ribs of varying strength. Few species in tropical Indo-Pacific.

Corculum cardissa Linnaeus   ▽×0.8
Heart Cockle

Compressed, heart-shaped shell with strong lateral keel which is usually ornamented with fine, pointed lamellae. Slightly convex posteriorly and anteriorly. Umbones strongly incurved and slightly overlapping each other. Numerous widely spaced radial

Below: *Acrosterigma elongatum*

ribs which are stronger on anterior side. Translucent and whitish yellow. 5–8cm. Indo-Pacific. Frequent.

Corculum impressum Lightfoot
Similar to *C. cardissa* but smaller, and thick keel has spiny nodules which diminish in size towards ventral margin. Yellowish. *c*3cm. Indo-Pacific (West Pacific). Frequent.

Genus NEMOCARDIUM Meek
Thin, inflated shells with broad, rounded umbones. Radial ornament assumes several distinct forms and has given rise to numerous subgenera or genera. Ornament usually strongest on posterior slope, but sometimes anterior slope has strong secondary riblets crossing radial ornament. Numerous species in warm and tropical seas.

Nemocardium aeolicum Born   ×0.6

Shell thin but solid, inflated. Umbonal area almost smooth, escutcheon smooth. Rest of shell with numerous fine radial ribs crossed on anterior half by raised concentric ridges which stop short at the midline. Whitish mottled with pinkish or reddish markings. Inside whitish flushed in the umbonal area with yellow. 4·5–6·0cm. West African. Common.

Nemocardium bechei Reeve   ×0.8
Medium-sized, solid, inflated shell with well rounded anterior margin, almost straight posterior margin and produced, rounded umbones. Median area and anterior side of valves with fine radial threads crossed by finer concentric striae; posterior side has crowded axial ribs bearing tiny, blunt prickles. Margins finely

serrated and interlocking. Shades of red and pink, the prickles being creamy yellow. Shiny brown periostracum. 5·5–6·5cm. Indo-Pacific (West Pacific), Japonic. Uncommon.

Nemocardium centifilosum Carpenter
Small, almost circular shell with radial and concentric ornament producing a cancellate effect on posterior slope. Anterior two-thirds of shell with fine radial ribs separated from posterior third by a single prominent rib. Greyish, greenish grey or brownish covered with thin periostracum. Inside white. Aleutian, Californian. Frequent.

Nemocardium lyratum Sowerby   ×0.9

Medium-sized, solid, inflated shell similar in outline to *N. aeolicum*, but with umbones slightly broader in relation to size of shell. Umbonal area almost smooth. Rest of shell with numerous fine, radial ribs, crossed on anterior half by raised concentric ridges which stop short at or before midline. Compared with *N. aeolicum*, the radial ribs of *N. lyratum* are less numerous and are scarcely apparent on anterior half; the concentric ridges of *N. lyratum* are less numerous and slant towards ventral margin. Purplish red, blotched with white. 4–6cm. Indo-Pacific (West Pacific). Japonic. Uncommon.

Genus CERASTODERMA Poli
Medium-sized, obliquely quadrangular shells with slightly arched hinge. Umbones

prominent. Numerous strong, low radial ribs, strongest on posterior slope. Moderately strong concentric threads cross ribs. Few species in European seas.

Cerastoderma edule Linnaeus   ×0.7
Common European Edible Cockle

Thick, solid, broadly oval shell with a prominent external ligament between well produced umbones. 22–28 strong radial ribs with numerous scaly spines and fine concentric lines. Prominent growth stages. Crenulations at margins continuous with furrows which continue inside shell for a short distance. Yellowish brown to whitish. Inside whitish with adductor muscle impression stained brownish. Brown periostracum. 2–5cm. Boreal, Mediterranean, West African. Common.

Cerastoderma glaucum Poiret
lamarcki Reeve.
Closely resembles *C. edule*, but thinner and the furrows continuous with marginal crenulations run well inside valves to umbones. 2–5cm. Boreal, Mediterranean. Frequent.

Cerastoderma pinnulatum Conrad
Smaller and thinner than *C. edule*, with 22–28 broad, flat ribs, bearing delicate scales on anterior slope. Creamy, with glossy white interior. 1·0–1·5cm. Boreal (East coast North America), Transatlantic. Common.

Superfamily
Tridacnacea

Family TRIDACNIDAE
Medium-sized to very large, thick and heavy shells which are usually strongly radially ribbed and may have larger, fluted

scales. Most species with byssal gape; some fastened to burrows in coral and some living unattached. The two genera are restricted to coral reefs in the Indo-Pacific.

Genus TRIDACNA Bruguière
Large, sometimes very large, massive shells with broad radial ribs, sometimes bearing large, fluted scales. Edges of valves usually scalloped. Valves equilateral or strongly inequilateral. Five species.

Tridacna crocea Lamarck   ×0.45
cumingii Reeve, *ferruginea* Reeve, *lamarcki* Hidalgo.

Large, thick, triangularly ovate shell, moderately or strongly inflated and with large byssal gape. 6–10 broad, flattened ribs with strong concentric ridges crossing them. Greyish white, flushed with yellow or pinkish orange. Inside white with pinkish margins. 6–15cm. Indo-Pacific (West Pacific). Common.

Tridacna derasa Röding
glabra Link, *serrifera* Lamarck, *obesa* Sowerby, *whitleyi* Iredale.
Very large, thick and heavy shell very similar to *T. gigas*, with massive umbones. 7–12 broad, low radial ribs and fine radial riblets on and between ribs. Concentric ornament of closely spaced, undulating growth lines which are often lamellate. Edges of valves gently or strongly scalloped. Small byssal gape surrounded by a few short plicae. Greyish white. Inside white. 6–50cm. Indo-Pacific (West Pacific). Frequent.

Tridacna gigas Linnaeus
Giant Clam
gigantea Perry, *cookiana* Iredale.

The largest bivalve in the world. Resembles *T. squamosa* in shape but lacks its scales. Has more central umbones than *T. squamosa* and *T. crocea*, and lacks a large byssal gape. On the other hand, closely resembles some forms of *T. derasa*, but is usually less inflated and its 4–6 radial ribs are more raised. Greyish white. Inside white. 12–13·5cm. Indo-Pacific (West Pacific). Frequent.

Tridacna maxima Röding
noae Röding, *elongata* Lamarck, *rudis* Reeve, *compressa* Reeve, *lanceolata* Sowerby, *acuticostata* Sowerby.
Distinguished from *T. gigas* and *T. squamosa* by being strongly inequilateral. Resembles *T. crocea*, but its 6–12 broad radial ribs have much more strongly developed concentric scales. Large byssal gape with distinct plicae at edges. Ventral margins of valves often deeply scalloped, the ends of the ribs being more or less pointed. Greyish white sometimes tinged with yellow or pinkish orange. Inside coloration similar to outside. 8–32cm. Indo-Pacific, Japonic, South African. Common.

Tridacna squamosa Lamarck   ×0.5
Scaly or Fluted Clam
imbricata Link, *elongatissima* Bianconi.

Large, thick, strongly inflated shell with small or medium-sized byssal gape. 4–12 strongly convex ribs with riblets in interspaces. Broad, sometimes long, fluted scales on ribs which may project beyond ventral margin considerably. Edge of byssal gape with evenly spaced plicae. Greyish white sometimes tinged with orange and yellow. Inside white tinged with yellow. 8–40cm. Indo-Pacific, Japonic, South African. Common.

Genus HIPPOPUS Lamarck
Resembles *Tridacna* in form but the byssal gape is closed when shell reaches maturity. The almost lozenge-shaped shell has no counterpart in the genus *Tridacna* but the great variation of the single species of *Hippopus*, particularly of old specimens, may lead to confusion with species of *Tridacna*. Posterior muscle impression is located centrally in valves of *Hippopus*, slightly posteriorly in those of *Tridacna*. One species.

Hippopus hippopus Linnaeus   ×0.45
Bear's Paw Clam
ungula Röding, *maculatus* Lamarck.

Large, thick, heavy, elongate-ovate, tri-angular to almost lozenge-shaped shell with tightly closed byssal area. 13–14 convex radial ribs with low riblets on and between ribs. Often covered with foliaceous or almost tube-like spines. Fine, wavy growth lines. Edge of byssal area with 6–12 plicae which are larger posteriorly. Greyish white with yellowish orange tinges. Often dark red patches on ribs arranged in irregular concentric bands. 8–39cm. Indo-Pacific (West Pacific). Common.

Superfamily
Mactracea

Family MACTRIDAE
Large family of thin, moderately inflated or compressed, triangular or elongate shells. Smooth or concentrically ornamented. External ligament small or altogether absent; internal ligament in a deep socket on the hinge below umbones. Valves slightly gaping. Well developed pallial sinus. Inverted V-shaped cardinal tooth in left valve, two cardinal teeth in right valve. Lateral teeth usually present. Most species are sand-dwellers and the well developed pallial sinus indicates long siphons which are usually required in this environment. About 20 genera in most seas.

Genus MACTRA Linnaeus
Large genus of thin, trigonal to oval, usually moderately inflated shells which are smooth or have weak or strong concentric ornament. Umbones about central on dorsal side. Smooth lateral teeth. Deep

pallial sinus, small or large. Hinge always well developed. Numerous species almost worldwide in distribution.

Mactra alata Spengler
Medium-sized, moderately thin, ovate-trigonal, inflated shell. Posterior dorsal slope is flattened, and bounded below by a strong ridge. Taller dorso-ventrally than *M. fragilis*. Fine, concentric growth lines. White. Thin, yellowish periostracum. 5–10cm. Caribbean. Frequent.

Mactra australis Lamarck
Thick, ovate-trigonal, moderately inflated shell with small, low umbones. Anterior end more rounded than posterior. Densely crowded concentric striae. Glossy, rayed with pale grey and violet. Umbones violet. Inside purplish. *c*4cm. Australian (South Australia, Tasmania). Common.

Mactra chinensis Philippi   ×0.6
sulcataria Reeve.

Thin but solid, rounded-trigonal, moderately inflated shell with almost central umbones. Irregular concentric ridges over whole shell except at umbones. Dull, white to pale brown, sometimes with irregularly spaced, narrow, whitish rays. Inside yellowish white. 6–7cm. Indo-Pacific (West Pacific), Japonic. Common.

Mactra corallina Linnaeus   ×0.9

Thin but solid, ovate-trigonal, moderately inflated shell with prominent, small, central umbones. Smooth. Creamy white, tinged with purple on umbones and with brown rays. Pale brown periostracum. Inside white or purple. 4–5cm. Boreal, Mediterranean, West African. Common.

Mactra dissimilis Reeve   ×1.1

Thin, stout shell with regular, deeply incised concentric striae. Yellowish or pale beige. Inside beige flushed with violet. 4·5–5·0cm. Australian. Frequent.

Mactra elongata Quoy & Gaimard   ×0.5

Large, thick shell with nearly straight ventral edge. Umbonal area smooth, becoming irregularly concentrically ribbed towards ventral edge. Yellowish with irregular, brown spotting. Inside creamy white. 7–9cm. Australian (New Zealand).

Mactra fragilis Gmelin
Medium-sized, relatively thin but solid, elongate-trigonal, rather inflated shell with moderately large posterior gape. Posterior dorsal slope with thin ridge near dorsal margin and more conspicuous ridge below it. Irregular, concentric growth lines. Creamy white. Thin, greyish periostracum. 5–10cm. Transatlantic, Caribbean. Frequent.

Mactra glabrata Linnaeus
Solid, triangularly ovate shell similar in shape to *M. chinensis* but not so strongly concentrically ridged, most of the shell being smooth. Greyish lilac with fine,

brown rays. Inside violet. Greyish yellow periostracum. 3·5–5·5cm. West African. Common.

Mactra glauca Born   ×0.4

Solid, broadly ovate-trigonal, moderately inflated, slightly inequilateral shell with small, low· umbones. Fine, concentric growth lines. Creamy white, sometimes with pale brown rays. Periostracum yellowish or greenish. Inside white. 10–12cm. Boreal, Mediterranean. Frequent.

Mactra maculata Gmelin
Solid, ovately trigonal shell with inflated umbones. Smooth. Yellowish with irregular, brownish spots all over. *c*4·5cm. Japonic. Common.

Mactra ornata Gray
Thin, ovately trigonal, moderately inflated shell similar in shape to *M. elongata*. Smooth, yellowish, heavily mottled with red blotches and occasionally rays of same colour. Yellowish brown periostracum. Umbones rosy. 4–5cm. Japonic. Uncommon.

Mactra pulchella Philippi
Very similar to *M. chinensis* but smaller, more solid and glossier. Yellowish with brown rays. *c*2cm. Indo-Pacific (West Pacific), Japonic. Common.

Mactra rufescens Lamarck
contraria Reeve.
Solid, triangularly, ovate and somewhat compressed shell with rounded anterior and more angled posterior end. Ventral margin gently curved. Irregularly and finely concentrically ridged. Pale fawn, sometimes stained orange on anterior and posterior slopes. Inside white. *c*4·5cm. Australian (Australia and Tasmania). Common.

Mactra veneriformis Reeve
Thin, rounded-trigonal, inflated shell with very broad umbones, giving shell more globose appearance than usual for genus. Growth lines distinct, otherwise no surface ornament. Yellowish covered by a brownish grey periostracum; ventral margin purplish. 3–4cm. Indo-Pacific (West Pacific). Japonic. Common.

Mactra violacea Gmelin   ×0.6

Shell fairly large, thin and fragile, with median umbones. Unicolorous violet. Pale brown periostracum. Inside violet, hinge white. c7·5cm. Indo-Pacific. Frequent.

Genus SCISSODESMA Gray
Schizodesma Gray.
Medium-sized, thin but strong, triangu-

Scissodesma spengleri

larly ovate shells with bluntly pointed anterior and posterior ends, small, pointed umbones and rounded ventral margin. Ligament seated in a deep slit. Posterodorsal slope bounded by sharp ridge. One species.

Scissodesma spengleri Linnaeus   ×0.5
For details see genus *Scissodesma*. Surface smooth but for posterior ridge. Whitish covered by thin, yellowish brown periostracum. Inside white. 7–9cm. South African. Uncommon.

Genus SPISULA Gray
Small to large, trigonal to ovate shells with posterior area sometimes delimited by sharp ridge, and with lunule and escutcheon also clearly delimited. No conspicuous surface ornament. Shell does not gape at margin. Numerous species in most seas.

Spisula dolabriformis Conrad
Elongate-trigonal shell which is compressed and smooth. Anterior end more elongate and less rounded than posterior end. Small gape at posterior end. White, covered by a dull, pale brown, thin periostracum. 8–10cm. Panamic. Frequent.

Spisula elliptica Brown   ×1.4

Solid, equivalve, equilateral and moderately inflated shell which is more elongate than *S. solida* and *S. subtruncata* which it otherwise resembles. Fine concentric lines and clear growth stages. Moderately deep pallial sinus. Dirty white inside and outside. Brown or greenish brown periostracum. 2·5–3·5cm. Boreal. Common.

Spisula sachalinensis Schrenk
Large, thick and heavy shell with broad umbones and well rounded posterior and anterior ends. Deep pallial sinus. Yellowish white, covered by a rough, brown periostracum. c10cm. Japonic. Common.

Spisula solida Linnaeus   ×0.8

Solid, mostly equilateral shell with umbones usually, but not invariably, central. Triangular in outline with rounded ends. Fine, irregular concentric grooves and lines. Clear growth stages. Deep pallial sinus. Off-white. Inside white. 4–5cm. Boreal, Mediterranean. Common.

Spisula solidissima Dillwyn
Very large, solid oval shell with broad umbones and short, broad hinge. Except for irregular growth lines the surface is smooth. Yellowish white with a thin, yellowish brown periostracum. 10–17cm. Boreal (East coast of North America). Transatlantic. Common.

Spisula subtruncata da Costa
Very similar to *S. solida* but much smaller and with more arched hinge. Pallial sinus shallower. c2·5cm. Boreal, Mediterranean. Common.

Genus LUTRARIA Lamarck
Medium-sized to large, usually fairly thin, elliptical, inequilateral, equivalve shells which gape at each end. No lunule or escutcheon. Hinge heavy and with a broadly open socket for reception of internal ligament. External ligament very thin. Pallial sinus very broad and deep extending to a position almost below umbonal cavity. No conspicuous surface ornament. Numerous species in most seas.

Lutraria lutraria Linnaeus   ×0.35
Common Otter Shell
Thin but solid, broadly elliptical shell with well rounded ends. Umbones low, scarcely projecting above hinge line. Hinge thick. Pallial sinus broad and very deep. White, pale yellow or pale brown, covered by an

olive brown periostracum. 10–13cm. Boreal, Mediterranean, West African, South African. Common.

Lutraria magna da Costa
Oblong Otter Shell
oblonga Gmelin.
Differs from *L. lutraria* by having umbones much nearer anterior end, by incurved dorsal margin and more rounded posterior end. Pallial sinus relatively deeper. Coloration and periostracum similar. 10–13cm. Boreal, Mediterranean, West African, South African. Common.

Lutraria maxima Jonas
Very large, narrowly elliptical, compressed shell with small, anteriorly placed umbones. White, covered by an olivaceous green periostracum. *c*11cm. Japonic. Uncommon.

Family MESODESMATIDAE
Small to medium-sized, elliptically triangular shells with fore-shortened posterior end and extended anterior end. Many species have a *Donax*-like outline. Compressed and almost smooth. Strong thick hinge with short internal ligament. Pallial sinus broad and moderately deep. Subdued colours. Moderately thick periostracum usually present. About ten genera in most seas.

Genus MESODESMA Deshayes
Amphidesma Lamarck (of many authors),
Ceronia Gray.
Elliptically triangular shells with short posterior end, strong, thick hinge, short internal ligament and well marked pallial sinus. Numerous species in warm and cool seas.

Mesodesma arctatum Conrad
Small, triangularly ovate, thick and compressed shell with rounded ends and gently rounded ventral margin. Fine growth lines. Small pallial sinus. Creamy, covered by a smooth, yellowish perostracum.

Inside creamy. 3–4cm. Arctic, Boreal (East coast North America), Transatlantic. Common.

Mesodesma cuneata Lamarck
Triangularly ovate, thick shell with posterior end more rounded than in *M. subtriangulatum*. Whitish inside and outside. *c*2·5cm. Australian (Australia and Tasmania). Common.

Mesodesma subtriangulatum Wood ×0.5

Elliptically triangular, compressed shell with small, pointed umbones which slope moderately steeply towards both ends. Ventral margin moderately rounded. Irregular growth lines. Yellowish white with yellowish periostracum. Inside white. 7–9cm. Australian (New Zealand). Common.

Superfamily
Solenacea

Family SOLENIDAE
Small family of medium-sized, cylindrical, compressed shells, widely gaping at both ends. Umbones very small and placed at or close to anterior end. One cardinal tooth in each valve. Lateral teeth very weak and thin and often absent. Pallial sinus usually short. Animals burrow vertically into sand. Two genera, widely distributed in most seas.

Genus SOLEN Linnaeus
For details see Family Solenidae. Numerous species in most seas.

Solen grandis Dunker ×0.4

Large, thin, very long and moderately broad shell with angled anterior end and rounded posterior end. Glossy and smooth. Creamy white. Thin, greenish brown periostracum. *c*12cm. Indo-Pacific. Uncommon.

Solen obliquus Spengler
Long, relatively broad shell with rounded anterior and straight, slightly angled posterior ends. White, rayed with light brown and covered by brown periostracum. 10–15cm. Caribbean. Common.

Solen sicarius Gould
Blunt Jacknife Clam
Medium-sized, relatively broad, slightly curved shell with well rounded posterior end and slightly angled, moderately rounded anterior end. Covered by a glossy, greenish periostracum. 5–10cm. Californian. Frequent.

Solen strictus Gould ▽ ×1.1
gouldi Conrad.
Long, narrow, rather fragile shell with slightly angled ends. Smooth, polished and covered by a thin, yellowish periostracum. 6–8cm. Indo-Pacific (West Pacific), Japonic. Common.

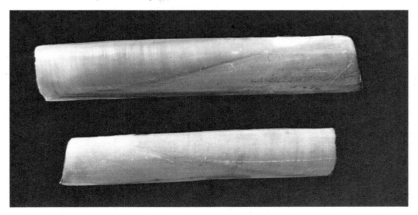

Solen truncatus Wood   ×0.6

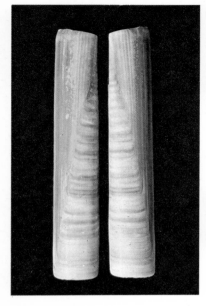

its length. 8–15cm. Boreal, Mediterranean (Atlantic coast of Iberian Peninsula). Frequent.

Ensis ensis

Long, relatively broad and thick shell with angled anterior end and abruptly cut away posterior end. Glossy and smooth. Creamy with reddish rays on postero-dorsal slope which stop abruptly along a diagonal line below which the rays run at right angles. Thin, greenish brown periostracum. *c*12 cm. Indo-Pacific (Sri Lanka). Uncommon.

Solen viridis Say
Green Jacknife Clam
Small, narrow shell with straight dorsal edge and slightly curved ventral edge. Posterior end slightly attenuate, anterior end widely angled and rounded. White, covered by a thin, light green or brownish periostracum. *c*5cm. Transatlantic, Caribbean. Frequent.

Family CULTELLIDAE
Members of this family resemble some of the Solenidae in shape but valves are often wider, umbones are mostly not at end and hinge may have up to three cardinal teeth, one in one valve and two in the other. About six genera widely distributed in most seas.

Genus ENSIS Schumacher
Long, thin, narrow shells with either straight or curved margins to the compressed valves. Umbones nearly at extreme anterior end. One cardinal tooth in right valve, two cardinal teeth in left valve. Anterior adductor muscle impression elongate. Few species in European and North American waters.

Ensis arcuatus Jeffreys
Similar in shape, colour and size to *E. directus*, but not quite so broad relative to

Ensis directus Conrad   ×0.5
Atlantic Jacknife Clam

Very long, thin, slightly curved shell with anterior end conspicuously raised up. Both ends rounded. White, covered by thin, glossy, brownish green periostracum. 9–15cm. Boreal (East coast North America). Transatlantic. Common.

Ensis ensis Linnaeus   ×1.2
Long, narrow, brittle shell with broadly curved dorsal and ventral margins. Anterior end more rounded than posterior. Creamy white with reddish brown streaks and blotches which are vertical in the postero-dorsal region and horizontal below, the two types of markings being delimited by diagonal line. Yellow green or dark green, glossy periostracum. 8–13 cm. Boreal, Mediterranean. Common.

Ensis myrae Berry
Similar in shape to *E. directus* and *E. ensis* but much smaller than either. Thin, glossy, greenish periostracum. *c*5cm. Californian (South California). Uncommon.

Ensis siliqua Linnaeus   ×0.3

Very long, relatively solid, brittle shell with straight and parallel margins and almost square-cut ends. Umbones very close to anterior end. Lateral teeth about one-third length of ligament. Clear growth stages and very fine growth lines between. White or creamy with reddish brown streaks or blotches, those on postero-dorsal side being vertical and those below horizontal, the two types of marking being divided by diagonal line. Covered by a dark green or yellowish green periostracum. 15–20cm. Boreal, Mediterranean. Common.

Genus PHAXAS Gray
Thin, fragile, oblong shells with well rounded ends and curved dorsal and ventral margins. Umbones near anterior end. Anterior muscle impression long and triangular, posterior muscle impression small. Short pallial sinus. Few species in Indo-Pacific and European seas.

Phaxas cultellus Linnaeus   ×1.0

Very thin, translucent shell, finely striate concentrically. Olive green mottled reddish brown. 3.5–5.0cm. Indo-Pacific. Common.

Phaxas pellucidus Pennant
Small, long, thin shell with rounded anterior end and slightly angulate posterior end. Dorsal margin straight, ventral margin gently curved. White or creamy white with occasional reddish brown streaks. Resembles *P. cultellus* in shape but much smaller and with different colour and pattern. 2.5–3.5cm. Boreal, Mediterranean, South African. Common.

Phaxas philippianus Dunker
Very similar to *P. cultellus* but not so broad. Glossy. Smooth. Yellowish mottled with brownish purple. *c*5cm. Indo-Pacific (West Pacific), Japonic. Uncommon.

Genus SILIQUA Megerle von Mühlfeld
Medium-sized to moderately large, thin, broadly elongate shells with umbones small and anteriorly placed. Easily distinguished from other Cultellidae by a strong internal rib from cardinal teeth vertically or obliquely downwards to pallial line or beyond. Widely rounded and deep pallial sinus. Numerous species in cold and warm seas.

254

Siliqua alta Broderip
Large, thick shell, much broader relative to length than most other species of genus. Prominent external ligament. Brownish periostracum wears off older shells. 10–13cm. Japonic. Common.

Siliqua costata Say
Atlantic Razor Clam
Medium-sized, fragile, smooth shell, elongate-oval in shape, with anterior end bluntly rounded and posterior end extended. Strong internal rib extends to middle of anterior end. Greenish periostracum. Inside purplish white. 5–6cm. Arctic, Boreal (East coast North America). Transatlantic. Common.

Siliqua japonica Dunker
Small, fragile, elongate-oval shell resembling a young *S. radiata* but less brightly coloured and with only two or three whitish rays. Internal white rib from cardinal teeth to ventral margin. *c*3cm. Indo-Pacific (West Pacific), Japonic. Uncommon.

Siliqua patula Dixon   ×0.4
Pacific Razor Clam

Large, thin, oval-oblong shell similar in shape to *S. radiata* but covered with a glossy, olive green periostracum. Also much larger. 12–15cm. Aleutian, Californian. Common.

Siliqua radiata Linnaeus   ×0.8

Thin, fragile, translucent shell. Purple or pale brown rayed with three or four broad, white lines. 4–8cm. Indo-Pacific. Common.

Superfamily
Tellinacea

Family TELLINIDAE
Large family of small to medium-sized, inequilateral shells usually with an external ligament and a more or less pronounced flexure or ridge posteriorly, especially on right valve. Valves often slightly unequal, umbones low and small. Shape varies from almost circular to very elongated. Margins smooth. Ornament usually concentric. Often brilliantly coloured and rayed. Narrow hinge plate with two, often bifid, cardinal teeth in each valve and well developed lateral teeth; posterior laterals further from cardinals than anterior laterals. Adductor muscle impressions connected by pallial line. Pallial sinus deep and often broad. Siphons are usually long and foot is large and laterally compressed as may be expected in a group which is characteristically sand-dwelling. Many genera and subgenera have been described for hundreds of living and fossil species but there is still wide disagreement among authorities about the most suitable classification to adopt. In particular, there is disagreement over the many names available for species allied to genus *Tellina*. A conservative approach is adopted here, the genus *Tellina* incorporating the majority of allied genera and subgenera, over 40 of them altogether.

Genus TELLINA Linnaeus
Very extensive genus which is here comprehended in its widest sense as explained under Family Tellinidae. Broadly speaking all the species are distinguished by being more or less elongate, having slightly unequal, inequilateral valves, usually with a posterior flexure and with predominantly concentric ornament. Hundreds of species in most seas.

Tellina agilis Stimpson
tenera Say, *tener* Say.
Small, thin and fragile, elongate-trigonal, compressed shell with prominent external ligament. Fine concentric lines on the otherwise smooth and glossy surface. Large pallial sinus almost reaches anterior adductor muscle impression. White to pink. Inside white. 0·5–1·3cm. Boreal (East coast North America), Transatlantic. Common.

Tellina albinella Lamarck
Ovate trigonal, slightly inequivalve, compressed shell with posterior side of dorsal margin straight and very oblique; strong fold from umbo just below. Anterior side well rounded. Crowded concentric striae which are slightly raised on posterior side dorsally. Very large, deep pallial sinus. Pale red, orange or white, but white form usually pale orange or yellowish

around umbones. *c*6·5cm. Australian (Australia, Tasmania). Common.

Tellina aldingensis Tate
Transversely elongate, compressed shell with umbones almost central and moderately pointed. Anterior end rounded, posterior end narrower and with flexure along its dorsal slope. Concentric growth lines are raised slightly on posterior slope. Yellowish white. *c*3cm. Australian (South Australia). Rare.

Tellina alternata Say   ×0.8

Solid, elongate-trigonal, compressed shell with small, pointed umbones. Posterior end slightly twisted and more angular than anterior end, Numerous, regularly spaced concentric grooves. Pallial sinus does not touch anterior muscle impression. Whitish, yellowish or pinkish. Inside yellowish or pinkish. Thin, yellowish brown periostracum. 5–7cm. Transatlantic, Caribbean. Common.

Tellina aurea Perry
Similar to *T. perrieri* but relatively narrower dorso-ventrally and with a longer posterior half. Orange red flushed with yellow or sometimes all yellow. 4–5cm. Indo-Pacific (West Pacific), Japonic. Uncommon.

Tellina balaustina Linnaeus
Small, rounded, compressed shell with umbones slightly towards posterior. Slightly twisted near posterior ventral margin. Prominent concentric ridges. White or pale yellow sometimes rayed with pink or reddish brown. Glossy, transparent periostracum. 1·5–2·5cm. Boreal, Mediterranean, West African. Common.

Tellina crassa Pennant   ×1.1

Solid, broadly oval, moderately inflated shell with slightly twisted posterior ventral border. Evenly spaced concentric ridges with fine radial lines between. Deep pallial sinus pointing diagonally upwards. Whitish, sometimes with orange or reddish brown rays and pale orange or pink umbones. 4·0–6·5cm. Boreal, Mediterranean (Atlantic coast), West African. Common.

Tellina donacina Linnaeus   ×1.3

Thin but solid, elongate-ovate, compressed shell with low umbones in posterior half. Posterior end slightly twisted. Evenly spaced, fine concentric ridges and clear growth stages. Whitish or pale yellow, with pink rays. Inside white, with external rays showing through. 2·0–2·5cm. Boreal, Mediterranean, West African. Common.

Tellina fausta Pulteney   ×0.7

Medium-sized, moderately thick, ovate-trigonal, moderately inflated shell with prominent external ligament. Weak ridge on posterior dorsal slope. Irregular concentric growth lines. White. Inside white, tinged with yellow. 5–10cm. Transatlantic. Caribbean. Common.

Tellina foliacea Linnaeus   ×0.5

Shell fairly large, thin with median umbones and pronounced posterior flexure. Striae coarser posteriorly. Outside yellowish orange faintly rayed with purple. Interior orange white dorsally, purplish ventrally. 6–9cm. Indo-Pacific. Common.

Tellina inflata Gmelin
Solid, inflated, roundly ovate shell with well rounded anterior slope and straight, steep posterior slope. Ventral margin well rounded. Smooth, polished. Unicolorous white. *c*3cm. Indo-Pacific, Japonic. Common.

Tellina laevigata Linnaeus   ×0.6

Moderately thick, rounded oval, compressed shell with steep posterior slope and well rounded anterior slope. Umbones nearer posterior end. Smooth except for very fine growth lines. Whitish with yellowish or orange rays and concentric bands. Inside shiny, white to yellow. 5–8cm. Caribbean. Common.

Tellina linguafelis Linnaeus   ×0.7
Cat's-tongue Tellin

Thick, moderately inflated, rounded oval shell with steep, gently curved posterior slope and well rounded anterior slope, umbones being nearer posterior end. Strong flexure on posterior dorsal slope. Whole surface roughened by tiny, raised scales suggestive of a cat's tongue. Whitish, delicately rayed and banded with rosy or pink hues. 4·0–6·5cm. Indo-Pacific. Common.

Tellina listeri Röding   ×0.6
interrupta Wood.

Fairly thick shell with median umbones and pronounced posterior flexure. Fine concentric ridges becoming broader and stronger posteriorly. Yellowish white mottled and rayed with pale brown. Inside yellowish, whitish towards margin. 6–8cm. Caribbean. Common.

Tellina lutea Wood
Strong, elongate-oval, compressed shell with prominent external ligament. Umbones median. Anterior and posterior dorsal slopes about equal. Smooth except

for growth ridges. White, or sometimes pink, covered by thick, greenish periostracum. Inside rosy. 6–10cm. Arctic, Aleutian, Japonic. Common.

Tellina magna Spengler ×0.4
Great Tellin

Medium-sized, thin but solid, elongate, compressed shell with pointed and only slightly elevated, almost central umbones. Weak ridge on posterior dorsal slope, with slight, broad furrow below it. Fine concentric striae. Glossy. Left valve white or faintly tinged yellow; right valve orange or pink. 7–12cm. Transatlantic, Caribbean. Uncommon.

Tellina perna Spengler ×0.7

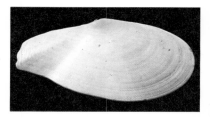

Thin, elongate, moderately inflated shell with attenuate posterior end. Ridge on posterior dorsal slope and furrow below it leading to pronounced constriction at ventral margin. Smooth and glossy. White or pale rose. Inside pale yellow. 6–7cm. Indo-Pacific (Pacific), Japonic. Uncommon.

Tellina perrieri Bertin ×0.7
consanguinea Sowerby.

Thin, elongate, compressed shell with attenuate posterior end. Ridge on posterior dorsal slope with broad furrow

below. Smooth and glossy. Red or pinkish, occasionally white. 5–6cm. Indo-Pacific, Japonic. Common.

Tellina pretium Salisbury
pretiosa Deshayes.
Small, thin, moderately inflated, roundly ovate shell which is well rounded anteriorly and more angled posteriorly. Distinguished from nearly all other tellins by being ornamented with numerous sharp radial ribs crossed by fine concentric lines forming a reticulated surface. White to pale reddish. *c*2cm. Indo-Pacific (West Pacific), Japonic. Uncommon.

Tellina pulcherrima Sowerby
Beautiful Tellin
Thin but strong, elliptical shell with median umbones and almost equally sloping posterior and anterior dorsal slopes. Prominent flexure on posterodorsal slope. Ornamented with numerous small, upright scales which are most strongly developed on posterior slope and weakest on median area. Dark red or purplish with narrow paler rays. *c*4cm. Indo-Pacific (West Pacific), Japonic. Uncommon.

Tellina punicea Born ×1.2

Thin, triangularly ovate, compressed shell similar in shape to *T. alternata*. Fine, regular concentric striae. Purplish red outside and inside. Pallial sinus touches anterior muscle impression which it does not in *T. alternata*. 2·5–6·0cm. Caribbean. Common.

Tellina radiata Linnaeus ×0.7
Sunrise Tellin

Moderately thick, elongate, somewhat inflated shell with prominent external ligament. Smooth and glossy. Creamy white, often with pale red or yellow rays.

Inside coloration the same, but also tinged with yellow. Umbones usually bright red. 5–10cm. Transatlantic, Caribbean. Common.

Tellina rastellum Hanley
Similar in shape to *T. virgata*. Dull cream with brownish yellow rays crossing concentric, pinkish bands. 5–8cm. Indo-Pacific (Indian Ocean). Uncommon.

Tellina rugosa Born ×0.5

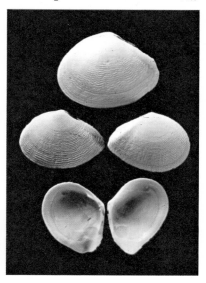

Fairly thin but strong, inflated shell with pronounced posterior flexure. Coarse, wavy concentric ridges. Unicolorous white, pink or yellowish inside and out. 4–6cm. Indo-Pacific. Common.

Tellina scobinata Linnaeus ×0.4

Shell thick, nearly circular with median umbones. Pronounced flexure posteriorly. Whole surface roughened with short, erect scales, those on the right valve being larger and less numerous than those on the left valve. Whitish, faintly rayed with pale brown. Inside white flushed with yellow. 6–7cm. Indo-Pacific. Common.

257

Tellina similis Sowerby
decora Say.
Small, thin, elongate, compressed shell with small but prominent external ligament. Concentric growth lines are crossed obliquely by fine threads. White, tinged with yellow and with unequally spaced, red rays. Inside pink or yellow, or yellowish with red rays. c2·5cm. Transatlantic (Florida), Caribbean. Common.

Tellina sowerbyi Hanleyi   ×0.6

Thin, fragile, elliptical shell with low flexure on posterior slope ending at a well marked angle at margin of shell. Umbones pointed. Anterior and ventral margins rounded. Very fine concentric striae. Glossy. Unicolorous white. 6–7cm. Australian (West Australia). Frequent.

Tellina tenuis da Costa   ×1.3

Small, thin, fragile, elongate-ovate, compressed shell with prominent, external ligament. Irregularly spaced, concentric growth lines and clear growth stages. White, pink, red, orange, yellow or shades of these colours, often in concentric bands;

occasionally colour of left valve does not match that of right. Inside colour same as outside. 2·0–2·5cm. Boreal, Mediterranean. Common.

Tellina virgata Linnaeus   ×0.6

Medium-sized, solid, elongate-ovate, moderately inflated shell which is attenuated posteriorly and well rounded anteriorly. Moderately strong flexure on posterior dorsal slope. Whole surface covered by numerous, regularly spaced concentric ridges. White to yellow, with numerous red or purplish rays. 6–8cm. Indo-Pacific. Common.

Genus STRIGILLA Turton
Small, triangularly rounded, equivalve, moderately compressed shells ornamented with fine, oblique riblets. Nearly always pink. Few species in temperate and tropical seas.

Strigilla carnaria Linnaeus   ×1.2

Small, triangularly rounded shell with long, steep posterior slope and short, rounded anterior slope. Ornamented with oblique radial lines in central and posterior areas of valves. Oblique lines wavy and orientated in contary direction. Pallial line reaches anterior muscle impression. Pinkish and white outside, purplish red inside. 1·5–2·5cm. Caribbean. Common.

Strigilla polyaulax Tomlin & Shackleford
senegalensis Hanley.
Similar in shape to *S. carnaria* but umbones broader and oblique lines confined to anterior portion of shell. Pale lilac or yellowish white. 2·0–2·5cm. West African. Uncommon.

Strigilla rombergi Mörch
Very similar to *S. carnaria* but radial lines finer. Pink outside with whitish growth lines, inside deep pink. Pallial line does not reach anterior muscle impression. c2cm. Caribbean. Uncommon.

Genus TELLIDORA H. & A. Adams
Medium-sized, very compressed, inequilateral, inequivalve, ovate-trigonal shells with acutely pointed, approximately central umbones. Ornamented with numerous coarse and fine concentric folds and lamellae. Dorsal margin on each side of umbones with few widely spaced, prominent serrations. Two species in American waters.

Tellidora burneti Broderip & Sowerby
×1.1

Thin, compressed, ovate-trigonal shell with steeply sloping anterior and posterior dorsal margins, each of which has widely spaced, prominent serrations. Left valve flat, right valve slightly convex. Prominent flexure on posterior dorsal slope. Ventral margin well rounded. Numerous coarse and fine concentric folds. Bluish white sometimes with pale mushroom concentric bands. 3·5–4·5cm. Panamic. Uncommon.

Tellidora cristata Recluz
Similar to *T. burneti* but umbones not so elevated and whole shell more ovate. Concentric folds occasionally developed into more elevated lamellae. Whitish. 2·5–4·0cm. Transatlantic, Caribbean. Uncommon.

Genus MACOMA Leach
Small to large, usually thin, rounded or elongate-oval, inequilateral and inequivalve shells, usually with posterior end slightly twisted. Usually lacking conspicuous ornament. Rarely colourful, or if coloured, without colour pattern. No lateral teeth. Pallial sinus larger in one valve than the other. Periostracum usually tends to flake off. Numerous species in nearly all seas but principally in temperate or very cold waters.

Macoma balthica Linnaeus   ×0.8

Small, solid, moderately inflated, almost equivalve shell with broad, low umbones centrally placed. Anterior slope well rounded and posterior slope steeply curved and slightly twisted to right. Ventral margin well rounded. Smooth but for fine concentric lines and clear growth stages. White, yellow, pink or purple, or shades of these sometimes arranged in concentric bands. Inside usually a shade of outside colour. 2·5–3·5cm. Arctic, Boreal, Mediterranean (Atlantic coast), Aleutian, Californian. Common.

Macoma calcarea Gmelin

Bears some resemblance in shape to *M. balthica* but much larger. Moderately compressed but relatively inflated at anterior half. Left valve flatter than right. Pallial sinus almost reaches anterior muscle impression. Chalky white. Periostracum flakes off except at margins. 4–5cm. Arctic, Aleutian, Transatlantic, Californian, Japonic. Common.

Macoma deltoidalis Lamarck

Similar in shape to *M. balthica*, but larger, more solid, with more rounded anterior slope and longer, straighter posterior slope. Ventral margin less rounded. Numerous very fine, closely spaced concentric striae. White or yellowish white. Thin periostracum which flakes off except at margins. 3·5–4·0cm. Australian (South Australia, Tasmania). Common.

Genus APOLYMETIS Salisbury

polymetis Salisbury.

Medium-sized, nearly circular, compressed shells with strongly twisted posterior end. Pronounced furrow on median portion of valves. Postero-dorsal slope bears strong, radial groove. Ornament of well spaced concentric ribs or growth lines. Ligament long and internal. Very large pallial sinus. Few species in cool and warm seas.

Apolymetis intastriata Say

Similar in shape and size to *A. senegamb-*

iensis, but umbones broader. Strong radial rib at posterior end of right valve and corresponding strong radial groove on left valve. Fine concentric grooves. Unicolorous white. 5–8cm. Caribbean. Frequent.

Apolymetis plicatus Valenciennes

Roundly ovate shell with well rounded anterior end and almost straight, steeply sloping posterior end. Two low ridges on postero-dorsal slope. Numerous lamellate growth lines cover whole shell. Unicolorous white. *c*3·5cm. Japonic. Frequent.

Apolymetis senegambiensis Salisbury ×0.7
listeri Hanley.

Medium-sized, solid, nearly circular, compressed shell with small umbones. Well rounded anterior end; posterior end more elongated and with a pronounced furrow on lower border of posterior dorsal margin. Fine concentric growth lines over whole surface. Unicolorous white. 5·5–7·5cm. West African. Uncommon.

Genus GASTRANA Schumacher

Thin, obliquely triangular, moderately inflated, inequilateral, equivalve shells ornamented with irregular concentric lamellae. No lateral teeth. Pallial sinus rounded and deep. About twelve species in African and European waters.

Gastrana fragilis Linnaeus   ×1.0

Small, thin, obliquely triangular, moderately inflated shell with well rounded anterior end and long, nearly straight posterior slope. Irregular concentric ridges and fine radial lines. Deep, narrow pallial sinus. Whitish outside and inside. 3·5–4·5cm. Boreal, Mediterranean. Frequent.

Gastrana matadoa Gmelin

Very similar to *G. fragilis* and differing principally in colour; *G. matadoa* is white outside but is yellowish inside in umbonal cavities. 2·5–3·5cm. West African, South African. Frequent.

Family DONACIDAE

Small to medium-sized, trigonal, solid, inequilateral shells. Antero-dorsal margin longer than postero-dorsal margin. Inner margins smooth or denticulate. Surface smooth or with radial or concentric ornament, sometimes both. Two cardinal teeth usually with lateral tooth on each side in each valve. Pallial sinus usually present. Often brightly coloured. Numerous genera and subgenera have been described, most of which are here conservatively treated as one (*Donax*). Three other genera are distinct enough to be placed apart from *Donax*. Inhabitants of warm and tropical seas mostly in sandy places.

Genus DONAX Linnaeus

For details see Family Donacidae. Always a lateral tooth on each side of cardinals in either valve or in both valves. Radial ornament present in most of the numerous species.

Donax californicus Conrad   ×1.1

Narrowly elongated shell moderately angulated at each end. Inner margins denticulate. Yellowish white, sometimes faintly rayed. Inside white with large purple areas, particularly around muscle impressions. Glossy, smooth. Greenish to pale brown periostracum. 2·5–3·0cm. Californian, Panamic. Common.

Donax deltoides Lamarck
Relatively large, thick, trigonal shell with steeply sloping anterior and posterior dorsal margins. Ventral margin slightly convex posteriorly and gently rounded anteriorly. Large external ligament. Smooth except for numerous fine radial striae and concentric growth stages. White tinged with rose or blue. Thin, brown periostracum. c6cm. Australian (South Australia). Common.

Donax denticulatus Linnaeus ×1.0
Common Caribbean Donax

Thick, wedge-shaped, inflated shell with abruptly truncated posterior slope and longer, straight anterior slope. Strong ridge delimits posterior slope. Minutely punctate radial grooves distinguish this species. Very variable colour and pattern. May be purple, pale brown or white; may be with or without rays. Usually conspicuous zigzag lines on posterior slope. Inside usually purplish. 2·0–2·5cm. Caribbean. Common.

Donax electilis Iredale
Small, trigonal shell with steeply angled anterior and posterior dorsal margins. Posterior side angularly truncate, anterior side produced, ventral edge well rounded. Ornamented with concentric grooves which are most pronounced towards posterior angle. On posterior slope grooves are strong and crossed by fine radial lines. Strongly denticulate ventral margin. Creamy white sometimes rayed with pink. Inside white occasionally with a purple area. c2·0cm. Australian (South and West Australia). Common.

Donax gouldi Dall
Bean Clam
Small, elongate-trigonal, inflated shell with short, truncate posterior slope and long anterior slope. Smooth but for fine radial lines anteriorly. Inner margins denticulate. Glossy. Creamy or white with pale brown rays and dark growth stages. Inside purple. 1·5–2·0cm. Panamic. Common.

Donax peruvianus Deshayes
Thick, trigonal shell resembling *D. denticulatus*. Fine radial grooves. Brownish yellow with brown concentric bands. c2cm. Peruvian. Common.

Donax rugosus Linnaeus
Solid, moderately inflated, trigonal shell with straight, steep posterior margin and longer, gently sloping anterior margin. Ventral margin almost straight. Posterior slope ornamented with fine concentrically arranged granulations. Rest of shell with fine radial striae. Posterior and ventral margins denticulate. Very variable colour, being white, violet and orange in about equal proportions. 4·5–6·0cm. West African. Common.

Donax scortum Linnaeus ×0.6

Large, thick, very inflated, broadly trigonal shell with large, heart-shaped escutcheon and smaller, narrower lunule. Strong concentric lamellae are crossed by finer radial lines which are weak or obsolete at centre. White with brownish periostracum. Inside violet. 6–9cm. Indo-Pacific (Indian Ocean). Frequent.

Donax trunculus Linnaeus ×1.1

Thick, elongate-trigonal shell with long, straight antero-dorsal margin and relatively short, steeply angled postero-dorsal slope. Both ends well rounded. Fine radial

striae. Inner margins strongly denticulate. Glossy. Yellowish white covered by a pale yellowish brown periostracum. Inside deep purple with white margins. 2·5–3·5cm. Mediterranean, Boreal (South West France). Common.

Donax variabilis Say
Florida Coquina
Small, solid, elongate-trigonal, moderately inflated shell with postero-dorsal margin short and steeply sloped, antero-dorsal margin almost parallel with the nearly straight ventral margin. Radial threads which are strongest posteriorly. Inner margins finely denticulate. Colour extremely variable, ranging from white and yellow to pink, purple, bluish or red, usually with dark rays. Inside similar to outside. 1·5–2·0cm. Transatlantic, Caribbean. Common.

Donax variegatus Gmelin
Similar to *D. vittatus* but umbones are less produced. Colour light yellow or olive sometimes rayed with white, pale yellow or reddish brown, usually broad ray from umbones running almost vertically downwards to ventral margin. Inside white, often with voilet stain. 2·5–4·0cm. Boreal, Mediterranean. Common.

Donax vittatus da Costa ×0.9
Banded Wedge Shell

Thin but solid, wedge-shaped, moderately inflated shell with umbones towards posterior. Dorsal margin straight and long anteriorly; shorter posteriorly. Ends rounded. Smooth except for very fine radial lines. Inner margins strongly denticulate. White, yellow, brown or purple or shades of these with occasional whitish rays. Inside white lightly stained purple. 3–4cm. Boreal, Mediterranean. Common.

Genus IPHIGENIA Schumacher
Thin, roundly trigonal to ovate, inequilateral shells without conspicuous orna-

ment. Two cardinal teeth in each valve and two lateral teeth in right valve. Short external ligament. Large pallial sinus. Few species in West African, and South and Central American waters.

Iphigenia brasiliana Lamarck   ×0.3

Thick, solid, roundly trigonal, moderately inflated shell with rounded ends and low, broad, almost central umbones. Slight furrow from umbo to posterior half of ventral margin. Smooth. Cream with purple-tipped umbones. Pale brown periostracum. 5–7cm. Caribbean. Frequent.

Iphigenia laevigata Gmelin
Very similar in most respects to *I. brasiliana* but slightly more elongate. Covered with olivaceous brown periostracum. Pale violet inside. 5–7cm. West African. Frequent.

Iphigenia rostrata Römer
Similar to *I. brasiliana* and *I. laevigata* but larger than either and with much more attenuated posterior end. Very rounded anteriorly. White. Covered by an olive brown periostracum. 6·5–8·5cm. West African. Frequent.

Family PSAMMOBIIDAE

Thin, elongate, roughly rectangular, compressed or moderately inflated shells usually with gaping ends, particularly posteriorly. Radial and concentric ornament usually delicate. 1–4 cardinal teeth. Lateral teeth weak or absent. Pallial sinus usually well developed. About six genera widespread in most seas.

Genus GARI Schumacher
Psammobia Lamarck.
Thin, elongate-ovate to quadrate, compressed shells. Smooth or moderately or strongly ornamented. Posterior end is wider than anterior. Often a strong or weak flexure on postero-dorsal slope. Pallial sinus short or long. Numerous species in most seas.

Gari anomala Deshayes
Thin, compressed, elongate shell similar in shape to *G. fervensis* but broader relative to length. Ventral margin more curved.

Fine oblique threads from anterior to posterior. Creamy white with pale reddish rays. 3–4cm. Indo-Pacific (West Pacific), Japonic. Frequent.

Gari californica Conrad
Moderately large, fairly strong, elongate-oval shell with low umbones and large external ligament. Bears some resemblance in shape to *G. depressa* but broader dorsoventrally. Ornamented with strong, irregular concentric growth lines. Cream or whitish sometimes with faint, narrow, purple rays. Inside whitish. Brownish, thin and wrinkled periostracum. 5–10cm. Aleutian. Californian, Japonic. Common.

Gari costulata Turton
Small, thin, compressed, elongate-oval shell resembling *G. depressa* in shape but with a relatively broader posterior half and more attenuate anterior half. Fine concentric ridges and, on posterior slope, strong radial ribs. Clear growth stages. White or pinkish, sometimes with purple or red areas, particularly on umbones. Occasionally with reddish brown rays. 2·0–2·5cm. Boreal, Mediterranean. South African. Common.

Gari depressa Pennant   ×0.7

Solid, almost equivalve, quadrangular shell with low umbones, broadly rounded anterior end and straight-sided posterior end. Numerous concentric lines, sometimes ridge-like. Clear growth stages. Cream or white with pale purple rays. Inside purple or white. 5–7cm. Boreal, Mediterranean, West African. Common.

Gari fervensis Gmelin   ×0.8
Solid, almost quadrangular, moderately compressed shell with right valve slightly more convex than left and just overlapping it. Umbones almost central. Anterior rounded. Posterior end bluntly angled, low fold on posterior slope from umbo to margin. Prominent external ligament. Well defined concentric ridges over whole shell. Clear growth stages. White, yellow, pink,

reddish brown or purple with a few whitish rays. Inside white flushed with pink or pale purple. 4–5cm. Boreal, Mediterranean, West African. Common.

Gari squamosa Lamarck
Small, thin, elongate with rounded anterior end and truncate posterior end. Ornamented with strong, oblique grooves extending from anterior side to posterior, becoming coarser posteriorly and producing a dentate posterior margin. Yellowish white. 2·5–3·0cm. Indo-Pacific (West Pacific). Uncommon.

Gari tellinella Lamarck   ×1.4

Solid, equivalve, compressed, almost equilateral shell, oval in outline. Fine concentric and radial lines. Clear growth stages. Cream or white tinted with orange, yellow, red or violet, sometimes in the form of rays. Inside white, pale orange or yellow. 2·5–3·0 cm. Boreal, Mediterranean. Common.

Genus ASAPHIS Modeer

Capsa Bruguière, *Psammocola* Blainville. Medium-sized, elongate-oval, moderately inflated, inequilateral, equivalve shells with well developed radial ribs distributed evenly over surface. Low, broad umbones. Moderately thick hinge. Some species have oblique ribs running in at an acute angle on anterior half. Often brightly coloured. Few species in Caribbean and Indo-Pacific.

Asaphis deflorata Linnaeus ×0.8

Moderately thick, elongate-oval, moderately inflated shell ornamented with numerous coarse, unequal radial ridges. Ridges tend to be slightly scaly on anterior and posterior slopes. Variable in colour and usually brighter inside. May be whitish, reddish, yellow, purple or pinkish. Caribbean form is definitely this species but it is probable that specimens from Indo-Pacific require another name. Specimen illustrated is from Singapore. 5·0–6·5cm. Caribbean, Indo-Pacific. Common.

Asaphis dichotoma Anton

Similar in general features to *A. deflorata* but more rounded and umbones broader. Ornament tends to be stronger. *c*3·5cm. Japonic. Common.

Genus SANGUINOLARIA Lamarck

Thin, elongate or rounded-oval shells bearing strong resemblance to *Tellina*. Inequilateral and mostly inequivalve. Valves usually slightly gaping. Posterior end often more or less pointed. Umbones small and low. Ventral margin often sinuate. Smooth or only weakly developed ornament. Pallial sinus well developed. Usually thin periostracum. Widely distributed in most seas.

Sanguinolaria diphos Linnaeus

Large, thin, elongate-elliptical shell with well rounded anterior end and obliquely truncated posterior end. Broad, low umbones. Gapes posteriorly. Fine concentric striae. Unicolorous purple outside and inside. Shiny, greenish brown periostracum. 6–8cm. Indo-Pacific (West Pacific). Japonic. Common.

Sanguinolaria nuttalli Conrad

Thin but strong, rounded oval shell with an almost flat right valve and a moderately inflated left valve. Prominent, thick, elevated external ligament. Smooth. Whitish with purple rays. Inside whitish usually flushed with rose or purple. Dark brown, glossy periostracum. 6–9cm. Californian. Common.

Sanguinolaria sanguinolenta Gmelin ×1.1

Thin, elongate-oval, compressed shell with well rounded anterior end and more attenuate posterior end. Slight posterior gape. Glossy, smooth except for fine concentric striae. White with bright red umbones fading to pink. 3·5–5·0cm. Caribbean. Uncommon.

Family SCROBICULARIIDAE

Small family of amost circular, compressed, smooth shells without a conspicuous flexure on posterior slope. Small cardinal teeth and no lateral teeth. Small, external ligament and larger internal ligament. Broad pallial sinus. One genus.

Genus SCROBICULARIA H. & A. Adams

For details see Family Scrobiculariidae. Few species in temperate waters.

Scrobicularia plana da Costa ×0.8

Solid, equivalve, almost circular shell with low, broad umbones. Irregular concentric lines and ridges. External ligament small, internal ligament large and situated in a spoon-shaped depression on the hinge plate. Two small cardinal teeth in right valve and one in left. No lateral teeth. Greyish white, pale brown or pale yellow. Inside white. 5·0–6·5cm. Boreal, Mediterranean, West African. Common.

Family SEMELIDAE

Small family of small to medium-sized shells. Larger forms usually strongly ornamented, smaller ones often smooth. Usually with a slight posterior flexure. External and internal ligament usually present. 2–3 cardinal teeth. Lateral teeth usually present. Pallial sinus large and rounded. About six genera, widely distributed in most seas.

Genus ABRA Lamarck

Thin, small, trigonal or rounded-trigonal shells with small, pointed umbones. Equivalve but inequilateral. Some species with divaricate ornament, but most are smooth or nearly so. Pallial sinus deep. Internal ligament in a spoon-shaped depression on hinge plate. Two cardinal teeth in right valve, one in left. Very weak lateral teeth. Numerous species in most seas.

Abra alba Wood ×2.3

Small, thin, almost equivalve, inequilateral shell with broadly rounded anterior end; posterior end narrowly rounded. Small pointed umbones. Fine concentric lines and clear growth stages. Pallial sinus deep, its lower border partly confluent with pallial line. Unicolorous white. 1·5–2·5cm. Boreal, Mediterranean, West African. Common.

Abra prismatica Montagu

More elongate than *A. alba*, the dorsal and ventral margins being almost parallel. Slightly attenuated posteriorly. Fine concentric lines and obscure growth stages. Pallial sinus deep, its lower border partly confluent with pallial line. Unicolorous white. 2·0–2·5cm. Boreal, Mediterranean. Frequent.

Family SOLECURTIDAE

Shells in this small family range in shape from quadrate to very elongate and *Solen*-like. Widely gaping at both ends, and more or less compressed. Smooth, or ornamented with widely spaced, oblique striae. Weak hinge plate. Usually three cardinal teeth. Lateral teeth absent or reduced. Large or small pallial sinus. Four genera, widely distributed in most seas.

Genus PHARUS Brown
Ceratisolen Forbes & Hanley.
Elongate-cylindrical shells superficially bearing a close resemblance to *Solen*, but quite different in several important respects. Valves are compressed and inequilateral; anterior end broader than posterior end. Ligament nearly central. Two cardinal teeth in left valve and one in right. Long, low anterior lateral tooth and short, projecting posterior lateral. Short pallial sinus. One species.

Pharus legumen Linnaeus   ×0.45

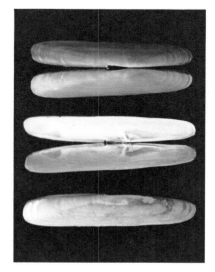

For details see genus *Pharus*. Shell is ornamented with fine concentric lines and is white or fawn in colour. Inside chalky white. Thin, pale yellow periostracum. 9–13cm. Boreal, Mediterranean. Common.

Superfamily
Arcticacea

Family ARCTICIDAE

As this family comprises predominantly fossil species, the description given here applies only to the genus *Arctica*, which contains the one living representative of the family. Large, thick, ovate, inflated shells with broad, elevated umbones and thick hinge plate. No lunule or escutcheon. Well developed cardinal and lateral teeth. No pallial sinus. Ornamented only with fine concentric lines. Prominent external ligament.

Genus ARCTICA Schumacher
Cyprina Lamarck.
For details see Family Arcticidae.

Arctica islandica Linnaeus   ×0.5
For details see Family Arcticidae. The white shell is covered by a thick, rather

glossy, brownish or blackish periostracum. 7–13cm. Arctic, Boreal, Transatlantic. Common.

Superfamily
Glossacea

Family GLOSSIDAE

Small to large, globose, mostly equivalve shells with prominent, usually inrolled umbones. Valves do not gape. Two thin cardinal teeth in each valve; lateral teeth variable in strength and disposition. Ornament varies from fine concentric lines to prominent concentric ridges. Ligament external. One genus.

Genus GLOSSUS Poli
Isocardia Lamarck, *Bucardia* Schumacher.
Small to large, globose, ovate shells with prominent inrolled umbones. No pallial sinus. Few species in temperate and tropical seas.

Glossus humanus Linnaeus   ×0.4
Heart Cockle
cor Linnaeus.

Solid but not heavy, equivalve and inequilateral shell with large, inrolled umbones which recurve away from hinge line. Very globose and almost circular in outline. Viewed dorsally, the shell is heart-shaped. Lunule wide and fan-shaped but not well defined. Fine concentric lines. Three cardinal teeth in each valve. A posterior lateral tooth in each valve. White or fawn. Inside white. Thick, dark green or brownish periostracum. 6–11cm. Boreal, Mediterranean. Frequent.

Superfamily
Veneracea

Family VENERIDAE

Very large family of equivalve, ovate to ovate-trigonal, or nearly circular shells. Thin to very thick, light or heavy, with predominantly concentric ornament, but radial ornament in some, or sometimes smooth. Umbones usually in anterior half, often produced and usually slightly or strongly curved towards anterior end. External ligament. Lunule and escutcheon usually well developed. Three cardinal teeth in each valve. Posterior lateral teeth weak or absent. Anterior lateral teeth present or absent. Pallial sinus variable but usually present to some degree. Many genera in nearly all seas.

Genus VENUS Linnaeus
Thick, ovate, inflated, shells with smooth, large escutcheon, coarse concentric ornament and short pallial sinus. Numerous species in temperate and tropical seas.

Venus lamellaris Schumacher   ×1.0

Thick, inflated, elongate-oval shell with broad, slightly incurved umbones. Prominent, raised lunule. Strong, widely spaced concentric lamellae with strong radial ridges between them. Creamy, with pale brown blotches. Pink and white inside. 4–5cm. Indo-Pacific (West Pacific), Japonic. Common.

Venus listeri Gray   ×0.6
Princess Venus
Moderately large, thick, ovate, inflated shell with broad umbones. Moderately long, almost straight posterior dorsal margin and straight posterior end. Rounded anterior margin. Strong concentric

263

lamellae which are serrated by fine radial riblets. Long, deep and narrow groove surrounds lunule. White. Inside white with brown, posterior muscle impression. 5–10 cm. Caribbean. Frequent.

Venus verrucosa Linnaeus   ×0.7

Thick, roundly ovate, inflated shell with prominent umbones. Strong concentric ridges are warty on anterior and posterior areas. Fine radial ribs give a slightly cancellate texture. White or brown. Inside white, sometimes with a pale purple or brown zone on posterior adductor muscle impression. Dark brown periostracum. 5·0–6·5cm. Boreal, Mediterranean, West African, South African. Common.

Genus CIRCE Schumacher
Thick, nearly equilateral, compressed shells, rounded-trigonal in outline with broad, low umbones. Lunule and escutcheon narrow. Deeply sunken ligament. Strong or weak concentric ornament but radial ornament always weak and usually confined to umbonal area. Few species in Indo-Pacific.

Circe corrugata Dillwyn
Thick, rounded-trigonal, compressed shell, smaller and more inflated than *C. scripta*. Coarse concentric ridges, fewer and larger than those of *C. scripta*. Umbonal area ornamented with wavy, oblique ridges. Inner margins crenulate. Moderately glossy. Yellowish, flushed with pink or pale purple and covered with fine, brown lines which form tented shapes. Lines thickest on lunule and escutcheon. Inside yellowish white flushed with pale purple centrally. 3·5–4·5cm. Indo-Pacific (Indian Ocean). Common.

Circe rivulare Born
Thick, heavy, very compressed shell with a more rounded outline than *C. scripta*. Coarse, irregular growth ridges are crossed by indistinct, wavy radial riblets on anterior and posterior slopes. Edges very sharp. Yellowish white, occasionally blotched with pink. Lunule and escutcheon have reddish brown lines. Thin, greenish brown periostracum wears off umbonal area. 4–5cm. Australian (East Coast). Common.

Circe scripta Linnaeus   ×1.0

Thick, rounded-trigonal, compressed shell with broad, low umbones and steeply sloping anterior and posterior dorsal margins. Numerous crowded, concentric ridges with weaker radial riblets around umbonal area. White to cream, with large, often zigzag, brown to purple blotches on lower two thirds of valves. 4–5cm. Indo-Pacific, Japonic. Common.

Genus GAFRARIUM Röding
Crista Römer.
Ovate to rounded-trigonal, compressed to moderately inflated shells with low, broad umbones and sunken ligament. Ornament of nodose radial ribs which tend to diverge towards anterior or posterior ends from the median area of valves. Small pallial sinus. Numerous species in Indo-Pacific.

Gafrarium divaricatum Gmelin   ×1.0

Thick, rounded ovate, compressed shell. Numerous divaricating radial ribs crossed, on anterior slope, by coarse concentric ribs. Creamy white, blotched and streaked with reddish brown, blotches often forming triangles. Inside whitish with purplish brown blotches. 3·5–4·5cm. Indo-Pacific, Japonic. Common.

Gafrarium pectinatum Linnaeus   ×1.0

Solid, oblong-ovate, somewhat compressed shell with umbones at anterior one third of dorsal margin. Numerous strong, nodose radial ribs which bifurcate on posterior and anterior slopes. Whitish, with concentric purplish brown blotches. Inside white with purplish brown blotches in umbonal cavities. 3–4cm. Indo-Pacific, Japonic. Common.

Gafrarium tumidum Röding   ×1.2
gibba Lamarck.

Similar to *G. pectinatum* in outline and ornament but more rounded, more inflated; the radial ribs are more nodulous and have narrower interstices. White with a few purplish streaks on posterior slope. Inside white with purple-stained hinge. 3–4cm. Indo-Pacific, Japonic. Common.

Genus SUNETTA Link
Meroë Schumacher.
Moderately thick, elongate-oval to rounded-trigonal shells with umbones to posterior of midline. Smooth or concentrically ribbed. Inner margins crenulate. Large, rounded pallial sinus. Ligament lies in a deeply excavated escutcheon. Numerous species in Indo-Pacific.

Sunetta scripta

Sunetta alicae Adams & Angas
Broad-hinged Venus
Well rounded, thick, solid, compressed shell with broad hinge. Escutcheon deeply sunken between valves with ligament at bottom of it. Smooth and glossy. Creamy or whitish, rayed and blotched with pale rose or purplish red. Inside white and pink. 2·5–3·0cm. Australian (South Australia). Common.

Sunetta concinna Dunker
Small, thick, ovate-trigonal shell which is nearly equilateral and has a more rounded ventral margin than *S. scripta*. The smooth, polished surface has purplish concentric lines and zigzag markings on a pale yellow or rosy background. *c*2·5cm. Japonic. Common.

Sunetta menstrualis Menke
Moderately large, thick, heavy, compressed, very roundly ovate shell. Escutcheon deeply sunken between valves with ligament visible at bottom of it. Lunule small and elongate. Smooth shiny surface only faintly ornamented with radial lines and

concentric growth lines. Inner margin crenulate. Creamy, rayed and concentrically banded with purple and purplish brown markings. Inside orange yellow with purplish orange muscle impressions. 5·0–7·5cm. Indo-Pacific (West Pacific), Japonic. Frequent.

Sunetta scripta Linnaeus   ×0.9
Rounded-trigonal, compressed shell with well produced anterior end and steeply sloping, slightly arched anterior slope. Strong, smooth concentric ridges with narrow, deep grooves between. Inner margins stained with pale purple. Creamy, with small, purplish brown blotches which are often arranged in a zigzag pattern. Inside white stained with pale purple. 4·0–6·5 cm. Indo-Pacific. Common.

Genus TIVELA Link
Medium-sized to large, trigonal, smooth shells with centrally placed umbones. Long cardinal teeth and deep pallial sinus. Thick external ligament. Numerous species in warm and tropical seas.

Tivela byronensis Gray
hindsii Hanley, *radiata* Sowerby, *solangensis* d'Orbigny.
Medium-sized, trigonal shell with well rounded anterior and posterior ends. Umbones prominent and inflated. Very similar to *T. mactroides*. Smooth. White, or shades of light or dark brown, strongly rayed with these colours. Inside white, with purple brown blotch in umbonal cavities. 3·0–3·5cm. Panamic, Peruvian. Common.

Tivela mactroides Born   ×0.9

Thick, inflated, trigonal shell with large rounded umbones making it almost as tall as it is wide. Creamy brown with darker brown rays. Surface smooth except for growth stages. 4·0–5·5cm. Caribbean. Common.

Tivela stultorum Mawe   ×0.8
Pismo Clam
crassatelloides Stearns.
Heavy, thick, trigonal shell with conspicuous external ligament. Surface smooth

except for occasional growth stages. Creamy brown, with or without mauve radial bands. Thin periostracum. Inside white stained mauve. 6–15cm. Californian. Common.

Genus PITAR Römer
Oval or trigonal, compressed or inflated, inequilateral shells with umbones towards anterior side of midline. Lunule and escutcheon poorly developed. Smooth, concentrically ribbed or lamellate, and sometimes with spines on posterior border. Pallial sinus usually deep. Numerous species in warm and tropical seas.

Pitar fulminata Menke
Lightning Venus
Rounded-ovate, inflated shell with large umbones and very large lunule. Numerous prominent growth lines. Whitish, with yellowish brown spots and zigzag or triangular markings often forming interrupted radial bands. 2·5–4·0cm. Transatlantic, Caribbean. Frequent.

Pitar lupanaria Lesson   ×0.9

Moderately thick, ovate-trigonal, moderately inflated shell with weak or strong concentric ribs or lamellae, which terminate on posterior border in a series of long and short, open spines. White, tinged with violet; dark purple blotches between spines. 5–8cm. Panamic, Peruvian. Uncommon.

Genus CALLISTA Poli
Thick, rounded-ovate to elongate-ovate, moderately inflated shells with broad, low umbones. Smooth, or strongly concentrically ribbed. Wide, deep pallial sinus. Glossy. Numerous species widespread in temperate, warm and tropical seas.

Callista chione Linnaeus ×0.7

Solid, broadly ovate, moderately inflated shell with small, prominent ligament. Lunule elongate, heart-shaped. No escutcheon. Smooth, glossy. Reddish or pinkish brown, with rays of deeper hue. Inside white. 6–9cm. Boreal, Mediterranean. Common.

Callista erycina Linnaeus ×0.5

Solid, broadly ovate, moderately inflated shell with posterior half much longer than anterior half. Strong flattened ribs have narrow grooves between them. Cream, fawn and brownish orange with darker and paler brown rays. 7–10cm. Indo-Pacific. Frequent.

Genus LIOCONCHA Mörch
Thick, roundly ovate, smooth or concentrically ribbed shells resembling *Pitar* in shape and with a prominent, elevated lunule. Shallow pallial sinus. Colour laid on in zigzag streaks or spots. Few species in Indo-Pacific waters.

Lioconcha castrensis Linnaeus ×0.8/1.0

Thick, roundly ovate, smooth shell with prominent, elevated lunule and prominent, fairly small umbones. Creamy with zigzag or smear-like streaks and spots. 3–5cm. Indo-Pacific, Japonic. Common.

Lioconcha picta Lamarck
Similar in general appearance and size to *L. castrensis* but more elongate and with more produced umbones. Lunule large and heart-shaped. Fine, irregular growth lines. Decorated with reddish brown lines, blotches, triangles and zigzags. 3–4cm. Indo-Pacific (Indian Ocean). Common.

Genus DOSINIA Scopoli
Medium-sized, solid, discus-shaped, very compressed, equivalve and inequilateral shells. Lunule well defined. Escutcheon either well defined or absent. Concentrically striate. Deep pallial sinus. Hinge strong. Great similarity between species, which are found in most seas.

Dosinia anus Philippi
Thick, compressed, almost circular shell with small umbones strongly directed towards anterior slope. Fine, strong concentric ridges. Very thick hinge. Dull, creamy with mushroom tinge. White inside. 7–8cm. Australian (New Zealand). Common.

Dosinia bilunulata Gray ×0.7

Moderately large shell characterised by having the prominent lunule surrounded by a raised, lamellate border representing the anterior dorsal ends of the strong concentric ribs, which cover the valves. Posterior dorsal ends of ribs also raised up

as lamellae. White with faint, brownish rays. 5–6cm. Japonic. Uncommon.

Dosinia discus Reeve ×0.7

Almost circular, with small, pointed umbones and small, heart-shaped lunule. Surface covered by very fine, regular, concentric, smooth ridges. Unicolorous white. Yellowish periostracum. 6–8cm. Transatlantic, Caribbean. Common.

Dosinia elegans Conrad ×0.7

Very similar to *D. discus*, but has fewer concentric ridges. 6–8cm. Transatlantic, Caribbean. Common.

Dosinia exoleta Linnaeus ×0.8

Almost circular, moderately inflated compared with other members of genus. Well defined, heart-shaped lunule with very fine radial ridges. Flat concentric ridges. Clear growth stages. White, yellowish white or pale brown, often rayed, blotched or streaked with brown or pink. Inside white. Yellow periostracum. 3·5–6·0cm. Boreal, Mediterranean, West African. Common.

Dosinia histrio Gmelin
Medium-sized, moderately inflated shell with well defined, heart-shaped lunule. Numerous coarse concentric ridges, absent from escutcheon which is smooth. Creamy with three broad, brown rays which are usually broken up into irregular blotches and streaks. Inside creamy, sometimes blotched with pale purple. 2·5–3·0cm. Indo-Pacific (Indian Ocean). Common.

Dosinia japonica Reeve
Similar to *D. bilunulata* but slightly smaller, more nearly circular in outline, and with a less prominent lunule. Also lacks elevated terminations of the concentric ridges on anterior and posterior dorsal margins. White. *c*5cm. Indo-Pacific (West Pacific), Japonic. Common.

Dosinia juvenilis Gmelin
Rather small, nearly circular, compressed shell distinguished from other species by the three broad, brown rays on a white background. Concentric growth lines are coarse. *c*2cm. Japonic. Common.

Dosinia ponderosa Gray ×0.35

Very large, thick and heavy, compressed shell with numerous irregular concentric ridges, which are strongest on posterior dorsal slope and almost obsolete on median portion of shell. White, covered by a thin, greenish brown periostracum. 11–15cm. Panamic. Common.

Genus TAPES Megerle von Mühlfeld
Medium-sized to large, ovate to elongate, sometimes rhomboidal shells with umbones well towards anterior end. Moderately compressed, with escutcheon bordered by a keel and a well defined lunule. Weak concentric ornament. Some-

times with radial ornament. Numerous species in Indo-Pacific and European waters.

Tapes literatus Linnaeus ×0.7

Ovate-rhomboidal, moderately compressed, thin shell with almost parallel ventral and posterior dorsal margins. Fine concentric grooves which are strongest posteriorly. Creamy, with fine, brown, zig-zag lines and irregular blotches. 4–9cm. Indo-Pacific. Common.

Tapes platyptychus Pilsbry
Similar in shape to *T. turgidus*, but umbones less prominent, and less broad dorso-ventrally. Concentric grooves shallower, particularly on median portion of valves. Pale yellowish brown, usually with a few blackish blotches and irregular rays. *c*5cm. Japonic. Frequent.

Tapes turgidus Lamarck ×0.7

Ovate-rhomboidal, moderately compressed, thin shell resembling *T. literatus* in shape but with shorter, posterior dorsal margin. Broader dorso-ventrally and with fewer, much stronger concentric grooves. Creamy, often with brownish to violet, zigzag streaks or blotches. Faint, broad radial bands. 6–8cm. Indo-Pacific. Common.

Genus PAPHIA Röding
Similar in general aspect to *Tapes*, but shells are more elongate, more compressed and glossier. Smooth or strongly concentrically ridged. Numerous species in Indo-Pacific waters.

Paphia amabilis Philippi
Similar to *P. textile* in outline but larger and ornamented with numerous strong ridges with deep grooves between. Ridges

are more densely crowded on the valves than they are on *P. euglypta*. Brownish, with darker brown interrupted rays which are narrower than those of *P. euglypta*. 7–8cm. Indo-Pacific (West Pacific), Japonic. Frequent.

Paphia euglypta Philippi
Similar in outline to *P. textile*, but larger, relatively broader dorso-ventrally, and ornamented with strong, flattened ridges with deep grooves between. Brownish, rayed with three or four interrupted, darker brown markings. *c*7cm. Indo-Pacific (West Pacific), Japonic. Common.

Paphia textile Gmelin ×1.1

Ovate-elliptical shell with long, straight posterior dorsal margin and gently curved ventral margin. Concentric growth lines, otherwise smooth. Very glossy. Creamy with fine, pale brown zigzag and lozenge-shaped markings. White inside. 4–5cm. Indo-Pacific (Indian Ocean). Common.

Genus VENERUPIS Lamarck
Ovate-elliptical shells bearing some resemblance to the genus *Tapes*. Ornamented with irregular, radial and concentric or slightly zigzag ribs. Some species distorted because they live and grow in crevices. Numerous species in temperate and warm waters.

Venerupis aurea Gmelin ×1.0
Golden Carpet Shell

Ovate, moderately inflated shell with broadly curved ventral margins. Prominent inset ligament. Well defined lunule. Numerous concentric ridges crossed by fine, distinct, radiating lines. Whitish or brownish, with purple or reddish brown streaks, lines, blotches or zigzag markings. Inside white, with purple, yellow or orange tints. 3·0–4·5cm. Boreal, Mediterranean. Common.

Venerupis decussata Linnaeus   ×0.7
Carpet Shell

Solid, broadly oval, moderately inflated shell with broad, low umbones and prominent, thick inset ligament. Lunule elongate and heart-shaped. Strong radial ribs and concentric grooves producing a decussate surface, particularly well defined anteriorly and posteriorly. Clear growth stages. Whitish, yellow or pale brown, sometimes with streaks, rays, blotches or zigzags of darker brown. Dull to moderately glossy. Inside white, sometimes tinged with orange or purple. 5–8cm. Boreal, Mediterranean, West African. Common.

Venerupis dura Gmelin
Thin but solid, elongate-ovate, inflated shell with broad, low umbones. Large, narrow lunule bounded by a fine, incised line and indistinct escutcheon containing a prominent ligament. Numerous smooth, rounded concentric ridges which are strongest posteriorly. Long, deep pallial sinus. Creamy yellow or pale brown, usually with three or four rays of interrupted, brown blotches and dots. Inside yellowish white. 4·5–7·5cm. Mediterranean (South Morocco), West African. Frequent.

Venerupis pullastra Montagu
Pullet Carpet Shell
Very similar in shape, size and ornament

to *V. rhomboides*, but lunule less well defined. Colour pattern, when present, similar to that of *V. rhomboides*. Pallial sinus deep, extending up to or beyond the midline, unlike that of *V. rhomboides*, which is short. 4–6cm. Boreal, Mediterranean. Common.

Venerupis rhomboides Pennant   ×0.9
Banded Carpet Shell

Broadly oval, moderately compressed shell with gently curved ventral margin and slightly angulated posterior end. Elongate lunule. Numerous smooth, concentric ridges. Glossy. Creamy, pale yellow or pinkish brown, often marked with brown or reddish brown rays, streaks, blotches or zigzags. Inside white, sometimes tinted with orange or pink. 5–7cm. Boreal, Mediterranean. Common.

Genus CHIONE Megerle von Mühlfeld
Ovate-trigonal, inequilateral, thick, solid shells with or without lunule and escutcheon. Ornamented with usually bold concentric ridges and much weaker radial riblets. Pallial sinus usually short. Well developed cardinal teeth. Usually a deep umbonal cavity in each valve. Numerous species in American and New Zealand waters.

Chione cancellata Linnaeus
Thick, solid, trigonal shell distantly similar to *C. paphia* in appearance, but the strong concentric ribs are thinner and there are also numerous coarse radial ribs. Escutcheon long and smooth. Whitish, sometimes blotched and rayed with brown. Escutcheon usually has six or seven brown stripes. Inside white tinged with purplish blue. 2·5–4·5cm. Transatlantic, Caribbean. Common.

Chione fluctifraga Sowerby
Similar in size and general appearance to *C. undatella*, but broader dorso-ventrally, with much more produced umbones and less rounded anterior end. Concentric ribs fewer, stronger and only weakly ribbed radially. Escutcheon less well defined. White, sometimes tinted blue grey. Inside white, with muscle impressions and hinge purple. 5–7cm. Californian. Common.

Chione gnidia Broderip & Sowerby
Large, thick, heavy, ovate-trigonal, inflated shell with large, heart-shaped lunule and

long, narrow escutcheon. Prominent, widely spaced, frilled lamellae with coarse, flattened radial ribs between them. Inner margins crenulate. Yellowish white. Inside yellowish white or white. 7–12cm. Panamic (Gulf of California). Common.

Chione paphia Linnaeus   ×1.0

Thick, solid, ovate-trigonal shell with produced umbones and steep posterior dorsal margin. Ornamented with 10–12 very pronounced concentric ribs which diminish in strength posteriorly. White or cream, mottled, streaked or shaded with reddish brown. Inside white, flushed with pale purple. 3·0–4·5cm. Caribbean. Uncommon.

Chione undatella Sowerby   ×0.7
Thick, rounded, trigonal shell with broadly rounded ventral margin and steep posterior dorsal slope. Numerous strong,

concentric ribs with broader, less elevated radial ribs showing in interstices only, giving cancellate texture. Inner ventral margin crenulate. Whitish, sometimes with purplish brown blotches. Inside white, with purplish blotch posteriorly. 5–10cm. Californian, Panamic. Common.

Genus ANOMALOCARDIA Schumacher

Thick, solid, trigonal, inflated shells with large, impressed lunule. Ornamented with strong or weak radial ribs and wavy concentric folds. Ventral margin sometimes crenulate within. Numerous species widely distributed in warm and tropical seas.

Anomalocardia flexuosa Linnaeus

Medium-sized, moderately thick, solid, inflated, elongate-trigonal shell with attenuated posterior end. Lunule ill-defined. Escutcheon long and narrow. Prominent external ligament. Coarse concentric ridges on median and anterior portions, fainter anteriorly. Strong radial ribs on posterior portion. Whitish, yellowish or pale brownish, usually with three or four broad, interrupted purplish rays. Inside creamy yellow, flushed with pale purple at margins. 3–4cm. Indo-Pacific. Common.

Anomalocardia kochii Philippi

alfredensis Bartsch.

Thin but solid, elongate-trigonal, inflated shell with attenuated posterior end. Anterior end narrowly rounded. Lunule and escutcheon ill-defined. Smooth except for fine concentric growth lines. Moderately glossy. Creamy, dotted, blotched, streaked and rayed with pale brown, yellowish brown, purplish or combinations of these. Inside creamy white, with purple staining below hinge. 3·0–3·5cm. Indo-Pacific (East Africa), South African. Common.

Anomalocardia squamosa Linnaeus ×1.5

Small, very thick, trigonal, inflated shell with a moderately pointed posterior end. Large, heart-shaped lunule. Ventral margin crenulate within. Numerous closely spaced radial ribs which are nodulous or scaly. Ribs become obsolete posteriorly. Yellowish white, sometimes tinged with yellow or brown. Inside white. 2–4cm.

Indo-Pacific (West Pacific), Japonic. Common.

Genus BASSINA Jukes-Brown

Rounded-trigonal or ovate to elongate-ovate shells with features similar to *Chione*, but without escutcheon. Thin, widely spaced concentric lamellae which may be turned upwards at their outer edges. Few species in West Pacific and Australasia.

Bassina disjecta Perry ×0.7

Wedding Cake Venus
lamellata Lamarck.

Thin, elongate-ovate, compressed shell with almost parallel ventral and posterior dorsal margins. About six thin, well developed concentric lamellae which are turned upwards at their outer edges. Creamy white, with pink lamellae. 6–7cm. Australian (South Australia, Tasmania). Frequent.

Bassina yatei Gray

Thick, ovate, compressed shell with umbones strongly recurved towards anterior. Escutcheon long and narrow. Lunule indistinct and narrow. Prominent, foliaceous, concentric lamellae are wider apart towards umbones than they are towards ventral margin. Lamellae more raised at anterior and posterior ends. Whitish or yellowish orange. Inside white, flushed with pale purple. 5–6cm. Australian (New Zealand). Common.

Genus CHAMELEA Mörch

Small, solid, ovate-trigonal shells ornamented with narrow, close-set, concentric ridges. No radial ornament. Lunule short

Chamelea gallina

and heart-shaped. Escutcheon elliptical. Usually three cardinal teeth in each valve and no lateral teeth. Pallial sinus shallow. Few species in European and Mediterranean waters.

Chamelea gallina Linnaeus ×1.6

Very similar to *C. striatula* and considered by some authorities to be conspecific. In most respects the two are identical, but in *C. gallina* the concentric ridges are more flattened and smoother, and are not so accentuated anteriorly. 2·5–4·5cm. Boreal, Mediterranean. Common.

Chamelea striatula da Costa ×1.5

Solid, thick, ovate-trigonal, moderately compressed shell with long, gently curved posterior slope. Escutcheon reaches almost to posterior margin. Numerous strong but thin concentric ridges. Fine concentric lines in grooves between ridges. White, cream or pale yellow, usually with three reddish brown rays. 2·5–4·5cm. Boreal, Mediterranean. Common.

Genus CLAUSINELLA Gray

Thick, ovate-trigonal, equivalve shells with umbones in anterior half. Escutcheon elliptical and long; lunule short and heart-shaped. Ornamented with broad, flat concentric ridges. Three cardinal teeth in each valve. No lateral teeth. Pallial sinus small. Inner margin crenulate. Colourful. One species.

Clausinella fasciata da Costa ×1.0

Solid, thick, ovate-trigonal, moderately compressed shell with small, prominent umbones inclined towards anterior. Well rounded ventral margin. Ligament deeply

inset in anterior half of escutcheon. Lunule short, heart-shaped, with indistinct border. Ornamented with a few, broad, flat concentric ridges which vary considerably in strength. Concentric lines in the intermediate grooves. Extremely variable in colour and pattern: every shade of yellow, white, pink, purple or brown, and patterned with lines, rays, blotches or streaks. Thin, pale brown periostracum. Inside white sometimes tinged with purple. 2·0–2·5cm. Boreal, Mediterranean. Common.

Genus MERCENARIA Schumacher

Resembles *Chione* in shape, but much larger. Lunule heart-shaped or elongated, and escutcheon long and narrow but border indistinct. Fine, sometimes lamellate, concentric ridges which are strongest around umbones. Radial ornament absent or limited to fine riblets between concentric ridges. Three cardinal teeth in each valve. No lateral teeth. Pallial sinus not very deep. Few species in cool and temperate waters.

Mercenaria campechiensis Gmelin
Southern Quahog

Very similar to *M. mercenaria* but much more inflated, heavier and strongly ridged concentrically over entire shell even in adult specimens. Same colour as *M. mercenaria*, but may have a purplish stain on escutcheon and brown mottlings elsewhere. Inside white, without purplish staining. 7–15cm. Transatlantic, Caribbean. Common.

Mercenaria mercenaria Linnaeus ×0.5
Northern Quahog

Thick, heavy, broadly ovate, moderately inflated shell with long, well curved posterior dorsal margin which meets dorsal margin at a rounded angle. Ligament deeply inset. Lunule well defined, heart-shaped. Escutcheon indistinct. Numerous, fine, crowded concentric lines which are more prominent and wider spaced on umbones. In adult specimens, the ridges are worn away on median area of valves. Whitish, pale brown, grey or greyish brown, sometimes with brown zigzag markings. Inside white, usually with purple staining in region of muscle impressions.

7–13cm. Boreal (East coast of North America, and introduced in Western European coastal waters), Transatlantic, Caribbean, Californian (introduced in Humboldt Bay, California). Common.

Mercenaria stimpsoni Gould
Large, thick, heavy, moderately compressed, ovate-trigonal shell resembling *M. mercenaria* in general appearance but more produced anteriorly, with more pointed umbones. Concentric ridges are more lamellate and there are radial riblets in the grooves between ridges. Whitish. 7–10cm. Japonic. Common.

Genus PLACAMEN Iredale

Small, rounded-trigonal, thick, very inequilateral, moderately inflated shells. Lunule deep and heart-shaped. Ornamented with widely spaced, upturned concentric lamellae which are smooth and blunt. No radial ornament. Ventral margin sometimes crenulate within. Few species in Indo-Pacific, Japanese and Australian waters.

Placamen flindersi Cotton & Godfrey
Similar in shape to *P. placidus* and *P. tiara*, but differs from both by its smaller size and especially by its ornament which consists of only 12 concentric lamellae which are much more strongly developed and more sharply curved upwards. The three lamellae furthest from umbo cover more than half the valve. Creamy, with pink rays sometimes present. 2·0–2·5cm. Australian (South Australia). Rare.

Placamen placidus Philippi ×1.7
Ovate-trigonal, almost heart-shaped in outline. Thick, moderately inflated shell with umbones almost in line with anterior

dorsal margin. About 23 strong, blunt, smooth, concentric lamellae which curve up and inwards. Ventral margin finely crenulate. Whitish. Inside whitish, stained with brown and purple. 2·0–2·5cm. Australian (South Australia, Tasmania). Common.

Placamen tiara Dillwyn
Small, rounded-trigonal shell similar in shape to *P. placidus*, but with fewer concentric lamellae. The white ground colour has three or four purplish brown rays which are most conspicuous on the lamellae. *c*3cm. Indo-Pacific, Japonic. Common.

Genus TIMOCLEA Brown
Small, rounded-trigonal, moderately compressed shells with small, almost central umbones. Escutcheon elongate or narrowly heart-shaped. Ornament predominantly radial but sometimes with concentric lamellae. Inner margins finely crenulate. Three cardinal teeth in each valve. No lateral teeth. Pallial sinus small. Numerous species widespread in most seas.

Timoclea arakanensis Nevill ×2.2

Thin, solid, trigonal, moderately compressed shell with slightly attenuated posterior end. Strong radial ribs at posterior and anterior ends, weaker in median portion where they are crossed by strong concentric ribs giving cancellate surface. Creamy yellow with occasional dark brown blotches. *cl*.5cm. Indo-Pacific (Indian Ocean). Frequent.

Timoclea layardi Reeve
Thin, elongate-trigonal, inequilateral, moderately inflated shell with narrowly heart-shaped lunule and ill-defined elliptical escutcheon. Similar in outline to *T. arakanensis*, but posterior end slightly more attenuate. Numerous strong, irregular concentric ribs which are lamellate at ends. Coarse radial ribs at ends and fine radial striae between concentric ribs on median portion of valves. Fawn, sometimes bearing dark brown streaks, blotches or zigzags. Inside white. 1·3–1·7cm. Indo-Pacific (Indian Ocean). Frequent.

Timoclea marica Linnaeus
Thin, solid, roundly trigonal, moderately compressed shell with elongate, narrow

lunule. Strong concentric ribs tend to be lamellate, particularly posteriorly. Strong radial grooves between ribs tend to give shell a cancellate appearance. Creamy white, with purplish brown blotches. Inside yellowish, flushed with purple. 1·5–2·0cm. Indo-Pacific. Common.

Timoclea ovata Pennant   ×1.6

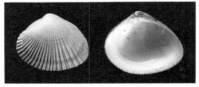

Thin, solid, trigonal, moderately compressed shell with ill-defined, narrowly heart-shaped lunule and elliptical escutcheon. Up to 50 radial ribs cut into by numerous fine concentric grooves, which are more pronounced posteriorly. Pale yellow or fawn, sometimes streaked and blotched with reddish brown. Inside white. 1·5–2·0cm. Boreal, Mediterranean, West African (Cape Verde Islands). Common.

Timoclea scabra Hanley
Small, thin, ovate-trigonal, moderately inflated shell, somewhat resembling *T. ovata* in outline, but more rounded posteriorly and ventrally. Strong radial ribs have fine, scaly concentric lamellae superimposed on them. Radial ribs strongest just anterior to posterior slope. Whitish, sometimes with a broad, brownish ray on posterior slope. 1·0–1·3cm. Indo-Pacific (Indian Ocean). Common.

Family PETRICOLIDAE
Thin, elongate or elongate-ovate shells without lunule or escutcheon and with hinge lacking lateral teeth. Three cardinal teeth in left valve and two in right. Pallial sinus deep. Radial ornament usually well developed. Shells often distorted to a certain extent because they bore into hard substances which inhibit free growth. Three genera widespread in most seas.

Genus PETRICOLA Lamarck
For details see Family Petricolidae. Numerous genera and subgenera have been proposed but, despite the very varied appearance of the species, they all seem close enough in essential features to be placed in one genus. The numerous species all bore into hard or soft substances such as limestone, mudstone, coral, clay and stiff mud.

Petricola lapicida Gmelin
Very different to *P. pholadiformis*, being ovate with well rounded ends and broadly curved ventral margin. Umbones much more centrally placed. Ornamented with divaricating radial ridges crossed by con-

centric growth lines. Chalky white. Ornamentation is not part of the shell proper but consists of mud particles deposited on the surface by the animal. 2·5–4·5cm. Caribbean. Common.

Petricola pholadiformis Lamarck   ×1.3

Thin, very inequilateral, elongate-oval, inflated shell with broad, low umbones and prominent external ligament. Numerous radial ribs which are much stronger and coarser anteriorly, where they bear prominent eave-shaped spines. Fine and coarse concentric growth lines. Deep pallial sinus. Unicolorous white or fawn. 4–7cm. Boreal, Mediterranean, West African, Transatlantic, Caribbean, Californian. Common.

Superfamily
Myacea

Family MYIDAE
Small to large, thin, elongate or ovate shells, inequivalve, the right valve being more convex than the left. A mainly internal ligament is attached to a large, spoon-shaped process on the thin hinge plate of both valves, this process being largest in the left valve. No true teeth on hinge plate. No lunule or escutcheon. Usually with a wide posterior gape. Shell not nacreous. Pallial sinus usually large, the siphons being very long and broad. Usually a thin periostracum which flakes off when dry. Most species burrow in sand and mud. Six genera widespread in cool and warm seas.

Genus MYA Linnaeus
Medium-sized to large, thin, porcellanous to chalky, elongate to ovate shells widely gaping posteriorly. Ligament mostly internal and attached to a large, spoon-shaped process in each valve. Large, deep pallial sinus. Few species in cool and temperate waters.

Mya arenaria Linnaeus   ×0.4
Sand Gaper, Soft-shell Clam, Soft Clam
Moderately thick, solid, inflated, oval shell with well rounded anterior end and narrower, rounded posterior end which is less gaping than in *M. truncata*. Numerous concentric lines and clear growth stages. Spoon-shaped process to which ligament

is attached is very large in left valve. Pallial sinus deep and V-shaped, containing large, broad siphons of living animal. White or fawn, covered by pale yellow or fawn periostracum. Inside white. 12–15cm. Boreal, Transatlantic, Aleutian, Californian, Japonic. Common.

Mya truncata Linnaeus   ×0.4
Blunt Gaper, Truncate Soft-shell Clam

Thin but solid, inflated shell with abruptly cut away posterior end and rounded anterior end. Right valve more convex than left. Broad, low umbones just posterior to midline. Posterior end widely gaping. Ligament attached to large, spoon-shaped process on hinge. Pallial sinus broadly U-shaped. Numerous, irregular concentric growth lines and clear growth stages. Whitish or cream, covered by pale or dark brown periostracum. Inside white. 5–8cm. (excluding siphons). Arctic, Boreal, Transatlantic, Aleutian, Californian, Japonic. Common.

Family CORBULIDAE
Small, thick, solid, strongly or slightly inequivalve, inequilateral, elongate-trigonal, inflated shells with very weakly developed hinge teeth. Ligament internal and attached to a spoon-shaped process in left valve and corresponding depression in right valve. Usually ornamented with strong concentric ridges. Pallial sinus small or absent. Many genera and subgenera have been proposed but seem to be reducible to about half a dozen genera. Found in nearly all seas.

Genus CORBULA Bruguière
Gloidis Megerle von Mühlfeld.
For details see Family Corbulidae. Left valve smaller than right, the two valves not meeting at their ventral margins. Posterior end usually attenuated and pointed. Many species in almost all seas.

Corbula erythrodon Lamarck
Thick, heavy, elongate-trigonal inflated shell. Well produced posteriorly and thick-

271

ened with a calcareous knob or callus terminally. Widely spaced concentric ridges. Muscle impressions deeply impressed. No pallial sinus. Whitish. Inside white, with margins stained bright red. c2·5cm. Japonic. Frequent.

Corbula gibba Olivi
Small, solid, trigonal, inflated and very inequilateral shell; right valve very much larger and more convex than left. Ventral margin of right valve overlaps that of left valve considerably. Numerous low, concentric ridges on each valve and few faint, radial lines on left valve. Clear growth stages. White or cream, covered by a greyish periostracum. Inside white, tinged with pink or blue. 1·0–1·3cm. Boreal, Mediterranean, West African. Common.

Corbula iredalei Cotton
Similar to *C. tunicata* but taller dorsoventrally, more coarsely ornamented and with right valve overlapping left to a greater extent posteriorly. White, covered by a thick, brown periostracum. c2cm. Australian (South Australia). Uncommon.

Corbula sulcata Lamarck   ×1.6

Shell small, thick and heavy, with broad, flattened umbones. Right valve with coarse, concentric ribbing. Left valve with less

Corbula tunicata

coarse ribbing. Right valve uniformly creamy white, left valve creamy white with brown lines between ribs. Inside yellowish white, with brown margin. c2·5cm. Indo-Pacific. Frequent.

Corbula tunicata Hinds   ×1.6
Small, solid, inflated shell with left valve considerably smaller than right. Umbones rounded or flattened. Left valve coarsely ribbed, concentrically. Right valve more prominently ribbed and ribs smoother. Whitish with brown stain ventrally. 2·5–3·0cm. Indo-Pacific (West Pacific). Uncommon.

Superfamily
Hiatellacea

Family HIATELLIDAE
Medium-sized to large, thin or thick shells, quadrate to trapezoidal, often irregular in outline, with valves slightly or widely gaping. Ligament external. No lateral teeth, and cardinal teeth weak or absent. Muscle impressions irregular and pallial line irregular or discontinuous. Pallial sinus, when present, may be wide or insignificant. The burrowing habits of some species affect overall shape considerably. Four genera, mostly in cool or very cold waters.

Genus HIATELLA Bosc
Saxicava Fleuriau de Bellevue.
Small, trapezoidal, usually irregular in shape due to nestling and boring habits. No well defined teeth on hinge of adult shells. Discontinuous pallial line. Muscle scars conspicuous and widely separated. Few species, widespread, mostly in cooler seas.

Hiatella arctica Linnaeus   ×2.0
rugosa Linnaeus, *pholadis* Linnaeus.

Shell solid, slightly inequivalve, usually more or less irregular in shape but generally elongate with approximately parallel dorsal and ventral margins. The two ends may be rounded or fairly straight. Irregular

concentric lines and folds with two ridges radiating from each umbo along posterior dorsal slope. In juvenile shells, these ridges bear small spines. Unicolorous white, covered by a yellowish brown periostracum. Deep pallial sinus. 2–7cm. Boreal, Mediterranean, Arctic, Transatlantic, Caribbean. Common.

Hiatella australis Lamarck
Very similar to *H. arctica*, but ornament tends to be stronger, the concentric ribs being sharply raised. As in *H. arctica*, the posterior adductor muscle impression is larger than the anterior, but differs from that species in having a shallow pallial sinus. 3–4cm. Australian, Indo-Pacific (West Pacific). Common.

Superfamily
Pholadacea

Family PHOLADIDAE
Elongate to globular, thin and brittle shells, equivalve and inequilateral, frequently gaping at both ends. Dorsal margin anterior to umbones reflected upwards. Differ from most other bivalve families in possessing variously shaped and positioned accessory plates which have specialised functions and technical names. The principal accessory plates are on the dorsal margin and comprise a protoplax (over and anterior to umbones), a mesoplax (a much smaller plate just posterior to the protoplax) and a metaplax (an elongate plate covering the posterior part of dorsal margin). Projecting from the umbonal cavity of each valve, there may be a fingerlike projection known as an apophysis. The three genera described below may be distinguished, in addition to other features, by the presence or absence of these structures. The other features peculiar to the shells of this family are ignored here because only a few well known species are dealt with, the identification of which is relatively easy. Surface of shells ornamented with strong concentric or radial ridges which are often scaly. About 16 genera in nearly all seas, the majority of them including species which bore into hard or soft substances.

Genus PHOLAS Linnaeus
Thin, elliptical or rounded, inflated shells with dorsal margin reflected over umbones, the reflected portion containing walled cavities. Protoplax thin and calcareous, divided longitudinally, mesoplax solid, calcareous and transverse; metaplax, long, thin and calcareous. An apophysis in each valve. Usually strongly ornamented. Numerous species, all of them rock-borers, in temperate and tropical seas.

Pholas campechiensis Gmelin
Similar to *P. dactylus*, but smaller, less

elongated posteriorly and wider anteriorly. Radial ridges stronger and covering median and anterior portion of shell. 7–10cm. Transatlantic, Caribbean. Uncommon.

Pholas dactylus Linnaeus   ×0.45
Common Piddock

Thin, brittle, elliptical shell with pointed anterior end, more rounded posteriorly, both ends gaping. Umbonal reflection has 9–14 walled cavities. Protoplax broad, mesoplax very small, metaplax long and thin. Small apophysis in each valve. Prominent concentric ridges crossed anteriorly by strong radial ribs, the intersections bearing short spines. Deep, broad pallial sinus. White or grey, covered by a pale yellow periostracum. Inside white. 10–15cm. Boreal, Mediterranean. Common.

Genus BARNEA Leach
Similar in general appearance to *Pholas* but lacking mesoplax and metaplax. Protoplax not divided longitudinally. Dorsal margin raised up above umbones as in *Pholas* but lacking walled cavities. Both ends gaping. Small apophysis in each valve. Ornamented with strong concentric and radial ridges. Numerous species in temperate waters; all bore into rock, peat, wood and other substances.

Barnea candida Linnaeus   ×0.9
White Piddock

Thin, brittle elongate-oval, inflated shell with rounded anterior end and narrower posterior end. Gaping posteriorly.

Umbonal reflection closely adhering to shell. Strong radial and concentric ridges over whole shell, strongest anteriorly, and spiny at intersections. Irregularly oval protoplax with shallow central groove. Small, thin apophysis in each valve. Deep pallial sinus. Unicolorous white. Thin, pale brown periostracum. 3·5–7·0cm. Boreal, Mediterranean, West African. Common.

Barnea parva Pennant
Little Piddock
Similar to *B. candida*, but broader dorso-ventrally and gaping at both ends. Umbonal reflection does not adhere so closely to shell. Protoplax longer and narrower. Apophysis long, broad and flat. Deep pallial sinus. 3·0–4·5cm. Boreal, Mediterranean. Frequent.

Barnea truncata Say
Differs from *B. candida* by its broader posterior end and by the anterior end which is attenuated and bears some resemblance to that of *Zirfaea*. Widely gaping at both ends. Posterior half almost smooth, rest of shell ornamented with concentric and radial ridges which are strongest anteriorly. Apophysis in each valve long and narrow. White. 5–7cm. Transatlantic. Common.

Genus ZIRFAEA Leach
Oval or broadly elongate-oval, inflated shells which are broader dorso-ventrally than *Pholas* and *Barnea*. Widely gaping at both ends. Protoplax and metaplax absent. Mesoplax small and triangular. Broad, spoon-shaped apophysis in each valve. Concentric ornament usually crossed by radial ornament anteriorly. Few species in Atlantic and North Pacific where they bore into soft rock and other substances.

Zirfaea crispata Linnaeus   ×0.9
Oval Piddock, Great Piddock

Solid, equivalve, broadly ovate, inflated shell with well rounded posterior end and triangular, pointed anterior end, both ends

widely gaping. Small triangular mesoplax. Entire anterior and umbonal dorsal margin reflected and adhering closely to shell for most of its length. Concentric ridges are weak on posterior half and strong and wavy on anterior half. Broad, flat long apophysis in each valve. Pallial sinus broad and deep. Median groove runs from each umbo to ventral margin. Unicolorous white. Brown periostracum. 4–9cm. Boreal, Transatlantic, Arctic.

Superfamily
Pandoracea

Family LYONSIIDAE
Small to medium-sized, thin, fragile, elongate or oval, inequilateral shells. Valves gaping posteriorly in most species. No hinge teeth. Ligament sunken and supported internally by a calcareous plate (the lithodesma). Ornament subdued or strong. Periostracum thin or thick. Pallial sinus distinct. About half a dozen genera widely distributed in most seas.

Genus LYONSIA Turton
For details see Family Lyonsiidae. Most species elongate, with attenuate, slightly gaping posterior end. Lithodesma large or small. Ornament fine, mostly radial. Deep pallial sinus. Few species, mostly in cooler waters.

Lyonsia hyalina Conrad
Similar to *L. norwegia* in general appearance, but smaller, more elongate and with more produced umbones. Posterior end more attenuate. Ornament similar to *L. norwegia*. Semi-translucent. Whitish. 1·5–2·0cm. Boreal (East coast of North America). Transatlantic. Common.

Lyonsia norwegica Gmelin   ×1.2

Thin, fragile, nearly equivalve shell with left valve slightly more convex than right. Anterior end well rounded, posterior end straight-sided and slightly narrowed. Shell surface coarsely granulated, the granulations assuming the form of radial lines or riblets. Also fine concentric ridges. No hinge teeth. Deep pallial sinus. Translucent white. Periostracum pale brown, often encrusted with sand grains. 3–4cm. Boreal, Mediterranean (Atlantic coasts and islands). Frequent.

Family MYOCHAMIDAE

Small family of small to medium-sized, strongly inequivalve shells. Some live attached to other objects and some are free-living. No hinge teeth. Dorsal margins of one valve overlap the other and fit into corresponding depressions in shell wall. Umbones usually acutely pointed. Ligament external or absent. Small pallial sinus. Two genera in Australasia and Indo-Pacific.

Genus MYADORA Gray

Small, thin, inequivalve, compressed, triangularly-ovate shells which do not attach themselves to other objects. Umbones usually acutely pointed. Right valve more convex than the left which is usually flat. Ornament mostly concentric. Small pallial sinus. Few species in Australasia and often in deep water.

Myadora elongata May

Very small, oblong-ovate, compressed shell with the longer anterior half rounded, and posterior half square-ended. Low ridge from umbo to posterior ventral edge of each valve. About eight strong, low, rounded concentric ribs. Unicolorous white. *c*0·6cm. Australia (South Australia, Tasmania). Uncommon.

Myadora iredalei Cotton

Small, elongate-ovate, compressed, thin shell with left valve smaller and flatter than right. Anterior end well rounded, posterior end attenuated and straight-edged. Acutely pointed, posteriorly directed umbones. Well defined ridge from umbo to base of straight posterior edge, less distinct on left valve than on right. Strong, regularly spaced concentric ribs. White. Inside glossy white. *c*1·5cm. Australian (South Australia). Uncommon.

Myadora striata Quoy   ×0.6

Thin, triangularly-ovate, compressed shell with flat left valve and moderately convex right valve. Ventral margin well rounded. Ridge on posterior dorsal slope. Irregular concentric ridges on both valves. Adductor muscle impressions and pallial line very clear. Yellowish white. Inside white. 3–4 cm. Australian (New Zealand). Frequent.

Family PERIPLOMATIDAE

Medium-sized, thin, strongly inequivalve, moderately inflated, ovate to elongate shells with a slit in umbones. No hinge teeth and no ligament. Internally there is a spoon-shaped process below umbo of each valve. Pallial sinus wide but usually shallow. Two genera, almost worldwide in distribution.

Genus PERIPLOMA Schumacher

For details see Family Periplomatidae. Right valve more convex than left and slightly overlapping it. Ornament mostly concentric and usually subdued. Pallial sinus shallow, rarely deep. Few species, widely distributed in most seas.

Periploma angasi Crosse & Fischer   × 0·6

Very thin, fragile, elongate-oval, strongly inequivalve shell with right valve more convex than the left, and with both ends gaping. Anterior end well rounded; posterior end attenuated, with dorsal margin not sloping and ventral margin sinuate. Umbones broad, each traversed from left to right by a thin, sealed-up slit. Fine, irregular concentric growth lines. Pallial sinus moderately deep and narrow. Nearly translucent, dull white. Inside white. 6·5–7·5cm. Australian (South Australia, Tasmania, New Zealand). Frequent.

Periploma inequale C. B. Adams

Thin, fragile, oblong shell, the left valve

more inflated and slightly overlapping the right. Umbones each have a slit running from left to right. Low ridge from each umbo to anterior ventral margin, grooved below ridge. Large, spoon-shaped process below umbones. V-shaped pallial sinus. Unicolorous white. Transatlantic, Caribbean. Common.

Family THRACIIDAE

Medium-sized to moderately large, ovate to elongate-ovate, mostly inequilateral, usually slightly gaping shells with right valve larger than the left and often overlapping it. No hinge teeth. External ligament sometimes present. Smooth or with mostly concentric ornament. Spoon-shaped process (lithodesma) inside shell under umbones. Pallial sinus usually broad and deep. Eight genera, widespread in nearly all seas.

Genus THRACIA Sowerby

Elongate-ovate or rounded-trigonal, inequivalve, nearly equilateral shells with rounded anterior end and slightly narrower, more or less straight-sided posterior end with a low ridge on posterior dorsal slope. No teeth on hinge. Internal ligament attached to small, spoon-shaped or triangular plate, the lithodesma, below umbones. Smooth or concentrically striate. Pallial sinus shallow. Numerous species, widespread in cooler waters of most seas.

Thracia conradi Couthouy

Larger than *T. pubescens*, more inflated and much more trigonal in shape, with more sloping dorsal margins and rounded, sinuate ventral margin. Umbo of right valve always pierced by umbo of left valve. Pallial sinus U-shaped but not deep. White, covered by a yellowish brown periostracum. 7–10cm. Boreal (East coast of North America). Transatlantic. Frequent.

Thracia pubescens Pulteney   ×0.5

Thin, elongate-oval, moderately inflated shell with right valve larger and more convex than left, umbo of left valve tucked into base of umbo of right valve. Irregular concentric lines and ridges on a finely granulated surface. White or cream, covered by a pale yellowish brown periostracum. Inside white. 7–9cm. Boreal, Mediterranean. West African. Common.

Class
CEPHALOPODA

A class small in members – about 400 species, all marine – but including the largest invertebrates in the world. Cephalopods, better known as squids, octopuses, cuttlefish and nautiluses, are mostly shell-less creatures, usually having 8 or 10 arms or tentacles. Squids have an internal, corneous structure, known as a pen from its resemblance to a feather quill pen.

Cuttlefish have an internal, calcareous structure, the cuttle-bone, well known as a food for cage birds. The coiled shell of *Spirula*, though internal, is a true shell. The Argonautidae secrete an external shell-like covering, but this is merely a case for the protection of eggs. Only in the Nautilidae do we find a true external shell. A radula is usually present as well as a beak resembl-

ing a parrot's which cephalopods use to tear up their living food – they are mostly voracious predators. The eyes are large and well developed. The tentacles often bear rows of suckers, and a funnel-shaped organ enables the animals to propel themselves through the water at speed. Cephalopods are pelagic creatures, some of them living at great depth.

Sub-Class
Nautiloidea

Family NAUTILIDAE

The only cephalopod family including species with external true shells. The shells are large, light in weight and resemble a round-bottomed boat. They are distinguished, above all, by being partitioned or chambered internally, the partitions being linked by a tube known as a siphuncle. The chambers are filled with a gas allowing the shell to float – the animal controls its buoyancy by introducing water into or removing it from the chambers. One genus, containing three or four species, all of them living in the Indo-Pacific region.

Genus NAUTILUS Linnaeus
For details see Family Nautilidae.

Nautilus pompilius Linnaeus ×0.4
Chambered Nautilus

Large, thin, inflated, boat-shaped, bilaterally symmetrical shell with large aperture enclosing rest of the regularly coiled whorls. No umbilicus. Internally shell is partitioned into regularly spaced chambers each joined by a tube, or siphuncle. White, with bold, zebra stripes which are usually absent from the last half of body whorl in adult shells. 15–20cm. Indo-Pacific. Frequent.

Nautilus scrobiculatus Lightfoot
Similar to *N. pompilius* but with a large, wide umbilicus on each side. 12–20cm. Indo-Pacific (Pacific). Rare.

Sub-Class
Coleoidea

Family ARGONAUTIDAE

Octopus-like molluscs which do not secrete true shells. The female argonaut has dorsal

Argonauta argo

arms expanded into glandular membranes which secrete a thin, fragile, calcareous 'false shell' for the retention of eggs. The false shell is laterally compressed, boat-shaped and consists almost entirely of a capacious body whorl. One genus with few species, most of which have a worldwide distribution in warm and tropical seas.

Genus ARGONAUTA Linnaeus
For details see Family Argonautidae.

Argonauta argo Linnaeus ×0.7
Thin, fragile, laterally compressed shell with double keel bearing numerous sharp nodules. Opaque, milky white with nodules on early part of shell stained dark purplish brown. 9–20cm. Worldwide in warm and tropical seas. Common.

Argonauta hians Lightfoot ×0.9
Similar to *A. argo*, but smaller, fatter with the two keels wider apart. Fewer nodules on keels. Brownish white with darker

brown on early part of shell. 5–7cm. Worldwide in warm and tropical seas. Uncommon.

Argonauta nodosa Lightfoot   ×0.4

Shell less elongate than *A. argo*, but much fatter and more solid. Two keels relatively wider apart and the nodules much stouter and more widely spaced. Whole shell covered with radiating rows of low tubercles. Tubercles coalesced to form ridges on earlier part of shell. Opaque, white with early part of shell stained dark brown, darkest on tubercles. 15–18cm. Worldwide in warm and tropical seas. Uncommon.

Family SPIRULIDAE

Small, squid-like animals. Coiled internal shell partitioned into chambers, as in *Nautilus*, has much the same function in buoyancy control. The shell is a loosely and flatly coiled spiral structure. The animal is rarely seen alive. One genus with one species of worldwide distribution in warm and tropical seas.

Genus SPIRULA Lamarck
For details see Family Spirulidae.

Spirula spirula Linnaeus   ×2.0
peroni Lamarck.
Small, thin, fragile shell loosely and regularly coiled in a flat spiral. Internally

partitioned into chambers by fragile shelly walls or septa. Externally the septa are discernible as shallow grooves. In section, shell tube is perfectly circular. A small tube, or siphuncle, connects the chambers. Unicolorous white. 2–3cm. Worldwide in warm and tropical seas. Common.

Glossary

adductor muscle In a bivalve, the muscle, either one or two, connecting valves and drawing them together.

adductor muscle impression Impression on inside of bivalve shell valves where adductor muscle was attached.

anterior The end of a shell nearest to the front of the mollusc when in motion.

anterior slope Surface of valve of bivalve shell from umbo to anterior ventral margin.

antero-dorsal surface Dorsal surface of bivalve shell anterior to umbones.

apertural Pertaining to aperture or on same side as aperture.

aperture Anterior opening of shell in univalve molluscs.

apex Earliest part of shell, usually pointed.

apophysis (plural **apophyses**) Projecting structure on inside of bivalve shell below umbo to which certain muscles are attached; also applied to projecting structure on inside of operculum in some gastropods, e.g. Neritidae.

arcuate Arched, or gently curved.

auricle *See* ear.

axial Parallel with shell axis of univalve molluscs.

axis Imaginary line through shell apex about which are coiled the whorls of most univalve shells.

base Last formed part of gastropod shell, opposite to apex.

bead Small rounded knob on a rib.

biconical Resembling two cones placed base to base.

bifurcate Branch; when ribs or other linear features originate close together and diverge, usually seen on bivalve shells.

bivalve Having a shell consisting of two pieces.

body whorl The last formed whorl of a shell.

byssal gape Opening between bivalve shell margins through which byssus is extruded.

byssal notch Indentation below anterior ear of right valve of Pectinidae for passage of byssus or protrusion of foot.

byssus Bunch of fine silky threads by which some bivalves are affixed to other objects.

calcareous Composed of calcium carbonate or lime, chalky.

callus A thickening of shelly material found principally on parietal region of gastropod shells.

canal Narrow extension of aperture through which siphon may be extruded.

canaliculate Gutter-like or channelled; applied to suture of some gastropod shells.

cancellate (ornament) Consisting of intersecting threads meeting more or less at right angles.

cardinal tooth Elevated process on hinge plate near umbo, usually with corresponding socket in opposite valve.

columella Pillar surrounding axis of gastropod shell.

columella fold Ridge winding round columella and projecting into interior of shell.

compressed Flattened.

concentric Coinciding in direction with growth lines on bivalve shells.

cord Line of coarse, elevated ornament with rounded top.

corneous Non-calcareous or horny.

coronate With tubercles or low spines at shoulder of whorls.

costa Line of ornament similar to, but of greater prominence than, cord.

crenate Notched – describing edge or crest of bivalve shells; notched or scalloped – outer lip of gastropod shells.

crenulate Notched – describing edge of inner margins of some bivalve shells; wrinkled – edge of outer lip margin of gastropod shells.

decollate With the earlier whorls detached.

decussate With lines of ornament crossing at right angle, like basket weave.

dentate (in gastropod shells) With tooth-like protuberances on inner side of outer lip.

denticle Small, rounded, tooth-like protuberance.

denticulate Bearing denticles.

depressed Low in relation to diameter.

dextral Right-handed – applied to a gastropod shell having its aperture on observer's right when shell apex is directed upwards; definition really depends on anatomical details.

digitation Finger-like projection outwards from outer lip.

discoidal Disc-like and more or less compressed.

divaricate When ridges, grooves or other types of ornament in bivalve shells change course and do not usually follow a concentric or radial growth pattern.

dorsal In the direction of hinge region of bivalves; also applied to uppermost side of certain gastropods, e.g. cowries.

dorsum Upper surface of certain gastropods, e.g. cowries.

dull Without sheen or gloss.

ear Small extension of dorsal region of bivalve shell, usually with a notch between it and main part of shell, as in Pectinidae.

elevated Raised up; high in proportion to diameter.

emarginate With margin, or edge, of shell cut into by a notch or notches or gently indented.

equilateral With portion of bivalve shell on anterior side of umbones approximately same size and shape as that on posterior side.

equivalve With valves of same shape and size.

escutcheon Depressed, elongate area behind umbones, encompassing ligament, if external, on one or both valves of bivalve shell; usually differing from rest of shell in ornament and/or colour.

false umbilicus Depression at base of gastropod shell not penetrating deeper than height of body whorl, as in some of the Trochidae.

fasciole Raised band, or a groove round basal portion of some gastropod shells.

flaring Widening outwards towards opening, usually applied to outer lip of gastropod shells.

fluted With rounded excavations resembling architectural flutings, found on some bivalve shells; also applied to scales which are arched.

fold *See* columella fold.

foliated Having branched or crimped outer ends; applied to the appearance of spines of certain gastropods such as some Muricidae.

fossula Shallow depression of inner lip in some cowries.

fusiform More or less spindle-shaped, as in the genus *Fusinus*.

gape Space between edge of valves of a closed bivalve shell; *see also* byssal gape.

girdle Muscular, plain or ornamented integument binding together and surrounding valves of chitons.

globose More or less spherical.

granulated Covered with granules or small tubercles.

growth lines Elevated and concentrically disposed lines or ridges indicating former growth margins.

growth stages Exaggerated growth lines indicating a cessation of growth.

hinge Thickened internal area in dorsal region of bivalve shells where ligament and interlocking teeth are situated.

hinge line Dorsal, or upper side of hinge.

hinge plate Part of hinge bearing teeth and sockets.

hinge tooth Structure projecting from hinge plate which, in conjunction with an opposing socket, is a strengthening device in bivalve shells.

imbricate (ornament) Overlapping, resembling tiles on a roof.

imperforate Lacking an umbilicus; an inexact term as its opposite, perforate, cannot be applied to possession of an umbilicus, which is not a perforation.

impressed (suture) More or less indented.

incurved Term used to indicate that a structure curves in upon itself, as do the umbones of certain bivalves, or the spines or lamellae of certain bivalves and gastropods.

inequilateral With the portions of shell on either side of umbones of unequal size and shape.

inequivalve With one valve larger than the other.

inflated or **ventricose** Swollen, or strongly convex.

inner lip Margin of aperture extending from base of columella to suture.

intermediate valve Any one of the valves between the head and tail valves of a chiton.

interspace The region between a pair of raised ridges or other linear surface ornament.

keel More or less sharp edge of gastropod shell periphery.

labial teeth Tooth-like processes around the aperture of some gastropods, notably cowries.

lamella Thin plate-like ridge.

last whorl *See* body whorl.

lateral tooth Tooth on bivalve hinge plate relatively distant from umbo, in contrast to cardinal teeth which are always near umbo.

left valve Valve situated on observer's left when bivalve shell is placed with anterior end pointing away from him and the hinge line uppermost.

ligament Elastic, corneous structure joining valves of bivalve shell dorsally and causing valves to open when adductor muscles are relaxed.

lira (plural **lirae**) Fine linear elevation of shelly material usually within outer lip of some gastropod shells.

lirate Bearing lirae.

lithodesma Calcareous structure supporting internal ligament in some bivalves.

lunule Usually heart-shaped depression anterior to umbones of many bivalves.

mantle Integument surrounding internal soft parts of a bivalve which secretes the shell and which is attached to inside of valves at pallial line.

margin Extreme edge of valve of bivalve shell; also the thickened periphery of base of some gastropods, notably cowries; sometimes used as equivalent to edge.

mesoplax Accessory plate lying across umbonal region of the Pholadidae.

metaplax Long, narrow accessory plate covering gap between the dorsal margins of valves behind umbones of the Pholadidae.

multispiral With numerous whorls, usually referring to spiral line on an operculum.

nacreous Lustrous in appearance, like mother-of-pearl, with structure comprising thin layers of aragonite parallel to inner surface of shell.

nodose With small lumpy protuberances.

nucleus Earliest-formed part of gastropod shell or its operculum.

operculate With an operculum.

operculum Calcareous or horny structure attached to foot of many gastropods and used to close aperture of shell, but sometimes too small to do so effectively.

ornament Surface sculpture standing out in relief on shell surface.

outer lip Outer margin of aperture extending from suture to base of columella.

ovate Egg-shaped, or with egg-shaped outline.

palatal Belonging to outer lip.

pallial line Impressed line on inside of each valve of a bivalve shell towards margin indicating former line of attachment of mantle muscle.

pallial sinus Embayment in pallial line indicating former line of attachment of siphonal retractor muscles.

parietal In a gastropod shell, describes the region just inside and just outside the aperture opposite to the outer lip.

patelliform Limpet-shaped, resembling shells of genus *Patella*.

paucispiral With relatively few whorls, usually referring to spiral lines on operculum.

periostracum Coating or skin of corneous material, known as conchiolin, covering calcareous shell of many molluscs.

periphery Outermost part of any whorl.

peristome Margin of aperture.

plica (plural **plicae**) Fold or ridge on columella, a less conspicuous feature than columella fold but the two terms are more or less interchangeable.

plicate Bearing plicae; also occasionally used here as equivalent to crenulate.

porcellaneous Having a translucent or porcelain-like appearance.

posterior The end of a shell nearest to the rear of the mollusc when it is in motion.

posterior ridge Ridge originating near or on umbo and running diagonally towards posterior end of ventral margin of a bivalve shell.

posterior slope Surface of valve of bivalve shell from umbo to posterior ventral margin.

postero-dorsal surface Dorsal surface of bivalve shell posterior to umbones.

protoplax Long, narrow accessory plate, in one piece or longitudinally divided into two at anterior end of dorsal margin of the Pholadidae.

punctate Pitted with minute depressions like pin-pricks or punctures, often occurring in lines.

pustule Small, rounded protuberance on shell surface, smaller than tubercle.

pyriform Pear-shaped.

quadrate Square or nearly so.

radial (surface feature) Directed from umbo towards margins.

recurved (of siphonal canal) Bent or curved away from central axis of shell.

reflected Turned outward and backwards at margin, usually referring to margin of outer lip.

reticulate Bearing reticulations.

reticulation Pattern formed by obliquely intersecting threads or linear ridges of ornament.

rhomboidal With four more or less equal sides and no right-angled corners.

rib Fairly broad and prominent elevation of shell surface, usually occurring as a continuous line.

riblet Same as rib but usually associated closely with rib which is obviously broader.

ridge Sharp-edged elevation of shell surface occurring as a single line.

right valve Valve situated on observer's right when bivalve shell is placed with anterior end pointing away from him and the hinge line uppermost.

scale Slightly or strongly raised ledge, usually very small and often on a rib.

scalloped With shell margin showing regular flutings.

sculpture Synonymous with ornament, the term preferred here.

septum Transverse plate sealing off chambers in some shells, notably in *Nautilus* and *Spirula*.

shoulder Angulation of whorl just below suture.

sinistral Left-handed – applied to a gastropod shell having its aperture on observer's left when shell apex is directed upwards; definition really depends on anatomical details.

sinus Embayment, notch or slit. In gastropod shells, sinus close to suture on upper part of outer lip is sometimes called the anal sinus. *See also* pallial sinus.

siphon Tubelike, protrusible organ of a gastropod, or similarly shaped extension of mantle of a bivalve; for passage of inhalant or exhalant current, sometimes for more specialised purposes.

siphonal canal Tubular or gutter-like extension of lower part of apertural margin often continuous with columella, also known as an anterior canal, for enclosure of anterior siphon.

siphonal notch Narrow or broad, shallow or deep, embayment in apertural margin near base of columella where anterior siphon protrudes.

spicules Small, usually spiny processes on girdle of a chiton.

spine Spiky or thorn-like protuberance on shell surface; may be flattened or rounded, foliated or pointed at outer end, solid or tubular.

spiral Passing continuously around whorls nearly parallel with suture.

spire The part of a gastropod shell preceding the body whorl.

stepped or **turreted** With whorls resembling a series of steps viewed in profile.

stria (plural **striae**) Incised groove or furrow anywhere on shell surface, sometimes called striation.

stromboid notch On shells of Strombidae, narrow or broad, shallow or deep, embayment in apertural margin additional to and above siphonal notch; the left eye stalk protrudes through it.

suture The continuous spiral line on gastropod shells where whorls join; in most books a coiled shell is considered to have more than one suture, but here it is treated as a single line.

teeth Term loosely applied to structures seen on inside of outer lip or on parietal region of gastropod shells; *see also* hinge tooth.

terminal At end of shell, as when umbones occur at anterior end of bivalve shell.

thread Fine raised line of ornament.

transverse Crossing direction of spiral growth in gastropod shells and crossing concentric growth lines in bivalves.

trigonal Three cornered.

trochoidal Like an inverted spinning top, or like the shell of a *Trochus* having a pointed spire, flat sides and flat base.

truncate Abruptly cut off; applied to the square-ended appearance of certain bivalve shells, and to the abrupt termination of the columella in some gastropod shells such as *Planaxis*.

tubercle Small rounded elevation on shell surface, larger than pustule.

turbinate Turban-shaped, with broadly conical spire and convex base, as in shell of *Turbo*.

turreted *See* stepped.

turriculate Having acutely pointed, elongate spire with many, rather flat-sided whorls, as in *Terebra*.

umbilicate Having an umbilicus.

umbilicus The hole around which the inner surface of a gastropod shell is coiled; imaginary axis passes through centre of umbilicus.

umbo (plural **umbones**) Earliest formed region of bivalve shell. The term 'beak', often used to describe its extremity, is not used here.

umbonal cavity The space inside valves within umbones and under hinge plate.

umbonal reflection When dorsal line is turned up and over and in front of umbo in each valve; found in Pholadidae.

univalve Mollusc with a one-piece shell.

valve One half of a bivalve shell or one of the eight pieces comprising a chiton's shell.

varicose Bearing a varix or varices.

varix (plural **varices**) An axial growth stage, usually very prominent, which is a former outer lip margin not fully covered by subsequent growth.

ventral In the region of a bivalve shell opposite to ligament, where valves open most widely; also the apertural side of a gastropod shell.

ventricose *See* inflated.

whorl One complete turn of a coiled, tubular gastropod shell around its imaginary axis.

wing Terminal part of dorsal region of bivalve shell which is more or less elongate or triangular; here used to denote elongate extension such as that on *Pteria* rather than the relatively shorter ear of *Chlamys*; also rarely used to denote an extension of outer lip margin of some gastropod shells.

Select Bibliography

Nearly all the titles on this list are in print, and most of them have provided information which is incorporated in this book. Nearly all of them contain descriptions and illustrations of species which are not featured here. The list is far from being a complete inventory of current literature, but includes most of the titles useful to collectors.

Abbott, R. T. 1954. *American Seashells*. Princeton.
—— (ed.). 1959 – (in progress). *Indo-Pacific Mollusca*. Delaware Museum of Natural History, Greenville, Delaware.
Allan, J. 1959. *Australian Shells*. Melbourne.
Barnard, K. H. 1953. *A Beginner's Guide to South African Shells*. Cape Town.
Burgess, C. M. 1970. *The Living Cowries*. South Brunswick, N.J.
Cernohorsky, W. O. 1967–72. *Marine Shells of the Pacific*. 2 vols. Sydney.
Dautzenberg, P. 1913. *Des Coquilles des côtes de France*. Paris.
Keen, A. M. 1971. *Seashells of Tropical West America*. Stanford.
Kira, T., & Habe, T. 1959–61. *Coloured Illustrations of the Shells of Japan*. 2 vols. Osaka.
Macpherson, J. H., & Gabriel, C. J. 1962. *Marine Molluscs of Victoria*. Melbourne.

Moore, R. C. (ed.). 1960 – (in progress). *Treatise on Invertebrate Paleontology*. Mollusca (several volumes already published including complete coverage of Bivalvia and Amphineura). Geological Society of America and University of Kansas Press.
Nicklés, M. 1950. *Mollusques Testacés Marins de la côte occidentale d'Afrique*. Paris.
Powell, A. W. P. 1961. *Shells of New Zealand*. Auckland.
Rios, E. de Carvalhos. 1970. *Coastal Brazilian Seashells*. North Myrtle Beach, S. Carolina.
Shikama, T., & Horikoshi, M. 1963. *Selected Shells of the World*. 2 vols. Tokyo.
Tebble, N. 1966. *British Bivalve Seashells*. London.
Thiele, J. 1929. *Handbuch der systematischen Weichtierkunde*. Jena.
Wagner, R. L. J., & Abbott, R. T. 1967. *Van Nostrand's Standard Catalog of Shells*. New York.
Warmke, G. L., & Abbott, R. T. 1961. *Caribbean Seashells*. Narberth.
Weaver, C. S., & du Pont, J. E. 1970. *The Living Volutes*. Greenville.
Wilson, B. R., & Gillett, K. 1971. *Australian Shells*. Sydney.
Woodward, S. P. 1851. *A Manual of the Mollusca*. London.
Zeigler, R. F., & Porreca, H. C. 1969. *Olive Shells of the World*. North Myrtle Beach, S. Carolina.

Index